Why You Need the New Edition

1. New chapter on Selecting Research Participants
2. Chapter on scientific writing updated to conform to 6th edition of APA style
3. New sample manuscript reflects recent changes in APA style
4. New section on resisting one's personal biases when conducting research
5. Expanded coverage of effect size indicators
6. Revision of sections on main effects and interactions
7. New coverage of confidence intervals and the use of error bars
8. Expanded sections on telephone surveys, experience sampling, and Internet research
9. Enhanced discussion (and case study) on neuroimaging methods (fMRI)
10. New section on cross-sequential cohort designs
11. New section on research with vulnerable populations
12. New section on using PsycInfo
13. New up-to-date Behavioral Research Case Studies throughout text
14. Expanded glossary

PEARSON

Sixth Edition

Introduction to Behavioral Research Methods

Mark R. Leary
Duke University

PEARSON

Boston   New York   San Francisco   Mexico City   Montreal
Toronto   London   Madrid   Munich   Paris   Hong Kong
Singapore   Tokyo   Cape Town   Sydney

Executive Editor: Stephen Frail
Editorial Assistant: Madelyn Schricker
Marketing Manager: Nicole Kunzmann
Production Manager: Meghan DeMaio
Creative Director: Jayne Conte
Cover Designer: Bruce Kenselaar
Cover Image: Kronick/iStockphoto
Editorial Production Service: Hemalatha/Integra Software Services
Printer/Binder: Courier Companies
Cover Printer: Moore Langen

Library of Congress Cataloging-in-Publication Data
Leary, Mark R.
  Introduction to behavioral research methods/Mark R. Leary. — 6th ed.
    p. cm.
  Includes bibliographical references and index.
  ISBN-13: 978-0-205-20398-7
  ISBN-10: 0-205-20398-1
  1. Psychology—Research—Methodology.   I. Title.
  BF76.5.L39 2012
  150.72'1—dc23
                                                    2011017850

ISBN 10: 0-205-20398-1
ISBN 13: 978-0-205-20398-7

CONTENTS

PREFACE

Regardless of how good a particular class is, the students' enthusiasm for the course material is rarely as great as the professor's. No matter how interesting the material, how motivated the students, or how skillful the instructor, those who take a course are seldom as enthralled with the content as those who teach it. We've all taken courses in which an animated, nearly zealous professor faced a classroom of only mildly interested students.

In departments founded on the principles of behavioral science—psychology, communication, human development, education, marketing, social work, and the like— this discrepancy in student and faculty interest is perhaps most pronounced in courses that deal with research design and analysis. On one hand, the faculty members who teach courses in research methods are usually quite enthused about research. Many have contributed to the research literature in their own areas of expertise, and some are highly regarded researchers within their fields. On the other hand, despite these instructors' best efforts to bring the course alive, many students dread taking methods courses. They expect that these courses will be dry and difficult and wonder why such courses are required as part of their curriculum. Thus, the enthusiastic, involved instructor is often confronted by a class of disinterested students, some of whom may begrudge the fact that they must study research methods at all.

In many ways, these attitudes are understandable. After all, students who choose to study psychology, education, human development, and other areas that rely on behavioral research rarely do so because they are enamored with research. And, in fact, many of them are initially surprised by the degree to which their courses are built around the results of scientific studies. (I certainly was.) Rather, such students either plan to enter a profession in which knowledge of behavior is relevant (such as professional psychology, social work, teaching, or public relations) or are intrinsically interested in the subject matter. Most students eventually come to appreciate the value of research to behavioral science, the helping professions, and society, although some continue to regard it as an unnecessary curricular diversion. For some students, being required to take courses in methodology and statistics supplants other courses in which they are more interested.

In addition, the concepts, principles, analyses, and ways of thinking central to the study of research methods are new to most students and, thus, require a bit of extra effort to comprehend and learn. Add to that the fact that the topics covered in research methods courses, on the whole, seem inherently less interesting than those covered in most other courses in psychology and related fields. Wouldn't most of us rather be sitting in a class in developmental psychology, neuroscience, social psychology, or human sexuality than one about research methods?

I wrote *Introduction to Behavioral Research Methods* because, as a teacher and as a researcher, I wanted a book that would help counteract students' natural tendencies to dislike and shy away from research—a book that would make research methodology as understandable, palatable, useful, and interesting for my students as it was for me. Thus, my primary goal was to write a book that is *readable.* Students should be able to understand most of the material in a book such as this without the course instructor having to serve as an interpreter. Enhancing comprehensibility can be achieved in two ways.

The less preferred way is simply to dilute the material by omitting complex topics and by presenting material in a simplified, "dumbed-down" fashion. The alternative that I chose to pursue in this text is to present the material with sufficient elaboration, explanation, and examples to render it understandable. The feedback that I have received about the five previous editions of this book give me the sense that I have succeeded in my goal to create a rigorous yet readable book.

A second goal was to integrate the various topics covered in the book to a greater extent than is done in most research methods texts, using the concept of variability as a unifying theme. From the development of a research idea, through measurement issues, to design and analysis, the entire research process is an attempt to understand variability in behavior. Because the concept of variability is woven throughout the research process, I've used it as a framework to provide coherence to the various topics in the book. Having taught research methods courses centered around the theme of variability for over 25 years, I can attest that students find the unifying theme very useful.

Third, I tried to write a book that is interesting—that presents ideas in an engaging fashion and uses provocative examples of real and hypothetical research. This edition of the book has even more examples of real research, tidbits about the lives of famous researchers, and intriguing controversies that have arisen in behavioral science than previous editions. Far from being icing on the cake, these features help to enliven the research enterprise. Research methods are essentially tools, and learning about tools is enhanced when students can see the variety of fascinating studies that behavioral researchers have built with them.

Courses in research methods differ widely in the degree to which statistics are incorporated into the course. My personal view is that students' understanding of research methodology is enhanced by familiarity with basic statistical principles. Without an elementary grasp of statistical concepts, students will find it very difficult to understand the research articles they read. Although this book is decidedly focused on research methodology and design, I've sprinkled essential statistical topics throughout the book. My goal is to help students understand statistics conceptually without asking them to actually complete the calculations. With a better understanding of what becomes of the data they collect, students should be able to design more thorough and reliable research studies. Knowing that instructors differ widely in the degree to which they incorporate statistics into their methods courses, I have made it easy for individual instructors to choose whether students will deal with the calculational aspects of the analyses that appear. For the most part, presentation of statistical calculations is confined to a few within-chapter boxes, Chapters 11 and 12, and Appendix B. These sections may easily be omitted if the instructor prefers.

This edition of *Introduction to Behavioral Research Methods* has benefitted from the comments I have received from both students and instructors who have used it, as well as from reviewers who provided extensive feedback on every chapter. Those who are familiar with the previous edition will find the organization of the book mostly unchanged. The changes in this edition involve adding new examples of real studies, adding and updating references, incorporating the 6th edition of APA style, and clarifying and elaborating sections that I thought could be improved.

As a teacher, researcher, and author, I know that there will always be some discrepancy between professors' and students' attitudes toward research methods, but I hope that the new edition of this book will help to narrow the gap.

SUPPLEMENTS

Instructor's Manual/Test Bank (download from www.pearsonhighered.com/IRC) Each chapter in this manual contains an outline of the chapter in the text, a list of key terms (in the order in which they appear in the text), ideas for course enhancement (including handouts that can be copied and given to students) and multiple choice, short answer, and application test questions.

MyTest (http://pearsonmytest.com/) The Test Bank is also available within Pearson MyTest, a powerful assessment generation program that helps instructors easily create and print quizzes and exams. Questions and tests can be authored online, allowing instructors ultimate flexibility and the ability to efficiently manage assessments anytime, anywhere.

PowerPoint Lecture Slides (download from www.pearsonhighered.com/IRC) Lecture outlines are provided in this set of PowerPoint files, compatible with Mac and PC.

MySearchLab (www.mysearchlab.com) MySearchLab delivers proven results in helping individual students succeed. Step by step tutorials present complete overviews of the writing process. Instructors and students receive access to the EBSCO ContentSelect database, census data from Social Explorer, Associated Press news feeds, and the Pearson bookshelf. Pearson SourceCheck helps students and instructors monitor originality and avoid plagiarism. MySearchLab also includes an eText version of the Leary text. Just like the printed text, students and instructors can highlight and add their own notes to their interactive text online. Chapter quizzes and flashcards offer immediate feedback and a gradebook allows both students, and instructors to monitor student progress throughout the course. An online laboratory manual, by Barney Beins and Jeffrey Holmes, both of Ithaca College, provides a series of labs students can complete to get hands on practice with scientific research methods.

ACKNOWLEDGMENTS

I would like to thank the following reviewers of this edition: Jonathan Amburgey– The University of Utah, Troy Beckert– Utah State University, Melina Bersamin– California State University, Sacramento, Michael Dudley– Southern Illinois University Edwardsville, Marie Helweg-Larsen– Dickinson College, Elizabeth Hennon Peters– University of Evansville, Evan Kleiman– George Mason University, Marianne Lloyd– Seton Hall University, David McCaffrey– The University of Mississippi, Amy Overman– Elon University, and Sarah Wood- University of Wisconsin-Stout.

1

RESEARCH IN THE BEHAVIORAL SCIENCES

Stop for a moment and imagine, as vividly as you can, a scientist at work. Let your imagination fill in as many details as possible regarding this scene. What does the imagined scientist look like? Where is the person working? What is the scientist doing?

When I asked a group of undergraduate students to imagine a scientist and tell me what they imagined, I found their answers to be quite intriguing. First, virtually every student said that their imagined scientist was male. This in itself is interesting given that a high percentage of scientists are, of course, women.

Second, most of the students reported that they imagined that the scientist was wearing a white lab coat and working in some kind of laboratory. The details regarding this laboratory differed from student to student, but the lab always contained technical scientific equipment of one kind or another. Some students imagined a chemist, surrounded by substances in test tubes and beakers. Other students thought of a biologist peering into a microscope. Still others conjured up a physicist working with sophisticated electronic equipment. One or two students imagined an astronomer peering through a telescope, and a few even imagined a "mad scientist" creating monsters in a shadowy dungeon lit by torches. Most interesting to me was the fact that although these students were members of a psychology class (in fact, most were psychology majors), not one of them thought of any kind of a *behavioral scientist* when I asked them to imagine a scientist.

Their responses were probably typical of what most people would say if asked to imagine a scientist. For most people, the prototypical scientist is a man wearing a white lab coat working in a laboratory filled with technical equipment. Most people do not think of psychologists and other behavioral researchers as scientists in the same way that they think of physicists, chemists, and biologists as scientists.

Instead, people tend to think of psychologists primarily in their roles as mental health professionals. If I had asked you to imagine a psychologist, you probably would have thought of a counselor talking with a client about his or her problems. You probably would not have imagined a behavioral researcher, such as a physiological psychologist studying startle responses, a social psychologist conducting an experiment on aggression, a developmental psychologist studying how children learn numbers, or an industrial psychologist interviewing the line supervisors at an automobile assembly plant.

Psychology, however, not only is a profession that promotes human welfare through counseling, psychotherapy, education, and other activities but also is a scientific discipline that studies behavior and mental processes. Just as biologists study living organisms and astronomers study the stars, behavioral scientists conduct research involving behavior and mental processes.

THE BEGINNINGS OF BEHAVIORAL RESEARCH

People have asked questions about the causes of behavior throughout written history. Aristotle (384–322 BCE) is sometimes credited for being the first individual to address systematically basic questions about the nature of human beings and why they behave as they do, and within Western culture this claim may be true. However, more ancient writings from India, including the *Upanishads* and the teachings of Gautama Buddha (563–483 BCE), offer equally sophisticated psychological insights into human thought, emotion, and behavior.

For over two millennia, however, the approach to answering these questions was entirely speculative. People would simply concoct explanations of behavior based on everyday observation, creative insight, or religious doctrine. For many centuries, people who wrote about behavior tended to be philosophers or theologians, and their approach was not scientific. Even so, many of these early insights into behavior were, of course, quite accurate.

However, many of these explanations of behavior were also completely wrong. These early thinkers should not be faulted for having made mistakes, for even modern researchers sometimes draw incorrect conclusions. Unlike behavioral scientists today, however, these early "psychologists" (to use the term loosely) did not rely on scientific research to answer questions about behavior. As a result, they had no way to test the validity of their explanations and, thus, no way to discover whether or not their ideas and interpretations were accurate.

Scientific psychology (and behavioral science more broadly) was born during the last quarter of the nineteenth century. Through the influence of early researchers such as Wilhelm Wundt, William James, John Watson, G. Stanley Hall, and others, people began to realize that basic questions about behavior could be addressed using many of the same methods that were used in more established sciences, such as biology, chemistry, and physics.

Today, more than 100 years later, the work of a few creative scientists has blossomed into a very large enterprise, involving hundreds of thousands of researchers around the world who devote part or all of their working lives to the scientific study of behavior. These include not only research psychologists but also researchers in other disciplines such as education, social work, family studies, communication, management, health and exercise science, marketing, and a number of medical fields (such as nursing, neurology, psychiatry, and geriatrics). What researchers in all of these areas of behavioral science have in common is that they apply scientific methodologies to the study of behavior, thought, and emotion.

Contributors to Behavioral Research
Wilhelm Wundt and the Founding of Scientific Psychology

Wilhelm Wundt (1832–1920) was the first research psychologist. Most of those before him who were interested in behavior identified themselves primarily as philosophers, theologians, biologists, physicians, or physiologists. Wundt, on the other hand, was the first to view himself as a research psychologist.

Wundt began studying medicine but switched to physiology after working with Johannes Müller, the leading physiologist of the time. Although his early research was in physiology rather than psychology, Wundt soon became interested in applying the methods of physiology to the study of psychology. In 1874, Wundt published a landmark text, *Principles of Physiological Psychology*, in which he boldly stated his plan to "mark out a new domain of science."

In 1875, Wundt established one of the first two psychology laboratories in the world at the University of Leipzig. Although it has been customary to cite 1879 as the year in which his lab was founded, Wundt was actually given laboratory space by the university for his laboratory equipment in 1875 (Watson, 1978). William James established a laboratory at Harvard University at about the same time, thus establishing the first psychological laboratory in the United States (Bringmann, 1979).

Beyond establishing the Leipzig laboratory, Wundt made many other contributions to behavioral science. He founded a scientific journal in 1881 for the publication of research in experimental psychology—the first journal to devote more space to psychology than to philosophy. (At the time, psychology was viewed as an area in the study of philosophy.) He also conducted research on a variety of psychological processes, including sensation, perception, reaction time, attention, emotion, and introspection. Importantly, he also trained many students who went on to make their own contributions to early psychology: G. Stanley Hall (who started the American Psychological Association and is considered the founder of child psychology); Lightner Witmer (who established the first psychological clinic); Edward Titchener (who brought Wundt's ideas to the United States); and Hugo Munsterberg (a pioneer in applied psychology). Also among Wundt's students was James McKeen Cattell who, in addition to conducting early research on mental tests, was the first to integrate the study of experimental methods into the undergraduate psychology curriculum (Watson, 1978). In part, you have Cattell to thank for the importance that colleges and universities place on courses in research methods.

GOALS OF BEHAVIORAL RESEARCH

Psychology and the other behavioral sciences are thriving as never before. Theoretical and methodological advances have led to important discoveries that have not only enhanced our understanding of behavior but also improved the quality of human life. Each year, behavioral researchers publish the results of tens of thousands of studies, each of which adds incrementally to what we know about the behavior of human beings and other animals.

Some researchers distinguish between two primary types of research that differ with respect to the researcher's primary goal. **Basic research** is conducted to understand psychological processes without regard for whether or not the knowledge is immediately applicable. The primary goal of basic research is to increase our knowledge. This is not to say that basic researchers are not interested in the applicability of their findings. They usually are. In fact, the results of basic research are usually quite useful, often in ways that were not anticipated by the researchers themselves. For example, basic research involving brain function has led to the development of drugs that control symptoms of mental illness, and basic research on cognitive development in children has led to educational innovations in schools. However, the immediate goal of basic research is to understand a psychological phenomenon rather than to solve a particular problem.

In contrast, the goal of **applied research** is to find solutions for certain problems rather than to enhance general knowledge about psychological processes. For example, industrial-organizational psychologists are often hired by businesses to study and solve problems related to employee morale, satisfaction, and productivity. Similarly, community psychologists are sometimes asked to investigate social problems such as racial tension, littering, and violence in a particular city, and researchers in human development and social work study problems such as child abuse and teenage pregnancy. These applied researchers use scientific approaches to understand and solve some problem of immediate concern (such as employee morale, prejudice, or child abuse). Other applied researchers conduct **evaluation research** (also called *program* *evaluation*), using behavioral research methods to assess the effects of social or institutional programs on behavior. When new programs are implemented—such as when new educational programs are introduced into the schools, new laws are passed, or new employee policies are implemented in a business organization—program evaluators are sometimes asked to determine whether the new program is effective in achieving its intended purpose. If so, the evaluator often tries to figure out precisely why the program works; if not, the evaluator tries to uncover why the program was unsuccessful.

Although the distinction between basic and applied research is sometimes useful, we must keep in mind that the primary difference between them lies in the researcher's purpose in conducting the research and not in the nature of the research itself. In fact, it is often difficult to know whether a particular study should be classified as basic or applied simply from looking at the design of the study.

Furthermore, the basic–applied distinction overlooks the intimate connection between research that is conducted to advance knowledge and research that is conducted to solve problems. Much basic research is immediately applicable, and much applied research provides information that enhances our basic knowledge. Furthermore, because applied research often requires an understanding of what people do and why, basic research provides the foundation on which much applied research rests. In return, applied research often provides important ideas and new questions for basic researchers. In the process of trying to solve particular problems, new questions and insights arise. Thus, although researchers may approach a particular study with one of these goals in mind, behavioral science as a whole benefits from the integration of both basic and applied research.

Whether behavioral researchers are conducting basic or applied research, they generally do so with one of three goals in mind—description, prediction, or explanation. That is, they design their research with the intent of describing behavior, predicting behavior, or explaining behavior. Basic researchers stop once they have adequately described, predicted, or explained the phenomenon of interest; applied researchers typically go one step further to offer suggestions and solutions based on their findings.

Describing Behavior

Some behavioral research focuses primarily on describing patterns of behavior, thought, or emotion. Survey researchers, for example, conduct large studies of randomly selected respondents to determine what people think, feel, and do. You are undoubtedly familiar with public opinion polls, such as those that dominate the news during elections, that describe people's attitudes and preferences for candidates. Some research in clinical psychology and psychiatry investigates the prevalence of certain psychological disorders. Marketing researchers conduct descriptive research to study consumers' preferences and buying practices. Other examples of descriptive studies include research in developmental psychology that describes age-related changes in behavior and studies from industrial psychology that describe the behavior of effective managers.

Predicting Behavior

Many behavioral researchers are interested in predicting people's behavior. For example, personnel psychologists try to predict employees' job performance from employment tests and interviews. Similarly, educational psychologists develop ways to predict academic performance from scores on standardized tests in order to identify students who might have learning difficulties in school. Likewise, some forensic psychologists are interested in understanding variables that predict which criminals are likely to be dangerous if released from prison. Developing ways to predict job performance, school grades, or violent tendencies requires considerable research. The tests to be used (such as employment or achievement tests) must be administered, analyzed, and refined to meet certain statistical criteria. Then data are collected and analyzed to identify the best predictors of the target behavior. Prediction equations are calculated and validated on other samples of participants to verify that they predict the behavior successfully. All along the way, the scientific prediction of behavior involves behavioral research methods.

Explaining Behavior

Most researchers regard explanation as the most important goal of scientific research. Although description and prediction are quite important, scientists usually do not feel that they really understand something until they can explain it. We may be able to describe patterns of violence among prisoners who are released from prison and even identify variables that allow us to predict, within limits, which prisoners are likely to be violent once released. However, until we can *explain* why certain prisoners are violent and others are not, the picture is not complete. As we will discuss later in this chapter, an important part of any science involves developing and testing theories that explain the phenomena of interest.

BEHAVIORAL SCIENCE AND COMMON SENSE

Unlike research in the physical and natural sciences, research in the behavioral sciences often deals with topics that are familiar to most people. For example, although few of us would claim to have personal knowledge of subatomic particles, cellular structure, or chloroplasts, we all have a great deal of experience with memory, prejudice, sleep, and emotion. Because they have personal experience with many of the topics of behavioral science, people sometimes maintain that the findings of behavioral science are mostly common sense—things that we all knew already.

In some instances, this is undoubtedly true. It would be a strange science indeed whose findings contradicted everything that laypeople believed about behavior, thought, and emotion. Even so, the fact that a large percentage of the population believes something is no proof of its accuracy. After all, most people once believed that the sun revolved around the Earth, that flies generated spontaneously from decaying meat, and that epilepsy was brought about by demonic possession—all formerly "commonsense" beliefs that were disconfirmed through scientific investigation.

Likewise, behavioral scientists have discredited many widely held beliefs about behavior: For example, parents should not respond too quickly to a crying infant because doing so will make the baby spoiled and difficult (in reality, greater parental responsiveness actually leads to less demanding babies); geniuses are more likely to be crazy or strange than people of average intelligence (on the contrary, exceptionally intelligent people tend to be more emotionally and socially adjusted); paying people a great deal of money to do a job increases their motivation to do it (actually high rewards can undermine intrinsic motivation); and most differences between men and women are purely biological (only in the past 40 years have we begun to understand fully the profound effects of socialization on gender-related behavior). Only through scientific investigation can we test popular beliefs to see which ones are accurate and which ones are myths.

To look at another side of the issue, common sense can interfere with scientific progress. Scientists' own commonsense assumptions about the world can blind them to alternative ways of thinking about the topics they study. Some of the greatest advances in the physical sciences have occurred when people realized that their commonsense notions about the world needed to be abandoned. The Newtonian revolution in physics, for example, was the "result of realizing that commonsense notions about change, forces, motion, and the nature of space needed to be replaced if we were to uncover the real laws of motion" (Rosenberg, 1995, p. 15).

Social and behavioral scientists often rely on commonsense notions regarding behavior, thought, and emotion. When these notions are correct, they guide us in fruitful directions, but when they are wrong, they prevent us from understanding how psychological processes actually operate. Scientists are, after all, just ordinary people who, like everyone else, are subject to biases that are influenced by culture and personal experience. However, scientists have a special obligation to question their commonsense assumptions and to try to minimize the impact of those assumptions on their work.

THE VALUE OF RESEARCH TO THE STUDENT

The usefulness of research for understanding behavior and improving the quality of life is rather apparent, but it may be less obvious that a firm grasp of basic research methodology has benefits for a student such as yourself. After all, most students who take courses in research methods have no intention of becoming researchers. Understandably, such students may wonder how studying research benefits them.

 A background in research has at least four important benefits. First, knowledge about research methods allows people to understand research that is relevant to their professions. Many professionals who deal with people—not only psychologists but also those in social work, nursing, education, management, medicine, public relations, coaching, communication, advertising, and the ministry—must keep up with advances in their fields. For example, people who become counselors and therapists are obligated to stay abreast of the research literature that deals with therapy and related topics. Similarly, teachers need to stay informed about recent research that might help improve their teaching. In business, many decisions that executives and managers make in the workplace must be based on the outcomes of research studies. However, most of this information is published in professional research journals, and, as you may have learned from experience, journal articles can be nearly incomprehensible unless the reader knows something about research methodology and statistics. Thus, a background in research provides you with knowledge and skills that may be useful in professional life.

 Related to this outcome is a second: A knowledge of research methodology makes one a more intelligent and effective "research consumer" in everyday life. Increasingly, we are asked to make everyday decisions on the basis of scientific research findings. When we try to decide which new car to buy, how much we should exercise, which weight-loss program to select, whether to enter our children in public versus private schools, whether to get a flu shot, or whether we should follow the latest fad to improve our happiness or prolong our life, we are often confronted with research findings that argue one way or the other. Similarly, when people serve on juries, they often must consider scientific evidence presented by experts. Unfortunately, studies show that most adults do not understand the scientific process well enough to weigh such evidence

intelligently and fairly. Less than half of American adults in a random nationwide survey understood the most basic requirement of a good experimental design, and only a third could explain "what it means to study something scientifically" (National Science Board, 2002). Without such knowledge, people are unprepared to spot shoddy studies, questionable statistics, and unjustified conclusions in the research they read or hear about. People who have a basic knowledge of research design and analyses are in a better position to evaluate the scientific evidence they encounter in everyday life than those without such knowledge.

A third outcome of research training involves the development of critical thinking. Scientists are a critical lot, always asking questions, considering alternative explanations, insisting on hard evidence, refining their methods, and critiquing their own and others' conclusions. Many people have found that a critical, scientific approach to solving problems is useful in their everyday lives.

Finally, a fourth benefit of learning about and becoming involved in research is that it helps one become an authority, not only on research methodology but also on particular topics. In the process of reading about previous studies, wrestling with issues involving research strategy, collecting data, and interpreting the results, researchers grow increasingly familiar with their topics. For this reason, faculty members at many colleges and universities urge their students to become involved in research, such as class projects, independent research projects, or a faculty member's research. This is also one reason why many colleges and universities insist that their faculty maintain ongoing research programs. By remaining active as researchers, professors engage in an ongoing learning process that keeps them at the forefront of their fields.

Many years ago, science fiction writer H. G. Wells predicted: "Statistical thinking will one day be as necessary for efficient citizenship as the ability to read and write." Although we are not at the point where the ability to think like a scientist and statistician is as important as reading or writing, knowledge of research methods and statistics is becoming increasingly important for successful living.

THE SCIENTIFIC APPROACH

I noted earlier that most people have greater difficulty thinking of psychology and other behavioral sciences as science than regarding chemistry, biology, physics, or astronomy as science. In part, this is because many people misunderstand what science is. Most people appreciate that scientific knowledge is somehow special, but they judge whether a discipline is scientific on the basis of the topics it studies. Research involving molecules, chromosomes, and sunspots seems more scientific to most people than research involving emotions, memories, or social interactions, for example.

Whether an area of study is scientific has little to do with the topics it studies, however. Rather, science is defined in terms of the approaches used to study the topic. Specifically, three criteria must be met for an investigation to be considered scientific: systematic empiricism, public verification, and solvability (Stanovich, 1996).

Systematic Empiricism

Empiricism refers to the practice of relying on observation to draw conclusions about the world. The story is told about two scientists who saw a flock of sheep standing in a field. Gesturing toward the sheep, one scientist said, "Look, all of those sheep have just been shorn." The other scientist narrowed his eyes in thought, then replied, "Well, on the side facing us anyway." Scientists insist that conclusions be based on what can be objectively observed and not on assumptions, hunches, unfounded beliefs, or the products of people's imaginations. Although most people today would agree that the best way to find out about something is to observe it directly, this was not always the case. Until the late sixteenth century, experts relied more heavily on reason, intuition, and religious doctrine than on observation to answer questions.

But observation alone does not make something a science. After all, everyone draws conclusions about human nature from observing people in everyday life. Scientific observation is *systematic*. Scientists structure their observations in systematic ways so that they can use them to draw valid conclusions about the nature of the world. For example,

a behavioral researcher who is interested in the effects of exercise on stress is not likely simply to chat with people who exercise about how much stress they feel. Rather, the researcher would design a carefully controlled study in which people are assigned randomly to different exercise programs, and then measure their stress using reliable and valid techniques. Data obtained through systematic empiricism allow researchers to draw much more confident conclusions than they can draw from casual observation alone.

Public Verification

The second criterion for scientific investigation is that the methods and results be available for **public verification**. In other words, research must be conducted in such a way that the findings of one researcher can be observed, replicated, and verified by others.

There are two reasons for this. First, the requirement of public verification ensures that the phenomena scientists study are real and observable and not one person's fabrications. Scientists disregard claims that cannot be verified by others. For example, a person's claim that he or she was kidnapped by Bigfoot makes interesting reading, but it is not scientific if it cannot be verified.

Second, public verification makes science self-correcting. When research is open to public scrutiny, errors in methodology and interpretation can be discovered and corrected by other researchers. The findings obtained from scientific research are not always correct, but the requirement of public verification increases the likelihood that errors and incorrect conclusions will be detected and corrected.

Public verification requires that researchers report their methods and their findings to the scientific community, usually in the form of journal articles or presentations of papers at professional meetings. In this way, the methods, results, and conclusions of a study can be examined and possibly challenged by others. As long as researchers report their methods in detail, other researchers can attempt to repeat, or replicate, the research. Replication not only catches errors but also allows researchers to build on and extend the work of others.

Solvable Problems

The third criterion for scientific investigation is that science deals only with *solvable problems*. Scientists can investigate only those questions that are answerable given current knowledge and research techniques.

This criterion means that many questions fall outside the realm of scientific investigation. For example, the question "Are there angels?" is not scientific: No one has yet devised a way of studying angels that is empirical, systematic, and publicly verifiable. This does not necessarily imply that angels do not exist or that the question is unimportant. It simply means that this question is beyond the scope of scientific investigation.

In Depth
Science and Pseudoscience

The results of scientific investigations are not always correct, but because researchers abide by the criteria of systematic empiricism, public verification, and solvable problems, scientific findings are the most trustworthy source of knowledge that we have. Unfortunately, not all research findings that appear to be scientific actually are, but people sometimes have trouble telling the difference. The term **pseudoscience** refers to claims of evidence that masquerade as science but in fact violate the basic criteria of scientific investigation that we just discussed (Radner & Radner, 1982).

NONSYSTEMATIC AND NONEMPIRICAL EVIDENCE

As we have seen, scientists rely on systematic observation. Pseudoscientific evidence, however, is often not based on observation, and when it is, the data are not collected in a systematic fashion that allows valid conclusions to be drawn. Instead, the evidence is based on myths, untested beliefs, anecdotes about people's personal experiences, the opinions of self-proclaimed "experts," or the results of poorly designed studies that do not meet minimum scientific standards. For example, von Daniken (1970) used biblical references to "chariots of fire" in *Chariots of the Gods?* as evidence for ancient spacecrafts. However, because biblical evidence of past events is neither systematic nor verifiable, it cannot be considered scientific. This is not to say that such evidence is necessarily inaccurate; it is simply not permissible in scientific investigation because its veracity cannot be determined conclusively. Similarly, pseudoscientists often rely on people's beliefs rather than on observation or accepted scientific fact to bolster their arguments. Scientists wait for the empirical evidence to come in rather than basing their conclusions on what others think might be the case.

When pseudoscience does rely on observed evidence, it tends to use data that are biased to support its case. For example, those who believe that people can see the future point to specific episodes in which people seemed to know in advance that something was going to happen. A popular tabloid once invited its readers to send in their predictions of what would happen during the next year. When the 1,500 submissions were opened a year later, one contestant was correct in all five of her predictions. The tabloid called this a "stunning display of psychic ability." Was it? Isn't it just as likely that, out of 1,500 entries, one person would, just by chance, make correct predictions? Scientific logic requires that the misses be considered evidence along with the hits. Pseudoscientific logic, on the other hand, is satisfied with a single (perhaps random) occurrence. Unlike the extrasensory perception (ESP) survey conducted by the tabloid, scientific studies of ESP test whether people can predict future events at better than chance levels.

NO PUBLIC VERIFICATION

Much pseudoscience is based on individuals' reports of what they have experienced—reports that are essentially unverifiable. If Mr. Smith claims to have been abducted by aliens, how do we know whether he is telling the truth? If Ms. Brown says she "knew" beforehand that her uncle had been hurt in an accident, who's to refute her? Of course, Mr. Smith and Ms. Brown might be telling the truth. On the other hand, they might be playing a prank, mentally disturbed, trying to cash in on the publicity, or sincerely confused. Regardless, because their claims are unverifiable, they cannot be used as scientific evidence.

Furthermore, when pseudoscientific claims appear to be based on research studies, one usually finds that the research was not published in scientific journals. In fact, it is often hard to find a report of the study anywhere, and when a report can be located, on the Web, for example, it has usually not been peer-reviewed by other scientists. You should be very suspicious of the results of any research that has not been submitted to other experts for review.

UNSOLVABLE QUESTIONS AND IRREFUTABLE HYPOTHESES

Pseudoscientific beliefs are often stated in such a way that they can never be tested. Those who believe in ESP, for example, sometimes argue that ESP cannot be tested empirically because the conditions necessary for the occurrence of ESP are compromised under controlled laboratory conditions. Similarly, some advocates of creationism claim that the Earth is much younger than it appears from geological evidence. When the Earth was created in the relatively recent past, they argue, God put fossils and geological formations in the rocks that only make it appear to be millions of years old. In both these examples, the claims are untestable and, thus, pseudoscientific.

THE SCIENTIST'S TWO JOBS: DETECTING AND EXPLAINING PHENOMENA

Scientists are in the business of doing two distinct things (Haig, 2002; Herschel, 1987; Proctor & Capaldi, 2001). First, they are in the business of discovering and documenting new phenomena, patterns, and relationships. Historically, analyses of the scientific method have neglected this crucial aspect of scientific investigation. Most descriptions of how scientists go about their work have assumed that all research involves testing theoretical explanations of phenomena.

Many philosophers and scientists now question this narrow view of science. In many instances, it is not reasonable for a researcher to propose a hypothesis before conducting a study because no viable theory yet exists and the researcher does not have enough information about the phenomenon to develop one (Kerr, 1998). Being forced to test hypotheses prematurely—before a coherent, viable theory exists—may lead to poorly conceived studies that test half-baked ideas. In the early stages of investigating a particular phenomenon, it may be better to design studies to detect and describe patterns and relationships before testing hypotheses about them. After all, without identifying and describing phenomena that need to be understood, neither theory-building nor future research can proceed in an efficient manner. Typically, research questions evolve from vague and poorly structured ideas to a point at which formal theories may be offered. Conducting research in the "context of discovery" (Herschel, 1987) allows researchers to collect data that describe phenomena, uncover patterns, and identify questions that need to be addressed.

The scientist's second job is to develop and evaluate explanations of the phenomena that they see. Once they identify phenomena to be explained and have collected sufficient information about them, they develop theories to explain the patterns they observe and then conduct research to test those theories. When you hear the word *theory*, you probably think of theories such as Darwin's theory of evolution or Einstein's theory of relativity. However, nothing in the concept of theory requires that it be as grand or all-encompassing as evolution or relativity. Most theories, whether in psychology or in other sciences, are much less ambitious, attempting to explain only a small and circumscribed range of phenomena.

A **theory** is a set of propositions that attempts to explain the relationships among a set of concepts. For example, Fiedler's (1967) contingency theory of leadership specifies the conditions in which certain kinds of leaders will be more effective in group settings. Some leaders are predominantly task-oriented; they keep the group focused on its purpose, discourage socializing, and demand that the members participate. Other leaders are predominantly relationship-oriented; these leaders are concerned primarily with fostering positive relations among group members and with group satisfaction. The contingency theory proposes three factors that determine whether a task-oriented or relationship-oriented leader will be more effective in a particular situation: the quality of the relationship between the leader and group members, the degree to which the group's task is structured, and the leader's power within the group. In fact, the theory specifies quite precisely the conditions under which certain leaders are more effective than others. The contingency theory of leadership fits our definition of a theory because it attempts to explain the relationships among a set of concepts (the concepts of leadership effectiveness, task versus interpersonal leaders, leader–member relations, task structure, and leader power).

Occasionally, people use the word *theory* in everyday language to refer to hunches or unsubstantiated ideas. For example, in the debate on whether to teach creationism or intelligent design as an alternative to evolution in public schools, creationists dismiss evolution because it's "only a theory." This use of the term *theory* is very misleading. Scientific theories are not wild guesses or unsupported hunches. On the contrary, theories are accepted as valid only to the extent that they are supported by empirical findings. Science insists that theories be consistent with the facts as they are currently known. Theories that are not supported by data are usually discarded or replaced by other theories.

Theory construction is a creative exercise, and ideas for theories can come from almost anywhere. Sometimes, researchers immerse themselves in the research literature and purposefully work toward developing a theory. In other instances, researchers construct theories to explain patterns they observe in data they have collected. Other theories have been developed on the basis of case studies or everyday observation. Sometimes, a scientist does not agree with another researcher's explanation of a phenomenon and sets out to develop a better theory to explain it. At other times, a scientist may get a fully developed theoretical insight at a time when he or she is not even working on research. Researchers are not constrained in terms of where they get their theoretical ideas, and there is no single way to develop a theory.

However, even though ideas for theories can come from anywhere, a good theory must meet several criteria (Fiske, 2004). Specifically, a good theory in psychology:

- proposes causal relationships, explaining how one or more variables cause or lead to particular cognitive, emotional, behavioral, or physiological responses;
- is coherent in the sense of being clear, straightforward, logical, and consistent;
- is parsimonious, using as few concepts and processes as possible to explain the target phenomenon;
- generates testable hypotheses that are able to be disconfirmed through research;
- stimulates other researchers to conduct research to test the theory; and
- solves an existing theoretical question.

Closely related to theories are models. In fact, researchers occasionally use the terms *theory* and *model* interchangeably, but we can make a distinction between them. Whereas a theory specifies both how and why concepts are related, a **model** describes only how they are related. We may have a model that describes how variables are related (such as specifying that X leads to Y, which then leads to Z) without having a theory that explains why these effects occur. Put differently, a model tries to *describe* the hypothesized relationships among variables, whereas a theory tries to *explain* those relationships.

For example, the assortative mating model postulates that people tend to select mates who are similar to themselves. This model has received overwhelming support from numerous research studies showing that for nearly every variable that has been examined—such as age, ethnicity, race, emotional stability, agreeableness, conscientiousness, and physical attractiveness—people tend to pair up with others who resemble them (Botwin, Buss, & Shackelford, 1997; Little, Burt, & Perrett, 2006). However, this model does not explain *why* assortative mating occurs. Various theories have been proposed to explain this effect. For example, one theory suggests that people tend to form relationships with people who live close to them, and we tend to live near those who are similar to us, and another theory proposes that interactions with

Source: SCIENCECARTOONSPLUS.COM © 2000 by Sidney Harris.

people who are similar to us are generally more rewarding and less conflicted than those with people who are dissimilar.

RESEARCH HYPOTHESES

On the whole, scientists are a skeptical bunch, and they are not inclined to accept theories and models that have not been supported by empirical research. Thus, a great deal of their time is spent testing theories and models to determine their usefulness in explaining and predicting behavior. Although theoretical ideas may come from anywhere, scientists are very constrained in the procedures they use to test their theories.

People can usually find reasons for almost anything *after* it happens. In fact, we sometimes find it equally easy to explain completely opposite occurrences. Consider Jim and Marie, a married couple I know. If I hear in five years that Jim and Marie are happily married, I'll be able to look back and find clear-cut reasons why their relationship worked out

so well. If, on the other hand, I learn in five years that they're getting divorced, I'll undoubtedly be able to recall indications that all was not well even from the beginning. As the saying goes, hindsight is 20/20. Nearly everything makes sense after it happens.

The ease with which we can retrospectively explain even opposite occurrences leads scientists to be skeptical of **post hoc explanations**—explanations that are made after the fact. In light of this, a theory's ability to explain occurrences in a post hoc fashion provides little evidence of its accuracy or usefulness. If scientists have no preconceptions about what should happen in a study, they can often explain whatever pattern of results they obtain in a post hoc fashion (Kerr, 1998). Of course, if a theory can't explain a particular finding, we can conclude that the theory is weak, but researchers can often explain findings post hoc that they would not have predicted in advance of conducting the study.

More informative is the degree to which a theory can successfully *predict* what will happen.

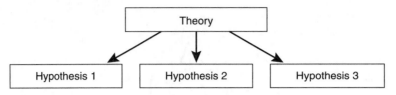

Deduction. When deduction is used, researchers start with a theory or model and then derive testable hypotheses from it. Usually, several hypotheses can be deduced form a particular theory.

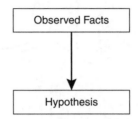

Induction. When induction is used, researchers develop hypotheses from observed facts, including previous research findings.

FIGURE 1.1   Developing Hypotheses through Deduction and Induction

To provide a convincing test of a theory, researchers make specific research hypotheses **a priori**—before collecting the data. By making specific predictions about what will occur in a study, researchers avoid the pitfalls associated with purely post hoc explanations. Theories that accurately predict what will happen in a research study are regarded much more positively than those that can only explain the findings afterward.

The process of testing theories is an indirect one. Theories themselves are not tested directly. The propositions in a theory are usually too broad and complex to be tested directly in a particular study. Rather, when researchers set about to test a theory, they do so indirectly by testing one or more hypotheses that are derived from the theory. (See Figure 1.1.)

Deriving hypotheses from a theory involves **deduction**, a process of reasoning from a general proposition (the theory) to specific implications of that proposition (the hypotheses). When deriving a hypothesis, the researcher asks, If the theory is true, what would we expect to observe? For example, one hypothesis that can be derived (or deduced) from the contingency model of leadership is that relationship-oriented leaders will be more effective when the group's task is moderately structured

rather than unstructured. If we do an experiment to test the validity of this hypothesis, we are testing part, but only part, of the contingency theory of leadership.

You can think of a **hypothesis** as an if–then statement of the general form, "If *a*, then *b*." Based on the theory, the researcher hypothesizes that *if* certain conditions occur, *then* certain consequences should follow. For example, a researcher studying the contingency model of leadership might deduce a hypothesis from the theory that says: If the group's task is unstructured, then a relationship-oriented leader will be more effective than a task-oriented leader. Although not all hypotheses are actually expressed in this manner, virtually all hypotheses are reducible to an if–then statement.

Not all hypotheses are derived deductively from theory. Often, scientists arrive at hypotheses through **induction**—abstracting a hypothesis from a collection of facts. Hypotheses that are based on previously observed patterns of results are sometimes called **empirical generalizations**. Having seen that certain variables repeatedly relate to certain other variables in a particular way, we can hypothesize that such patterns will occur in the future. In the case of an empirical generalization, we often have no theory to explain why the variables are related but nonetheless can make predictions about them.

Whether derived deductively from a theory or inductively from observed facts, hypotheses must be formulated precisely in order to be testable. Specifically, hypotheses must be stated in such a way that leaves them open to the possibility of being falsified by the data that we collect. A hypothesis is of little use unless it has the potential to be found false (Popper, 1959). In fact, some philosophers have suggested that empirical **falsification** is the central hallmark of science—the characteristic that distinguishes science from other ways of seeking knowledge, such as philosophical argument, personal experience, casual observation, or religious insight. In fact, one loose definition of science is that science is "knowledge about the universe on the basis of explanatory principles subject to the possibility of empirical falsification" (Ayala & Black, 1993, p. 230).

One criticism of Freud's psychoanalytic theory, for example, is that many of Freud's hypotheses are difficult to falsify. Although psychoanalytic theory can explain virtually any behavior after it has occurred, researchers have found it difficult to derive specific falsifiable hypotheses from the theory that predict how people will behave under certain circumstances. For example, Freud's theory relies heavily on the concept of repression—the idea that people push anxiety-producing thoughts into their unconscious—but such a claim is exceptionally difficult to falsify. According to the theory itself, anything that people can report to a researcher is obviously not unconscious, and anything that is unconscious cannot be reported. So how can the hypothesis that people repress undesirable thoughts and urges ever be falsified? Because parts of the theory do not easily generate falsifiable hypotheses, most behavioral scientists regard aspects of psychoanalytic theory as inherently nonscientific. Ideas that cannot be tested, with the possibility of falsification, may be interesting and even true, but they are not scientific.

The amount of support for a theory or hypothesis depends not only on the number of times it has been supported by research but also on the stringency of the tests it has survived. Some studies provide more convincing support for a theory than other studies do

(Ayala & Black, 1993; Stanovich, 1996). Not surprisingly, seasoned researchers try to design studies that will provide the strongest, most stringent tests of their hypotheses. The findings of tightly conceptualized and well-designed studies are simply more convincing than the findings of poorly conceptualized and weakly designed ones. In addition, the greater the variety of the methods and measures that are used to test a theory in various experiments, the more confidence we can have in their accumulated findings. Thus, researchers often aim for **methodological pluralism**—using many different methods and designs—as they test theories. Throughout this book, you will learn how to design rigorous, informative studies using a wide array of research approaches.

Some of the most compelling evidence in science is obtained from studies that directly pit the predictions of one theory against the predictions of another theory. Rather than simply testing whether the predictions of a particular theory are or are not supported, researchers often design studies to test simultaneously the opposing predictions of two theories. Such studies are designed so that, depending on how the results turn out, the data will confirm one of the theories while disconfirming the other. This head-to-head approach to research is sometimes called the **strategy of strong inference** because the findings of such studies allow researchers to draw stronger conclusions about the relative merits of competing theories than do studies that test a single theory (Platt, 1964).

An example of the strategy of strong inference comes from research on self-evaluation. For many years, researchers have disagreed regarding the primary motive that affects people's perceptions and evaluations of themselves: self-enhancement (the motive to evaluate oneself favorably), self-assessment (the motive to see oneself accurately), and self-verification (the motive to maintain one's existing self-image). And, over the years, a certain amount of empirical support has been obtained for each of these motives and for the theories on which they are based. Sedikides (1993) conducted six experiments that placed each of these theories in direct opposition with one another. In these studies, participants indicated the kinds of questions they would ask themselves if they wanted to know whether they possessed a particular characteristic (such as whether they were open-minded, greedy, or selfish). Participants could choose questions that varied according to the degree to which the question would lead to information about themselves that was (1) favorable (reflecting a self-enhancement motive); (2) accurate (reflecting a desire for accurate self-assessment); or (3) consistent with their current self-views (reflecting a motive for self-verification). Results of the six studies provided overwhelming support for the precedence of the self-enhancement motive. When given the choice, people tend to ask themselves questions that allow them to evaluate themselves positively rather than choosing questions that either support how they already perceive themselves or that lead to accurate self-knowledge. By using the strategy of strong inference, Sedikides was able to provide a stronger test of these three theories than would have been obtained from research that focused on any one of them alone.

CONCEPTUAL AND OPERATIONAL DEFINITIONS

For a hypothesis to be falsifiable, the terms used in the hypothesis must be clearly defined. In everyday language, we usually don't worry about how precisely we define the terms we use. If I tell you that the baby is hungry, you understand what I mean without my specifying the criteria I'm using to conclude that the baby is, indeed, hungry. You are unlikely to ask detailed questions about what I mean exactly by *baby* or *hunger;* you understand well enough for practical purposes.

More precision is required of the definitions we use in research, however. If the terms used in research are not defined precisely, we may be unable to determine whether the hypothesis is supported. Suppose that we are interested in studying the effects of hunger on attention in infants. Our hypothesis is that babies' ability to pay attention decreases as they become more hungry. We can study this topic only if we define clearly what we mean by *hunger* and *attention*. Without clear definitions, we won't know whether the hypothesis has been supported.

Researchers use two kinds of definitions in their work. On one hand, they use **conceptual definitions**. A conceptual definition is more or less like the definition we might find in a dictionary. For example, we might define hunger as *having a desire for food*. Although conceptual definitions are necessary, they are seldom specific enough for research purposes.

A second way of defining a concept is by an **operational definition**. An operational definition defines a concept by specifying precisely how the concept is measured or induced in a particular study. For example, we could operationally define hunger in our study as *being deprived of food for 12 hours*. An operational definition converts an abstract conceptual definition into concrete, situation-specific terms.

There are potentially many operational definitions of a single construct. For example, we could operationally define hunger in terms of hours of food deprivation. Or we could define hunger in terms of responses to the question: How hungry are you at this moment? Consider a scale composed of the following responses: (1) *not at all*, (2) *slightly*, (3) *moderately*, and (4) *very*. We could classify people as hungry if they answered *moderately* or *very* on this scale.

One study of the incidence of hunger in the United States defined hungry people as those who were eligible for food stamps but who didn't get them. This particular operational definition is a poor one, however. Many people with low income living in a farming area would be classified as hungry, no matter how much food they raised on their own.

Operational definitions are essential so that researchers can replicate one another's studies. Without knowing precisely how hunger was induced or measured in a particular study, other researchers have no way of replicating the study in precisely the same manner that it was conducted originally. For example, if I merely tell you that I measured "hunger" in a study, you would have no idea what I actually did. If I tell you my *operational definition*, however—that I instructed parents not to feed their infants for six hours before the study—you not only know what I did but also can replicate my procedure exactly. In addition, using operational definitions forces researchers to clarify their concepts precisely (Underwood, 1957), thereby allowing scientists to communicate clearly and unambiguously.

Developing Your Research Skills
Getting Ideas for Research

The first and perhaps most important step in the research process is to get a good research idea. Researchers get their ideas from almost everywhere. Sometimes the ideas come easily, but at other times they emerge slowly. Some suggestions of ways to stimulate ideas for research follow (see also McGuire, 1997).

Read some research articles on a topic that interests you. Be on the lookout for unanswered questions and conflicting findings. Often, the authors of research articles offer their personal suggestions for future research.

Deduce hypotheses from an existing theory. Read about a theory and ask yourself, If this theory is true, what are some implications for behavior, thought, or emotion? State your hypotheses in an if–then fashion. Traditionally, this has been the most common way for behavioral researchers to develop ideas for research.

Apply an old theory to a new phenomenon. Often, a theory that was developed originally to explain one kind of behavior can be applied to an entirely different topic.

Perform an intensive case study of a particular animal, person, group, or event. Such case studies invariably raise interesting questions about behavior. For example, Irving Janis's study of the Kennedy administration's ill-fated Bay of Pigs invasion in 1962 led to his theory of groupthink (Janis, 1982). Similarly, when trying to solve an applied problem, researchers often talk to people who are personally familiar with the problem.

Reverse the direction of causality for a commonsense hypothesis. Think of some behavioral principle that you take for granted. Then reverse the direction of causality to see whether you construct a plausible new hypothesis. For example, most people think that people daydream when they are bored. Is it possible that people begin to feel bored when they start to daydream?

Break a process down into its subcomponents. What are the steps involved in learning to ride a bicycle? Deciding to end a romantic relationship? Choosing a career? Identifying a sound?

Think about variables that might mediate a known cause-and-effect relationship. Behavioral researchers are interested in knowing more than that a particular variable affects a particular behavior; they want also to understand the psychological processes that mediate the connection between the cause and the effect. For example, we know that people are more likely to be attracted to others who are similar to them, but why? What mediating variables are involved?

Analyze a puzzling behavioral phenomenon in terms of its functions. Look around at all the seemingly incomprehensible things people and other animals do. Instead of studying, John got drunk the night before the exam. Gwen continues to date a guy who always treats her like dirt. The family dog keeps running into the street even though he's punished each time he does. Why do these behaviors occur? What functions might they serve?

Imagine what would happen if a particular factor were reduced to zero in a given situation. What if nobody ever cared what other people thought of them? What if there were no leaders? What if people had no leisure time? What if people did not know that they will someday die? Such questions often raise provocative insights and questions about behavior.

Once you have a few possible ideas, critically evaluate them to see whether they are worth pursuing. Four major questions will help you to decide.

Does the idea have the potential to advance our understanding of behavior? Assuming that the study is conducted and the expected patterns of results are obtained, will we have learned something new about behavior?

Is the knowledge that may be gained potentially important? A study can be important in several ways: (a) It tests hypotheses derived from a theory (thereby providing evidence for or against the theory);

(continued)

(continued)

(b) it identifies a qualification to a previously demonstrated finding; (c) it demonstrates a weakness in a previously used research method or technique; (d) it documents the effectiveness of procedures for modifying a behavioral problem (such as in counseling, education, or industry, for example); (e) it demonstrates the existence of a phenomenon or effect that had not been previously recognized. Rarely does a single study provide earthshaking information that revolutionizes the field, so don't expect too much. Ask yourself whether this idea is likely to provide information that other behavioral researchers or practitioners (such as practicing psychologists) would find interesting or useful.

Do you find the idea interesting? No matter how important an idea might be, it is difficult to do research that one finds boring. This doesn't mean that you have to be fascinated by the topic, but if you really don't care about the area and aren't interested in the answer to the research question, consider getting a different topic.

Is the idea researchable? Can the idea be investigated according to the basic criteria and standards of science? Also, many research ideas are not viable because they are ethically questionable or because they require resources that the researcher cannot possibly obtain.

PROOF, DISPROOF, AND SCIENTIFIC PROGRESS

As we have seen, the validity of scientific theories can be assessed only indirectly by testing hypotheses. One consequence of this approach to testing theories is that no theory can be proved or disproved by the data from research. In fact, scientists virtually never speak of *proving* a theory. Instead, they often talk of theories being *confirmed* or *supported* by their research findings.

The claim that theories cannot be proved may strike you as bizarre; what's the use of testing theories if we can't actually prove or disprove them anyway? Before answering this question, let me explain why theories cannot be proved or disproved.

The Logical Impossibility of Proof

Theories cannot be proved because obtaining empirical support for a hypothesis does not necessarily mean that the theory from which the hypothesis was derived is true. For example, imagine that we want to test Theory A. To do so, we logically deduce an implication of the theory that we'll call Hypothesis H. (We could state this implication as an if–then statement: If Theory A is true, then Hypothesis H is true.) We then collect data to see whether Hypothesis H is, in fact, correct. If we find that Hypothesis H is supported by the data, can we conclude that Theory A is true? The answer is no. Hypothesis H may be supported even if the theory is completely wrong. In logical terminology, it is invalid to prove the antecedent of an argument (the theory) by affirming the consequent (the hypothesis).

To show that this is true, imagine that we are detectives trying to solve a murder that occurred at a large party. In essence, we're developing and testing "theories" about the identity of the murderer. I propose the theory that Jake is the murderer. One hypothesis that can be deduced from this theory is that, if Jake is the murderer, then Jake must have been at the party. (Remember the if–then nature of hypotheses.) We check on Jake's whereabouts on the night in question, and, sure enough, he was at the party! Given that my hypothesis is supported, would you conclude that the fact that Jake was at the party proves my theory that Jake is, in fact, the murderer? Of course not. Why not? Because we can't logically prove a theory (Jake was the murderer) by affirming hypotheses that are derived from it (Jake must have been at the party).

This state of affairs is one reason that we sometimes find that several theories appear to do an equally good job of explaining a particular behavior. Hypotheses derived from each of the theories have been empirically supported in research studies, yet this support does not *prove* that any one of the theories is better than the others. For example, during the 1970s, a great deal of research was conducted to test explanations of attitude change provided by cognitive dissonance theory versus self-perception theory. By and large, researchers found that the data supported the hypotheses derived from both theories. Yet, for the reasons we discussed previously, this support did not prove either theory.

The Practical Impossibility of Disproof

Unlike proof, disproof is a *logically* valid operation. If I deduce Hypothesis H from Theory A, then find that Hypothesis H is not supported by the data, Theory A must be false by logical inference. Imagine again that we hypothesize that, if Jake is the murderer, then Jake must have been at the party. If our research subsequently shows that Jake was not at the party, our theory that Jake is the murderer is logically disconfirmed.

However, testing hypotheses in real-world research involves a number of practical difficulties that may lead a hypothesis to be disconfirmed by the data even when the theory is true. Failing to find empirical support for a hypothesis can be due to a number of factors other than the fact that the theory is incorrect. For example, using poor measuring techniques may result in apparent disconfirmation of a hypothesis, even though the theory is actually valid. (Maybe Jake slipped into the party, undetected, for only long enough to commit the murder.) Similarly, obtaining an inappropriate or biased sample of participants, failing to account for or control extraneous variables, and using improper research designs or statistical analyses can produce negative findings. Much of this book focuses on ways to eliminate problems that hamper researchers' ability to produce strong, convincing evidence that would allow them to disconfirm their hypotheses.

Because there are many ways in which a research study can go wrong, the failure of a study to support a particular hypothesis seldom, if ever, means the death of a theory (Hempel, 1966). With so many possible reasons why a particular study might have failed to support a theory, researchers typically do not abandon a theory after only a few disconfirmations (particularly if it is *their* theory).

This is also the reason that scientific journals are reluctant to publish the results of studies that fail to support a theory. You might think that results showing that certain variables are *not* related to behavior—so-called **null findings**—would provide important information. After all, if we predict that certain psychological variables are related, but our data show that they are not, haven't we learned something important?

The answer is "not necessarily" because, as we have seen, data may fail to support our research hypotheses for reasons that have nothing to do with the validity of a particular hypothesis. As a result, null findings are usually uninformative regarding the hypothesis being tested. Was the hypothesis disconfirmed, or did we simply design a lousy study? Because we can never know for certain, journals generally will not publish studies that fail to obtain effects. The failure to confirm one's research hypotheses can occur for many reasons other than the invalidity of the theory.

One drawback of this policy, however, is that researchers may design studies to test a theory, unaware of the fact that the theory has already been disconfirmed in dozens of earlier studies. However, because of the difficulties in interpreting null findings (and journals' reluctance to publish them), none of those previous studies were published. The failure to publish studies that obtain null findings is often called the **file-drawer problem** because of the possibility that researchers' files contain many unpublished studies that failed to support a particular predicted finding. Many scientists have expressed the need for ways to disseminate information about unsuccessful studies.

If Not Proof or Disproof, Then What?

If proof is logically impossible and disproof is pragmatically impossible, how does science advance? How do we ever decide which theories are good ones and which are not? This question has provoked considerable interest among both philosophers and scientists (Feyerabend, 1965; Kuhn, 1962; Popper, 1959).

In practice, the merit of theories is judged, not on the basis of a single research study but instead on the accumulated evidence of several studies. Although any particular piece of research that fails to support a theory may be disregarded because it might be poorly designed, the failure to obtain support in many studies provides evidence that the theory has problems. Similarly, a theory whose hypotheses are repeatedly corroborated by research is considered supported by the data.

The Scientific Filter

Another way to think about scientific progress is in terms of a series of filters by which science separates valid from invalid ideas (Bauer, 1992). Imagine a giant funnel that contains four filters through which ideas may pass, each with successively smaller holes than the one before, as in Figure 1.2.

At the top of the funnel is a hopper that contains all of the ideas, beliefs, and hunches held by people at any particular period of time. Some of these notions are reasonable, well-informed, and potentially useful, but the vast majority of them are incorrect, if not preposterous. Imagine, for example, convening a randomly selected group of people from your hometown and asking them to speculate about

the functions of dreaming. You would get a very wide array of ideas of varying degrees of reasonableness. Science begins with this unfiltered mess of untested ideas, which it then passes through a series of knowledge filters (Bauer, 1992).

Only a fraction of all possible ideas in the hopper would be seriously considered by scientists. By virtue of their education and training, scientists will immediately disregard certain ideas as untenable because they are clearly ridiculous or inconsistent with what is already known. Thus, a large number of potential ideas are immediately filtered out of consideration. Furthermore, researchers' concerns with their professional reputations and their need to obtain funding for their research will limit the approaches they will even consider investigating. The ideas that pass through Filter 1 are not necessarily valid, but they are not obviously wrong and probably not blatant nonsense.

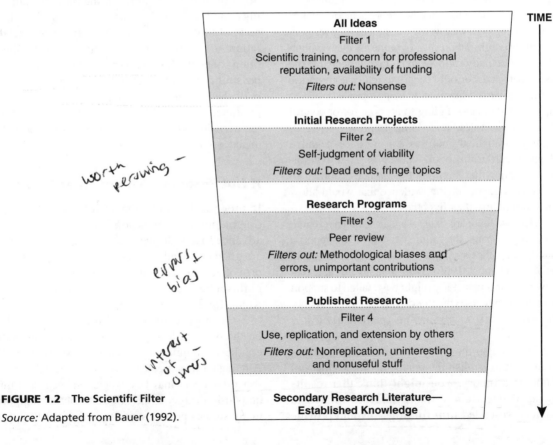

FIGURE 1.2 The Scientific Filter
Source: Adapted from Bauer (1992).

A great deal of research is focused on the ideas that have passed through Filter 1, ideas that are plausible but not always widely accepted by other scientists. Researchers may recognize that some of these ideas are long shots, yet they pursue their hunches to see where they lead. Many of these research projects die quickly when the data fail to support them, but others seem to show some promise. If the researcher surmises that a line of research may ultimately lead to interesting and important findings (and to scientific publication), he or she may decide to pursue it. But if not, the idea may be dropped, never making it to the research literature. Each scientist serves as his or her own filter at this stage (Filter 2) as he or she decides whether a particular idea is worth pursuing.

As researchers pursue a potentially viable research question, simply knowing that a successful, published study must eventually pass the methodological standards of their peers provides another filter on the ideas that they address and the approaches they use to study them. Then, should the results of a particular line of research appear to make a contribution to knowledge, the research will be subjected directly to the scrutiny of reviewers and editors who must decide whether it should be published. Filter 3 screens out research that is not methodologically sound, as well as findings that are not judged to be sufficiently important to the scientific community. Filter 3 will not eliminate all flawed or useless research, but a great deal of error, bias, and pablum will be filtered out at this stage through the process of peer review.

Research that is published in scientific, peer-reviewed journals has passed the minimum standards of scientific acceptability, but that does not necessarily mean that it is correct or that it will have an impact on the field. Other researchers may try to replicate or build on a piece of research and thereby provide additional evidence that either supports or refutes it. Studies found to be lacking in some way are caught by Filter 4, as are ideas and results that do not attract the interest of other scientists. Only research that is cited and used by other researchers and that continues to pass the test of time becomes part of the established scientific literature—those things that most experts in the field accept.

Although you may be tempted to regard any knowledge that makes it through all four filters as "true," most scientists deny that they are uncovering the truth about the world and rarely talk about their findings as being "true." Of course, the empirical findings of a specific study are true in some limited sense, but there will never be the point at which a scientist decides that he or she knows the truth, the whole truth, and nothing but the truth. Not only may any particular theory or finding be refuted by future research, but also most scientists see their job as developing, testing, and refining theories and models that provide a viable understanding of how the world works rather than discovering preexisting truth. As Powell (1962) put it:

> The scientist, in attempting to explain a natural phenomenon, does not look for some underlying true phenomenon but tries to invent a hypothesis or model whose behavior will be as close as possible to that of the observed natural phenomenon. As his techniques of observation improve, and he realizes that the natural phenomenon is more complex than he originally thought, he has to discard his first hypothesis and replace it with another, more sophisticated one, which may be said to be "truer" than the first, since it resembles the observed facts more closely. (pp. 122–123)

No intellectual system of understanding based on words or mathematical equations can ever really capture the whole truth about how the universe works. Any explanation, conclusion, or generalization we develop is, by necessity, too limited to be completely true. All we can really do is to develop increasingly sophisticated perspectives and explanations that help us to make sense out of things the best we can and pass those perspectives and explanations through the scientific filter.

Throughout the process of scientific investigation, theory and research interact to advance science. Research is often conducted explicitly to test theoretical propositions; then the findings obtained in that research are used to further develop, elaborate, qualify, or fine-tune the theory. Then more research is conducted to test hypotheses derived from the refined theory, and the theory is further modified on the basis of new data. This process typically continues until researchers tire of the theory (usually because most of the interesting and important issues seem to have been addressed) or until a new theory, with the potential to explain the phenomenon more fully, gains support.

Science advances most rapidly when researchers work on the fringes of what is already known about a phenomenon. Not much is likely to come of devoting oneself to continuous research on topics that are already reasonably well understood. As a result, researchers tend to gravitate toward areas in which we have more questions than answers. This is one reason that researchers often talk more about what they don't know rather than what is already known (Stanovich,

1996). In fact, scientists sometimes seem uncertain and indecisive, if not downright incompetent, to the lay public. However, as McCall (1988) noted, we must realize that,

> by definition, professionals on the edge of knowledge do *not* know what causes what. Scientists, however, are privileged to be able to say so, whereas business executives, politicians, and judges, for example, sometimes make decisions in audacious ignorance while appearing certain and confident. (p. 88)

Developing Your Research Skills
Resisting Personal Biases

A central characteristic of a good scientist is to be a critical thinker with the desire and ability to evaluate carefully the quality of ideas and research designs, question interpretations of data, and consider alternative explanations of findings, and as you learn more about research methodology, you will increasingly hone your critical thinking skills. But there's a problem: People find it very easy to critically evaluate other people's ideas, research designs, and conclusions, but they find it very difficult to be equally critical of their own.

In a classic paper on biased interpretations of research evidence, Lord, Ross, and Lepper (1979) obtained a group of people who were in favor of the death penalty and another group who opposed it. Then they presented each participant with bogus scientific evidence that supported their existing attitude as well as bogus evidence that challenged it. For example, participants read about a study that supposedly showed that the murder rate went up when capital punishment was abolished in a state (supporting the deterrence function of executions) and another study showing that murder rates went down when states got rid of the death penalty (a finding against the usefulness of the death penalty). Participants were asked to evaluate the quality of the studies on which these findings were based. The results showed that participants found extensive methodological flaws in the studies whose conclusions they disagreed with, but they ignored the same problems if the evidence supported their views.

In another study, Munro (2010) told participants that they were participating in a study that involved judging the quality of scientific information. He first measured the degree to which participants believed that homosexuality might be associated with mental illness. Then he had half of each group read bogus research studies suggesting that homosexuality was associated with greater mental illness, and half of each group read five studies showing that homosexuality was not associated with greater psychological problems. (After the study was finished, participants were told that all of these research papers were fake.) Participants were then asked questions about the research and rated the degree to which they agreed with the statement "The question addressed in the studies summarized . . . is one that cannot be answered using scientific methods."

Results showed that participants whose existing views had been challenged by the bogus scientific studies were more likely to say that science simply cannot answer the question of whether homosexuality is associated with mental illness. More surprisingly, these participants were also more likely to say that science cannot answer questions about a wide range of topics, including the effects of televised violence on aggression, the effects of spanking to discipline children, and the mental and physical effects of herbal medicines. In other words, participants whose stereotypes about homosexuality had been challenged by the bogus scientific evidence were then more likely to conclude that science had nothing to offer on any question—not just on homosexuality—when compared to participants whose views about homosexuality had been supported by the research.

From the standpoint of science, these findings are rather disturbing. They show that people not only judge research that supports their beliefs less critically than research that opposes their beliefs (Lord et al., 1979), but they may also dismiss the usefulness of science entirely when it contradicts their beliefs (Munro, 2010). Although scientists genuinely try to be as unbiased as possible when evaluating evidence, they too are influenced by their own biases, and you should be vigilant for any indication that your personal beliefs and biases are influencing your scientific judgment.

STRATEGIES OF BEHAVIORAL RESEARCH

Roughly speaking, all behavioral research can be classified into four broad methodological categories that reflect descriptive, correlational, experimental, and quasi-experimental approaches. Although we will return to each of these research strategies in later chapters, it will be helpful for you to understand the differences among them from the beginning.

Descriptive Research

Descriptive research describes the behavior, thoughts, or feelings of a particular group of individuals. Perhaps the most common example of purely descriptive research is public opinion polls, which describe the attitudes or political preferences of a particular group of people. Similarly, in developmental psychology, the purpose of some studies is to describe the typical behavior of children of a certain age. Along the same lines, naturalistic observation describes the behavior of nonhuman animals in their natural habitats. In descriptive research, researchers make little effort to relate the behavior under study to other variables or to examine or explain its causes systematically. Rather, the purpose is, as the term indicates, to describe.

Some research in clinical psychology, for example, is conducted to describe the prevalence, severity, or symptoms of certain psychological problems. In a descriptive study of the incidence of emotional and behavioral problems among high school students (Lewinsohn, Hops, Roberts, Seeley, & Andrews, 1993), researchers obtained a representative sample of students from high schools in Oregon. Through personal interviews and the administration of standard measures of psychopathology, the researchers found that nearly 10% of the students had a recognized psychiatric disorder at the time of

the study—most commonly depression. Furthermore, 33% of the respondents had experienced a disorder at some time in their lives. Female respondents were more likely than male respondents to experience unipolar depression, anxiety disorders, and eating disorders, whereas males had higher rates of problems related to disruptive behavior.

Descriptive research, which we will cover in greater detail in Chapter 6, provides the foundation on which all other research rests. However, it is only the beginning.

Correlational Research

If behavioral researchers only described how human and nonhuman animals think, feel, and behave, they would provide us with little insight into the complexities of psychological processes. Thus, most research goes beyond mere description to an examination of the correlates or causes of behavior. **Correlational research** investigates the relationships among various psychological variables. Is there a relationship between self-esteem and shyness? Does parental neglect in infancy relate to particular problems in adolescence? Do certain personality characteristics predispose people to abuse drugs? Is the ability to cope with stress related to physical health? Each of these questions asks whether there is a relationship—a *correlation*—between two variables.

Health psychologists have known for many years that people who are Type A—highly achievement-oriented and hard-driving—have an exceptionally high risk of heart disease. More recently, research has suggested that Type A people are most likely to develop coronary heart disease if they have a tendency to become hostile when their goals are blocked. In a correlational study designed to explore this issue, Kneip et al. (1993) asked the spouses of 185 cardiac patients to rate these patients on their tendency to become hostile and angry. They also conducted scans of the patients' hearts to measure the extent of their heart disease. The data showed not only that spouses' ratings of the patients' hostility correlated with heart disease but also that hostility predicted heart disease above and beyond traditional risk factors such as age, whether the patient smoked, and high blood pressure. Thus, the data supported the hypothesis that hostility is correlated with coronary heart disease.

Correlational studies provide valuable information regarding the relationships between variables. However, although correlational research can establish that certain variables are related to one another, it cannot tell us whether one variable actually *causes* the other. We'll return to a full discussion of correlational research strategies in Chapters 7 and 8.

Experimental Research

When researchers are interested in determining whether certain variables cause changes in behavior, thought, or emotion, they turn to **experimental research**. In an experiment, the researcher manipulates or changes one variable (called the *independent variable*) to see whether changes in behavior (the *dependent variable*) occur as a consequence. If behavioral changes occur when the independent variable is manipulated, we can conclude that the independent variable caused changes in the dependent variable (assuming certain conditions are met).

For example, Terkel and Rosenblatt (1968) were interested in whether maternal behavior in rats is caused by hormones in the bloodstream. They injected virgin female rats with either blood plasma from rats who had just given birth or blood plasma from rats who were not mothers. They found that the rats who were injected with the blood of mother rats showed more maternal behavior toward rat pups than those who were injected with the blood of nonmothers, suggesting that the presence of hormones in the blood of mother rats is partly responsible for maternal behavior. In this study, the nature of the injection (blood from mothers versus blood from nonmothers) was the independent variable, and maternal behavior was the dependent variable. We'll spend four chapters (Chapters 9–12) on the design and analysis of experiments such as this one.

Note that the term *experiment* applies to only one kind of research—a study in which the researcher controls an independent variable to assess its effects on behavior. Thus, it is incorrect to use the word *experiment* as a synonym for *research* or *study*.

Quasi-Experimental Research

When behavioral researchers are interested in understanding cause-and-effect relationships, they prefer to use experimental designs in which they vary an independent variable while controlling other extraneous factors that might influence the results of the study. However, in many cases, researchers are not able to manipulate the independent variable or control all other factors. When this is the case, a researcher may conduct **quasi-experimental research**. In a quasi-experimental design, such as those we'll study in Chapter 13, the researcher either studies the effects of some variable or event that occurs naturally (and does not vary an independent variable) or else manipulates an independent variable but does exercise the same control over extraneous factors as in a true experiment.

Many parents and teachers worry that students' schoolwork will suffer if students work at a job each day after school. Indeed, previous research has shown that part-time employment in adolescence is correlated with a number of problems, including lower academic achievement. What is unclear, however, is whether employment causes these problems or whether students who choose to have an after-school job tend to be those who are already doing poorly in school. Researchers would find it difficult to conduct a true experiment on this question because they would have to manipulate the independent variable of employment by randomly requiring certain students to work after school while prohibiting other students from having a job.

Because a true experiment was not feasible, Steinberg, Fegley, and Dornbusch (1993) conducted a quasi-experiment. They tested high school students during the 1987–88 school year and the same students again in 1988–89. They then compared those students who had started working during that time to those who did not take a job. As they expected, even before starting to work, students who later became employed earned lower grades and had lower academic expectations than those who later did not work. Even so, the researchers found clear effects of working above and beyond these preexisting differences. Compared to students who did not work, those who took a job subsequently spent less time on homework, cut class more frequently, and had lower academic expectations. Although quasi-experiments do not allow the same degree of confidence in interpretation as do true experiments, the data from this study appear to show that after-school employment can have deleterious effects on high school students.

Each of these basic research strategies— descriptive, correlational, experimental, and quasi-experimental—has its uses. One task of behavioral researchers is to select the strategy that will best address their research questions given the limitations imposed by practical concerns (such as time, money, and control over the situation) as well as ethical issues

(the manipulation of certain independent variables would be ethically indefensible). By the time you reach the end of this book, you will have the background to make informed decisions regarding how to choose the best strategy for a particular research question.

DOMAINS OF BEHAVIORAL SCIENCE

The breadth of behavioral science is staggering, ranging from researchers who study microscopic biochemical processes in the brain to those who investigate the broad influence of culture. What all behavioral scientists have in common, however, is an interest in behavior, thought, and emotion.

Regardless of their specialties and research interests, virtually all behavioral researchers rely on the methods that we will examine in this book. To give you a sense of the variety of specialties that comprise behavioral science, Table 1.1 provides

TABLE 1.1 Primary Specialties in Behavioral Science	
Specialty	**Primary Focus of Theory and Research**
Developmental psychology	Description, measurement, and explanation of age-related changes in behavior, thought, and emotion across the life span
Personality psychology	Description, measurement, and explanation of psychological differences among individuals
Social psychology	The influence of social environments (particularly other people) on behavior, thought, and emotion; interpersonal interactions and relationships
Experimental psychology	Basic psychological processes, including learning and memory, sensation, perception, motivation, language, and physiological processes; the designation *experimental psychology* is sometimes used to include subspecialties such as physiological psychology, cognitive psychology, and sensory psychology
Neuroscience; psychophysiology; physiological psychology	Relationship between bodily structures and processes, particularly those involving the nervous system, and behavior
Cognitive psychology	Thinking, learning, and memory
Industrial–organizational psychology	Behavior in work settings and other organizations; personnel selection
Environmental psychology	Relationship between people's environments (whether natural, built, or social) and behavior
Educational psychology	Processes involved in learning (particularly in educational settings) and the development of methods and materials for educating people

(continued)

TABLE 1.1 continued	
Specialty	**Primary Focus of Theory and Research**
Clinical psychology	Causes and treatment of emotional and behavioral problems; assessment of psychopathology
Counseling psychology	Causes and treatment of emotional and behavioral problems; promotion of normal human functioning
School psychology	Intellectual, social, and emotional development of children, particularly as it affects performance and behavior in school
Community psychology	Normal and problematic behaviors in natural settings, such as the home, workplace, neighborhood, and community; prevention of problems that arise in these settings
Family studies	Relationships among family members; family influences on child development
Interpersonal communication	Verbal and nonverbal communication; group processes

brief descriptions of some of the larger areas. Keep in mind that these labels often tell us more about particular researchers' academic degrees or the department in which they work than about their research interests. Researchers in different domains often have very similar research interests, whereas those within a domain may have quite different interests.

BEHAVIORAL RESEARCH ON HUMAN AND NONHUMAN ANIMALS

Although most research in the behavioral sciences is conducted on human beings, about 8% of psychological studies use nonhuman animals as research participants. Most of the animals used in research are mice, rats, and pigeons, with monkeys and apes used much less often. (Dogs and cats are very rarely studied.) The general public, particularly people who are concerned about the welfare and treatment of animals, sometimes wonders about the merits of animal research and whether it provides important knowledge that justifies the use of animals in research. We will discuss the ethical issues involved in animal research in Chapter 15 but, for now, let's look at ways in which animal research contributes to our understanding of thought, emotion, behavior, and psychophysiology.

Ever since Charles Darwin alerted scientists to the evolutionary connections between human beings and other animals, behavioral researchers have been interested in understanding the basic processes that underlie the behavior of all animals—from flatworms to human beings (Coon, 1992). Although species obviously vary from one another, a great deal can be learned by studying the similarities and differences in how human and nonhuman animals function.

Nonhuman animals provide certain advantages as research participants over human beings. For example, they can be raised under controlled laboratory conditions, thereby eliminating many of the environmental effects that complicate human behavior. They can also be studied for extended periods of time under controlled conditions—for several hours each day for many weeks—whereas human beings cannot. Furthermore, researchers are often willing to test the effects of psychoactive drugs or surgical procedures on mice or rats that they would not test on human beings. And, although some people disagree with the practice, nonhuman animals can be sacrificed at the end of an experiment so that their brains can be studied, a procedure that is not likely to attract many human volunteers.

But what do we learn from nonhuman animals? Can research that is conducted on animals tell us anything about human behavior? Many important advances in behavioral science have come from research on animals (for discussions of the benefits of animal research, see Baldwin, 1993; Domjan & Purdy, 1995). For example, most of our knowledge regarding basic motivational systems—such as those involved in hunger, thirst, and sexual behavior—has come from animal research. Animal research has also provided a great deal of information about the processes involved in vision, hearing, taste, smell, and touch and has been essential in understanding pain and pain relief. Research on animal cognition (how animals think) has provided an evolutionary perspective on mind and intelligence, showing how human behavior resembles and differs from that of other animals (see Behavioral Research Case Study: *Chimpanzees Select the Best Collaborators* below). Through research with animals, we have also learned a great deal about emotion and stress that has been used to help people cope with stress and emotional problems.

Animal research has helped us understand basic learning processes (classical and operant conditioning operate quite similarly across species) and has paved the way for interventions that enhance learning, promote self-reliance (through token economies, for example), and facilitate the clinical treatment of substance abuse, phobias, self-injurious behavior, stuttering, social skills deficits, and other problems among human beings.

Much of what we know about the anatomy and physiology of the nervous system has come from animal research. Animal studies of neuroanatomy, recovery after brain damage, physiological aspects

of emotional states, mechanisms that control eating, and the neurophysiology of memory, for example, contribute to our understanding of psychological processes. Because this research often requires researchers to surgically modify or electrically stimulate areas of the brain, much of it could not have been conducted using human participants.

Because researchers can administer drugs to animals that they would hesitate to give to people, animal research has been fundamental to understanding the effects of psychoactive drugs, processes that underlie drug dependence and abuse, and the effects of new pharmacological treatments for depression, anxiety, alcoholism, Alzheimer's disease, and other problems. Likewise, behavioral genetics research has helped us to understand genetic vulnerability to drug dependence because researchers can breed strains of mice and rats that are low or high in their susceptibility to becoming dependent on drugs. Finally, animal research has contributed to our efforts to help animals themselves, such as in protecting endangered species, improving the well-being of captive animals (such as in zoos), and developing ways to control animal populations in the wild.

Of course, using animals as research participants raises a number of ethical issues that we will examine later. But few would doubt that animal research has contributed in important ways to the scientific understanding of thought, emotion, and behavior.

Behavioral Research Case Study
Chimpanzees Select the Best Collaborators

When you need help performing a task, you naturally pick someone who you think will be able to help to accomplish your goal. Furthermore, if the person you asked to help you did not perform well, you would be unlikely to choose that individual again if you needed assistance in the future.

Melis, Hare, and Tomasello (2006) had the suspicion that the ability to select helpful collaborators might be a primitive cognitive skill that evolved millions of years ago—perhaps even before the appearance of human beings—because it promoted survival and reproduction. If so, we might expect to see evidence of this same ability among our closest animal relatives—the chimpanzees. To see whether, like us, chimpanzees select the best collaborators for tasks that require cooperation between individuals, Melis and her colleagues constructed a feeding platform that their chimps could access only if two of them cooperated by simultaneously pulling a rope that was connected to the platform.

The researchers first taught six chimpanzees how to cooperate to access the food platform by pulling on the rope, as well as how to use a key to open doors that connected the testing room to two adjacent cages that

(continued)

(continued)

housed other chimps who could help them. In one room was a chimp who the researchers knew was very good at helping to pull the rope. The other room contained a chimp who was much less effective at pulling the rope to retrieve the food tray.

The study was conducted on two successive days, with six trials each day. On each trial, the chimpanzee participant was given the opportunity to release one of the two other chimpanzees from its cage to help pull the food tray. Given that they were unfamiliar with the two potential helpers on Day 1, the participants initially selected them as helpers at random on the first day. However, on the second day, the chimpanzees chose the more effective rope-pulling partner significantly more often than the ineffective one (see Figure 1.3). In fact, during the test session on Day 2, the participants chose the more effective partner on nearly all six trials.

Presumably, if the helper that the participant chose on Day 1 was helpful in getting food, the participant chose that chimp again on Day 2. However, if the helper that the participant chose on Day 1 was not helpful in accessing the food tray, the participant switched to the other, more effective helper on Day 2. These results suggest not only that chimpanzees know when it is necessary to recruit a collaborator to help them to perform a task, but also that they realize that some helpers are better than others and reliably choose the more effective of two collaborators after only a few encounters with each one.

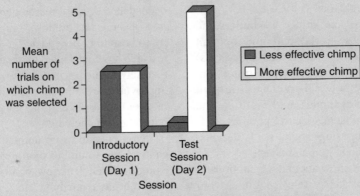

FIGURE 1.3   **Selection of Less and More Effective Chimpanzees as Helpers**   *Source*: From "Chimpanzees Recruit the Best Collaborators," by A. P. Melis, B. Hare, and M. Tomasello, 2006, *Science, 111*. pp. 1297–1300. Reprinted with permission from AAAS.

A PREVIEW

The research process is a complex one. In every study researchers must address many questions:

- How should I measure participants' thoughts, feelings, behavior, or physiological responses in this study?
- How do I obtain a sample of participants for my research?
- Given my research question, what is the most appropriate research strategy?
- How can I be sure my study is as well designed as possible?
- What are the most appropriate and useful ways of analyzing the data?
- How should my findings be reported?
- What are the ethical issues involved in conducting this research?

Each chapter in this book deals with an aspect of the research process. Now that you have an overview of the research process, Chapter 2 sets the stage for the remainder of the book by discussing what is perhaps the central concept in research design and analysis—variability. Armed with an understanding of behavioral variability, you will be better equipped to understand many of the issues we'll address in later chapters.

Chapters 3 and 4 deal with how researchers measure behavior and psychological processes. Chapter 3 focuses on basic issues involved in psychological measurement, and Chapter 4 examines specific types of measures used in behavioral research. In Chapter 5, we examine the ways in which researchers select participants for their studies.

After covering basic topics that are relevant to all research in Chapters 1 through 5, we turn to specific research strategies. Chapter 6 deals with descriptive research methods, including surveys, epidemiological studies, and demographic research. In Chapters 7 and 8, you will learn about correlational research strategies—not only correlation per se but also regression, partial correlation, factor analysis, and other procedures that are used to investigate how naturally occurring variables are related to one another.

Chapters 9 and 10 will introduce you to experimental design; Chapters 11 and 12 will then go into greater detail regarding the design and analysis of experiments. In these chapters, you'll learn not only how to design experiments but also how to analyze experimental data.

Chapter 13 deals with quasi-experimental designs and Chapter 14 with single-case designs. The complex ethical issues involved in conducting behavioral research are discussed in Chapter 15. Finally, in Chapter 16, we'll take a look at how research findings are disseminated and discuss how to write research reports.

At the end of the book are three appendixes containing statistical tables and formulas and guidelines for choosing statistical analysis, as well as a glossary and list of references.

Summary

1. Psychology is both a profession that promotes human welfare through counseling, psychotherapy, education, and other activities, as well as a scientific discipline that is devoted to the study of behavior and mental processes.

2. Interest in human behavior can be traced to ancient times, but the study of behavior became scientific only in the late 1800s, stimulated in part by the laboratories established by Wilhelm Wundt in Germany and William James in the United States.

3. Behavioral scientists work in many disciplines, including psychology, education, social work, family studies, communication, management, health and exercise science, marketing, psychiatry, neurology, and nursing.

4. Behavioral scientists conduct research to describe, explain, and predict behavior, as well as to solve applied problems.

5. Although the findings of behavioral researchers often coincide with common sense, many commonly held beliefs have been disconfirmed by behavioral science.

6. To be considered scientific, observations must be systematic and empirical, research must be conducted in a manner that is publicly verifiable, and the questions addressed must be potentially solvable given current knowledge. Science is defined by its adherence to these criteria and not by the topics that it studies.

7. Pseudoscience involves evidence that masquerades as science but that fails to meet one or more of the three criteria of scientific investigation.

8. Scientists do two distinct things: They discover and document new phenomena, and they develop and test explanations of the phenomena that they observe.

9. Much research is designed to test the validity of theories and models. A theory is a set of propositions that attempts to specify the interrelationships among a set of concepts; a theory specifies how and why concepts are related to one another. A model describes how concepts are related but does not explain why they are related to one another as they are.

10. Researchers assess the usefulness of a theory by testing hypotheses. Hypotheses are propositions that are either deduced logically from a theory or developed inductively from observed

facts. To be tested, hypotheses must be stated in a manner that is potentially falsifiable.

11. By stating their hypotheses a priori, researchers avoid the risks associated with post hoc explanations of patterns that have already been observed.

12. Researchers use two distinct kinds of definitions in their work. Conceptual definitions are much like dictionary definitions. Operational definitions, on the other hand, define concepts by specifying precisely how they are measured or manipulated in the context of a particular study. Operational definitions are essential for replication, as well as for clear communication among scientists.

13. Strictly speaking, theories can never be proved or disproved by research. Proof is logically impossible because it is invalid to prove the antecedent of an argument by showing that the consequent is true. Disproof, though logically possible, is impossible in a practical sense; failure to obtain support for a theory may reflect more about the research procedure than about the accuracy of the hypothesis. Because of this, the failure to obtain hypothesized findings (null findings) is usually uninformative regarding the validity of a hypothesis.

14. Even though a particular study cannot prove or disprove a theory, science progresses on the basis of accumulated evidence across many investigations.

15. Behavioral research falls into four broad categories: descriptive, correlational, experimental, and quasi-experimental.

16. Although most behavioral research uses human beings as participants, about 8% studies nonhuman animals. Animal research has yielded important findings involving the anatomy and physiology of the nervous system, motivation, emotion, learning, and drug dependence, as well as similarities and differences in cognitive, emotional, and behavioral processes between human beings and other animals.

Key Terms

applied research (p. 3)
a priori prediction (p. 12)
basic research (p. 3)
conceptual definition (p. 14)
correlational research (p. 21)
deduction (p. 12)
descriptive research (p. 21)
empirical generalization (p. 12)
empiricism (p. 7)

evaluation research (p. 3)
experimental research (p. 22)
falsification (p. 13)
file-drawer problem (p. 17)
hypothesis (p. 12)
induction (p. 12)
methodological pluralism (p. 13)
model (p. 10)
null finding (p. 17)

operational definition (p. 14)
post hoc explanation (p. 11)
pseudoscience (p. 8)
public verification (p. 7)
quasi-experimental research (p. 22)
strategy of strong inference (p. 13)
theory (p. 9)

Questions for Review

1. In what sense is psychology both a science and a profession?

2. Describe the development of psychology as a science.

3. What was Wilhelm Wundt's primary contribution to behavioral research?

4. Name at least 10 academic disciplines in which behavioral scientists do research.

5. What are the three basic goals of behavioral research?

6. Distinguish between basic and applied research. In what ways are basic and applied research interdependent?

7. In what ways is the study of research methods valuable to students like you?

8. Discuss the importance of systematic empiricism, public verification, and solvability to the scientific method.

9. In what ways does pseudoscience differ from true science?

10. Is it true that most of the findings of behavioral research are just common sense?

11. What are the two primary jobs that characterize scientific investigation?

12. What are the properties of a good theory?
13. Describe how researchers use induction versus deduction to generate research hypotheses.
14. Describe the process by which hypotheses are developed and tested.
15. Why must hypotheses be falsifiable?
16. One theory suggests that people feel socially anxious or shy in social situations when two conditions are met: (a) They are highly motivated to make a favorable impression on others who are present, but (b) they doubt that they will be able to do so. Suggest at least three research hypotheses that can be derived from this theory. Be sure your hypotheses are falsifiable.
17. Why are scientists skeptical of post hoc explanations?
18. Why are operational definitions important in research?
19. Suggest three operational definitions for each of the following constructs:
    a. aggression
    b. patience
    c. test anxiety
    d. memory
    e. smiling
20. What are some ways in which scientists get ideas for their research?
21. Why can theories not be proved or disproved by research?
22. Given that proof and disproof are impossible in science, how does scientific knowledge advance?
23. Why are scientific journals reluctant to publish null findings? In what way does this policy create the file-drawer problem?
24. Distinguish among descriptive, correlational, experimental, and quasi-experimental research.
25. Distinguish between an independent and dependent variable.
26. Tell what researchers study in each of the following fields:
    a. developmental psychology
    b. experimental psychology
    c. industrial-organizational psychology
    d. social psychology
    e. cognitive psychology
    f. personality psychology
    g. family studies
    h. interpersonal communication
    i. psychophysiology
    j. school psychology
    k. counseling psychology
    l. community psychology
    m. clinical psychology
    n. educational psychology
    o. neuroscience
    p. environmental psychology
27. Describe some of the topics that have benefitted from research conducted on animals.

Questions for Discussion

1. Why do you think behavioral sciences such as psychology developed later than other sciences, such as chemistry, physics, astronomy, and biology?
2. Why do you think many people have difficulty seeing psychologists and other behavioral researchers as scientists?
3. How would today's world be different if the behavioral sciences had not developed?
4. Develop your own idea for research. If you have trouble thinking of a research idea, use one of the tactics described in the box, "Getting Ideas for Research." Choose your idea carefully as if you were actually going to devote a great deal of time and effort to carrying out the research.
5. After researchers formulate an idea, they must evaluate its quality to decide whether the idea is really worth pursuing. Evaluate the research idea you developed in Question 4 using the following four criteria. If your idea fails to meet one or more of these criteria, think of another idea.

- **Does the idea have the potential to advance our understanding of behavior?** Assuming that the study is conducted and the expected patterns of results are obtained, will we have learned something new about behavior?
- **Is the knowledge that may be gained potentially important?** Importance is, of course, in the eye of the beholder. A study can be important in several ways: (a) It tests hypotheses derived from a theory (thereby providing evidence for or against the theory); (b) it identifies a qualification to a previously demonstrated finding; (c) it demonstrates a weakness in a previously used research method or technique; (d) it documents the effectiveness of procedures for modifying a behavioral problem (such as in counseling, education, or industry, for example); or (e) it demonstrates the existence of a phenomenon or effect that had not been previously recognized. Rarely does a single study provide earthshaking information that revolutionizes the field, so don't

expect too much. Ask yourself whether your idea is likely to provide information that other behavioral researchers or practitioners (such as practicing psychologists) would find interesting or useful.

- **Do I find the idea interesting?** No matter how important an idea might be, it is difficult to do research that one finds boring. This doesn't mean that you have to be fascinated by the topic, but if you really don't care about the area and aren't interested in the answer to the research question, consider getting a different topic.
- **Is the idea researchable?** Many research ideas are not viable because they are ethically questionable or because they require resources that the researcher cannot possibly obtain.

6. We noted that research falls into four basic categories, depending on whether the goal is to describe patterns of behavior, thought, or emotion (descriptive research); to examine the relationship among naturally occurring variables (correlational research); to test cause-and-effect relationships by experimentally manipulating an independent variable to examine its effects on a dependent variable (experimental research); or to examine the possible effects of an event that cannot be controlled by the researcher (quasi-experimental research). For each of the following research questions, indicate which kind of research—descriptive, correlational, experimental, or quasi-experimental—would be most appropriate.

   a. What percentage of college students attend church regularly?
   b. Does the artificial sweetener aspartame cause dizziness and confusion in some people?
   c. What personality variables are related to depression?
   d. What is the effect of a manager's style on employees' morale and performance?
   e. Do SAT scores predict college performance?
   f. Do state laws that mandate drivers to wear seat belts reduce traffic fatalities?
   g. Does Prozac (a popular antidepression medication) help insomnia?
   h. Does getting married make people happier?
   i. Do most U.S. citizens support stronger gun control laws?

7. Go to the library and locate several journals in psychology or other behavioral sciences. A few journals that you might look for include the *Journal of Experimental Psychology, Journal of Personality and Social Psychology, Developmental Psychology, Journal of Abnormal Psychology, Health Psychology, Journal of Applied Psychology, Journal of Clinical and Consulting Psychology, Journal of Counseling Psychology*, and *Journal of Educational Psychology*. Look through the table of contents in several of these journals to see the diversity of the research that is currently being published. If an article title looks interesting, read the abstract (the article summary) that appears at the beginning of the article.

8. Read one entire article. You will undoubtedly find parts of the article difficult (if not impossible) to understand, but do your best to understand as much as you can. As you stumble on the methodological and statistical details of the study, tell yourself that, by the time you are finished with this book, you will understand the vast majority of what you read in an article such as this. (You might even want to copy the article so that you can underline the methodological and statistical items that you do not understand. Then, after finishing this book, read the article again to see how much you have learned.)

9. Parapsychology—the study of anomalous mental phenomena such as telepathy (mind-to-mind communication), precognition (knowing the future), and psychokinesis (influencing physical events with one's mind)—is a very controversial area of investigation. Its critics often characterize parapsychology as a pseudoscience, implying that parapsychological research does not meet the basic criteria for scientific investigation. However, parapsychologists insist that, aside from the fact that they are studying phenomena that cannot be explained according to known physical or psychological processes, not only are their studies scientific but also their research designs are virtually indistinguishable from those of mainline psychological researchers. Read "Does Psi Exist" by Bem and Honorton, published in *Psychological Bulletin* (1994), and discuss whether parapsychology appears to be a science or a pseudoscience. (Don't get hung up on the statistical details.) If you think parapsychology is a pseudoscience, discuss whether you think psychic phenomena can ever be studied scientifically. If you think it is a science, discuss why you think parapsychology is so controversial and why it is often regarded as pseudoscientific.

10. In this chapter, we discussed the importance of scientists keeping an open mind and not allowing their personal preferences and biases to influence their evaluation of scientific evidence. Of course, everyone—scientists included—often has great difficulty setting aside their personal biases. Imagine that you were hired to help scientists avoid being influenced by their personal biases. What strategies could you develop to help people be more objective and unbiased?

2 BEHAVIORAL VARIABILITY AND RESEARCH

Psychologists use the word *schema* to refer to a cognitive generalization that organizes and guides the processing of information. You have schemas about many categories of events, people, and other stimuli that you have encountered in life. For example, you probably have a schema for the concept *leadership*. Through your experiences with leaders of various sorts, you have developed a generalization of what a good leader is. Similarly, you probably have a schema for *big cities*. What do you think of when I say, "New York, Los Angeles, and Atlanta"? Some people's schemas of large cities include generalizations such as "crowded and dangerous," whereas other people's schemas include attributes such as "interesting and exciting." We all have schemas about many categories of stimuli.

Researchers have found that people's reactions to particular stimuli and events are strongly affected by the schemas they possess. For example, if you were a business executive, your decisions about whom to promote to a managerial position would be affected by your schema for leadership. You would promote a very different kind of employee to manager if your schema for leadership included attributes such as caring, involved, and people-oriented than if you saw effective leaders as autocratic, critical, and aloof. Similarly, your schema for large cities would affect your reaction to receiving a job offer in Miami or Dallas.

Importantly, when people have a schema, they more easily process and organize information relevant to that schema. Schemas provide us with frameworks for organizing, remembering, and acting on the information we receive. It would be difficult for executives to decide whom to promote to manager if they didn't have schemas for leadership, for example. Even though schemas sometimes lead us to wrong conclusions when they are not rooted in reality (as when our stereotypes about a particular group bias our perceptions of a particular member of that group), they allow us to process information efficiently and effectively. If we could not rely on the generalizations of our schemas, we would have to painstakingly consider every new piece of information when processing information and making decisions.

By now you are probably wondering how schemas relate to research methods. Having taught courses in research methods and statistics for many years, I have come to the conclusion that, for most students, the biggest stumbling block to understanding behavioral research is their failure to develop a schema for the material. Many students have little difficulty mastering specific concepts and procedures, yet they complete their first course in research methods without seeing the big picture. They learn many concepts, facts, principles, designs, analyses, and skills, but they do not develop an overarching framework for integrating and organizing all of the information they learn. Their lack of a schema impedes their ability to process, organize, remember, and use information about research methods. In contrast, seasoned researchers have a well-articulated schema for the research process that facilitates their research activities and helps them to make methodological decisions.

The purpose of this chapter is to provide you with a schema for thinking about the research process. By giving you a framework for thinking about research, I hope that you will find the rest of the book easier to comprehend and remember. In essence, this chapter will give you pegs on which to hang what you learn about behavioral research. Rather than dumping all of the new information you learn in a big heap on the floor, we'll put schematic hooks on the wall for you to use in organizing the incoming information.

The essence of this schema is that, at the most basic level, all behavioral research attempts to answer questions about *behavioral variability*—that is, how and why behavior varies across situations, differs among individuals, and changes over time. The concept of variability underlies many of the topics we will discuss in later chapters and provides the foundation on which much of this book rests. The better you understand this basic concept now, the more easily you will grasp many of the topics we will discuss later in the book.

VARIABILITY AND THE RESEARCH PROCESS

All aspects of the research process revolve around the concept of **variability**. The concept of variability runs through the entire enterprise of designing and analyzing research. To show what I mean, let me describe five ways in which variability is central to the research process.

1. Psychology and other behavioral sciences involve the study of behavioral variability. Psychology is often defined as the study of behavior and mental processes. However, what psychologists and other behavioral researchers actually study is behavioral variability. That is, they want to know how and why behavior varies across situations, among people, and over time. Put differently, understanding behavior and mental processes really means understanding what makes behavior, thought, and emotion vary.

Think about the people you interact with each day and about the variation you see in their behavior. First, their behavior varies *across situations*. People feel and act differently on sunny days than when it is cloudy, and differently in dark settings than when it is light. College students are often more nervous when interacting with a person of the other sex than when interacting with a person of their own sex. Children behave more aggressively after watching violent TV shows than they did before watching them. A hungry pigeon that has been reinforced for pecking when a green light is on pecks more in the presence of a green light than a red light. In brief, people and other animals behave differently in different situations. Behavioral researchers are interested in how and why features of the situation cause this variability in behavior, thought, and emotion.

Second, behavior varies *among individuals*. Even in similar situations, not everyone acts the same. At a party, some people are talkative and outgoing, whereas others are quiet and shy. Some people are more conscientious and responsible than others. Some individuals generally appear confident and calm whereas others seem nervous. And certain animals, such as dogs, display marked differences in behavior depending on their breed. Thus, because of differences in their biological makeup and previous experience, different people and different animals behave differently. A great deal of behavioral research focuses on understanding this variability across individuals.

Third, behavior also varies *over time*. A baby who could barely walk a few months ago can run today. An adolescent girl who two years ago thought boys were "gross" now has romantic fantasies about them. A task that was interesting an hour ago has become boring. Even when the situation remains constant, behavior may change as time passes. Some of these changes, such as developmental changes that occur with age, are permanent; other changes, such as boredom or sexual drive, are temporary. Behavioral researchers are often interested in understanding how and why behavior varies over time.

2. Research questions in all behavioral sciences are questions about behavioral variability. Whenever behavioral scientists design research, they are interested in answering questions about behavioral variability (whether they think about it that way or not). For example, suppose we want to know the extent to which sleep deprivation affects performance on cognitive tasks (such as deciding whether a blip on a radar screen is a flock of geese or an incoming enemy aircraft). In essence, we are asking how the amount of sleep people get causes their performance on the task to change or vary. Or imagine that we're interested in whether a particular form of counseling reduces family conflict. Our research centers on the question of whether counseling causes changes or variation in a family's interactions. Any specific research question we might develop can be phrased in terms of behavioral variability.

3. Research should be designed in a manner that best allows the researcher to answer questions about behavioral variability. Given that all behavioral research involves understanding variability,

research studies must be designed in a way that allows us to identify, as unambiguously as possible, factors related to the behavioral variability we observe. Viewed in this way, a well-designed study is one that permits researchers to describe and account for the variability in the behavior of their research participants. A poorly designed study is one in which researchers have difficulty answering questions about the source of variability they observe.

As we'll see in later chapters, flaws in the design of a study can make it impossible for a researcher to determine why participants behaved as they did. At each step of the design and execution of a study, researchers must be sure that their research will permit them to answer their questions about behavioral variability.

4. The measurement of behavior involves the assessment of behavioral variability. All behavioral research involves the measurement of some behavior, thought, emotion, or physiological process. Our measures may involve the number of times a rat presses a bar, a participant's heart rate, the score a child obtains on a memory test, or a person's rating of how tired he or she feels on a scale of 1 to 7. In each case, we're assigning a number to a person's or animal's behavior: 15 bar presses, 65 heartbeats per minute, a test score of 87, a tiredness rating of 5, or whatever.

No matter what is being measured, we want the number we assign to a participant's behavior to correspond in a meaningful way to the behavior being measured. Put another way, we would like the variability *in the numbers we assign* to various participants to correspond to the actual variability *in participants' behaviors, thoughts, emotions, or physiological reactions*. We must have confidence that the scores we use to capture participants' responses reflect the true variability in the behavior we are measuring. If the variability in the scores does not correspond, at least roughly, to the variability in the attribute we are measuring, the measurement technique is worthless and our research is doomed.

5. Statistical analyses are used to describe and account for the observed variability in the behavioral data. No matter what the topic being investigated or the research strategy being used, one phase of the research process always involves analyzing the data that are collected. Thus, the study of research methods necessarily involves an introduction to statistics. Unfortunately, many students are initially intimidated by statistics and sometimes wonder why they are so important. The reason is that statistics are necessary for us to understand behavioral variability.

After a study is completed, all we have is a set of numbers that represent the responses of our research participants. These numbers vary, and our goal is to understand something about why they vary. The purpose of statistics is to summarize and answer questions about the behavioral variability we observe in our research. Assuming that the research was competently designed and conducted, statistics help us account for or explain the behavioral variability we observed. Does a new treatment for depression cause an improvement in mood? Does a particular drug enhance memory in mice? Is self-esteem related to the variability we observe in how hard people try when working on difficult tasks? We use statistics to answer questions about the variability in our data.

As we'll see in greater detail in later chapters, statistics serve two general purposes for researchers. **Descriptive statistics** are used to summarize and describe the behavior of participants in a study. They are ways of reducing a large number of scores or observations to interpretable numbers such as averages and percentages.

Inferential statistics, on the other hand, are used to draw conclusions about the reliability and generalizability of one's findings. They are used to help answer questions such as, How likely is it that my findings are due to random extraneous factors rather than to the variables of central interest in my study? How representative are my findings of the larger population from which my sample of participants came?

Descriptive and inferential statistics are simply tools that researchers use to interpret the behavioral data they collect. Beyond that, however, understanding statistics provides insight into what makes some research studies better than others. As you learn about how statistical analyses are used to study behavioral variability, you'll develop a keener sense of how to design powerful, well-controlled studies.

In brief, the concept of variability accompanies us through the entire research process: Our research questions concern the causes and correlates of behavioral variability. We try to design studies that best help us to describe and understand variability in a particular behavior. The measures we use are an attempt to capture numerically the variability we observe in participants' behavior. And our statistics help us to analyze the variability in our data to answer the questions we began with. Variability is truly the thread that runs throughout the research process. Understanding variability will provide you with a schema for understanding, remembering, and applying what you learn about behavioral research. For this reason, we will devote the remainder of this chapter to the topic of variability and return to it continually throughout the book.

VARIANCE: AN INDEX OF VARIABILITY

Given the importance of the concept of variability in designing and analyzing behavioral research, researchers need a way to express how much variability there is in a set of data. Not only are researchers interested simply in knowing the amount of variability in their data, but also they need a numerical index of the variability in their data to conduct certain statistical analyses that we'll examine in later chapters. Researchers use a statistic known as **variance** to indicate the amount of observed variability in participants' behavior. We will confront variance in a variety of guises throughout this book, so we need to understand it well.

Imagine that you conducted a very simple study in which you asked 6 participants to describe their attitudes about capital punishment on a scale of 1 to 5 (where 1 indicates strong opposition and 5 indicates strong support for capital punishment). Suppose you obtained:

Participant	Response
1	4
2	1
3	2
4	2
5	4
6	3

For a variety of reasons (that we'll discuss later), you may need to know how much variability there is in these data. Can you think of a way of expressing how much these responses, or scores, vary from one person to the next?

A Conceptual Explanation of Variance

One possibility is simply to take the difference between the largest and the smallest scores. In fact, this number, the **range**, is sometimes used to express variability. If we subtract the smallest from the largest score above, we find that the range of these data is $3 (4 - 1 = 3)$. Unfortunately, the range has limitations as an indicator of the variability in our data. The problem is that the range tells us only how much the largest and smallest scores vary but does not take into account the other scores and how much they vary from each other.

Consider the two distributions of data in Figure 2.1. These two sets of data have the same range. That is, the difference between the largest and smallest scores is the same in each set. However, the variability in the data in Figure 2.1 (a) is smaller than the variability in Figure 2.1 (b). That is, most of the scores in 2.1(a) are more tightly clustered together than the scores in 2.1(b), which are more spread out. What we need is a way of expressing variability that includes information about all of the scores.

When we talk about things varying, we usually do so in reference to some standard. A useful standard for this purpose is the average or mean of the scores in our data set. Researchers use the term **mean** as a synonym for what you probably call the average—the sum of a set of scores divided by the number of scores you have.

The mean stands as a fulcrum around which all of the other scores balance. So we can express the variability in our data in terms of how much the scores vary around the mean. If most of the scores in a set of data are tightly clustered around the mean (as in Figure 2.1[a]), then the variance of the data will be small. If, however, our scores are more spread out (as in Figure 2.1[b]), they will vary a great deal around the mean, and the variance will be large. So, the variance is nothing more than an indication of how tightly or loosely a set of scores clusters around the

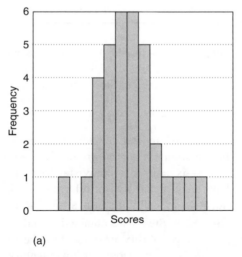

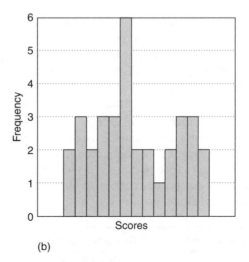

(a)   (b)

FIGURE 2.1   Distributions with Low and High Variability.   The two sets of data shown in these graphs contain the same number of scores and have the same range. However, the variability in the scores in Graph (a) is less than the variability in Graph (b). Overall, most of the participants' scores are more tightly clustered in (a)—that is, they vary less among themselves (and around the mean of the scores) than do the scores in (b). By itself, the range fails to reflect the difference in variability in these two sets of scores.

mean of the scores. As we will see, this provides a very useful indication of the amount of variability in a set of data. And, again, we need to know how much variability there is in our data in order to answer questions about the causes of that variability.

A Statistical Explanation of Variance

You'll understand more precisely what the variance tells us about our data if we consider how variance is expressed statistically. At this point in our discussion of variance, the primary goal is to help you to better understand what variance is from a conceptual standpoint, not to teach you how to calculate it. The following statistical description will help you get a clear picture of what variance tells us about our data.

We can see what the variance is by following five simple steps. We will refer here to the scores or observations obtained in our study of attitudes on capital punishment.

Step 1. As we saw earlier, variance refers to how spread out the scores are around the mean of the data. So to begin, we need to calculate the mean of our data. Just sum the numbers (4 + 1 + 2 + 2 + 4 + 3 = 16) and divide by the number of scores you have (16/6 = 2.67). Note that statisticians usually use the symbol $\bar{y}$ or $\bar{x}$ to represent the mean of a set of data (although the symbol M is often used in scientific writing). In short, all we do on the first step is calculate the mean of the six scores.

Step 2. Now we need a way of expressing how much the scores vary around the mean. We do this by subtracting the mean from each score. This difference is called a *deviation score*.

Let's do this for our data involving people's attitudes toward capital punishment:

Participant	Deviation Score
1	4 − 2.67 = 1.33
2	1 − 2.67 = −1.67
3	2 − 2.67 = −0.67
4	2 − 2.67 = −0.67
5	4 − 2.67 = 1.33
6	3 − 2.67 = 0.33

Step 3. By looking at these deviation scores, we can see how much each score varies or deviates from the mean. Participant 2 scores furthest from the mean (1.67 units below the mean), whereas Participant 6 scores closest to the mean (0.33 unit above it). Note that a positive number indicates that the person's score fell above the mean, whereas a negative sign (−) indicates a score below the mean. (What would a deviation score of zero indicate?)

You might think we could add these six deviation scores to get a total variability score for the sample. However, if we sum the deviation scores for all of the participants in a set of data, they always add up to zero. So we need to get rid of the negative signs. We do this by squaring each of the deviation scores.

Participant	Deviation Score	Deviation Score Squared
1	1.33	1.77
2	−1.67	2.79
3	−0.67	0.45
4	−0.67	0.45
5	1.33	1.77
6	0.33	0.11

Step 4. Now we add the squared deviation scores. If we add all of the squared deviation scores obtained in Step 3, we get

1.77 + 2.79 + 0.45 + 1.77 + 0.11 = 7.34.

As we'll see in later chapters, this number—the *sum of the squared deviations of the scores from the mean*—is central to many statistical analyses. We have a shorthand way of referring to this important quantity; we call it the **total sum of squares**.

Step 5. In Step 4 we obtained an index of the total variability in our data—the total sum of squares. However, this quantity is affected by the number of scores we have; the more participants in our sample, the larger the total sum of squares will be. However, just because we have a larger number of participants does not necessarily mean that the variability of our data will be greater.

Because we do not want our index of variability to be affected by the size of the sample, we divide the sum of squares by a function of the number of participants in our sample. Although you might suspect that we would divide by the actual number of participants from whom we obtained data, we usually divide by one less than the number of participants. (Don't concern yourself with why this is the case.) This gives us the variance of our data, which is indicated by the symbol s^2. If we do this for our data, the variance (s^2) is 1.47.

To review, we calculate variance by (1) calculating the mean of the data, (2) subtracting the mean from each score, (3) squaring these differences or deviation scores, (4) summing these squared deviation scores (this, remember, is the total sum of squares), and (5) dividing by the number of scores minus 1. By following these steps, you should be able to see precisely what the variance is. It is an index of the average amount of variability in a set of data expressed in terms of how much the scores differ from the mean in squared units. Again, variance is important because virtually every aspect of the research process will lead to the analysis of behavioral variability, which is expressed in the statistic known as *variance*.

Developing Your Research Skills
Statistical Notation

Statistical formulas are typically written using **statistical notation**. Just as we commonly use symbols such as a plus sign (+) to indicate *add* and an equal sign (=) to indicate *is equal to*, we'll be using special symbols—such as Σ, n, and s^2—to indicate statistical terms and operations. Although some of these symbols may be new to you, they are nothing more than symbolic representations of variables or mathematical operations, all of which are elementary.

For example, the formula for the mean, expressed in statistical notation, is

$$\bar{y} = \Sigma y_i / n$$

The uppercase Greek letter sigma (Σ) is the statistical symbol for summation and tells us to add what follows. The symbol y_i is the symbol for each individual participant's score. So the operation Σy_i simply tells us to add up all of the scores in our data. That is,

$$\Sigma y_i = y_1 + y_2 + y_3 + \dots + y_n$$

where n is the number of participants. Then the formula for the mean tells us to divide Σy_i by n, the number of participants. Thus, the formula $\bar{y} = \Sigma y_i / n$ indicates that we should add all of the scores and divide by the number of participants.

Similarly, the variance can be expressed in statistical notation as

$$s^2 = \Sigma(y_i - \bar{y})^2 / (n - 1).$$

Look back at the steps for calculating the variance on the preceding pages and see whether you can interpret this formula for s^2.

Step 1 Calculate the mean, $\bar{y}$.
Step 2 Subtract the mean from each participant's score to obtain the deviation scores, $(y_i - \bar{y})$.
Step 3 Square each participant's deviation score, $(y_i - \bar{y})^2$.

Step 4 Sum the squared deviation scores, $\Sigma (y_i - \bar{y})^2$.
Step 5 Divide by the number of scores minus 1, $n - 1$.

As we will see throughout the book, statistical notation will allow us to express certain statistical constructs in a shorthand and unambiguous manner.

SYSTEMATIC AND ERROR VARIANCE

So far, our discussion of variance has dealt with the **total variance** in the responses of participants in a research study—the total variability in a set of data. However, the total variance in a set of data can be split into two parts:

$$\text{Total variance} = \text{systematic variance} + \text{error variance.}$$

The distinction between systematic and error variance will appear throughout the chapters of this book. In fact, at one level, answering questions about behavioral variability always involves distinguishing between the systematic and error variance in a set of data and then figuring out what variables in our study are related to the systematic portion of the variance. Because systematic and error variance are important to the research process, developing a grasp of the concepts now will allow us to use them as needed throughout the book. We'll explore them in greater detail in later chapters.

Systematic Variance

Most research is designed to determine whether there is a relationship between two or more variables. For example, a researcher may wish to test the hypothesis that self-esteem is related to drug use or that changes in office illumination cause systematic changes in on-the-job performance. Put differently, researchers usually are interested in whether variability in one variable (self-esteem, illumination) is related *in a systematic fashion* to variability in other variables (drug use, on-the-job performance).

Systematic variance is that part of the total variability in participants' behavior that is related in an orderly, predictable fashion to the variables the researcher is investigating. If the participants' behavior varies in a systematic way as certain other variables change, the researcher has evidence that those variables are related to behavior. In other words, when some of the total variance in participants' behavior is found to be associated with certain variables in an orderly, systematic fashion, we can conclude that those variables are related to participants' behavior. The portion of the total variance in

participants' behavior that is related systematically to the variables under investigation is systematic variance. Two examples may help clarify the concept of systematic variance.

TEMPERATURE AND AGGRESSION. In an experiment that examined the effects of temperature on aggression, Baron and Bell (1976) led participants to believe that they would administer electric shocks to another person. (In reality, that other person was an accomplice of the experimenter and was not actually shocked.) Participants performed this task in a room in which the ambient temperature was 73 degrees, 85 degrees, or 95 degrees F. To determine whether temperature did, in fact, affect aggression, the researchers had to determine how much of the variability in participants' aggression was related to temperature. That is, they needed to know how much of the total variance in the aggression scores (that is, the shocks) was *systematic variance* due to temperature. We wouldn't expect all of the variability in participants' aggression to be a function of temperature. After all, participants entered the experiment already differing in their tendencies to respond aggressively. In addition, other factors in the experimental setting may have affected aggressiveness. What the researchers wanted to know was whether *any* of the variance in how aggressively participants responded was due to differences in the temperatures in the three experimental conditions (73°, 85°, and 95°). If systematic variance related to temperature was obtained, they could conclude that changes in temperature affected aggressive behavior. Indeed, this and other research has shown that the likelihood of aggression is greater when the temperature is moderately hot than when it is cool, but that aggression decreases under extremely high temperatures (Anderson, 1989).

OPTIMISM AND HEALTH. In a correlational study of the relationship between optimism and health, Scheier and Carver (1985) administered to participants a measure for optimism. Four weeks later, the same participants completed a checklist on which they indicated the degree to which they had experienced each of 39 physical symptoms.

Of course, there was considerable variability in the number of symptoms that participants reported. Some indicated that they were quite healthy, whereas others reported many symptoms. Interestingly, participants who scored high on the optimism scale reported fewer symptoms than did less optimistic participants; that is, there was a correlation between optimism scores and the number of symptoms that participants reported. In fact, approximately 7% of the total variance in reported symptoms was related to optimism; in other words, 7% of the variance in symptoms was systematic variance related to participants' optimism scores. Thus, optimism and symptoms were related in an orderly, systematic fashion.

In both of these studies, the researchers found that some of the total variance was systematic variance. Baron and Bell found that some of the total variance in aggression was systematic variance related to temperature; Scheier and Carver found that some of the total variance in physical symptoms was systematic variance related to optimism. Finding evidence of systematic variance indicates that variables are related to one another—that room temperature is related to aggression, and optimism is related to physical symptoms, for example. Uncovering relationships in research is always a matter of seeing whether part of the total variance in participants' scores is systematic variance.

As we'll see in detail in later chapters, researchers must design their studies so that they can tell how much of the total variance in participants' behavior is systematic variance associated with the variables they are investigating. If they don't, the study will fail to detect relationships among variables that are, in fact, related. Poorly designed studies do not permit researchers to conclude confidently which variables were responsible for the systematic variance they obtained. We'll return to this important point in later chapters as we learn how to design good studies.

Error Variance

Not all of the total variability in participants' behavior is systematic variance. Factors that the researcher is *not* investigating may also be related to participants'

behavior. In the Baron and Bell experiment, not all of the variability in aggression across participants was due to temperature. And in the Scheier and Carver study only 7% of the variance in the symptoms that participants reported was related to optimism; the remaining 93% of the variance in symptoms was due to other things.

Clearly, then, other factors are at work. Much of the variance in these studies was not associated with the primary variables of interest (temperature and optimism). For example, in the experiment on aggression, some participants may have been in a worse mood than others, leading them to behave more aggressively for reasons that had nothing to do with room temperature. Similarly, some participants may have come from aggressive homes, whereas others may have been raised by parents who were pacifists. The experimenter may have unintentionally treated some subjects more politely than others, thereby lowering their aggressiveness. A few participants may have been unusually hostile because they had just failed an exam. Each of these factors may have contributed to the total variability in participants' aggression, but none of them is related to the variable of interest in the experiment—the temperature.

Even after a researcher has determined how much of the total variance is related to the variables of interest in the study (that is, how much of the total variance is systematic), some variance remains unaccounted for. Variance that remains unaccounted for is called **error variance**. Error variance is that portion of the total variance that is unrelated to the variables under investigation in the study (see Figure 2.2).

Do not think of the term *error* as indicating errors or mistakes in the usual sense of the word. Although error variance may be due to mistakes in recording or coding the data, more often it is simply the result of factors that remain unidentified in a study. No single study can investigate every factor that is related to the behavior under investigation. Rather, a researcher chooses to investigate the impact of only one or a few variables on the target behavior. Baron and Bell chose to study temperature, for example, and ignored other variables that might influence aggression. Scheier and Carver focused on

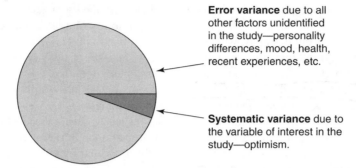

Error variance due to all other factors unidentified in the study—personality differences, mood, health, recent experiences, etc.

Systematic variance due to the variable of interest in the study—optimism.

FIGURE 2.2   Variability in Physical Symptoms.   If we draw a circle to represent the total variability in the physical symptoms reported by participants in the Scheier and Carver (1985) study, systematic variance is that portion of the variance that is related to the variable under investigation, in this case optimism. Error variance is that portion of the total variability that is not related to the variable(s) being studied.

optimism but not on other variables related to physical symptoms. All of the other unidentified variables that the researchers did not study contributed to the total variance in participants' responses, and the variance that is due to these unidentified variables is called error variance.

Distinguishing Systematic from Error Variance

To answer questions about behavioral variability, researchers must determine whether any of the total variance in the data they collect is related in a systematic fashion to the variables they are investigating. If the participants' behavior varies in a systematic way as certain other variables change, systematic variance is present, providing evidence that those variables are related to the behavior under investigation.

As they analyze their data, researchers always face the task of distinguishing the systematic variance from the error variance in their data. In order to determine whether variables are related to one another, they must be able to tell how much of the total variability in the behavior being studied is systematic variance versus error variance. This is the point at which statistics are indispensable. Researchers use certain statistical analyses to partition the total variance in their data into components that reflect systematic versus error variance. These analyses

allow them not only to calculate how much of the total variance is systematic versus error variance but also to test whether the amount of systematic variance in the data is large enough to conclude that the effect is real (as opposed to being due to random influences). We will return to some of these analyses later in the book. For now, the important point to remember is that, in order to draw conclusions from their data, researchers must statistically separate systematic from error variance.

Unfortunately, error variance can mask or obscure the effects of the variables in which researchers are primarily interested. The more error variance in a set of data, the more difficult it is to determine whether the variables of interest are related to variability in behavior. For example, the more participants' aggression in an experiment is affected by extraneous factors, such as their mood or how the researcher treats them, the more difficult it is to determine whether room temperature affected their aggression.

The reason that error variance can obscure the systematic effects of other variables is analogous to the way in which noise or static can cover up a song that you want to hear on the radio. In fact, if the static is too loud (because you are sitting beside an electrical device, for example), you might wonder whether a song is playing at all. Similarly, you can think of error variance as noise or static—unwanted, annoying variation that, when too strong, can mask the real "signal" produced by the variables in which the researcher is interested.

In the same way that we can more easily hear a song on the radio when the static is reduced, researchers can more easily detect systematic variance produced by the variables of interest when error variance is minimized. They can rarely eliminate error variance entirely, both because the behavior being studied is almost always influenced by unknown factors and because the procedures of the study itself can create error variance. But researchers strive to reduce error variance as much as possible. A good research design is one that minimizes error variance so that the researcher can detect any systematic variance that is present in the data. We will discuss the ways in which researchers try to reduce error variance in later chapters.

To review, the total variance in a set of data contains both systematic variance due to the variables of interest to the researcher and error variance due to everything else (that is, total variance = systematic variance + error variance). The analysis of data from a study always requires us to separate systematic from error variance and thereby determine whether a relationship between our variables exists.

EFFECT SIZE: ASSESSING THE STRENGTH OF RELATIONSHIPS

Researchers are interested not only in whether certain variables are related to participants' responses but also in *how strongly* they are related. Sometimes variables are associated only weakly with particular cognitive, emotional, behavioral, or physiological responses, whereas at other times, variables are strongly related to thoughts, emotions, and behavior. For example, in a study of variables that predict workers' reactions to losing their jobs, Prussia, Kinicki, and Bracker (1993) found that the degree to which respondents were emotionally upset about losing their jobs was strongly related to how much effort they expected they would have to exert to find a new job but only weakly related to their expectations of actually finding a new job.

Measures of the strength or magnitude of relationships among variables show us how important particular variables are in producing a particular behavior, thought, emotion, or physiological response. Researchers assess the strength of

the empirical relationships they discover by determining the proportion of the total variability in participants' responses that is systematic variance related to the variables under study. As we saw, the total variance of a set of data is composed of systematic variance and error variance. Once we calculate these types of variance, we can easily determine the *proportion* of the total variance that is systematic (that is, the proportion of total variance that is systematic variance = systematic variance/total variance).

Researchers use measures of **effect size** to show them how strongly variables in a study are related to one another. How researchers calculate effect sizes is a topic for later chapters. For now, it is enough to understand that one index of the strength of the relationship between variables involves the proportion of total variance that is systematic variance. That is, we can see how strongly two variables are related by calculating the proportion of the total variance that is systematic variance. For example, we could calculate the proportion of the total variance in people's ratings of how upset they are about losing their job that is systematic variance related to their expectations of finding a new one.

At one extreme, if the proportion of the total variance that is systematic variance is .00, *none* of the variance in participants' responses in a study is systematic variance. When this is the case, we know there is absolutely no relationship between the variables under study and participants' responses. At the other extreme, if *all* of the variance in participants' responses is systematic variance (that is, if systematic variance/total variance = 1.00), then all of the variability in the data can be attributed to the variables under study. When this is the case, the variables are as strongly related as they possibly can be (in fact, this is called a *perfect relationship*). When the ratio of systematic to total variance is between .00 and 1.00, the larger the proportion, the stronger the relationship between the variables.

When we view effect size as a proportion, we can compare the strength of different relationships directly. For example, in the study of reactions to job loss described earlier, 26% of the total variance in emotional upset after being fired was related to how much effort the respondents expected they would have to exert to find a new job. In contrast, only 5% of the variance in emotional upset was related to their expectations of finding a new job. Taken together, these findings suggest that, for people who lose their jobs, it is not the possibility of being forever unemployed that is most responsible for their upset but rather the expectation of how difficult things will be in the short run while seeking reemployment. In fact, by comparing the strength of association for the two findings, we can see that the person's expectations about the effort involved in looking for work (which accounted for 26% of the total variance in distress) was over five times more strongly related to their emotional upset than their expectation of finding a new job (which accounted for only 5% of the variance).

In Depth
Types of Effect Size Indicators

Researchers use several different statistics to indicate effect size depending on the nature of their data. Roughly speaking, these effect size statistics fall into three broad categories. Some effect size indices, sometimes called d-based effect sizes, are based on the size of the difference between the means of two groups, such as the difference between the average scores of men and women on some measure or the differences in the average scores that participants obtained in two experimental conditions. The larger the difference between the means, relative to the total variability of the data, the stronger the effect and the larger the effect size statistic.

The r-based effect size indices are based on the size of the correlation between two variables. The larger the correlation, the more strongly two variables are related and the more of the total variance in one variable is systematic variance related to the other variable.

A third category of effect sizes index involves the odds-ratio, which tells us the ratio of the odds of an event occurring in one group to the odds of the event occurring in another group. If the event is equally likely in both groups, the odds ratio is 1.0. An odds ratio greater than 1.0 shows that the odds of the event is greater in one group than in another, and the larger the odds ratio, the stronger the effect. The odds ratio is used when the variable being measured has only two levels. For example, imagine doing research in which first-year students in college are either assigned to attend a special course on how to study or not assigned to attend the study skills course, and we wish to know whether the course reduces the likelihood that students will drop out of college. We could use the odds ratio to see how much of an effect the course had on the odds of students dropping out.

You do not need to understand the statistical differences among these effect size indices, but you will find it useful in reading journal articles to know what some of the most commonly used effect sizes are called. These are all ways of expressing how strongly variables are related to one another—that is, the effect size.

Symbol	Name
d	Cohen's d
g	Hedge's g
η^2	eta squared
ω^2	omega squared
r or r^2	correlation effect size
OR	odds ratio

The strength of the relationships between variables varies a great deal across studies. In some studies, as little as 1% of the total variance may be systematic variance, whereas in other contexts, the proportion of the total variance that is systematic variance may be quite large, sometimes (though rarely) as high as 80%.

Generally, researchers prefer that their research findings have relatively large effect sizes because a large effect size usually indicates that they have identified an important correlate, predictor, or cause of the phenomenon they are studying. In reality, however, studies in behavioral science rarely account for more than 40% of the total variance with any single variable, and most effects are far smaller. In fact, one study of three leading journals in psychology showed that the average effect sizes were in the .10 to .20 range (Ward, 2002). And, we must remember that published studies typically have stronger effects than unpublished ones.

Many students are initially surprised, and even troubled, to learn how "weak" many research findings are. For example, a national survey of a representative sample of nearly 5,000 adults by DeVoe and Pfeffer (2009) showed that people who had higher annual incomes reported being happier than people who made less money. But how much of the total variance in happiness do you think was accounted for by income? Less than 3%! (That is, less than 3% of the total variance in happiness was systematic variance due to income.) That's not a very large effect size.

Yet, perhaps we should not be surprised that any particular variable is only weakly related to whatever phenomenon we are studying. After all, most psychological phenomena are multiply determined—the result of a large number of factors. In light of this, we should not expect that *any single variable* investigated in a particular study would be systematically related to a large portion of the total variance in the phenomenon being investigated. For example, think of all of the factors that contribute to variability in happiness and unhappiness, such as a person's health, relationship satisfaction, family situation, financial difficulties, job satisfaction, difficulties at school, the well-being of loved ones, legal problems, and so on. Viewed in this way, explaining even a small percentage of the total variance in a particular response, such as happiness, in terms of only one variable may be an important finding. Seemingly small effects can be interesting and important.

Consider another example—the fact that people's romantic partners tend to be about the same level of physical attractiveness as they are. Highly attractive people tend to have relationship partners who are high in attractiveness, moderately attractive people tend to pair with moderately attractive partners, and unattractive people tend to have less attractive partners. But how much of the total variance in the attractiveness of people's relationship partners is systematic variance related to the attractiveness of the people themselves? Research shows that it is only about 16% (Meyer et al., 2001). That may not seem like a very strong association, yet the effect is strong enough to be seen easily in everyday life and it shows that something involving physical appearance influences people's choices of relationship partners.

In Depth

Effect Sizes in Psychology, Medicine, and Baseball

Behavioral researchers have sometimes been troubled by the small effect sizes they often obtain in their research. In fact, however, the sizes of the effects obtained in behavioral research are comparable to those obtained in other disciplines. For example, many effects in medicine that are widely regarded as important are smaller than those typically obtained in psychological research (Meyer et al., 2001).

Research has shown, for example, that taking aspirin daily helps to reduce the risk of death by heart attack, and many people regularly take aspirin for this purpose. But aspirin usage accounts for less than 1% of the risk of having a heart attack. This should not deter you from taking aspirin if you wish; yours may be one of the lives that are saved. But the effect is admittedly small. Similarly, many people take ibuprofen to reduce the pain of headaches, sore muscles, and injuries, and ibuprofen's effectiveness is well-documented. Even so, taking ibuprofen accounts for only about 2% of the total variance in pain reduction. The effect of Viagra is somewhat more impressive; Viagra accounts for about 14% of the improvement in men's sexual functioning.

To look at another well-known effect, consider the relationship between a major league baseball player's batting skill (as indicated by his RBI) and the probability that he will get a hit on a given instance at

(continued)

(continued)

bat. You might guess that RBI bears a very strong relationship to success-at-bat. A player with a higher RBI surely has a much greater chance of getting a hit than one with a lower RBI. (Why else would players with higher RBIs be paid millions of dollars more than those with lower RBIs?) But if we consider the question from the standpoint of variance, the answer may surprise you. RBI accounts for only .0036% of the total variance in a batter's success at a given instance at bat! The small size of this effect stands in contrast to the importance of RBI and makes an important point: Small effects can add up. Although a higher RBI gives a batter only a slight edge at any given time at bat, over the course of a season or a career, the cumulative effects of slight differences in batting average may be dramatic. (Hence, the large salaries.) The same is true of certain psychological variables as well.

My point is not to glorify the size of effects in behavioral research relative to other domains. Rather, my point is twofold: The effects obtained in behavioral research are no smaller than those in most other fields, and even small effects can be important.

META-ANALYSIS: SYSTEMATIC VARIANCE ACROSS STUDIES

As we've seen, researchers are typically interested in the strength of the relationships they uncover in their studies. However, any particular piece of research can provide only a rough estimate of the "true" proportion of the total variance in a particular behavior that is systematically related to other variables. The effect size obtained in a particular study is only a rough estimate of the true effect size because the strength of the relationship obtained in a study is affected not only by the relationship between the variables but also by the characteristics of the study itself—the sample of participants who were studied, the particular measures used, and the research procedures, for example. Thus, although Prussia et al. (1993) found that 26% of the variance in their respondents' emotional upset was related to their expectations of how much effort they would need to exert to find a new job, the strength of the relationship between expectations and emotional upset in their study may have been affected by the particular participants, measures, and procedures the researchers used. We may find a somewhat stronger or weaker relationship if we conducted a similar study using different participants, measures, or methods.

For this reason, behavioral scientists have become increasingly interested in examining the strength of relationships between particular variables *across many studies*. Although any given study provides only a rough estimate of the strength of a particular relationship, averaging these estimates over many studies that used different participants, measures, and procedures should provide a more accurate indication of how strongly the variables are "really" related.

A procedure known as **meta-analysis** is used to analyze and integrate the results from a large set of individual studies (Cooper, 1990). When researchers conduct a meta-analysis, they examine every study that has been conducted on a particular topic to assess the relationship between whatever variables are the focus of their analysis. Using information provided in the journal article or report of each study, the researcher calculates the effect size in that study, which, as we have seen, is an index of the strength of the relationship between the variables. These effect sizes from different studies are then statistically combined to obtain a general estimate of the strength of the relationship between the variables. By combining information from many individual studies, researchers assume that the resulting estimate of the average strength of the relationship will be more accurate than the estimate provided by any particular study.

Let's consider a meta-analysis of the psychological effects of punishment on children. Parents and psychologists have long debated the immediate effectiveness and long-term impact of using corporal punishment, such as spanking, to discipline children. Some have argued that physical punishment is not only effective but also desirable, but others have concluded that it is ineffective if not ultimately harmful. In an effort to address this controversy, Gershoff (2002) conducted a meta-analysis of 88 studies that investigated various effects of corporal punishment. These studies spanned more than 60 years (1938 to 2000) and involved more than 36,000 participants. Clearly, conclusions based on such a massive amount of data should be more conclusive than those obtained by any single study. Gershoff's statistical analyses of these studies showed that, considered as a whole, corporal punishment was associated with all of the 11 outcome behaviors she examined, which included childhood aggression and antisocial behavior, decreased quality of the relationship between child and parents, poorer mental health during both childhood and adulthood, and increased risk of later abusing a child or a spouse.

In most meta-analyses, researchers not only determine the degree to which certain variables are related (that is, the overall effect) but also explore the factors that affect their relationship. For example, in looking across many studies, they may find that the relationship was generally stronger for male than for female participants, that it was stronger when certain kinds of measures were used, or that it was weaker when particular experimental conditions were present. For example, Gershoff (2002) found that the more girls that were included in a study, the less corporal punishment was associated with aggression and antisocial behavior (suggesting that the effect of punishment on increased aggression is stronger for boys). Furthermore, although corporal punishment was associated with negative effects for all age groups, the negative effects were strongest when the mean age of the participants was between 10 and 12, suggesting that corporal punishment has a stronger effect on middle school children than on other ages. Thus, meta-analysis is used not only to document relationships across studies but also to explore factors that affect the strength of those relationships.

For many years, researchers who conducted meta-analyses were frustrated by the fact that many authors did not report information regarding the effect sizes of their findings in journal articles and other research reports. However, new guidelines from the American Psychological Association now require researchers to report effect sizes in their publications and papers (APA Publications and Communications Board Working Group, 2008). With this information more readily available, the quality and usefulness of meta-analyses will improve in the future.

Behavioral Research Case Study
Meta-Analyses of Gender Differences in Math Ability

Meta-analyses have been conducted on many areas of the research literature, including factors that influence the effectiveness of psychotherapy, gender differences in sexuality, the effects of rejection on emotion and self-esteem, personality differences in prejudice, helping behavior, and employees' commitment to their jobs. However, by far, the most popular topic for meta-analysis has been gender differences.

Although many studies have found that men and women differ on a variety of cognitive, emotional, and behavioral variables, researchers have been quick to point out that the differences obtained in these studies are often quite small (and typically smaller than popular stereotypes of men and women assume). Furthermore, some studies have obtained differences between men and women, whereas others have not. This is fertile territory for meta-analyses, which can combine the findings of many studies to show us whether, in general, men and women differ on particular variables. Researchers have conducted meta-analyses of research on gender differences to answer the question of whether men and women really differ in regard to certain behaviors and, if so, to document the strength of the relationship between gender and these behaviors. Using the concepts we have learned in this chapter, we can rephrase these questions as: Is any of the total variability in people's behavior related to their gender, and, if so, what proportion of the total variance is systematic variance due to gender?

Hyde, Fennema, and Lamon (1990) conducted a meta-analysis to examine gender differences in mathematics performance. Based on analyses of 100 individual research studies (that involved over 3 million

(continued)

(continued)

participants), these researchers concluded that, overall, the relationship between gender and math performance is very weak. Put differently, the meta-analysis showed that very little of the total variance in math performance is systematic variance related to gender. Analyses did show that girls slightly outperformed boys in mathematic computation in elementary and middle school but that boys tended to outperform girls in math problem solving in high school. By statistically comparing the effect sizes for studies that were conducted before versus after 1974, they also found that the relationship between gender and math ability has weakened over time.

More recently, Else-Quest, Hyde, and Linn (2010) conducted a meta-analysis of gender differences in mathematics achievement and attitudes using data from 69 countries. Their analysis, which was based on nearly 500,000 students ranging in age from 14 to 16 years old, found that the average effect sizes for the differences between boys and girls were very small, sometimes favoring one gender and sometimes the other. In fact, the effect sizes for gender differences in the United States hovered around .00, showing no overall difference in math achievement between boys and girls. Further analyses showed that the effect size differed somewhat by country, but overall, the data provided no evidence for strong and consistent differences in the math abilities of boys and girls. Even so, the meta-analysis showed that boys *thought* they were better at math than girls did.

THE QUEST FOR SYSTEMATIC VARIANCE

In the final analysis, virtually all behavioral research is a quest for systematic variance. No matter what specific questions researchers may want to answer, they are trying to account for (or explain) the variability they observe in some thought, emotion, behavior, or physiological reaction that is of interest to them. Does the speed with which people process information decrease as they age? What effect does the size of a reward have on the extinction of a response once the reward is stopped? Are women more empathic than men? What effect does alcohol have on the ability to pay attention? Why do people who score high in rejection sensitivity have less satisfying relationships? To address questions such as these, researchers design studies to determine whether certain variables relate to the observed variability in the phenomenon of interest in a systematic fashion. If so, they will explore precisely *how* the variables are related; but the first goal is always to determine whether any of the total variance is systematic.

Keeping this goal in mind as you move forward in your study of research methods will give you a framework for thinking about all stages of the research process. From measurement to design to data collection to analysis, a researcher must remember at each juncture that he or she is on a quest for systematic variance.

Summary

1. Psychology and other behavioral sciences involve the study of behavioral variability. Most aspects of behavioral research are aimed at explaining variability in behavior: (a) Research questions are about the causes and correlates of behavioral variability; (b) researchers try to design studies that will best explain the variability in a particular behavior; (c) the measures used in research attempt to capture numerically the variability in participants' behavior; and (d) statistics are used to analyze the variability in our data.

2. Descriptive statistics summarize and describe the behavior of research participants. Inferential statistics analyze the variability in the data to answer questions about the reliability and generalizability of the findings.

3. Variance is a statistical index of variability. Variance is calculated by subtracting the mean of the data from each participant's score, squaring these differences, summing the squared difference scores, and dividing this sum by the number of participants minus 1. In statistical notation, the variance is expressed as: $s^2 = \Sigma(y_i - \bar{y})^2/(n - 1)$.

4. The total variance in a set of data can be broken into two components. Systematic variance is that part of the total variance in participants' responses that is related in an orderly fashion to the variables under investigation in a particular study. Error variance is variance that is due to unidentified sources and, thus, remains unaccounted for in a study.

5. To examine the strength of the relationships they study, researchers determine the proportion of the total variability in behavior that is systematic variance associated with the variables under study. The larger the proportion of the total variance that is systematic variance, the stronger the relationship between the variables. Statistics that express the strength of relationships are called measures of effect size.

6. Meta-analysis is used to examine the nature and strength of relationships between variables across many individual studies. By averaging effect sizes across many studies, a more accurate estimate of the relationship between variables can be obtained.

Key Terms

descriptive statistics (*p. 34*)
effect size (*p. 41*)
error variance (*p. 39*)
inferential statistics (*p. 34*)
mean (*p. 35*)

meta-analysis (*p. 44*)
range (*p. 35*)
statistical notation (*p. 37*)
systematic variance (*p. 38*)

total sum of squares (*p. 36*)
total variance (*p. 38*)
variability (*p. 32*)
variance (*p. 34*)

Questions for Review

1. Discuss how the concept of behavioral variability relates to the following topics:
a. the research questions that interest behavioral researchers
b. the design of research studies
c. the measurement of behavior
d. the analysis of behavioral data

2. Why do researchers care how much variability exists in a set of data?

3. Distinguish between descriptive and inferential statistics.

4. Conceptually, what does the variance tell us about a set of data?

5. What is the range, and why is it not an ideal index of variability?

6. Give a definition of variance and then explain how you would calculate it.

7. How does variance differ from the total sum of squares?

8. What does each of the following symbols mean in statistical notation?
a. Σ
b. $\bar{x}$
c. s^2
d. $\Sigma y_i/n$
e. $\Sigma(y_i - \bar{y})^2$

9. The total variance in a set of scores can be partitioned into two components. What are they, and how do they differ?

10. What are some factors that contribute to error variance in a set of data?

11. Generally, do researchers want systematic variance to be large or small? Explain.

12. Why are researchers often interested in knowing the proportion of total variance that is systematic variance?

13. What would the proportion of total variance that is systematic variance indicate if it were .25? .00? .98?

14. Why do researchers want the error variance in their data to be small?

15. Why is effect size important in scientific investigations?

16. What are the three general types of effect size indicators that researchers use?

17. If the proportion of systematic variance to total variance is .08, would you characterize the relationship as small, medium, or large? What if the proportion were .72? .00?

18. Why do researchers use meta-analysis? In what way are meta-analyses more informative than the results of a particular study?

19. In a meta-analysis, what does the effect size indicate?

Questions for Discussion

1. Restate each of the following research questions as a question about behavioral variability.
   a. Does eating too much sugar increase children's activity level?
   b. Do continuous reinforcement schedules result in faster learning than intermittent reinforcement schedules?
   c. Do people who are depressed sleep more or less than those who are not depressed?
   d. Are people with low self-esteem more likely than those with high self-esteem to join cults?
   e. Does caffeine increase the startle response to loud noise?

2. Simply from inspecting the following three data sets, which would you say has the largest variance? Which has the smallest?
   a. 17, 19, 17, 22, 17, 21, 22, 23, 18, 18, 20
   b. 111, 132, 100, 122, 112, 99, 138, 134, 116
   c. 87, 42, 99, 27, 35, 37, 92, 85, 16, 22, 50

3. A researcher conducted an experiment to examine the effects of distracting noise on people's ability to solve anagrams (scrambled letters that can be unscrambled to make words). Participants worked on anagrams for 10 minutes while listening to the sound of jackhammers and dissonant music that was played at one of four volume levels (quiet, moderate, loud, or very loud).

After analyzing the number of anagrams that participants solved in the four conditions, the researcher concluded that loud noise did, in fact, impede participants' ability to solve anagrams. In fact, the noise conditions accounted for 23% of the total variance in the number of anagrams that participants solved.
   a. Is this a small, medium, or large effect?
   b. What proportion of the total variance was error variance?
   c. List at least 10 things that might have contributed to the error variance in this study.

4. Several years ago, Mischel (1968) pointed out that, on average, only about 10% of the total variance in a particular behavior is systematic variance associated with another variable being studied. Reactions to Mischel's observation were of two varieties. On one hand, some researchers concluded that the theories and methods of behavioral science must somehow be flawed; surely, if our theories and methods were better we would obtain stronger relationships. However, others argued that accounting for an average of 10% of the variability in a particular behavior with any single variable is not a bad track record at all. Where do you stand on this issue? How much of the total variability in a particular phenomenon should we expect to explain with some other variable?

3 | THE MEASUREMENT OF BEHAVIOR

In 1904, the French minister of public education decided that children of lower intelligence required special education, so he hired Alfred Binet to design a procedure to identify children in the Paris school system who needed special attention. Binet faced a complicated task. Previous attempts to measure intelligence had been notably unsuccessful. Earlier in his career, Binet had experimented with craniometry, which involved estimating intelligence (as well as personality characteristics) from the size and shape of people's heads. Craniometry was an accepted practice at the time, but Binet became skeptical about its usefulness as a measure of intelligence. Other researchers had tried using other aspects of physical appearance, such as facial features, to measure intelligence, but these also were unsuccessful. Still others had used tests of reaction time under the assumption that more intelligent people would show faster reaction times than would less intelligent people. However, evidence for a link between intelligence and reaction time also was weak.

Thus, Binet rejected the previous methods and set about designing a new technique for measuring intelligence. His approach involved a series of short tasks requiring basic cognitive processes such as comprehension and reasoning. For example, children would be asked to name objects, answer commonsense questions, and interpret pictures. Binet published the first version of his intelligence test in 1905 in collaboration with one of his students, Theodore Simon.

When he revised the test 3 years later, Binet proposed a new index of intelligence that was based on an age level for each task on the test. The various tasks were arranged sequentially in the order in which a child of average intelligence could pass them successfully. For example, average 4-year-olds know their sex, are able to indicate which of two lines is longer, and can name familiar objects (such as a key), but cannot say how two abstract terms (such as *pride* and *pretension*) differ. By seeing which tasks a child could or could not complete, one could estimate the "mental age" of a child—the intellectual level at which the child is able to perform. Later, the German psychologist William Stern recommended dividing a child's mental age (as measured by Binet's test) by his or her chronological age to create the intelligence quotient, or IQ.

Binet's work provided the first useful measure of intelligence and set the stage for the widespread use of tests in psychology and education. Furthermore, it developed the measurement tools behavioral researchers needed to conduct research on intelligence, a topic that continues to attract a great deal of research attention today. Although contemporary intelligence tests continue to have their critics, the development of adequate measures was a prerequisite to the scientific study of intelligence.

All behavioral research involves the measurement of some behavioral, cognitive, emotional, or physiological response. Indeed, it would be inconceivable to conduct a study in which nothing was measured. Importantly, a particular piece of research is only as good as the measuring techniques that are used; poor measurement can doom a study. In this and the following chapter, we will look at how researchers measure behavioral, cognitive, emotional, and physiological events by examining the types of measures that behavioral scientists commonly use, the properties of such measures, and the characteristics that distinguish good measures from bad ones. In addition, we will discuss ways to develop the best possible measures for research purposes. As we will see, throughout the process of selecting or designing measures for use in research, our goal will be to use measures for which the variability in participants' scores on those measures reflects, as closely as possible, the variability in the behavior, thought, emotion, or physiological response being measured.

TYPES OF MEASURES

The measures used in behavioral research fall roughly into three categories: observational measures, physiological measures, and self-reports. **Observational measures** involve the direct observation of behavior. Observational measures, therefore, can be used to measure anything a participant does that researchers can observe—a rat pressing a bar, eye contact between people in conversation, fidgeting by a person giving a speech, aggression in children on the playground, the time it takes a worker to complete a task. In each case, researchers either observe participants

directly or else make audio or video recordings from which information about the participants' behavior is later coded.

Behavioral researchers who are interested in the relationship between bodily processes and behavior use **physiological measures**. Internal processes that are not directly observable—such as heart rate, brain activity, and hormonal changes—can be measured with sophisticated equipment. Some physiological processes, such as facial blushing and muscular reflexes, are potentially observable with the naked eye, but specialized equipment is needed to measure them accurately.

Self-report measures involve the replies people give to questionnaires and interviews. Self-report measures may provide information about the respondent's thoughts, feelings, or behavior. *Cognitive self-reports* measure what people *think* about something. For example, a developmental psychologist may ask a child which of two chunks of clay is larger—one rolled into a ball or one formed in the shape of a hot dog. Or a survey researcher may ask people about their attitudes about a political issue. *Affective self-reports* involve participants' responses regarding how they *feel*. Many behavioral researchers are interested in emotional reactions, such as depression, anxiety, stress, grief, and happiness, and in people's evaluations of themselves and others. The most straightforward way of assessing these kinds of affective responses is to ask participants to report on them. *Behavioral self-reports* involve participants' reports of how they *act*. Participants may be asked how often they read the newspaper, go to church, or have sex, for example. Similarly, many personality inventories ask participants to indicate how frequently they engage in certain behaviors.

As I noted, the success of every research study depends heavily on the quality of the measures used. Measures of behavior that are flawed in some way can distort our results and lead us to draw erroneous conclusions about the data. Because measurement is so important to the research process, an entire specialty known as **psychometrics** is devoted to the study of psychological measurement. Psychometricians investigate the properties of the measures used in behavioral research and work toward improving psychological measurement.

> ### Behavioral Research Case Study
> *Converging Operations in Measurement*
>
> Because any particular measurement procedure may provide only a rough and imperfect measure of a given construct, researchers sometimes measure a given construct in several different ways. By using several types of measures—each coming at the construct from a different angle—researchers can more accurately assess the variable of interest. When different kinds of measures provide the same results, we have more confidence in their validity. This approach to measurement is called **converging operations** or *triangulation*. (In the vernacular of navigation and land surveying, triangulation is a technique for determining the position of an object based on its relationship to points whose positions are known.)
>
> A case in point involves Pennebaker, Kiecolt-Glaser, and Glaser's (1988) research on the effects that writing about one's experiences has on health. On the basis of previous studies, these researchers hypothesized that people who wrote about traumatic events they had personally experienced would show an improvement in their physical health. To test this idea, they conducted an experiment in which 50 university students were instructed to write for 20 minutes a day for 4 days about either a traumatic event they had experienced (such as the death of a loved one, child abuse, rape, or intense family conflict) or superficial topics.
>
> Rather than rely on any single measure of physical health—which is a complex and multifaceted construct—Pennebaker and his colleagues used converging operations to assess the effects of writing on participants' health. First, they obtained *observational measures* involving participants' visits to the university health center. Second, they used *physiological measures* to assess directly the functioning of participants' immune systems. Specifically, they collected samples of participants' blood three times during the study and tested the lymphocytes, or white blood cells. Third, they used *self-report measures* to assess how distressed participants later felt—1 hour, 6 weeks, and 3 months after the experiment.
>
> Together, these triangulating data supported the experimental hypothesis. Compared to participants who wrote about superficial topics, those who wrote about traumatic experiences visited the health center less frequently, showed better functioning of their immune systems (as indicated by the action of the lymphocytes), and reported they felt better. This and other studies by Pennebaker and his colleagues were among the first to demonstrate the beneficial effects of expressing one's thoughts and feelings about troubling events (Pennebaker, 1990).

SCALES OF MEASUREMENT

Regardless of what kind of measure is used—observational, physiological, or self-report—the goal of measurement is to assign numbers to participants' responses so that they can be summarized and analyzed. For example, a researcher may convert participants' marks on a questionnaire to a set of numbers (from 1 to 5, perhaps) that meaningfully represent the participants' responses. These numbers are then used to describe and analyze participants' answers.

However, in analyzing and interpreting research data, not all numbers can be treated the same way. As we'll see, some numbers used to represent participants' responses are, in fact, "real" numbers that can be added, subtracted, multiplied, and divided. Other numbers, however, have special characteristics and require special treatment.

Researchers distinguish among four different levels or **scales of measurement.** These scales of measurement differ in the degree to which the numbers being used to represent participants' responses correspond to the real number system. Differences among these scales of measurement are important because they have implications for what a particular number indicates about a participant and how one's data may be analyzed.

The simplest type of scale is a **nominal scale**. With a nominal scale, the numbers that are assigned to participants' behaviors or characteristics are essentially labels. For example, for purposes of analysis, we may assign all boys in a study the number 1 and all girls the number 2. Or we may indicate whether participants are married by designating 1 if they have never been married, 2 if they are currently married, 3 if they were previously married but are not married now, or 4 if they were married but their spouse is deceased. Numbers on a nominal scale indicate attributes of our participants, but they are labels, descriptions, or names rather than real numbers. Thus, they do not have many of the properties of real numbers and it often makes no sense to perform mathematical operations on them.

An **ordinal scale** involves the rank ordering of a set of behaviors or characteristics. Measures that use ordinal scales tell us the relative order of our participants on a particular dimension but do not indicate the distance between participants on the dimension being measured. Imagine being at a talent contest in which the winner is the contestant who receives the loudest applause. Although we might be able to rank the contestants by the applause they receive, we would find it difficult to judge precisely how much more the audience liked one contestant than another. Likewise, we can record the order in which runners finish a race, but these numbers do not indicate how much faster one person was than another. The person who finished first (whom we label *1*) is not 1/10th as fast as the person who came in tenth (whom we label *10*).

When an **interval scale** of measurement is used, equal differences between the numbers reflect equal differences between participants in the characteristic being measured. On an IQ test, for example, the difference between scores of 90 and 100 (10 points) is the same as the difference between scores of 130 and 140 (10 points). However, an interval scale does not have a true zero point that indicates the absence of the quality being measured. An IQ score of 0 does not necessarily indicate that no intelligence is present, just as on the Fahrenheit thermometer (which is an interval scale), a temperature of zero degrees does not indicate the absence of temperature. Because an interval scale has no true zero point, the numbers cannot be multiplied or divided. It makes no sense to say that a temperature

of 100 degrees is twice as hot as a temperature of 50 degrees or that a person with an IQ of 60 is one-third as intelligent as a person with an IQ of 180.

The highest level of measurement is the **ratio scale**. Because a ratio scale has a true zero point, ratio measurement involves real numbers that can be added, subtracted, multiplied, and divided. Many measures of physical characteristics, such as weight, are on a ratio scale. Because weight has a true zero point (indicating no weight), it makes sense to talk about 100 pounds being twice as heavy as 50 pounds.

Scales of measurement are important to researchers for two reasons. First, the measurement scale determines the amount of information provided by a particular measure. Nominal scales usually provide less information than ordinal, interval, or ratio scales. When asking people about their opinions, for example, simply asking whether they agree or disagree with particular statements (which is a nominal scale) does not capture as much information as an interval scale that asks *how much* they agree or disagree. In many cases, choice of a measurement scale is determined by the characteristic being measured; it would be difficult to measure gender on anything other than a nominal scale, for example. However, given a choice, researchers prefer to use the highest level of measurement scale possible because it will provide the most pertinent and precise information about participants' responses or characteristics.

The second important feature of scales of measurement involves the kinds of statistical analyses that can be performed on the data. Certain mathematical operations can be performed only on numbers that conform to the properties of a particular measurement scale. The more useful and powerful statistical analyses, such as *t*-tests and *F*-tests (which we'll meet in later chapters), generally require that numbers be on interval or ratio scales. As a result, researchers try to choose scales that allow them to use the most informative statistical tests.

In Depth
Scales, Scales, and Scales

To avoid confusion, I should mention that the word **scale** has at least three meanings among behavioral researchers. Setting aside the everyday meaning of *scale* as an instrument for measuring weight, researchers use the term in three different ways.

First, as we have just seen, the phrase *scale of measurement* is used to indicate whether a variable is measured at the nominal, ordinal, interval, or ratio level. So, for example, a researcher might say that a particular response was measured on a nominal scale or a ratio scale of measurement.

Second, researchers sometimes use *scale* to refer to the way in which a participant indicates his or her answer on a questionnaire or in an interview. For example, researchers might say that they used a "true-false scale" or that participants rated their attitudes on a "5-point scale that ranged from strongly disagree to strongly agree." We will use the term *response format* to refer to this use of the word *scale*.

Third, *scale* can refer to a set of questions that all assess the same construct. Typically, using several questions to measure a construct—such as mood, self-esteem, attitudes toward a particular topic, or an evaluation of another person—provides a better measure than asking only a single question. For example, a researcher who wanted to measure self-compassion (the degree to which people treat themselves with kindness and concern when things go badly in their life) might use a scale consisting of several items such as *When I'm going through a very hard time, I give myself the caring and tenderness I need* and *I try to be understanding and patient towards those aspects of my personality I don't like* (Neff, 2003). The researcher would add participants' ratings of the statements on this scale to obtain a self-compassion score.

ASSESSING THE RELIABILITY OF A MEASURE

The goal of measurement is to assign numbers to people, behaviors, objects, or events so that the numbers correspond in a meaningful way to the attribute that we are trying to measure. Whatever we are measuring in a study, all we have in the end are numbers that correspond to information about participants' characteristics and responses. In order for those numbers to be useful in answering our research questions, we must be certain that they accurately reflect the characteristics and responses that we intended to measure. Put differently, we want the variability in those numbers to reflect, as closely as possible, the variability in the characteristic or response being measured.

In fact, a perfect measure would be one for which the variability in the numbers provided by our measuring technique perfectly matched the true variability in whatever we are trying to measure. As you might guess, however, our measures of people's thoughts, emotions, behaviors, and physiological responses are never perfect. So, the variability in our data rarely reflects the variability in participants' responses perfectly. Given that no measure captures the true variability in whatever we are measuring, how do we know whether a particular measurement technique provides us with scores that reflect what we want to measure closely enough to be useful in our research? How can we tell whether the variability in the numbers produced by a particular measure does, in fact, adequately reflect the actual variability in the characteristic or response we want to measure? To answer this question, we must examine two attributes of the measures that we use in research—reliability and validity.

The first characteristic that any good measure must possess is reliability. **Reliability** refers to the consistency or dependability of a measuring technique. If you weigh yourself on a bathroom scale three times in a row, you expect to obtain the same weight each time. If, however, you weigh 140 pounds the first time, 108 pounds the second time, and 162 pounds the third time, then the scale is *unreliable*—it can't be trusted to provide consistent weights. Similarly, measures used in research must be reliable. When they aren't, we can't trust them to provide meaningful data regarding our participants.

Measurement Error

To understand reliability, let's consider why a particular participant obtains the score that he or she obtains on a particular measure. A participant's score on any measure consists of two components:

the true score and measurement error. We can portray this by the equation:

$$\text{Observed score} = \text{True score} + \text{Measurement error}$$

The **true score** is the score that the participant would have obtained if our measure were perfect and we were able to measure whatever we were measuring without error. If researchers were omniscient beings, they would know exactly what a participant's score should be—that Susan's IQ is *exactly* 138, that Sean's score on a measure of prejudice is *genuinely* 43, or that the rat pressed the bar *precisely* 52 times, for example.

However, the measures used in research are seldom that precise. Virtually all measures contain **measurement error**. This component of the participant's observed score is the result of factors that distort the observed score so that it isn't precisely what it should be (i.e., it doesn't perfectly equal the participant's true score). If Susan was anxious and preoccupied when she took the IQ test, for example, her observed IQ score might be lower than 138. If Sean was in a really bad mood when he participated in the study, he might score as more prejudiced than he really is. If the counter on the bar in a Skinner box malfunctioned, it might record that the rat pressed the bar only 50 times instead of 52. Each of these factors would introduce measurement error, making the observed score on each measure different from the true score.

Many factors can contribute to measurement error, but they fall into five major categories. First, measurement error is affected by *transient states* of the participant. For example, a participant's mood, health, level of fatigue, and feelings of anxiety can all contribute to measurement error so that the observed score on some measure does not perfectly reflect the participant's true characteristics or reactions.

Second, *stable attributes* of the participant can lead to measurement error. For example, paranoid or suspicious participants may purposefully distort their answers, and less intelligent participants may misunderstand certain questions. Individual differences in motivation can affect test scores; on tests of ability, motivated participants will score more highly than unmotivated participants regardless of their real level of ability. Both transient and stable characteristics can produce lower or higher observed scores than participants' true scores would be.

Third, *situational factors* in the research setting can create measurement error. If the researcher is particularly friendly, a participant might try harder; if the researcher is stern and aloof, participants may be intimidated, angered, or unmotivated. Rough versus tender handling of experimental animals can change their behavior. Room temperature, lighting, noise, and crowding also can artificially affect people's scores by introducing measurement error.

Fourth, *characteristics of the measure* itself can create measurement error. For example, ambiguous questions create measurement error because they can be interpreted in more than one way. And measures that induce fatigue (such as tests that are too long) or fear (such as intrusive or painful physiological measures) also can affect observed scores.

Finally, actual *mistakes* in recording participants' responses can make the observed score different from the true score. If a researcher sneezes while counting the number of times a rat presses a bar, he may lose count; if a careless researcher writes 3s that look like 5s, the person entering the data into the computer may enter a participant's score incorrectly; a participant might write his or her answer to question 17 in the space provided for question 18. In each case, the observed score that is ultimately analyzed contains error.

Whatever its source, measurement error undermines the reliability of the measures researchers use. In fact, the reliability of a measure is an inverse function of measurement error: The more measurement error present in a measuring technique, the less reliable the measure is. Anything that increases measurement error decreases the consistency and dependability of the measure.

The relationship between measurement error and reliability is shown in Figure 3.1. Imagine that we want to measure some variable (reaction time, intelligence, extraversion, or physical strength, for example) on five research participants. Ideally, we would like our measure to perfectly capture the participants' actual standing on this variable as shown by their true scores at the left side of the figure. Put differently, we

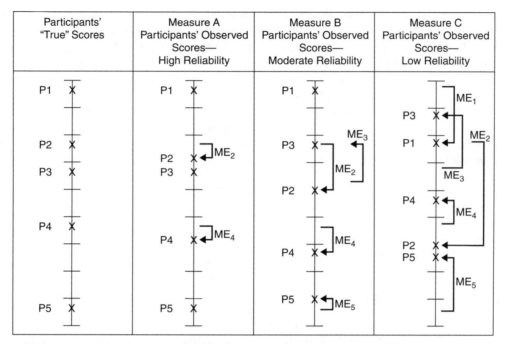

FIGURE 3.1   A Portrayal of High, Moderate, and Low Reliability   The five participants' true scores—the scores we would obtain if we could measure without error—are shown in the left-hand panel. Measure A has high reliability. Participants 1, 3, and 5 obtained scores that perfectly reflect their true scores (i.e., there is no measurement error). The observed scores for Participants 2 and 4 are very close to their true scores, and the measurement errors for these two participants (indicated by the arrows labeled ME) are small. Measure B has more measurement error, but participants' observed scores still reflect their true scores reasonably well. The reliability of Measure C is quite low because measurement errors are quite large, and the participants' observed scores are quite different from their true scores.

want the variability in the observed scores on our measure to mirror the variability in participants' true scores. Of course, we do not know what their true scores are and must rely on a potentially fallible instrument to assess them as best we can.

Imagine that we used a measure that was highly reliable. As you can see by comparing participants' scores on Measure A to their true scores in Figure 3.1, the observed scores we obtain with Measure A are quite close to participants' true scores. In fact, the observed scores for Participants 1, 3, and 5 are identical to their true scores; there is no measurement error whatsoever. For Participants 2 and 4, a little measurement error has crept into the observed scores, as indicated by the arrows labeled ME_2 and ME_4. These measurement errors show that

the observed scores for Participants 2 and 4 differ slightly from their true scores.

Next, look at what might happen if we used a moderately reliable measure. Comparing the scores on Measure B to the true scores shows that the observed scores for Participants 2, 3, 4, and 5 differ somewhat from their true scores. Participants 2 and 4 have obtained observed scores that underestimate their true scores, and Participants 3 and 5 have observed scores that overestimate their true scores. Even so, the observed scores fall roughly in the proper order, so this measure would allow us to get a pretty good idea of the participants' standing on whatever variable we were measuring.

Measure C on the right side of Figure 3.1 has very low reliability. As you can see, participants' observed scores differ markedly from their true scores. The measurement errors, as indicated by the arrows labeled ME, are quite large, showing that the observed scores are contaminated by a large amount of measurement error. A great deal of the variability among the participants' observed scores on Measure C is due to measurement error rather than the variable we are trying to assess. In fact, the measurement errors are so large that the participants' observed scores don't even fall in the same rank order as their true scores.

We would obviously prefer to use Measure A rather than Measure B or Measure C because the observed scores are closer to the truth. But, given that we don't really know what participants' true scores are, how can we tell if our measures are reliable?

Reliability as Systematic Variance

Researchers never know for certain precisely how much measurement error is contained in a particular participant's score or what the participant's true score really is. In fact, in many instances, researchers have no way of knowing for sure whether their measure is reliable and, if so, how reliable it is. However, for certain kinds of measures, researchers have ways of *estimating* the reliability of the measures they use. If they find that a measure is not acceptably reliable, they may take steps to increase its reliability. If the reliability cannot be increased, they may decide not to use it at all.

Assessing a measure's reliability involves an analysis of the variability in a set of scores. We saw earlier that each participant's observed score is composed of a true-score component and a measurement-error component. If we combine the scores of many participants and calculate the variance, the total variance of the *set of scores* is composed of the same two components:

$$\text{Total variance in a set of scores} = \text{Variance due to true scores} + \text{Variance due to measurement error.}$$

Stated differently, the portion of the total variance in a set of scores that is associated with participants'

true scores is *systematic variance* because the true-score component is related in a systematic fashion to the actual attribute that is being measured. The variance due to measurement error is *error variance* because it is *not* related to the attribute being measured. (See Chapter 2 for a review of systematic and error variance.) To assess the reliability of a measure, researchers estimate the proportion of the total variance in the data that is true-score (systematic) variance versus measurement error. Specifically,

Reliability = True-score variance/Total variance.

Thus, reliability is the proportion of the total variance in a set of scores that is systematic variance associated with participants' true scores.

The reliability of a measure can range from .00 (indicating no reliability) to 1.00. (indicating perfect reliability). As the preceding equation shows, the reliability is .00 when none of the total variance in a set of scores is true-score variance. When the reliability coefficient is zero, the scores reflect nothing but measurement error, and the measure is totally worthless. At the other extreme, a reliability coefficient of 1.00 would be obtained if all of the total variance were true-score variance. A measure is perfectly reliable if there is no measurement error. With a perfectly reliable measure, all of the variability in the observed scores reflects the actual variability in the characteristic or response being measured.

Although researchers prefer that their measures be as reliable as possible, a measure is usually considered sufficiently reliable for research purposes if at least 70% of the total variance in scores is systematic, or true-score, variance. That is, if we can trust that at least 70% of the total variance in our scores reflects the true variability in whatever we are measuring (and no more than 30% of the total variance is due to measurement error), the measure is reliable enough to use.

Types of Reliability

Researchers use three methods to estimate the reliability of their measures: test–retest reliability, interitem reliability, and interrater reliability. All three methods are based on the same general logic. To the extent that two measurements of the same characteristic or response yield similar scores, we can assume that both measurements are tapping into the same true score. However, if two measurements of something yield very different scores, the measures must contain a high degree of measurement error. Thus, by statistically testing the degree to which the two measurements yield similar scores, we can estimate the proportion of the total variance that is systematic true-score variance versus measurement-error variance, thereby estimating the reliability of the measure.

Most estimates of reliability are obtained by examining the correlation between what are supposed to be two measures of the same characteristic, behavior, or event. We'll discuss correlation in considerable detail in Chapter 7. For now, all you need to know is that a **correlation coefficient** is a statistic that expresses the strength of the relationship between two measures on a scale from .00 (no relationship between the two measures) to 1.00 (a perfect relationship between the two measures). Correlation coefficients can be positive, indicating a direct relationship between the measures, or negative, indicating an inverse relationship.

If we square a correlation coefficient, we obtain the proportion of the total variance in one set of scores that is systematic variance related to another set of scores. As we saw in Chapter 2, the proportion of systematic variance to total variance (i.e., systematic variance/total variance) is an index of the strength of the relationship between the two variables. Thus, the higher the correlation (and its square), the more closely the two variables are related. In light of this relationship, correlation is a useful tool in estimating reliability because it reveals the degree to which two measurements yield similar scores.

TEST–RETEST RELIABILITY. **Test–retest reliability** refers to the consistency of participants' responses on a measure over time. Assuming that the characteristic being measured is relatively stable and does not change over time, participants should obtain approximately the same score each time they are measured. If a person takes an intelligence test twice 8 weeks apart, we would expect his or her two test scores to be similar. Because there is some measurement error in even well-designed tests, the scores probably won't be exactly the same, but they should be close. If the two scores are not reasonably similar, the

measurement error must be distorting the scores, and the test is unreliable.

Test–retest reliability is determined by measuring participants on two occasions, usually separated by a few weeks. Then the two sets of scores are correlated to see how highly the second set of scores correlates to the first. If the two sets of scores correlate highly (at least .70), the scores must not contain much measurement error, and the measure has good test–retest reliability. If they do not correlate highly, participants' scores must be distorted upward and downward by too much measurement error. If so, the measure is not adequately reliable and should not be used. Low and high test–retest reliability are shown pictorially in Figure 3.2.

Assessing test–retest reliability makes sense only if the attribute being measured would not be expected to change between the two measurements. We would generally expect high test–retest reliability on measures of intelligence, attitudes, or personality, for example, but not on measures of hunger or fatigue.

INTERITEM RELIABILITY. A second kind of reliability is relevant for measures that consist of more than one item. (Recall that measures that contain multiple items measuring the same construct are often called scales.) **Interitem reliability** assesses the degree of consistency among the items on a scale. Personality inventories, for example, typically consist of several questions that are summed to provide a single score that reflects the respondent's extraversion, self-esteem, shyness, paranoia, or whatever. Similarly, on a scale used to measure depression, participants may be asked to rate themselves on several mood-related items (sad, unhappy, blue, helpless, etc.) that are then added together to provide a single depression score. Scores on attitude scales are also calculated by summing a respondent's responses to several questions about a particular topic.

When researchers sum participants' responses to several questions or items to obtain a single score, they must be sure that all of the items are tapping into the same construct (such as a particular trait, emotion, or attitude). On an inventory to measure

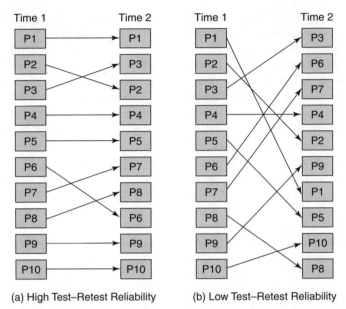

(a) High Test–Retest Reliability   (b) Low Test–Retest Reliability

FIGURE 3.2   Test–Retest Reliability   High test–retest reliability indicates that participants' scores are consistent across time and, thus, the rank order of participants is roughly the same at Time 1 and Time 2. In Figure 3.2 (a), for example, participants' scores are relatively consistent from Time 1 to Time 2. If they are not consistent across time, as in Figure 3.2 (b), test–retest reliability is low.

extraversion, for example, researchers want all of the items to measure some aspect of extraversion. Including items on a scale that don't measure the construct of interest increases measurement error. Researchers check to see that the items on such a scale measure the same general construct by examining interitem reliability.

First, researchers typically look at the **item-total correlation** for each question or item on the scale. An item-total correlation is the correlation between a particular item and the sum of all other items on the scale. So, for example, if you had a 10-item measure of hostility, you could look at the item-total correlations between each of the items and the sum of people's scores on the other nine items. (You would have 10 item-total correlations—one for each item.) If a particular item measures the same construct as the rest of the items, it should correlate at least moderately with the sum of those items. How people respond to one of the hostility items ought to

be related to how they respond to the others. People who score high in hostility on any particular question ought to have a relatively high score if we summed their responses on the other items, and people who score low on one item ought to score relatively low on the others as well. Thus, each item on the scale should correlate with the sum of the others. If this is not the case for a particular item, that item must not be measuring what the others are measuring, and it doesn't belong on the scale. When this is the case, including that "bad" item on the scale adds measurement error to the observed score, reducing its reliability.

Generally, researchers want the item-total correlation between each item and the sum of the other items to exceed .30. If a particular item does not correlate with the sum of the other items (i.e., its item-total correlation is low), it must not be tapping into the same "true score" as the other items. For example, every item on a hostility scale should assess some aspect of hostility, and a low item-total correlation tells us that an item is not really measuring hostility like the other items are. Thus, if combined with scores on the other items, that item would add only measurement error—and no true score variance—to the total hostility score.

In addition to knowing how well each item correlates with the rest of the items, researchers also need to know how reliable the measure is as a whole. Historically, researchers used **split-half reliability** as an index of interitem reliability. With split-half reliability, the researcher would divide the items on the scale into two sets. Sometimes the first and second halves of the scale were used, sometimes the odd-numbered items formed one set and even-numbered items formed the other, or sometimes items were randomly put into one set or the other. Then a total score was obtained for *each set* by adding the items within each set, and the correlation between these two sets of scores was calculated. If the items on the scale measure the same construct (and, thus, estimate the true score consistently), scores obtained on the two halves of the measure should correlate highly (> .70). However, if the split-half correlation is

small, the two halves of the scale are not measuring the same thing and, thus, the total score contains a great deal of measurement error.

There is one drawback to the use of split-half reliability, however. The reliability coefficient one obtains depends on how the items are split. Using a first-half/second-half split is likely to provide a slightly different estimate of interitem reliability than an even/odd split. What, then, is the *real* interitem reliability? To get around this ambiguity, researchers now use **Cronbach's alpha coefficient** (Cronbach, 1970). Cronbach's alpha coefficient is equivalent to the average of all possible split-half reliabilities (although it can be calculated directly from a simple formula). As a rule of thumb, researchers consider a measure to have adequate interitem reliability if Cronbach's alpha coefficient exceeds .70. This is because a coefficient of .70 indicates that 70% of the total variance in participants' scores on the measure is systematic, true-score variance. In other words, when Cronbach's alpha coefficient exceeds .70, we know that the items on the measure are systematically assessing the same construct and that less than 30% of the variance in people's scores on the scale is measurement error.

| **Behavioral Research Case Study**
Interitem Reliability and the Construction of Multi-Item Measures

As noted, whenever researchers calculate a score by summing respondents' answers across a number of questions, they must be sure that all of the items on the scale measure the same construct because items that do not measure the construct add measurement error and decrease reliability. Thus, when researchers develop new multi-item measures, they use item-total correlations to help them select items for the measure. Several years ago, I developed a new measure of the degree to which people tend to feel nervous in social interactions (Leary, 1983). I started this process by writing 87 self-report items (such as "I often feel nervous even in casual get-togethers," "Parties often make me feel anxious and uncomfortable," and "In general, I am a shy person"). Then, two students and I narrowed these items down to what seemed to be the best 56 items. We administered those 56 items to 112 respondents, asking them to rate how characteristic or true each statement was of them on a 5-point scale (where 1 = *not at all,* 2 = *slightly,* 3 = *moderately,* 4 = *very,* and 5 = *extremely*). We then calculated the item-total correlation for each item—the correlation between the respondents' answers on each item and their total score on all of the other items. Because a low item-total correlation indicates that an item is not measuring what the rest of the items are measuring, we eliminated all items for which the item-total correlation was less than .40. A second sample then responded to the reduced set of items, and we looked at the item-total correlations again. Based on these correlations, we retained 15 items for the final version of our Interaction Anxiousness Scale (IAS).

(continued)

(continued)

To be sure that our final set of items was sufficiently reliable, we administered these 15 items to a third sample of 363 respondents. All 15 items on the scale had item-total correlations greater than .50, demonstrating that all items were measuring aspects of the same construct. Furthermore, we calculated Cronbach's alpha coefficient to examine the interitem reliability of the scale as a whole. Cronbach's alpha was .89, which exceeded the minimum criterion of .70 that most researchers use to indicate acceptable reliability.

Because social anxiety is a relatively stable characteristic, we examined the test–retest reliability of the IAS as well. Eight weeks after they had completed the scale the first time, 74 participants answered the items again, and we correlated the scores they obtained on the two administrations. The test–retest reliability was .80, again above the desired minimum of .70. Together, these data showed us that the new measure of social anxiety was sufficiently reliable to use in research.

INTERRATER RELIABILITY. **Interrater reliability** (also called *interjudge* or *interobserver reliability*) involves the consistency among two or more researchers who observe and record participants' behavior. Obviously, when two or more observers are involved, we want their ratings to be consistent. If one observer records that a participant nodded her head 15 times and another observer records 18 head nods, the difference between their observations represents measurement error and lowers the reliability of the observational measure.

For example, Gottschalk, Uliana, and Gilbert (1988) analyzed presidential debates for evidence that the candidates were cognitively impaired at the time of the debates. They coded what the candidates said during the debates using the Cognitive Impairment Scale. In their report of the study, the authors presented data to support the interrater reliability of their procedure. The reliability analysis demonstrated that the raters agreed sufficiently among themselves and that measurement error was acceptably low.

Researchers use two general methods for assessing interrater reliability. If the raters are simply recording whether a behavior occurred, we can calculate the percentage of times they agreed. Alternatively, if the raters are rating the participants' behavior on a scale (an anxiety rating from 1 to 5, for example), we can correlate their ratings across participants. If the observers are making similar ratings, we should obtain a relatively high correlation (at least .70) between them.

Increasing the Reliability of Measures

Unfortunately, researchers cannot always assess the reliability of measures they use in research. For example, if we ask a person to rate on a scale from 1 to 7 how happy he or she feels at the moment, we have no direct way of testing the reliability of the response. Test–retest reliability is inappropriate because the state we are measuring changes over time; interitem reliability is irrelevant because there is only one item; and, because others cannot observe and rate the participant's feelings of happiness, we cannot assess interrater reliability. Even though researchers assess the reliability of their measuring techniques whenever possible, the reliability of some measures cannot be determined.

In light of this, often the best that researchers can do is to make every effort to maximize the reliability of their measures by eliminating possible sources of measurement error. The following list offers a few ways of increasing the reliability of behavioral measures.

- *Standardize administration of the measure.* Ideally, every participant should be tested under precisely the same conditions. Differences in how the measure is given can contribute to measurement error. If possible, have the same researcher administer the measure to all participants in precisely the same setting.
- *Clarify instructions and questions.* Measurement error results when some participants do not fully understand the instructions or

questions. When possible, questions to be used in interviews or questionnaires should be pilot tested to be sure participants understand them.

- *Train observers.* If participants' behavior is being observed and rated, train the observers carefully. Observers should also be given the opportunity to practice using the rating technique.
- *Minimize errors in coding data.* No matter how reliable a measuring technique is, error is introduced if researchers make mistakes in recording, coding, tabulating, or computing the data.

In summary, reliable measures are a prerequisite of good research. A reliable measure is one that is relatively unaffected by sources of measurement error and thus is consistent and dependable. More specifically, reliability reflects the proportion of the total variance in a set of scores that is systematic, true-score variance. The reliability of measures is estimated in three ways: test–retest reliability, interitem reliability, and interrater reliability. In instances in which the reliability of a technique cannot be determined, steps should be taken to minimize sources of measurement error.

ASSESSING THE VALIDITY OF A MEASURE

The measures used in research not only must be reliable but also must be valid. **Validity** refers to the extent to which a measurement procedure actually measures what it is intended to measure rather than measuring something else (or nothing at all). Validity is the degree to which variability in participants' scores on a particular measure reflects variability in the characteristic we want to measure. Do scores on the measure relate to the behavior or attribute of interest? Are we measuring what we think we are measuring? If a researcher is interested in the effects of a new drug on obsessive-compulsive disorder, for example, the measure for obsession-compulsion must reflect differences in the degree to which participants actually have the disorder. That is, to be valid, the measure must assess what it is supposed to measure.

Note that a measure can be highly reliable but not valid. That is, a measure might provide consistent, dependable scores yet not measure what we want to measure. For example, the cranial measurements that early psychologists used to assess intelligence were very reliable. When measuring a person's skull, two researchers would arrive at very similar measurements—that is, interrater reliability was quite high. Skull size measurements also demonstrate high test–retest reliability; they can be recorded consistently over time with little measurement error. However, no matter how reliable skull measurements may be, they are not a valid measure of intelligence. They are not valid because they do not measure the construct of intelligence.

Thus, high reliability tells us that a measuring technique is measuring *something*, as opposed to being plagued by measurement error. But reliability does not tell us precisely what the technique is measuring. Thus, researchers must take care to be certain that their measures are both reliable (relatively free of measurement error) and valid (measuring the construct that they are intended to measure).

Types of Validity

When researchers refer to a measure as valid, they do so in terms of a particular scientific or practical purpose. Validity is not a property of a measuring technique per se but rather an indication of the degree to which the technique measures a particular construct in a particular context. Thus, a measure may be valid for one purpose but not for another. Cranial measurements, for example, are valid measures of hat size, but they are not valid measures of intelligence.

In assessing a measure's validity, the question is how to determine whether the measure actually assesses what it's supposed to measure. To do this, researchers refer to three types of validity: face validity, construct validity, and criterion-related validity.

FACE VALIDITY. Face validity refers to the extent to which a measure appears to measure what it's supposed to measure. Rather than being a technical or statistical procedure, face validation involves the judgment of the researcher or of research participants.

A measure has face validity if people think it does. Although this may seem a rather loose way to establish a measure's validity, in many cases, the judgments of experts may provide useful information about a measure's validity. For example, if a committee of clinical psychologists agrees that the items on a questionnaire assess the central characteristics of a certain personality disorder, their judgment provides some support for its validity. Face validity is never enough evidence, but it's a start.

In general, a researcher is more likely to have faith in an instrument whose content obviously taps into the construct he or she wants to measure than in an instrument that is not face valid. Furthermore, if a measuring technique, such as a test, does not have face validity, participants, clients, job applicants, and other laypeople are likely to doubt its relevance and importance (Cronbach, 1970). In addition, they are likely to be resentful if they are affected by the results of a test whose validity they doubt. A few years ago, a national store chain paid $1.3 million to job applicants who sued the company because they were required to take a test that contained bizarre personal items such as "I would like to be a florist" and "Evil spirits possess me sometimes." The items on this test were from commonly used, well-validated psychological measures, such as the Minnesota Multiphasic Personality Inventory (MMPI) and the California Personality Inventory (CPI), but they lacked face validity. Thus, all other things being equal, it is usually better to have a measure that is face valid than one that is not; it simply engenders greater confidence by the public at large.

Although face validity is often desirable, three qualifications must be kept in mind. First, just because a measure has face validity doesn't necessarily mean that it is actually valid. There are many cases of face-valid measures that do not measure what they appear to measure. For researchers of the nineteenth century, skull size measurements seemed to be a face-valid measure of intelligence because they assumed that bigger heads indicated bigger brains and that bigger brains reflected higher intelligence. (What could be more obvious?)

Second, many measures that lack face validity are, in fact, valid. For example, the MMPI and CPI mentioned earlier—measures of personality that are used in practice, research, and business—contain many items that are not face valid, yet scores on these measures predict various behavioral patterns and psychological problems. For example, responses indicating an interest in being a florist or believing that one is possessed by evil spirits are, when combined with responses to other items, valid indicators of certain attributes, even though these items are by no means face valid.

Third, researchers sometimes want to disguise the purpose of their tests. If they think that respondents will hesitate to answer sensitive questions honestly, they may design instruments that lack face validity and thereby conceal the purpose of the test.

CONSTRUCT VALIDITY. Much behavioral research involves the measurement of **hypothetical constructs**—entities that cannot be directly observed but are inferred on the basis of empirical evidence. Behavioral science abounds with hypothetical constructs such as intelligence, attraction, status, schema, self-concept, moral maturity, motivation, satiation, learning, self-efficacy, ego-threat, and so on. None of these entities can be observed directly, but they are hypothesized to exist on the basis of indirect evidence. In studying these kinds of constructs, researchers must use valid measures. But how does one go about validating the measure of a hypothetical (and invisible) construct?

In an important article, Cronbach and Meehl (1955) suggested that the validity of a measure of a hypothetical construct can be assessed by studying the relationship between the measure of the construct and scores on other measures. We can specify what the scores on any particular measure should be related to if that measure is valid. For example, scores on a measure of self-esteem should be positively related to scores on measures of confidence and optimism but negatively related to measures of insecurity and anxiety. We assess **construct validity** by seeing whether a particular measure relates as it should to other measures.

Researchers typically examine construct validity by calculating correlations between the measure they wish to validate and other measures. Because correlation coefficients describe the strength and direction of relationships between variables, they can tell us whether a particular measure is related to other measures as it should be. Sometimes we expect the correlations between one measure and measures of other constructs to be high, whereas in other instances we expect only moderate or weak relationships or none at all. Thus, unlike in the case of reliability (where we want correlations to exceed .70), no general criteria can be specified for evaluating the size of correlations when assessing construct validity. The size of each correlation coefficient must be considered relative to the correlation we would expect to find if our measure were valid and measured what it was intended to measure.

To have construct validity, a measure should both correlate with other measures that it should correlate with (**convergent validity**) and *not* correlate with measures that it should not correlate with (**discriminant validity**). When measures correlate highly with measures they should correlate with, we have evidence of convergent validity. When measures correlate weakly (or not at all) with conceptually unrelated measures, we have evidence of discriminant validity. Thus, we can examine the correlations between scores on a test and scores from other measures to see whether the relationships converge and diverge as predicted. In brief, both convergent and discriminant validity provide evidence that the measure is related to other measures as it should be and supports its construct validity.

Behavioral Research Case Study
Construct Validity

Earlier I described the development of a measure of social anxiety—the Interaction Anxiousness Scale (IAS)—and data attesting to the scale's interitem and test–retest reliability. Before such a measure can be used, its construct validity must be assessed by seeing whether it correlates with other measures as it should. To examine the construct validity of the IAS, we determined what scores on our measure should be related to if it was a valid measure of social anxiety. Most obviously, scores on the IAS should be related to scores on existing measures of social anxiety. In addition, because feeling nervous in social encounters is related to how easily people become embarrassed (and blush), scores on the IAS ought to correlate with measures of embarrassability and blushing. Given that social anxiety arises from people's concerns with other people's perceptions and evaluations of them, IAS scores should also correlate with the degree to which people fear negative evaluations. We might also expect negative correlations between IAS scores and self-esteem because people with lower self-esteem should be prone to be more nervous around others. Finally, because people who often feel nervous in social situations tend to avoid them when possible, IAS scores should be negatively correlated with sociability and extraversion.

We administered the IAS and measures of these other constructs to more than 200 respondents and calculated the correlations between the IAS scores and the scores on other measures. As shown in the accompanying table, the data were consistent with all of these predictions. Scores on the IAS correlated positively with measures of social distress, embarrassability, blushing propensity, and fear of negative evaluation, but negatively with measures of self-esteem, sociability, and extraversion. Together, these data supported the construct validity of the IAS as a measure of the tendency to experience social anxiety (Leary & Kowalski, 1993).

Scale	Correlation with IAS
Social Avoidance and Distress	.71
Embarrassability	.48
Blushing Propensity	.51
Fear of Negative Evaluation	.44
Self-Esteem	−.36
Sociability	−.39
Extraversion	−.47

CRITERION-RELATED VALIDITY. A third type of validity is criterion-related validity. **Criterion-related validity** refers to the extent to which a measure allows us to distinguish among participants on the basis of a particular behavioral criterion. For example, do scores on the Scholastic Aptitude Test (SAT) permit us to distinguish students who will do well in college from those who will not? Does a self-report measure of marital conflict actually correlate with the number of fights that married couples have? Do scores on a depression scale discriminate between people who do and do not show depressive patterns of behavior? Note that the issue in each case is not one of assessing the link between the SAT, marital conflict, or depression and other constructs (as in construct validity) but of assessing the relationship between each measure and a relevant *behavioral criterion*.

When examining criterion-related validity, researchers identify behavioral outcomes that the measure should be related to if the measure is valid. Finding that the measure does, in fact, correlate with behaviors as it theoretically should supports the criterion-related validity of the measure. If the measure does not predict behavioral criteria as one would expect, either the measure lacks criterion-related validity or we were mistaken in our assumptions regarding the behaviors that the measure should predict. This point is important: A test of criterion-related validity is only useful if we identify a behavioral criterion that really should be related to the measure we are trying to validate.

Researchers distinguish between two primary kinds of criterion validity: concurrent validity and predictive validity. The major difference between them involves the amount of time that elapses between administering the measure to be validated and the measure of the behavioral criterion. In **concurrent validity**, the two measures are administered at roughly the same time. The question is whether the measure being validated distinguishes successfully between people who score low versus high on the behavioral criterion at the present time. When scores on the measure are related to behaviors that they should be related to *right now,* the measure possesses concurrent validity.

In the case of predictive validity, the time that elapses between administering the measure to be validated and the measure of the behavioral criterion is longer, often a matter of months or even years. **Predictive validity** refers to a measure's ability to distinguish between people on a relevant behavioral criterion at some time in the future. For the SAT, for example, the important issue is one of predictive validity. No one really cares whether high school seniors who score high on the SAT are better prepared for college than low scorers at the time they take the test (concurrent validity). Instead, college admissions officers want to know whether SAT scores predict academic performance one to four years later (predictive validity).

Imagine that we are examining the criterion-related validity of a self-report measure of hypochondriasis—the tendency to be overly concerned with one's health and to assume that one has many health-related problems. To assess criterion-related validity, we would first identify behaviors that should unquestionably distinguish between people who are high versus low in hypochondriasis. Some of these may involve behaviors that we can measure now and, thus, can be used to examine concurrent validity. For example, we could videotape participants in an unstructured conversation with another person and record the number of times that the individual mentions his or her health. Presumably, people scoring high on the hypochondriasis scale should talk about their health more than people who score low in hypochondriasis. If we find that this is the case, we would have evidence to support the measure's concurrent validity. We could also ask participants to report the medical symptoms that they are currently experiencing. A valid measure of hypochondriasis should correlate with the number of symptoms people report right now.

In addition, we may identify behaviors that should distinguish between people who are high versus low in hypochondriasis at some time in the future. For example, we might expect that hypochondriacs would see their doctors more often during the coming year. If we were able to predict visits to the doctor from scores on the hypochondriasis measure, we would have evidence for its predictive validity.

Criterion-related validity is often of interest to researchers in applied research settings. In educational research, for example, researchers are often interested in the degree to which tests predict academic performance. Similarly, before using tests to select new employees, personnel psychologists must demonstrate that the tests successfully predict future on-the-job performance—that is, that they possess predictive validity.

To sum up, validity refers to the degree to which a measuring technique measures what it's intended to measure. Although face-valid measures are often desirable, construct and criterion-related validity are much more important. Construct validity is assessed by seeing whether scores on a measure are related to other measures as they should be. A measure has criterion-related validity if it correctly distinguishes between people on the basis of a relevant behavioral criterion either at present (concurrent validity) or in the future (predictive validity).

Behavioral Research Case Study
Criterion-Related Validity

Establishing criterion-related validity involves showing that scores on a measure are related to people's behaviors as they should be. In the case of the Interaction Anxiousness Scale described earlier, scores on the IAS should be related to people's reactions in real social situations. For example, as a measure of the general tendency to feel socially anxious, scores on the IAS should be correlated with how nervous people feel in actual interpersonal encounters. In several laboratory studies, participants completed the IAS, then interacted with another individual. Participants' reported feelings of anxiety before and during these interactions correlated with IAS scores as expected. Furthermore, IAS scores correlated with how nervous the participants were judged to be by people who observed them during these interactions.

We also asked participants who completed the IAS to keep track for about a week of all social interactions they had that lasted more than 10 minutes. For each interaction, they completed a brief questionnaire that assessed, among other things, how nervous they felt. Not only did participants' scores on the IAS correlate with how nervous they felt in everyday interactions, but participants who scored high on the IAS had fewer interactions with people whom they did not know well (presumably because they were uncomfortable in interactions with people who were unfamiliar) than did people who scored low on the IAS. These data showed that scores on the IAS related to people's real reactions and behaviors as they should, thereby supporting the criterion-related validity of the scale.

FAIRNESS AND BIAS IN MEASUREMENT

In recent years, a great deal of public attention and scientific research have been devoted to the possibility that certain psychological and educational measures, particularly tests of intelligence and academic ability, are biased against certain groups of individuals. **Test bias** occurs when a particular measure is not equally valid for everyone who takes the test. That is, if test scores more accurately reflect the true ability or characteristics of one group than another, the test is biased.

Identifying test bias is difficult. Simply showing that a certain gender, racial, or ethnic group performs worse on a test than other groups does not necessarily indicate that the test is unfair. The observed difference in scores may reflect a true difference between the groups in the attribute being measured (which would indicate that the test is valid). Bias exists only if groups that do not differ on the attribute or ability being measured obtain different scores on the test.

Bias can creep into psychological measures in very subtle ways. For example, test questions sometimes refer to objects or experiences that are more familiar to members of one group than to those of another. If those objects or experiences are not relevant to the attribute being measured (but rather are being used only as examples), some individuals may be unfairly disadvantaged. Consider, for example, this sample analogy from the SAT:

Strawberry:Red

(A) peach:ripe   (B) leather:brown   (C) grass:green
(D) orange:round   (E) lemon:yellow

The correct answer is (E) because a *strawberry* is a *fruit* that is *red,* and a *lemon* is a *fruit* that is *yellow.* However, statistical analyses showed that Hispanic test takers missed this particular item notably more often than members of other groups. Further investigation suggested that the difference occurred because some Hispanic test takers were familiar with green rather than yellow lemons. As a result, they chose *grass:green* as the analogy to *strawberry:red,* a very reasonable response for an individual who does not associate lemons with the color yellow ("What's the DIF?," 1999). Along the same lines, a geometry question on a standardized test was identified as biased when it became clear that women missed it more often than did men because it referred to the dimensions of a football field. In these two cases, the attributes being measured (analogical reasoning and knowledge about geometry) had nothing to do with one's experience with yellow lemons or football, yet those experiences led some test takers to perform better than others.

Test bias is hard to demonstrate because it is often difficult to determine whether the groups truly differ on the attribute in question. One way to document the presence of bias is to examine the predictive validity of a measure separately for different groups. A biased test will predict future outcomes better for one group than another. For example, imagine that we find that Group X performs worse on the SAT than Group Y. Does this difference reflect test bias or is Group X actually less well prepared for college than Group Y? By using SAT scores to predict how well Group X and Group Y subsequently perform in college, we can see whether the SAT predicts college grades equally well for the two groups (i.e., whether the SAT has predictive validity for both groups). If it does, the test is probably not biased even though the groups perform differently on it. However, if SAT scores predict college performance less accurately for Group X than Group Y—that is, if the predictive validity of the SAT is worse for Group X—then the test is likely biased.

"YOU CAN'T BUILD A HUT, YOU DON'T KNOW HOW TO FIND EDIBLE ROOTS AND YOU KNOW NOTHING ABOUT PREDICTING THE WEATHER. IN OTHER WORDS, YOU DO TERRIBLY ON OUR I.Q. TEST."

An Example of a Biased Test

Source: SCIENCECARTOONSPLUS.COM © 2000 by Sidney Harris.

Test developers often examine individual test items for evidence of bias. One method of doing this involves matching groups of test takers on their total test scores, then seeing whether the groups performed comparably on particular test questions. The rationale is that if test takers have the same overall knowledge or ability, then on average they should perform similarly on individual questions regardless of their sex, race, or ethnicity. So, for example, we might take all individuals who score between 500 and 600 on the verbal section of the SAT and compare how different groups performed on the *strawberry:red* analogy described earlier. If the item is unbiased, an approximately equal proportion of

each group should get the analogy correct. However, if the item is biased, we would find that a disproportionate number of people in one of the groups got it "wrong."

All researchers and test developers have difficulty setting aside their own experiences and biases. However, they must make every effort to reduce the impact of their biases on the measures they develop. By collaborating with investigators of other genders, races, ethnic groups, and cultural backgrounds, potential sources of bias can be identified as tests are constructed. And by applying their understanding of validity, they can work together to identify biases that do creep into their measures.

In Depth
The Reliability and Validity of College Admission Exams

Most colleges and universities use applicants' scores on entrance examinations as one criterion for making admissions decisions. By far the most frequently used exam for this purpose is the Scholastic Aptitude Test (SAT), developed by the Educational Testing Service.

Many students are skeptical of the SAT and similar exams. Many claim, for example, that they don't perform well on standardized tests and that their scores indicate little, if anything, about their ability to do well in college. No doubt, there are many people for whom the SAT does not predict performance well. Like all tests, the SAT contains measurement error and, thus, underestimates and overestimates some people's true aptitude scores. (Interestingly, I've never heard anyone criticize the SAT because they scored *higher* than they should have. From a statistical perspective, measurement error should lead as many people to obtain scores that are higher than their true ability as to obtain scores lower than their ability.) However, a large amount of data attest to the overall reliability and validity of the SAT. The psychometric data regarding the SAT are extensive, based on tens of thousands of scores over a span of many years.

The reliability of the SAT is impressive in comparison with most psychological tests. The SAT possesses high test–retest reliability as well as high interitem reliability. Reliability coefficients average around .90 (Kaplan, 1982), easily exceeding the standard criterion of .70. Over 90% of the total variance in SAT scores is systematic, true-score variance.

In the case of the SAT, *predictive validity* is of paramount importance. Many studies have examined the relationship between SAT scores and college grades. These studies have shown that the criterion-related validity of the SAT depends, in part, on one's major in college; SAT scores predict college performance better for some majors than for others. In general, however, the predictive validity of the SAT is fairly good. On the average, about 16% of the total variance in first-year college grades is systematic variance accounted for by SAT scores (Kaplan, 1982). Sixteen percent may not sound like a great deal until one considers all of the other factors that contribute to variability in college grades, such as motivation, health, personal problems, the difficulty of one's courses, the academic ability of the student body, and so on. Given everything that affects performance in college, it is not too surprising that a single test score does not predict with greater accuracy.

Of course, most colleges and universities also use criteria other than entrance exams in the admissions decision. The Educational Testing Service advises admissions offices to consider high school grades, activities, and awards, as well as SAT scores, for example. Using these other criteria further increases the validity of the selection process.

This is not to suggest that the SAT and other college entrance exams are infallible or that certain people do not obtain inflated or deflated scores. But such tests are not as unreliable or invalid as many students suppose.

Summary

1. Measurement lies at the heart of all research. Behavioral researchers have a wide array of measures at their disposal, including observational, physiological, and self-report measures. Psychometrics is a specialty devoted to the study and improvement of psychological tests and other measures.

2. Because no measure is perfect, researchers sometimes use several different measures of the same variable, a practice known as *converging operations* (or *triangulation*).

3. The word *scale* is used in several ways in research—to refer to whether a variable is measured on a nominal, ordinal, interval, or ratio scale of measurement; the way in which participants indicate their responses (also called a response format); and a set of questions that all measure the same construct.

4. A measure's scale of measurement—whether it is measured at the nominal, ordinal, interval, or ratio level—has implications for the kind of information that the instrument provides, as well as for the statistical analyses that can be performed on the data.

5. Reliability refers to the consistency or dependability of a measuring technique. Three types of reliability can be assessed: test–retest reliability (consistency of the measure across time), interitem reliability (consistency among a set of items intended to assess the same construct), and interrater reliability (consistency between two or more researchers who have observed and recorded participants' behavior).

6. All observed scores consist of two components—the true score and measurement error. The true-score component reflects the score that would have been obtained if the measure were perfect; measurement error reflects the effects of factors that make the observed score lower or higher than it should be. The more measurement error a score contains, the less reliable the measure will be.

7. Factors that increase measurement error include transient states (such as mood, fatigue, health), stable personality characteristics, situational factors, features of the measure itself (such as confusing questions), and researcher mistakes.

8. A correlation coefficient is a statistic that expresses the direction and strength of the relationship between two variables.

9. Reliability is tested by examining correlations between (a) two administrations of the same measure (test–retest), (b) items on a questionnaire (interitem), or (c) the ratings of two or more observers (interrater).

10. Reliability can be enhanced by standardizing the administration of the measure, clarifying instructions and questions, training observers, and minimizing errors in coding and analyzing data.

11. Validity refers to the extent to which a measurement procedure measures what it's intended to measure.

12. Three basic types of validity are: face validity (does the measure appear to measure the construct of interest?), construct validity (does the measure correlate with measures of other constructs as it should?), and criterion-related validity (does the measure correlate with measures of current or future behavior as it should?).

13. Test bias occurs when scores on a measure reflect the true ability or characteristics of one group of test takers more accurately than the ability or characteristics of another group—that is, when validity is better for one group than another.

Key Terms

concurrent validity (p. 64)
construct validity (p. 62)
convergent validity (p. 63)
converging operations (p. 51)

correlation coefficient (p. 57)
criterion-related validity (p. 64)
Cronbach's alpha coefficient (p. 59)

discriminant validity (p. 63)
face validity (p. 61)
hypothetical construct (p. 62)
interitem reliability (p. 57)

interrater reliability (p. 60)
interval scale (p. 52)
item-total correlation (p. 58)
measurement error (p. 54)
nominal scale (p. 51)
observational measure (p. 50)
ordinal scale (p. 52)

physiological measure (p. 50)
predictive validity (p. 64)
psychometrics (p. 50)
ratio scale (p. 52)
reliability (p. 53)
scale (p. 52)
scales of measurement (p. 51)

self-report measure (p. 50)
split-half reliability (p. 59)
test bias (p. 65)
test–retest reliability
    (p. 57)
true score (p. 54)
validity (p. 61)

Questions for Review

1. Distinguish among observational, physiological, and self-report measures.
2. What do researchers interested in psychometrics study?
3. Why do researchers use converging operations?
4. Distinguish among nominal, ordinal, interval, and ratio scales of measurement. Why do researchers prefer to use measures that are on interval and ratio scales when possible?
5. Researchers use the word *scale* in three very different ways. What are the three meanings of *scale* (aside from an instrument for measuring weight)?
6. Why must measures be reliable? What is the main consequence of using an unreliable measure in a study?
7. What is measurement error, and what are some things that cause it?
8. Why is it virtually impossible to eliminate all measurement error from the measures we use in research?
9. What is the relationship between the reliability of a measure and the degree of measurement error it contains?
10. What does the reliability of a measure indicate if it is .60? .00? 1.00?
11. What does a correlation coefficient tell us? Why are correlation coefficients useful when assessing reliability?
12. What are the three ways in which researchers assess the reliability of their measures? Be sure that you understand the differences among these three approaches to reliability.
13. When would you calculate Cronbach's alpha coefficient? What does it tell you?
14. What is the minimum reliability coefficient that researchers consider acceptable? Why do researchers use this minimum criterion for reliability?
15. For what kind of measure is it appropriate to examine test–retest reliability? Interitem reliability? Interrater reliability?
16. Why are researchers sometimes not able to test the reliability of their measures?
17. What steps can be taken to increase the reliability of measuring techniques?
18. What is validity?
19. Distinguish among face validity, construct validity, and criterion-related validity. In general, which kind of validity is least important to researchers?
20. Can a measurement procedure be valid but not reliable? Reliable but not valid? Explain.
21. Distinguish between construct and criterion-related validity.
22. Distinguish between convergent and discriminant validity. Do these terms refer to types of construct validity or criterion-related validity (or both)?
23. Distinguish between concurrent and predictive validity.
24. How can we tell whether a particular measure is biased against a particular group?
25. How do researchers identify biased test items on tests of intelligence or ability?

Questions for Discussion

1. Many students experience a great deal of anxiety whenever they take tests. Imagine that you conduct a study of test anxiety in which participants take tests and their reactions are measured. Suggest how you would apply the idea of converging operations using observational, physiological, and self-report measures to measure test anxiety in such a study.
2. For each measure in the following list, indicate whether it is measured on a nominal, ordinal, interval, or ratio scale of measurement.
   a. body temperature
   b. sexual orientation
   c. the number of times that a baby smiles in 5 minutes
   d. the order in which 160 runners finish a race

e. the number of books on a professor's shelf
f. ratings of happiness on a scale from 1 to 7
g. religious preference

3. If the measures used in research had no measurement error whatsoever, would researchers obtain weaker or stronger findings in their studies? (This one may require some thought.)

4. Hypochondriacs are obsessed with their health, talk a great deal about their real and imagined health problems, and visit their physician frequently. Imagine that you developed an 8-item self-report measure of hypochondriacal tendencies. Tell how you would examine the (a) test–retest reliability and (b) interitem reliability of your measure.

5. Imagine that the test–retest reliability of your hypochondriasis scale was .50, and Cronbach's alpha coefficient was .62. Comment on the reliability of your scale.

6. Now explain how you would test the validity of your hypochondriasis scale. Discuss how you would examine both construct validity and criterion-related validity.

7. Imagine that you calculated the item-total correlations for the eight items on your scale and obtained these correlations:

Item 1 .42	Item 5 .37
Item 2 .50	Item 6 −.21
Item 3 .14	Item 7 .30
Item 4 .45	Item 8 .00

Discuss these item-total correlations, focusing on whether any of the items on the scale are problematic.

8. Some scientists in the physical sciences (such as physics and chemistry) argue that hypothetical constructs are not scientific because they cannot be observed directly. Do you agree or disagree with this position? Why?

9. Imagine that we found that women scored significantly lower than men on a particular test. Would you conclude that the test was biased against women? Why or why not?

10. Imagine that you want to know whether the SAT is biased against Group X and in favor of Group Y. You administer the SAT to members of the two groups; then, 4 years later, you examine the correlations between SAT scores and college grade point average (GPA) for the two groups. You find that SAT scores correlate .45 with GPA for both Group X and Group Y. Would you conclude that the test was biased? Explain.

4 APPROACHES TO PSYCHOLOGICAL MEASUREMENT

Observational Approaches	Archival Data
Physiological and Neuroscience Approaches	Content Analysis
Self-Report Approaches: Questionnaires and Interviews	

Evidence suggests that certain people who are diagnosed as schizophrenic (though by no means all) *want* other people to view them as psychologically disturbed because being perceived as "crazy" has benefits for them. For example, being regarded as mentally incompetent frees people from normal responsibilities at home and at work, provides an excuse for their failures, and may even allow people living in poverty to improve their living conditions by being admitted to a mental institution. Indeed, Braginsky, Braginsky, and Ring (1982) suggested that some very poor people use mental institutions as "resorts" where they can rest, relax, and escape the stresses of everyday life. This is not to say that people who display symptoms of schizophrenia are not psychologically troubled, but it suggests that psychotic symptoms sometimes reflect patients' attempts to manage the impressions others have of them rather than underlying psychopathology per se (Leary, 1995).

Imagine that you are a member of a research team that is investigating the hypothesis that some patients use psychotic symptoms as an impression-management strategy. Think for a moment about how you would measure these patients' behavior to test your hypothesis. Would you try to observe the patients' behavior directly and rate how disturbed it appeared? If so, which of their behaviors would you focus on, and how would you measure them? Or would you use questionnaires or interviews to ask patients how disturbed they are? If you used questionnaires, would you design them yourself or rely on existing scales? Would hospitalized schizophrenics be able to complete questionnaires, or would you need to interview them personally instead? Alternatively, would it be useful to ask other people who know the patients well—such as family members and friends—to rate the patients' behavior, or perhaps use ratings of the patients made by physicians, nurses, or psychologists? Could you obtain useful information by examining transcripts of what the patients talked about during psychotherapy sessions or by examining medical records and case reports? Could you assess how disturbed the patients were trying to appear by looking at the pictures they drew or the letters they wrote? If so, how would you convert their drawings and writings to numerical data that could be analyzed? Would physiological measures—of heart rate, brain waves, or autonomic arousal, for example—be useful to you?

Researchers face many such decisions each time they design a study. They have at their disposal a diverse array of techniques to assess behavior, thought, emotion, and physiological responses, and the decision regarding the best, most effective measures to use is not always easy. In this chapter, we will examine four general types of psychological measures in detail: observational methods (in which participants' overt behaviors are observed and recorded), physiological measures (that record activity in the body), self-report measures (in which participants report on their own behavior), and archival methods (in which existing data, not collected specifically for the study, are used). Because some of these measures involve things that research participants say or write, we will also delve into content analysis, which converts spoken or written text to numerical data.

Importantly, each of these types of measures—observational, physiological, self-report, and archival—may be used in conjunction with any of the four research strategies described in Chapter 1 (that is, descriptive, correlational, experimental, or quasi-experimental). Any kind of research may utilize any kind of measure. So, for example, a researcher who is conducting a correlational study of shyness may observe participants' behavior (observational measure), measure their physio-logical responses during a social interaction (physiological measure), ask them to answer items on a questionnaire (self-report measure), and/or content-analyze the entries in their diaries (archival measure). Likewise, a researcher conducting an experimental study of the effects of a stress-reduction program may assign participants either to participate or not participate in a stress-reduction program (the independent variable), then observe them working on a stressful task (observation), measure their level of arousal (physiological), ask them how much stress they feel (self-report), and/or later examine their medical records for stress-related problems (archival). Regardless of the kind of study being conducted, researchers try to select the types of measures that will provide the most useful information.

OBSERVATIONAL APPROACHES

A great deal of behavioral research involves the direct observation of human or nonhuman behavior. Behavioral researchers have been known to observe and record behaviors as diverse as eating, arguing, bar pressing, blushing, smiling, helping, food salting, hand clapping, running, eye blinking, mating, typing, yawning, conversing, and even urinating. Roughly speaking, researchers who use **observational approaches** to measure behavior must make three decisions about how they will observe and record participants' behavior in a particular study: (1) Will the observation occur in a natural or contrived setting? (2) Will the participants know they are being observed? and (3) How will participants' behavior be recorded?

Naturalistic Versus Contrived Settings

In some studies, researchers observe and record behavior in real-world settings. **Naturalistic observation** involves the observation of ongoing behavior as it occurs naturally with no intrusion or intervention by the researcher. In naturalistic studies, the participants are observed as they engage in ordinary activities in settings that have not been arranged specifically for research purposes. For example, researchers have used naturalistic observation to study behavior during riots and other mob events, littering, nonverbal behavior, and parent–child interactions on the playground.

Researchers who are interested in the behavior of animals in their natural habitats—ethologists and comparative psychologists—also use naturalistic observation methods. Animal researchers have studied a wide array of behaviors under naturalistic conditions, including tool use by elephants, mating among iguana lizards, foraging in squirrels, and aggression among monkeys (see, for example, Chevalier-Skolnikoff & Liska, 1993). Jane Goodall and Dianne Fossey used naturalistic observation of chimpanzees and gorillas in their well-known field studies.

Participant observation is one type of naturalistic observation. In participant observation, the researcher engages in the same activities as the people he or she is observing. In a classic example of participant observation, social psychologists infiltrated a doomsday group that prophesied that much of the world would soon be destroyed (Festinger, Riecken, & Schachter, 1956). The researchers, who were interested in how such groups react when their prophecies are disconfirmed (as the researchers assumed they would be), concocted fictitious identities to gain admittance to the group, then observed and recorded the group members' behavior as the time for the cataclysm came and went. In other studies involving participant observation, researchers have posed as cult members, homeless people, devil worshipers, homosexuals, African Americans (in this case, a white researcher tinted his skin and passed as black for several weeks), salespeople, and gang members.

Participating in the events they study can raise special problems for researchers who use participant observation. To the extent that researchers become immersed in the group's activities and come to identify with the people they study, they may lose their ability to observe and record others' behavior objectively. In addition, in all participant observation studies, the researcher runs the risk of influencing the behavior of the individuals being studied. To the extent that the researcher interacts with the participants, helps to make decisions that affect the group, and otherwise participates in the group's activities, he or she may unwittingly affect participants' behavior in ways that make it unnatural.

In contrast to naturalistic observation, **contrived observation** involves the observation of behavior in settings that are arranged specifically for observing and recording behavior. Often such studies are conducted in laboratory settings in which participants know they are being observed, although the observers are usually concealed, such as behind a one-way mirror, or the behavior is video-recorded for later analysis. For example, to study parent–child relationships, researchers often observe parents interacting with their children in laboratory settings. In one such study (Rosen & Rothbaum, 1993), parents brought their children to a laboratory "playroom." Both parent and child behaviors were videotaped as the child explored the new environment with the parent present, as the parent left the

child alone for a few minutes, and again when the parent and child were reunited. In addition, parents and their children were videotaped playing, reading, cleaning up toys in the lab, and solving problems. Analyses of the videotapes provided a wealth of information about the relationship between the quality of the care parents provided their children and the nature of the parent–child bond.

In other cases, researchers use contrived observation in the "real world." In these studies, researchers set up situations outside of the laboratory to observe people's reactions. For example, field experiments on determinants of helping behavior have been conducted in everyday settings. In one such study, researchers interested in factors that affect helping staged an "emergency" on a New York City subway (Piliavin, Rodin, & Piliavin, 1969). Over more than two months, researchers staged 103 accidents in which a researcher staggered and collapsed on a moving subway car. Sometimes the researcher carried a cane and acted as if he were injured or infirm; at other times he carried a bottle in a paper bag and pretended to be drunk. Two observers then recorded bystanders' reactions to the "emergency."

Disguised Versus Nondisguised Observation

The second decision a researcher must make when using observational methods is whether to let participants know they are being observed. Sometimes the individuals who are being studied know that the researcher is observing their behavior (**undisguised observation**). As you might guess, the problem with undisguised observation is that people often do not respond naturally when they know they are being scrutinized. When they react to the researcher's observation, their behaviors are affected. Researchers refer to this phenomenon as **reactivity**.

When they are concerned about reactivity, researchers may conceal the fact that they are observing and recording participants' behavior (**disguised observation**). Festinger and his colleagues (1956) used disguised observation when studying the doomsday group because they undoubtedly would not have been allowed to observe the group otherwise. Similarly, the subway passengers studied by Piliavin et al. (1969) did not know their reactions to the staged emergency were being observed. However, disguised observation raises ethical issues because researchers may invade participants' privacy as well as violate participants' right to decide whether to participate in the research (the right of *informed consent*). As long as the behaviors under observation occur in public and the researcher does not unnecessarily inconvenience or upset the participants, the ethical considerations are small. However, if the behaviors are not public or the researcher intrudes uninvited into participants' everyday lives, then disguised observation may be problematic.

In some instances, researchers compromise by letting participants know they are being observed while withholding information regarding precisely what aspects of the participants' behavior are being recorded. This *partial concealment* strategy (Weick, 1968) lowers, but does not eliminate, the problem of reactivity while avoiding ethical questions involving invasion of privacy and informed consent. We will return to the ethical issues involved in disguised observation in Chapter 15.

Because people often behave unnaturally when they know they are being watched, researchers sometimes measure behavior indirectly rather than actually observing it. For example, researchers occasionally recruit **knowledgeable informants**—people who know the participants well—to observe and rate their behavior (Moscowitz, 1986). Typically, these individuals are people who play a significant role in the participants' lives, such as best friends, parents, romantic partners, coworkers, or teachers.

For example, in a study of factors that affect the degree to which people's perceptions of themselves are consistent with others' perceptions of them, Cheek (1982) obtained ratings of 85 college men by three of their fraternity brothers. Because the participants are being observed during the course of everyday life, they are more likely to behave naturally.

Another type of disguised observation involves unobtrusive measures. **Unobtrusive measures** involve measures that can be taken without participants knowing that they are being studied. Rather than asking participants to answer questions or observing them directly, researchers can assess their behaviors and attitudes indirectly without intruding on them in any way. For example, because he was concerned that people might lie about how much alcohol they drink, Sawyer (1961) counted the number of empty liquor bottles in neighborhood garbage cans rather than asking residents to report on their alcohol consumption directly or trying to observe them actually drinking. Similarly, we could find out which parts of a textbook students consider important by examining the sections that they underlined or highlighted. Or to assess people's preferences for particular radio stations, we could visit auto service centers, inspect the radio dials of the cars being serviced, and record the radio station to which each car's radio was tuned. Researchers have used unobtrusive measures as varied as the graffiti on the walls of public restrooms, the content of people's garbage cans, the amount of wear on library books, and the darkness of people's tans (as an unobtrusive measure of the time they spend in the sun or tanning booths without sunscreen).

Behavioral Research Case Study
Disguised Observation in Laboratory Settings

Researchers who use observation to measure participants' behavior face a dilemma. On one hand, they are most likely to obtain accurate, unbiased data if participants do not know they are being observed. In studies of interpersonal interaction, for example, participants have a great deal of difficulty acting naturally when they know their behavior is being observed or videotaped for analysis. On the other hand, failing to obtain participants' prior approval to be observed violates their right to choose whether they wish to participate in the research and, possibly, their right to privacy.

Researcher William Ickes devised an ingenious solution to this dilemma (Ickes, 1982). His approach has been used most often to study dyadic, or two-person, social interactions (hence, it is known as the *dyadic interaction paradigm*), but it could be used to study other behavior as well. Pairs of participants reporting for an experiment are escorted to a waiting room and seated on a couch. The researcher excuses him- or herself to complete preparations for the experiment and leaves the participants alone. Unknown to the participants, their behavior is then recorded by means of a concealed video-recorder.

But how does this subterfuge avoid the ethical issues we just posed? Haven't we just observed participants' behavior without their consent and thereby invaded their privacy? The answer is no because, although the participants' behavior was recorded, *no one has yet observed their behavior or seen the video-recording.* Their conversation in the waiting room is still as private and confidential as if it hadn't been recorded at all.

After a few minutes, the researcher returns and explains to the participants that their behavior was video-taped. The purpose of the study is explained, and the researcher asks the participants for permission to code and analyze the recording. However, participants are free to deny their permission, in which case the recording is erased in the participants' presence or, if they want, given to them. Ickes reports that most participants are willing to let the researcher analyze their behavior.

This observational paradigm has been successfully used in studies of sex role behavior, empathy, shyness, Machiavellianism, interracial relations, social cognition, and birth-order effects. Importantly, this approach to disguised observation in laboratory settings can be used to study not only overt social behavior but also covert processes involving thoughts and feelings. In some studies, researchers have shown participants the video-recordings of their own behavior and asked them to report the thoughts or feelings they had at certain points during their interaction in the waiting room (see Ickes, Bissonnette, Garcia, & Stinson, 1990).

Behavioral Recording

The third decision facing the researcher who uses observational methods involves precisely how the participants' behavior will be recorded. When researchers observe behavior, they must devise ways of recording what they see and hear. Sometimes the behaviors being observed are relatively simple and easily recorded, such as the number of times a pigeon pecks a key or the number of M&Ms eaten by a participant (which might be done in a study of social influences on eating).

In other cases, the behaviors are more complex. When observing complex, multifaceted reactions such as embarrassment, group discussion, or union–management negotiations, researchers spend a great deal of time designing and pretesting the system they will use to record their observations. Although the specific techniques used to observe and record behavioral data are nearly endless, most fall into four general categories: narrative records, checklists, temporal measures, and rating scales.

NARRATIVES. Although rarely used in psychological research, **narrative records** (sometimes called *specimen records*) are common in other social and behavioral sciences. A narrative or specimen record is a full description of a participant's behav-ior. The intent is to capture, as completely as possible, everything the participant said and did during a specified period of time. Although researchers once wrote handwritten notes as they observed participants in person, today they are more likely to produce written narratives from audio- or video-recordings or to record a spoken narrative into an audio recorder as they observe participants' behavior; the recorded narrative is then transcribed.

One of the best known uses of narrative records is Piaget's groundbreaking studies of children's cognitive development. As he observed children, Piaget kept a running account of precisely what the child said and did. For example, in a study of Jacqueline, who was about to have her first birthday, Piaget (1951) wrote

. . . when I seized a lock of my hair and moved it about on my temple, she succeeded for the first time in imitating me. She suddenly took her hand from her eyebrow, which she was touching, felt above it, found her hair and took hold of it, quite deliberately. (p. 55)

Narrative records differ in their explicitness and completeness. Sometimes researchers try to record verbatim virtually everything the participant says or does. More commonly, researchers take **field notes** that include summary descriptions of the participant's behaviors but with no attempt to record every behavior.

Although narrative records provide the most complete description of a researcher's observations, they cannot be analyzed quantitatively until they are *content analyzed.* As we'll discuss later in this chapter, content analysis involves classifying or rating behavior numerically so that it can be analyzed.

CHECKLISTS.   Narrative records are classified as *unstructured* observation methods because of their open-ended nature. In contrast, most observation methods used by behavioral researchers are *structured.* A structured observation method is one in which the observer records, times, or rates behavior on dimensions that have been decided upon in advance.

The simplest structured observation technique is a **checklist** (or tally sheet) on which the researcher records attributes of the participants (such as sex, age, and race) and whether particular behaviors were observed. In some cases, researchers are interested only in whether a single particular behavior occurred. For example, in a study of helping, Bryan and Test (1967) recorded whether passersby donated to a Salvation Army kettle at Christmas time. In other cases, researchers record whenever one of several behaviors is observed. For example, many researchers have used the Interaction Process Analysis (Bales, 1970) to study group interaction. In this checklist system, observers record whenever any of 12 behaviors is observed: seems friendly, dramatizes, agrees, gives suggestion, gives opinion, gives information, asks for information, asks for opinion, asks for suggestion, disagrees, shows tension, and seems unfriendly.

Although checklists may seem an easy and straightforward way of recording behavior, researchers often struggle to develop clear, explicit operational definitions of the target behaviors. Whereas we may find it relatively easy to determine whether a passerby dropped money into a Salvation Army kettle, we may have more difficulty defining explicitly what we mean by "seems friendly" or "shows tension." As we discussed in Chapter 1, researchers use *operational definitions* to define unambiguously how a particular construct will be measured in a particular research setting. Clear operational definitions are essential anytime researchers use structured observational methods.

TEMPORAL MEASURES: LATENCY AND DURATION. Sometimes researchers are interested not only in whether a behavior occurred but also in *when* it occurred and *how long* it lasted. Researchers are often interested in how much time elapsed between a particular event and a behavior, or between two behaviors (**latency**). The most obvious and commonplace measure of latency is **reaction time**—the time that elapses between the presentation of a stimulus and the participant's response (such as pressing a key). Reaction time is used by cognitive psychologists as an index of how much processing of information is occurring in the nervous system; the longer the reaction time, the more internal processing must be occurring.

Another measure of latency is **task completion time**—the length of time it takes participants to solve a problem or complete a task. In a study of the effects of altitude on cognitive performance, Kramer, Coyne, and Strayer (1993) tested climbers before, during, and after climbing Mount Denali in Alaska. Using portable computers, the researchers administered several perceptual, cognitive, and sensorimotor tasks, measuring both how well the participants performed and how long it took them to complete the task (i.e., task completion time). Compared to a control group, the climbers showed deficits in their ability to learn and remember information, and they performed more slowly on most of the tasks.

Other measures of latency involve **inter-behavior latency**—the time that elapses between the performance of two behaviors. For example, in a study of emotional expressions, Asendorpf (1990) observed the temporal relationship between smiling and gaze during embarrassed and nonembarrassed smiling. Observation of different smiles showed that nonembarrassed smiles tend to be followed by immediate gaze aversion (people look away briefly right as they stop smiling), but when people are embarrassed, they avert their gaze 1.0 to 1.5 seconds before they stop smiling.

In addition to latency measures, a researcher may be interested in how long a particular behavior lasted—its **duration.** For example, researchers interested in social interaction often measure how long people talk during a conversation or how long people look at one another when they interact (eye contact). Researchers interested in infant behavior have studied the temporal patterns in infant crying—for example, how long bursts of crying last (duration) and how much time elapses between bursts (interbehavior latency) (Zeskind, Parker-Price, & Barr, 1993).

OBSERVATIONAL RATING SCALES.   For some purposes, researchers are interested in measuring the *quality* or *intensity* of a behavior. For example, a developmental psychologist may want to know not only whether a child cried when teased but *how hard* he or she cried. Or a counseling psychologist may want to assess *how anxious* speech-anxious participants appeared while giving a talk. In such cases, observers go beyond recording the presence of a behavior to judging its intensity or quality. The observer may rate the child's crying on a 3-point scale (1 = slight, 2 = moderate, 3 = extreme) or how nervous a public speaker appeared on a 5-point scale (1 = not at all, 2 = slightly, 3 = moderately, 4 = very, 5 = extremely).

Because these kinds of ratings necessarily entail a certain degree of subjective judgment, special care must be devoted to defining clearly the rating scale categories. Unambiguous criteria must be established so that observers know what distinguishes "slight crying" from "moderate crying" from "extreme crying," for example.

Increasing the Reliability of Observational Methods

To be useful, observational coding strategies must demonstrate adequate interrater reliability. As we saw in the previous chapter, *interrater reliability* refers to the degree to which the observations of two or more independent raters or observers agree. Low interrater reliability indicates that the raters are not using the observation system in the same manner and that their ratings contain excessive measurement error.

The reliability of observational systems can be increased in two ways. First, as noted earlier, clear and precise operational definitions must be provided for the behaviors that will be observed and recorded. All observers must use precisely the same criteria in recording and rating participants' behaviors.

Second, raters should practice using the coding system, comparing and discussing their practice ratings with one another before observing the behavior to be analyzed. In this way, they can resolve differences in how they are using the observation system. This also allows researchers to check the interrater reliability to be sure that the observational coding system is sufficiently reliable before the observers observe the behavior of the actual participants.

Behavioral Research Case Study
An Observational Study: Predicting Divorce from Observing Husbands and Wives

To provide insight into the processes that lead many marriages to dissolve, Gottman and Levenson (1992) conducted an observational study of 79 couples who had been married an average of 5.2 years. The couples reported to a research laboratory where they participated in three 15-minute discussions with one another about the events of the day, a problem on which they disagreed, and a pleasant topic. Two video cameras, partially concealed behind dark glass, recorded the individuals as they talked.

Raters later coded these videotapes using the Rapid Couples Interaction Scoring System (RCISS). This coding system classifies people's communication during social interactions according to both positive categories (such as neutral or positive problem description, assent, and humor-laugh) and negative categories (such as complain, criticize, put down, and defensive). The researchers presented evidence showing that interrater reliability for the RCISS was sufficiently high (.72). On the basis of their scores on the RCISS, each couple was classified as either regulated or nonregulated. Regulated couples were those who showed more positive than negative responses as reflected on the RCISS, and nonregulated couples were those who showed more negative than positive responses.

When these same couples were contacted again four years later, 49.3% reported that they had considered dissolving their marriage, and 12.5% had actually divorced. Analyses showed that whether a couple was classified as regulated or nonregulated based on their interaction in the laboratory four years earlier significantly predicted what

(continued)

(continued)

had happened to their relationship. Whereas 71% of the nonregulated couples had considered marital dissolution in the four years since they were first observed, only 33% of the regulated couples had thought about breaking up. Furthermore, 36% of the nonregulated couples had separated compared to 16.7% of the regulated couples. And perhaps most notably, 19% of the nonregulated couples had actually divorced compared to 7.1% of the regulated couples! The data showed that as long as couples maintained a ratio of positive to negative responses of at least 5 to 1 as they interacted, their marriages fared much better than if the ratio of positive to negative responses fell below 5:1. The short snippets of behavior that Gottman and Levenson had observed four years earlier clearly predicted the success of these couples' relationships.

PHYSIOLOGICAL AND NEUROSCIENCE APPROACHES

Some behavioral researchers work in areas of **neuroscience**—a broad, interdisciplinary field that studies biochemical, anatomical, physiological, genetic, and developmental processes involving the nervous system. Some neuroscience research focuses on molecular, genetic, and biochemical properties of the nervous system and thus lies more within the bio-logical than the behavioral sciences. However, many neuroscientists (including researchers that refer to themselves as psychophysiologists, cognitive neuroscientists, and behavioral neuroscientists) study how processes occurring in the brain and other parts of the nervous system relate to psychological phenomena such as sensation, perception, thought, emotion, and behavior. In particular, cognitive, affective, and social neuroscience deal with the relationships between psychological phenomena (such as attention, thought, memory, and emotion) and activity in the nervous system.

Psychophysiological and **neuroscientific measures** can be classified into five general types: measures of neural electrical activity, neuroimaging, measures of autonomic nervous system activity, blood and saliva assays, and precise measurement of overt reactions.

Measures of Neural Electrical Activity

Measures of neural activity are used to investigate the electrical activity of the nervous system and other parts of the body. For example, researchers who study sleep, dreaming, and other states of consciousness use the electroencephalogram (EEG) to measure brain waves. Electrodes are attached to the outside of the head to record the brain's patterns of electrical activity. Other researchers implant electrodes directly into areas of the nervous system to measure the activity of specific neurons or groups of neurons. The electromyograph (EMG) measures electrical activity in muscles and, thus, provides an index of physiological activity related to emotion, stress, reflexes, and other reactions that involve muscular tension or movement.

Neuroimaging

One of the most powerful measures of neural activity is **neuroimaging** (or brain imaging). Researchers use two basic types of neuroimaging—structural and functional. Structural neuroimaging is used to examine the physical structure of the brain. For example, computerized axial tomography, commonly known as CAT scan, uses x-rays to get a detailed picture of the interior structure of the brain (or other parts of the body). CAT scans can be used to identify tumors or other physical abnormalities in the brain.

Functional neuroimaging is used to examine activity within the brain. In **fMRI** (or functional magnetic resonance imaging), a research participant's head is placed in an fMRI chamber, which exposes the brain to a strong magnetic field and low power radio waves (see Figure 4.1[a]). Precise measurements are made of the relative amount of oxygenated blood flowing to different parts of the brain. More oxygenated blood in a particular region is associated with higher neural activity in that part of the brain, thus allowing the researcher to identify the regions of the brain that are most active and, thus, the areas in which certain psychological functions occur. In essence, fMRI images are pictures that show which parts of the brain "light up" when participants perform certain mental functions such as looking at stimuli or remembering words. An example of an fMRI image is shown in Figure 4.1 (b).

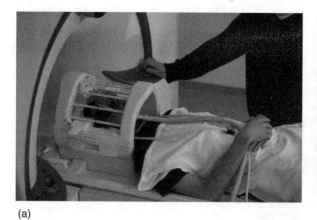
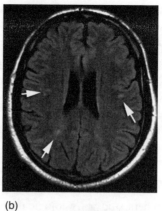

(a)   (b)

FIGURE 4.1   Functional Magnetic Resonance Imaging (fMRI).   (a) A research participant
is being inserted into a functional magnetic resonance imaging (fMRI) machine. The
participant in this picture wears special glasses that deliver visual stimulation. fMRI is used
to investigate brain function by providing images of brain activity. (b) This fMRI scan shows
brain activity as a research participant experiences a migraine headache. The white spots
on this image signify abnormal blood flow.

Source: (a) Mark Hamel/Photo Researchers, Inc. (b) Custom Medical Stock Photo

Behavioral Research Case Study
Neuroimaging: Judging Other People's Trustworthiness

People form impressions of one another very quickly when they first meet, usually on the basis of very little information. One of the most important judgments that we make about other people involves whether or not we can
trust them. Research shows that people make judgments about others' trustworthiness very quickly, often on the
basis of nothing more than the person's appearance. How do we do that? What parts of the brain are involved?

Engell, Haxby, and Todorov (2007) explored the role of the amgdala, an almond-shaped group of nuclei
located in the temporal lobes of the brain, in judging other people's trustworthiness. They were interested specifically in the amygdala because, among its other functions, the amygdala is involved in vigilance to threats of various
kinds. Given that untrustworthy people constitute a threat to our well-being, perhaps the amygdala is involved in
assessing trustworthiness. To examine this hypothesis, Engell and his colleagues tested 129 participants in an fMRI
scanner so that their brains could be imaged as they looked at photographs of faces. When participants are studied
in an fMRI scanner, they lie on their back inside the unit, which allows them to view a computer monitor mounted
above them on which visual stimuli can be presented. They can also hold a controller in their hand that allows them
to press a response button without otherwise moving their body.

The participants viewed photographs of several faces that had been selected to have neutral expressions
that conveyed no emotion. In the first part of the study, participants lay in the fMRI scanner as they indicated
whether each face was among a set of pictures they had viewed earlier. Then, in the second part of the study,
participants were removed from the scanner and asked to view each picture again, this time rating how trustworthy each face appeared to them.

The question is whether participants' amygdalas responded differently to faces that they later rated as
truthworthy than to faces that they thought were untrustworthy. Analysis of the fMRI data showed that activity
in the amygdala was greater for faces that participants rated as less trustworthy. In other words, the amygdala
appeared to be particularly responsive to faces that seemed untrustworthy. The researchers concluded that,
among its other functions, the amydala rapidly assesses other people's trustworthiness. Of course, this finding
does not indicate that people are accurate in their judgments of trustworthiness, but it does show that the amygdala is involved in the process.

Measures of Autonomic Nervous System Activity

Physiological techniques are also used to measure activity in the autonomic nervous system, that portion of the nervous system that controls involuntary responses of the visceral muscles and glands. For example, measures of heart rate, respiration, blood pressure, skin temperature, and electrodermal response all reflect activity in the autonomic nervous system.

Blood and Saliva Assays

Some researchers study physiological processes by analyzing participants' blood or saliva. For example, certain hormones, such as adrenalin and cortisol, are released in response to stress; other hormones, such as testosterone, are related to activity level and aggression. As one example, Dabbs, Frady, Carr, and Besch (1987) measured testosterone in saliva samples taken from 89 male prison inmates and found that prisoners with higher concentrations of testosterone were significantly more likely to have been convicted of violent rather than nonviolent crimes. (In fact, whereas 10 out of the 11 inmates with the highest testosterone concentrations had committed violent crimes, only 2 of the 11 inmates with the lowest testosterone concentrations had committed violent crimes.) Researchers can also study the relationship between psychological processes and physical health by measuring properties of blood that relate to health and illness. In their research on the beneficial effects of writing about personally traumatic experiences (see Chapter 3), Pennebaker Kiecolt-Glaser, and Glaser (1988) analyzed white blood cells to assess the functioning of participants' immune systems.

Precise Measurement of Overt Reactions

Finally, some physiological measures are used to measure bodily reactions that, although sometimes observable, require specialized equipment for precise measurement. For example, in studies of embarrassment, special sensors can be attached to the face to measure blushing; and in studies of sexual arousal, special sensors can be used to measure blood flow to the vagina (the plethysmograph) or the penis (the penile strain gauge).

Often, physiological and neuroscientific measures are used not because the researcher is interested in the physiological reaction per se but rather because the measures are a known marker or indicator of some other phenomenon. For example, because the startle response—a reaction that is mediated by the brainstem—is associated with a defensive eyeblink (that is, people blink when they are startled), a researcher studying startle may use EMG to measure the contraction of the muscles around the eyes. In this case, the researcher really does not care about muscles in the face but rather measures the eyeblink response with EMG to assess activity elsewhere in the brain. Similarly, researchers may use facial EMG to measure facial expressions associated with emotional reactions such as tension, anger, and happiness.

SELF-REPORT APPROACHES: QUESTIONNAIRES AND INTERVIEWS

Behavioral researchers generally prefer to observe behavior directly rather than to rely on participants' reports of how they behave. However, practical and ethical issues often make direct observation implausible or impossible. Furthermore, some information—such as about past experiences, feelings, and attitudes—is most directly assessed through self-report measures such as questionnaires and interviews. On **questionnaires**, participants respond by writing their answers; in **interviews**, participants respond orally to an interviewer.

Although researchers loosely refer to the items to which people respond on questionnaires and in interviewers as "questions," in fact, they are often not actually questions. Of course, sometimes questionnaires and interviewers actually ask questions, such as "How old are you?" or "Have you ever sought professional help for a psychological problem?" But, often researchers obtain information about research participants not by asking questions but rather by instructing participants to rate statements about their attitudes or personal characteristics. For example, participants may be instructed to rate how much they agree with statements such as, "Most people cannot be trusted" or "I am a religious person." At other times, researchers may instruct participants to make lists—of what they ate yesterday or all of the people that they have ever

hated. Questionnaires and interviews may ask participants to rate how they feel (tense–relaxed, happy–sad,
interested–bored) or ask them to describe their feelings
in their own words. As you can see, not all "questions"
that are used on questionnaires and interviews are
actually questions. In light of that, I will use the word
item to refer to any prompt that leads a participant to
provide an answer, rating, or other verbal response on
a questionnaire or in an interview.

Single-Item and Multi-item Measures

The items that are used in questionnaires and
interviews are usually specifically designed to be
analyzed either by themselves as a single-item
measure or as part of a multi-item scale. **Single-item
measures** are intended to be analyzed by themselves. Obviously, when items ask participants to
indicate their gender or their age, these responses are
intended to be used as a single response and not
combined with responses to other questions. Or, if
we ask elementary school students, "How much do
you like school? (with possible answers of n*ot at all,
a little, somewhat,* or *a great deal*) or ask older adults
how lonely they feel (with response options *not at
all, slightly, moderately, very*, or *extremely*), we will
treat their answers to those questions as a single measure of liking for school or loneliness, respectively.

Other items are designed to be used together to
create a **multi-item scale**. You may recall from
Chapter 3 that a scale is a set of items that all assess
the same construct. As we discussed, using several
items often provides a more reliable and valid measure than using a single-item measure. For example, if
we wanted to measure how satisfied people are with
their lives, we could ask them to rate their satisfaction
with eight different areas of life such as finances,
physical health, job, social life, family, romantic relationships, living conditions, and leisure time. Then we
could sum their satisfaction ratings across all the eight
items and use this single score as our measure of life
satisfaction. Or, if we wanted a measure of religiosity,
we could ask respondents to write down how many
hours they spent in each of several religious activities
in the past week—attending religious services, pray-
ing or meditating, reading religious material, attending other religious group meetings, and so on. Then

we would add up their hours across these activities to
get a religiosity score. And, of course, measures of
personality and attitudes very often consist of multiple
items that are summed to provide a single score.

Writing Items

Researchers spend a great deal of time working on
the wording of the items that they use in their questionnaires and interviews. Misconceived and poorly
worded items can doom a study, so considerable
work goes into the content and phrasing of self-
report items. Following are some guidelines for
writing good questionnaire and interview items.

**BE SPECIFIC AND PRECISE IN PHRASING THE
ITEMS.**   Be certain that your respondents will interpret each item exactly as you intended and understand
the kind of response that you desire. What reply
would you give, for example, to the question, "What
kinds of drugs do you take?" One person might list the
recreational drugs he or she has tried, such as marijuana or cocaine. Other respondents, however, might
interpret the question to be asking what kinds of
prescription drugs they are taking and list things such
as penicillin or insulin. Still others might try to recall
the brand names of the various over-the-counter remedies in their medicine cabinets. Similarly, if asked,
"How often do you get really irritated?," different
people may interpret "really irritated" differently.
Write items in such a way that all respondents will
understand and interpret them precisely the same.

**WRITE THE ITEMS AS SIMPLY AS POSSIBLE,
AVOIDING DIFFICULT WORDS, UNNECESSARY
JARGON, AND CUMBERSOME PHRASES.**   Many
respondents would stumble over instructions such
as, "Rate your self-relevant affect on the following
scales." Why not just say, "Rate how you feel about
yourself"? Keep the items short and uncomplicated.
Testing experts recommend limiting each item to no
more than 20 words.

**AVOID MAKING UNWARRANTED ASSUMPTIONS
ABOUT THE RESPONDENTS.**   We often tend to
assume that most other people are just like us, and so
we write items that make unjustified assumptions

based on our own experiences. The question, "How do you feel about your mother?," for example, assumes that the participant knows his or her mother, which might not be the case. Or, what if the respondent is adopted? Should he or she describe feelings about his or her birth mother or adopted mother? Similarly, consider whether respondents have the necessary knowledge to answer each item. A respondent who does not know the details of a new international treaty would not be able to give his or her attitude about it, for example.

CONDITIONAL INFORMATION SHOULD PRECEDE THE KEY IDEA OF THE ITEM.   When a question contains conditional or hypothetical information, that information should precede the central part of the question. For example, it would be better to ask, "If a good friend were depressed for a long time, would you suggest he or she see a therapist?" rather than "Would you suggest a good friend see a therapist if he or she were depressed for a long time?" When the central idea in a question is presented first, respondents may begin formulating an answer before considering the essential conditional element.

DO NOT USE DOUBLE-BARRELED QUESTIONS. A double-barreled question asks more than one question but provides the respondent with the opportunity for only one response. Consider the question, "Do you eat healthfully and exercise regularly?" How should I answer the question if I eat healthfully but don't exercise, or vice versa? Rewrite double-barreled questions as two separate questions.

CHOOSE AN APPROPRIATE RESPONSE FORMAT. The **response format** refers to the manner in which the participant indicates his or her answer to the item. There are three basic response formats, each of which works better for some research purposes than for others.

In a **free-response format** (or open-ended item), the participant provides an unstructured response. In simple cases, the question may ask for a single number, as when respondents are asked how many siblings they have or how many minutes they think have passed as they worked on an experimental task. In more complex cases, respondents may be asked to write an essay or give a long verbal answer. For example, respondents might be asked to describe themselves.

Open-ended items can provide a wealth of information but they have two drawbacks. First, open-ended items force the respondent to figure out the kind of response that the researcher desires as well as how extensive the answer should be. If a researcher interested in the daily lives of college students were to ask you to give her a list of "everything you did today," how specific would your answer be? Would it involve the major activities of your day (such as got up, ate breakfast, went to class . . .) or would you include minor things as well (took a shower, put on my clothes, looked for my missing shoe . . .). Obviously, the quality of the results depends on respondents providing the researcher with the desired kinds of information. Second, if verbal (as opposed to numerical) responses are obtained, the answers must be coded or content-analyzed before they can be statistically analyzed and interpreted. As we will see later in the chapter, doing content analysis raises many other methodological questions. Open-ended items are often very useful, but they must be used with care.

When questions are about behaviors, thoughts, or feelings that can vary in frequency or intensity, a **rating scale response format** should be used. Often, a 5-point scale is used, as in the following example.

To what extent do you oppose or support capital punishment?

_____ Strongly oppose

_____ Moderately oppose

_____ Neither oppose nor support

_____ Moderately support

_____ Strongly support

However, other length scales are also used, as in this example of a 4-point rating scale:

How depressed did you feel after failing the course?

_____ Not at all

_____ Slightly

_____ Moderately

_____ Very

When participants are asked to rate themselves, other people, or objects on descriptive adjectives, respondents are sometimes asked to write an *X* in one of seven spaces to indicate their answer.

Not lonely:___:___:___:___:___:___:___: Lonely

Depressed:___:___:___:___:___:___:___: Not depressed

This kind of measure is often called a *bipolar adjective scale* because each item consists of an adjective and its opposite.

In Depth
How Many Response Options Should Be Offered?

When using a rating scale response format, many researchers give the respondent no more than seven possible response options to use in answering the question. This rule of thumb arises from the fact that human short-term memory can hold only about seven pieces of information at a time (seven plus or minus two, to be precise). Some researchers believe that using response formats that have more than seven options exceeds the number of responses that a participant can consider simultaneously and undermines the quality of their answers. For example, consider this response scale:

Rate how tired you feel right now:

:___:
  1   2   3   4   5   6   7   8   9 10 11 12 13 14 15 16 17 18 19 20 21

On this 21-point scale, can you really distinguish a tiredness rating of 16 from a rating of 17? If not, your decision of whether to mark a 16 or a 17 to indicate that you feel somewhat tired may reflect nothing but measurement error. The difference between a 16 and a 17 doesn't really map on to differences in how people feel.

Although the 21-point scale above has too many response options, I think that researchers can often use scales with more than 7 points. My sense is that in answering questions, participants quickly gravitate to one area of the response scale and do not actually consider all possible options. For example, rate your current level of anxiety on the following scale:

Not at all anxious:_____:_____:_____:_____:_____:_____:_____:_____: Extremely anxious

Did you actually consider all nine possible response options, or did you immediately go to one general area of the scale (perhaps the *not at all* end or somewhere near the middle), then fine-tune your answer within that relatively small range? If you did the latter (and I suspect you did), we need not worry too much about exceeding the capacity of your short-term memory.

In my own research, I capitalize on the fact that participants appear to answer questions such as these in two stages—first deciding on a general area of the scale, then fine-tuning their response. I often use 12-point scales with five scale labels, such as these:

• How anxious do you feel right now?

:_____._____._____:_____._____._____:_____._____._____:_____._____._____:
Not at all   Slightly   Moderately   Very   Extremely

• I am an outgoing, extraverted person.

:_____._____._____:_____._____._____:_____._____._____:_____._____._____:
Strongly   Moderately   Neither agree   Moderately   Strongly
disagree   disagree   nor disagree   agree   agree

When using scales such as these, participants seem to look first at the five verbal labels and decide which one best reflects their answer. Then they fine-tune their answer by deciding which of the options around that label most accurately indicates their response. At both stages of the answering process, the participant is confronted with only a few options—choosing first among five verbal labels, then picking which of the three or four blanks closest to that level best conveys his or her answer.

When using rating scales, researchers must pay very close attention to the labels or numbers that are used to describe the points on the scale because people answer the same item differently depending on the labels that are provided. For example, researchers in one study asked respondents, "How successful would you say you have been in life?" and gave them one of two scales for answering the question. Some respondents saw a scale that ranged from 0 (*not at all successful*) to 10 (*extremely successful*), whereas other respondents saw a scale that ranged from –5 (*not at all successful*) to +5 (*extremely successful*). Even though both were 11-point scales and used the same verbal labels, participants rated themselves as much more successful on the scale that ranged from 0 to 10 than on the scale that went from –5 to +5 (Schwarz, Knäuper, Hippler, Noelle-Neumann, & Clark, 1991).

Finally, sometimes respondents are asked to choose one response from a set of possible alternatives—the **multiple choice** or **fixed-alternative response format**.

What is your attitude toward abortion?

_____ Disapprove under all circumstances

_____ Approve only under special circumstances, such as when the woman's life is in danger

_____ Approve whenever a woman wants one

As with rating scales, the answers that respondents give to multiple choice questions are affected by the alternatives that are presented. For example, in reporting the frequency of certain behaviors, respondents' answers may be strongly influenced by the available response options. Researchers in one study asked respondents to indicate how many hours they watch television on a typical day by checking one of six answers. Half of the respondents were given the options: (1) up to $\frac{1}{2}$ hour, (2) $\frac{1}{2}$ to 1 hour, (3) 1 to $1\frac{1}{2}$ hour, (4) $1\frac{1}{2}$ to 2 hours, (5) 2 to $2\frac{1}{2}$ hours, or (6) more than $2\frac{1}{2}$ hours. The other half of the respondents were

given these six options: (1) up to $2\frac{1}{2}$ hours, (2) $2\frac{1}{2}$ to 3 hours, (3) 3 to $3\frac{1}{2}$ hours, (4) $3\frac{1}{2}$ to 4 hours, (5) 4 to $4\frac{1}{2}$ hours, or (6) more than $4\frac{1}{2}$ hours. When respondents saw the first set of response options, only 16.2% indicated that they watched television more than $2\frac{1}{2}$ hours a day. However, among respondents who got the second set of options, 37.5% reported that they watched TV more than $2\frac{1}{2}$ hours per day (Schwarz, Hippler, Deutsch, & Strack, 1985)! Researchers must be aware that the way in which they ask questions may shape the nature of respondents' answers.

The *true–false response format* is a special case of the fixed-alternative format in which only two responses are available—"true" and "false." A true–false format is most useful for questions of fact (for example, "I attended church last week") but is not recommended for measuring attitudes and feelings. In most cases, people's subjective reactions are not clear-cut enough to fall neatly into a true or false category. For example, if asked to respond true or false to the statement, "I feel nervous in social situations," most people would have difficulty answering either true or false and would probably say, "It depends."

Researchers should consider various options when deciding on a response format and then choose the one that provides the most useful information for their research purposes. Perhaps most importantly, researchers should be on guard for ways in which the questions themselves influence the nature of respondents' answers (Schwarz, 1999).

PRETEST THE ITEMS.   Whenever possible, researchers pretest their items before using them in a study. Items are pretested by administering the questionnaire or interview and instructing respondents to tell the researcher what they think each item is asking, report on difficulties they have understanding the items or using the response formats, and express other reactions to the items. Based on participants' responses during pretesting, the items can be revised before they are actually used in research.

Developing Your Research Skills
Anti-Arab Attitudes in the Wake of 9/11

Shortly after the terrorist attacks of September 11, 2001, a nationwide poll was conducted that concluded that "A majority of Americans favor having Arabs, even those who are U.S. citizens, subjected to separate, more intensive security procedures at airports." Many people were surprised that most Americans would endorse such a policy, particularly for U.S. citizens. But looking carefully at the question that respondents were asked calls the poll's conclusion into question.

Specifically, respondents were instructed as follows:

Please tell me if you would favor or oppose each of the following as a means of preventing terrorist attacks in the United States.

They were then asked to indicate whether they supported or opposed a number of actions, including

Requiring Arabs, including those who are U.S. citizens, to undergo special, more intensive security checks before boarding airplanes in the U.S.

The results showed that 58% of the respondents said that they supported this action. Stop for a moment and see if you can find two problems in how this item was phrased that may have affected respondents' answers (Frone, 2001).

First, the question's stem asks the respondent whether they favored this action "as a means of preventing terrorist attacks." Presumably, if one assumed that taking the action of subjecting all Arabs to special scrutiny would, in fact, prevent terrorist attacks, many people, including many Arabs, might agree with it. But in reality we have no such assurance. Would respondents have answered differently if the stem of the question had asked whether they favored the action "in an effort to lower the likelihood of terrorist attacks" rather than as a means of preventing them? Or, what if respondents had simply been asked, "Do you support requiring all Arabs to undergo special, more intensive security checks before flying?," without mentioning terrorist attacks at all? My hunch is that far fewer respondents would have indicated that they supported this action.

Second, the question itself is double-barreled because it refers to requiring *Arabs, including those who are U.S. citizens,* to undergo special searches. How would a person who favored closer scrutiny of Arabs who were not citizens but opposed it for those who were U.S. citizens answer the question? Such a person—and many Americans probably supported this view—would neither fully agree nor fully disagree with the statement. Because of this ambiguity, we do not know precisely what respondents' answers indicated they were endorsing.

Questionnaires

Questionnaires are perhaps the most ubiquitous of all psychological measures. Many dependent variables in experimental research are assessed via questionnaires on which participants provide information about their cognitive or emotional reactions to the independent variable. Similarly, many correlational studies ask participants to complete questionnaires about their thoughts, feelings, and behaviors. Likewise, survey researchers often ask respondents to complete questionnaires about their attitudes, lifestyles, or behaviors. Even researchers who typically do not use questionnaires to measure dependent variables, such as physiological psychologists and neuroscientists, may use them to ask about participants' reactions to the study. Questionnaires are used at one time or another not only by most researchers who study human behavior but also by clinical psychologists to obtain information about their clients, by companies to collect data on applicants and employees, by members of Congress to poll their constituents, by restaurants to assess the quality of their food and service, and by colleges to obtain students' evaluations of their teachers. You have undoubtedly completed many questionnaires.

Although researchers must often design their own questionnaires, they usually find it worthwhile to look for existing questionnaires before investing time and energy into designing their own. Existing measures often have a strong track record that gives us confidence in their psychometric properties. Particularly when using questionnaires to measure attitudes or personality, the chances are good that relevant measures already exist, although it sometimes takes a little detective work to track down measures that are relevant to a particular research topic. Keep in mind, however, that just because a questionnaire has been published does not necessarily indicate that it has adequate reliability and validity. Be sure to examine the available psychometric data for any measures you plan to use.

Four sources of information about existing measures are particularly useful. First, many psychological measures were initially published in journal articles, and you can locate these measures using the same kinds of strategies you use to search for articles on any topic (such as the computerized search service PsycInfo). Second, many books have been published that describe and critically evaluate measures used in behavioral and educational research. Some of these compendia of questionnaires and tests—such as *Mental Measurements Yearbook, Tests in Print*, and the *Directory of Unpublished Experimental Mental Measures*—include many different kinds of measures; other books focus on measures that are used primarily in certain kinds of research, such as personality psychology or health psychology (Robinson, Shaver, & Wrightsman, 1991). Third, several data-bases can be found on the World Wide Web that describe psychological tests and measures, such as ERIC's Clearing House on Assessment and Educa-tion, and Educational Testing Service's Test Collecting Catalog. Fourth, some questionnaires may be purchased from commercial publishers. In the case of commercially published scales, be aware that you must have certain professional credentials to purchase many measures, and you are limited in how you may use them.

Although they often locate existing measures for their research, researchers sometimes must design measures "from scratch" either because appropriate measures do not exist or because they believe that the existing measures will not adequately serve their research purpose. But because new measures are time-consuming to develop and risky to use (in the sense that we do not know how well they will perform), researchers usually check to see whether relevant measures have already been published.

Behavioral Research Case Study
Experience Sampling Methods

One shortcoming of some self-report questionnaires is that respondents have difficulty remembering the details needed to answer the questions accurately. Suppose, for example, that you are interested in whether lonely people have fewer contacts with close friends than nonlonely people. The most accurate way to examine this question would be to administer a measure of loneliness and then follow participants around for a week and directly observe with whom they interact. Obviously, practical and ethical problems preclude such an approach, not to mention the fact that people would be unlikely to behave naturally with a researcher trailing them 24 hours a day.

Alternatively, you could measure participants' degree of loneliness and then ask participants to report how many times (and for how long each time) they interacted with certain friends and acquaintances during the past week. If participants' memories were infallible, this would be a reasonable way to address the research question, but people's memories are simply not that good. Can you really recall everyone you interacted with during the past seven days, and how long you interacted with each person? Thus, neither observational methods nor retrospective self-reports are likely to yield valid data in a case such as this.

One approach for solving this problem involves **experience sampling methods** or **ESM**. Several different experience sampling methods have been developed, but all of them ask participants to record information about their thoughts, emotions, or behaviors as they occur in everyday life. Instead of asking participants to recall their past reactions as most questionnaires do, ESM asks them to report what they are thinking, feeling, or doing *right now*. Although ESM is a self-report method, it does not require participants to remember details of past experiences, thereby reducing memory biases.

The earliest ESM studies involved a **diary methodology.** Participants were given a stack of identical questionnaires that they were to complete one or more times each day for several days. For example, Wheeler, Reis, and Nezlek (1983) used a diary approach to study the question posed above involving the relationship between loneliness and social interaction. In this study, participants completed a standard measure of loneliness and kept a daily record of their social interactions for about two weeks. For every interaction they had that lasted 10 minutes or longer, the participants filled out a short form on which they recorded with whom they had interacted, how long the interaction lasted, the gender of the other interactant(s), and other information such as who had initiated the interaction and how pleasant the encounter was. By having participants record this information soon after each interaction, the researchers decreased the likelihood that the data would be contaminated by participants' faulty memories.

The results showed that, for both male and female participants, loneliness was negatively related to the amount of time they interacted with women; that is, spending more time with women was associated with lower loneliness. Furthermore, although loneliness was not associated with the number of different people participants interacted with, lonely participants rated their interactions as less meaningful than less lonely participants did. In fact, the strongest predictor of loneliness was how meaningful participants found their daily interactions.

More recently, researchers have started using **computerized experience sampling methods** (Barrett & Barrett, 2001). Computerized experience sampling involves the use of portable, handheld computers or personal digital assistants that are programmed to ask participants about their experiences during everyday life. Participants carry these small units with them each day (they fit easily in a backpack, pocket, or purse), answering items either when signaled to do so by the unit or when certain kinds of events occur. Items are presented on the unit's screen, and participants answer by selecting from a set of response options. The unit stores the participant's data for several days, after which it is uploaded for analysis. In another variation of computerized experience sampling, participants may be instructed to log onto a research Web site one or more times each day to answer questions about their daily experiences.

In addition to avoiding memory biases that may arise when participants are asked to recall their behaviors, computerized ESM can ensure that participants answer the questions at specified times by time-stamping participants' responses (unlike pencil-and-paper ESM studies in which the researcher cannot be sure that participants completed the questionnaires at the proper times). Most importantly, ESM allows researchers to measure experiences as they arise naturally in real-life situations. As a result, data obtained from ESM studies can provide insight into processes that are difficult to study under controlled laboratory conditions. ESM has been used to study a large number of everyday phenomena including academic performance, behavior in romantic relationships, social support, alcohol use, self-presentation in everyday life, the "flow" experience, the role of physical attractiveness in social interactions, effects of wearing cologne or perfume, and friendship processes (Bolger, Davis, & Rafaeli, 2003; Green, Rafaeli, Bolger, Shrout, & Reis, 2006; Reis & Gable, 2000; Reis & Wheeler, 1991).

Consider a study of smoking relapse among smokers who were in a smoking-cessation program (Shiffman, 2005). Participants carried a palmtop computer on which they answered questions about their smoking, mood, daily stresses, and self-esteem when "beeped" to do so by the computer. The results showed that, although daily changes in mood and stress did not predict smoking relapse, many episodes of smoking relapse were preceded by a spike in strong negative emotions during the six hours leading up to the relapse. Findings such as these would have been impossible to obtain without using computerized ESM to track participants' emotions and behavior as their daily lives unfolded.

Interviews

For some research purposes, participants' answers are better obtained in face-to-face or telephone interviews rather than on questionnaires. Each of the guidelines for writing questionnaire items discussed earlier is equally relevant for designing an **interview schedule**—the series of items that is used in an interview.

In addition, the researcher must consider how the interview process itself—the interaction between the interviewer and respondent—will affect participants' responses. Following are a few suggestions of ways for interviewers to improve the quality of the responses they receive from interviewees.

Create a Friendly Atmosphere. The interviewer's first goal should be to put the respondent at ease. Respondents who like and trust the interviewer will be more open and honest in their answers than those who are intimidated or angered by the interviewer's style.

Maintain an Attitude of Friendly Interest. The interviewer should appear truly interested in the respondent's answers rather than mechanically recording the responses in a disinterested manner.

Conceal Personal Reactions to the Respondent's Answers. At the same time, however, the interviewer should not react to the respondents' answers. The interviewer should never show surprise, approval, disapproval, or other reactions to what the respondent says. Do not imitate the interviewer in the cartoon on the next page.

Order the Sections of the Interview to Facilitate Building Rapport and to Create a Logical Sequence. Start the interview with the most basic and least threatening topics, and then move slowly to more specific and sensitive items as the respondent becomes more relaxed.

Ask Questions Exactly as They are Worded. In most instances, the interviewer should ask each question in precisely the same way to all respondents. Impromptu wordings of the questions introduce differences in how various respondents are interviewed, thereby increasing measurement error and lowering the reliability of participants' responses.

Don't Lead the Respondent. In probing the respondent's answer—asking for clarification or details—the interviewer must be careful not to put words in the respondent's mouth.

Behavioral Research Case Study
An Interview Study: Runaway Adolescents

Why do some adolescents run away from home, and what happens to them after they leave? Thrane, Hoyt, Whitbeck, and Yoder (2006) conducted a study in which they interviewed 602 runaway adolescents ranging in age from 12 to 22 in four Midwestern states. Each runaway was interviewed by a staff member who was trained to interview runway and homeless youth. During the interview, participants were asked the age at which they first ran away from home, whether they had engaged in each of 15 deviant behaviors in order to subsist after leaving their family (such as using sex to get money, selling drugs, or stealing), and whether they had been victimized after leaving home, for example by being robbed, beaten, or sexually assaulted. To understand why they had run away, participants were also asked questions about their home life, including sexual abuse, physical abuse, neglect, and changes in the family (such as death, divorce, and remarriage). They were also asked about the community in which their family lived so that the researchers could examine differences between runaways who had lived in urban versus rural areas.

Results showed that, not surprisingly, adolescents who experienced neglect and sexual abuse ran away from home at an earlier age than those who were not neglected or abused. Adolescents from rural areas who experienced high levels of physical abuse reported staying at home longer before running away than urban adolescents. Furthermore, family abuse and neglect also predicted the likelihood that a runaway would be victimized on the street after leaving home. After running away, rural youth were more likely to rely on deviant subsistence strategies than their urban counterparts, possibly because rural areas have fewer social service agencies to which they can turn. The authors concluded that rural youth who have experienced a high level abuse at home have a greater risk of using deviant subsistence strategies, which increase the likelihood that they will be victimized after they run away.

Advantages of Questionnaires Versus Interviews

Both questionnaires and interviews have advantages and disadvantages, and researchers must decide which strategy will best serve a particular research purpose. On one hand, because questionnaires require less extensive training of researchers and can be administered to groups of people simultaneously, they are usually less expensive and time-consuming than interviews. Furthermore, if the topic is a sensitive one, participants can be assured that their responses to a questionnaire will be anonymous, whereas anonymity is impossible in a face-to-face interview. Thus, participants may be more honest on questionnaires than in interviews.

On the other hand, if respondents are drawn from the general population, questionnaires are inappropriate for those who are functionally illiterate—approximately 10% of the adult population of the United States. Similarly, interviews are necessary for young children, people who are cognitively impaired, severely disturbed individuals, and others who are incapable of completing questionnaires on their own. Also, interviews allow the researcher to be sure respondents understand each item before answering. We have no way

"That's the worst set of opinions I've heard in my entire life."

Source: © Robert Weber/The New Yorker Collection/www.cartoonbank.com

of knowing whether respondents understand all of the items on a questionnaire. Perhaps the greatest advantage of interviews is that detailed information can be obtained about complex topics. A skilled interviewer can probe respondents for elaboration of details in a way that is impossible on a questionnaire.

Biases in Self-Report Measurement

Although measurement in all sciences is subject to biases of various sorts (for example, all scientists are prone to see what they expect to see), the measures used in behavioral research are susceptible to certain biases that those in many other sciences are not. Unlike the objects of study in the physical sciences, for example, the responses of the participants in behavioral research are sometimes affected by the research process itself. A piece of crystal will not change how it responds while being studied by a geologist, but a human being may well act differently when being studied by a psychologist or other behavioral researcher. In this section, we briefly discuss two measurement biases that may affect self-report measures.

THE SOCIAL DESIRABILITY RESPONSE BIAS. Research participants are often concerned with how they will be perceived and evaluated by the researcher or by other participants. As a result, they sometimes respond in a socially desirable manner rather than naturally and honestly. People are hesitant to admit that they do certain things, have certain problems, feel certain emotions, or hold certain attitudes, for example. This **social desirability response bias** can lower the validity of certain measures. When people bias their answers or behaviors in a socially desirable direction, the instrument no longer measures whatever it was supposed to measure; instead, it measures participants' proclivity for responding in a socially desirable fashion.

Social desirability biases can never be eliminated entirely, but steps can be taken to reduce their effects on participants' responses. First, items

should be worded as neutrally as possible, so that concerns with social desirability do not arise. Second, when possible, participants should be assured that their responses are anonymous, thereby lowering their concern with others' evaluations. (As I noted, this is easier to do when information is obtained on questionnaires rather than in interviews.) Third, in observational studies, observers should be as unobtrusive as possible to minimize participants' concerns about being watched.

ACQUIESCENCE AND NAY-SAYING RESPONSE STYLES.   Some people show a tendency to agree with statements regardless of the content (**acquiescence**), whereas others tend to express disagreement (**nay-saying**). These response styles were discovered during early work on authoritarianism. Two forms of a measure of authoritarian attitudes were developed, with the items on one form written to express the opposite of the items on the other form. Given that the forms were reversals of one another, people's scores on the two forms should be inversely related; people who score low on one form should score high on the other, and vice versa. Instead, scores on the two forms were positively related, alerting researchers to the fact that some respondents were consistently agreeing or disagreeing with the statements regardless of what the statement said!

Fortunately, years of research suggest that the tendency toward acquiescence and nay-saying has only a very minor effect on the validity of self-report measures as long as one essential precaution is taken—any measure that asks respondents to indicate agreement or disagreement (or true versus false) to various statements should have an approximately equal number of items on which people who score high on the construct would indicate *agree* versus *disagree* (or *true* versus *false*) (Nunnally, 1978). For example, on a measure of the degree to which people's feelings are easily hurt, we would need an equal number of items that express a high tendency toward hurt feelings ("My feelings are easily hurt") and items that express a low tendency ("I am thick-skinned").

| **In Depth** |
| *Asking for More Than Participants Can Report* |

When using self-report measures, researchers should be alert to the possibility that they may sometimes ask questions that participants cannot answer accurately. In some cases, participants *know* they do not know the answer to a particular question, such as "How old were you, in months, when you were toilet-trained?" When they know they don't know the answer to a question, participants may indicate that they do not know the answer or they may simply guess. Unfortunately, as many as 30% of respondents will answer questions about completely fictitious issues, presumably because they do not like to admit they don't know something. (This is an example of the social desirability bias discussed earlier.) Obviously, researchers who treat participants' guesses as accurate responses are asking for trouble.

In other cases, participants *think* they know the answer to a question—in fact, they may be quite confident of their response—yet they are entirely wrong. Research shows, for example, that people often are not aware that their memories of past events are distorted; nor do they always know why they behave or feel in certain ways. Although we often assume that people know why they do what they do, people can be quite uninformed regarding the factors that affect their behavior. In a series of studies, Nisbett and Wilson (1977) showed that participants were often ignorant of why they behaved as they did, yet they confidently gave what sounded like cogent explanations. In fact, some participants vehemently denied that the factor that the researchers *knew* had affected the participant's responses had, in fact, influenced them.

People's beliefs about themselves are important to study in their own right, regardless of the accuracy of those beliefs. But behavioral researchers should not blithely assume that participants are always able to report accurately the reasons they act or feel certain ways.

ARCHIVAL DATA

In most studies, measurement is contemporaneous— it occurs at the time the research is conducted. A researcher designs a study, recruits participants, and then collects data about those participants using a predesigned observational, physiological, or self-report measure.

However, some research uses data that were collected prior to the time the research was designed. In **archival research**, researchers analyze data pulled from existing records, such as census data, court records, personal letters, newspaper reports, magazine articles, government documents, economic data, and so on. In most instances, archival data were collected for purposes other than research. Like contemporaneous measures, archival data may involve information about observable behavior (such as immigration records, school records, marriage statistics, and sales figures), physiological processes (such as hospital and other medical records), or self-reports (such as personal letters and diaries).

Archival data are particularly suited for studying certain kinds of questions. First, they are uniquely suited for studying social and psychological phenomena that occurred in the historical past. We can get a glimpse of how people thought, felt, and behaved by analyzing records from earlier times. Jaynes (1976), for example, studied writings from several ancient cultures to examine the degree to which people of earlier times were self-aware. Cassandro (1998) used archival data to explore the question of why eminent creative writers tend to die younger than do eminent people in other creative and achievement domains.

Second, archival research is useful for studying social and behavioral changes over time. Researchers have used archival data to study changes in race relations, gender roles, patterns of marriage and child-rearing, male–female relationships, and so on. For example, Sales (1973) used archival data to test the hypothesis that the prevalence of authoritarianism—a personality constellation that involves rigid adherence to group norms (and punishment of those who break them), toughness, respect for authority, and cynicism—

increases during periods of high social threat, such as during economic downturns. Sales obtained many kinds of archival data going back to the 1920s, including budgets for police departments (authoritarian people should want to crack down on rule-breakers), crime rates, popular books and articles, and applications for various kinds of jobs. His analyses showed that, as predicted, authoritarianism increased when economic times turned bad.

Third, certain research topics require an archival approach because they inherently involve existing documents such as newspaper articles, magazine advertisements, or campaign speeches. For example, in a study that examined differences in how men and women are portrayed pictorially, Archer, Iritani, Kimes, and Barrios (1983) examined pictures of men and women from three different sources: American periodicals, publications from other cultures, and artwork from the past six centuries. Their analyses of these pictures documented what they called "face-ism"—the tendency for men's faces to be more prominent than women's faces in photographs and drawings, and this difference was found both across cultures and over time.

Fourth, researchers sometimes use archival sources of data because they cannot conduct a study that will provide the kinds of data they desire or because they realize a certain event needs to be studied after it has already occurred. For example, we would have difficulty designing and conducting studies that investigate relatively rare events—such as riots, suicides, mass murders, and school shootings—because we would not know in advance who to study as "participants." After such events occur, however, we can turn to existing data regarding the people involved in these events. Similarly, researchers have used archival data involving past events—such as elections, natural disasters, and sporting events—to test hypotheses about behavior.

Fifth, to study certain phenomena, resear-chers sometimes need a large amount of data about events that occur in the real world. For example, Baumeister and Steinhilber (1984) used many years of data involving professional baseball and basketball championships to test hypotheses about why athletes "choke under pressure," and Frank and Gilovich (1988) used archival data from professional football and ice hockey to show that wearing black uniforms is associated with higher aggression during games. Archival research has also been conducted on the success of motion pictures, using several types of archival data in an effort to understand variables that predict a movie's financial success, critical acclaim, and receipt of movie awards, such as an Oscar (Simonton, 2009). Some of these studies showed that the cost of making a movie was uncorrelated with the likelihood that it would be nominated for or win a major award, was positively correlated with box office receipts (although not with profitability), and negatively correlated with critical acclaim. Put simply, big-budget films bring movie goers into the theatre, but they are not judged as particularly good by critics or the movie industry itself and do not necessarily turn a profit, partly because they cost so much to make.

The major limitation of archival research is that the researcher must make do with whatever measures are already available. Sometimes, the existing data are sufficient to address the research question, but often, important measures simply do not exist. Even when the data contain the kinds of measures that the researcher needs, the researcher often has questions about how the information was initially collected and, thus, concerns about the reliability and validity of the data.

Behavioral Research Case Study
Archival Research: Predicting Greatness

Although archival measures are used to study a wide variety of topics, they are indispensable when researchers are interested in studying people and events in the past. Simonton (1994) has relied heavily on archival measures in his extensive research on the predictors of greatness. In trying to understand the social and psychological variables that contribute to notable achievements in science, literature, politics, and the arts, Simonton has used archival data regarding famous and not-so-famous people's lives and professional contributions.

In some of this work, Simonton (1984) examined the age at which notable nineteenth-century scientists (such as Darwin, Laplace, and Pasteur) and literary figures (such as Dickens, Poe, and Whitman) made their major contributions. In examining the archival data, he found that, for both groups, the first professional contribution—a scientific finding or work of literature—occurred in their mid-twenties on average. After that, the productivity of these individuals rose quickly, peaking around age 40 (±5 years). (See accompanying graph.) Then their productivity declined slowly for the rest of their careers.

When only the most important and creative contributions—those that had a major impact on their fields—were examined, the curve followed the same pattern. Both scientists and literary figures made their most important contributions around age 40. There were, of course, exceptions to this pattern (Darwin was 50 when he published *The Origin of Species,* and Hugo was 60 when he wrote *Les Misérables*), but most eminent contributions occurred around age 40. This archival research seems to support Oliver Wendell Holmes, Jr.'s observation that "If you haven't cut your name on the door of fame by the time you've reached 40, you might as well put up your jackknife."

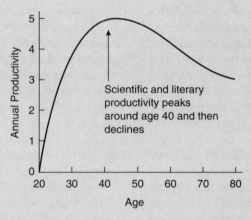

Source: Adapted from *Greatness* by D. K. Simonton, 1994, by permission of Guilford Press.

CONTENT ANALYSIS

In many studies that use observational, self-report, or archival measures, the data of interest involve the *content* of people's speech or writing. For example, behavioral researchers may be interested in what children say aloud as they solve difficult problems, what shy strangers talk about during a getting-acquainted conversation, or what married couples discuss during marital therapy. Similarly, researchers may want to analyze the content of essays that participants write about themselves or the content of participants' answers to open-ended questions. In other cases, researchers want to study existing archival data such as newspaper articles, letters, or personal diaries.

Researchers interested in such topics are faced with the task of converting written or spoken material to meaningful data that can be analyzed. In such situations, researchers turn to **content analysis**, a set of procedures designed to convert textual information to numerical data that can be analyzed (Berelson, 1952; Rosengren, 1981; Weber, 1990). Content analysis has been used to study topics as diverse as historical changes in the lyrics of popular songs, differences in the topics men and women talk about in group discussions, suicide notes, racial and sexual stereotypes reflected in children's books, election campaign speeches, biases in newspaper coverage of events, television advertisements, the content of the love letters of people in troubled and untroubled relationships, and psychotherapy sessions.

The central goal of content analysis is to classify words, phrases, or other units of text into a limited number of meaningful categories that are relevant to the researcher's hypothesis. Any text can be content analyzed, whether it is written material (such as answers, essays, or articles) or transcripts of spoken material (such as conversations, public speeches, or talking aloud).

The first step in content analysis is to decide what units of text will be analyzed—words, phrases, sentences, or some other unit. Often the most useful unit of text is the *utterance* (or theme), which corresponds, roughly, to a simple sentence having a noun, a verb, and supporting parts of speech (Stiles, 1978). For example, the statement, "I hate my mother," is a single utterance. In contrast, the statement, "I hate my mother and father," reflects two utterances: "I hate my mother" and "[I hate] my father." The researcher goes through the text or transcript, marking and numbering every discrete utterance.

The second step is to define how the units of text will be coded. At the most basic level, the researcher must decide whether to (1) *classify* each unit of text into one of several mutually exclusive categories or (2) *rate* each unit on some specified dimensions. For example, imagine that we were interested in people's responses to others' complaints. On one hand, we could classify people's reactions to another's complaints into one of four categories, such as disinterest (simply not responding to the complaint), refutation (denying that the person has a valid complaint), acknowledgment (simply acknowledging the complaint), or validation (agreeing with the complaint). On the other hand, we could rate participants' responses on the degree to which they are supportive. For example, we could rate participants' responses to complaints on a 5-point scale where 1 = *nonsupportive* and 5 = *extremely supportive.*

Whichever system is used, clear rules must be developed for classifying or rating the text. These rules must be so explicit and clear that two raters using the system will rate the material in the same way. To maximize the degree to which their ratings agree,

raters must discuss and practice the system before actually coding the textual material from the study. Also, researchers assess the interrater reliability of the system by determining the degree to which the raters' classifications or ratings are consistent with one another (see Chapter 3). If the reliability is low, the coding system is clarified or redesigned.

After the researcher is convinced that interrater reliability is sufficiently high, raters code the textual material for all participants. They must do so independently and without conferring with one another so that interrater reliability can again be assessed based on ratings of the material obtained in the study.

Although researchers must sometimes design a content analysis coding system for use in a particular study, they should always explore whether a system already exists that will serve their purposes. Coding schemes have been developed for analyzing everything from newspaper articles to evidence of inner psychological states (such as hostility and anxiety) to group discussions and conversations (Bales, 1970; Rosengren, 1981; Stiles, 1978; Viney, 1983).

A number of computer software programs have been designed to content analyze textual material. The text is typed into a text file, which the software searches for words or phrases of interest to the researcher. For example, the Linguistic Inquiry and Word Count (LIWC) program calculates the percentage of words in a text file that fits into each of 72 language categories, such as negative emotion words, positive emotion words, first-person pronouns, words that convey uncertainty (such as "maybe" and "possibly"), words related to topics such as sex or death, and so on (Pennebaker, Francis, & Booth, 2001). (Researchers can create their own word categories as well.) Another widely used program, NUD*IST (which stands for Non-numerical Unstructured Data with powerful processes of Indexing, Searching, and Theorizing) helps the researcher to identify prevailing categories of words and themes in participants' responses. Then, once those categories are identified, NUD*IST content analyzes the data by searching participants' responses for those categories (Gahan & Hannibal, 1998).

Behavioral Research Case Study

What Makes People Boring? A Content Analysis

Several years ago, I conducted a series of studies to identify the behaviors that lead people to regard other individuals as boring (Leary, Rogers, Canfield, & Coe, 1986). In one of these studies, 52 pairs of participants interacted for 5 minutes in an unstructured laboratory conversation, and their conversations were tape-recorded. After these 52 conversations were transcribed (converted from speech to written text), 12 raters read each transcript and rated how interesting versus boring each participant was on a 5-point scale. These 12 ratings were then averaged to create a "boringness index" for each participant.

Two trained raters then used the Verbal Response Mode (VRM) Taxonomy (Stiles, 1978) to content analyze the conversations. The VRM coding scheme classifies each utterance a person makes into one of several, mutually-exclusive verbal response modes such as disclosures (first-person declarative statements, such as "I failed the test"), edifications (statements of fact), acknowledgments (utterances that convey understanding of information, such as "uh-huh"), and questions. Preliminary analyses confirmed that interrater reliability was sufficient for most of the verbal response modes. (The ones that were not acceptably reliable involved verbal responses that occurred very infrequently. It is often difficult for raters to reliably detect very rare behaviors.)

We then correlated participants' boringness index scores with the frequency with which they used various verbal responses during the conversation. Results showed that ratings of boringness correlated positively with the number of a person's utterances that were questions and acknowledgments, and negatively with the number of utterances that were edifications. Although asking questions and acknowledging others' contributions are important in conversations, people who ask too many questions and use too many acknowledgments are seen as boring, as are those who don't contribute enough information. The picture of a boring conversationalist that emerges from this content analysis is a person whose verbal responses do not absorb the attention of other people.

Summary

1. Most measures used in behavioral research involve either observations of overt behavior, physiological measures and neuroimaging, self-report items (on questionnaires or in interviews), or archival data.

2. Researchers who use observational measures must decide whether the observation will occur in a natural or contrived setting. Naturalistic observation involves observing behavior as it occurs naturally with no intrusion by the researcher. Contrived observation involves observing behavior in settings that the researcher has arranged specifically for observing and recording behavior.

3. Participant observation is a special case of naturalistic observation in which researchers engage in the same activities as the people they are studying.

4. When researchers are concerned that behaviors may be reactive (affected by participants' knowledge that they are being observed), they sometimes conceal from participants the fact they are being observed. However, because disguised observation sometimes raises ethical issues, researchers often use undisguised observation or partial concealment strategies, rely on the observations of knowledgeable informants, or use unobtrusive measures.

5. Researchers record the behaviors they observe in four general ways: narrative records (relatively complete descriptions of a participant's behavior), checklists (tallies of whether certain behaviors were observed), temporal measures (such as measures of latency and duration), and observational rating scales (on which researchers rate the intensity or quality of participants' reactions).

6. Interrater reliability can be increased by developing precise operational definitions of the behaviors being observed and by giving

observers the opportunity to practice using the observational coding system.

7. Physiological measures are used to measure processes occurring in the participant's body. Such measures can be classified into five general types that assess neural electrical activity (such as brain waves, the activity of specific neurons, or muscle firing), neuroimaging (to get "pictures" of the structure and activity of the brain), autonomic arousal (such as heart rate and blood pressure), biochemical processes (through blood and saliva assays of hormones and neurotransmitters), and observable physical reactions (such as blushing or reflexes).

8. People's self-reports can be obtained using either questionnaires or interviews, each of which has advantages and disadvantages. Some self-report measures consist of a single item or question (single-item measures), whereas others consist of sets of questions or items that are summed to measure a single variable (multi-item scales).

9. To write good items for questionnaires and interviews, researchers should use precise terminology, write the items as simply as possible, avoid making unwarranted assumptions about the respondents, put conditional information before the key part of the question, avoid double-barreled questions,

choose an appropriate response format, and pretest the items.

10. Self-report measures use one of three general response formats: free response, rating scale, and fixed alternative (or multiple choice).

11. Before designing new questionnaires, researchers should always investigate whether validated measures already exist that will serve their research needs.

12. When experience sampling methodology (ESM) is used, respondents keep an ongoing record of certain target behaviors.

13. When interviewing, researchers must structure the interview setting in a way that increases the respondents' comfort and promotes the honesty and accuracy of their answers.

14. Whenever self-report measures are used, researchers must guard against the social desirability response bias (the tendency for people to respond in ways that convey a socially desirable impression), and acquiescence and nay-saying response styles.

15. Archival data are obtained from existing records, such as census data, newspaper articles, research reports, and personal letters.

16. If spoken or written textual material is collected, it must be content analyzed. The goal of content analysis is to classify units of text into meaningful categories or to rate units of text along specified dimensions.

Key Terms

acquiescence (*p. 90*)
archival research (*p. 91*)
checklist (*p. 76*)
computerized experience sampling methods (*p. 87*)
content analysis (*p. 93*)
contrived observation (*p. 73*)
diary methodology (*p. 87*)
disguised observation (*p. 73*)
duration (*p. 76*)
experience sampling methods (*p. 87*)

field notes (*p. 75*)
fixed-alternative response format (*p. 84*)
fMRI (*p. 78*)
free response format (*p. 82*)
interbehavior latency (*p. 76*)
interview (*p. 80*)
interview schedule (*p. 88*)
knowledgeable informant (*p. 74*)
latency (*p. 76*)
multi-item scale (*p. 81*)

multiple choice response format (*p. 84*)
narrative record (*p. 75*)
naturalistic observation (*p. 72*)
nay-saying (*p. 90*)
neuroimaging (*p. 78*)
neuroscience (*p. 78*)
neuroscientific measure (*p. 78*)
observational method (*p. 72*)
participant observation (*p. 72*)
psychophysiological measure (*p. 78*)

questionnaire (*p. 80*)
rating scale response format (*p. 82*)
reaction time (*p. 76*)
reactivity (*p. 73*)

response format (*p. 82*)
single-item measure (*p. 81*)
social desirability response bias
    (*p. 90*)

task completion time (*p. 76*)
undisguised observation
    (*p. 73*)
unobtrusive measure (*p. 74*)

Questions for Review

1. Discuss the pros and cons of using naturalistic versus contrived observation.
2. What special opportunities and problems does participant observation create for researchers?
3. What does it mean if a behavior is reactive?
4. What are three ways in which researchers minimize reactivity?
5. What is the right of informed consent?
6. Explain how Ickes's dyadic interaction paradigm helps to avoid the problem of reactivity.
7. What are the advantages and disadvantages of using narrative records in observational research?
8. Distinguish between a structured and unstructured observation method.
9. When would you use a checklist versus an observational rating scale to record behavior?
10. Distinguish among the four types of temporal measures—reaction time, task completion time, interbehavior latency, and duration—and give three examples of when each might be used in research.
11. What are some ways that you can increase the interrater reliability of observational methods?
12. Give an example of each of the five general types of physiological and neuroscience measures.
13. What is the difference between structural and functional neuroimaging?
14. When might you decide to use a single-item measure versus a multi-item scale?
15. List at least five considerations that researchers should keep in mind when writing items to be used on a questionnaire or in an interview.

16. What is a double-barreled question? Give an example.
17. Describe each of the three basic types of response formats—free response, rating scale, and multiple choice.
18. Which of the three response formats would be most useful in obtaining the following information?
    a. to ask whether the respondent's maternal grandfather is still living
    b. to measure the degree to which participants liked another person with whom they had just interacted
    c. to find out whether the participant was single, married, divorced, or widowed
    d. to find out how happy the participants felt
    e. to ask participants to describe why a recent romantic breakup had occurred
19. How might you find information about measures that have been developed by other researchers?
20. What are experience sampling methodologies, and why are they used?
21. Discuss ways in which interviewers can increase the reliability and validity of the information they obtain from respondents.
22. Discuss the advantages and disadvantages of using questionnaires versus interviews to obtain self-report data.
23. How can researchers minimize the effects of the social desirability response bias on participants' self-reports?
24. List as many sources of archival data as you can.
25. What four kinds of research questions are particularly suited for the use of archival data?
26. Describe how you would conduct a content analysis.

Questions for Discussion

1. Design a questionnaire that assesses people's eating habits. Your items could address topics such as what they eat, when they eat, how much they eat, with whom they eat, where they eat, how healthy their eating habits are, and so on. In designing your questionnaire, be sure to consider the issues discussed throughout this chapter.
2. Pretest your questionnaire by giving it to three people. Ask for their reactions to each item, looking for potential

problems in how the items are worded and in the response formats that you used.

3. Do you think that people's responses on your questionnaire might be affected by response biases? If so, what steps could you take to minimize them?

4. Obtain two textbooks—one in a social or behavioral science (such as psychology, sociology, communication, or anthropology) and the other in a natural science (such as biology, chemistry, or physics). Pick a page from each at random (but be sure to choose a page that is all text, with no figures or tables). Do a content analysis of the text on these pages that will address the question, "Are textbooks in behavioral and social science written in a more personal style than textbooks in natural science?" You will need to (a) decide what unit of text will be analyzed, (b) operationally define what it means for something to be written in a "personal style," (c) develop your coding system, (d) code the material on the two pages of text, and (e) describe the differences you discovered between the two texts. (Note: Because there will likely be a different number of units of text on the two pages, you will need to adjust the scores for the two pages by the number of units on that page.)

5. Using the approaches discussed in this chapter, identify as many existing multi-item scales as possible that measure one of the constructs below. That is, pick one topic below and then find as many measures of it as possible. You will have to think about what terms might be used to describe the construct that you choose. Locate actual copies of two or three of these scales (online or in the library, for example).
   a. attitudes toward people of other races
   b. religiosity
   c. agreeableness
   d. loneliness

5 SELECTING RESEARCH PARTICIPANTS

A Common Misconception	Nonprobability Samples
Probability Samples	How Many Participants?

In 1936, the magazine *Literary Digest* surveyed more than 2 million voters regarding their preference for Alfred Landon versus Franklin Roosevelt in the upcoming presidential election. Based on the responses they received, the *Digest* predicted that Landon would defeat Roosevelt in a landslide by approximately 15 percentage points. When the election was held, however, not only was Roosevelt elected president, but his margin of victory was overwhelming. Roosevelt received 62% of the popular vote, compared to only 38% for Landon. What happened? How could the pollsters have been so wrong?

As we will see later, the problem with the *Literary Digest* survey involved how the researchers selected respondents for the survey. Among the decisions that researchers face every time they design a study is selecting research participants. Researchers can rarely examine every individual in the population who is relevant to their interests—all newborn babies, all paranoid schizophrenics, all color-blind adults, all registered voters, all female chimpanzees, or whomever. Fortunately, there is absolutely no need to study *every* individual in the population of interest. Instead, researchers collect data from a subset, or **sample**, of individuals in the population. Just as a physician can learn a great deal about a patient by analyzing a small sample of the patient's blood (and does need not need to drain every drop of blood for analysis), researchers can learn about a population by analyzing a relatively small sample of individuals. **Sampling** is the process by which a researcher selects a sample of participants for a study. In this chapter, we focus on the various ways that researchers select samples of participants to study, problems involved in recruiting participants, and questions about the number of participants that we need to study.

A COMMON MISCONCEPTION

To get you off on the right foot with this chapter, I want first to disabuse you of a very common misconception—that most behavioral research uses *random* samples. On the contrary, the vast majority of research does not use random samples, researchers couldn't use random samples even if they wanted to in most studies, and using random samples in most research is not necessarily a good idea anyway. As we will see, random samples are absolutely essential for certain kinds of research questions, but most research in psychology and other behavioral sciences does not address questions for which random sampling is needed or even desirable.

At the most general level, samples can be classified as probability samples or nonprobability samples. A **probability sample** is a sample that is selected in such a way that the likelihood that any particular individual in the population will be selected for the sample can be specified. Although we will discuss several kinds of probability samples later in the chapter, the best known probability sample is the simple random sample. A simple random sample is one in which every possible sample of the desired size has the same chance of being selected from the population and, by extension, every individual in the population has an equal chance of being selected for the sample. Thus, if we have a simple random sample, we know precisely the likelihood that any particular individual in the population will end up in our sample.

When a researcher is interested in accurately describing the behavior of a particular population from a sample, probability samples are essential. For example, if we want to know the percentage of voters who prefer one candidate over another, the number of children in our state who are living with only one parent, or how many veterans show signs of post traumatic stress disorder, we must obtain probability samples from the relevant populations. Without probability sampling, we cannot be sure of the degree to which the data provided by the sample approximate the behavior of the larger population.

However, except when researchers are trying to estimate the number of people in a population who display certain attitudes, behaviors, or problems, probability samples are virtually never used in psychological research. The goal of most behavioral research is *not* to describe how a population behaves but rather to test hypotheses regarding how certain psychological variables relate to one another. If the data are consistent with our hypotheses, they provide evidence in support of the theory regardless of the nature of our sample. Of course, we may wonder whether the results generalize to other samples, and we can assess the generalizability of the findings by trying to replicate the study on other samples of participants who differ in age, education level, socioeconomic status, geographic region, and other psychological and personal characteristics. If similar

findings are obtained using several different samples, we can have confidence that our results hold for different kinds of people. But we do not need to use random samples in most studies.

We are fortunate that random samples are not needed for many kinds of research because, as we will see, probability sampling is very time-consuming, expensive, and difficult. Imagine, for example, that a developmental psychologist is interested in studying language development among 2-year-olds and wants to test a sample of young children on a set of computer-administered tasks under controlled conditions. How could the researcher possibly obtain a random sample of 2-year-olds from all children of that age in the country (or even a smaller geographical unit such as a state or city)? And, how could he or she induce the parents of these children to bring them to the laboratory for testing? Or, imagine a clinical psychologist studying people's psychological reactions to learning that they are HIV+. Where could he or she get a random sample of people with HIV? Similarly, researchers who study animals could never obtain a random sample of animals of the desired species but instead study individuals that are housed in colonies (of rats, chimpanzees, lemurs, bees, or whatever) for research use. Thus, in most research contexts, it is impossible, impractical, or unnecessary for a researcher to obtain a random sample.

PROBABILITY SAMPLES

Even so, a probability sample is essential for certain kinds of research questions. When the purpose of a study is to accurately describe the behavior, thoughts, or feelings of a particular group, researchers must ensure that the sample they select is representative of the population at large. A **representative sample** is one from which we can draw accurate, unbiased estimates of the characteristics of the larger population. We can draw accurate inferences about the population from data obtained from a sample only if it is representative.

The Error of Estimation

Unfortunately, samples rarely mirror their parent populations in every respect. The characteristics of the individuals selected for the sample always differ somewhat from the characteristics of the general population. This difference, called **sampling error**, causes results obtained from a sample to differ from what would have been obtained had the entire population been studied. If you calculate the average grade point average of a representative sample of 200 students at your college or university, the mean for this sample will not perfectly match the average that you would obtain if you had used the grade point averages of *all* students in your school. If the sample is truly representative, however, the value obtained on the sample should be very close to what would be obtained if the entire population were studied.

Fortunately, when probability sampling techniques are used, researchers can estimate how much their results are affected by sampling error. The **error of estimation** (also called the **margin of error**) indicates the degree to which the data obtained from the sample are expected to deviate from the population as a whole. For example, you may have heard newscasters report the results of a political opinion poll and then add that the results "are accurate within 3 percentage points." What this means is that if 45% of the respondents in the sample endorsed Smith for president, we know that there is a 95% probability that the true percentage of people in the population who support Smith is between 42% and 48% (that is, 45% ± 3%). By allowing researchers to estimate the sampling error in their data, probability samples permit them to specify how confident they are that the results obtained on the sample accurately reflect the behavior of the population. Their confidence is expressed in terms of the error of estimation.

The smaller the error of estimation, the more closely the results from the sample estimate the behavior of the larger population. For example, if the limits on the error of estimation are only ±1%, the sample data are a better indicator of the population than if the limits on the error of estimation are ±10%. So, if the error of estimation in the opinion poll was 1%, we are rather confident that the true population value falls between 44% and 46% (that is, 45% ± 1%). But if the error of estimation is 10%, the true population has a 95% probability of being anywhere between 35% and 55% (that is, 45% ± 10%). Obviously, researchers prefer the error of estimation to be as small as possible.

The error of estimation is a function of three things: the sample size, the population size, and the variance of the data. First, the larger a probability sample, the more similar the sample tends to be to the population (that is, the smaller the sampling error) and the more accurately the sample data estimate the population's characteristics. You would estimate the average grade point average at your school more closely with a sample of 400 than with a sample of 50, for example, because larger sample sizes have a lower error of estimation.

The error of estimation also is affected by the size of the population from which the sample was drawn. Imagine we have two samples of 200 respondents. The first was drawn from a population of 400, the second from a population of 10 million. Which sample would you expect to mirror more closely the population's characteristics? I think you can guess that the error of estimation will be lower when the population contains 400 cases than when it contains 10 million cases.

The third factor that affects the error of estimation is the variance of the data. The greater the variability in the data, the more difficult it is to estimate the population values accurately. We saw in Chapter 2 that the larger the variance, the less representative the mean is of the set of scores as a whole. As a result, the larger the variance in the data, the larger the sample needs to be to draw accurate inferences about the population.

The error of estimation is meaningful only when we have a **probability sample**—a sample for which the researcher knows the mathematical probability that any individual in the population is included in the sample. Only with a probability sample do we know that the statistics that we calculate from the sample data reflect the true values in the parent population, at least within the margin defined by the error of estimation. If we do not have a probability sample, the characteristics of the sample may not reflect those of the population, so we cannot trust that the sample statistics tell us anything at all about the population. In this case, the error of estimation is irrelevant because the data cannot be used to draw inferences about the population anyway.

Thus, when researchers want to draw inferences about a population from a sample, they must select a probability sample. Probability samples may be obtained in several ways, but four basic methods involve simple random sampling, systematic sampling, stratified random sampling, and cluster sampling.

Simple Random Sampling

When a sample is chosen in such a way that every possible sample of the desired size has the same chance of being selected from the population, the sample is a **simple random sample**. For example, suppose we want to select a sample of 200 participants from a school district that has 5,000 students. If we wanted a simple random sample, we would select our sample in such a way that every possible combination of 200 students has the same probability of being chosen.

To obtain a simple random sample, the researcher must have a **sampling frame**—a list of the population from which the sample will be drawn. Then participants are chosen randomly from this list. If the population is small, one approach is to write the name of each case in the population on a slip of paper, shuffle the slips of paper, then pull slips out until a sample of the desired size is obtained. For example, we could type each of the 5,000 students' names on cards, shuffle the cards, then randomly pick 200. However, with larger populations, pulling names "out of a hat" becomes unwieldy.

The primary way that researchers select a random sample is to number each person in the sampling frame from 1 to N, where N is the size of the population. Then they pick a sample of the desired size by selecting numbers from 1 to N by some random process. Traditionally, researchers have used a **table of random numbers**, which contains long rows of numbers that have been generated in a random order. (Tables of random numbers can be found in many statistics books and on the Web.) Today, researchers more commonly use computer programs to generate lists of random numbers, and you can find Web sites that allow you to generate lists of random numbers from 1 to whatever sized population you might have. Whether generated from a table or by a computer, the idea is the same. Once we have numbered our sampling frame from 1 to N and generated as many random numbers as needed for the desired sample size, the individuals in our sampling frame who have the randomly generated numbers are selected for the sample.

In Depth
Random Telephone Surveys: The Problem of Cell Phones

Not too many years ago, almost all American households had a single telephone line. As a result, phone numbers provided a convenient sampling frame from which researchers could choose a random sample of households for surveys. Armed with a population of phone numbers, researchers could easily draw a random sample. Although researchers once used phone books to select their samples, for the past few decades they have relied upon random digit dialing. **Random digit dialing** is a method for selecting a random sample for telephone surveys by generating telephone numbers at random. Random digit dialing is better than choosing numbers from a phone book because it will generate unlisted numbers as well as listed ones.

However, the spread of cell phones has created a number of problems for researchers who rely on random digit dialing to obtain random samples. First, the Telephone Consumer Protection Act prohibits using an automatic dialer to call cell phone numbers. Researchers could dial them manually, but then the advantages of using automated dialing are lost. Second, because many households have both a landline and one or more cell phones, households differ in the likelihood that they will be contacted for the study. (Households with more phone numbers are more likely to be sampled.) As we saw earlier, a probability sample requires that researchers estimate the probability that a particular case will be included in the sample, but this is not possible if households differ in the number of phones they have. Third, researchers often want to confine their probability sample to a particular geographical region—a particular city or state, for example. But because people can keep their cell phone number when they move, the area code for a cell phone does not reflect the person's location as it does with landline phone numbers. Finally, people may be virtually anywhere when they answer their cell phone. Researchers worry that the quality of the data they collect as people are driving, standing in line, shopping, sitting in the bathroom, visiting, and multitasking in other ways is not as good as when people are in the privacy of their own homes (Keeter, Kennedy, Clark, Tompson, & Mokrzycki, 2007; Link, Battaglia, Frankel, Osborn, & Mokdad, 2007).

On top of these methodological issues, evidence suggests that people who use only a cell phone differ on average from those who have only a landline phone or both landlines and cell phones. This fact was discovered during the 2004 presidential election when phone surveys underestimated the public's support for John Kerry in his campaign against George W. Bush. The problem arose because people who had only a cell phone (but no landline phone) were more likely to support Kerry than those who had landline phones. Not only do they differ in their demographic characteristics (for example, they are younger and more likely to be unmarried), but they hold different political attitudes, watch different TV shows, and are more likely to use computers to get the news. Not surprisingly, then, the results of cell phone surveys often differ from the results of landline phone surveys. And to make matters worse, among people who have both cell phones and landlines, those who are easier to reach on their cell phone differ from those who are easier to reach on their landline phone at home (Link et al., 2007). Fortunately, because the number of people who have a cell phone but no landline home phone remains small, using random digit dialing to contact people with landline phones may not influence the results of telephone surveys much for now (Keeter et al., 2007). But as the number of cell phones grows and home-based landline phones continue to disappear, researchers will need to find new ways to grapple with this problem.

Systematic Sampling

One major drawback of simple random sampling is that we must know how many individuals are in the population and have a sampling frame that lists all of them before we begin. Imagine that we wish to study people who use hospital emergency rooms for psychological rather than medical problems. We cannot use simple random sampling because at the time that we start the study, we have no idea how many people might come through the emergency room during the course of the study and don't have a sampling frame. In such a situation, we might choose to use **systematic sampling**. Systematic sampling involves taking every so many individuals for the sample. For example, we could decide that we would interview every 8th person who came to the ER for care until we obtained a sample of whatever size we desired. When the study is over, we will know how many people came through the emergency room and how many we

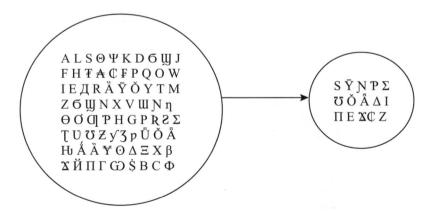

FIGURE 5.1 Simple Random Sampling. In this figure, the population is represented by the large circle, the sample is represented by the small circle, and the letters are individual people. In simple random sampling, cases are sampled at random directly from the population in such a way that every possible sample of the desired size has an equal probability of being chosen.

selected and, thus, we would also know the probability that any person who came to the ER during the study would be in our sample.

You may be wondering why this is not a simple random sample. The answer is that, with a simple random sample, every possible sample of the desired size has the same chance of being selected from the population. In systematic sampling this is not the case. After we select a particular participant, the next several people have no chance at all of being in the sample. For example, if we are selecting every 8th person for the study, the 9th through the 15th persons to walk into the ER have no chance of being chosen, and our sample could not possibly include, for example, both the 8th and the 9th person. In a simple random sample, all possible samples have an equal chance of being used, so this combination would be possible.

Stratified Random Sampling

Stratified random sampling is a variation of simple random sampling. Rather than selecting cases directly from the population, we first divide the population into two or more subgroups or strata. A **stratum** is a subset of the population that shares a particular characteristic. For example, we might divide the population into men and women, into different racial groups, or into six age ranges (20–29, 30–39, 40–49, 50–59, 60–69, over 69). Then cases are randomly sampled from each of the strata.

Stratification ensures that researchers have adequate numbers of participants from each stratum so that they can examine differences in responses among the various strata. For example, the researcher might want to compare younger respondents (20–29 years old) with older respondents (60–69 years old). By first stratifying the sample, the researcher ensures that there will be an ample number of both young and old respondents in the sample.

In many cases, researchers use a **proportionate sampling method** in which cases are sampled from each stratum in proportion to their prevalence in the population. For example, if the registered voters in a city are 55% Democrats and 45% Republicans, a researcher studying political attitudes may wish to sample proportionally from those two strata to be sure that the sample is also composed of 55% Democrats and 45% Republicans. When this is done, stratified random sampling can increase the probability that the sample we select will be representative of the population.

Cluster Sampling

Although they provide us with very accurate pictures of the population, simple and stratified random sampling have a major drawback: They require that we have a sampling frame of all cases in the population before we begin. Obtaining a list of small, easily identified populations is no problem. You would find it relatively easy to obtain a list of all students in your

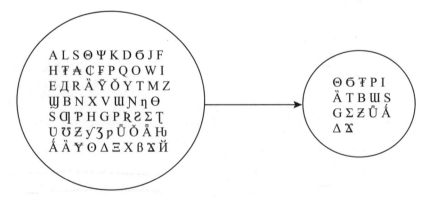

FIGURE 5.2   Systematic Sampling.   In this figure, the population is represented by the large circle, the sample is represented by the small circle, and the letters are individual people. In systematic sampling, every *n*th person is selected from a list. In this example, every 4th person has been chosen.

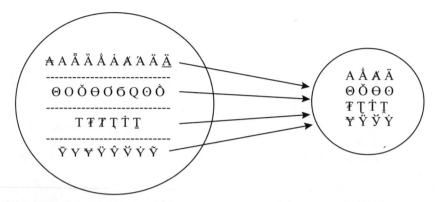

FIGURE 5.3   Stratified Random Sampling.   In this figure, the population is represented by the large circle, the sample is represented by the small circle, and the letters are individual people. In stratified random sampling, the population is first divided into strata composed of individuals who share a particular characteristic. In this example, the population is divided into four strata. Then cases are randomly selected from each of the strata.

college or all members of the Association for Psychological Science, for example. Unfortunately, not all populations are easily identified. Could we, for example, obtain a list of every person in the United States or, for that matter, in New York City or Miami? Could we get a sampling frame of all Hispanic 3-year-olds, all people who are deaf who know sign language, or all single-parent families in Canada headed by the father? In cases such as these, random sampling is not possible because without a list we cannot locate potential participants or specify the probability that a particular case will be included in the sample.

In such instances, **cluster sampling** is often used. To obtain a cluster sample, the researcher first samples not participants but rather groupings or *clusters* of participants. These clusters are often based on naturally occurring groupings, such as geographical areas or particular institutions. For example, if we wanted a sample of elementary school children in West Virginia, we might first randomly sample from the 55 county school systems in West Virginia. Perhaps we would pick 15 counties at random. Then, after selecting this small random sample of counties, we could get lists of students for those counties and obtain random samples of students from the selected counties.

Often cluster sampling involves a **multistage cluster sampling** process in which we begin by sampling large clusters, then we sample smaller clusters from within the large clusters, then we sample even smaller clusters, and finally we obtain our sample of participants. For example, we could randomly pick counties and then randomly choose several particular schools from the selected counties. We could then randomly select particular classrooms from the schools we selected, and finally randomly sample students from each classroom.

Cluster sampling has two advantages. First, a sampling frame of the population is not needed to begin sampling—only a list of the clusters. In this example, all we would need to start is a list of counties in West Virginia, a list that would be far easier to obtain than a census of all children enrolled in West Virginia schools. Then, after sampling the clusters, we can get lists of students within each cluster (that is, county) that was selected, which is much easier than getting a list of the entire population of students in West Virginia. The second advantage is that, if each cluster represents a grouping of participants that are close together geographically (such as students in a certain county or school), less time and effort are required to contact the participants. Focusing on only 15 counties would require considerably less time, effort, and expense than sampling students from all 55 counties in the state.

In Depth
To Sample or Not to Sample: The Census Debate

Since the first U.S. census in 1790, the Bureau of the Census has struggled to find ways to account for every person in the country. For a variety of reasons, many citizens are miscounted by census-takers. The population of the United States is not only large, but it is also moving, changing, and partially hidden, and any effort to count the entire population will both overcount and undercount certain groups. In the 2000 census, for example, an estimated 6.4 million people were not counted, and approximately 3.1 million people appear to have been counted twice. The challenge that faces the Census Bureau is to design and administer the census in a way that provides the most accurate data. To do so, the Census Bureau has proposed to rely on sampling procedures rather than to try to track down each and every person.

The big problem that compromises the validity of the census is that a high percentage of people either do not receive the census questionnaire or, if they receive it, do not complete and return it as required by law. So, how can we track these nonresponders down? Knowing that it will be impossible to visit every one of the millions of households that did not respond to the mailed questionnaire or follow-up call, the bureau proposed that census-takers visit a **representative sample** of the addresses that do not respond. The rationale is that, by focusing their time and effort on this representative sample rather than trying to contact every household that is unaccounted for (which previous censuses showed is fruitless), they could greatly increase their chances of obtaining the missing information from these otherwise uncounted individuals. Then, using the data from the representative sample of nonresponding households, researchers could estimate the size and demographic characteristics of other missing households. Once they know the racial, ethnic, gender, and age composition of this representative sample of people who did not return the census form, statistical models can be used to estimate the characteristics of the entire population that did not respond.

Statisticians overwhelmingly agree that sampling will dramatically improve the accuracy of the census. A representative sample of nonresponding individuals provides far more accurate data than an incomplete set of households that is biased in unknown ways. However, despite its statistical merit, the plan met stiff opposition in Congress, and the Supreme Court ruled that sampling techniques could not be used to reapportion seats in the House of Representatives. Many people have trouble believing that contacting a probability sample of nonresponding households provides far more accurate data than trying (and failing) to locate them all, although you should now be able to see that this is the case. In addition, many politicians worry that the sample would be somehow biased (resulting perhaps in loss of federal money to their districts), would underestimate members of certain groups, or would undermine public trust in the census. Such concerns reflect misunderstandings about probability sampling.

Despite the fact that sampling promised to both improve the accuracy of the census and lower its cost, Congress denied the Census Bureau's request to use sampling in the 2000 and 2010 census. However, although the bureau was forced to attempt a full-scale enumeration of every individual in the country (a challenge that was doomed to failure from the outset), it was allowed to study sampling procedures to document their usefulness. Unfortunately, politics have prevailed over reason and science, and opponents have blocked the use of sampling procedures that would undoubtedly provide a better estimate of the population's characteristics.

The Problem of Nonresponse

The **nonresponse problem** is the failure to obtain responses from individuals that researchers select for a sample. In practice, researchers are rarely able to obtain perfectly representative samples because some people who are initially selected for the sample either cannot be contacted or refuse to participate. For example, when households or addresses are used as the basis of sampling, interviewers may repeatedly find that no one is at home when they visit the address. Or, in the case of mailed surveys, the person selected for the sample may have moved and left no forwarding address. If the people who can easily be located differ from those who cannot be found, the people who can be found may not be representative of the population as a whole and the results of the study may be biased in unknown ways.

Even when people who are selected for the sample are contacted, a high proportion of them do not

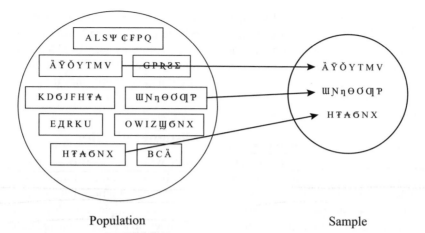

Population   Sample

FIGURE 5.4   Cluster Sampling.   In this figure, the population is represented by the large circle, the samle is represented by the small circle, and the letters are individual people. In cluster sampling, the population is divided into groups, usually based on geographical proximity. In this example, the population is divided into eight clusters of varying sizes. A random sample of clusters is then selected. In this example, three clusters were chosen at random.

want to participate in the study, and, to the extent that those who agree to participate differ from those who don't, nonresponse destroys the benefits of probability sampling. As a result, the final set of respondents we contact may not be representative of the population.

Imagine, for example, that we wish to obtain a representative sample of family physicians for a study of professional burnout. We design a survey to assess burnout and, using a professional directory to obtain names, mail this questionnaire to a random sample of family physicians in our state. To obtain a truly representative sample, *every* physician we choose for our sample must complete and return the questionnaire. If our return rate is less than 100%, the data we obtain may be biased in ways that are impossible to determine. For example, physicians who are burned out may be unlikely to take the time to complete and return our questionnaire. Or perhaps those who do return it are highly conscientious or have especially positive attitudes toward behavioral research. In any case, if some individuals who were initially chosen for the sample decline to participate, the representativeness of our sample is compromised.

A similar problem arises when telephone surveys are conducted. Aside from the fact that some American households do not have a telephone, the nonresponse rate is often high in telephone surveys, and it is particu-

larly high when people are contacted on their cell phones (Link et al., 2007). If the people who decline to participate differ in important ways from those who agree, these differences can bias our results.

Researchers tackle the nonresponse problem in a number of ways depending on why they think people are refusing to participate in a particular study (Biemer & Lyberg, 2003). Some of the factors that contribute to nonresponse include:

- Lack of time
- Being contacted at an inconvenient time
- Illness
- Other responsibilities
- Literacy or language problems
- Fear of being discovered by authorities (e.g., people who have violated parole or are illegal immigrants)
- Disinterest
- Study involves a sensitive topic
- Sense of being used without being compensated
- Suspiciousness about researcher's motives

First, researchers can take steps to increase the number of people in the sample who are contacted successfully. For example, they can try contacting the person at different times of day, leave messages for the person to contact the researcher, or find other ways to track him or her down. When mail surveys are used, researchers often follow up the initial mailing of the questionnaire with telephone calls or postcards to urge people to complete and return them. Of course, many people become irritated by researchers' persistent efforts to contact them, so there's a limit to how much pestering should be done.

Second, researchers often offer incentives for participation such as small payments, a gift, or entry into a random drawing for a large prize. Sometimes mail surveys include a small "prepaid incentive"— a few dollars that may make people more likely to complete and return the survey. Offering incentives certainly increases people's willingness to participate in research, but it may be more effective with certain groups of people than with others. For example, we might imagine that people with lower incomes will be swayed more by a small payment than wealthy people.

Third, they can try to make participation as easy for participants as possible by designing studies that require as little time to complete as possible, using interviewers who speak second languages, or asking whether they can call back at a more convenient time. The amount of time required is a particularly important consideration for respondents.

Fourth, evidence suggests that telling people in advance that they will be contacted for the study increases the likelihood that people will participate when they receive the questionnaire in the mail or are called on the phone.

Whether nonresponse biases a study's findings depends on the degree to which people who respond differ from those who don't. If responders and nonresponders are very similar, then nonresponse does not impair our ability to draw valid, unbiased conclusions from the data. However, if responders and nonresponders differ in important ways that are relevant to our study, a high nonresponse rate can essentially ruin a study. Thus, researchers usually try to determine whether respondents and nonrespondents differ in any systematic ways. Based on what they know about the sample they select, researchers can see whether those who did and did not respond differ. For example, the professional directory we use to obtain a sample of physicians may provide their birthdates, the year in which they obtained their

medical degrees, their workplaces (hospital versus private practice), and other information. Using this information, we may be able to show that those who returned the survey did not differ from those who did not. (Of course, they may differ on dimensions about which we have no information.)

Misgeneralization

Even when probability sampling is used, results may be misleading if the researcher generalizes them to a population that differs from the one from which the sample was drawn, an error known as **misgeneralization**. For example, a researcher studying parental attitudes may study a random sample of parents who have children in the public school system. So far, so good. But if the researcher uses his or her data to make generalizations about *all* parents, misgeneralization may occur because parents whose children attend private schools or who are home-schooled were not included in the sample.

This was essentially the problem with the *Literary Digest* poll described at the start of this chapter, the poll that failed miserably in its attempt to predict the outcome of the presidential election between Roosevelt and Landon in 1936. To obtain voters for the survey, the researchers sampled names from telephone directories and automobile registration lists. This sampling procedure had yielded accurate predictions in the presidential elections of 1920, 1924, 1928, and 1932. However, by 1936, in the aftermath of the Great Depression, people who had telephones and automobiles were not representative of the country at large. Thus, the respondents who were selected for the survey tended to be wealthier, Republican, and more likely to support Landon rather than Roosevelt for president. Thus, the survey vastly underestimated Roosevelt's popularity, misjudging the eventual winner's margin of victory by 39 points in the wrong direction! The researchers misgeneralized the results, believing that they were representative of all voters when, in fact, they were representative only of voters who had telephones or automobiles.

Another interesting case of misgeneralization occurred in several studies of sexual behavior. Studies around the world consistently show that men report having more sexual partners than women do.

This pattern is, of course, impossible: For every woman with whom a man reports having sex, some woman should also report having sex with a man. (Even if a small number of women are having sex with lots of men, the total numbers of partners that men and women report should be equal overall.) Clearly, something is amiss here, but researchers could not determine whether this pattern reflected a self-report bias (perhaps men report having more partners than they actually do and/or women under-report their number of partners) or a problem with how the studies were conducted. As it turns out, the illogical discrepancy between the number of men's and women's partners was a sampling problem that led to misgeneralization. Specifically, prostitutes are dramatically underrepresented in most studies of sexual behavior because respondents for those studies have been obtained by sampling households (as I described earlier when discussing random digit dialing), and many prostitutes live in motels, homeless shelters, boarding houses, jails, and other locations that would not be considered "households" by survey researchers. If we take into account prostitutes that are not included in probability samples of households and the number of men with whom they have sex, this number accounts entirely for the discrepancy between men's and women's reported numbers of sexual partners (Brewer et al., 2000). In other words, the extra partners that men report relative to women in previous surveys can be entirely explained by the relative absence of prostitutes from the samples. This is a case of misgeneralization because researchers erroneously generalized results obtained on samples that included too few prostitutes to the population of "all women." As a consequence, results appeared to show that women had fewer sexual partners than men.

NONPROBABILITY SAMPLES

As I explained earlier, most behavioral research does not use probability samples such as random, systematic, stratified, and cluster samples. Instead, research relies on nonprobability samples. With a **nonprobability sample**, researchers have no way of knowing the probability that a particular case will be chosen for the sample. As a result, they cannot calculate the error of estimation to determine precisely how representative the sample is of the population. However, as I mentioned earlier, this is not necessarily a problem when researchers are not trying to describe precisely what a population thinks, feels, or does.

The three primary types of nonprobability samples are convenience, quota, and purposive samples.

Convenience Sampling

The most common type of sample in psychological research is the **convenience sample**, which includes participants that are readily available. For example, we could stop people we encounter on a downtown street, recruit people from the local community, study patients at a local hospital or clinic, test children at a nearby school, or use a sample of students at our own college or university.

The primary benefit of convenience samples is that they are far easier to obtain than representative samples. Imagine for a moment trying to recruit a representative sample for a controlled, laboratory experiment. Whether you want a representative sample of 10-year-old children, pregnant women, people diagnosed with social anxiety disorder, unemployed men in their 50s, or unselected ordinary adults, you would find it virtually impossible to select a representative sample of participants who would be able and willing to travel to your lab for the study. Instead, you would recruit whatever participants you can from the appropriate group, usually people living in the local community.

Many people automatically assume that using a convenience sample creates a serious problem, but it doesn't. If we were trying to describe the characteristics of the population from which our participants came, we could not use a convenience sample. But most experimental research is not trying to describe a population. Instead, experimental studies test hypotheses about how variables relate to one another, and we can test these relationships on any sample that we choose. Although the sample is not representative of any particular population, we can nonetheless test hypotheses about relationships among variables.

Of course, we might wonder whether the relationships that we uncover with a particular convenience sample also occur in other groups.

But we can test the generalizability of our findings by replicating the experiment on other convenience samples. The more different those convenience samples are from one another, the better we can see whether our findings generalize across different groups of people.

In Depth
College Students as Research Participants

By far, the most common type of sample used in behavioral research is a convenience sample composed of college students. The practice of using students as research participants began more than 100 years ago. Initially, students were recruited primarily for medical research, including studies of student health, but by the 1930s, researchers in psychology departments were also using large numbers of students in their studies. One interesting, albeit bigoted, justification for doing so was that college students of the day best represented psychologically "normal" human beings because they were predominately white, upper-class, and male (Prescott, 2002).

The field's heavy reliance on college students as research participants has been discussed for many years (Wintre, North, & Sugar, 2001). Most researchers agree that students offer a convenient source of participants and that much research could not be conducted without using student samples. Yet, the question that troubles most researchers involves the degree to which studies of students tell us about psychological processes more generally. Students differ from the "average person" in a number of ways. For example, they tend to be more intelligent than the general population, are more likely to come from middle- and upper-class backgrounds, and are more likely to hold liberal attitudes than the population at large. The question is whether these kinds of characteristics are related to the psychological processes that we study. To the extent that many basic psychological processes are universal, there is often little reason to expect different samples to respond differently, and it may matter little what kind of sample one uses. But, we really don't know much about the degree to which college students differ from other samples in ways that might limit the conclusions we can draw about people in general.

To tackle this question, Peterson (2001) examined meta-analyses of studies that included samples of both college students and nonstudents. (Remember that meta-analyses calculate the average effect size of a finding across many studies.) His findings presented a mixed picture of the degree to which research findings using student and nonstudent samples are similar. For approximately 80% of the effects tested, the direction of the effect was the same for students and nonstudents, showing that most of the time, patterns of relationships between variables operate in the same direction for students and nonstudents. However, the size of the effects sometimes differed a great deal. So, for example, in studies of the relationship between gender and assertiveness, the effect size for this relationship was much larger for nonstudent samples than for student samples. In normal language, men and women differ more on measures of assertiveness in studies conducted on nonstudents than in studies that used students.

Frankly, I am not particularly bothered by differences in effect sizes between student and nonstudent samples as long as the same general relationship between two variables is obtained across samples. We should not be surprised that the strength of various effects is moderated by other variables that differ between the groups. For example, there are many reasons why differences in male and female assertiveness is lower among college students than among nonstudents.

Perhaps more troubling is the fact that in 1 out of 5 cases, variables related in different directions for students and nonstudents (Peterson, 2001). Even this might not be as problematic as it first seems, however, because in some cases, at least one effect was close to .00. For example, for student samples, the correlation between blood pressure and certain aspects of personality was negative ($-.01$) whereas for students it was positive ($+.03$). But, although $-.01$ and $+.03$ technically show opposite effects, neither is significantly different from .00. In reality, both student and nonstudent samples showed no correlation.

So, the picture is mixed: Research on student and nonstudent samples generally show the same patterns, but the sizes of the effects sometimes differ, and occasionally effects are in different directions. Researcher should be cautious when using college students to draw conclusions about people in general. This is true, of course, no matter what kind of convenience sample is being used.

Quota Sampling

A **quota sample** is a convenience sample in which the researcher takes steps to ensure that certain kinds of participants are obtained in particular proportions. The researcher specifies in advance that the sample will contain certain percentages of particular kinds of participants. For example, if researchers wanted to obtain an equal proportion of male and female participants, they might decide to obtain 20 women and 20 men in a sample from a psychology class rather than simply select 40 people without regard to gender.

Purposive Sampling

For a **purposive sample**, researchers use past research findings or their judgment to decide which participants to include in the sample, trying to choose respondents who are typical of the population they want to study. One area in which purposive sampling has been used successfully involves forecasting the results of national elections. Based on previous elections, researchers have identified particular areas of the country that tend to vote like the country as a whole. Voters from these areas are then interviewed and their political preferences used to predict the outcome of an upcoming election. Although these are not probability samples, they appear to be reasonably representative of the country as a whole. Unfortunately, researchers' judgments cannot be relied on as a trustworthy basis for selecting samples, and purposive sampling should not generally be used.

Behavioral Research Case Study
Sampling and Sex Surveys

People appear to have an insatiable appetite for information about other people's sex lives. The first major surveys of sexual behavior were conducted by Kinsey and his colleagues in the 1940s and 1950s (Kinsey, Pomeroy, & Martin, 1948; Kinsey, Pomeroy, Martin, & Gebhard, 1953). Kinsey's researchers interviewed more than 10,000 American men and women, asking about their sexual practices. You might think that with such a large sample, Kinsey would have obtained valid data regarding sexual behavior in the United States. Unfortunately, although Kinsey's data were often cited as if they reflected the typical sexual experiences of Americans, his sampling techniques do not permit us to draw conclusions about people's sexual behavior.

Rather than using a probability sample that would have allowed him to calculate the error of estimation in his data, Kinsey relied on convenience samples (or what he called "100 percent samples"). His researchers would contact a particular group, such as a professional organization or sorority, and then obtain responses from 100% of its members. However, these groups were not selected at random (as they would be in the case of cluster sampling). As a result, the sample contained a disproportionate number of respondents from Indiana, college students, Protestants, and well-educated people (Kirby, 1977). In an analysis of Kinsey's sampling technique, Cochran, Mosteller, and Tukey (1953) concluded that, because he had not used a probability sample, Kinsey's results "must be regarded as subject to systematic errors of unknown magnitude due to selective sampling" (p. 711).

Other surveys of sexual behavior have encountered similar difficulties. In Hunt's (1974) survey, names were chosen at random from the phone books of 24 selected American cities. This technique produced three sampling biases. First, the cities were not selected randomly. Second, by selecting names from the phone book, the survey overlooked people without phones and those with unlisted numbers. Third, only 20% of the people who were contacted agreed to participate in the study; how these respondents differed from those who declined is impossible to judge.

Several popular magazines—such as *McCall's, Psychology Today,* and *Redbook*—have also conducted large surveys of sexual behavior. Again, probability samples were not obtained and, thus, the accuracy of their data is questionable. The most obvious sampling bias in these surveys is that readers of particular magazines are unlikely to be representative of the population at large, and those readers who complete and return a questionnaire about their sex lives may be different than the average reader.

(continued)

(continued)

In 1987, Hite published a book entitled *Women in Love* that reported the findings of a nationwide study of women and their relationships with men. To ensure anonymity, questionnaires were sent to organizations rather than to individuals, with the idea that the organizations would distribute the questionnaires to their members. Thus, the sample included primarily women who belonged to some kind of organization. Furthermore, out of the 100,000 questionnaires that were sent out, only 4,500 completed surveys were returned—a return rate of only 4.5%. How respondents differed from nonrespondents is impossible to determine, but the nonresponsiveness of the sample should make us very hesitant to generalize the findings to the population at large.

The only national study of sexual behavior that used a probability sample was the National Health and Social Life Survey, which used cluster sampling to obtain a representative sample of Americans (Laumann, Gagnon, Michael, & Michaels, 1994). To begin, the entire United States was broken into geographical areas that consisted of all Standard Metropolitan Statistical Areas, counties, and independent cities. Eighty-four of these areas were then randomly selected, and a sample of districts (either city blocks or enumeration districts) were chosen from each of the selected areas. Then, for each of the 562 districts that were selected, a sample of households was selected. The final sample included 1,749 women and 1,410 men.

Among other things, the study revealed that sex is unevenly distributed in America. About 15% of adults have 50% of all sexual encounters. Interestingly, people with only a high school education are more sexually active than those with advanced degrees. (And it's not because well-educated people are too busy with demanding jobs to have sex. After work hours were taken into account, education was still negatively related to sexual activity.) Furthermore, income was largely unrelated to sex. One of the oddest findings was that people who prefer jazz over other kinds of music are, on average, 30% more sexually active than other people. Jazz was the only musical genre that was associated with sexual behavior.

The data replicated previous research showing that people who are Jewish and agnostic are more sexually active than members of other religions. Liberals were more sexually active than conservatives, but strangely, both liberals and conservatives beat out political moderates. Married couples have sex one time less per month on average than couples who are cohabiting, but a higher percentage of married men and women find their sex lives physically and emotionally satisfying. Importantly, the results of this study suggest that the nonrepresentive samples used in previous surveys may have included a disproportionate number of sexually open people. For example, data from the new survey obtained a lower incidence of marital infidelity than earlier research.

This was an exceptionally complex, time-consuming, and expensive sample to obtain, but it is about as representative of the United States as a whole as a sample can possibly be. Only by having a representative sample can we obtain accurate data regarding sexual behavior of the population at large.

HOW MANY PARTICIPANTS?

As researchers select their samples, they must decide how many participants they will ultimately need for their study. Several considerations come into play when selecting a sample size.

Error of Estimation

For studies that use probability samples, the key issue when determining sample size is the error of estimation (or margin of error). As we discussed earlier in this chapter, when researchers plan to use data from their sample to draw conclusions about the population (as in the case of opinion polling or studies of the prevalence of certain psychological problems, for example), they want the error of estimation to be reasonably small, usually a few percentage points. We also learned that the error of estimation decreases as sample size increases so that larger samples estimate the population's characteristics more accurately. When probability samples are used, researchers can calculate how many participants are needed to achieve the desired error of estimation.

Although you might expect that researchers always obtain as large a sample as possible, this is usually not the case. Rather, researchers opt for an **economic sample**—one that provides a reasonably accurate estimate of the population (within a few percentage points) at reasonable effort and cost. After a sample of a certain size is obtained, collecting additional data adds little to the accuracy of the results. For example, if we are trying to estimate the percentage of voters in a population of 10,000 who will vote for a particular candidate in a close election, interviewing a sample of 500 will allow us to estimate the percentage of voters in the population who will support each candidate within 9 percentage points (which is not sufficiently accurate). Increasing the sample size to 1,000 (an increase of 500 respondents) lowers the error of estimation from ±9% to only ±3%, a rather substantial improvement in accuracy. However, adding an additional 500 participants beyond that to the sample helps relatively little; with 1,500 respondents in the sample, the error of estimation drops only to 2.3%. In this instance, it may make little practical sense to increase the sample size beyond 1,000 respondents.

In deciding on a sample size, researchers must keep in mind that they may want to estimate the characteristics of certain groups within the population in addition to the population at large. If so, they need to be concerned about the error of estimation for those subgroups as well. For example, although 1,000 respondents might be enough to estimate the percentage of voters who will support each candidate, if we want to estimate the percentage of men and women who support the candidate separately, we might need a total sample size of 2,000 so that we have 1,000 of each gender. If not, the error estimation might be acceptable for making inferences about the population but too large for drawing conclusions about men and women separately.

Power

In statistical terminology, **power** refers to the ability of a research design to detect any effects of the variables being studied that exist in the data. A design with high power will detect whatever actual effects

are present, whereas a design with low power may fail to pick up effects that are actually there. As we will discuss later, many things can affect a study's power, but one of them is sample size. All other things being equal, the larger the sample size, the more likely a study will detect effects that are actually present.

For example, imagine that you want to know whether there is a correlation between the accuracy of people's self-concepts and their overall level of happiness. If these two variables are actually correlated, you will be much more likely to detect that correlation in a study with a sample size of 150 than a sample size of 20, for example. Or, imagine that you are conducting an experiment on the effects of people's moods on their judgments of others. So, you put some participants in a good mood and some participants in a bad mood, and then have them rate another person. If mood influences judgments of other people, your experiment will be more likely to detect the effect with a sample of 50 than a sample of 10.

A central consideration in the power of a design involves the size of the effects that researchers expect to find in their data. Strong effects are obviously easier to detect than weak ones, so a particular study might be powerful enough to detect strong effects but not powerful enough to detect weak effects. Because the power of a study increases with its sample size, larger samples are needed when the expected effects are weaker.

Researchers obviously want to detect any effects that actually exist, so they should make every effort to have a sample that is large enough to provide adequate power and, thus, have a reasonable chance of getting results. Although the details go beyond the scope of this book, statistical procedures exist that allow researchers to estimate the sample size needed to detect effects of the size they expect to find. In fact, agencies and foundations that fund behavioral research usually insist that researchers who are applying for research grants demonstrate that their sample sizes are sufficiently large to provide adequate power. There's no reason to support a study that is not likely to detect whatever effects are present!

In Depth

Most Behavioral Studies are Underpowered

Fifty years ago, Cohen (1962) warned that most studies in psychology are underpowered and thus unable to detect any but the strongest effects. His analyses showed that, although most studies were capable of detecting large effects, the probability of detecting medium-sized effects was only about 50:50 and the probability of detecting small effects was only about 1 out of 5 (.18 to be exact). Since then, many other researchers have conducted additional investigations of studies published in various journals with similar results. Yet there has been little or no change in the power of most psychological studies over the past 50 years (except perhaps in health psychology), which led Sedlmeier and Gigerenzer (1989) to wonder why all these studies about low power have not changed how researchers do their work.

Think for a moment about what these studies of power tell us: Most studies in the published literature are likely to detect only the strongest effects and miss many other effects that might, in fact, be present in the data. Most researchers shoot themselves in the foot by designing studies that may not find effects that are really there. Furthermore, the situation is even worse than that because these studies of power have not examined all of the studies that were conducted but not published, often because they failed to obtain predicted effects. How many of those failed, unpublished studies were victims of insufficient power?

In addition to the lost opportunities to uncover effects, underpowered studies may also contribute to inconsistencies in the research literature and to failures to replicate previous findings (Maxwell, 2004). If I obtain a particular finding in a study, you may not find the same effect (even though it's there) if you design a study that is underpowered.

As we will learn later, there are many ways to increase the power of a study—for example, by increasing the reliability of the measures we use and designing studies with tight experimental control. From the standpoint of this chapter, however, a key solution is to use a sufficiently large sample.

Summary

1. Sampling is the process by which a researcher selects a group of participants (the sample) from some larger population of individuals.

2. Very few studies use random samples. Fortunately, for most research questions, a random sample is not necessary. Rather, studies are conducted on samples of individuals who are readily available, and the generalizability of research findings is tested by replicating them on other nonrandom samples.

3. When a probability sample is used, researchers can specify the probability that any individual in the population will be included in the sample. With a probability sample, researchers can calculate the error of estimation, allowing them to know how accurately the data they collect from the sample describe the population.

4. The error of estimation—the degree to which data obtained from the sample are expected to differ from the population as a whole—is a function of the size of the sample, the size of the population, and the variance of the data.

Researchers usually opt for an economical sample that provides an acceptably low error of estimation at reasonable cost and effort.

5. Simple random samples, which are one type of probability sample, are selected in such a way that every possible sample of the desired size has an equal probability of being chosen. To select a simple random sample, researchers must have a sampling frame—a list of everyone in the population from which the sample will be drawn.

6. When using a systematic sample, researchers select every kth individual on a list, who arrives at a location, or that they encounter.

7. A stratified random sample is chosen by first dividing the population into subsets or strata that share a particular characteristic (such as sex, age, or race). Then participants are sampled randomly from each stratum.

8. In cluster sampling, the researcher first samples groupings or clusters of participants and then samples participants from the selected clusters. In multistage sampling, the

researcher sequentially samples clusters from within clusters before choosing the final sample of participants.

9. When the response rate for a probability sample is less than 100%, the findings of the study may be biased in unknown ways because the people who responded may differ from those who did not respond. Because of this, researchers using probability samples put a great deal of effort into ensuring that the people who are selected for the sample agree to participate.

10. Misgeneralization occurs when a researcher generalizes the results obtained on a sample to a population that differs from the actual population from which the sample was selected.

11. When nonprobability samples—such as convenience, quota, and purposive samples—are used, researchers have no way of determining the degree to which they are representative of any particular population. Even so, nonprobability samples are used far more often in behavioral research than probability samples are.

12. The most common type of sample in psychological research is the convenience sample, which consists of people who are easy to contact and recruit. The college students who participate in many psychological studies are convenience samples. Quota and purposive samples are used less frequently.

13. In deciding how large the sample for a particular study should be, researchers using a probability sample are primarily concerned with having enough participants to make the error of estimation acceptably low (usually less than ±3 percent).

14. In addition, researchers want to have a large-enough sample so that the study has sufficient power—the ability to detect relationships among variables. Most behavioral studies do not have adequate power to detect small effects, often because their samples are too small.

Key Terms

cluster sampling (*p. 105*)	nonresponse problem (*p. 106*)	sample (*p. 99*)
convenience sample (*p. 109*)	power (*p. 113*)	sampling (*p. 99*)
economic sample (*p. 113*)	probability sample (*p. 100*)	sampling error (*p. 101*)
error of estimation (*p. 101*)	proportionate sampling method	sampling frame (*p. 102*)
margin of error (*p. 101*)	(*p. 104*)	simple random sample (*p. 102*)
misgeneralization (*p. 108*)	purposive sample (*p. 111*)	stratified random sample (*p. 104*)
multistage cluster	quota sample (*p. 111*)	stratum (*p. 104*)
sampling (*p. 105*)	random digit dialing (*p. 102*)	systematic sampling (*p. 103*)
nonprobability sample (*p. 109*)	representative sample (*p. 106*)	table of random numbers (*p. 102*)

Questions For Review

1. Why do so few studies in the behavioral sciences use random samples?

2. What is a probability sample, and for what kinds of research questions are probability samples absolutely essential?

3. What is sampling error? What statistic indicates the degree to which findings obtained from a sample are influenced by sampling error?

4. What does the error of estimation tell us about the results of a study conducted using probability sampling? Would we prefer our error of estimation to be small or large? Why?

5. What happens to the error of estimation as one's sample size increases? Why does this happen?

6. What is a simple random sample? What is the central difficulty involved in obtaining simple random samples from large populations?

7. Is a systematic sample also a simple random sample? Why or why not?

8. What is the drawback of obtaining random samples by telephone?

9. How does cluster sampling solve the practical problems involved in simple random sampling?

10. What is the difference between a stratum and a cluster?

11. In what way would the use of sampling improve the accuracy of the United States Census?
12. What is the nonresponse problem, and what difficulties does it create for interpreting findings obtained on probability samples? What steps do researchers take to minimize nonresponse?
13. What type of sample is used most frequently in behavioral research? Why?
14. What problems are associated with the widespread use of convenience samples of college students?
15. Is it true that valid conclusions cannot be drawn from studies that are conducted on convenience samples? Explain your answer.
16. Distinguish between a quota sample and a purposive sample.
17. What are two primary considerations when determining how large one's sample should be?
18. What does it mean to say that a study is "underpowered"? Discuss the problem of low power in behavioral science and how the problem can be solved.

Questions for Discussion

1. Suppose that you wanted to obtain a simple random sample of kindergarten children in your state. How might you do it?
2. Suppose that you wanted to study children who have Down syndrome. How might you use cluster sampling to obtain a probability sample of children under the age of 18 with Down syndrome in your state?
3. In defending the sampling methods used for *Women in Love* (described on p. 111), Hite (1987) wrote: "Does research that is not based on a probability or random sample give one the right to generalize from the results of the study to the population at large? If a study is large enough and the sample is broad enough, and if one generalizes carefully, yes" (p. 778). Do you agree with Hite? Why or why not?
4. Imagine that you were appointed to prepare a presentation to Congress to convince them that sampling should be used to conduct the United States Census (see p. 106). How would you explain to them why sampling would produce a more accurate enumeration of the characteristics of the population of the United States? What arguments would you present to make your case? In developing your case, assume that your audience knows nothing whatsoever about sampling.
5. How do you feel about the use of college students as research participants? To examine both sides of the issue fully, first argue for the position that *college students should not be used as research participants*. Then, argue just as strongly for the position that *using college students as research participants is essential to behavioral science*.

6 | DESCRIPTIVE RESEARCH

Each year, the Federal Interagency Forum on Child and Family Statistics releases a report that describes the results of studies dealing with crime, smoking, illicit drug use, nutrition, and other topics relevant to the well-being of children and adolescents in the United States. The most recent report painted a mixed picture of how American youth are faring. On one hand, studies showed that many American high school students engage in behaviors that may have serious consequences for their health. For example, 11.4% of high school seniors in a nationwide survey reported that they smoked daily, 24.6% indicated that they had drunk heavily in the past 2 weeks, and 22.3% said that they had used illicit drugs in the previous 30 days. The percentages for younger adolescents, although lower, also showed a high rate of risky behavior: The data for eighth grade students showed that 3.1% smoked regularly, 8.1% drank heavily, and 7.6% had used illicit drugs in the previous month. On the other hand, the studies also showed improvements in the well-being of young people. In particular, the number of youth between the ages of 12 and 17 who were victims of violent crime (such as robbery, rape, aggravated assault, and homicide) had declined markedly in the last decade.

The studies that provided these results involved descriptive research. The purpose of **descriptive research** is to describe the characteristics or behaviors of a given population in a systematic and accurate fashion. Typically, descriptive research is not designed to test hypotheses but rather is conducted to provide information about the physical, social, behavioral, economic, or psychological characteristics of some group of people. The group of interest may be as large as the population of the world or as small as the students in a particular class. Descriptive research may be conducted to obtain basic information about the group of interest or to provide to government agencies and other policy-making groups specific data concerning social problems.

TYPES OF DESCRIPTIVE RESEARCH

Although several kinds of descriptive research may be distinguished, we will examine three that psychologists and other behavioral researchers often use—survey, demographic, and epidemiological research.

Survey Research

Surveys are, by far, the most common type of descriptive research. They are used in virtually every area of social and behavioral science. For example, psychologists use surveys to inquire about people's attitudes, lifestyles, behaviors, and problems; sociologists use surveys to study political preferences and family systems; political scientists use surveys to study political attitudes and predict the outcomes of elections; government researchers use surveys to understand social problems; and advertisers conduct survey research to understand consumers' attitudes and buying patterns. In each case, the goal is to provide a description of people's behaviors, thoughts, or feelings.

Some people loosely use the term *survey* as a synonym for *questionnaire,* as in the sentence "Fifty-five of the respondents completed the survey that they received in the mail." Technically speaking, however, surveys and questionnaires are different things. Surveys are a type of descriptive research that may utilize questionnaires, interviews, or observational techniques to collect data. Be careful not to confuse the use of *survey* as a type of a research design that tries to describe people's thoughts, feelings, or behavior with the use of *survey* to mean questionnaire.

In most survey research, respondents provide information about themselves by completing a questionnaire or answering an interviewer's questions. (We discussed questionnaires versus interviews in Chapter 4.) Many surveys are conducted face-to-face, as when people are recruited to report to a survey research center or pedestrians are stopped on the street to answer questions, but some are conducted by phone, through the mail, or on Web sites.

Most surveys involve a **cross-sectional survey design** in which a single group of respondents—a "cross-section" of the population—is surveyed. These one-shot studies can provide important information about the characteristics of the group and, if more than one group is surveyed, about how various groups differ in their characteristics, attitudes, or behaviors.

Behavioral Research Case Study
Cross-sectional Survey Design: Adolescents' Reactions to Divorce

A good deal of research has examined the effects of divorce on children, but little attention has been paid to how adolescents deal with the aftermath of divorce. To correct this deficiency, Buchanan, Maccoby, and Dornbusch (1996) conducted an extensive survey of 10- to 18-year-old adolescents whose parents were divorced. Approximately $4\frac{1}{2}$ years later after their parents filed for divorce, 522 adolescents from 365 different families were interviewed.

Among the many questions that participants were asked during the interview was how they felt about their parents' new partners, if any. To address this question, the researchers asked the adolescents whether their parents' new partner was mostly like a parent, a friend, just another person, or someone the adolescents wished weren't part of their lives. The respondents were also asked whether they thought that the parent's new partner had the right to set up rules for the respondents or tell them what they could and couldn't do. The results for these two questions are shown in Figure 6.1.

As can be seen in the left-hand graph, the respondents generally felt positively about their parents' new partners; approximately 50% characterized the partner as being like a friend. However, only about a quarter of the adolescents viewed the new partner as a parent. Thus, most adolescents seemed to accept the new partner yet not accord him or her full parental status. The right-hand graph shows that respondents were split on the question of whether the parent's new partner had the right to set rules for them. Contrary to the stereotype that children have greater difficulty getting along with stepmothers than stepfathers (a stereotype fueled perhaps by the wicked stepmothers that appear in many children's stories), respondents tended to regard mothers' and fathers' new partners quite similarly. The only hint of a difference in reactions to stepmothers and stepfathers is reflected in the repeated response that fathers' new partners (i.e., stepmothers) did not have the right to tell respondents what to do.

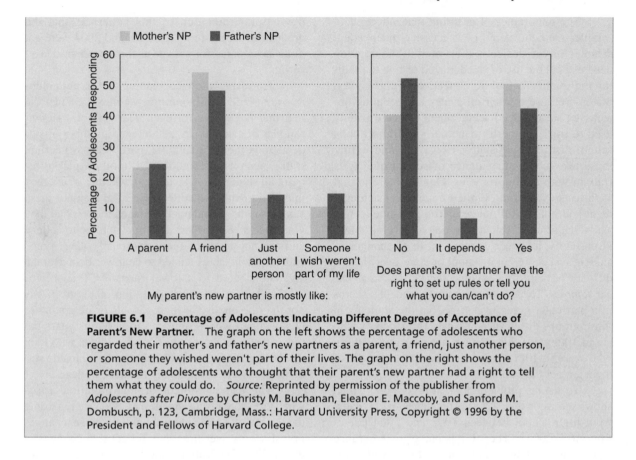

FIGURE 6.1   Percentage of Adolescents Indicating Different Degrees of Acceptance of Parent's New Partner.   The graph on the left shows the percentage of adolescents who regarded their mother's and father's new partners as a parent, a friend, just another person, or someone they wished weren't part of their lives. The graph on the right shows the percentage of adolescents who thought that their parent's new partner had a right to tell them what they could do.   *Source:* Reprinted by permission of the publisher from *Adolescents after Divorce* by Christy M. Buchanan, Eleanor E. Maccoby, and Sanford M. Dombusch, p. 123, Cambridge, Mass.: Harvard University Press, Copyright © 1996 by the President and Fellows of Harvard College.

Changes in attitudes or behavior can be examined if a cross-section of the population is studied more than once. In a **successive independent samples survey design**, two or more samples of respondents answer the same questions at different points in time. Even though the samples are composed of different individuals, conclusions can be drawn about how people have changed if the respondents are selected in the same manner each time. For example, since 1939, the Gallup organization has asked successive independent random samples of Americans, "Did you happen to attend a church or synagogue service in the last seven days?" As the data in Table 6.1 show, the percentage of Americans who attend religious services weekly has remained remarkably constant over a 70-year span. The validity of a successive independent samples design depends on the samples being comparable, so researchers must be sure that each sample is selected in precisely the same way.

TABLE 6.1	Percentage of Americans Who Say They Attended Religious Services in the Past Week
Year	**Percent**
1939	41
1950	39
1962	46
1972	40
1981	41
1990	40
1999	40
2008	42

Source: Gallup Organization Web site.

The importance of ensuring that independent samples are equivalent in a successive independent samples survey design is illustrated in the ongoing debate about the use of standardized testing to monitor the quality of public education in the United States. Because of their efficiency and seeming objectivity, standardized achievement tests are widely used to track the performance of specific schools, school districts, and states. However, interpreting these test scores as evidence of school quality is fraught with many problems. One problem is that such tests assess only limited domains of achievement and not the full range of complex intellectual skills that schools should be trying to develop. More importantly, however, making sense of changes in student test scores in a school or state over time is difficult because they involve *successive independent samples.* These studies compare student's scores in a particular grade over time, but the students in those groups differ year-by-year. The students who are in 10th grade this year are not the same as those who were in 10th grade last year (at least most of them are not the same.)

To see the problem, look at Figure 6.2, which shows scores on the ACT for students who graduated from high school between 1998 and 2004 (*News from ACT,* 2004). (The ACT is one of two entrance exams that colleges and universities require for admission, the other being the SAT.) As you can see, ACT scores stayed constant for students who graduated in 1998 through 2001, then dropped in 2002 and stayed lower than they were previously. The most obvious interpretation of this pattern is that the graduating classes of 2002, 2003, and 2004 were not quite as prepared for college as those who graduated earlier.

However, before concluding that recent graduates are academically inferior, we must consider the fact that the scores for each year reflect different samples of students. In fact, a record number of students took the ACT in 2002, partly because certain states, such as Colorado and Illinois, began to require all students to take the test, whether or not they intended to apply to college. Because many of these students (who would not have taken the test had they graduated a year earlier) did not plan to go to college and had not taken the more rigorous "college-prep" courses, their scores tended to be lower than average and contributed to a lower mean ACT score for 2002. Thus, a better interpretation of Figure 6.2 is not that the quality of high schools or of graduates has declined when compared to previous years but rather that a higher proportion of students who took the ACT in 2002 through 2005 were less capable students who were not planning to attend college.

The same problem of interpretation arises when test score results are used as evidence regarding the quality of a particular school. Of course, changes in test scores over time may reflect real changes in the quality of education. However, they may also reflect changes in the nature of the students in a particular sample. If a school's population changes over time, rising or declining test scores may reflect nothing more than a change in the kinds of students who

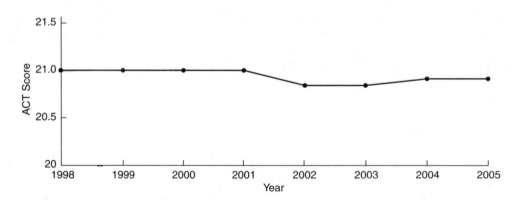

FIGURE 6.2 Average ACT Scores, 1998–2004.

live in the community. It is important to remember that a successive independent samples design can be used to infer changes over time only if we know that the samples are comparable.

In a **longitudinal** or **panel survey design**, a single group of respondents is questioned more than once. If the same sample is surveyed on more than one occasion, changes in their behavior can be studied. However, problems arise with a panel survey design when, as usually happens, not all respondents who were surveyed initially can be reached for later follow-up sessions. When some respondents drop out of the study—for example, because they have moved, died, or simply refuse to participate further—the sample is no longer the same as before. As a result, we do not know for certain whether changes we observe in the data over time reflect real changes in people's behavior or simply changes in the kinds of people who comprise our sample.

In Depth
Conducting Surveys on the Internet

As the number of people who have access to the Internet has increased, many researchers have turned to the Internet to collect data. Sometimes the online questionnaire is available to anyone who wishes to answer it; in other cases, researchers e-mail potential respondents a password to access the site that contains the questionnaire.

Internet surveys (or *e-surveys*) have many advantages, as well as some distinct disadvantages, when compared to other ways of conducting surveys (Anderson & Kanuka, 2003). On the positive side, Internet surveys are relatively inexpensive because, unlike mail surveys, they do not have to be printed and mailed, and unlike interview surveys, they do not require a team of interviewers to telephone or meet with the respondents. Internet surveys also bypass the step of entering respondents' data into the computer because the survey software automatically records respondents' answers. This lowers the cost and time of data entry, as well as the possibility that researchers will make mistakes when entering the data (because respondents enter their data directly). Internet surveys may also allow researchers to contact respondents who would be difficult to reach in person and allow respondents to reply at their convenience, often at times when the researcher would not normally be available (such as late at night or on weekends).

On the negative side, a researcher who uses Internet surveys often has little control over the selection of his or her sample. Not only are people without Internet access unable to participate, but also certain kinds of people are more likely to respond to Internet surveys. Thus, the researcher often cannot be certain of the nature of the sample. It is also very difficult to verify who actually completed the survey, as well as whether a particular person responded more than once. E-research is in its infancy and, with time, researchers may find ways to deal with many of these problems.

Demographic Research

Demographic research is concerned with describing and understanding patterns of basic life events and experiences such as birth, marriage, divorce, employment, migration (movement from one place to another), and death. For example, demographic researchers study questions such as why people have the number of children they do, socioeconomic factors that predict death rates, the reasons that people move from one location to another, and social predictors of divorce.

Although most demographic research is conducted by demographers and sociologists, psychologists and other behavioral scientists sometimes become involved in demography because they are interested in the psychological processes that underlie major life events. For example, a psychologist may be interested in understanding demographic variables that predict differences in family size, marriage patterns, or divorce rates among various groups. Furthermore, demographic research is sometimes used to forecast changes in society that will require governmental attention or new programs, as described in the following case study.

Behavioral Research Case Study

Demographic Research: Predicting Population Growth

Over the past 100 years, life expectancy in the United States has increased markedly. Scientists, policy-makers, and government officials are interested in forecasting future trends in longevity because changes in life expectancy have consequences for government programs (such as social security and Medicare), tax revenue (retired people don't pay many taxes), the kinds of problems for which people will need help (more gerontologists and geriatric psychologists will be needed, for example), business (the demand for products for older people will increase), and changes in the structure of society (more residential options for the elderly are needed).

Using demographic data from a number of sources, Olshansky, Goldman, Zheng, and Rowe (2009) estimated patterns of birth, migration, and death to make new forecasts about the growth of the population of the United States, particularly with respect to older people.

Their results predicted that the size of the U. S. population will increase from its current level (just over 310 million) to between 411 and 418 million by the year 2050. More importantly from the standpoint of understanding aging, the size of the population aged 65 and older will increase from about 40 million to over 100 million by 2050, and the population over age 85 will increase from under 6 million people today to approximately 30 million people. Olshansky et al.'s statistical models suggest that previous government projections may have underestimated the growth of the population, particularly the increase in the number of older people.

Epidemiological Research

Epidemiological research is used to study the occurrence of disease and death in different groups of people. Most epidemiological research is conducted by medical and public health researchers who study patterns of health and illness, but psychologists are often interested in epidemiology for two reasons. First, many illnesses and injuries are affected by people's behavior and lifestyles. For example, skin cancer is directly related to how much people expose themselves to the sun, and one's chances of contracting a sexually transmitted disease is related to practicing safe sex. Thus, epidemiological data can provide information regarding groups that are at risk of illness or injury, thereby helping health psychologists target certain groups for interventions to reduce their risk.

Second, some epidemiological research deals with describing the prevalence and incidence of psychological disorders. (Prevalence refers to the proportion of a population that has a particular disease or disorder at a particular point in time; incidence refers to the rate at which new cases of the disease or disorder occur over a specified period.)

Behavioral researchers are interested in documenting the occurrence of psychological problems—such as depression, alcoholism, child abuse, schizophrenia, and personality disorders—and they conduct epidemiological studies to do so.

For example, data released by the National Institute of Mental Health (2006) showed that 32,439 people died from suicide in the United States in 2004. Of those, the vast majority had a diagnosable psychological disorder, most commonly depression or substance abuse. Men were four times more likely to commit suicide than were women, and the highest suicide rate in the United States was among white men over the age of 65. Of course, many young people also commit suicide; in the most recent year for which statistics are available, suicide was the third leading cause of death among 15- to 24-year-olds. Descriptive, epidemiological data such as these provide important information about the prevalence of psychological problems in particular groups, thereby raising questions for future research and suggesting groups to which mental health programs should be targeted.

Behavioral Research Case Study
Epidemiological Research: Why Do More Men than Women Die Prematurely?

At nearly every age, men are more likely to die than women. Kruger and Neese (2004) conducted a multi-country epidemiological study in an effort to explore possible reasons why. They examined the male–to–female mortality ratio, the ratio of the number of men to the number of women who die at each age, for 11 leading causes of death. Their results confirmed that men had higher mortality rates than women, especially in early adulthood, when three men die for every woman who dies. This discrepancy in male and female mortality rates was observed across 20 countries, although the size of the male–to–female mortality ratio varied across countries, raising questions about the social and cultural causes of those differences.

When the data were examined to identify the causes of this discrepancy, the leading causes of death that contributed to a higher mortality rate for men were cardiovascular diseases, non automobile accidents, suicide, auto-accidents, and malignant neoplasms (cancer). Kruger and Neese concluded that "being male is now the single largest demographic risk factor for early mortality in developed countries" (p. 66).

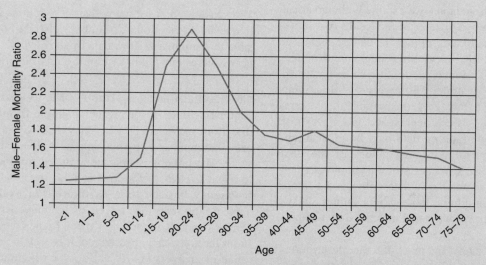

FIGURE 6.3   Differences in the Male–to–Female Mortality Ratio Across Age.   A ratio of 1 (at the bottom of the graph) would indicate that men and women were dying at the same rate—that is, 1 man for every woman. The fact that the plotted values are all above 1 shows that more men die than women at every age. The peak in the 20–24 year range shows that, between the ages of 20 and 24, 2.9 men die for every woman who dies.

Although psychologists are less likely to conduct descriptive research than other kinds we will discuss in this book (correlational, experimental, and quasi-experimental research), descriptive research plays an important role in behavioral science. Survey, demographic, and epidemiological research provide a picture of how large groups of people tend to think, feel, and behave. Thus, descriptive data can help point researchers to topics and problems that need attention and suggest hypotheses that can be examined in future research. If descriptive research shows that the attitudes, behaviors, or experiences of people in different groups differ in important ways, researchers can begin to explore the psychological processes that are responsible for those differences. For example, knowing that the male–female mortality ratio is highest in young adulthood (Figure 6.3), researchers can design studies that try to understand why.

AND PRESENTING DATA

...icular study was not designed ...tive research, researchers usually ...scribe their participants' characteristics, thoughts, emotions, behaviors, or physiological responses. Thus, in virtually all studies, researchers must find ways to describe and present their data in the most accurate, clear, useful, and convincing manner. An important part of all research involves describing and presenting the results to other people, so researchers must always decide how to summarize and describe their data in the most meaningful and useful fashion possible. In the remainder of this chapter, we explore both numerical and graphical ways to describe the results of a study.

To be useful, descriptions of data should meet three criteria: accuracy, conciseness, and understandability. Obviously, data must be summarized and described accurately. Some ways of describing the findings of a study are more accurate than others. For example, as we'll see later, certain ways of describing and graphing data may be misleading. Similarly, depending on the nature of the data (whether extreme scores exist, for example), certain statistics may summarize and describe the data more accurately than others. Researchers should always present their data in ways that most accurately represent the data.

Unfortunately, the most accurate descriptions of data are often the least useful because they overwhelm the reader with information. Strictly speaking, the most accurate description of a set of data would involve a table of the **raw data**—all participants' scores on all measures. A table of the raw data is accurate because there is virtually no possibility that data in this raw form will be distorted. However, to be interpretable, data must be summarized in a concise and meaningful form. It is during this process that distortions can occur. Researchers must be selective in the data they choose to present, presenting only the data that most clearly describe the results.

Third, the description of one's data must be easily understood. Overly complicated tables, graphs, or statistics can obscure the findings and lead to confusion. Having decided which aspects of the data best portray the findings of a study, researchers must then choose the clearest, most straightforward manner of describing the data.

Methods of summarizing and describing sets of numerical data can be classified as either **numerical methods** or **graphical methods**. Numerical methods summarize data in the form of numbers such as percentages or means. Graphical methods involve the presentation of data in graphical or pictorial form, such as graphs.

FREQUENCY DISTRIBUTIONS

The starting point for many data descriptions is the frequency distribution. A **frequency distribution** is a table that summarizes raw data by showing the number of scores that fall in each of several categories.

SIMPLE FREQUENCY DISTRIBUTIONS. One way to summarize data is to construct a **simple frequency distribution**. A simple frequency distribution indicates the number of participants who obtained each score. The possible scores are arranged from lowest to highest. Then, in a second column, the number or **frequency** of each score is shown. For example, Table 6.2 presents the answers of 168 university students when asked to tell how many friends they had. From the frequency distribution, it is easy to see the range of answers (1–40) and to see which answer occurred most frequently (7).

GROUPED FREQUENCY DISTRIBUTIONS. In many instances, simple frequency distributions provide a meaningful, easily comprehended summary of the data. However, when there are many possible scores, it is difficult to make much sense out of a simple frequency distribution. In these cases, researchers use a **grouped frequency distribution** that shows the frequency of *subsets of scores*. To make a grouped frequency distribution, you first break the range of scores into several subsets, or **class intervals**, of equal size. For example, to create a grouped frequency distribution of the data in Table 6.2, we could create eight class intervals: 1–5, 6–10, 11–15, 16–20, 21–25, 26–30, 31–35, and 36–40. We could

TABLE 6.2	A Simple Frequency Distribution: Number of Reported Friends				
Friends	**Frequency**	**Friends**	**Frequency**	**Friends**	**Frequency**
1	2	16	2	31	0
2	0	17	4	32	1
3	9	18	4	33	1
4	7	19	3	34	0
5	13	20	3	35	4
6	12	21	2	36	0
7	19	22	2	37	0
8	10	23	2	38	0
9	7	24	0	39	1
10	13	25	3	40	2
11	9	26	1		
12	6	27	0		
13	6	28	0		
14	7	29	0		
15	9	30	4		

then indicate the frequency of scores in each of the class intervals, as shown in Table 6.3.

Often researchers also include relative frequencies in a table such as this. The **relative frequency** of each class is the proportion or percentage of the total number of scores that falls in each class interval. It is calculated by dividing the frequency for a class interval by the total number of scores. For example, the relative frequency for the class interval 1–5 in Table 6.3 is 31/168 or 18.5%. If you'll compare the grouped frequency distribution (Table 6.3) to the simple frequency distribution (Table 6.2), you will see that the

grouped frequency distribution more clearly shows the number of friends that respondents reported having.

You should notice three features of the grouped frequency distribution. First, the class intervals are mutually exclusive. A person could not fall into more than one class interval. Second, the class intervals capture all possible responses; every score can be included in one of the class intervals. Third, all of the class intervals are the same size. In this example, each class interval spans five scores. All grouped frequency distributions must have these three characteristics.

FREQUENCY HISTOGRAMS AND POLYGONS. In many cases, the information given in a frequency distribution is more easily and quickly grasped when presented graphically rather than in a table. Frequency distributions are often portrayed graphically in the form of **histograms** and **bar graphs**. The horizontal x-axis of histograms and bar graphs presents the class intervals, and the vertical y-axis shows the number of scores in each class interval (the frequency). Bars are drawn to a height that indicates the frequency of cases in each response category. For example, if we graphed the data in Table 6.2, the histogram would look like the graph in Figure 6.4.

TABLE 6.3	A Grouped Frequency Distribution: Number of Reported Friends	
Class Interval	**Frequency**	**Relative Frequency**
1–5	31	18.5
6–10	61	36.3
11–15	37	22.0
16–20	16	9.5
21–25	9	5.4
26–30	5	2.9
31–35	6	3.6
36–40	3	1.8

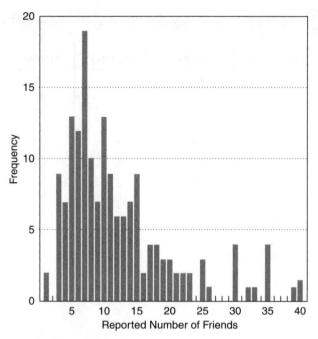

FIGURE 6.4   Histogram of Number of Friends Reported by College Students

Although histograms and bar graphs look similar, they differ in an important way. A histogram is used when the variable on the *x*-axis is on an interval or ratio scale of measurement. Because the variable is continuous and equal differences in the scale values represent equal differences in the attribute being measured, the bars on the graph touch one another (as in Figure 6.4). However, when the variable on the *x*-axis is on a nominal or ordinal scale (and, thus, equal differences in scale values do not reflect equal differences in the characteristic being measured), a *bar graph* is used in which the bars are separated to avoid implying that the variable is continuous.

Researchers also present frequency data as a **frequency polygon**. The axes on the frequency polygon are labeled just as they are for the histogram, but rather than using bars (as in the histogram), lines are drawn to connect the frequencies of the class intervals. Typically, this type of graph is used only for data that are on an interval or ratio scale. The data from Table 6.2, which were shown in Figure 6.4 as a histogram, look like Figure 6.5 when illustrated as a frequency polygon.

MEASURES OF CENTRAL TENDENCY

Frequency distributions, however they are portrayed, convey important information about participants' responses. However, researchers typically present descriptive statistics as well—numbers that summarize the data for an entire group of participants.

Much information can be obtained about a distribution of scores by knowing only the average or typical score in the distribution. For example, rather than presenting you with a table showing the number of hospitalized mental patients per state last year, I might simply tell you that there were an average of 4,282 patients per state. Or, rather than drawing a frequency polygon of the distribution of students' IQ scores in my city's school system, I might simply tell you that the average IQ is 104.6. **Measures of central tendency** convey information about a distribution by providing information about the average or most typical score. Three measures of central tendency are used most often, each of which tells us something different about the data.

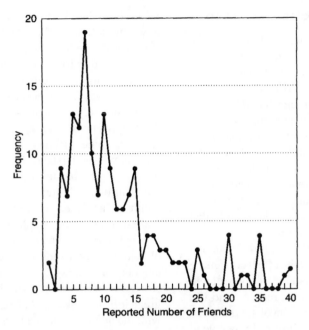

FIGURE 6.5 **Frequency Polygon of Number of Friends Reported by College Students**

THE MEAN.   The most commonly used measure of central tendency is the **mean**, or average. As we saw in Chapter 2, the mean is calculated by summing the scores for all cases, then dividing by the number of cases, as expressed by the formula, $\bar{x} = \sum x_i/n$. In general, the mean is the most common and useful measure of central tendency, but it can sometimes be misleading. Consider, for example, that the mean of the data in Table 6.2 is 12.2. Yet, as you can see from the data in the table, this value does not well reflect how many friends most of the respondents said they had (most of them fell in the 5–10 range). In cases when the mean does not accurately represent the average or typical case, researchers also report the median and the mode of the distribution.

THE MEDIAN.   The **median** is the middle score of a distribution. If we rank-order the scores, the median is the score that falls in the middle. Put another way, it is the score below which 50% of the measurements fall. For example, if we rank-order

the data in Table 6.2, we find that the median is 10, which more closely represents the typical score than the mean of 12.2. The advantage of the median over the mean is that it is less affected by extreme scores, or **outliers**. In the data shown in Table 6.2, the respondents who said that they had 39 or 40 friends are outliers.

The median is easy to identify when there is an odd number of scores because it is the middle score. When there is an even number of scores, however, there is no middle score. In this case, the median falls halfway between the two middle scores. For example, if the two middle scores in a distribution were 48 and 50, the median would be 49 even though no participant actually obtained that score.

THE MODE.   The **mode** is the most frequent score. The mode of the distribution in Table 6.2 is 7. That is, more students indicated that they had 7 friends than any other number. If all of the scores in the distribution are different, there is no mode. Occasionally, a distribution may have more than one mode.

Presenting Means in Tables and Graphs

When researchers wish to present only one or two means, they usually do so in sentence form. For example, a researcher might write that "The average score for male participants ($M = 56.7$) was lower than the average score for female participants ($M = 64.9$)," using an italicized *M* as the symbol for *mean*. However, often researchers want to present many means—for different samples, different experimental groups, or different variables—and doing so in sentence form would be confusing to read. When researchers wish to present many means, they often do so either in a table of numbers or in a figure that displays the results in graphical form.

For example, Löckenhoff et al. (2009) studied how people in 26 countries view the effects of getting older on nine dimensions (such as age-related changes in attractiveness, wisdom, respect, and life satisfaction). Their major findings involved the mean ratings on each of these nine dimensions for people in each of the 26 countries. Think for a moment about how you would present these findings. You can probably see that it would not be feasible to describe the results in sentence form because they involve 234 means (9 dimensions × 26 countries)! Löckenhoff and her colleagues wisely decided to present the means in a table. To do so, they listed the 26 countries down the left side of the table and the nine dimensions across the top of the table. Then, they reported the mean rating for each country for each dimension in each of the 234 cells of the table. Even when a study involves far fewer means, presenting them in a table is not only efficient but can also help readers see the patterns more clearly.

In some instances, researchers decide that readers will understand their results most clearly if they are presented in graphical form. For example, the National Center for Educational Statistics conducts analyses of student achievement in the United States. The graph in Figure 6.6 shows the average scores on a national reading test for 13-year-olds and 17-year-olds who reported doing varying amounts of homework, from none at all to more than two hours of homework per night. This graph does a great job of showing that reading scores increase with the amount of homework that students reported doing for both 13-year-olds and 17-year-olds.

ERROR BARS.   Sometimes you will see graphs of means that include I-shaped vertical lines extending through the tops of the bars as in Figure 6.7. These **error bars** provide information about the researcher's

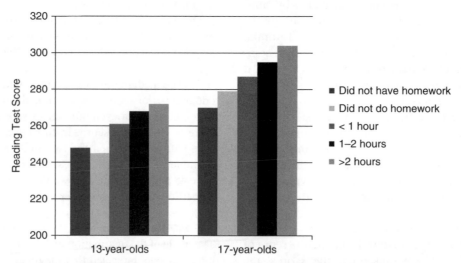

FIGURE 6.6   Mean Reading Test Scores for Students Who Do Varying Amounts of Homework.   This graph presents 10 means in a concise and easy-to-grasp fashion. Clearly, students who do more homework score higher on a standardized reading test than students who do less homework.

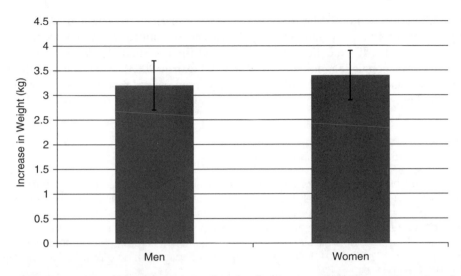

FIGURE 6.7 Average Weight Gain During the First Semester of College. These data show that male students gained an average of 3.2 kg (7 pounds) and female students gained an average of 3.4 kg (7.5 pounds) between September and December of their first year of college. The error bars on the graph show the 95% confidence interval for each mean. If mean weight gain was calculated for 100 samples drawn from this population, the true population mean would fall in 95% of the confidence intervals for the 100 samples. (Data are from Lloyd-Richardson, Bailey, Fava, & Wing, 2009).

confidence in the value of each mean. We learned in Chapter 5 that the mean of a sample only *estimates* the true value of the mean of the population from which the sample was drawn. Because no sample perfectly reflects its parent population, the sample mean is not likely to hit the population mean perfectly, and the means of different samples drawn from the same population will usually differ from one another because of sampling error (see p. 101). As a result, simply presenting a mean, either as a number or as a bar on a graph, is potentially misleading because the value of the mean is not likely to be the true population average.

Because we know that the mean calculated on a sample will probably differ from the population mean, we want to have a sense of how accurately the mean we calculate in our study estimates the population mean. To do this, researchers use a statistic called the **confidence interval** or **CI**, and most use what's called a 95% confidence interval. To understand what the 95% confidence interval tells us, imagine that we conduct a study and calculate both the mean, M, and the 95% confidence interval, CI. (Don't concern yourself with how the CI is calculated.) If we subtract the CI from the mean ($M - CI$) and add the CI to the mean ($M + CI$), we get the

lower and upper values for a range or span of scores with the mean at the center of that range.

And here's the important thing: If we conducted the same study 100 times and calculated the CIs for each of those 100 means, the true population mean would fall in 95% of the CIs that we calculated. Thus, the confidence interval gives us a good idea of the range in which the population mean is likely to fall. If the CI is relatively small, then the sample mean is more likely to be a better estimate of the population mean than if the CI is larger.

To see confidence intervals in action, let's examine the results of a study that examined the average weight gain for male and female students during their first semester of college. In Figure 6.7, you can see that the men gained an average of 3.2 kg (7 pounds) between September and December of their first year of college, whereas women gained an average of 3.4 kg (7.5 pounds) during the same time period. (Clearly, the "Freshman-15" is a real phenomenon.)

You can also see the 95% confidence interval for each mean indicated by the I-shaped vertical lines slicing through the top of each bar. We know that the average weight gain in the population is probably not precisely 3.2 kg for men or 3.4 kg for women. But the CI provides information regarding what the true value is likely to be. If we collected data on many samples from this population, the true population means for men and women will fall within the CIs for 95% of those samples.

The American Psychological Association publishes an exceptionally useful guide to preparing tables and figures titled *Displaying Your Findings* (Nicol & Pexman, 2003). When you have the need to present data in papers, reports, posters, or presentations, I highly recommend this book.

Developing Your Research Skills
How to Lie with Statistics: Bar Charts and Line Graphs

Many years ago, Darrell Huff published a humorous look at the misuse of statistics entitled *How to Lie with Statistics*. Among the topics Huff discussed was what he called the "gee-whiz graph." A gee-whiz graph, although technically accurate, is constructed in such a way as to give a misleading impression of the data—usually to catch the reader's attention or to make the data appear more striking than they really are.

Consider the graph in Figure 6.8(a), which shows the number of violent crimes (murder, rape, robbery, and assault) in the United States from 1994 to 2001. From just glancing at the graph, it is obvious that violent crime has dropped sharply from 1994 to 2001. Or has it?

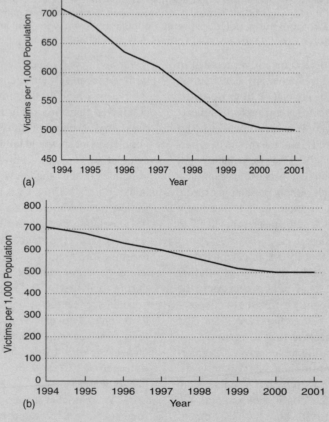

FIGURE 6.8   Did the Crime Rate Plummet or Decline Slightly?
Source: Federal Bureau of Investigation Web site.

Let's look at another graph of the same data. In the graph in Figure 6.8(b), we can see that the crime rate has indeed declined between 1994 and 2001. However, its rate of decrease is nowhere near as extreme as implied by the first graph.

If you'll look closely, you'll see that the two graphs present *exactly the same data;* technically speaking, they both portray the data accurately. The only difference between these graphs involves the units along the *y*-axis. The first graph used very small units and no zero point to give the impression of a large change in the murder rate. The second graph provided a more accurate perspective by using a zero point.

A similar tactic for misleading readers employs bar graphs. Again, the *y*-axis can be adjusted to give the impression of more or less difference between categories than actually exists. For example, the bar graph in Figure 6.9 (a) shows the effects of two different anti-anxiety drugs on people's ratings of anxiety. From this graph it appears that participants who took Drug B expressed much less anxiety than those who took Drug A. Note, however, that the actual difference in anxiety ratings is quite small. This fact is seen more clearly when the scale on the *y*-axis is extended (Figure 6.9[b]).

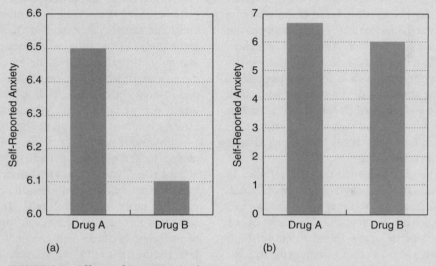

(a)   (b)

FIGURE 6.9   Effects of Drugs on Anxiety

Misleading readers with such graphs is common in advertising. However, because the goal of scientific research is to express the data as accurately as possible, researchers should present their data in ways that most clearly and honestly portray their findings.

MEASURES OF VARIABILITY

In addition to knowing the average or typical score in a data distribution, it is helpful to know how much the scores in the distribution vary. We noted in Chapter 2 that, because the entire research enterprise is oriented toward accounting for behavioral variability, researchers often use statistics that indicate the amount of variability in the data.

Among other things, knowing about the variability in a distribution tells us how typical the mean is of the scores as a set. If the variability in a set of data is very small, the mean is representative of the scores as a whole, and the mean tells us a great deal about the typical participant's score. On the other hand, if the variability is large, the mean is not very representative of the scores as a set. Guessing the mean for a particular participant would probably miss his or her score by a wide margin if the scores showed a great deal of variability.

To examine the extent to which scores in a distribution vary from one another, researchers use **measures of variability**—descriptive statistics that convey information about the spread or variability of a set of data. As we saw in Chapter 2, the **range** is the difference between the largest and smallest scores in a distribution. The range of the data in Table 6.2 is 39 (i.e., 40-1). The range is the least useful of the measures of variability because it is based entirely on two extreme scores and does not take the variability of the remaining scores into account. Although researchers often report the range of their data, they more commonly provide information about the **variance** and its square root, the **standard deviation**. The advantage of the variance and standard deviation is that, unlike the range, the variance and standard deviation take into account *all* of the scores when calculating the variability in a set of data.

In Chapter 2, we learned that the variance is based on the sum of the squared differences between each score and the mean. You may recall that we can calculate the variance by subtracting the mean of our data from each participant's score, squaring these differences (or deviation scores), summing the squared deviation scores, and dividing by the number of scores minus 1. The variance is an index of the average amount of variability in a set of data—the average amount that each participant's score differs from the mean of the data—expressed in squared units.

Variance is the most commonly used measure of variability for purposes of statistical analysis. However, when researchers simply want to *describe* how much variability exists in their data, it has a shortcoming—it is expressed in terms of squared units and thus is difficult to interpret conceptually. (You may recall that we squared the deviation scores as we calculated the variance.) For example, if we are measuring systolic blood pressure in a study of stress, the variance is expressed not in terms of the original blood pressure readings but in terms of *blood pressure squared!* When researchers want to express behavioral variability in

the original units of their data, they use the standard deviation. A great deal can be learned from knowing only the mean and standard deviation of the data.

Standard Deviation and the Normal Curve

In the nineteenth century, the Belgian statistician and astronomer Adolphe Quetelet demonstrated that many bodily measurements, such as height and chest circumference, showed identical distributions when plotted on a graph. When plotted, such data form a curve, with most of the points on the graph falling near the center, and fewer and fewer points lying toward the extremes. Sir Francis Galton, an eminent British scientist and statistician, extended Quetelet's discovery to the study of psychological characteristics. He found that no matter what attribute he measured, graphs of the data nearly always followed the same bell-shaped distribution. For example, Galton showed that scores on university examinations fell into this same pattern. Four such curves are shown in Figure 6.10.

Many, if not most, of the variables that psychologists and other behavioral scientists study fall, at least roughly, into a **normal distribution**. A normal distribution rises to a rounded peak at its center, and then tapers off at both tails. This pattern indicates that most of the scores fall toward the middle of the range of scores (i.e., around the mean), with fewer scores toward the extremes. That many data distributions approximate a normal curve is not surprising because, regardless of what attribute we measure, most people are about average, with few people having extreme scores.

Occasionally, however, our data distributions are nonnormal, or skewed. In a **positively skewed distribution** such as Figure 6.11(a), there are more low scores than high scores in the data; if data are positively skewed, one observes a clustering of scores toward the lower, left-hand end of the scale, with the tail of the distribution extending to the right. (The distribution of the data involving students' self-reported number of friends is also positively skewed; see Figure 6.5.) In a **negatively skewed distribution** such as Figure 6.11(b), there are more high scores than low scores; the hump is to the right of the graph, and the tail of the distribution extends to the left.

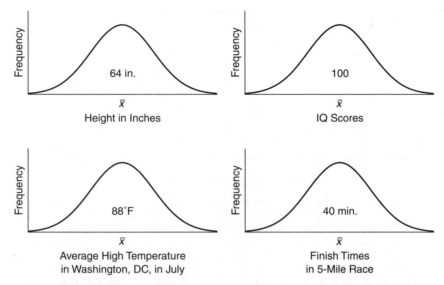

FIGURE 6.10 Normal Distributions. Figure 6.10 shows four idealized normal distributions. In normal distributions such as these, most scores fall toward the middle of the range, with the greatest number of scores falling at the mean of the distribution. As we move in both directions away from the mean, the number of scores tapers off symmetrically, indicating an equal number of low and high scores.

Assuming that we have a roughly normal distribution, we can estimate the percentage of participants who obtained certain scores just by knowing the mean and standard deviation of the data. For example, in any normally distributed set of data, approximately 68% of the scores (68.26%, to be exact) will fall in the range defined by ±1 standard deviation from the mean. In other words, roughly 68% of the participants will have scores that fall between 1 standard deviation below the mean and 1 standard deviation above the mean. Let's consider IQ scores, for example. One commonly used IQ test has a mean of

100 and a standard deviation of 15. The score falling 1 standard deviation below the mean is 85 (i.e., 100 − 15) and the score falling 1 standard deviation above the mean is 115 (i.e., 100 + 15). Thus, approximately 68% of all people have IQ scores between 85 and 115.

Figure 6.12 shows this principle graphically. As you can see, 68.26% of the scores fall within 1 standard deviation (±1 *s*) from the mean. Furthermore, approximately 95% of the scores in a normal distribution fall ±2 standard deviations from the mean. On an IQ test with a mean of 100 and standard

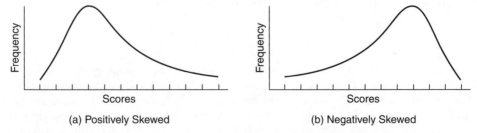

FIGURE 6.11 Skewed Distributions. In skewed distributions, most scores fall toward one end of the distribution. In a positively skewed distribution (a), there are more low scores than high scores. In a negatively skewed distribution (b), there are more high scores than low scores.

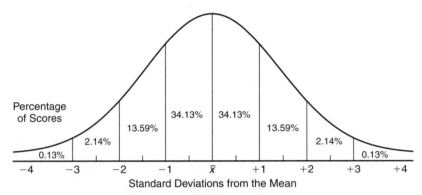

FIGURE 6.12 Percentage of Scores Under Ranges of the Normal Distribution.
This figure shows the percentage of participants who fall in various portions of the normal distribution. For example, 34.13% of the scores in a normal distribution will fall between the mean and 1 standard deviation above the mean. Similarly, 13.59% of participants' scores will fall between 1 and 2 standard deviations below the mean. By adding ranges, we can see that approximately 68% fall between −1 and +1 standard deviations from the mean, and approximately 95% fall between −2 and +2 standard deviations from the mean.

deviation of 15, 95% of people score between 70 and 130. Less than 1% of the scores fall further than 3 standard deviations below or above the mean. If you have an IQ score below 55 or above 145 (i.e., more than 3 standard deviations from the mean of 100), you are quite unusual in that regard.

It is easy to see why the standard deviation is so useful. By knowing the mean and standard devi-

ation of a set of data, we can tell not only how much the data vary but also how they are distributed across various ranges of scores. With real data, which are seldom perfectly normally distributed, these ranges are only approximate. Even so, researchers find the standard deviation very useful as they try to describe and understand the data they collect.

Developing Your Research Skills
Calculating the Variance and Standard Deviation

Although most researchers rely heavily on computers to conduct statistical analyses, you may occasionally have reason to calculate certain statistics by hand using a calculator. A description of how to calculate the variance and the standard deviation by hand follows.

The formula for the variance, expressed in statistical notation, is

$$S^2 = \frac{\sum y_i^2 - [(\sum y_i)^2/n]}{n-1}$$

Remember that $\sum$ is summation, y_i refers to each participant's score, and n reflects the number of participants.

To use this formula, you first square each score (y_i^2) and add these squared scores together ($\sum y_i^2$). Then, add up all of the original scores ($\sum y_i$) and square the sum $[(\sum y_i)^2]$. Finally, plug these numbers into the formula, along with the sample size (n), to get the variance. It simplifies the calculations if you set up a table with two columns—one for the raw scores and one for the square of the raw scores. If we do this for the data we analyzed in Chapter 2 dealing with attitudes about capital punishment, we get:

Participant #	y_i	y_i^2
1	4	16
2	1	1
3	2	4
4	2	4
5	4	16
6	3	9

$$\sum y_i = 16 \quad \sum y_i^2 = 50$$
$$(\sum y_i)^2 = 256$$

Then,

$$s^2 = \frac{50 - 256/6}{6 - 1} = \frac{50 - 42.67}{5} = 1.47$$

Thus, the variance (s^2) of these data is 1.47. To obtain the standard deviation (s), we simply take the square root of the variance. The standard deviation of these data is the square root of 1.47, or 1.21.

THE *Z*-SCORE

In some instances, researchers need a way to describe where a particular participant falls in the data distribution. Just knowing that a certain participant scored 47 on a test does not tell us very much. Knowing the mean of the data tells us whether the participant's score was above or below average, but without knowing something about the variability of the data, we still cannot tell how far above or below the mean the participant's score was, relative to other participants.

The **z-score**, or *standard score,* is used to describe a particular participant's score relative to the rest of the data. A participant's z-score indicates how far from the mean in terms of standard deviations the participant's score falls. For example, if we find that a participant has a z-score of −1.00, we know that his or her score is 1 standard deviation below the mean. By referring to Figure 6.12, we can see that only about 16% of the other participants scored lower than this person. Similarly, a z-score of +2.9 indicates a score

nearly 3 standard deviations above the mean—one that is in the uppermost ranges of the distribution.

If we know the mean and standard deviation of a sample, a participant's z-score is easy to calculate:

$$z = (y_i - \bar{y})/s$$

where y_i is the participant's score, $\bar{y}$ is the mean of the sample, and s is the standard deviation of the sample.

Sometimes researchers standardize an entire set of data by converting all of the participants' raw scores to z-scores. This is a useful way to identify extreme scores or outliers. An outlier can be identified by a very low or very high z-score—one that falls below −3.00 or above +3.00, for example. Also, certain statistical analyses require standardization prior to the analysis. When a set of scores is standardized, the new set of z-scores always has a mean equal to 0 and a standard deviation equal to 1 regardless of the mean and standard deviation of the original data.

Developing Your Research Skills
A Descriptive Study of Pathological Video-Game Use

To wrap up this chapter, let us look at a study that exemplifies many of the concepts we have covered in this chapter (and in the last chapter on sampling). Many parents worry about the amount of time that their children play video games, sometimes remarking that their child seems "addicted" to them. Are they really addicted to video

(continued)

(continued)

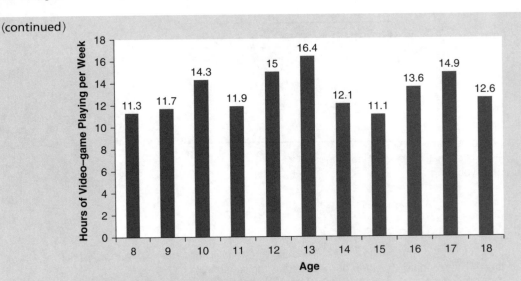

FIGURE 6.13 Average hours of video-game playing per week

games, or do they simply really like to play them? How many children play video games to such an extent that their behavior appears to be pathological and interferes with many areas of their life as true addictions do?

To find out, Gentile (2009) analyzed data from a national sample of 8- to 18-year-olds. This was a stratified random sample of 588 boys and 590 girls, which was large enough to provide results with an error of estimation of +/−3%. (See Chapter 5 for information on stratified sampling and the error of estimation.) The study was conducted online via a Web-based questionnaire. Respondents answered questions about their use of video games, including indicators of pathological use, such as playing games when one should be studying, feeling restless or irritable when one does not get to play games as much as desired, and trying to cut back on how much one plays but being unable to do so.

Overall, 88% of the sample played video games at least occasionally, with boys playing more hours per week on average ($M = 16.4$ hours/week, SD = 14.1) than girls ($M = 9.2$ hours/week, SD = 10.2). Adolescents reported playing video games fewer times per week as they got older, but they played longer during each session so their total game usage did not change much between age 8 and age 18 on average. Figure 6.13 shows how much time children of various ages spent playing video games.

TABLE 6.4 Symptoms of Pathological Video-Game Use

	Percentage	
	Boys	**Girls**
Need to spend more time or money on video games to feel same excitement	12	3
Spent too much money on video games or equipment	13	4
Play video games to escape from problems or bad feelings	29	19
Lied about how much you play video games	17	10
Skip doing homework to play video games	29	15
Done poorly on school assignment or test because spent too much time playing video games	26	11

But did any of the participants show signs of pathological game playing? Among participants who were identified as "pathological gamers," the average number of hours of video-game play was 24.6 hours per week (SD = 16)—that's a full 24-hour day of game playing each week! The author of the article presented a table listing 11 symptoms of pathological game use and the percentage of respondents who indicated that they exhibited each symptom. The table below shows the results for only a few of the symptoms.

Now let's see how well you understand the concepts used in this study and can present descriptive data:

1. Would you characterize this study as an example of survey research, demographic research, epidemiological research, or some combination? Why?
2. Is this a cross-sectional, successive independent samples, or longitudinal design? Explain.
3. Imagine that you wanted to use a table rather than a figure to present the average amount of time that participants of different ages played video games each week. Design a table that presents the data in Figure 6.13 above.
4. Table 6.4 shows that 26% of boys reported that they had done poorly on a school assignment or test because they spent too much time playing video games. What does the margin of error in this study tell us about this percentage? (If needed, review the material on margin of error on page 101 in Chapter 5.)
5. In the description of the results above, you can see that boys not only played video games more hours per week on average than girls but also that the standard deviation (SD) was larger for boys than for girls. What does this indicate about differences in patterns of video game playing for boys and girls?
6. Imagine that you wanted to use a graph rather than a table to present the percentage of boys and girls who experience each symptom of pathological video game use in Table 6.4. Create a bar graph that presents the data in Table 6.4 in graphical form.

Summary

1. Descriptive research is designed to describe the characteristics or behaviors of a particular population in a systematic and accurate fashion.
2. Survey research uses questionnaires or interviews to collect information about people's attitudes, beliefs, feelings, behaviors, and lifestyles. A cross-sectional survey design studies a single group of respondents, whereas a successive independent samples survey design studies different samples at two or more points in time. A longitudinal or panel survey design studies a single sample of respondents on more than one occasion.
3. Demographic research describes patterns of basic life events, such as births, marriages, divorces, migration, and deaths.
4. Epidemiological research studies the occurrence of physical and mental health problems.
5. Researchers attempt to describe their data in ways that are accurate, concise, and easily understood.

6. Data can be summarized and described using either numerical methods or graphical methods.
7. A simple frequency distribution is a table that indicates the number (frequency) of participants who obtained each score. Often the relative frequency (the proportion of participants who obtained each score) is also included.
8. A grouped frequency distribution indicates the frequency of scores that fall in each of several mutually exclusive class intervals.
9. Histograms, bar graphs, and frequency polygons (line graphs) are common graphical methods for describing data.
10. A full statistical description of a set of data usually involves measures of both central tendency (mean, median, mode) and variability (range, variance, standard deviation).
11. The mean is the numerical average of a set of scores, the median is the middle score when a set of scores is rank-ordered, and the mode is the most frequent score. The mean is the most

commonly used measure of central tendency, but it can be misleading if the data are skewed or outliers are present.

12. Researchers often present confidence intervals (which are shown in graphs as error bars) to indicate the range of values in which the means of other samples drawn from the population would be likely to fall.

13. The range is the difference between the largest and smallest scores. The variance and its square root (the standard deviation) indicate the total variability in a set of data. Among other things, the variability in a set of data indicates how representative the mean is of the scores as a whole.

14. When plotted, distributions may be either normally distributed (roughly bell-shaped) or skewed.

15. In a normal distribution, approximately 68% of scores fall within 1 standard deviation of the mean, approximately 95% of scores fall within 2 standard deviations of the mean, and over 99% of scores fall within 3 standard deviations of the mean. Scores that fall more than 3 standard deviations from the mean are often regarded as outliers.

16. A z-score describes a particular participant's score relative to the rest of the data in terms of its distance from the mean in standard deviations.

Key Terms

bar graph (*p. 125*)
class interval (*p. 124*)
confidence interval (*p. 129*)
cross-sectional survey
    design (*p. 118*)
demographic research (*p. 121*)
descriptive research (*p. 117*)
epidemiological research (*p. 122*)
frequency (*p. 124*)
frequency distribution (*p. 124*)
frequency polygon (*p. 126*)
graphical method (*p. 124*)
grouped frequency
    distribution (*p. 124*)

histogram (*p. 125*)
internet surveys (*p. 121*)
longitudinal survey design (*p. 121*)
mean (*p. 127*)
measures of central
    tendency (*p. 126*)
measures of variability (*p. 132*)
median (*p. 127*)
mode (*p. 127*)
negatively skewed distribution
    (*p. 132*)
normal distribution (*p. 132*)
numerical method (*p. 124*)
outlier (*p. 127*)

panel survey design (*p. 121*)
positively skewed
    distribution (*p. 132*)
range (*p. 132*)
raw data (*p. 124*)
relative frequency (*p. 125*)
simple frequency distribution
    (*p. 124*)
standard deviation (*p. 132*)
successive independent
    samples survey design
    (*p. 119*)
variance (*p. 132*)
z-score (*p. 135*)

Questions for Review

1. How does descriptive research differ from other kinds of research strategies, such as correlational, experimental, and quasi-experimental research?

2. What is the most common type of survey research design?

3. A successive independent samples survey design is used to examine changes in attitudes or behaviors over time, but results from such designs are often difficult to interpret. Describe the successive independent samples survey design and discuss why it is sometimes difficult to draw clear conclusions about

the changes in attitudes or behavior that are observed.

4. How does the longitudinal (or panel) survey design help researchers to draw clearer conclusions about changes over time? What problem arises when respondents drop out of a longitudinal study?

5. What are some pros and cons of conducting descriptive research using the Internet?

6. Why are psychologists sometimes interested in (a) demographic and (b) epidemiological research?

7. What three criteria characterize good descriptions of data?

8. What is raw data? What are the best seasonings to use when it is cooked? (Just kidding.)

9. Under what conditions is a grouped frequency distribution more useful as a means of describing a set of scores than a simple frequency distribution? Why do researchers often add relative frequencies to their tables?

10. What three rules govern the construction of a grouped frequency distribution?

11. What is the difference between a histogram and a bar graph?

12. Distinguish among the median, mode, and mean.

13. Under what conditions is the median a more meaningful measure of central tendency than the mean?

14. What does the confidence interval tell us?

15. How are error bars interpreted?

16. Why do researchers prefer the standard deviation as a measure of variability over the range?

17. In a normal distribution, what percentage of scores falls between -1 and $+1$ standard deviations from the mean? Between the mean and -2 standard deviations? Between the mean and $+3$ standard deviations? Within the range of ± 3 standard deviations?

18. Draw a negatively skewed distribution.

19. What does it indicate if a participant has a z-score of 2.5? $-.80$? .00?

7 | CORRELATIONAL RESEARCH

My grandfather, a farmer for over 60 years, told me on several occasions that the color and thickness of a caterpillar's coat are related to the severity of the coming winter. When "woolly worms" have dark, thick, furry coats, he said that we can expect an unusually harsh winter.

Whether this bit of folk wisdom is true, I don't know. But like my grandfather, we all hold many beliefs about associations between events in the world. Many people believe, for instance, that hair color is related to personality—that people with red hair have fiery tempers and that blondes are of less-than-average intelligence. Others think that geniuses are particularly likely to suffer from mental disorders or that people who live in large cities are apathetic and uncaring. Racial stereotypes involve beliefs about the characteristics that are associated with people of different races. Those who believe in astrology claim that the date on which a person is born is associated with the person's personality later in life. Sailors capitalize on the relationship between the appearance of the sky and approaching storms, as indicated by the old saying: "Red sky at night, sailor's delight; red sky at morning, sailors take warning." You probably hold many such beliefs about things that tend to go together.

Like all of us, behavioral researchers also are interested in whether certain variables are related to each other. Is outside temperature related to the incidence of urban violence? To what extent are children's IQ scores related to the IQs of their parents? Is shyness associated with low self-esteem? What is the relationship between the degree to which students experience test anxiety and their performance on exams? Are SAT scores related to college grades? Each of these questions asks whether two variables (such as SAT scores and grades) are related and, if so, how strongly they are related.

We determine whether one variable is related to another by seeing whether scores on the two variables *covary*—whether they *vary or change together*. If self-esteem is related to shyness, for example, we should find that scores on measures of self-esteem and shyness vary together. Higher self-esteem scores should be associated with lower shyness scores, and lower self-esteem scores should be associated with greater shyness.

Such a pattern would indicate that scores on the two measures covary—that they vary, or go up and down, together. On the other hand, if self-esteem and shyness scores bear no consistent relationship to one another—if we find that high self-esteem scores are as likely to be associated with high shyness scores as with low shyness scores—the scores do not vary together, and we will conclude that no relationship exists between self-esteem and shyness.

When researchers are interested in questions regarding whether variables are related to one another, they often conduct **correlational research**. Correlational research is used to describe the relationship between two or more naturally occurring variables.

Before delving into details regarding correlational research, let's look at an example of a correlational study. Since the earliest days of psychology, researchers have debated the relative importance of genetic versus environmental influences on behavior—often dubbed the *nature–nurture controversy*. Scientists have disagreed about whether people's behaviors are more affected by their inborn biological makeup or by their experiences in life. Most psychologists now agree that the debate is a complex one; behavior and mental ability are a product of *both* inborn and environmental factors. So rather than discuss whether a particular behavior should be classified as inherited or acquired, researchers have turned their attention to studying the interactive effects of nature and nurture on behavior, and to identifying aspects of behavior that are more affected by nature than nurture, and vice versa.

Part of this work has focused on the relationship between the personalities of children and their parents. Common observation reveals that children display many of the psychological characteristics of their parents. But is this similarity due to genetic factors or to the particular way parents raise their children? Is this resemblance due to nature or to nurture?

If we only study children who were raised by their natural parents, we cannot answer this question; both genetic and environmental influences can explain why children who are raised by their biological parents are similar to them. For this reason, many researchers have turned their attention to children who were adopted in infancy. Because any resemblance between children and their adoptive parents is unlikely to be due to genetic factors, it must be due to environmental variables.

In one such study, Sandra Scarr and her colleagues administered several personality measures to 120 adolescents and their natural parents and to 115 adolescents and their adoptive parents (Scarr, Webber, Weinberg, & Wittig, 1981). These scales measured a number of personality traits, including extraversion (the tendency to be sociable and outgoing) and neuroticism (the tendency to be anxious and insecure). The researchers wanted to know whether children's personalities were related more closely to their natural parents' personalities or to their adoptive parents' personalities.

This study produced a wealth of data, a small portion of which is shown in Table 7.1. This table shows *correlation coefficients* that express the nature of the relationships between the children's and parents' personalities. These correlation coefficients indicate both the strength and direction of the relationship between parents' and children's scores on the two personality measures. One column lists the correlations between children and their biological parents, and the other column lists correlations between children and their adoptive parents. This table can tell us a great deal about the relationship between children's and parents' personalities, but first we must learn how to interpret correlation coefficients.

TABLE 7.1	Correlations Between Children's and Parents' Personalities	
Personality Measure	**Biological Parents**	**Adoptive Parents**
Extraversion	.19	.00
Neuroticism	.25	.05

Source: Adapted from Scarr, Webber, Weinberg, and Wittig (1981).

THE CORRELATION COEFFICIENT

A **correlation coefficient** is a statistic that indicates the degree to which two variables are related to one another in a linear fashion. In the study just described, the researchers were interested in the relationship between children's personalities and those of their parents. Any two variables can be correlated: self-esteem and shyness, the amount of time that people listen to rock music and hearing damage, marijuana use and scores on a test of memory, children's extraversion scores and parents' extraversion scores, and so on. We could even do a study on the correlation between the thickness of caterpillars' coats and winter temperatures. The only requirement for a correlational study is that we obtain scores on two variables for each participant in our sample.

The **Pearson correlation coefficient**, designated by the letter *r*, is the most commonly used measure of correlation. The numerical value of a correlation coefficient always ranges between −1.00 and +1.00. When interpreting a correlation coefficient, a researcher considers two aspects of the coefficient: its sign and its magnitude.

The *sign* of a correlation coefficient (+ or −) indicates the *direction* of the relationship between the two variables. Variables may be either positively or negatively correlated. A **positive correlation** indicates a direct, positive relationship between the two variables. If the correlation is positive, scores on one variable tend to increase as scores on the other variable increase. For example, the correlation between SAT scores and college grades is a positive one; people with higher SAT scores tend to have higher grades, whereas people with lower SAT scores tend to have lower grades. Similarly, the correlation between educational attainment and income is positive; better-educated people tend to make more money. In Chapter 2, we saw that optimism and health are positively correlated; more optimistic people tend to be healthier, and less optimistic people tend to be less healthy.

A **negative correlation** indicates an inverse, negative relationship between two variables. As values of one variable increase, values of the other variable decrease. For example, the correlation between self-esteem and shyness is negative. People with higher self-esteem tend to be less shy, whereas people with lower self-esteem tend to be more shy. The correlation between alcohol consumption and college grades is also negative. On the average, the more alcohol students consume in a week, the lower their grades are likely to be. Likewise, the degree to which people have a sense of control over their lives is negatively correlated with depression; lower perceived control is associated with greater depression, whereas greater perceived control is associated with lower depression.

The *magnitude of the correlation*—its numerical value, ignoring the sign—expresses the strength of the relationship between the variables. When a correlation coefficient is zero ($r = .00$), we know that the variables are not linearly related. As the numerical value of the coefficient increases, so does the strength of the linear relationship. Thus, a correlation of +.78 indicates that the variables are more strongly related than does a correlation of +.30.

Keep in mind that the sign of a correlation coefficient indicates only the direction of the relationship and tells us nothing about its strength. Thus, a correlation of −.78 indicates a larger correlation (and a stronger relationship) than a correlation of +.40, but the first relationship is negative, whereas the second one is positive.

A GRAPHIC REPRESENTATION OF CORRELATIONS

The relationship between any two variables can be portrayed graphically on *x*- and *y*-axes. For each participant, we can plot a point that represents his or her combination of scores on the two variables (which we can designate *x* and *y*). When scores for an entire sample are plotted, the resulting graphical representation of the data is called a **scatter plot**. A scatter plot of the relationship between depression and anxiety is shown in Figure 7.1.

Figure 7.2 shows several scatter plots of relationships between two variables. Positive correlations can be recognized by their upward slope to the right, which indicates that participants with high values on one variable (*x*) also tend to have high values on the other variable (*y*), whereas low values on one variable are associated with low values on the other. Negative correlations slope downward to the right, indicating that participants who score high on one variable tend to score low on the other variable, and vice versa.

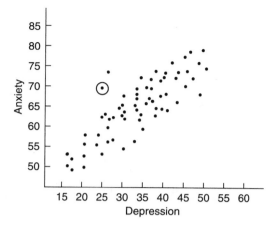

FIGURE 7.1   A Linear Relationship: Depression and Anxiety.   This graph shows subjects' scores on two measures (depression and anxiety) plotted on an axis, where each dot represents a single subject's score. For example, the circled subject scored 25 on depression and 70 on anxiety. As you can see from this scatter plot, depression and anxiety are linearly related; that is, the pattern of the data tends to follow a straight line.

The stronger the correlation, the more tightly the data are clustered around an imaginary line running through them. When we have a **perfect correlation** (−1.00 or +1.00), all of the data fall in a straight line, as in Figure 7.2(e). At the other extreme, a zero correlation appears as a random array of dots because the two variables bear no relationship to one another (see Figure 7.2(f)).

As noted, a correlation of zero indicates that the variables are not linearly related. However, it is possible that they are related in a curvilinear fashion. Look, for example, at Figure 7.3. This scatter plot shows the relationship between physiological arousal and performance; people perform better when they are moderately aroused than when arousal is either very low or very high. If we calculate a correlation coefficient for these data, r will be nearly zero. Can we conclude that arousal and performance are unrelated? No, for as Figure 7.3 shows, they are closely related. But the relationship is curvilinear, and correlation tells us only about linear relationships. Many researchers regularly examine a scatter plot of their data to be sure that the variables are not curvilinearly related. Statistics exist for measuring the degree of curvilinear relationship between two variables, but those statistics do not concern us here. Simply remember that correlation coefficients tell us only about linear relationships between variables.

You should now be able to make sense out of the correlation coefficients in Table 7.1. First, we see that the correlation between the extraversion scores of children and their natural parents is +.19. This is a positive correlation, which means that children who scored high in extraversion tended to have natural parents who also had high extraversion scores. Conversely, children with lower scores tended to be those whose natural parents also scored low. The correlation is only .19, however, which indicates a relatively weak relationship between the scores of children and their natural parents.

The correlation between the extraversion scores of children and their adoptive parents, however, was .00; there was no relationship. Considering these two correlations together suggests that a child's level of extraversion is more closely related to that of his or her natural parents than to that of his or her adoptive parents. The same appears to be true of neuroticism. The correlation for children and their natural parents was +.25, whereas the correlation for children and adoptive parents was only +.05. Again, these positive correlations are small, but they are stronger for natural than for adoptive parents. Taken together, these correlations suggest that both extraversion and neuroticism may be more a matter of nature than nurture.

THE COEFFICIENT OF DETERMINATION

We've seen that the correlation coefficient, r, expresses the direction and strength of the relationship between two variables. But what, precisely,

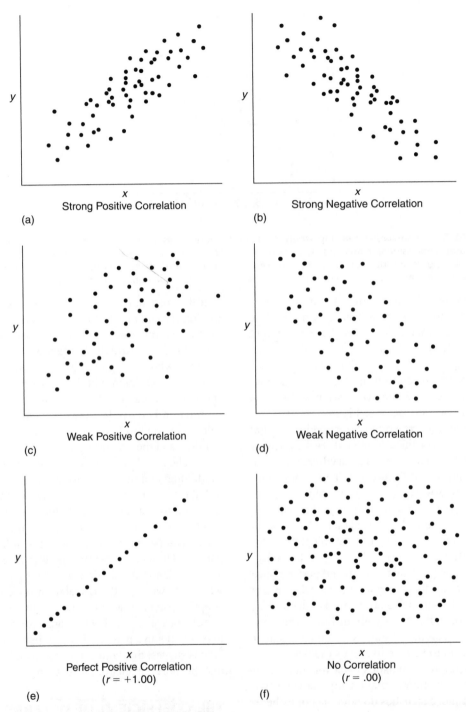

FIGURE 7.2   Scatter Plots and Correlations

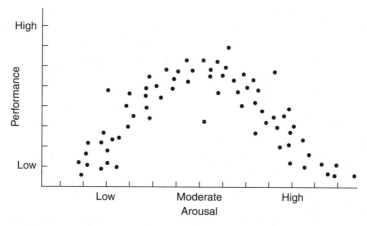

FIGURE 7.3 A Curvilinear Relationship: Arousal and Performance. This is a scatter plot of 70 participants' scores on a measure of arousal (*x*-axis) and a measure of performance (*y*-axis). The relationship between arousal and performance is curvilinear; participants with moderate arousal performed better than those with low or high arousal. Because *r* is a measure of linear relationships, calculating a correlation coefficient for these data would yield a value of *r* that was approximately zero. Obviously, this cannot be taken to indicate that arousal and performance are unrelated.

does the value of *r* indicate? If children's neuroticism scores correlate +.25 with the scores of their parents, we know there is a positive relationship, but what does the number itself tell us?

To interpret a correlation coefficient fully, we must first square it. This is because the statistic, *r,* is not on a ratio scale. As a result, we can't add, subtract, multiply, or divide correlation coefficients, nor can we compare them directly. Contrary to how it appears, a correlation of .80 is *not* twice as large as a correlation of .40! To make *r* easier to interpret, we square it to obtain the **coefficient of determination**, which is easily interpretable as the proportion of variance in one variable that is explained or accounted for by the other variable. To understand what this means, let us return momentarily to the concept of variance.

We learned in Chapter 2 that variance indicates the amount of variability in a set of data. We learned also that the total variance in a set of data can be partitioned into systematic variance and error variance. Systematic variance is that part of the total variability in participants' responses that is related to variables the researcher is investigating. Error variance is that portion of the total variance that is unrelated to the variables under investigation in the study. We also learned that researchers can assess the strength of the relationships they study by determining the proportion of the total variance in participants' responses

that is systematic variance related to other variables under study. (This proportion equals the quantity, systematic variance/total variance.) The higher the proportion of the total variance in one variable that is systematic variance related to another variable, the stronger the relationship between them is.

The squared correlation coefficient (or coefficient of determination) tells us the proportion of variance in one of our variables that is accounted for by the other variable. Viewed another way, the coefficient of determination indicates the proportion of the total variance in one variable that is systematic variance shared with the other variable. For example, if we square the correlation between children's neuroticism scores (.25) and the neuroticism scores of their biological parents (.25 × .25), we obtain a coefficient of determination of .0625. This tells us that 6.25% of the variance in children's neuroticism scores can be accounted for by their parents' scores, or, to say it differently, 6.25% of the total variance in children's scores is systematic variance, which is variance related to the parents' scores.

When two variables are uncorrelated—when *r* is .00—they are totally independent and unrelated, and we cannot account for any of the variance in one variable with the other variable. When the correlation coefficient is .00, the coefficient of determination is also .00 (because .00 × .00 = .00), so the proportion of the total variance in one variable that can be accounted for by the other variable is zero. If the correlation between x and y is .00, we cannot explain any of the variability that we see in people's scores on y by knowing their scores on x (and vice versa). To say it differently, there is no systematic variance in the data.

However, if two variables are correlated with one another, scores on one variable *are* related to scores on the other variable, and systematic variance is present. The existence of a correlation (and, thus, systematic variance) means that we can account for, or explain, some of the variance in one variable by the other variable. And, we can learn the proportion of variance in one variable that we can explain with the other variable by squaring their correlation to get the coefficient of determination. If x and y correlate .25, we can account for 6.25% of the variance in one variable with the other variable.

If we knew everything there is to know about neuroticism, we would know *all* of the factors that account for the variance in children's neuroticism scores, such as genetic factors, the absence of a secure home life, neurotic parents who provide models of neurotic behavior, low self-esteem, frightening life experiences, and so on. If we knew everything about neuroticism, we could account for 100% of the variance in children's neuroticism scores.

But we are not all-knowing. The best we can do is to conduct research that looks at the relationship between neuroticism and a handful of other variables. In the case of the research conducted by Scarr and her colleagues (1981) described earlier, we can account for only a relatively small portion of the variance in children's neuroticism scores—that portion that is associated with the neuroticism of their natural parents. Given the myriad of factors that influence neuroticism, it is not surprising that one particular factor, such as parental neuroticism, can account for only 6.25% of the variance in children's neuroticism scores.

The square of a correlation coefficient—its coefficient of determination—is a very important statistic that expresses the effect size for relationships between variables that are correlated with each other. As we discussed in Chapter 2, the goal of behavioral research is to understand variability in thoughts, feelings, behaviors, and physiological reactions, and the squared correlation coefficient tells us the proportion of variance in one variable that can be accounted for by another variable. If r is zero, we can account for none of the variance. If r equals -1.00 or +1.00, we can perfectly account for 100% of the variance. And if r is in between, the more variance we account for, the stronger the relationship.

Developing Your Research Skills
Calculating the Pearson Correlation Coefficient

Now that we understand what a correlation coefficient tells us about the relationship between two variables, let's take a look at how it is calculated. To calculate the Pearson correlation coefficient (r), we must obtain scores on two variables for a sample of several individuals.

THE FORMULA
The equation for calculating r is

$$r = \frac{\sum xy - \frac{\left(\sum x\right)\left(\sum y\right)}{n}}{\sqrt{\left(\sum x^2 - \frac{\left(\sum x\right)^2}{n}\right)\left(\sum y^2 - \frac{\left(\sum y\right)^2}{n}\right)}}.$$

In this equation, x and y represent participants' scores on the two variables of interest, for example, shyness and self-esteem, or neuroticism scores for children and their parents. The term $\sum xy$ indicates that we multiply each participant's x- and y-scores together, then sum these products across all participants. Likewise, the term $\left(\sum x\right)\left(\sum y\right)$

indicates that we sum all participants' x-scores, sum all participants' y-scores, then multiply these two sums. The rest of the equation should be self-explanatory. Although calculating r may be time-consuming with a large number of participants, the math involves only simple arithmetic.

AN EXAMPLE

Many businesses use ability and personality tests to help them hire the best employees. Before they may legally use such tests, however, employers must demonstrate that scores on the tests are related to job performance. Psychologists are often called on to validate employment tests by showing that test scores correlate with performance on the job.

Suppose we are interested in whether scores on a particular test relate to job performance. We obtain employment test scores for 10 employees. Then, 6 months later, we ask these employees' supervisors to rate their employees' job performance on a scale of 1 to 10, where a rating of 1 represents extremely poor job performance and a rating of 10 represents superior performance.

TABLE 7.2 Calculating the Pearson Correlation Coefficient

Employee	Test Score (x)	Job Performance Rating (y)	x^2	y^2	xy
1	85	9	7,225	81	775
2	60	5	3,600	25	300
3	45	3	2,025	9	135
4	82	9	6,724	81	738
5	70	7	4,900	49	490
6	80	8	6,400	64	640
7	57	5	3,249	25	285
8	72	4	5,184	16	288
9	60	7	3,600	49	420
10	65	6	4,225	36	390
	$\Sigma x = 676$ $(\Sigma x)^2 = 456,976$	$\Sigma y = 63$ $(\Sigma y)^2 = 3,969$	$\Sigma x^2 = 47,132$	$\Sigma y^2 = 435$	$\Sigma xy = 4,451$

Table 7.2 shows the test scores and ratings for the 10 employees, along with some of the products and sums we need in order to calculate r. In this example, two scores have been obtained for 10 employees: an employment test score (x) and a job performance rating (y). We wish to know whether the test scores correlate with job performance.

As you can see, we've obtained x^2, y^2, and the product of x and y (xy) for each participant, along with the sums of x, y, x^2, y^2, and xy. Once we have these numbers, we simply substitute them for the appropriate terms in the formula for r:

$$ r = \frac{\Sigma xy - \dfrac{\left(\Sigma x\right)\left(\Sigma y\right)}{n}}{\sqrt{\left(\Sigma x^2 - \dfrac{\left(\Sigma x\right)^2}{n}\right)\left(\Sigma y^2 - \dfrac{\left(\Sigma y\right)^2}{n}\right)}}. $$

(continued)

(continued)

Entering the appropriate numbers into the formula yields:

$$r = \frac{4{,}451 - (676)(63)/10}{\sqrt{(47{,}132 - 456{,}976/10)(435 - 3{,}969/10)}}$$

$$r = \frac{4{,}451 - 4{,}258.8}{\sqrt{(47{,}132 - 456{,}976.6)(435 - 396.9)}}$$

$$= \frac{192.2}{\sqrt{(1{,}434.4)(38.1)}} = \frac{192.2}{\sqrt{54{,}650.64}} = \frac{192.2}{233.77} = .82$$

The obtained correlation for the example in Table 7.2 is +.82.

Can you interpret this number? First, the sign of r is positive, indicating that test scores and job performance are directly related; employees who score higher on the test tend to be evaluated more positively by their supervisors, whereas employees with lower test scores tend to be rated less positively. The value of r is .82, which is a strong correlation. To see precisely how strong the relationship is, we square .82 to get the coefficient of determination, .67. This indicates that 67% of the variance in employees' job performance ratings can be accounted for by knowing their test scores. The test seems to be a valid indicator of job performance.

Contributors to Behavioral Research
The Invention of Correlation

The development of correlation as a statistical procedure began with the work of Sir Francis Galton. Intrigued by the ideas of his cousin, Charles Darwin, regarding evolution, Galton began investigating human heredity. One aspect of his work on inheritance involved measuring various parts of the body in hundreds of people and their parents. In 1888, Galton introduced the "index of co-relation" as a method for describing the degree to which two such measurements were related. Rather than being a strictly mathematical formula, Galton's original procedure for estimating co-relation (which he denoted by the letter r) involved inspecting data that had been graphed on x- and y-axes (Cowles, 1989; Stigler, 1986).

Galton's seminal work provoked intense excitement among three British scientists who further developed the theory and mathematics of correlation. Walter Weldon, a Cambridge zoologist, began using Galton's ideas regarding correlation in his research on shrimps and crabs. In the context of his work examining correlations among various crustacean body parts, Weldon first introduced the concept of *negative correlation*. (Weldon tried to name r after Galton, but the term *Galton's function* never caught on; Cowles, 1989.)

In 1892 Francis Edgeworth published the first mathematical formula for calculating the coefficient of correlation directly. Unfortunately, Edgeworth did not initially recognize the importance of his work, which was buried in a more general, "impossibly difficult to follow paper" on statistics (Cowles, 1989, p. 139).

Thus, when Galton's student Karl Pearson derived a formula for calculating r in 1895, he didn't know that Edgeworth had obtained an essentially equivalent formula a few years earlier. Edgeworth himself notified Pearson of this fact in 1896, and Pearson later acknowledged that he had not carefully examined others' previous work. Even so, Pearson recognized the importance of the discovery and went ahead to make the most of it, applying his formula to research problems in both biology and psychology (Pearson & Kendall, 1970; Stigler, 1986). Because Pearson was the one to popularize the formula for calculating r, the coefficient became known as the *Pearson correlation coefficient*, or *Pearson r*.

STATISTICAL SIGNIFICANCE OF *r*

When calculating a correlation between two variables, researchers are interested not only in the value of the correlation coefficient but also in whether the value of *r* they obtain is statistically significant. **Statistical significance** exists when a correlation coefficient calculated on a sample has a very low probability of being zero in the population.

To understand what this means, let's imagine for a moment that we are all-knowing beings, and that, as all-knowing beings, we know for certain that if we tested every person in a particular population, we would find that the correlation between two particular variables, *x* and *y*, was absolutely zero (that is, *r* = .00). Now, imagine that a mortal behavioral researcher wishes to calculate the correlation between these two variables. Of course, as a mortal, this researcher usually cannot collect data on a very large population, so she obtains a sample of 200 respondents, measures *x* and *y* for each respondent, and calculates *r*. Will the value of *r* she obtains be .00? I suspect that you can guess that the answer is probably not. Because of sampling error, measurement error, and other sources of error variance, she will probably obtain a nonzero correlation coefficient *even though the true correlation in the population is zero.*

Of course, this discrepancy creates a problem. When we calculate a correlation coefficient, how do we know whether we can trust the value we obtain or whether the true value of *r* in the population may, in fact, be zero? As it turns out, we can't know for certain, but we can estimate the probability that the value of *r* we obtain in our research would really be zero if we had tested the entire population from which our sample was drawn. And, if the probability that our correlation is truly zero in the population is sufficiently low (usually less than .05), we refer to it as *statistically significant.* Only if a correlation is statistically significant—and unlikely to be zero—do researchers treat it as if it is a real correlation.

The statistical significance of a correlation coefficient is affected by three factors. First is the sample size. Assume that, unbeknown to each other, you and I independently calculated the correlation between shyness and self-esteem and that we both obtained a correlation of −.50. However, your calculation was based on data from 300 participants, whereas my calculation was based on data from 30 participants. Which of us should feel more confident that the true correlation between shyness and self-esteem in the population is not .00? You can probably guess that your sample of 300 should give you more confidence in the value of *r* you obtained than my sample of 30. Thus, all other things being equal, we are more likely to conclude that a particular correlation is statistically significant the larger our sample size.

Second, the statistical significance of a correlation coefficient depends on the magnitude of the correlation. For a given sample size, the larger the value of *r* we obtain, the less likely it is to be .00 in the population. Imagine you and I both calculated a correlation coefficient based on data from 300 participants; your calculated value of *r* was .75, whereas my value of *r* was .20. You would be more confident that your correlation was not .00 in the population than I would be.

Third, statistical significance depends on how careful we want to be not to draw an incorrect conclusion about whether the correlation we obtain could be zero in the population. The more careful we want to be, the larger the correlation must be to be declared "significant." Typically, researchers decide that they will consider a correlation to be significantly different from zero if there is less than a 5% chance (that is, less than 5 chances out of 100) that a correlation as large as the one they obtained could have come from a population with a true correlation of zero.

Formulas and tables for testing the statistical significance of correlation coefficients can be found in many statistics books as well as online. Table 7.3 shows part of one such table. This table shows the minimum value of *r* that would be considered statistically significant if we set the chances of making an incorrect decision at 5%. To use the table, we need to know three things: (1) the sample size—how many participants were used to calculate the correlation (*n*), (2) the absolute value of the correlation coefficient that was calculated (|*r*|), and (3) whether we have made a directional or nondirectional hypothesis about the correlation. The first two things—sample size and the magnitude of *r*—are pretty straightforward, but the third consideration requires some explanation.

TABLE 7.3	Critical Values of r	
	Minimum Value of ∣r∣ that is Significant	
Number of Participants (n)	**Directional Hypothesis**	**Nondirectional Hypothesis**
10	.55	.63
20	.38	.44
30	.31	.36
40	.26	.31
50	.24	.28
60	.21	.25
70	.20	.24
80	.19	.22
90	.17	.21
100	.17	.20
200	.12	.14
300	.10	.11
400	.08	.10
500	.07	.09
1000	.05	.06

These are the minimum values of r that are considered statistically significant, with less than a 5% chance that the correlation in the population is zero.

You have already learned that correlations can be either positive or negative, reflecting either a positive or an inverse relationship between the two variables. When conducting a correlational study, a researcher can make one of two kinds of hypotheses about the correlation that he or she expects to find between the variables. On one hand, a **directional hypothesis** predicts the direction of the correlation—that is, whether the correlation will be positive or negative. On the other hand, a **nondirectional hypothesis** predicts that two variables will be correlated but does not specify whether the correlation will be positive or negative. Typically, most hypotheses about correlations are directional because it would be quite strange for a researcher to be convinced that two variables are correlated but be unable to predict whether they are positively or negatively related to one another. In some instances, however, different theories may make different predictions about the direction of a correlation, so a nondirectional hypothesis would be used.

To understand how to use Table 7.3, let's consider a study that examined the relationship between the degree to which people believe that closeness and intimacy are risky and their romantic partners' ratings of the quality of their relationship (Brunell, Pilkington, & Webster, 2007). In this study, the two members of 64 couples completed a measure of risk in intimacy as well as measures of the quality of their relationship. The results showed that the women's risk in intimacy scores correlated −.41 with their male partner's ratings of the quality of their relationship. However, the correlation between men's risk in intimacy scores and their female partner's ratings of the relationship was only −.10. That is, the more that people believe that intimacy is risky, the less satisfied their partners are with the relationship, but this effect is stronger for women than for men.

Let's assume that the hypothesis is directional. Specifically, we predict that the correlation will be negative because people who think that intimacy is risky will behave in ways that lower their partner's satisfaction with the relationship. Look down the column for directional hypotheses to find the number of participants ($n = 64$). Because this exact number does not appear, you will need to extrapolate based on the values for sample sizes of 60 and 70. We see that the minimum value of r that is significant with 64 participants lies between .20 and .21. Because the absolute value of the correlation between women's risk in intimacy scores and their male partner's ratings of the quality of their relationship ($|-.41|$) exceeds this critical value, we conclude that the population correlation is very unlikely to be zero (in fact, there is less than a 5% chance that the population correlation is zero). Thus, we can treat this $-.41$ correlation as "real."

However, the correlation between men's risk in intimacy scores and their female partner's ratings of the relationship was $-.10$, which is less than the critical value in the table. So, we conclude that this correlation could have easily come from a population in which the correlation between risk in intimacy and relationship satisfaction is .00. Thus, the effect is not statistically significant, and we must treat it as if it were zero.

Keep in mind that, with large samples, even very small correlations are statistically significant. Thus, finding that a particular r is significant tells us only that it is very unlikely to be .00 in the population; it does not tell us whether the relationship between the two variables is a strong or an important one. The strength of a correlation is assessed only by its magnitude, not whether it is statistically significant. Although only a rule of thumb, behavioral researchers tend to regard correlations at or below about .10 as *weak* in magnitude (they account for only 1% of the variance), correlations around .30 as *moderate* in magnitude, and correlations over .50 as *strong* in magnitude.

FACTORS THAT DISTORT CORRELATION COEFFICIENTS

Correlation coefficients do not always accurately reflect the relationship between two variables. Many factors can distort coefficients so that they either underestimate or overestimate the true degree of relationship between two variables. Therefore, when interpreting correlation coefficients, one must be on the lookout for three factors that may artificially inflate or deflate the magnitude of correlations.

Restricted Range

Look for a moment at Figure 7.4(a). From this scatter plot, do you think SAT scores and grade point averages are related? There is an obvious positive linear trend to the data, which reflects a moderately strong positive correlation. Now look at Figure 7.4(b). In this set of data, are SAT scores and grade point average (GPA) correlated? In this case, the pattern, if there is one, is much less pronounced. It is difficult to tell whether there is a relationship between SAT scores and GPA or not.

If you'll now look at Figure 7.4(c), you will see that Figure 7.4(b) is actually taken from a small section of Figure 7.4(a). However, rather than representing the full range of possible SAT scores and grade point averages, the data shown in Figure 7.4(b) represents a quite narrow or **restricted range**. Instead of ranging from 200 to 1,600, the SAT scores fall only in the range from 1,000 to 1,150.

These figures show graphically what happens to correlations when the range of scores is restricted. Correlations obtained on a relatively homogeneous group of participants whose scores fall in a narrow range are smaller than those obtained from a heterogeneous sample with a wider range of scores. If the range of scores is restricted, a researcher may be misled into concluding that the two variables are only weakly correlated, if at all. However, had people with a broader range of scores been studied, a strong relationship would have emerged. The lesson here is to examine one's raw data to be sure the range of scores is not artificially restricted.

The problem may be even more serious if the two variables are curvilinearly related *and* the range of scores is restricted. Look, for example, at Figure 7.5. This graph shows the relationship between anxiety and performance on a task that we examined earlier, and the relationship is obviously curvilinear. Now imagine that you selected a sample of 200 respondents from a phobia treatment center and examined the relationship

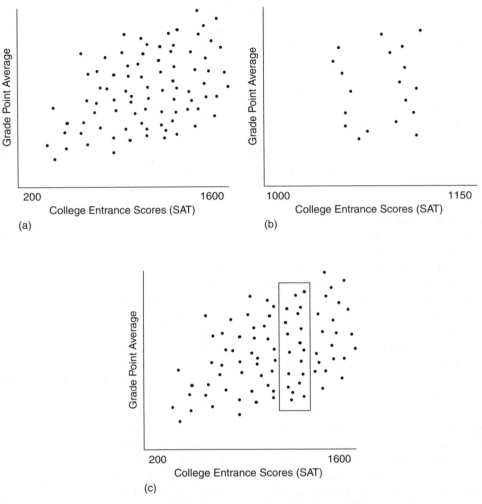

FIGURE 7.4   Restricted Range and Correlation.   Scatter plot (a) shows a distinct positive correlation between SAT scores and grade point averages when the full range of SAT scores (from 200 to 1,700) is included. However, when a more restricted range of scores is examined (those from 1,000 to 1,150), the correlation is less apparent (b). Scatter plot (c) graphically displays the effects of restricted range on correlation.

between anxiety and performance for these 200 participants. Because your sample had a restricted range of scores (being phobic, these participants were higher than average in anxiety), you would likely detect a negative *linear* relationship between anxiety and performance, not a curvilinear relationship. You can see this graphically in Figure 7.5 if you look only at the data for participants who scored above average in anxiety. For these individuals, there is a strong, negative relationship between their anxiety scores and their scores on the measure of performance.

Outliers

Outliers are scores that are so obviously deviant from the remainder of the data that one can question whether they belong in the data set at all. Many researchers consider a score to be an outlier if it is farther than 3 standard deviations from the mean of the data. You may remember from Chapter 6 that, assuming we have a roughly normal distribution, scores that fall more than 3 standard deviations below the mean are smaller than more than 99% of

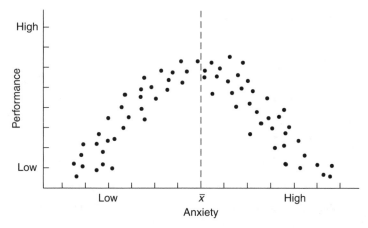

FIGURE 7.5   Restricted Range and a Curvilinear Relationship.   As shown here, the relationship between anxiety and performance is curvilinear, and, as we have seen, the calculated value of *r* will be near .00. Imagine what would happen, however, if data were collected on only highly anxious participants. If we calculate *r* only for participants scoring above the mean of the anxiety scores, the obtained correlation will be strong and negative.

the scores; a score that falls more than 3 standard deviations above the mean is larger than more than 99% of the scores. Clearly, scores that deviate from the mean by more than ±3 standard deviations are very unusual.

Figure 7.6 shows two kinds of outliers. Figure 7.6(a) shows two *on-line outliers*. Two participants' scores, although falling in the same pattern as the rest of the data, are extreme on both variables. On-line outliers tend to artificially inflate correlation coefficients, making them larger than is warranted by the rest of the data. Figure 7.6(b) shows two *off-line outliers*. Off-line outliers tend to artificially deflate the value of *r*. The presence of even a few off-line outliers will cause *r* to be smaller than indicated by most of the data.

Because outliers can lead to erroneous conclusions about the strength of the correlation between variables, researchers should examine scatter plots of their data to look for outliers. Some researchers exclude outliers from their analyses, arguing that such extreme scores are flukes that don't really - belong in the data. Other researchers change outliers' scores to the value of the variable that is 3 standard deviations from the mean. By making the outlier less extreme, the researcher can include the participant's data in the analysis while minimizing

the degree to which they distort the correlation coefficient. You need to realize that, whereas many researchers regularly eliminate or rescore the outliers they find in their data, other researchers discourage modifying data in these ways. However, because only one or two extreme outliers can badly distort correlation coefficients and lead to incorrect conclusions, typically researchers must take some action to deal with outliers.

Reliability of Measures

Unreliable measures attenuate the magnitude of correlation coefficients. All other things being equal, the less reliable our measures, the lower the correlation coefficients we will obtain. (You may wish to review the section on reliability in Chapter 3.)

To understand why this is so, let us again imagine that we are omniscient. In our infinite wisdom, we know that the real correlation between a child's neuroticism and the neuroticism of his or her parents is, say, +.45. However, let's also assume that a poorly trained, fallible researcher uses a measure of neuroticism that is totally unreliable. That is, it has absolutely no test–retest or interitem reliability. If the researcher's measure is completely unreliable, what value of *r* will he or she obtain between

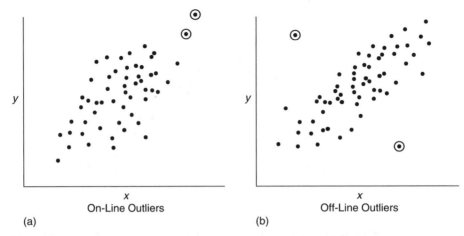

FIGURE 7.6   Outliers. Two on-line outliers are circled in (a). On-line outliers lead to inflated correlation coefficients. Off-line outliers, such as those circled in (b), tend to artificially deflate the magnitude of *r*.

parents' and children's scores? Not +.45 (the true correlation) but rather .00. Of course, researchers seldom use measures that are totally unreliable. Even so, the less reliable the measure, the lower the correlation will be.

CORRELATION AND CAUSALITY

Perhaps the most important consideration in interpreting correlation coefficients is that *correlation does not imply causality.* Often people will conclude that because two phenomena are related, they must be *causally* related in some way. This is not necessarily so; one variable can be strongly related to another yet not cause it. The thickness of caterpillars' coats may correlate highly with the severity of winter weather, but we cannot conclude that caterpillars *cause* blizzards, ice storms, and freezing temperatures. Even if two variables are perfectly correlated ($r = -1.00$ or $+1.00$), we cannot infer that one of the variables causes the other. This point is exceptionally important, so I will repeat it: A correlation can never be used to conclude that one of the variables causes or influences the other.

For us to conclude that one variable causes or influences another variable, three criteria must be met: covariation, directionality, and elimination of extraneous variables. However, most correlational research satisfies only the first of these criteria unequivocally.

First, to conclude that two variables are causally related, they first must be found to covary, or correlate. If one variable causes the other, then changes in the values of one variable should be associated with changes in values of the other variable. Of course, this is what correlation means by definition, so if two variables are found to be correlated, this first criterion for inferring causality is met.

Second, to infer that two variables are causally related, we must show that the presumed cause precedes the presumed effect in time. However, in most correlational research, both variables are measured at the same time. For example, if a researcher correlates participants' scores on two personality measures that were collected at the same time, there is no way to determine the direction of causality. Does variable *x* cause variable *y,* or does variable *y* cause variable *x* (or, perhaps, neither)?

The third criterion for inferring causality is that all extraneous factors that might influence the relationship between the two variables are controlled or eliminated. Correlational research never satisfies this requirement completely. Two variables may be correlated not because they are causally related to one another but because they are both related to a third variable. For example,

Levin and Stokes (1986) were interested in correlates of loneliness. Among other things, they found that loneliness correlated +.60 with depression. Does this mean that being lonely makes people depressed or that being depressed makes people feel lonely? Perhaps neither. Another option is that both loneliness and depression are due to a third variable, such as the quality of a person's social network. Having a large number of friends and acquaintances, for example, may reduce both loneliness and depression.

The inability to draw conclusions about causality from correlational data is the basis of the tobacco industry's insistence that no research has produced evidence of a causal link between smoking and lung cancer in humans. Plenty of research shows that smoking and the incidence of cancer are *correlated* in humans; more smoking is associated with a greater likelihood of getting lung cancer. But because the data are correlational, we cannot infer a causal link between smoking and health. Research *has* established that smoking causes cancer in laboratory animals, however, because animal research can use experimental designs that allow us to infer cause-and-effect relationships. However, conducting experimental research on human beings would require randomly assigning people to smoke heavily. Not only would such a study be unethical, but would you volunteer to participate in a study that might give you cancer? Because we are limited to doing only correlational research on smoking in humans, we cannot infer causality from our results.

Behavioral Research Case Study
Correlates of Satisfying Relationships

Although relationships are an important part of most people's lives, behavioral researchers did not begin to study processes involved in liking and loving seriously until the 1970s. Since that time, we have learned a great deal about factors that affect interpersonal attraction, relationship satisfaction, and people's decisions to end their romantic relationships. However, researchers have focused primarily on the relationships of adults and have tended to ignore adolescent love experiences.

To remedy this shortcoming in the research, Levesque (1993) conducted a correlational study of the factors associated with satisfying love relationships in adolescence. Using a sample of more than 300 adolescents between the ages of 14 and 18 who were involved in dating relationships, Levesque administered measures of relationship satisfaction and obtained other information about the respondents' perceptions of their relationships.

A small portion of the results of the study is shown in Table 7.4. This table shows the correlations between respondents' ratings of the degree to which they were having certain experiences in their relationships and their satisfaction with the relationship.

Correlations with an asterisk (*) were found to be significantly different from zero; the probability that these correlations are .00 in the population is less than 5%. All of the other, nonasterisked correlations must be treated as if they were zero because the likelihood of their being .00 in the population is unacceptably high. Thus, we do not interpret these nonsignificant correlations.

As you can see from the table, several aspects of relationships correlated with relationship satisfaction, and, in most instances, the correlations were similar for male and female respondents. Looking at the magnitude of the correlations, we can see that the most important correlates of relationship satisfaction were the degree to which the adolescents felt that they were experiencing togetherness, personal growth, appreciation, exhilaration or happiness, and emotional support. By squaring the correlations (and thereby obtaining the coefficients of determination), we can see the proportion of variance in relationship satisfaction that can be accounted for by each variable. For example, ratings of togetherness accounted for 23% of the variance in satisfaction for male respondents ($.48^2 = .23$). From the reported data, we have no way of knowing whether the correlations are distorted by restricted range, outliers, or unreliable measures, but we trust that Levesque examined scatter plots of the data and took the necessary precautions.

(*continued*)

(continued)

These results show that adolescents' perceptions of various aspects of their relationships correlate with how satisfied they feel. However, because these data are correlational, we cannot conclude that their perceptions of their relationships *cause* them to be satisfied or dissatisfied. It is just as likely that feeling generally satisfied with one's relationships may cause people to perceive specific aspects of the relationships more positively. It is also possible that these results are due to participants' personalities: Happy, optimistic people perceive life, including their relationships, positively and are generally satisfied; unhappy, pessimistic people see everything more negatively and are dissatisfied. Thus, although we know that perceptions of relationships are correlated with relationship satisfaction, these data do not help us to understand why they are related.

TABLE 7.4   Correlates of Relationship Satisfaction Among Adolescents

	Correlation with Satisfaction	
Experiences in Relationships	**Males**	**Females**
Togetherness	.48[*]	.30[*]
Personal Growth	.44[*]	.22[*]
Appreciation	.33[*]	.21[*]
Exhilaration/Happiness	.46[*]	.39[*]
Painfulness/Emotional Turmoil	−.09	−.09
Passion/Romance	.19	.21[*]
Emotional Support	.34[*]	.23[*]
Good Communication	.13	.17

Source: Levesque, R. J. R. (1993). The romantic experience of adolescents in satisfying love relationships. *Journal of Youth and Adolescence, 22,* 219–251. With kind permission of Springer Science and Business Media.

PARTIAL CORRELATION

Although we can never conclude that two correlated variables cause one another, researchers sometimes use research strategies that allow them to make informed guesses about whether correlated variables might or might not be causally related. These strategies cannot provide definitive causal conclusions, but they can give us evidence that either does or does not support a particular causal explanation of the relationship between two correlated variables. Although researchers can never conclude that one correlated variable absolutely causes another, they may be able to conclude that a particular causal explanation of the relationship between the variables is more likely to be correct than are other causal explanations, and they can certainly use correlational data to conclude that two variables are *not* causally related.

If we find that two variables, *x* and *y,* are correlated, there are three general causal explanations of their relationship: *x* may cause *y, y* may cause *x,* or some other variable or variables (*z*) may cause both *x* and *y.* Imagine that we find a negative correlation between alcohol consumption and college grades—the more alcohol students drink per week, the lower their grades are likely to be. Such a correlation could be explained in three ways. On one hand, excessive alcohol use may cause students' grades to go down (because they are drinking instead of studying, missing class because of hangovers, or whatever). Alternatively, obtaining poor grades may cause students to drink (to relieve the stress of failing, for example).

A third possibility is that the correlation between alcohol consumption and grades is spurious. **A spurious correlation** is a correlation between two variables that is not due to any direct relationship between them but rather to their relation to other variables. When researchers believe that a correlation is spurious, they try to determine what other variables might cause x and y to correlate with each other. In the case of the correlation between alcohol consumption and grades, perhaps depression is the culprit: Students who are highly depressed do not do well in class, and they may try to relieve their depression by drinking. Thus, alcohol use and grades may be correlated only indirectly—by virtue of their relationship with depression. Alternatively, the relationship between alcohol and grades may be caused by the value that students place on social relationships versus academic achievement. Students who place a great deal of importance on their social lives may study less and party more. As a result, they coincidentally receive lower grades *and* drink more alcohol, but the grades and drinking are not directly related. (Can you think of third variables other than depression and sociability that might mediate the relationship between alcohol consumption and grades?)

Researchers can test hypotheses about the possible effects of third variables on the correlations they obtain by using a statistical procedure called *partial correlation*. Partial correlation allows researchers to examine a third variable's possible influence on the correlation between two other variables. Specifically, a **partial correlation** is the correlation between two variables with the influence of one or more other variables statistically removed. That is, we can calculate the correlation between x and y while removing any influence that some third variable, z, might have on the correlation between them to see whether removing z makes any difference in the correlation between x and y.

Imagine that we obtain a correlation between x and y, and we want to know whether the relationship between x and y is due to the fact that x and y are both caused by some third variable, z. We can statistically remove the variability in x and y that is associated with z and see whether x and y are still correlated. If x and y still correlate after we partial out the influence of z, we can conclude that the relationship between x and y is not likely to be due to z. Stated differently, if x and y are correlated even when systematic variance due to z is removed, z is unlikely to be causing the relationship between x and y.

However, if x and y are no longer correlated after the influence of z is statistically removed, we have evidence that the correlation between x and y is due to z or to some other variable that is associated with z. That is, systematic variance associated with z must be responsible for the relationship between x and y.

Let's return to our example involving alcohol consumption and college grades. If we wanted to know whether a third variable, such as depression, was responsible for the correlation between alcohol and grades, we could calculate the partial correlation between alcohol use and grade point average while statistically removing (partialing out) the variability related to depression scores. If the correlation between alcohol use and grades remains unchanged when depression is partialed out, we will have good reason to conclude that the relationship between alcohol use and grades is *not* due to depression. However, if removing depression from the correlation led to a partial correlation between alcohol and grades that was substantially lower than their Pearson correlation, we would conclude that depression—or something else associated with depression—may have mediated the relationship.

The formulas used to calculate partial correlations do not concern us here. The important thing is to recognize that, although we can never infer causality from correlation, we can tentatively test causal hypotheses using partial correlation as well as other techniques that we will discuss in Chapter 8.

Behavioral Research Case Study
Partial Correlation: Depression, Loneliness, and Social Support

Earlier I mentioned a study by Levin and Stokes (1986) that found a correlation of +.60 between loneliness and depression. These researchers hypothesized that one reason that lonely people tend to be more depressed is that they have smaller social support networks; people who have fewer friends are more likely to feel lonely *and* are

(continued)

(continued)

more likely to be depressed (because they lack social and emotional support). Thus, the relationship between loneliness and depression may be a spurious relationship due to a third variable, lack of social support.

To test this possibility, Levin and Stokes calculated the partial correlation between loneliness and depression, removing the influence of participants' social networks. When they removed the variability due to social networks, the partial correlation was .39, somewhat lower than the correlation between loneliness and depression without variability due to social networks partialed out. This pattern of results suggests that some of the relationship between loneliness and depression may be partly mediated by social network variables. However, even with the social network factor removed, loneliness and depression were still correlated, which suggests that factors other than social network also contribute to the relationship between them.

OTHER INDICES OF CORRELATION

We have focused in this chapter on the Pearson correlation coefficient because it is the most commonly used index of correlation. The Pearson correlation is appropriate when both variables, *x* and *y*, are on an interval or ratio scale of measurement (as most variables studied by behavioral researchers are). Recall from Chapter 3 that for both interval and ratio scales, equal differences between the numbers assigned to participants' responses reflect equal differences between participants in the characteristic being measured. (Interval and ratio scales differ in that ratio scales have a true zero point, whereas interval scales do not.)

When one or both variables are measured on an ordinal scale—in which the numbers reflect the rank ordering of participants on some attribute—the **Spearman rank-order correlation** coefficient is used. For example, suppose that we want to know how well teachers can judge the intelligence of their students. We ask a teacher to rank the 30 students in the class from 1 to 30 in terms of their general intelligence. Then we obtain students' IQ scores on a standardized intelligence test. Because the teacher's judgments are on an ordinal scale of measurement, we calculate a Spearman rank-order correlation coefficient to examine the correlation between the teacher's rankings and the student's real IQ scores.

Other kinds of correlation coefficients are used when one or both of the variables are dichotomous, such as gender (male vs. female), handedness (left- vs. right-handed), or whether a student has passed a course (yes vs. no). (A dichotomous variable is measured on a nominal scale but has only two

levels.) When correlations are calculated on dichotomous variables, the variables are assigned arbitrary numbers, such as male = 1 and female = 2. When both variables being correlated are dichotomous, a **phi coefficient** correlation is used; if only one variable is dichotomous (and the other is on an interval or ratio scale), a **point biserial correlation** is used. Thus, if we were looking at the relationship between gender and virginity, a phi coefficient is appropriate because both variables are dichotomous. However, if we were correlating gender (a dichotomous variable) with height (which is measured on a ratio scale), a point biserial correlation would be calculated. Once calculated, the Spearman, phi, and point biserial coefficients are interpreted precisely like a Pearson coefficient.

Importantly, sometimes relationships between variables are examined using statistics other than correlation coefficients. For example, imagine that we want to know whether women are more easily embarrassed than men. One way to test the relationship between gender and embarrassability would be to calculate a point biserial correlation as described in the previous paragraph. (We would use a point biserial correlation because gender is a dichotomous variable whereas embarrassability is measured on an interval scale.) However, a more common approach would be to test whether the average embarrassability scores of men and women differ significantly. Even though we have not calculated a correlation coefficient, finding a significant difference between the scores for men and women would demonstrate a correlation between gender and embarrassability. If desired, we could also calculate the effect size to determine the proportion of variance in embarrassability that is accounted for by gender (see page 41). This effect size would provide the same information as if we had squared a correlation coefficient. We will examine statistics such as these later in the book. For now, the important point is that we do not always use correlation coefficients to analyze correlational data.

Developing Your Research Skills
Single People Attract Crime

Statistics from the U.S. Justice Department's National Crime Victimization Survey (2005) show that people who are not married are three to four times more likely to be victims of violent crime as people who are married. The number of violent crimes per 1,000 people age 12 years or older are shown in the following list. Clearly, marital status correlates with victimization.

Marital Classification	Violent Crimes per 1,000 People
Married	10.0
Widowed	5.0
Divorced or separated	32.3
Never married	38.4

1. Speculate regarding possible explanations of this relationship. Suggest at least five reasons that marital status and victimization may be linked.
2. Consider how you would conduct a correlational study to test each of your explanations. You will probably want to design studies that allow you to partial out variables that may mediate the relationship between marital status and victimization.

Summary

1. Correlational research is used to describe the relationship between two variables.
2. A correlation coefficient (r) indicates both the direction and magnitude of the relationship.
3. If the scores on the two variables tend to increase and decrease together, the variables are positively correlated. If the scores vary inversely, the variables are negatively correlated.
4. The magnitude of a correlation coefficient indicates the strength of the relationship between the variables. A correlation of zero indicates that the variables are not related; a correlation of ± 1.00 indicates that they are perfectly related.
5. The square of the correlation coefficient, the coefficient of determination (r^2), reflects the proportion of the total variance in one variable that can be accounted for by the other variable.
6. Researchers test the statistical significance of correlation coefficients to gauge the likelihood that the correlation they obtained in their research might have come from a population in which the true correlation was zero. A correlation is usually considered statistically significant if there is less than a 5% chance that the true population correlation is zero. Significance is affected by sample size, magnitude of the correlation, and degree of confidence the researcher wishes to have.
7. When interpreting correlations, researchers look out for factors that may artificially inflate and deflate the magnitude of the correlation coefficient—restricted range, outliers, and low reliability.
8. Correlational research seldom if ever meets all three criteria necessary for inferring causality—

covariation, directionality, and elimination of extraneous variables. Thus, the presence of a correlation does not imply that the variables are causally related to one another.

9. A partial correlation is the correlation between two variables with the influence of one or more other variables statistically removed.

Partial correlation is used to examine whether the correlation between two variables might be due to certain other variables.

10. The Pearson correlation coefficient is most commonly used, but the Spearman, phi, and point biserial coefficients are used under special circumstances.

Key Terms

coefficient of determination (p. 144)
correlational research (p. 141)
correlation coefficient (p. 142)
negative correlation (p. 142)
outlier (p. 152)
partial correlation (p. 157)

Pearson correlation coefficient (p. 142)
perfect correlation (p. 143)
phi coefficient (p. 158)
point biserial correlation (p. 158)
positive correlation (p. 142)

restricted range (p. 151)
scatter plot (p. 142)
Spearman rank-order correlation (p. 158)
spurious correlation (p. 156)
statistical significance (p. 149)

Questions for Review

1. The correlation between self-esteem and shyness is −.50. Interpret this correlation.
2. Which is larger—a correlation of +.45 or a correlation of −.60? Explain.
3. Tell whether each of the following relationships reflects a positive or a negative correlation:
   a. the amount of stress in people's lives and the number of colds they get in the winter
   b. the amount of time that people spend suntanning and a dermatological index of skin damage due to ultraviolet rays
   c. happiness and suicidal thoughts
   d. blood pressure and a person's general level of hostility
   e. the number of times that a rat has run a maze and the time it takes to run it again
4. Why do researchers often examine scatter plots of their data when doing correlational research?
5. The correlation between self-esteem and shyness is −.50, and the correlation between self-consciousness and shyness is +.25. How much stronger is the first relationship than the second? (Be careful on this one.)
6. Why do researchers calculate the coefficient of determination?
7. What does a coefficient of determination of .40 indicate?

8. Why can it be argued that the formula for calculating r should be named the Edgeworth, rather than the Pearson, correlation coefficient?
9. Why may we not interpret or discuss a correlation coefficient that is not statistically significant?
10. Using Table 7.3 ("Critical Values of r"), indicate whether each of the following correlation coefficients is statistically significant:
    a. $r = .05$, $n = 300$, directional hypothesis
    b. $r = .00$, $n = 1,000$, nondirectional hypothesis
    c. $r = -.26$, $n = 50$, nondirectional hypothesis
    d. $r = -.15$, $n = 100$, directional hypothesis
    e. $r = .42$, $n = 112$, directional hypothesis
    f. $r = .25$, $n = 60$, nondirectional hypothesis
11. What is a restricted range, and what effect does it have on correlation coefficients? How would you detect and correct a restricted range?
12. How do we know whether a particular score is an outlier?
13. Do outliers increase or decrease the magnitude of correlation coefficients?
14. What impact does reliability have on correlation?
15. Why can't we infer causality from correlation?
16. How can partial correlation help researchers explore possible causal relationships among correlated variables?
17. When is the Spearman rank-order correlation used?
18. What is a dichotomous variable? What correlations are used for dichotomous variables?

Questions for Discussion

1. Imagine that you predicted a moderate correlation between people's scores on a measure of anxiety and the degree to which they report having insomnia. You administered measures of anxiety and insomnia to a sample of 30 participants, and obtained a correlation coefficient of .28. Because this correlation is not statistically significant (the critical value is .31), you must treat it as if it were zero. Yet you still think that anxiety and insomnia are correlated. If you were going to conduct the study again, what could you do to provide a more powerful test of your hypothesis?

2. Following the rash of school shootings that occurred in the late 1990s, some individuals suggested that violent video games were making children and adolescents more aggressive. Imagine that you obtained a sample of 150 15-year-old males and correlated their level of aggressiveness with the amount of time per week that they played violent video games. The correlation coefficient was .56 (and statistically significant). Does this finding provide support for the idea that playing violent video games increases aggression? Explain your answer.

3. A researcher obtained a sample of 180 participants between the ages of 18 and 24 and calculated the phi coefficient between whether they smoked cigarettes and whether they used marijuana (yes vs. no). Because the correlation between smoking and marijuana use was .45, the researcher concluded that cigarette smoking leads to marijuana use. Do you agree with the researcher's conclusion? Explain your answer.

4. Imagine you obtained a point biserial correlation of .35 between gender and punctuality, showing that men arrived later to class than did women. You think that this correlation might be due to the fact that more women than men wear watches, so you calculate the partial correlation between gender and punctuality while removing the influence of watch-wearing. The resulting partial correlation was .35. Interpret this partial correlation.

5. A study published in the *Archives of General Psychiatry* (Brennan, Grekin, & Mednick, 1999) found that babies whose mothers smoke are at a higher risk for criminal behavior in adulthood than babies of mothers who do not smoke. The researchers examined the arrest histories for over 4,000 34-year-old men. The number of cigarettes their mothers smoked while pregnant was related to the probability that the men were later arrested for violent and nonviolent crimes. The researchers tried to eliminate the possible influence of other factors such as mother's alcohol and drug use, income, divorce, and home environment, but the relationship between maternal smoking and the men's criminality remained even after these variables were partialed out. Can we conclude that smoking leads to criminal behavior in one's offspring? Design additional correlational research to examine this question more fully.

Exercises

1. Imagine that you are a college professor. You notice that fewer students appear to attend class on Friday afternoons when the weather is warm than when it is cold outside. To test your hunch, you collect data regarding outside temperature and attendance for several randomly selected weeks during the academic year. Your data are as listed in the adjacent table.
   a. Draw a scatter plot of the data.
   b. Do the data appear to be roughly linear?
   c. Do you see any evidence of outliers?
   d. From examining the scatter plot, does there appear to be a correlation between temperature and attendance? If so, is it positive or negative?
   e. Calculate *r* for these data.

Temperature (degrees F)	Attendance (number of students)
58	85
62	83
78	64
77	62
67	66
50	86
80	60
85	82
70	65
75	62

f. Is this correlation statistically significant? (You'll need to decide whether this is a directional or a nondirectional hypothesis.)

g. Interpret *r*. What does *r* tell you about the relationship between temperature and attendance?

2. A researcher was interested in whether people tend to marry individuals who are about the same level of physical attractiveness as they are. She took individual photographs of 14 pairs of spouses. Then she had 10 participants rate the attractiveness of these 28 pictures on a 10-point scale (where 1 = *very unattractive* and 10 = *very attractive*). She averaged the 10 participants' ratings to get an attractiveness score for each photograph. Her raw data are in the adjacent table.

a. Is the researcher expecting a positive or a negative correlation?

b. Draw a scatter plot of the data.

c. Do the data appear to be roughly linear?

d. From examining the scatter plot, does there appear to be a correlation between the physical attractiveness of husbands and wives? If so, is it positive or negative?

e. Calculate *r* for these data.

Score for Wife's Photograph	Score for Husband's Photograph
5	6
9	7
4	4
2	4
7	5
6	5
5	5
9	8
8	4
10	8
4	3
5	4
7	7
8	7

f. Is this correlation statistically significant?

g. Interpret *r*. What does *r* tell you about the relationship between the attractiveness of wives and husbands?

8 | ADVANCED CORRELATIONAL STRATEGIES

Predicting Behavior: Regression Strategies	Analyzing Nested Data: Multilevel Modeling
Assessing Directionality: Cross-Lagged and Structural Equations Analysis	Uncovering Underlying Dimensions: Factor Analysis

Knowing whether variables are related to one another provides the cornerstone for a great deal of scientific investigation. Typically, the first step in understanding any psychological phenomenon is to document that certain variables are somehow related; correlational research methods are indispensable for this purpose. However, as we saw in Chapter 7, correlational research can provide only tentative conclusions about cause-and-effect relationships, and simply demonstrating that variables are correlated is only the first step. Once they know that variables are correlated, researchers usually want to understand *how* and *why* they are related.

In this chapter, we take a look at four advanced correlational strategies that researchers use to explore how and why variables are related to one another. These methods allow researchers to go beyond simple correlations to a fuller and more precise understanding of how particular variables are related to one another. Specifically, these methods allow researchers to (1) develop equations that describe how variables are related and that allow us to predict one variable from one or more other variables (regression analysis); (2) explore the likely direction of causality between two or more variables that are correlated (cross-lagged panel and structural equations analysis); (3) examine relationships among variables that are measured at different levels of analysis (multilevel modeling); and (4) identify basic dimensions that underlie sets of correlations (factor analysis).

Our emphasis in this chapter is on understanding what each of these methods can tell us about the relationships among correlated variables and *not* on how to actually use them. Each of these strategies utilizes relatively sophisticated statistical analyses that would take us beyond the scope of this book. But you need to understand what these methodological approaches are so that you can understand studies that use them.

PREDICTING BEHAVIOR: REGRESSION STRATEGIES

Regression analyses are often used to extend the findings of correlational research. Once we know that certain variables are correlated with a particular psychological response or trait, regression analysis allows us to develop equations that describe precisely how those variables relate to that response. These regression equations both provide us with a mathematical description of how the variables are related and allow us to predict one variable from the others.

For example, imagine that you are an industrial-organizational psychologist who works for a large company. One of your responsibilities is to develop better ways of selecting employees from the large number of people who apply for jobs with your company. You have developed a job aptitude test that is administered to everyone who applies for a job. When you looked at the relationship between scores on this test and how employees were rated by their supervisors after working for the company for 6 months, you found that scores on the aptitude test correlated positively with ratings of job performance.

Armed with this information, you should be able to *predict* applicants' future job performance, allowing you to make better decisions about whom to hire. One consequence of two variables being correlated is that knowing a person's score on one variable allows us to predict his or her score on the other variable. Our prediction is seldom perfectly accurate, but if the two variables are correlated, we can predict scores at better than chance levels.

Linear Regression

This ability to predict scores on one variable from one or more other variables is accomplished through **regression analysis**. The goal of regression analysis is to develop a **regression equation** from which we can predict scores on one variable on the basis of scores on one or more other variables. This procedure is quite useful in situations in which psychologists must make predictions. For example, regression equations are used to predict students' college performance from entrance exams and high school grades. They are also used in business and industrial settings to predict a job applicant's potential job performance on the basis of test scores and other factors. Regression analysis is also widely used in basic research settings to describe how variables are related to one another. Understanding how one variable is predicted by other variables can help us understand the psychological processes that are involved. The precise manner in which a regression equation is calculated does not concern us here. What is important is that you know what a regression analysis is and the rationale behind it, should you encounter one in the research literature.

You will recall that correlation indicates a *linear* relationship between two variables. If the relationship between two variables is linear, a straight line can be drawn through the data to represent the relationship between the variables. For example, Figure 8.1 shows the scatter plot for the relationship between the employees' test scores and job performance ratings for which we calculated the correlation in Chapter 7. (Remember that we found that the correlation between the test scores and job performance was +.82; see page 148.) The line drawn through the scatter plot portrays the nature of the relationship between test scores and performance ratings. In following the trend in the data, this line reflects how test scores and job performance tend to be related.

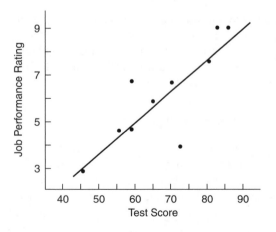

FIGURE 8.1   A Regression Line.   This is a scatter plot of the data in Table 6.2. The x-axis shows scores on an employment test, and the y-axis shows employees' job performance ratings 6 months later. The line running through the scatter plot is the regression line for the data—the line that best represents, or fits, the data. A regression line such as this can be described mathematically by the equation for a straight line. The equation for this particular regression line is $y = -2.76 + .13x$.

The goal of regression analysis is to find the equation for the line that best fits the pattern of the data. If we can find the equation for the line that best portrays the relationship between the two variables, this equation will provide us with a useful mathematical description of how the variables are related and also allow us to predict one variable from the other.

You may remember from high school geometry class that a line can be represented by the equation $y = mx + b$, where m is the slope of the line and b is the y-intercept. In linear regression, the symbols are different and the order of the terms is reversed, but the equation is the same:

$$y = \beta_0 + \beta_1 x.$$

In a regression equation, y is the variable we would like to predict. The variable we want to predict is called the **dependent variable**, **criterion variable**, or **outcome variable**. The lowercase x represents the variable we are using to predict y; x is called the **predictor variable**. β_0 is called the **regression constant** (or *beta-zero*) and is the y-intercept of the line that best fits the data in the scatter plot; it is equivalent to b in the formula you learned in geometry class. The **regression coefficient**, β_1, is the slope of the line that best represents the relationship between the predictor variable (x) and the criterion variable (y). It is equivalent to m in the formula for a straight line. The regression equation for the line for the data in Figure 8.1 is

$$y = -2.76 + .13x$$

or

Job performance rating $= -2.76 + .13$(test score).

If x and y represent any two variables that are correlated, we can predict a person's y-score by plugging his or her x-score into the equation. For example, suppose a job applicant obtained a test score of 75. Using the regression equation for the scatter plot in Figure 8.1, we can solve for y (job performance rating):

$$y = -2.76 + .13(75) = 6.99.$$

On the basis of knowing how well he or she performed on the test, we would predict this applicant's job performance rating after 6 months will be 6.99. Thus, if job ability scores and job performance are correlated, we can, within limits, predict an applicant's future job performance from the score he or she obtains on the employment test.

We can extend the idea of linear regression to include more than one predictor variable. For example, you might decide to predict job performance on the basis of four variables: aptitude test scores, high school grade point average (GPA), a measure of work motivation, and an index of physical strength. Using **multiple regression analysis**, you could develop a regression equation that includes all four predictors. Once the equation is determined, you could predict job performance from an applicant's scores on the four predictor variables. Typically, using more than one predictor improves the accuracy of our prediction over using only one.

Types of Multiple Regression

Researchers distinguish among three primary types of multiple regression procedures: standard, stepwise, and hierarchical multiple regression. These types of analyses differ with respect to how the predictor variables are entered into the regression equation as the equation is constructed. The predictor variables may be entered all at once (standard), based on the strength of their ability to help predict the criterion variable (stepwise), or in an order predetermined by the researcher (hierarchical).

STANDARD MULTIPLE REGRESSION. In **standard multiple regression** (also called **simultaneous multiple regression**), all of the predictor variables are entered into the regression analysis at the same time. So, for example, we could create a regression equation to predict job performance by entering simultaneously into the analysis employees' aptitude test scores, high school GPA, a measure of work motivation, and an index of physical strength. The resulting regression equation would provide a regression constant, as well as separate regression coefficients for each predictor. For example, the regression equation might look something like this:

Job performance rating =
$$-2.79 + .17 \text{ (test score)} + 1.29(\text{GPA}) + .85$$
(work motivation) + .04 (physical strength).

By entering into the equation particular applicants' scores, we will get a predicted value for their job performance rating.

Behavioral Research Case Study
Standard Multiple Regression Analysis: Do You Know How Smart You Are?

Researchers sometimes use standard or simultaneous multiple regression simply to see whether a set of predictor variables (a set of *x*'s) is related to some outcome variable (*y*). Paulhus, Lysy, and Yik (1998) used it in a study that examined the usefulness of self-report measures of intelligence. Because administering standardized IQ tests is time-consuming and expensive, Paulhus et al. wondered whether researchers could simply rely on participants' ratings of how intelligent they are; if so, self-reported intelligence could be used instead of real IQ scores in some research settings. After obtaining two samples of more than 300 participants each, they administered four measures that asked participants to rate their own intelligence, along with an objective IQ test.

They then conducted a standard multiple regression analysis to see whether scores on these four self-report measures of intelligence predicted real IQ scores. In this regression analysis, all four self-report measures were entered simultaneously as predictors of participants' IQ scores. The results of their analyses showed that, as a set, the four self-report measures of intelligence accounted for only 10% to 16% of the variance in real intelligence scores (depending on the sample). Clearly, asking people to rate their intelligence is no substitute for assessing intelligence directly with standardized IQ tests.

STEPWISE MULTIPLE REGRESSION.   Rather than entering the predictors all at once, **stepwise multiple regression** analysis builds the regression equation by entering the predictor variables one at a time. In the first step of the analysis, the predictor variable that, by itself, most strongly predicts the criterion variable is entered into the equation. For reasons that should be obvious, the predictor variable that enters into the equation in Step 1 will be the variable that correlates most highly with the criterion variable that we are trying to predict (in the example used earlier, job performance rating). Then, in Step 2, the equation adds the predictor variable that contributes most strongly to the prediction of the outcome variable *given that the first predictor variable is already in the equation.* The predictor variable that is entered in Step 2 will be the one that helps to account for the greatest amount of variance in the criterion variable above and beyond the variance that was accounted for by the predictor that was entered in Step 1.

Importantly, the variable that enters the analysis in Step 2 may or may not be the variable that has the second highest Pearson correlation with the criterion variable. If the predictor variable that entered the equation in Step 1 is highly correlated with other predictors, it may already account for the variance that they could account for in the criterion variable; if so, the other predictors may not be needed. A stepwise regression analysis enters predictor variables into the equation based on their ability to predict *unique* variance in the outcome variable—variance that is not already predicted by predictor variables that are already in the equation.

To understand this point, let's return to our example of predicting job performance from aptitude test scores, high school GPA, work motivation, and physical strength. Let's imagine that test scores and GPA correlate highly with each other ($r = .75$), and that the four predictor variables correlate with job performance as shown here:

Correlation with Job Performance	
Aptitude test scores	.68
High school GPA	.55
Work motivation	.40
Physical strength	.22

In a stepwise regression analysis, aptitude test scores would enter the equation in Step 1 because this predictor correlates most highly with job performance;

by itself, aptitude test scores account for the greatest amount of variance in job performance ratings. But which predictor will enter the equation in the second step? Although GPA has the second highest correlation with job performance, it might not enter the equation in Step 2 because it correlates highly with aptitude test scores. If aptitude test scores have already accounted for the variance in job performance that GPA can also predict, GPA is no longer a useful predictor. Put differently, if we calculated the partial correlation between GPA and job performance while statistically removing (partialing out) the influence of aptitude test scores (see Chapter 7, p. 156), we would find that the partial correlation would be small or nonexistent, showing that GPA is not needed to predict job performance if we are already using aptitude test scores as a predictor.

The stepwise regression analysis will proceed step by step, entering predictor variables according to their ability to add uniquely to the prediction of the criterion variable. The stepwise process will stop when one of two things happens. On one hand, if each of the predictor variables can make a unique contribution to the prediction of the criterion variable, all of them will end up in the regression equation. On the other hand, the analysis may reach a point at which, with only some of the predictors in the equation, the remaining predictors cannot uniquely predict any remaining variance in the criterion variable. If this happens, the analysis stops without entering all of the predictors (and this may happen even if those remaining predictors are correlated with the variable being predicted). To use our example, perhaps after aptitude test scores and work motivation are entered into the regression equation, neither GPA nor physical strength can further improve the prediction of job performance. In this case, the final regression equation would include only two predictors because the remaining two variables do not enhance our ability to predict job performance.

Behavioral Research Case Study
Stepwise Multiple Regression: Predictors of Blushing

I once conducted a study in which we were interested in identifying factors that predict the degree to which people blush (Leary & Meadows, 1991). We administered a Blushing Propensity Scale to 220 participants, along with measures of 13 other psychological variables. We then used stepwise multiple regression analysis, using the 13 variables as predictors of blushing propensity.

The results of the regression analysis showed that blushing propensity was best predicted by embarrassability (the ease with which a person becomes embarrassed), which entered the equation in the first step. Social anxiety (the tendency to feel nervous in social situations) entered the equation in Step 2 because, with embarrassability in the equation, it made the greatest unique contribution of the remaining 12 predictors to the prediction of blushing scores. Self-esteem entered the equation in Step 3, followed in Step 4 by the degree to which a person is repulsed or offended by crass and vulgar behavior. After four steps, the analysis stopped and entered no more predictors even though six additional predictor variables (such as fear of negative evaluation and self-consciousness) correlated significantly with blushing propensity. These remaining variables did not enter the equation because, with the first four variables already in the equation, none of the others predicted unique variance in blushing propensity scores.

HIERARCHICAL MULTIPLE REGRESSION. In **hierarchical multiple regression**, the predictor variables are entered into the equation in an order that is predetermined by the researcher based on hypotheses that he or she wants to test. As predictor variables are entered one by one into the regression analysis, their unique contributions to the prediction of the outcome variable can be assessed at each step. That is, by entering the predictor variables in some prespecified order, the researcher can determine whether particular predictors can account for unique variance in the outcome variable with the effects of other predictor variables statistically removed. Hierarchical multiple regression partials out or removes the effects of the predictor variables entered on earlier steps to see whether predictors that are entered later make unique contributions to the outcome variable. Hierarchical multiple regression is a very versatile analysis that can be used to answer many kinds of questions. Two common uses are to eliminate confounding variables and to test mediational hypotheses.

One of the reasons that we cannot infer causality from correlation is that, because correlational research cannot control or eliminate extraneous variables, correlated variables are naturally confounded. Confounded variables are variables that tend to occur together, making their distinct effects on behavior difficult to separate. For example, we know that depressed people tend to blame themselves for bad things that happen more than nondepressed people; that is, depression and self-blame are correlated. For all of the reasons discussed earlier, we cannot conclude from this correlation that depression causes people to blame themselves or that self-blame causes depression. One explanation of this correlation is that depression is confounded with low self-esteem. Depression and low self-esteem tend to occur together, so it is difficult to determine whether things that are correlated with depression are a function of depression per se or whether they might be due to low self-esteem. A hierarchical regression analysis could provide a partial answer to this question. We could conduct a two-step hierarchical regression analysis in which we entered self-esteem as a predictor of self-blame in the first step. Of course, we would find that self-esteem predicted self-blame. More importantly, however, the relationship between self-esteem and self-blame would be partialed out in Step 1. Now, when we add depression to the regression equation in Step 2, we can see whether depression predicts self-blame *above and beyond* low self-esteem. If depression predicts self-blame even after self-esteem was entered into the regression equation (and its influence on self-blame was statistically removed), we can conclude that the relationship between depression and self-blame is not likely due to the fact that depression and low self-esteem

are confounded. However, if depression no longer predicts self-blame when it is entered in Step 2, with self-esteem in the equation, the results will suggest that the relationship between depression and self-blame may be due to its confound with self-esteem.

A second use of hierarchical multiple regression is to test mediational hypotheses. Many hypotheses specify that the effects of a predictor variable on a criterion variable are mediated by one or more other variables. Mediation effects occur when the effect of x on y occurs because of an intervening variable, z. For example, we know that regularly practicing yoga reduces stress and promotes a sense of calm. To understand why yoga has these effects, we could conduct hierarchical regression analyses in which we enter possible mediators of the effect in Step 1. For example, we might hypothesize that some of the beneficial effects of yoga are mediated by its effects on the amount of mental "chatter" that goes on in the person's mind. That is, yoga helps to reduce mental chatter, which then leads to greater relaxation (because the person isn't thinking as much about worrisome things). To test whether mental chatter does, in fact, mediate the relationship between yoga and relaxation, we would enter measures of mental chatter (such as indices of obsessional tendencies, self-focused thinking, and worry) in Step 1 of the analysis. Of course, these measures will probably predict low relaxation, but that's not our focus. Rather, we are interested in what happens when we enter the amount of time that people practice yoga in Step 2 of the analysis. If the variables entered in Step 1 mediate the relationship between yoga and relaxation, then yoga should no longer predict relaxation when it is entered in the second step. Removing variance that is due to the mediators in Step 1 would eliminate yoga's ability to predict relaxation. However, if yoga practice predicts relaxation just as strongly with the influence of the hypothesized mediator variables removed in Step 1, then we conclude that yoga's effects are not mediated by reductions in mental chatter. Researchers are often interested in the processes that mediate the influence of one variable on another, and hierarchical regression can help them to test hypotheses about these mediators.

Behavioral Research Case Study
Hierarchical Regression: Personal and Interpersonal Antecedents of Peer Victimization

Hodges and Perry (1999) conducted a study to investigate factors that lead certain children to be victimized—verbally or physically assaulted—by their peers at school. Data were collected from 173 preadolescent children who completed several measures of personality and behavior, some of which involved personal factors (such as depression) and other measures involved interpersonal factors (such as difficulty getting along with others). They also provided information regarding the victimization of other children they knew. The participants completed these measures two times spaced one year apart.

Multiple regression analyses were used to predict victimization from the various personal and interpersonal factors. Of course, personal and interpersonal factors are likely to be confounded because certain personal difficulties may lead to social problems, and vice versa. Thus, the researchers wanted to test the separate effects of personal and interpersonal factors on victimization while statistically removing the effects of the other set. They used hierarchical regression to do this because it allowed them to enter predictors into the regression analysis in any order they desired. Thus, one hierarchical regression analysis was conducted to predict victimization scores at Time 2 (the second administration of the measures) from personal factors measured at Time 1, while removing the influence of interpersonal factors (also at Time 1). To do this, interpersonal factors were entered as predictors (and their influence on victimization removed) before the personal factors were entered into the regression equation. Another regression analysis reversed the order in which predictors were entered, putting personal factors in the regression equation first, then testing the unique effects of interpersonal factors. In this way, the effects of each set of predictors could be tested while eliminating the confounding influence of the other set.

Results showed that both personal and interpersonal factors measured at Time 1 predicted the degree to which children were victimized a year later. Personal factors such as anxiety, depression, social withdrawal, and peer hovering (standing around without joining in) predicted victimization, as did scoring low on a measure of physical strength (presumably because strong children are less likely to be bullied). The only interpersonal factor that predicted victimization after personal problems were partialed out was the degree to which the child was rejected by his or her peers. In contrast, being aggressive, argumentative, disruptive, and dishonest were unrelated to victimization. Using hierarchical regression analyses allows researchers to get a clearer picture of the relationships between particular predictors and a criterion variable, uncontaminated by confounding variables.

Multiple Correlation

When researchers use multiple regression analyses, they not only want to develop an equation for predicting people's scores but also need to know *how well* the predictor, or *x*, variables predict *y*. After all, if the predictors do a poor job of predicting the outcome variable, we wouldn't want to use the equation to make decisions about job applicants, students, or others. To express the usefulness of a regression equation for predicting a criterion variable, researchers calculate the **multiple correlation coefficient**, symbolized by the letter *R*. *R* describes the degree of relationship between the criterion variable (*y*) and the *set* of predictor variables (the *x*'s). Unlike the Pearson *r*, multiple correlation coefficients

range only from .00 to 1.00. The larger *R* is, the better job the equation does of predicting the outcome variable from the predictor variables.

Just as a Pearson correlation coefficient can be squared to indicate the percentage of variance in one variable that is accounted for by another, a multiple correlation coefficient can be squared to show the percentage of variance in the criterion variable (*y*) that can be accounted for by the *set* of predictor variables. In the study of blushing described previously, the multiple correlation, *R*, between the set of four predictors and blushing propensity was .63. Squaring *R* (.63 × .63) gives us an R^2 value of .40, indicating that 40% of the variance in participants' blushing propensity scores was accounted for by the set of four predictors.

ASSESSING DIRECTIONALITY: CROSS-LAGGED AND STRUCTURAL EQUATIONS ANALYSIS

We've stressed several times that researchers cannot infer causality from correlation. In Chapter 7, we saw how partial correlation can be used to tentatively test whether certain third variables are responsible for the correlation between two other variables, and in this chapter, we discussed how hierarchical regression analysis can help disentangle confounded variables. But even if we conclude that the correlation between *x* and *y* is unlikely to be due to certain other variables, we still cannot determine from a correlation whether *x* causes *y* or *y* causes *x*. Fortunately, researchers have developed procedures for testing the viability of their causal hypotheses. Although these procedures cannot tell us *for certain* whether *x* causes *y* or *y* causes *x*, they can give us more or less confidence in one causal direction than the other.

Cross-Lagged Panel Design

A simple case involves the **cross-lagged panel correlation design** (Cook & Campbell, 1979). In this design, the correlation between two variables, *x* and *y*, is calculated at two different points in time. Then correlations are calculated between measurements of the two variables across time. For example, we would correlate the scores on *x* taken at Time 1 with the scores on *y* taken at Time 2. Likewise, we would calculate the scores on *y* at Time 1 with those on *x* at Time 2. If *x* causes *y*, we should find that the correlation between *x* at Time 1 and *y* at Time 2 is larger than the correlation between *y* at Time 1 and *x* at Time 2. This is because the relationship between a cause (variable *x*) and its effect (variable *y*) should be stronger if the causal variable is measured before rather than after its effect.

A cross-lagged panel design was used to study the link between violence on television and aggressive behavior. More than 40 years of research has demonstrated that watching violent television programs is associated with aggression. For example, the amount of violence a person watches on TV correlates positively with the person's level of aggressiveness. However, we should not infer from this correlation

that television violence *causes* aggression. It is just as plausible to conclude that people who are naturally aggressive simply like to watch violent TV shows.

Eron, Huesmann, Lefkowitz, and Walder (1972) used a cross-lagged panel correlation design to examine the direction of the relationship between television violence and aggressive behavior. These researchers studied a sample of 427 participants twice: once when the participants were in the third grade and again 10 years later. On both occasions, participants provided a list of their favorite TV shows, which were later rated for their violent content. In addition, participants' aggressiveness was rated by their peers.

Correlations were calculated between TV violence and participants' aggressiveness across the two time periods. The results for the male participants are shown in Figure 8.2. The important correlations are on the diagonals of Figure 8.2—the correlations between TV violence at Time 1 and aggressiveness at Time 2, and between aggressiveness at Time 1 and TV violence at Time 2. As you can see, the correlation between earlier TV violence and later aggression (*r* = .31) is larger than the correlation between earlier aggressiveness and later TV violence (*r* = .01). This pattern is consistent with the idea that watching televised violence causes participants to become more aggressive rather than the other way around.

Structural Equations Modeling

A more sophisticated way to test causal hypotheses from correlational data is provided by **structural equations modeling**. Given the pattern of correlations among a set of variables, certain causal explanations of the relationships among the variables are more logical or likely than others. Given the pattern of correlations among the variables, certain causal relationships may be virtually impossible, whereas other causal relationships are plausible.

To use a simple example, imagine that we are trying to understand the causal relationships among three variables—*X, Y,* and *Z*. If we predict that *X* causes *Y* and then *Y* causes *Z*, then we should find not only that *X* and *Y* are correlated but also that the relationship between *X* and *Y* is stronger than the correlation between *X* and *Z*. (Variables that are directly linked in

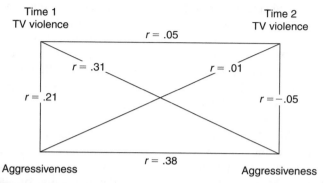

FIGURE 8.2 **A Cross-Lagged Panel Design.** The important correlations in this cross-lagged panel design are on the diagonals. The correlation between the amount of TV violence watched by the children at Time 1 and aggressiveness 10 years later ($r = .31$) was larger than the correlation between aggressiveness at Time 1 and TV watching 10 years later ($r = .01$). This pattern is more consistent with the notion that watching TV violence causes aggressive behavior than with the idea that being aggressive disposes children to watch TV violence. Strictly speaking, however, we can never infer causality from correlational data such as these.

Source: Eron, L. D., Huesmann, L. R., Lefkowitz, M. M., & Walder, L. O. (1972). Does television violence cause aggression? *American Psychologist, 27,* 253–263. Copyright © 1972 by the American Psychological Association. Adapted with permission.

a causal chain should correlate more highly than variables that are more distally related.) If either of these findings does not occur, then our hypothesis that $X \rightarrow Y \rightarrow Z$ would appear to be false.

To perform structural equations modeling, the researcher makes precise predictions regarding how three or more variables are causally related. (In fact, researchers often devise two or more competing predictions based on different theories.) Each prediction (or model) implies that the variables should be correlated in a particular way. Imagine that we have two competing predictions about the relationships among X, Y, and Z as shown in Figure 8.3. Hypothesis A says that X causes Y and then Y causes Z. In contrast, Hypothesis B predicts that X causes Z, and then Z causes Y.

We would expect X, Y, and Z to correlate with each other differently if Hypothesis A were true than if Hypothesis B were true. Thus, Hypothesis A predicts that the correlation matrix for X, Y, and Z will show a different pattern of correlations than Hypothesis B. For example, Hypothesis B predicts that variables X and Z should correlate more strongly than Hypothesis A does. This is because Hypothesis A assumes that X and Z are not directly

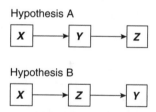

FIGURE 8.3 **Two Possible Models of the Causal Relationships Among Three Variables.** If we know that variables X, Y, and Z are correlated, they may be causally related in a number of ways, two of which are shown here. Hypothesis A suggests that variable X causes Y, which then causes Z. Hypothesis B suggests that variable X causes Z, and Z causes Y.

related, being mediated only by their relationships with variable Y. In contrast, Hypothesis B assumes a direct causal relationship between X and Z, which should lead X and Z to be more strongly correlated.

Structural equations modeling mathematically compares the correlation matrix implied by a particular hypothesized model to the real correlation matrix based on the data that we collect. The analysis examines the degree to which the pattern of correlations generated from our predicted model matches or fits the correlation matrix based on the data. If the correlation matrix predicted by our model closely resembles the real correlation matrix, then we have a certain degree of support for the hypothesized model. Structural equations analyses provide a **fit index** that indicates how well the hypothesized model fits the data. By comparing the fit indexes for different predicted models, we can determine whether one of our models fits the data better than other alternative models. Structural equations models can get very complex, adding not only more variables but also multiple measures of each variable to improve our measurement of the constructs we are studying.

When single measures of each construct are used, researchers sometimes call structural equations analysis *path analysis.* In a more complex form of structural equations modeling, sometimes called *latent variable modeling*, each construct in the model is assessed by two or more measures. Using multiple measures of each construct not only provides a better, more accurate measure of the underlying, or latent, variable than any single

measure can, but also allows us to account for measurement error in our model. You may recall from Chapter 3 that all measures contain a certain amount of measurement error that lowers their reliability. By using several measures of each construct, structural equations modeling (specifically latent variable modeling) can estimate measurement error and deal with it more effectively than most other statistical analyses can.

It is important to remember that structural equations modeling cannot provide us with confident conclusions about causality. We are, after all, still dealing with correlational data, and as I've stressed again and again, we cannot infer causality from correlation. However, structural equations modeling can provide information regarding the *plausibility* of causal hypotheses. If the analysis indicates that the model fits the data, then we have reason to regard that model as a reasonable causal explanation (though not necessarily the one and only correct explanation). Conversely, if the model does not fit the data, then we can conclude that the hypothesized model is not likely to be correct.

Behavioral Research Case Study
Structural Equations Modeling: Partner Attractiveness and Intention to Practice Safe Sex

Since the beginning of the AIDS epidemic in the 1980s, health psychologists have devoted a great deal of attention to ways of increasing condom use. Part of this research has focused on understanding how people think about the risks of having unprotected sexual intercourse. Agocha and Cooper (1999) were interested specifically in the effects of a potential sexual partner's sexual history and physical attractiveness on people's willingness to have unprotected sex. In this study, 280 college-age participants were given information about a member of the other sex that included a description of the person's sexual history (indicating that the person had between 1 and 20 previous sexual partners) as well as a yearbook-style color photograph of either an attractive or unattractive individual. Participants then rated the degree to which they were interested in dating or having sexual intercourse with the target person, the likelihood of getting AIDS or other sexually transmitted diseases from this individual, the likelihood that they would discuss sex-risk issues with the person prior to having sex, and the likelihood of using a condom if intercourse were to occur.

Among many other analyses, Agocha and Cooper conducted a path analysis (a structural equations model with one measure of each variable) to examine the effects of the target's sexual history and physical attractiveness on perceived risk and intention to use a condom. The path diagram shown in Figure 8.4 fits the data well, indicating that it is a plausible model of how these variables are related. The arrows in the diagram indicate the presence of statistically significant relationships. The numbers beside each arrow are path coefficients; they are analogous to the regression coefficients discussed earlier and reflect the strength of the relationship for each effect.

Examine the path diagram as I describe a few of the findings. First, participants' interest in dating or having sex with the target were predicted by both gender (male participants were more interested than females) and, not

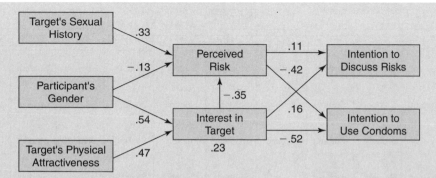

FIGURE 8.4 Structural Diagram from the Agocha and Cooper Study. The results of structural equations modeling are often shown in path diagrams such as this one. Arrows indicate significant relationships; the numbers are path coefficients that reflect the strength of the relationships. This model fits the data well, suggesting that it is a plausible model of how the variables might be related. However, because the data are correlational, any causal conclusions we draw are tentative.

Source: Agocha, V. B., & Cooper, M. L. (1999). Risk perceptions and safer-sex intentions: Does a partner's physical attractiveness undermine the use of risk-relevant information? *Personality and Social Psychology Bulletin, 25,* 746–759, copyright © 1999 by Sage. Reprinted by permission of Sage Publications, Inc.

surprisingly, the target's physical attractiveness. However, the target's sexual history did not predict interest in dating or sex (there is no arrow going from *Target's Sexual History* to *Interest in Target*).

Second, perceived risk of getting AIDS was predicted by gender (women were more concerned than men), target's sexual history (more sexually active targets were regarded as greater risks), and participants' interest in the target. The latter finding is particularly interesting: Participants rated having sex with targets in whom they were more interested as less risky, which is, of course, not particularly rational.

If we look at predictors of the intention to use condoms, we see that the intention to practice safe sex is predicted not only by perceived risk but also by the degree to which the participant was interested in the target. Regardless of the perceived risk, participants were less likely to intend to use a condom the more interested they were in the target and the more attractive the target was! Agocha and Cooper concluded that nonrational factors, such how appealing and attractive one finds a potential sexual partner, can undermine more rational concerns for one's health and safety.

ANALYZING NESTED DATA: MULTILEVEL MODELING

Many data sets in the behavioral and social sciences have a "nested" structure. To understand what nested data are like, imagine that you are interested in variables that predict academic achievement in elementary school. You pick a number of elementary schools in your county and then choose certain classrooms from each school. Then, to get your sample, you select students from each classroom to participate in your study. In this example, each participant is a student in a particular classroom that is located in a particular school. Thus, we can say that the students are "nested" within classrooms and

that the classrooms are "nested" within schools (see Figure 8.5). Or, imagine that you are conducting an experiment on decision-making in small groups. You have 18 groups of four participants each work on a laboratory task after receiving one of three kinds of experimental instructions. In this case, the participants are nested within the four-person groups, and the groups are nested within one of the three experimental conditions. Data that have this kind of nested structure present both special problems and special opportunities for which researchers use an approach called **multilevel modeling**.

The special problem with **nested designs** is that the responses of the participants within any particular group are not independent of one

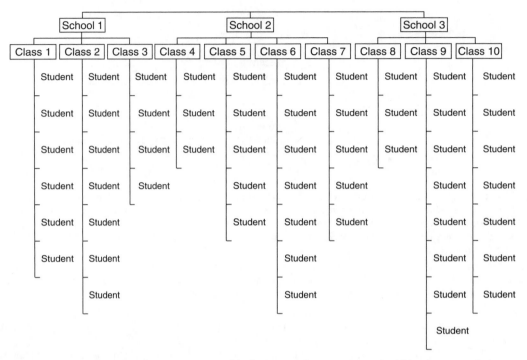

FIGURE 8.5 A Nested Data Structure. In this design, students are nested within classes, and classes are nested within schools.

another. For example, students in a particular classroom share a single teacher, cover precisely the same course material, and also influence one another directly. Similarly, participants who work together in a four-person laboratory group obviously influence one another's reactions. Yet, most statistical analyses require that each participant's responses on the dependent variables are independent of all other participants' responses, an assumption that is violated when data are nested. Multilevel modeling can deal with the problem of nonindependence of participants' responses within each nested group.

The special opportunity that nested data offer is the ability for researchers to study variables that operate at different levels of analysis. For example, a student's academic performance is influenced by variables that operate at the level of the individual participant (the student's ability, motivation,

personality, and past academic experiences, for example); at the level of the classroom (class size, the teacher's style, and the proportion of low-performing students in the class, for example); and at the level of the school (such as policies, programs, and budgetary priorities that are unique to a particular school). Multilevel modeling allows us to tease apart these various influences on student performance by analyzing variables operating at all levels of the nested structure simultaneously. It also permits researchers to explore the possibility that variables operating at one level of the nested structure have different effects depending on variables that are operating at other levels. So, for example, perhaps a certain school program (a school-level variable) affects students who have a particular level of ability but does not affect students who have another level of ability (a student-level variable). Multilevel modeling allows us to capitalize on the opportunity to examine relationships among variables across the levels of the design.

Multilevel modeling is known by a number of names, including multilevel random coefficient analysis and hierarchical linear modeling. The statistics underlying multilevel modeling are complex, but the general idea is simply to analyze the relationships among variables both within and across the nested levels.

Behavioral Research Case Study
Multilevel Modeling: Birth Order and Intelligence

Several studies have shown that intelligence is negatively related to birth order. These studies show that, on average, first-born children have higher IQ scores than second-born children, who have higher IQ's than children who were born third, who have higher IQs than fourth-born children, and so on. One explanation of this effect is that each additional child born into a family dilutes the intellectual environment in the home. For example, a first-born child sees and participates in many interactions with adults (at least until a sibling is born later), whereas a later-born child sees and participates in many more interactions with other children from the day they are born, interactions that are obviously at a lower intellectual level. As a result, later-born children are not exposed to as many adult-level interactions and end up with lower intelligence.

Before those of you who are first-borns start feeling good about yourselves or those of you who are later-born children become defensive, consider a study by Wichman, Rodgers, and MacCallum (2006) that examined this issue. Wichman and his colleagues pointed out that virtually all studies of this phenomenon are fundamentally flawed. Previous researchers would obtain a large sample of children, find out their birth order, and obtain their scores on a measure of intelligence. And, typically, the sample would contain many sets of siblings who were from the same family. From the standpoint of understanding family influences on intelligence, these designs have two problems—they fail to distinguish influences that occur within families from those that occur between families, and they violate the statistical requirement that each participant's scores are independent of all other participants' scores (because data for children from the same family cannot be considered independent).

The data used to study birth order effects have a nested structure in which children are nested within families and, thus, multilevel modeling should be used to analyze them. Using data from the National Longitudinal Survey of Youth, the researchers obtained birth order and intelligence data for 3,671 children. When they tested the relationship between birth order and intelligence without taking into account the nested structure of the data (i.e., without considering whether certain children were from the same family), their results confirmed previous studies showing that birth order is inversely related to intelligence. But when they analyzed the data properly using multilevel modeling, no relationship between birth order and intelligence was obtained.

Why would multilevel modeling produce different findings than previous analyses? When other researchers have analyzed children's data without taking into account the fact that the children were nested within families, differences in the children's intelligence could be due either to birth order or to differences in the families from which the children came. If any differences among their families were confounded with birth order, researchers might mistakenly conclude that differences in intelligence were due to birth order rather than to differences between families. Consider, for example, that children from larger families are more likely to have higher birth orders (such as being the sixth- or seventh-born child) than children from small families. If family size is associated with other variables that influence intelligence—such as socioeconomic status, the IQ or educational level of the parents, or the mother's age when she started having children—then it will appear that higher birth order leads to lower intelligence when, in fact, the lower intelligence is due to these other variables that predict having very large families.

By accounting for the fact that children were nested within families, multilevel modeling separated birth order from other family influences. Although other researchers raised questions about their analyses and conclusions, Wichman, Rodgers, and MacCallum (2007) published a second article that rebutted those arguments, justified the use of multilevel modeling, and provided analyses of new data to show that birth order is unrelated to intelligence.

UNCOVERING UNDERLYING DIMENSIONS: FACTOR ANALYSIS

Factor analysis refers to a class of statistical techniques that are used to analyze the interrelationships among a large number of variables. Its purpose is to identify the underlying dimensions or factors that account for the relationships that are observed among the variables.

If we look at the correlations among a large number of variables, we typically see that certain sets of variables correlate highly among themselves but weakly with other sets of variables. Presumably, these patterns of correlations occur because the highly correlated variables measure the same general construct, but the uncorrelated variables measure different constructs. That is, the presence of correlations among several variables suggests that the variables are each related to aspects of a more basic underlying factor. Factor analysis is used to identify the underlying factors (also called *latent variables*) that account for the observed patterns of relationships among a set of variables.

An Intuitive Approach

Suppose for a moment that you obtained participants' scores on five variables that we'll call *A, B, C, D,* and *E.* When you calculated the correlations among these five variables, you obtained the following correlation matrix:

	A	**B**	**C**	**D**	**E**
A	1.00	.78	.85	.01	−.07
B	—	1.00	.70	.09	.00
C	—	—	1.00	−.02	.04
D	—	—	—	1.00	.86
E	—	—	—	—	1.00

Look closely at the pattern of correlations. Based on the pattern, what conclusions would you draw about the relationships among variables *A, B, C, D,* and *E*? Which variables seem to be related to each other?

As you can see, variables *A, B,* and *C* correlate highly with each other, but each correlates weakly with variables *D* and *E.* Variables *D* and *E,* on the other hand, are highly correlated. This pattern suggests that these five variables may be measuring only

two different constructs: *A, B,* and *C* seem to measure aspects of one construct, whereas *D* and *E* measure something else. In the language of factor analysis, two **factors** underlie these data and account for the observed pattern of correlations among the variables.

Basics of Factor Analysis

Although identifying the factor structure may be relatively easy with a few variables, imagine trying to identify the factors in a data set that contained 20 or 30 or even 100 variables! Factor analysis identifies and expresses the factor structure by using mathematical procedures rather than by eyeballing the data as we have just done.

The mathematical details of factor analysis are complex and don't concern us here, but let us look briefly at how factor analyses are conducted and what they tell us. The grist for the factor analytic mill consists of correlations among a set of variables. Factor analysis attempts to identify the minimum number of factors or dimensions that will do a reasonably good job of accounting for the observed relationships among the variables. At one extreme, if all of the variables are highly correlated with one another, the analysis will identify a single factor; in essence, all of the observed variables are measuring aspects of the same thing. At the other extreme, if the variables are totally uncorrelated, the analysis will identify as many factors as there are variables. This makes sense; if the variables are not at all related, there are no underlying factors that account for their interrelationships. Each variable is measuring something different, and there are as many factors as variables.

The solution to a factor analysis is presented in a **factor matrix**. Table 8.1 shows the factor matrix for the variables we examined in the preceding correlation matrix. Down the left column of the factor matrix are the original variables—*A, B, C, D,* and *E.* Across the top are the factors that have been identified from the analysis. The numerical entries in the table are **factor loadings**, which are the correlations of the variables with the factors. A variable that correlates with a factor is said to *load* on that factor. (Do not confuse these factor loadings with the correlations among the original set of variables.)

TABLE 8.1	A Factor Matrix	
	Factor	
Variable	**1**	**2**
A	.97	−.04
B	.80	.04
C	.87	.00
D	.03	.93
E	−.01	.92

This is the factor matrix for a factor analysis of the correlation matrix on the previous page. Two factors were obtained, suggesting that the five variables measure two underlying factors. A researcher would interpret the factor matrix by looking at the variables that loaded highest on each factor. Factor 1 is defined by variables A, B, and C. Factor 2 is defined by variables D and E.

Researchers use these factor loadings to interpret and label the factors. By seeing which variables load on a factor, researchers can usually identify the nature of a factor. In interpreting the factor structure, researchers typically consider variables that load at least ±.30 on each factor. That is, they look at the variables that correlate at least ±.30 with a factor and try to discern what those variables have in common. By examining the variables that load on a factor, they can usually determine the nature of the underlying construct.

For example, as you can see in Table 8.1, variables A, B, and C each load greater than .30 on Factor 1, whereas the factor loadings of variables D and E with Factor 1 are quite small. Factor 2, on the other hand, is defined primarily by variables D and E. This pattern indicates that variables A, B, and C reflect aspects of a single factor, whereas D and E reflect aspects of a different factor. In a real factor analysis, we would know what the original variables (A, B, C, D, and E) were measuring, and we would use that knowledge to identify and label the factors we obtained. For example, we might know that variables A, B, and C were all related to language and verbal ability, whereas variables D and E were measures of conceptual ability and reasoning. Thus, Factor 1 would be a verbal ability factor and Factor 2 would be a conceptual ability factor.

Uses of Factor Analysis

Factor analysis has three basic uses. First, it is used to study the underlying structure of psychological constructs. Many questions in behavioral science involve the structure of behavior and experience. How many distinct mental abilities are there? What are the basic traits that underlie human personality? What are the primary emotional expressions? What factors underlie job satisfaction? Factor analysis is used to answer such questions, thereby providing a framework for understanding behavioral phenomena. This use of factor analysis is portrayed in the accompanying Behavioral Research Case Study box, "Factor Analysis: The Five-Factor Model of Personality."

Second, researchers use factor analysis to reduce a large number of variables to a smaller, more manageable set of data. Often a researcher measures a large number of variables, knowing that these variables measure only a few basic constructs. For example, participants may be asked to rate their current mood on 40 mood-relevant adjectives (such as happy, hostile, pleased, nervous). Of course, these do not reflect 40 distinct moods; instead, several items are used to measure each mood. So, a factor analysis may be performed to reduce these 40 scores to a small number of factors that reflect basic emotions. Once the factors are identified, common statistical procedures may be performed on the factors rather than on the original items. Not only does this approach eliminate the redundancy involved in analyzing many measures of the same thing, but analyses of factors are usually more powerful and reliable than measures of individual items.

Third, factor analysis is commonly used in the development of self-report measures of attitudes and personality. As we learned when discussing interitem reliability (Chapter 3), when questionnaire items are summed to provide a single score, we must ensure that all of the items are measuring the same construct. Thus, in the process of developing a new multi-item measure, researchers often factor analyze the items to be certain that they all measure the same construct. If all of the items on an attitude or personality scale are measuring the same construct, a factor analysis should reveal the presence of only one underlying factor on which all of the items load.

However, if a factor analysis reveals more than one factor, the items are not assessing a single, unidimensional construct, and the scale probably needs additional work before it is used.

Behavioral Research Case Study

Factor Analysis: The Five-Factor Model of Personality

How many basic personality traits are there? Obviously, people differ on dozens, if not hundreds, of attributes, but presumably many of these variables are aspects of broader and more general traits. Factor analysis has been an indispensable tool in the search for the basic dimensions of personality. By factor-analyzing people's ratings of themselves, researchers have been able to identify the basic dimensions of personality and to see which specific traits load on these basic dimensions. In several studies of this nature, factor analyses have obtained five fundamental personality factors: extraversion, agreeableness, conscientiousness, emotional stability (or neuroticism), and openness.

In a variation on this work, McCrae and Costa (1987) asked whether the same five factors would be obtained if we analyzed other people's ratings of an individual rather than the individual's self-reports. Some 274 participants were rated on 80 adjectives by a person who knew them well, such as a friend or coworker. When these ratings were factor analyzed, five factors were obtained that closely mirrored the factors obtained when people's self-reports were analyzed.

A portion of the factor matrix follows. (Although the original matrix contained factor loadings for all 80 dependent variables, the portion of the matrix shown here involves only 15 variables.) Recall that the factor loadings in the matrix are correlations between each item and the factors.

Factors are interpreted by looking for items that load at least ±.30 with a factor; factor loadings meeting this criterion are in bold. Look, for example, at the items that load greater than ±.30 in Factor 1: calm–worrying, at ease–nervous, relaxed–high-strung. These adjectives clearly have something to do with the degree to which a person feels nervous. McCrae and Costa called this factor *neuroticism*. Based on the factor loadings, how would you interpret each of the other factors?

	Factor				
Adjectives	**I**	**II**	**III**	**IV**	**V**
Calm–worrying	**.79**	.05	−.01	−.20	.05
At ease–nervous	**.77**	−.08	−.06	−.21	−.05
Relaxed–high-strung	**.66**	.04	.01	−**.34**	−.02
Retiring–sociable	−.14	**.71**	.08	.08	.08
Sober–fun-loving	−.08	**.59**	.12	.14	−.15
Aloof–friendly	−.16	**.58**	.02	**.45**	.06
Conventional–original	−.06	.12	**.67**	.08	−.04
Uncreative–creative	−.08	.03	**.56**	.11	.25
Simple–complex	.16	−.13	**.49**	−.20	.08
Irritable–good-natured	−.17	**.34**	.09	**.61**	.16
Ruthless–soft-hearted	.12	.27	.01	**.70**	.11
Selfish–selfless	−.07	−.02	.04	**.65**	.22
Negligent–conscientious	−.01	.02	.08	.18	**.68**
Careless–careful	−.08	−.07	−.01	.11	**.72**
Undependable–reliable	−.07	.04	.05	.23	**.68**

Source: Adapted from McCrae and Costa (1987).

On the basis of their examination of the entire factor matrix, McCrae and Costa (1987) labeled the five factors as follows:

1. Neuroticism (worrying, nervous, high-strung)
2. Extraversion (sociable, fun-loving, friendly, good-natured)
3. Openness (original, creative, complex)
4. Agreeableness (friendly, good-natured, soft-hearted)
5. Conscientiousness (conscientious, careful, reliable)

These five factors, obtained from peers' ratings of participants, mirror closely the five factors obtained from factor analyses of participants' self-reports and lend further support to the five-factor model of personality.

Summary

1. Regression analysis is used to develop a regression equation that describes how variables are related and allows researchers to predict people's scores on one variable (the outcome or criterion variable) based on their scores on other variables (the predictor variables). A regression equation provides a regression constant (equivalent to the *y*-intercept) as well as a regression coefficient for each predictor variable.

2. When constructing regression equations, a researcher may enter all of the predictor variables at once (simultaneous or standard regression), allow predictor variables to enter the equation based on their ability to account for unique variance in the criterion variable (stepwise regression), or enter the variables in a manner that allows him or her to test particular hypotheses (hierarchical regression).

3. Multiple correlation expresses the strength of the relationship between one variable and a set of other variables. Among other things, it provides information about how well a set of predictor variables can predict scores on a criterion variable in a regression equation.

4. Cross-lagged panel correlation designs and structural equations modeling are used to test the plausibility of causal relationships among a set of correlated variables. Both analyses can provide evidence for or against causal hypotheses, but our conclusions are necessarily tentative because the data are correlational.

5. Multilevel modeling is used to analyze the relationships among variables that are measured at different levels of analysis. For example, when several preexisting groups of participants are studied, multilevel modeling allows researchers to examine processes that are occurring at the level of the groups and at the level of the individuals.

6. Factor analysis refers to a set of procedures for identifying the dimensions or factors that account for the observed relationships among a set of variables. A factor matrix shows the factor loadings for each underlying factor, which are the correlations between each variable and the factor. From this matrix, researchers can identify the basic factors in the data.

Key Terms

criterion variable (*p. 165*)
cross-lagged panel correlation
   design (*p. 170*)
dependent variable (*p. 165*)

factor (*p. 176*)
factor analysis (*p. 176*)
factor loading (*p. 176*)
factor matrix (*p. 176*)

fit index (*p. 172*)
hierarchical multiple regression
   (*p. 167*)
multilevel modeling (*p. 173*)

multiple correlation coefficient (p. 169)
multiple regression analysis (p. 165)
nested design (p. 173)
outcome variable (p. 165)

predictor variable (p. 165)
regression analysis (p. 164)
regression coefficient (p. 165)
regression constant (p. 165)
regression equation (p. 163)
simultaneous multiple regression (p. 165)

standard multiple regression (p. 165)
stepwise multiple regression (p. 166)
structural equations modeling (p. 170)

Questions for Review

1. When do researchers use regression analysis?
2. Write the general form of a regression equation that has a single predictor variable. Identify the criterion variable, the predictor variable, the regression constant, and the regression coefficient.
3. A regression equation is actually the equation for a straight line. What line is described by the regression equation calculated for a set of data?
4. Imagine that the equation for predicting y from x is $y = 1.12 - .47x$. How would you use this equation to predict a particular individual's score?
5. What is multiple regression analysis?
6. Distinguish among simultaneous (or standard), stepwise, and hierarchical regression.
7. Of the three kinds of regression analyses, which would you use to
   a. build the best possible prediction equation from the least number of predictor variables?
   b. test a mediational hypothesis?
   c. determine whether a set of variables predicts a criterion variable?
   d. eliminate a confounding variable as you test the effects of a particular predictor variable?

8. In stepwise regression, why might a predictor variable that correlates highly with the criterion variable not enter into the regression equation?
9. Explain how you would use regression analysis to see whether variable Z mediates the effect of variable X on variable Y.
10. When would you calculate a multiple correlation coefficient? What do you learn if you square a multiple correlation?
11. How does a cross-lagged panel correlation design provide evidence to support a causal link between two variables?
12. Describe how structural equations modeling works.
13. Distinguish between latent variable modeling and path analysis as types of structural equations modeling.
14. What special problems do nested designs create for researchers? What special opportunities do they offer for understanding how variables relate to one another?
15. Why do researchers use multilevel modeling?
16. Why do researchers use factor analysis?
17. Imagine that you conducted a factor analysis on a set of variables that were uncorrelated with one another. How many factors would you expect to find? Why?

Questions for Discussion

1. In one of the exercises at the end of Chapter 7, you calculated the correlation between outside temperature and class attendance. The regression equation for the data in that exercise is

   Attendance $= 114.35 - .61$(temperature)

   Imagine that the weather forecaster predicts that next Friday's temperature will be 82 degrees F. How many students would you expect to attend class on that day?
2. One of the Behavioral Research Case Studies in this chapter involved Agocha and Cooper's (1999) study of partner characteristics and intentions to practice safe sex. Following are the Pearson correlations

   between the likelihood that participants would discuss risks before having sex and several other variables.
   a. In a stepwise regression analysis, which variable would enter the equation first? Why?
   b. Can you tell which variable will enter the equation second? Why or why not?
   c. Which variable is least likely to be included as a predictor in the final equation?
   d. If a standard or simultaneous regression analysis was conducted on these data, what is the smallest that the multiple correlation between the five predictor variables and the criterion variable could possibly be? (This one will take some thought.)

	Correlation with Likelihood of Discussing Risks
Target's physical attractiveness	−.14
Perceived desirability of target	.21
Target's sexual history	−.02
Perceived risk of sexually transmitted disease	.24
Participant's gender	−.29

3. Data show that narcissistic people (who have a grandiose, inflated perception of themselves) often fly into a "narcissistic rage" when things don't go their way. (In other words, they throw a temper tantrum.) A researcher hypothesized that this reaction occurs because narcissists think they are entitled to be treated as though they are special. Thus, she measured narcissism, the tendency to fly into a rage when frustrated by other people, and the degree to which people feel entitled to be treated well. Her data showed that narcissism by itself accounted for 24% of the variance in rage. She then conducted a hierarchical regression analysis in which she tested whether entitlement mediates the relationship between narcissism and rage. After entitlement was entered in Step 1 of the regression equation, narcissism accounted for 3% of the variance in rage when it was entered in Step 2. Does entitlement appear to mediate the effects of narcissism on rage? Why or why not?

4. In the following cross-lagged panel design, does X appear to cause Y, does Y appear to cause X, do both variables influence each other, or are X and Y unrelated?

Mood Rating	Factor 1	Factor 2	Factor 3
Happy	.07	.67	.03
Angry	.82	−.20	.11
Depressed	.12	−.55	.20
Nervous	.00	−.12	.67
Relaxed	.07	−.09	−.72

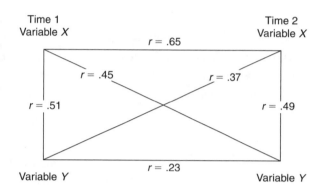

5. A researcher conducted a factor analysis of five items on which participants rated their current mood. Interpret the factor matrix that emerged from this factor analysis. Specifically, what do the three factors appear to be?

6. Researchers use hierarchical regression, cross-lagged panel designs, and structural equations modeling to partly resolve the problems associated with inferring causality from correlation.

   a. Describe how each of these analyses can be used to untangle the direction of the relationships among correlated variables.

   b. Explain why the causal inferences researchers draw from these analyses can be considered only tentative and speculative.

9

BASIC ISSUES IN EXPERIMENTAL RESEARCH

Manipulating the Independent Variable	Error Variance
Assigning Participants to Conditions	Experimental Control and Generalizability: The Experimenter's Dilemma
Experimental Control	Web-Based Experimental Research
Eliminating Confounds	

I have always been a careful and deliberate decision-maker. Whether I'm shopping for a new television, deciding where to go on vacation, or merely buying a shirt, I like to have as much information as possible as well as plenty of time to think through my options. Thus, I was surprised to learn about research suggesting that this might not always be the most optimal way to make complex decisions. After all, people can hold only a certain amount of information in working memory and can consciously think about only one thing at a time. Thus, trying to consider all of the features of 10 home entertainment systems simultaneously might be a lost cause.

Some researchers have suggested that making decisions nonconsciously rather than consciously will often lead to better decisions. According to this view, a person should soak up as much information about a decision as possible and then *not* think about it. By not thinking consciously about the decision, the person allows processes working below conscious awareness to solve the problem. Freud (1915/1949) shared this view, writing, "When making a decision of minor importance, I have always found it advantageous to consider all the pros and cons. In vital matters however . . . the decision should come from the unconscious, from somewhere within ourselves." Likewise, when people say they are going to "sleep on" a decision or problem, they are taking this approach—stopping deliberate thought by falling asleep and then seeing how they feel about things in the morning.

The idea that some decisions are best made by the nonconscious mind is intriguing, but how could we test whether or not it is correct? Dijksterhuis (2004) devised a method of testing the advantages of conscious versus unconscious thought in a series of experiments. In one of his studies, participants were provided with information to use in deciding which of four hypothetical apartments to rent. Twelve separate pieces of information about each of the four apartments (its size, location, cost, noisiness, and so on) were presented on a computer screen in random order so that each participant saw 48 pieces of information in all. The information that was presented about one apartment was predominately positive (with 8 positive and 4 negative characteristics described), information about one apartment was predominately negative (with 4 positive and 8 negative characteristics), and the information about the other two apartments was mixed (with 6 positive and 6 negative characteristics).

Participants were assigned randomly to one of three experimental conditions. After reading the 48 bits of information, participants in the *immediate decision condition* were immediately asked to rate their attitude toward each of the four apartments. In contrast, participants in the *conscious thought condition* were asked to think carefully about the four apartments for three minutes before rating them. Participants in the *unconscious thought condition* were given a distractor task for three minutes that prevented them from thinking consciously about the apartments (although presumably nonconscious processes were working), and then asked to rate the four apartments.

Dijksterhuis reasoned that we can tell which experimental condition led to the best decision by comparing participants' ratings of the most and least attractive apartments. The more differently participants rated the two apartments that were described as having the best and worst features, the better they must have processed the information they read about them. So, he subtracted each participant's rating of the unattractive apartment (the one with 8 negative characteristics) from the participant's rating of the attractive apartment (the one with 8 positive characteristics). A large difference score indicated

that the participant accurately distinguished between the best and worst apartments, whereas a difference score near zero showed that the participant didn't rate the objectively attractive and unattractive apartments differently.

The results of the experiment are shown in Table 9.1. As you can see, participants in the immediate decision condition and the conscious thought condition performed poorly. In fact, the differences between their ratings of the attractive and unattractive apartments, although slightly positive, did not differ statistically from .00. In other words, participants in these two conditions did not show a clear preference for the apartment that was actually described in more positive terms. However, in the unconscious thought condition—in which participants were prevented from thinking consciously about their decision—participants rated the attractive apartment significantly more positively than the unattractive apartment. Clearly, participants made a better decision in terms of preferring the objectively better apartment when they did not think consciously about their decision.

So far, we have discussed two general kinds of research strategies in this book: descriptive and correlational. Descriptive and correlational studies are important, but they have a shortcoming. They do not allow us to test directly hypotheses about the *causes* of behaviors, thoughts, and emotions.

TABLE 9.1   Results of Conscious and Unconscious Decision-making

Experimental Condition	Difference Between Ratings of Attractive and Unattractive Apartment
Immediate decision condition	0.47
Conscious thought condition	0.44
Unconscious thought (distraction) condition	1.23

Participants in the unconscious thought condition, who were distracted from thinking about the decision, did the best job of distinguishing between the attractive and unattractive apartments. Specifically, they rated the attractive and unattractive apartments more differently than participants who made their decision immediately after reading about the apartments or who thought about the decision for three minutes.

Source: Data are from "Think Different: The Merits of Unconscious Thought in Preference Development and Decision Making" by A. Dijksterhuis (2004). *Journal of Personality and Social Psychology, 87,* 586–598.

Descriptive research allows us to describe how our participants think, feel, and behave; correlational research allows us to see whether certain variables are related to one another. Although descriptive and correlational research can provide hints about possible causes of behavior, we can never be sure from such studies that a particular variable does, in fact, cause changes in thought, behavior, or emotion. Experimental designs, on the other hand, allow researchers to draw conclusions about cause-and-effect relationships. Thus, when Dijksterhuis wanted to know whether distracting people from thinking consciously about the apartments *caused* them to make better decisions, he conducted an **experiment**.

Does the presence of other people at an emergency deter people from helping the victim? Does eating sugar increase hyperactivity and hamper school performance in children? Do stimulants affect the speed at which rats learn? Does playing aggressive video games cause young people to behave more aggressively? Do people make better decisions when they don't think consciously about them? These kinds of questions about causality are ripe topics for experimental investigations. This chapter deals with the basic ingredients of a well-designed experiment. Chapter 10 will examine specific kinds of experimental designs, and Chapter 11 will study how data from experimental designs are analyzed.

A well designed experiment has three essential properties: (1) The researcher must *vary at least one independent variable* to assess its effects on participants' responses; (2) the researcher must have the power to assign participants to the various experimental conditions *in a way that ensures their initial equivalence;* and (3) the researcher must *control all extraneous variables* that may influence participants' responses. We discuss each of these elements of an experiment next.

MANIPULATING THE INDEPENDENT VARIABLE

The logic of experimentation stipulates that researchers vary conditions that are under their control to assess the effects of those different conditions on participants' behavior. By seeing how participants' behavior varies with changes in the conditions controlled by the experimenter, we can then determine whether those variables affect participants' behavior.

This is a very different strategy than that used with correlational research. In correlational studies, all of the variables of interest are measured and the relationships between these measured variables are examined. In experimental research, in contrast, at least one variable is varied (or manipulated) by the researcher to examine its effects on participants' thoughts, feelings, behaviors, or physiological responses.

Independent Variables

In every experiment, the researcher varies or manipulates one or more **independent variables** to assess their effects on participants' behavior. For example, a researcher interested in the effects of caffeine on memory would vary how much caffeine participants receive in the study; some participants might get capsules containing 100 milligrams (mg) of caffeine, some might get 300 mg, some 600 mg, and others might get capsules that contained no caffeine. After allowing time for the caffeine to enter the bloodstream, the participants' memory for a list of words could be assessed. In this experiment the independent variable is the amount of caffeine that participants received.

An independent variable must have two or more **levels**. The levels refer to the different values of the independent variable. For example, the independent variable in the experiment just described had four levels: Participants received doses of 0, 100, 300, or 600 mg of caffeine. Often researchers refer to the different levels of the independent variable as the experimental **conditions**. There were four conditions in this experiment. Dijksterhuis's unconscious thought experiment, on the other hand, had three experimental conditions; participants rated the apartments immediately, after thinking about them, or after performing a distracting task (see Table 9.1).

Sometimes the levels of the independent variable involve *quantitative differences* in the independent variable. In the experiment on caffeine and memory, for example, the four levels of the independent variable reflect differences in the *quantity* of caffeine participants received: 0, 100, 300, or 600 mg. In other experiments, the levels involve *qualitative differences* in the independent variable. In the experiment involving unconscious decision-making, participants were treated qualitatively differently by being given one of three sets of instructions.

TYPES OF INDEPENDENT VARIABLES.   Independent variables in behavioral research can be roughly classified into three types: environmental, instructional, and invasive.

Many questions in the behavioral sciences involve ways in which particular stimuli, situations, or events influence people's reactions, so researchers often want to vary features of the physical or social environment to study their effects. **Environmental manipulations** involve experimental modifications of aspects of the research setting. For example, a researcher interested in visual perception might vary the intensity of illumination, a study of learning might manipulate the amount of reinforcement that a pigeon receives, an experiment investigating attitude change might vary the characteristics of a persuasive message, and a study of emotions might have participants view pleasant or unpleasant photographs.

To study people's reactions to various kinds of social situations, researchers sometimes use environmental manipulations that vary the nature of the social setting that participants confront in the study. In these experiments, researchers have people participate in a social interaction—such as a group discussion, a conversation with another person, or a task on which they evaluate another individual—and then vary aspects of the situation. For example, they might vary whether participants believe that they are going to compete or cooperate with the other people, whether the other people appear to like or dislike them, or whether they are or are not similar to the other people.

In social, developmental, and personality psychology, **confederates**—accomplices of the researcher who pose as other participants or as uninvolved bystanders—are sometimes used to manipulate features of the participant's social environment. For example, confederates have been used to study participants' reactions to people of different races or genders (by using male and female or black and white confederates), reactions to being rejected (by having confederates treat participants in an accepting vs. rejecting manner), reactions to directive and nondirective leaders (by training confederates to take a directive or nondirective approach), and reactions to emergencies (by having confederates pretend to need help of various kinds).

Instructional manipulations vary the independent variable through instructions or information that participants receive. For example, participants in a study of creativity may be given one of several different instructions regarding how they should solve a particular task. In a study of how people's expectancies affect their performance, participants may be led to expect that the task will be either easy or difficult. A study of test-taking strategies may instruct participants to focus either on trying to get as many questions correct as possible or on trying to avoid getting questions incorrect.

Studies of interventions that are designed to change people's thoughts, emotions, or behaviors often involve what are essentially elaborate instructional manipulations. For example, research in health psychology that aims to change people's diets, exercise habits, alcohol use, or risky sexual behaviors often involve giving people new strategies for managing their behavior and instructing them about how to implement these strategies in their daily lives. Likewise, research on the effectiveness of interventions in clinical and counseling psychology often involves therapeutic approaches that aim to change how people think, feel, or behave by providing them with information, advice, and instructions.

Invasive manipulations involve creating physical changes in the participant's body through physical stimulation (such as in studies of pain), surgery, or the administration of drugs. In studies that test the effects of chemicals on emotion and behavior, for example, the independent variable is often the type or amount of drug given to the participant. In physiological psychology, surgical procedures may be used to modify animals' nervous systems to assess the effects of such changes on behavior.

> ## Behavioral Research Case Study
> *Emotional Contagion*
>
> Few experiments use all three types of independent variables just described. One well-known piece of research that used environmental, instructional, and invasive independent variables in a single study was a classic experiment on emotion by Schachter and Singer (1962).
>
> In this study, participants received an injection of either epinephrine (which causes a state of physiological arousal) or an inactive placebo (which had no physiological effect). Participants who received the epinephrine injection then received one of three explanations about the effect of the injection. Some participants were accurately informed that the injection would cause temporary changes in arousal such as shaking hands and increased heart rate. Other participants were misinformed about the effects of the injection, being told either that the injection would cause, among other things, numbness and itching, or that it would have no effect at all.
>
> Participants then waited for the injection to have an effect in a room with a confederate who posed as another participant. This confederate was trained to behave in either a playful, euphoric manner or an upset, angry manner. Participants were observed during this time, and they completed self-report measures of their mood as well.
>
> Results of the study showed that participants who were misinformed about the effects of the epinephrine injection (believing it would either cause numbness or have no effect at all) tended to adopt the mood of the happy or angry confederate. In contrast, those who received the placebo or who were accurately informed about the effects of the epinephrine injection showed no emotional contagion. The researchers interpreted this pattern of results in terms of the inferences that participants made for the way they felt. Participants who received an injection of epinephrine but did not know that the injection caused their arousal seemed to infer that their feelings were affected by the confederate's behavior. As a result, when the confederate was happy, they inferred that the confederate was causing them to feel happy, whereas when the confederate was angry, they labeled their feelings as anger. Participants who knew the injection caused their physiological changes, on the other hand, attributed their feelings to the injection rather than to the confederate and, thus, showed no mood change. And those who received the placebo did not feel aroused at all.
>
> As you can see, this experiment involved an invasive independent variable (injection of epinephrine vs. placebo), an instructional independent variable (information that the injection would cause arousal, numbness, or no effect), and an environmental independent variable (the confederate acted happy or angry).

EXPERIMENTAL AND CONTROL GROUPS. In some experiments, one level of the independent variable involves the absence of the variable of interest. Participants who receive a nonzero level of the independent variable compose the **experimental groups**, and those who receive a zero level of the independent variable make up the **control group**. In the caffeine-and-memory study described earlier, there were three experimental groups (those participants who received 100, 300, or 600 mg of caffeine) and one control group (those participants who received no caffeine).

Although control groups are useful in many experimental investigations, they are not always used or even necessary. For example, if a researcher is interested in the effects of audience size on performers' stage fright, she may have participants perform in front of audiences of 1, 3, or 9 people. In this example, there is no control group of participants who perform without an audience. Similarly, a researcher who is studying the impact of time pressure on decision-making may have participants work on a complex decision while knowing that they have 10, 20, or 30 minutes to complete the task. It would not make sense to have a control group in which participants had 0 minutes to do the task.

Researchers must decide whether a control group will help them interpret the results of a particular study. Control groups are particularly important when the researcher wants to know the *baseline* level of a behavior in the absence of the independent variable. For example, if we are interested in the effects of caffeine on memory, we would probably want a control group to determine how well participants remember words when they do not have any caffeine in their systems. Without such a control condition, we would have no way of knowing whether the lowest amount of caffeine produced any effect on memory. Likewise, if we are studying the effects of mood on consumers' judgments of products, we might want to have some participants view photographs that will make them feel sad, some participants view photographs that will make them feel happy, as well as a control condition in which some participants do not view emotionally evocative pictures at all. This control condition will allow us to understand the effects of sad and happy moods more fully. Without it, we might learn that people judge products differently when they feel happy as opposed to sad, but we would not know exactly how happiness and sadness influenced judgments compared to baseline mood.

ASSESSING THE IMPACT OF INDEPENDENT VARIABLES.

Many experiments fail, not because the hypotheses being tested are incorrect but rather because the independent variable was not manipulated successfully. If the independent variable is not strong enough to produce the predicted effects, the study is doomed from the outset.

Imagine, for example, that you are studying whether the brightness of lighting affects people's work performance. To test this, you have some participants work at a desk illuminated by a 75-watt light bulb, whereas others work at a desk illuminated by a 100-watt bulb. Although you have experimentally manipulated the brightness of the lighting, we might guess that the difference in brightness between the two conditions (75-watt vs. 100-watt bulbs) is probably not great enough to produce any detectable effects on behavior. In fact, participants in the two conditions may not even perceive the amount of lighting as noticeably different.

Researchers often **pilot test** the levels of the independent variables they plan to use, trying them out on a handful of participants before actually starting the experiment. The purpose of pilot testing is not to see whether the independent variables produce hypothesized effects on participants' behavior (that's for the experiment itself to determine) but rather to ensure that the levels of the independent variable are different enough to be detected by participants. If we are studying the effects of lighting on work performance, we could try out different levels of brightness to find out what levels of lighting pilot participants perceive as dim versus adequate versus blinding. By pilot testing

their experimental manipulations on a small number of participants, researchers can ensure that the independent variables are sufficiently strong before investing the time, energy, and money required to conduct a full-scale experiment. There are few things more frustrating (and wasteful) in research than conducting an experiment only to find out that the data do not test the research hypotheses because the independent variable was not manipulated successfully.

In addition to pilot testing levels of the independent variable while designing a study, researchers often use manipulation checks in the experiment itself. A **manipulation check** is a question (or set of questions) that is designed to determine whether the independent variable was manipulated successfully. For example, we might ask participants to rate the brightness of the lighting in the experiment. If participants in the various experimental conditions rate the brightness of the lights differently, we would know that the difference in brightness was perceptible. However, if participants in different conditions do not rate the brightness of the lighting differently, we would question whether the independent variable was successfully manipulated, and our findings regarding the effects of brightness on work performance would be suspect. Although manipulation checks are not always necessary (and, in fact, they are often not possible to use), researchers should always consider whether they are needed to document the strength of the independent variable in a particular study.

INDEPENDENT VARIABLES VERSUS SUBJECT VARIABLES.

As we've seen, in every experiment, the researcher varies or manipulates one or more independent variables to assess their effects on the dependent variables. However, researchers sometimes include other variables in their experimental designs that they do not manipulate. For example, a researcher might be interested in the effects of violent and nonviolent movies on the aggression of male versus female participants, or in the effects of time pressure on the test performance of people who are first-born, later-born, or only children. Although researchers could experimentally manipulate the violence of the movies that participants viewed or the amount of time pressure they were under as they took a test, they obviously cannot manipulate participants' gender or birth order. These kinds of nonmanipulated variables are not "independent variables" (even though some researchers loosely refer to them as such) because they are not experimentally manipulated by the researcher. Rather, they are **subject or participant variables** that reflect existing characteristics of the participants. Designs that include both independent and subject variables are common and quite useful, as we'll see in the next chapter. But we should be careful to distinguish the true independent variables that are manipulated in such designs from the subject variables that are measured but not manipulated.

Dependent Variables

In an experiment, the researcher is interested in the effect of the independent variable(s) on one or more **dependent variables**. A dependent variable is the response being measured in the study—the reaction that the researcher believes might be affected by the independent variable. In behavioral research, dependent variables typically involve either observations of actual behavior, self-report measures (of participants' thoughts, feelings, or behavior), or measures of physiological reactions (see Chapter 4). In the experiment involving caffeine, the dependent variable might involve how many words participants remember. In the Dijksterhuis study of nonconscious decision making, the dependent variable was participants' ratings of the apartments. Most experiments have several dependent variables. Few researchers are willing to expend the effort needed to conduct an experiment, then collect data regarding only one behavior.

Developing Your Research Skills
Identifying Independent and Dependent Variables

Study 1. Does Exposure to Misspelled Words Make People Spell More Poorly?   Research suggests that previous experience with misspelled words can undermine a person's ability to spell a word correctly. For example, teachers report that they sometimes become confused about the correct spelling of certain words after grading the spelling tests of poor spellers. To study this effect, Brown (1988) used 44 university students. In the first phase of the study, the participants took a spelling test of 26 commonly misspelled words (such as *adolescence*, *convenience*, and *vacuum*). Then half of the participants were told to purposely generate two incorrect spellings for 13 of these words. (For example, a participant might write *vacume* or *vaccum* for *vacuum*.) The other half of the participants were not asked to generate misspellings; rather, they performed an unrelated task. Finally, all participants took another test of the same 26 words as before but presented in a different order. As Brown had predicted, participants who generated the incorrect spellings subsequently switched from correct to incorrect spellings on the final test at a significantly higher frequency than participants who performed the unrelated task.

   1. What is the independent variable in this experiment?
   2. How many levels does it have?
   3. How many conditions are there, and what are they?
   4. What do participants in the experimental group(s) do?
   5. Is there a control group?
   6. What is the dependent variable?

Study 2. Do Guns Increase Testosterone?   Studies have shown that the mere presence of objects that are associated with aggression, such as a gun, can increase aggressive behavior in men. Klinesmith, Kasser, and McAndrew (2006) wondered whether this effect is due, in part, to the effects of aggressive stimuli on men's level of testosterone, a hormone that has been linked to aggression. They hypothesized that simply handling a gun would increase men's level of testosterone. To test this hypothesis, they recruited 30 male college students. When the participant arrived at the study, he was first asked to spit into a cup so that his saliva could later be analyzed to determine his testosterone level. The participant was then left alone for 15 minutes with either a pellet gun that resembled an automatic handgun or the children's game Mouse Trap™. Participants were told to handle the object (the gun or the game) in order to write a set of instructions about how to assemble and disassemble it. After 15 minutes, the researcher returned and collected a second saliva sample. Results showed that, as predicted, participants who interacted with the toy gun showed a significantly greater increase in testosterone from the first to the second saliva sample than participants who interacted with the children's game.

1. What is the independent variable in this experiment?
2. How many levels does it have?
3. How many conditions are there, and what are they?
4. What do participants in the experimental group(s) do?
5. Is there a control group?
6. What is the dependent variable?

The answers to these questions appear on page 211.

ASSIGNING PARTICIPANTS TO CONDITIONS

We've seen that, in an experiment, participants in different conditions receive different levels of the independent variable. At the end of the experiment, the responses of participants in the various experimental and control groups are compared to see whether their responses differ across the conditions. If so, we have evidence that they were affected by the manipulation of the independent variable.

Such a strategy for testing the effects of independent variables on behavior makes sense only if we can assume that our groups of participants are roughly equivalent at the beginning of the study. If we see differences in the behavior of participants in various experimental conditions at the end of the experiment, we want to have confidence that these differences were produced by the independent variable. The possibility exists, however, that the differences we observe at the end of the study are due to the fact that the groups of participants differed at the *start* of the experiment—even before they received one level or another of the independent variable.

For example, in our study of caffeine and memory, perhaps the group that received no caffeine was, on the average, simply more intelligent than

the other groups and, thus, these participants remembered more words than participants in the other conditions. For the results of the experiment to be interpretable, we must be able to assume that participants in our various experimental groups did not differ from one another before the experiment began. We would want to be sure, for example, that participants in the four experimental conditions did not differ markedly in average intelligence as a group. Thus, an essential ingredient for every experiment is that the researcher takes steps to ensure the initial equivalence of the groups before the introduction of the independent variable.

Simple Random Assignment

The easiest way to be sure that the experimental groups are roughly equivalent before manipulating the independent variable is to use **simple random assignment**. Simple random assignment involves placing participants in conditions in such a way that every participant has an equal probability of being placed in any experimental condition. For example, if we have an experiment with only two conditions— the simplest possible experiment—we can flip a coin to assign each participant to one of the two groups. If the coin comes up heads, the participant will be assigned to one experimental group; if it comes up tails, the participant will be placed in the other experimental group.

Random assignment ensures that, on the average, participants in the groups do not differ. No matter what personal attribute we might consider, participants with that attribute have an equal probability of being assigned to both groups. So, on average, the groups should be equivalent in intelligence, personality, age, attitudes, appearance, self-confidence, ability, anxiety, and so on. When random assignment is used, researchers have confidence that their experimental groups are roughly equivalent at the beginning of the experiment.

Matched Random Assignment

Research shows that simple random assignment is very effective in equating experimental groups at the start of an experiment, particularly if the number of participants assigned to each experimental condition is sufficiently large. However, there is always a small possibility that random assignment will not produce roughly equivalent groups.

Researchers sometimes try to increase the similarity among the experimental groups by using **matched random assignment**. When matched random assignment is used, the researcher obtains participants' scores on a measure known to be relevant to the outcome of the experiment. Typically, this variable is a pretest measure of the dependent variable. For example, if we were doing an experiment on the effects of a counseling technique on math anxiety, we could pretest our participants before the experiment using a math anxiety scale.

Then participants are ranked on this measure from highest to lowest. The researcher then matches participants by putting them in clusters or blocks of size k, where k is the number of conditions in the experiment. The first k participants with the highest scores are matched together into a cluster, the next k participants are matched together, and so on. Then the researcher randomly assigns the k participants in each cluster to each of the experimental conditions.

For example, assume we wanted to use matched random assignment in our study of caffeine and memory. We would obtain pretest scores on a

memory test for 40 individuals and then rank these 40 participants from highest to lowest. Because our study has four conditions (i.e., $k = 4$), we would take the four participants with the highest memory scores and randomly assign each participant to one of the four conditions (0, 100, 300, or 600 mg of caffeine). We would then take the four participants with the next highest scores and randomly assign each to one of the conditions, followed by the next block of four participants, and so on until all 40 participants were assigned to an experimental condition. This procedure ensures that each experimental condition contains participants who possess comparable memory ability.

Repeated Measures Designs

When different participants are assigned to each of the conditions in an experiment, as when we use simple and matched random assignment, the design is called a **randomized groups design**. This kind of study is also sometimes called a **between-subjects or between-groups design** because we are interested in differences in behavior *between* different groups of participants.

In some studies, however, a single group of participants serves in all conditions of the experiment. For example, rather than randomly assigning participants into four groups, each of which receives one of four dosages of caffeine, a researcher may test a single group of participants under each of the four dosage levels. Such an experiment uses a **within-subjects design** in which we are interested in differences in behavior across conditions within a single group of participants. This is also commonly called a **repeated measures design** because each participant is measured more than once.

Using a within-subjects or repeated measures design eliminates the need for random assignment because every participant is tested under every level of the independent variable. What better way is there to be sure the groups do not differ than to use the same participants in every experimental condition? In essence, each participant in a repeated measures design serves as his or her own control.

Behavioral Research Case Study
A Within-Subjects Design: Sugar and Behavior

Many parents and teachers are concerned about the effects of sugar on children's behavior. The popular view is that excessive sugar consumption results in behavioral problems ranging from mild irritability to hyperactivity and attention disturbances. Interestingly, few studies have tested the effects of sugar on behavior, and those that have studied its effects have obtained inconsistent findings.

Against this backdrop of confusion, Rosen, Booth, Bender, McGrath, Sorrell, and Drabman (1988) used a within-subjects design to examine the effects of sugar on 45 preschool and elementary school children. All 45 participants served in each of three experimental conditions. In the high sugar condition, the children drank an orange-flavored breakfast drink that contained 50 g of sucrose (approximately equal to the sucrose in two candy bars). In the low sugar condition, the drink contained only 6.25 g of sucrose. And in the control group, the drink contained aspartame (Nutrasweet™), an artificial sweetener.

Each child was tested five times in each of the three conditions. Each morning for 15 days each child drank a beverage containing either 0 g, 6.25 g, or 50 g of sucrose. To minimize order effects, the order in which participants participated in each condition was randomized across those 15 days.

Several dependent variables were measured. Participants were tested each day on several measures of cognitive and intellectual functioning. In addition, their teachers (who did not know what each child drank) rated each student's behavior every morning. Observational measures were also taken of behaviors that may be affected by sugar, such as activity level, aggression, and fidgeting.

The results showed that high amounts of sugar caused a slight increase in activity, as well as a slight decrease in cognitive performance for girls. Contrary to the popular view, however, the effects of even excessive consumption of sugar were quite small in magnitude. The authors concluded that "the results did not support the view that sugar causes major changes in children's behavior" (Rosen et al., 1988, p. 583). Interestingly, parents' expectations about the effects of sugar on their child were uncorrelated with the actual effects. Apparently, parents often attribute their children's misbehavior to excessive sugar consumption when sugar is not really the culprit.

ADVANTAGES OF WITHIN-SUBJECTS DESIGNS. The primary advantage of a within-subjects design is that it is more *powerful* than a between-subjects design. In statistical terminology, the **power** of an experimental design refers to its ability to detect effects of the independent variable. A powerful design is able to detect effects of the independent variable more easily than less powerful designs can. Within-subjects designs are more powerful because the participants in all experimental conditions are identical in every way (after all, they are the same individuals). When this is the case, none of the observed differences in responses to the various conditions can be due to preexisting differences between participants in the groups. Because we have repeated measures on every participant, we can more easily detect the effects of the independent variable on participants' behavior.

A second advantage of within-participants designs is that they require fewer participants. Because each participant is used in every condition, fewer are needed.

DISADVANTAGES OF WITHIN-SUBJECTS DESIGNS. Despite their advantages, within-subjects designs also create some special problems. Because each participant receives all levels of the independent variable, **order effects** can arise when participants' behavior is affected by the order in which they participate in the various conditions of the experiment. When order effects occur, the effects of a particular condition are contaminated by its order in the sequence of experimental conditions that participants receive. Researchers distinguish among three types of order effects—practice, fatigue, and sensitization. In addition, carryover effects may occur in within-subjects designs.

Practice effects occur when participants' performance improves merely because they complete the dependent variable several times. For example, if we use a within-subjects design for our study of caffeine and memory, participants will memorize and be tested on groups of words four times—once in each of the four experimental conditions. Because of the opportunity to practice memorizing lists of words, participants' performance may improve as the experiment progresses. As a result, they might perform better in the condition that they receive last than in the condition they receive first regardless of how much caffeine they ingest.

Alternatively, **fatigue effects** may occur if participants become tired, bored, or less motivated as the experiment progresses. With fatigue effects, treatments that occur later in the sequence of conditions may appear to be less effective than those that occurred earlier. In our example, participants may become tired, bored, or impatient over time and, thus, perform least well in the experimental condition they receive last.

A third type of order effect involves **sensitization**. After receiving several levels of the independent variable and completing the dependent variable several times, participants in a within-subjects design may begin to realize what the hypothesis is. As a result, participants may respond differently than they did before they were sensitized to the purpose of the experiment.

To guard against the possibility of order effects, researchers use **counterbalancing**. Counterbalancing involves presenting the levels of the independent variable in different orders to different participants. When feasible, all possible orders are used. In the caffeine and memory study, for example, there were 24 possible orders in which the levels of the independent variable could be presented, as shown below.

	Order			
	1st	**2nd**	**3rd**	**4th**
1	0 mg	100 mg	300 mg	600 mg
2	0 mg	100 mg	600 mg	300 mg
3	0 mg	300 mg	100 mg	600 mg
4	0 mg	300 mg	600 mg	100 mg
5	0 mg	600 mg	100 mg	300 mg
6	0 mg	600 mg	300 mg	100 mg
7	100 mg	0 mg	300 mg	600 mg
8	100 mg	0 mg	600 mg	300 mg
9	100 mg	300 mg	0 mg	600 mg
10	100 mg	300 mg	600 mg	0 mg
11	100 mg	600 mg	0 mg	300 mg
12	100 mg	600 mg	300 mg	0 mg
13	300 mg	0 mg	100 mg	600 mg
14	300 mg	0 mg	600 mg	100 mg
15	300 mg	100 mg	0 mg	600 mg
16	300 mg	100 mg	600 mg	0 mg
17	300 mg	600 mg	0 mg	100 mg
18	300 mg	600 mg	100 mg	0 mg
19	600 mg	0 mg	100 mg	300 mg
20	600 mg	0 mg	300 mg	100 mg
21	600 mg	100 mg	0 mg	300 mg
22	600 mg	100 mg	300 mg	0 mg
23	600 mg	300 mg	0 mg	100 mg
24	600 mg	300 mg	100 mg	0 mg

If you look closely, you'll see that all possible orders of the four conditions are listed. Furthermore, every level of the independent variable appears in each order position an equal number of times.

In this example, all possible orders of the four levels of the independent variable were used. However, complete counterbalancing becomes unwieldy when the number of conditions is large because of the sheer number of possible orders. Instead, researchers sometimes randomly choose a smaller subset of these possible orderings. For example, a researcher might randomly choose orders 2, 7, 9, 14, 19, and 21 from the set of 24 and then randomly assign each participant to one of these six orders.

Alternatively, a Latin Square design may be used to control for order effects. In a **Latin Square design**, each condition appears once at each ordinal position (1st, 2nd, 3rd, etc.), and each condition precedes and

follows every other condition once. For example, if a within-subjects design has four conditions, as in our example of a study on caffeine and memory, a Latin Square design would involve administering the conditions in four different orders as shown here.

As you can see, each dosage condition appears once at each ordinal position, and each condition precedes and follows every other condition just once. Our participants would be randomly assigned to four groups, and each group would receive a different order of the dosage conditions.

Carryover effects occur when the effect of a particular treatment condition persists even after the condition ends. Carryover effects occur when the effects of one level of the independent variable are still present when another level of the independent variable is introduced. Carryover effects create problems for within-subjects designs because a researcher might conclude that participants' behavior is due to the level of the independent variable that was just administered when the behavior is actually due to the lingering effects of a level administered earlier. In the experiment involving caffeine, for example, a researcher would have to be sure that the caffeine from one dosage wears off before giving participants a different dosage.

	Order			
	1st	**2nd**	**3rd**	**4th**
Group 1	0 mg	100 mg	600 mg	300 mg
Group 2	100 mg	300 mg	0 mg	600 mg
Group 3	300 mg	600 mg	100 mg	0 mg
Group 4	600 mg	0 mg	300 mg	100 mg

Behavioral Research Case Study
Carryover Effects in Cognitive Psychology

Cognitive psychologists often use within-subjects designs to study the effects of various conditions on how people process information. Ferraro, Kellas, and Simpson (1993) conducted an experiment that was specifically designed to determine whether within-subjects designs produce undesired carryover effects in which participating in one experimental condition affects participants' responses in other experimental conditions. Thirty-six participants completed three reaction-time tasks in which (a) they were shown strings of letters and indicated as quickly as possible whether each string of letters was a real word (primary task); (b) they indicated as quickly as possible when they heard a tone presented over their headphones (secondary task); or (c) they indicated when they both heard a tone and saw a string of letters that was a word (combined task). Although all participants completed all three tasks (80 trials of each), they did so in one of three orders: primary–combined–secondary, combined–secondary–primary, or secondary–primary–combined. By comparing how participants responded to the same task when it appeared in different orders, the researchers could determine whether carryover effects had occurred.

The results showed that participants' reaction times to the letters and tones differed depending on the order in which they completed the three tasks. Consider the implications of this finding: A researcher who had conducted this experiment using only one particular order for the three tasks (for example, primary–secondary–combined) would have reached different conclusions than a researcher who conducted the same experiment but used a different task order. Clearly, researchers must guard against, if not test for, carryover effects whenever they use within-subjects designs.

EXPERIMENTAL CONTROL

The third critical ingredient of a good experiment is **experimental control**. Experimental control refers to eliminating or holding constant extraneous factors that might affect the outcome of the study. If the effects of such factors are not eliminated, it will be difficult, if not impossible, to determine whether the independent variable had an effect on participants' responses.

Systematic Variance Revisited

To understand why experimental control is important, let's return to the concept of variance. You will recall from Chapter 2 that variance is an index of how much participants' scores differ or vary from one another. Furthermore, you may recall that the total variance in a set of data can be broken into two components—systematic variance and error variance.

In the context of an experiment, **systematic variance** (often called **between-groups variance**) is that part of the total variance that reflects differences among the experimental groups. The question to be addressed in every experiment is whether any of the total variability we observe in participants' scores is systematic variance due to the independent variable. If the independent variable affected participants' responses, then we should find that some of the variability in participants' scores is associated with the manipulation of the independent variable.

Put differently, if the independent variable had an effect on behavior, we should observe *systematic differences* between the scores in the various experimental conditions. If scores differ systematically between conditions—if participants remember more words in some experimental groups than in others, for example—systematic variance exists in the scores. This systematic or between-groups variability in the scores may come from two sources: the independent variable (in which case it is called *treatment variance*) and extraneous variables (in which case it is called *confound variance*).

TREATMENT VARIANCE. The portion of the variance in participants' scores that is due to the independent variable is called **treatment variance** (or sometimes **primary variance**). If nothing other than the independent variable affected participants' responses in an experiment, then all of the variance in the data would be treatment variance. This is rarely the case, however. As we will see, participants' scores typically vary for other reasons as well. Specifically, we can identify two other sources of variability in participants' scores other than the independent variable: confound variance (which we must eliminate from the study) and error variance (which we must minimize).

CONFOUND VARIANCE. Ideally, other than the fact that participants in different conditions receive different levels of the independent variable, all participants in the various experimental conditions should be treated in precisely the same way. The only thing that may differ between the conditions is the independent variable. Only when this is so can we conclude that changes in the dependent variable were caused by manipulation of the independent variable.

Unfortunately, researchers sometimes design faulty experiments in which something other than the independent variable differs among the conditions. For example, if in a study of the effects of caffeine on memory, all participants who received 600 mg of caffeine were tested at 9:00 A.M. and all participants who received no caffeine were tested at 3:00 P.M., the groups would differ not only in how much caffeine they received but also in the time at which they participated in the study. In this experiment, we would be unable to tell whether differences in memory between the groups were due to the fact that one group ingested caffeine and the other one didn't or to the fact that one group was tested in the morning and the other in the afternoon.

When a variable other than the independent variable differs between the groups, **confound variance** is produced. Confound variance, which is sometimes called **secondary variance**, is that portion of the variance in participants' scores that is due to extraneous variables that differ systematically between the experimental groups.

Confound variance must be eliminated at all costs. The reason is clear: It is impossible for researchers to distinguish treatment variance from confound variance. Although we can easily determine how much systematic variance is present in our data, we cannot tell how much of the systematic variance is treatment variance (due to the independent variable) and how much, if any, is confound variance (due to extraneous variables that differ systematically between conditions). As a result, the researcher will find it impossible to tell whether differences in the dependent variable between conditions were due to the independent variable or to this unwanted, confounding variable. As we'll discuss in detail later in the chapter, confound variance is eliminated through careful experimental control in which all factors other than the independent variable are held constant or allowed to vary nonsystematically between the experimental conditions.

Error Variance

Error variance (also called **within-groups variance**) is the result of *unsystematic* differences among participants. Not only do participants differ at the time they enter the experiment in terms of ability, personality, mood, past history, and so on, but also chances are that the experimenter will treat individual participants in slightly different ways. In addition, measurement error contributes to error variance by introducing random variability into participants' scores (see Chapter 3).

In our study of caffeine and memory, we would expect to see differences in the number of words recalled by participants who were in the same experimental condition; not all of the participants in a particular experimental condition will remember precisely the same number of words. This variability in scores within an experimental condition is not due to the independent variable because all participants in a particular condition receive the same level of the independent variable. Nor is this within-groups variance due to confounding variables because all participants within a group would experience any confound that existed. Rather, this variability—the error variance—is due to differences among participants within the group, to random variations in the experimental setting and procedure (time of

testing, weather, researcher's mood, and so forth), and to other unsystematic influences.

Unlike confound variance, error variance does not invalidate an experiment. This is because, unlike confound variance, we have statistical ways to distinguish between treatment variance (due to the independent variable) and error variance (due to unsystematic extraneous variables). Even so, the more error variance, the more difficult it is to detect effects of the independent variable. Because of this, researchers take steps to control the sources of error variance in an experiment, although they recognize that error variance will seldom be eliminated. We'll return to the problem of error variance in a moment.

An Analogy

To summarize, the total variance in participants' scores at the end of an experiment may be composed of three components:

$$\underbrace{\begin{matrix} \text{Total} \\ \text{variance} \end{matrix} = \begin{matrix} \text{Treatment} \\ \text{variance} \end{matrix} + \begin{matrix} \text{Confound} \\ \text{variance} \end{matrix}}_{\begin{matrix} \text{Systematic} \\ \text{variance} \end{matrix}} + \underbrace{\begin{matrix} \text{Error} \\ \text{variance} \end{matrix}}_{\begin{matrix} \text{Unsystematic} \\ \text{variance} \end{matrix}}$$

Together, the treatment and confound variance constitute systematic variance (creating systematic differences among experimental conditions), and the error variance is unsystematic variability within the various conditions. In an ideal experiment, researchers maximize the treatment variance, eliminate confound variance, and minimize error variance. To understand this point, we'll use the analogy of watching television.

When you watch television, the image on the screen constantly varies or changes. In the terminology we have been using, there is *variance* in the picture on the screen. Three sets of factors can affect the image on the screen.

The first is the signal being sent from the television station or cable network. This, of course, is the only source of image variance that you're really interested in when you watch TV. Ideally, you would like the image on the screen to change only as a function of the signal being received from the source of the program. Systematic changes in the picture that are due to changes in the signal from the TV station or cable network are analogous to treatment variance due to the independent variable.

Unfortunately, the picture on the screen may be altered in one of two ways. First, the picture may be systematically altered by images other than those of the program you want to watch. Perhaps "ghost figures" from another channel interfere with the image on the screen. This interference is much like confound variance because it distorts the primary image in a *systematic* fashion. In fact, depending on what you were watching, you might have difficulty distinguishing which images were from the program you wanted to watch and which were from the interfering signal. That is, you might not be able to distinguish the true signal (treatment variance) from the interference (confound variance).

The primary signal can also be weakened by static, fuzz, or snow. Static produces *unsystematic* changes in the TV picture. It dilutes the image without actually distorting it. If the static is extreme enough, you may not be able to recognize the real picture at all. Similarly, error variance in an experiment clouds the signal produced by the independent variable.

To enjoy TV, you want the primary signal to be as strong as possible, to eliminate systematic distortions entirely, and to have as little static as possible. Only then will the program you want to watch come through loud and clear. In an analogous fashion, researchers want to maximize treatment variance, eliminate confound variance, and reduce error variance. The remainder of this chapter deals with the ways researchers use experimental control to eliminate confound variance and minimize error variance.

ELIMINATING CONFOUNDS

Internal Validity

At the end of every experiment, we want to have confidence that any differences we observe between the experimental and control groups resulted from our manipulation of the independent variable rather than from extraneous variables. **Internal validity** is the degree to which a researcher draws accurate conclusions about the effects of the independent variable. An experiment is internally valid when it eliminates all potential sources of confound variance. When an experiment has internal validity, a researcher can confidently conclude that observed differences were due to the independent variable.

To a large extent, internal validity is achieved through experimental control. The logic of experimentation requires that nothing can differ systematically between the experimental conditions other than the independent variable. If something other than the independent variable differs in some systematic way, we say that **confounding** has occurred. When confounding occurs, there is no way to know whether the results were due to the independent variable or to the confound. Confounding is a fatal flaw in experimental designs, one that makes the findings worthless. As a result, possible threats to internal validity must be eliminated at all costs.

One well-publicized example of confounding involved the "Pepsi Challenge" (see Huck & Sandler, 1979). The Pepsi Challenge was a taste test in which people were asked to taste two cola beverages and indicate which they preferred. As it was originally designed, glasses of Pepsi were always marked with a letter *M*, and glasses of Coca-Cola were marked with a *Q*. People seemed to prefer Pepsi over Coke in these tests, but a confound was present. Do you see it? The letter on the glass was confounded with the beverage in it. Thus, we don't know for certain whether people preferred Pepsi over Coke or the letter *M* over *Q*. As absurd as this possibility may sound, later tests demonstrated that participants' preferences *were* affected by the letter on the glass. No matter which cola was in which glass, people tended to indicate a preference for the drink marked *M* over the one marked *Q*.

Before discussing some common threats to the internal validity of experiments, see if you can find the threat to internal validity in the hypothetical experiment described in the following box.

Developing Your Research Skills
Confounding: Can You Find It?

A researcher was interested in how people's perceptions of others are affected by the presence of a physical handicap. Research suggests that people may rate those with physical disabilities less positively than those without disabilities. Because of the potential implications of this bias for job discrimination against people with disabilities, the researcher wanted to see whether participants responded less positively to job applicants with disabilities.

The participant was asked to play the role of an employer who wanted to hire a computer programmer, a job in which physical disability is largely irrelevant. Participants were shown one of two sets of bogus job application materials prepared in advance by the experimenter. Both sets of application materials included precisely the same information about the applicant's qualifications and background (such as college grades, extracurricular activities, experience, test scores, and so on). The only difference in the two sets of materials involved a photograph attached to the application. In one picture, the applicant was shown seated in a wheelchair, thereby making the presence of a disability obvious to participants. The other photograph did not show the wheelchair; in this picture, only the applicant's head and shoulders were shown. Other than the degree to which the applicant's disability was apparent, the content of the two applications was identical in every respect.

In the experiment, 20 participants saw the photo in which the disability was apparent, and 20 participants saw the photo in which the applicant did not appear disabled. Participants were randomly assigned to one of these two experimental conditions. After viewing the application materials, including the photograph, each participant completed a questionnaire on which they rated the applicant on several dimensions. For example, participants were asked how qualified for the job the applicant was, how much they liked the applicant, and whether they would hire him.

1. What was the independent variable in this experiment?
2. What were the dependent variables?
3. The researcher made a critical error in designing this experiment, one that introduced confounding and compromised the internal validity of the study. Can you find the researcher's mistake?
4. How would you redesign the experiment to eliminate this problem?

Answers to these questions appear on page 211.

Threats to Internal Validity

The reason that threats to internal validity, such as those in the Pepsi Challenge taste test and the study of reactions to disabled job applicants, are so damaging is that they introduce alternative explanations for the results of an experiment. Instead of confidently concluding that differences among the conditions are due to the independent variable, the researcher must concede that there are alternative explanations for the results. When this happens, the results are highly suspect, and no one is likely to take them seriously. Although it would be impossible to list all potential threats to internal validity, a few of the more common threats are discussed next. (For complete coverage of these and other threats to internal validity, see Campbell and Stanley [1966] and Cook and Campbell [1979].)

BIASED ASSIGNMENT OF PARTICIPANTS TO CONDITIONS. We've already discussed one common threat to internal validity. If the experimental conditions are not equalized before participants receive the independent variable, the researcher may conclude that the independent variable caused differences between the groups when, in fact, those differences were due to **biased assignment**. Biased assignment of participants to conditions (which is often referred to as the *selection threat* to internal validity) introduces the possibility that the effects are due to nonequivalent groups rather than to the independent variable. We've seen that this problem is generally eliminated through simple or matched random assignment or use of within-subjects designs.

This confound poses a problem for research that compares the effects of an independent variable on preexisting groups of participants. For example, if researchers are interested in the effects of a particular curricular innovation in elementary schools, they might want to compare students in a school that uses the innovative curriculum with those in a school that uses a traditional curriculum. But, because the students are not randomly assigned to one school or the other, the groups will differ in many ways other than in the curriculum being used. As a result, the study possesses no internal validity, and no conclusions can be drawn about the effects of the curriculum.

Biased assignment can also arise when efforts to randomly assign participants to conditions fail to create experimental conditions that are equivalent prior to the manipulation of the independent variable. Every so often, random processes do not produce random results. For example, even if a coin is perfectly unbiased, tossing it 50 times will not necessarily yield 25 heads and 25 tails. In the same way, randomly assigning participants to conditions will not always yield perfectly equivalent groups. (See Figure 9.1.) Fortunately, random assignment usually works and, as we will see in later chapters, our statistical analyses are designed to protect us from less-than-perfect randomness to some degree. Even so, it is possible that, despite randomly assigning participants to conditions,

(a) Successful Random Assignment

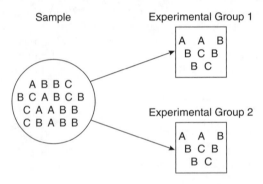

(b) Biased Assignment

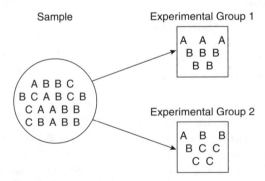

FIGURE 9.1   Biased Assignment.   Imagine that you conducted a two-group experiment with eight participants in each experimental condition. In Figure 9.1(a), random assignment distributed different kinds of participants in the original sample (indicated by A, B, and C) into the two experimental groups in an unbiased fashion. However, in Figure 9.1(b), biased assignment led Group 1 to have too many participants with A and B characteristics, whereas Group 2 consisted of too many Cs. If, after manipulating the independent variable, we found that the dependent variable differed for Group 1 and Group 2, we wouldn't know whether the independent variable caused the difference or whether the groups had differed from the outset because of biased assignment.

our experimental groups differ in some important respect before the independent variable in manipulated.

DIFFERENTIAL ATTRITION. **Attrition** refers to the loss of participants during a study. For example, some participants may be unwilling to complete the experiment because they find the procedures painful, difficult, objectionable, or embarrassing. When studies span a long period of time or involve people who are already very ill (as in some research in health psychology), participants may become unavailable due to death. (Because some attrition is caused by death, some researchers refer to this confound as *subject mortality*.)

When attrition occurs in a random fashion and affects all experimental conditions equally, it is only a minor threat to internal validity. However, when the rate of attrition differs across the experimental conditions, a bias known as **differential attrition**, internal validity is weakened. If attrition occurs at a different rate in different conditions, the independent variable may have caused the loss of participants. As a result, the experimental groups are no longer equivalent; differential attrition has destroyed the benefits of random assignment.

For example, suppose we are interested in the effects of physical stressors on intellectual performance. To induce physical stress, participants in the experimental group will be asked to immerse their right arm to the shoulder in a container of ice water, a procedure that is quite painful but not damaging. Participants in the control condition will put their arms in water that is at room temperature. While their arms are immersed, participants in both groups will complete a set of mental tasks. For ethical reasons, we must let participants choose whether to participate in this study. Let's assume, however, that, whereas all of the participants who are randomly assigned to the room-temperature water condition agree to participate, 15% of those assigned to the experimental ice-water condition decline. Differential attrition has occurred, and the two groups are no longer equivalent.

If we assume that participants who drop out of the ice-water condition are more fearful than those who agree to participate, then the average participant who remains in the ice-water condition is probably less fearful than the average participant in the

room-temperature condition, creating a potential bias. If we find a difference in performance between the two conditions, how do we know whether the difference is due to differences in physical stress or to differences in the characteristics of the participants who agree to participate in the two conditions? We don't, so differential attrition has created a confound that ruins our ability to draw meaningful conclusions from the results.

PRETEST SENSITIZATION. In some experiments, participants are pretested to obtain a measure of their behavior before receiving the independent variable. Although pretests provide useful baseline data, they have a drawback. Taking a pretest may lead participants to react differently than they would have if they had not been pretested. When **pretest sensitization** occurs, the researcher may conclude that the independent variable has an effect when, in reality, the effect is influenced by the pretest.

For example, imagine that a teacher designs a program to raise students' cultural literacy—their knowledge of common facts that are known by most literate, educated people within a particular culture (for example, what happened in 1492 or who Thomas Edison was). To test the effectiveness of this program, the teacher administers a pretest of such knowledge to 100 students. Fifty of these students then participate in a two-week course designed to increase their cultural literacy, whereas the remaining 50 students take another course. Both groups are then tested again, using the same test they completed during the pretest.

Assume that the teacher finds that students who take the cultural literacy course show a significantly greater increase in knowledge than students in the control group. Is the course responsible for this change? Possibly, but pretest sensitization may also be involved. When students take the pretest, they undoubtedly encounter questions they can't answer. When this material is covered during the course itself, students may be more attentive to it *because of their experience on the pretest*. As a result, they learn more than they would have had they not taken the pretest. Thus, the pretest sensitizes them to the experimental treatment and thereby affects the results of the study.

When researchers are concerned about pretest sensitization, they sometimes include conditions in their design in which some participants take the pretest whereas other participants do not. If the participants who are pretested respond differently in one or more experimental conditions than those who are not pretested, pretest sensitization has occurred.

HISTORY. The results of some studies are affected by extraneous events that occur outside of the research setting. As a result, the obtained effects are due not to the independent variable itself but to an interaction of the independent variable and **history effects**.

For example, imagine that we are interested in the effects of filmed aggression toward women on attitudes toward sexual aggression. Participants in one group watch a 30-minute movie that contains a realistic depiction of rape, whereas participants in another group watch a film about wildlife conservation. We then measure both groups' attitudes toward sexual aggression. Let's imagine, however, that a female student was sexually assaulted on campus the week before we conducted the study. It is possible that participants who viewed the aggressive movie would be reminded of the attack and that their subsequent attitudes would be affected by the *combination* of the film and their thoughts about the campus assault. That is, the movie may have produced a different effect on attitudes given the fact that a real assault had occurred recently. Participants who watched the wildlife film, however, would not be prompted to think about rape during their 30-minute film. Thus, the differences we obtain between the two groups could be due to this interaction of history (the real assault) and treatment (the film).

MISCELLANEOUS DESIGN CONFOUNDS. Many of the confounds just described are difficult to control or even to detect. However, one common type of confound is entirely within the researcher's control and, thus, can always be eliminated if sufficient care is taken as the experiment is designed. Ideally, every participant in an experiment should be treated in precisely the same way except that participants in different conditions will receive different levels of the independent variable. Of course, it is virtually impossible to treat each participant exactly the same. Even so, it is essential that no *systematic* differences

occur other than the different levels of the independent variable. When participants in one experimental condition are treated differently than those in another condition, confounding destroys our ability to identify effects of the independent variable and introduces an alternative rival explanation of the results. The study involving reactions to job applicants with disabilities provided a good example of a design confound, as did the case of the Pepsi Challenge.

These by no means exhaust all of the factors that can compromise the internal validity of an experiment, but they should give you a feel for unwanted influences that can undermine the results of experimental studies. When critiquing the quality of an experiment, ask yourself, "Did the experimental conditions differ systematically in any way other than the fact that the participants received different levels of the independent variable?" If so, confounding may have occurred and we cannot draw any conclusions about the effects of the independent variable.

Experimenter Expectancies, Demand Characteristics, and Placebo Effects

The validity of researchers' interpretations of the results of a study are also affected by the researcher's and participants' beliefs about what *should* happen in the experiment. In this section, I'll discuss three potential problems in which people's expectations affect the outcome of an experiment: experimenter expectancies, demand characteristics, and placebo effects.

EXPERIMENTER EXPECTANCY EFFECTS. Researchers usually have some idea about how participants will respond and often have an explicit hypothesis regarding the results of the study. Unfortunately, experimenters' expectations can distort the results of an experiment by affecting how they interpret participants' behavior.

A good example of the **experimenter expectancy effect** (sometimes called the *Rosenthal effect*) is provided in a study by Cordaro and Ison (1963). In this experiment, psychology students were taught to classically condition a simple response in *Planaria* (flatworms). Some students were told that the planarias had been previously conditioned and should show a high rate of response. Other students were told that the planarias had not been conditioned; thus, they thought their worms would show a low rate of response. In reality, both groups of students worked with identical planarias. Despite the fact that their planarias did not really differ in responsiveness, the students who expected responsive planarias recorded 20 times more responses than the students who expected unresponsive planarias!

Did the student experimenters in this study intentionally distort their observations? Perhaps, but more likely their observations were affected by their expectations. People's interpretations are often affected by their beliefs and expectations; people often see what they expect to see. Whether such effects involve intentional distortion or an unconscious bias, experimenters' expectancies may affect their perceptions, thereby compromising the validity of an experiment.

DEMAND CHARACTERISTICS. Participants' assumptions about the nature of a study can also affect the outcome of research. If you have ever participated in research, you probably tried to figure out what the study was about and how the researcher expected you to respond.

Demand characteristics are aspects of a study that indicate to participants how they should behave. Because many people want to be good participants who do what the experimenter wishes, their behavior is affected by demand characteristics rather than by the independent variable itself. In some cases, experimenters unintentionally communicate their expectations in subtle ways that affect participants' behavior. In other instances, participants draw assumptions about the study from the experimental setting and procedure.

A good demonstration of demand characteristics was provided by Orne and Scheibe (1964). These researchers told participants they were participating in a study of stimulus deprivation. In reality, participants were not deprived of stimulation at all but rather simply sat alone in a small, well-lit room for four hours. To create demand characteristics, however, participants in the experimental group were asked to sign forms that released the researcher from liability if the experimental procedure harmed the participant. They were also shown a "panic button" they could push if they could not stand the deprivation any longer. Such cues would likely raise in participants' minds the possibility that

they might have a severe reaction to the study. (Why else would release forms and a panic button be needed?) Participants in the control group were told that they were serving as a control group, were not asked to sign release forms, and were not given a panic button. Thus, the experimental setting would not lead control participants to expect extreme reactions.

As Orne and Scheibe expected, participants in the experimental group showed more extreme reactions during the deprivation period than participants in the control group even though they all underwent *precisely the same experience* of sitting alone for four hours. The only difference between the groups was the presence of demand characteristics that led participants in the experimental group to expect more severe reactions. Given that early studies of stimulus deprivation were plagued by demand characteristics such as these, Orne and Scheibe concluded that many so-called effects of deprivation were, in fact, the result of demand characteristics rather than of stimulus deprivation per se.

To eliminate demand characteristics, experimenters often conceal the purpose of the experiment from participants. In addition, they try to eliminate any cues in their own behavior or in the experimental setting that would lead participants to draw inferences about the hypotheses or about how they should act.

Perhaps the most effective way to eliminate both experimenter expectancy effects and demand characteristics is to use a **double-blind procedure**. With a double-blind procedure, neither the participants nor the experimenters who interact with them know which experimental condition a participant is in at the time the study is conducted. The experiment is supervised by another researcher, who assigns participants to conditions and keeps other experimenters "in the dark." This procedure ensures that the experimenters who interact with the participants will not subtly and unintentionally influence participants to respond in a particular way.

PLACEBO EFFECTS. Conceptually related to demand characteristics are placebo effects. A **placebo effect** is a physiological or psychological change that occurs as a result of the mere suggestion that the change will occur. In experiments that test the effects of drugs or therapies, for example, changes in health or behavior may occur because participants *think* that the treatment will work.

Imagine that you are testing the effects of a new drug, Mintovil, on headaches. One way you might design the study would be to administer Mintovil to one group of participants (the experimental group) but not to another group of participants (the control group). You could then measure how quickly the participants' headaches disappear.

Although this may seem to be a reasonable research strategy, this design leaves open the possibility that a placebo effect will occur, thereby jeopardizing internal validity. The experimental conditions differ in two ways. Not only does the experimental group receive Mintovil, but they *know* they are receiving some sort of drug. Participants in the control group, in contrast, receive no drug and know they have received no drug. If differences are obtained in headache remission for the two groups, we do not know whether the difference is due to Mintovil itself (a true treatment effect) or to the fact that the experimental group receives a drug they expect might reduce their headaches whereas the control group does not (a placebo effect). A placebo effect occurs when a treatment is confounded with participants' knowledge that they are receiving a treatment.

When a placebo effect is possible, researchers use a **placebo control group**. Participants in a placebo control group are administered an ineffective treatment. For example, in the preceding study, a researcher might give the experimental group a pill containing Mintovil and give the placebo control group a pill that contains an inactive substance. Both groups would believe they were receiving medicine, but only the experimental group would receive a pharmaceutically active drug. The children who received the aspartame-sweetened beverage in Rosen et al.'s (1988) study of the effects of sugar on behavior were in a placebo control group.

The presence of placebo effects can be detected by using both a placebo control group and a true control group in the experimental design. Whereas participants in the placebo control group receive an inactive substance (the placebo), participants in the true control group receive no pill and no medicine. If participants in the placebo control group (who received the inactive substance) improve more than those in the true control group (who received nothing), a placebo effect is operating. If this occurs but the researcher wants to conclude that the treatment was effective, he or she must demonstrate that the experimental group improved more than the placebo control group.

Behavioral Research Case Study
The Kind of Placebo Matters

As we have seen, researchers who are concerned that the effects of an independent variable might be due to a placebo effect often add a placebo control condition to their experimental design. Importantly, researchers should consider the precise nature of the placebos that they use because recent research suggests that different placebos can have different effects.

Kaptchuk and his colleagues (2006) tested a sample of 270 adults who had chronic arm pain due to repetitive use, such as tendonitis. Participants received either sham acupuncture in which a trick acupuncture needle retracts into a hollow shaft rather than penetrating the skin or a placebo pill, neither of which should actually affect chronic pain. Over a 2-week period, arm pain decreased in both the sham acupuncture and placebo pill conditions, but participants in the placebo pill condition reported that they were able to sleep, write, and open jars better than those in the sham acupuncture condition. Over 10 weeks, however, the sham acupuncture group reported a greater drop in reported pain than the placebo pill group.

Interestingly, the "side effects" that participants in each group experienced were consistent with the possible side effects that had been described to them at the start of the study. Twenty-five percent of the sham acupuncture group reported experiencing side effects from the nonexistent needle pricks (such as pain and red skin), and 31% of the placebo pill group reported side effects from the imaginary drug (such as dry mouth and fatigue). Findings such as these highlight the power of placebo effects in research and, ironically, also show that different kinds of ineffective treatments can have different effects.

"FIND OUT WHO SET UP THIS EXPERIMENT. IT SEEMS THAT HALF OF THE PATIENTS WERE GIVEN A PLACEBO, AND THE OTHER HALF WERE GIVEN A DIFFERENT PLACEBO."

Source: SCIENCECARTOONSPLUS.COM © 2000 by Sidney Harris.

ERROR VARIANCE

Error variance is a less "fatal" problem than confound variance, but it creates its own set of difficulties. By decreasing the power of an experiment, error variance reduces researchers' ability to detect effects of the independent variable on the dependent variable. Error variance is seldom eliminated from experimental designs. However, researchers try hard to minimize it.

Sources of Error Variance

Recall that error variance is the "static" in an experiment. It results from all of the unsystematic, uncontrolled, and unidentified variables that affect participants' behavior in large and small ways.

INDIVIDUAL DIFFERENCES. The most common source of error variance is preexisting individual differences among participants. When participants enter an experiment, they already differ in a variety of ways—cognitively, physiologically, emotionally, and behaviorally. As a result of their preexisting differences, even participants who are in the same experimental condition respond differently to the independent variable, creating error variance.

Of course, nothing can be done to eliminate individual differences among people. However, one partial solution to this source of error variance is to use a homogeneous sample of participants. The more alike participants are, the less error variance is produced by their differences, and the easier it is to detect effects of the independent variable.

This is one reason that researchers who use animals as participants prefer samples composed of littermates. Littermates are genetically similar, are of the same age, and have usually been raised in the same environment. As a result, they differ little among themselves. Similarly, researchers who study human behavior often prefer homogeneous samples. For example, whatever other drawbacks they may have as research participants, college students at a particular university are often a relatively homogeneous group.

TRANSIENT STATES.   In addition to differing on the relatively stable dimensions already mentioned, participants differ in terms of *transient states* that they may be in at the time of the study. At the time of the experiment, some are healthy whereas others are ill. Some are tired; others are well rested. Some are happy; others are sad. Some are enthusiastic about participating in the study; others resent having to participate. Participants' current moods, attitudes, and physical conditions can affect their behavior in ways that have nothing to do with the experiment.

About all a researcher can do to reduce the impact of these factors is to avoid creating different transient reactions in different participants during the course of the experiment itself. If the experimenter is friendlier toward some participants than toward others, for example, error variance will increase.

ENVIRONMENTAL FACTORS.   Error variance is also affected by differences in the environment in which the study is conducted. For example, participants who come to the experiment drenched to the skin are likely to respond differently than those who saunter in under sunny skies. External noise may distract some participants. Collecting data at different times during the day may create extraneous variability in participants' responses.

To reduce error variance, researchers try to hold the environment as constant as possible as they test different participants. Of course, little can be done about the weather, and it may not be feasible to conduct the study at only one time each day. However, factors such as laboratory temperature and noise should be held constant. Experimenters try to be sure that the experimental setting is as invariant as possible while different participants are tested.

DIFFERENTIAL TREATMENT.   Ideally, researchers should treat each and every participant within each condition exactly the same in all respects. However, as hard as they may try, experimenters find it difficult to treat all participants in precisely the same way during the study.

For one thing, experimenters' moods and health are likely to differ across participants. As a result, they may respond more positively toward some participants than toward others. Furthermore, experimenters are likely to act differently toward different kinds of participants. Experimenters are likely to respond differently toward participants who are pleasant, attentive, and friendly than toward participants who are unpleasant, distracted, and belligerent. Even the participants' physical appearance can affect how they are treated by the researcher. Furthermore, experimenters may inadvertently modify the procedure slightly, by using slightly different words when giving instructions, for example. Also, male and female participants may respond differently to male and female experimenters, and vice versa.

Even slight differences in how participants are treated can introduce error variance into their responses. One solution is to automate the experiment as much as possible, thereby removing the influence of the researcher to some degree. To eliminate the possibility that experimenters will vary in how they treat participants, many researchers record the instructions for the study rather than deliver them in person, and many experiments are administered entirely by computer. Similarly, animal researchers automate their experiments, using programmed equipment to deliver food, manipulate variables, and measure behavior, thereby minimizing the impact of the human factor on the results.

MEASUREMENT ERROR.   We saw in Chapter 3 that all behavioral measures contain measurement error to some degree. Measurement error contributes to error variance because it causes participants' scores to vary in unsystematic ways. Researchers should make every effort to use only reliable techniques and take steps to minimize the influence of factors that create measurement error.

Developing Your Research Skills
Tips for Minimizing Error Variance

1. Use a homogeneous sample.
2. Aside from differences in the independent variable, treat all participants precisely the same at all times.
3. Hold all laboratory conditions (heat, lighting, noise, and so on) constant.
4. Standardize all research procedures.
5. Automate the experiment as much as possible.
6. Use only reliable measurement procedures.

Many factors can create extraneous variability in behavioral data. Because the factors that create error variance are spread across all conditions of the design, they do not create confounding or produce problems with internal validity. Rather, they simply add static to the picture produced by the independent variable. They produce unsystematic, yet unwanted, changes in participants' scores that can cloud the effects the researcher is studying. After reading Chapter 11, you'll understand more fully why error variance increases the difficulty of detecting effects of the independent variable. For now, simply understand what error variance is, the factors that cause it, and how it can be minimized through experimental control.

In Depth
The Shortcomings of Experimentation

Experimental designs are preferred by many behavioral scientists because they allow us to determine causal relationships. However, there are many topics in psychology for which experimental designs are inappropriate. Sometimes researchers are not interested in cause-and-effect relationships. Survey researchers, for example, often want only to describe people's attitudes and aren't interested in *why* people hold the attitudes they do.

In other cases, researchers are interested in causal effects but find it impossible or unfeasible to conduct a true experiment. As we've seen, experimentation requires that the researcher be able to control aspects of the research setting. However, researchers are often unwilling or unable to manipulate the variables they study. For example, to do an experiment on the effects of facial deformities on people's self-concepts would require randomly assigning some people to have their faces disfigured. Likewise, to conduct an experiment on the effects of oxygen deprivation during the birth process on later intellectual performance, we would have to deprive newborns of oxygen for varying lengths of time. As we saw in Chapter 8, experiments have not been conducted on the effects of smoking on humans because such studies would assign some nonsmokers to smoke heavily. Despite the fact that experiments can provide clear evidence of causal processes, descriptive and correlational studies, as well as quasi-experimental designs (which we'll examine in Chapter 13), are sometimes more appropriate and useful.

EXPERIMENTAL CONTROL AND GENERALIZABILITY: THE EXPERIMENTER'S DILEMMA

We've seen that experimental control involves treating all participants precisely the same, with the exception of giving participants in different conditions different levels of the independent variable. The tighter the experimental control, the more internally valid the experiment will be. And the more internally valid the experiment, the stronger, more definitive conclusions we can draw about the causal effects of the independent variables.

However, experimental control is a two-edged sword. Tight experimental control means that the researcher has created a highly specific and often artificial situation. The effects of extraneous variables that affect behavior in the real world have been eliminated or held at a constant level. The result is that the more controlled a study is, the more difficult it is to generalize the findings.

External validity refers to the degree to which the results obtained in one study can be replicated or generalized to other samples, research settings, and procedures. External validity refers to the *generalizability* of the research results to other settings (Campbell & Stanley, 1966).

To some extent the internal validity and external validity of experiments are inversely related; high internal validity tends to produce lower external validity, and vice versa. The conflict between internal and external validity has been called the **experimenter's dilemma** (Jung, 1971). The more tightly the experimenter controls the experimental setting, the more internally valid the results but the lower the external validity. Thus, researchers face the dilemma of choosing between internal and external validity.

When faced with this dilemma, virtually all experimental psychologists opt in favor of internal validity. After all, if internal validity is weak, then they cannot draw confident conclusions about the effects of the independent variable, and the findings should not be generalized anyway.

Furthermore, in experimental research, the goal is seldom to obtain results that generalize to the real world. The goal of experimentation is not to make generalizations but rather to test them (Mook, 1983). Most experiments are designed to test hypotheses about the effects of certain variables on behavior, thought, emotion, or physiological responses. Researchers develop hypotheses, and then design studies to determine whether those hypotheses are supported by the data. If they are supported, evidence is provided that supports the theory. If they are not supported, the theory is called into question.

The purpose of most experiments is not to discover what people do in real-life settings or to create effects that will necessarily generalize to other settings or to the real world. In fact, the findings of any single experiment should *never* be generalized—no matter how well the study is designed, who its participants are, or where it is conducted. The results of any particular study depend too strongly on the context in which it is conducted to allow us to generalize its findings.

Instead, the purpose of experimentation is to test general propositions about the determinants of behavior. If the theory is supported by data, we may then try to generalize the theory, not the results, to other contexts. We determine the generalizability of a theory through replicating experiments in other contexts, with different participants, and using modified procedures. Replication tells us about the generality of our hypotheses.

Many people do not realize that the artificiality of many experiments is their greatest asset. As Stanovich (1996) noted, "contrary to common belief, the artificiality of scientific experiments is not an accidental oversight. Scientists *deliberately* set up conditions that are unlike those that occur naturally because this is the only way to separate the many inherently correlated variables that determine events in the world" (p. 90). He described several phenomena that would have been impossible to discover under real-world, natural conditions—phenomena ranging from subatomic particles in physics to biofeedback in psychology.

In brief, although important, external validity is not a crucial consideration in most behavioral studies (Mook, 1983). The comment "but it's not real life" is not a valid criticism of experimental research (Stanovich, 1996).

WEB-BASED EXPERIMENTAL RESEARCH

Many of you reading this book cannot remember a time when the Internet did not exist. Yet, the World Wide Web is a relatively recent innovation, becoming widely available only in the mid-1990s. In addition to the widespread changes that the Web brought in marketing, banking, personal communication, news, and entertainment, the Internet has opened up new opportunities for behavioral scientists by allowing researchers to conduct studies online without having participants come to a laboratory or even interact with a researcher. Behavioral researchers now use the Web to conduct surveys, correlational studies, and experiments, and investigators are working hard to understand the consequences of doing online research as well as ways to improve the validity of **Web-based research** (Anderson & Kanuka, 2003; Gosling, Vazire, Srivastava, & John, 2004; Kraut et al. 2004).

Like all research approaches, conducting research via the World Wide Web has both advantages and limitations. Among the advantages are the following:

- Using the Web, researchers can usually obtain much larger samples with a lower expenditure of time and money than with conventional studies. For example, using a Web site, social psychologists collected over 2.5 million responses to tests of implicit attitudes and beliefs in only five years (Nosek, Banaji, & Greenwald, 2002).
- The samples that are recruited for Web-based studies are often more diverse than those in many other studies. The convenience samples typically used in experimental research do not reflect the diversity of age, race, ethnicity, and education that we find in the general population. Internet samples are more diverse than traditional samples, although they are certainly not truly representative of the population because of differences in people's access to, interest in, and use of the Internet.
- Researchers who conduct Web-based studies find it reasonably easy to obtain samples with very specific characteristics by targeting groups through Web sites, newsgroups, and

organizations. Whether a researcher wants a sample of high school teachers, snake owners, people who play paintball, or patients with a particular disease, he or she can usually reach a large sample online.
- Because no researcher is present, data obtained from Web studies may be less susceptible to social desirability biases and experimenter expectancies than traditional studies.

Despite these advantages, Web-based studies also have some notable disadvantages compared to other kinds of research:

- Researchers have difficulty identifying and controlling the nature of the sample. Researchers have no way of confirming the identity of people who participate in a Web-based study nor any way of ensuring that a participant does not complete the study multiple times. Although cookies (files that identify a particular computer) can tell us whether a particular computer previously logged onto the research site, we do not know when someone participates more than once using different computers or whether several different people used the same computer to participate.
- As we have seen, researchers try to control the setting in which research is conducted to minimize error variance. However, the situations in which people complete Web-based studies—in their homes, apartments, dorm rooms, offices, and Internet cafes—vary greatly from one another in terms of background noise, lighting, the presence of other people, distractions, and so on.
- Participants frequently fail to complete Web studies that they start. A potential participant may initially find a study interesting and begin to participate but then lose interest and stop before finishing.
- Web studies are limited in the research paradigms that may be used. They work reasonably well for studies in which participants merely answer questions or respond to written stimuli, but they do not easily allow face-to-face interaction, independent variables involving

modification of the physical situation or the administration of drugs, experiments with multiple sessions, or experiments that require a great deal of staging of the social situation. Furthermore, because participants' individual computers differ in speed, hardware, and screen resolution, researchers may find it difficult to present visual stimuli or measure reaction times precisely.

Of course, all studies, including those conducted under controlled laboratory conditions, have advantages and limitations, so the big questional is whether Web-based studies are as valid as studies that are conducted in traditional settings. The jury is still out on this question, but studies that have compared the findings of laboratory studies to the results of similar studies conducted on the Internet have found a reassuring amount of convergence (Gosling, et al., 2004; Musch & Reips, 2000).

Summary

1. Of the four types of research (descriptive, correlational, experimental, and quasi-experimental), only experimental research provides conclusive evidence regarding cause-and-effect relationships.

2. In a well-designed experiment, the researcher varies at least one independent variable to assess its effects on participants' behavior, assigns participants to the experimental conditions in a way that ensures the initial equivalence of the conditions, and controls extraneous variables that may influence participants' behavior.

3. An independent variable must have at least two levels; thus, every experiment must have at least two conditions. The control group in an experiment, if there is one, gets a zero-level of the independent variable.

4. Researchers may vary an independent variable through environmental, instructional, or invasive manipulations.

5. To ensure that their independent variables are strong enough to produce the hypothesized effects, researchers often pilot test their independent variables and use manipulation checks in the experiment itself.

6. In addition to independent variables manipulated by the researcher, experiments sometimes include subject (or participant) variables that reflect characteristics of the participants.

7. The logic of the experimental method requires that the various experimental and control groups be equivalent before the levels of the independent variable are introduced.

8. Initial equivalence of the various conditions is accomplished in one of three ways. In between-subjects designs, researchers use simple or matched random assignment. In within-subjects or repeated measures designs, all participants serve in all experimental conditions, thereby ensuring their equivalence.

9. Within-subjects designs are more powerful and economical than between-subjects designs, but order effects and carryover effects are sometimes a problem.

10. Nothing other than the independent variable may differ systematically among conditions. When something other than the independent variable differs among conditions, confounding occurs, destroying the internal validity of the experiment and making it difficult, if not impossible, to draw conclusions about the effects of the independent variable.

11. Researchers try to minimize error variance. Error variance is produced by unsystematic differences among participants within experimental conditions. Although error variance does not undermine the validity of an experiment, it makes detecting effects of the independent variable more difficult.

12. Researchers' and participants' expectations about an experiment can bias the results. Thus, efforts must be made to eliminate the influence of experimenter expectancies, demand characteristics, and placebo effects.

13. Attempts to minimize the error variance in an experiment may lower the study's external

validity—the degree to which the results can be generalized. However, most experiments are designed to test hypotheses about the causes of behavior. If the hypotheses are supported, then they—not the particular results of the study—are generalized.

14. Behavioral researchers use the World Wide Web to conduct surveys, correlational studies, and experiments, allowing them to obtain larger and more diverse samples with a lower expenditure of time and money. However, researchers who conduct Web-based research often have difficulty identifying and controlling the nature of the sample, and they cannot control the search setting.

Key Terms

attrition (*p. 199*)
between-groups variance (*p. 194*)
between-subjects or between-groups design (*p. 190*)
biased assignment (*p. 197*)
carryover effects (*p. 193*)
condition (*p. 184*)
confederate (*p. 185*)
confounding (*p. 196*)
confound variance (*p. 194*)
control group (*p. 186*)
counterbalancing (*p. 192*)
demand characteristics (*p. 201*)
dependent variable (*p. 188*)
differential attrition (*p. 199*)
double-blind procedure (*p. 201*)
environmental manipulation (*p. 185*)
error variance (*p. 195*)

experiment (*p. 184*)
experimental control (*p. 194*)
experimental group (*p. 185*)
experimenter expectancy effect (*p. 200*)
experimenter's dilemma (*p. 206*)
external validity (*p. 206*)
fatigue effects (*p. 192*)
history effects (*p. 200*)
independent variable (*p. 184*)
instructional manipulation (*p. 185*)
internal validity (*p. 196*)
invasive manipulation (*p. 185*)
Latin Square design (*p. 193*)
level (*p. 184*)
manipulation check (*p. 187*)
matched random assignment (*p. 190*)
order effects (*p. 191*)

pilot test (*p. 187*)
placebo control group (*p. 202*)
placebo effect (*p. 201*)
power (*p. 190*)
practice effects (*p. 191*)
pretest sensitization (*p. 199*)
primary variance (*p. 194*)
randomized groups design (*p. 190*)
repeated measures design (*p. 190*)
secondary variance (*p. 194*)
sensitization (*p. 192*)
simple random assignment (*p. 189*)
subject or participant variable (*p. 188*)
systematic variance (*p. 194*)
treatment variance (*p. 194*)
Web-based research (*p. 207*)
within-groups variance (*p. 195*)
within-subjects design (*p. 190*)

Questions for Review

1. What advantage do experiments have over descriptive and correlational studies?
2. A well-designed experiment possesses what three characteristics?
3. Distinguish between qualitative and quantitative levels of an independent variable.
4. True or false: Every experiment has as many conditions as there are levels of the independent variable.
5. Give your own example of an environmental, instructional, and invasive experimental manipulation.
6. Must all experiments include a control group? Explain.
7. In what way do researchers take a risk if they do not pilot test the independent variable they plan to use in an experiment?

8. Explain how you would use a manipulation check to determine whether you successfully manipulated room temperature in a study of temperature and aggression.
9. Distinguish between an independent variable and a subject variable.
10. Why must researchers ensure that their experimental groups are roughly equivalent before manipulating the independent variable?
11. Imagine that you were conducting an experiment to examine the effect of generous role models on children's willingness to share toys with another child. Explain how you would use (a) simple random assignment and (b) matched random assignment to equalize your groups at the start of this study.

12. Explain how you would conduct the study in Question 11 as a within-subjects design.
13. Discuss the relative advantages and disadvantages between within-subjects designs and between-subjects designs.
14. What are order effects, and how does counterbalancing help us deal with them?
15. Distinguish among treatment, confound, and error variance.
16. Which is worse—confound variance or error variance? Why?
17. What is the relationship between confounding and internal validity?
18. Define the confounds in the following list and explain why each confound undermines the internal validity of an experiment:
    a. biased assignment of participants to conditions
    b. differential attrition
    c. pretest sensitization
    d. history
    e. miscellaneous design confounds
19. What are experimenter expectancy effects, and how do researchers minimize them?
20. Should demand characteristics be eliminated or strengthened in an experiment? Explain.
21. How do researchers detect and eliminate placebo effects?
22. What effect does error variance have on the results of an experiment?
23. What can researchers do to minimize error variance?
24. Discuss the trade-off between internal and external validity. Which is more important? Explain.
25. What advantages are there to conducting research using the World Wide Web? Disadvantages?

Questions for Discussion

1. Psychology developed primarily as an experimental science. However, during the past 20–25 years, non experimental methods (such as correlational research) have become increasingly popular. Why do you think this change has occurred? Do you think an increasing reliance on nonexperimental methods is beneficial or detrimental to the field?
2. Imagine that you are interested in the effects of background music on people's performance at work. Design an experiment in which you test the effects of classical music (played at various decibels) on employees' job performance. In designing the study, you will need to decide how many levels of loudness to use, whether to use a control group, how to assign participants to conditions, how to eliminate confound variance and minimize error variance, and how to measure job performance.
3. For each experiment described after the bulleted list, answer the following questions:
   • What is the independent variable?
   • How many levels does it have?
   • What did the participants in the experimental group(s) do?
   • Was there a control group? If so, what did participants in the control group experience?
   • What is the dependent variable?
   a. A pharmaceutical company developed a new drug to relieve depression and hired a research organization to investigate the potential effectiveness of the drug. The researchers contacted a group of psychiatric patients who were experiencing chronic depression and randomly assigned half of the patients to the drug group and half of the patients to the placebo group. To avoid any possible confusion in administering the drug or placebo to the patients, one psychiatric nurse always administered the drug and another nurse always administered the placebo. However, to control experimenter expectancy effects, the nurses did not know which drug they were administering. One month later the drug group had dramatically improved compared to the placebo group, and the pharmaceutical company concluded that the new antidepressant was effective.
   b. An investigator hypothesized that people in a fearful situation desire to be with other individuals. To test her hypothesis, the experimenter randomly assigned 50 participants to either a high or low fear group. Participants in the low fear group were told that they would be shocked but that they would experience only a small tingle that would not hurt. Participants in the high fear group were told that the shock would be quite painful and might burn the skin but would not cause any permanent damage. After being told this, eight participants in the high fear group declined to participate in the study. The experimenter released

them (as she was ethically bound to do) and conducted the experiment. Each group of participants was then told to wait while the shock equipment was being prepared and that they could wait either in a room by themselves or with other people. No difference was found in the extent to which the high and low fear groups wanted to wait with others.

c. A study was conducted to investigate the hypothesis that watching televised violence increases aggression in children. Fifty kindergarten children were randomly assigned to watch either a violent or a nonviolent television program. After watching the television program, the children were allowed to engage in an hour of free play while trained observers watched for aggressive behavior and recorded the frequency with which aggressive acts took place. To avoid the possibility of fatigue setting in, two observers observed the children for the first 30 minutes, and two other observers observed the children for the second 30 minutes. Results showed that children who watched the violent program behaved more aggressively than those who watched the nonviolent show.

4. Now go back through the three experiments just described, looking for any confounds that might be present. (Be careful not to identify things as confounds that are not.) Then redesign each study to eliminate any confounds that you find. Write a short paragraph for each case, identifying the confound and how you would eliminate it.

5. The text discusses the trade-off between internal and external validity, known as the *experimenter's dilemma*. Speculate on things a researcher can do to increase internal and external validity simultaneously, thereby designing a study that ranks high on both.

6. Why is artificiality sometimes an asset when designing an experiment?

Answers to In-Chapter Questions

IDENTIFYING INDEPENDENT AND DEPENDENT VARIABLES (P. 188)

Study 1

1. The independent variable is whether participants generated incorrectly spelled words.
2. It has two levels.
3. The experiment has two conditions—one in which participants generated incorrect spellings for 13 words and one in which participants performed an unrelated task.
4. They generate incorrectly spelled words.
5. Yes.
6. The frequency with which participants switched from correct to incorrect spellings on the final test.

Study 2

1. The independent variable is whether participants were exposed to a gun.
2. It has two levels.
3. The experiment has two conditions—one in which participants interacted with the gun and another in which participants interacted with the game.
4. In one experimental group, participants interacted with the gun, and in the other experimental group participants interacted with the game.
5. No.
6. The testosterone level in participants' saliva.

Confounding: Can You Find It? (p. 197)

1. The independent variable was whether the applicant appeared to have a disability.
2. The dependent variables were participants' ratings of the applicant (such as ratings of how qualified the applicant was, how much the participant liked the applicant, and whether the participant would hire the applicant).
3. The experimental conditions differed not only in whether the applicant appeared to have a disability (the independent variable) but also in the nature of the photograph that participants saw. One photograph showed the applicant's entire body, whereas the other photograph showed only his head and shoulders. This difference creates a confound because participants' ratings in the two experimental conditions may be affected by the nature of the photographs rather than by the apparent presence or absence of a disability.
4. The problem could be corrected in many ways. For example, full-body photographs could be used in both conditions. In one photograph, the applicant could be shown seated in a wheelchair, whereas in the other photograph, the person could be shown in a chair. Alternatively, identical photographs could be used in both conditions, with the disability listed in the information that participants receive about the applicant.

10 | EXPERIMENTAL DESIGN

People are able to remember verbal material better if they understand what it means than if they don't. For example, people find it difficult to remember seemingly meaningless sentences like *The notes were sour because the seams had split*. However, once they comprehend the sentence (it refers to a bagpipe), they remember it easily.

Bower, Karlin, and Dueck (1975) were interested in whether comprehension aids memory for pictures as it does for verbal material. These researchers designed an experiment to test the hypothesis that people remember pictures better if they comprehend them than if they don't comprehend them. In this experiment, participants were shown a series of "droodles." A droodle is a picture that, on first glance, appears meaningless but that has a humorous interpretation. An example of a droodle is shown in Figure 10.1. Participants were assigned randomly to one of two experimental conditions. Half of the participants were given an interpretation of the droodle as they studied each picture. The other half simply studied each picture without being told what it was supposed to be.

After viewing 28 droodles for 10 seconds each, participants were asked to draw as many of the droodles as they could remember. Then, one week later, the participants returned for a recognition test. They were shown 24 sets of three pictures; each set contained one droodle that the participants had seen the previous week, plus two pictures they had not seen previously. Participants rated the three pictures in each set according to how similar each was to a picture they had seen the week before. The two dependent variables in the experiment, then, were the number of droodles the participants could draw immediately after seeing them and the number of droodles that participants correctly recognized the following week.

The results of this experiment supported the researchers' hypothesis that people remember pictures better if they comprehend them than if they don't comprehend them. Participants who received an interpretation of each droodle accurately recalled significantly more droodles than those who did not receive interpretations. Participants in the interpretation condition recalled an average of 70% of the droodles, whereas participants in the no-interpretation condition recalled only 51% of the droodles. We'll return to the droodles study as we discuss basic experimental designs in this chapter.

We'll begin by looking at experimental designs that involve the manipulation of a single independent variable, such as the design of the droodles experiment. Then we'll turn

FIGURE 10.1 Example of a Droodle. What is it?
Answer: An early bird who caught a very strong worm.

Source: From "Comprehension and Memory for
Pictures," by G. H. Bower,
M. B. Karlin, and A. Dueck, 1975, *Memory and
Cognition, 3,* p. 217.

our attention to experimental designs that involve the
manipulation of two or more independent variables.

ONE-WAY DESIGNS

Experimental designs in which only one independent
variable is manipulated are called **one-way designs**.
The simplest one-way design is a **two-group experimental design** in which there are only two levels of
the independent variable (and, thus, two conditions).
A minimum of two conditions is needed so that we
can compare participants' responses in one experi-

mental condition with those in another condition.
Only then can we determine whether the different
levels of the independent variable led to differences
in participants' behavior. (A study that has only one
condition cannot be classified as an experiment at all
because no independent variable is manipulated.)
The droodles study was a two-group experimental
design; participants in one condition received interpretations of the droodles, whereas participants in
the other condition did not receive interpretations.

At least two conditions are necessary in an
experiment, but experiments typically involve more
than two levels of the independent variable. For
example, in a study designed to examine the effectiveness of weight-loss programs, Mahoney, Moura,
and Wade (1973) randomly assigned 53 obese adults
to one of five conditions: (1) One group rewarded
themselves when they lost weight; (2) another
punished themselves when they didn't lose weight;
(3) a third group used both self-reward and self-
punishment; (4) a fourth group monitored their
weight but did not reward or punish themselves; and
(5) a control group did not monitor their weight. This
study involved a single independent variable that had
five levels (the various weight-reduction strategies).
(In case you're interested, the results of this study are
shown in Figure 10.2. As you can see, self-reward
resulted in significantly more weight loss than the
other strategies.)

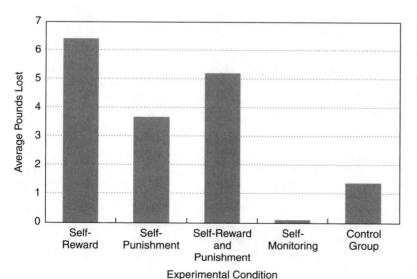

**FIGURE 10.2 Average Pounds Lost
by Participants in Each Experimental
Condition**

Source: Adapted from Mahoney,
Moura, and Wade (1973).

Assigning Participants to Conditions

One-way designs come in three basic varieties, each of which we discussed briefly in Chapter 9: the randomized groups design, the matched-subjects design, and the repeated measures or within-subjects, design. As we learned in Chapter 9, the **randomized groups design** is a between-subjects design in which participants are randomly assigned to one of two or more conditions. A randomized groups design was used for the droodles experiment described earlier (see Figure 10.3).

You learned in Chapter 9 that matched random assignment is sometimes used to increase the similarity of the experimental groups prior to the manipulation of the independent variable. In a **matched-subjects design**, participants are matched into blocks on the basis of a variable the researcher believes relevant to the experiment. Then participants in each matched block are randomly assigned to one of the experimental or control conditions.

Recall that, in a **repeated measures** (or within-subjects) **design**, each participant serves in all experimental conditions. To redesign the droodles study as a repeated measures design, we would provide interpretations for *half* of the droodles each participant saw but not for the other half. In this way, each participant would serve in *both* the interpretation and no-interpretation conditions, and we could see whether participants remembered more of the droodles that were accompanied by interpretations than droodles without interpretations.

Condition

Received interpretation of droodles	Did not receive interpretation of droodles

FIGURE 10.3 A Randomized Two-Group Design. In a randomized groups design such as this, participants are randomly assigned to one of the experimental conditions.

Source: Bower, Karlin, and Dueck (1975).

Developing Your Research Skills
Design Your Own Experiments

Read the following research questions. For each question, design an experiment in which you manipulate a single independent variable. Your independent variable may have as many levels as necessary to address the research question.

1. Timms (1980) suggested that people who try to keep themselves from blushing when embarrassed may actually blush more than if they don't try to stop blushing. Design an experiment to determine whether this is true.
2. Design an experiment to determine whether people's reaction times are shorter to red stimuli than to stimuli of other colors.
3. In some studies, participants are asked to complete a large number of questionnaires over the span of an hour or more. Researchers sometimes worry that completing so many questionnaires may make participants tired, frustrated, or angry. If so, the process of completing the questionnaires may actually change participants' moods. Design an experiment to determine whether participants' moods are affected by completing lengthy questionnaires.

In designing each experiment, did you use a randomized groups, matched-subjects, or repeated measures design? Why? Whichever design you chose for each research question, redesign the experiment using each of the other two kinds of one-way designs. Consider the relative advantages and disadvantages of using each of the designs to answer the research questions.

Posttest and Pretest–Posttest Designs

The three basic one-way experimental designs just described are diagrammed in Figure 10.4. Each of these three designs is called a **posttest-only design** because, in each instance, the dependent variable is measured only *after* the experimental manipulation has occurred.

In some cases, however, researchers measure the dependent variable twice—once before the independent variable is manipulated and again afterward. Such designs are called **pretest–posttest designs**. Each of the three posttest-only designs we described can be converted to a pretest–posttest design by measuring the dependent variable both before and after manipulating the independent variable. Figure 10.5 shows the pretest–posttest versions of the randomized groups, matched-subjects, and repeated measures designs.

Many students mistakenly assume that both a pretest and a posttest are needed in order to determine whether the independent variable affected participants' responses. They reason that we can test the effects of the independent variable only by seeing whether participants' scores on the dependent variable change from the pretest to the posttest. However,

you should be able to see that this is not true. As long as researchers make the experimental and control groups equivalent by using simple random assignment, matched random assignment, or a within-subjects design as we discussed in Chapter 9, they can test the effects of the independent variable using only a posttest measure of the dependent variable. If participants' scores on the dependent variable differ significantly between the conditions, researchers can conclude that the independent variable caused those differences without having pretested the participants beforehand. So, posttest–only designs are perfectly capable of identifying effects of the independent variable and, in fact, most experiments use posttest-only designs.

Even so, researchers sometimes use pretest-posttest designs because, depending on the nature of the experiment, they offer three advantages over posttest-only designs. First, by obtaining pretest scores on the dependent variable, the researcher can verify that participants in the various experimental conditions did not differ with respect to the dependent variable at the beginning of the experiment.

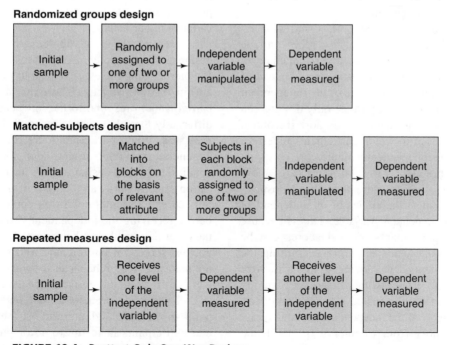

FIGURE 10.4 Posttest-Only One-Way Designs

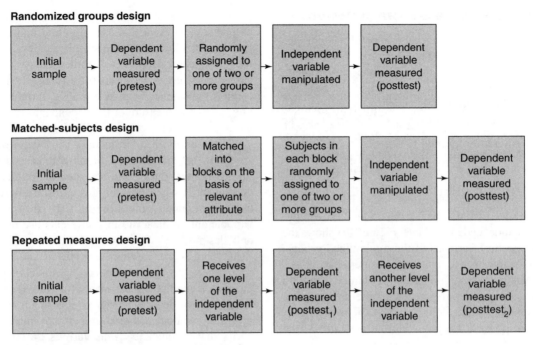

FIGURE 10.5 Pretest–Posttest One-Way Designs

In this way, the effectiveness of random or matched assignment can be documented.

Second, by comparing pretest and posttest scores on the dependent variable, researchers can see exactly *how much* the independent variable changed participants' behavior. Pretests provide useful baseline data for judging the size of the independent variable's effect. However, posttest-only designs can also provide baseline data of this sort if control conditions are used in which participants receive a zero level of the independent variable.

Third, pretest–posttest designs are more powerful; that is, they are more likely than a posttest-only design to detect the effects of the independent variable on the dependent variable. This is because variability in participants' pretest scores can be removed from the analyses before examining the effects of the independent variable. In this way, error variance due to pre-existing differences among participants can be eliminated from the analyses, making the effects of the independent variable easier to see. Remember from Chapter 9 (p. 195) that minimizing error variance makes the effects of the

independent variable stand out more clearly, and pretest–posttest designs allow us to lower the error variance in our data.

Despite these advantages, pretest–posttest designs also have potential drawbacks. As we saw in Chapter 9, using pretests can lead to **pretest sensitization**. Administering a pretest may sensitize participants to respond to the independent variable differently than they would respond if they are not pretested. When participants are pretested on the dependent variable, researchers sometimes add conditions to their design to look for pretest sensitization effects. For example, half of the participants in each experimental condition could be pretested before receiving the independent variable, whereas the other half would not be pretested. By comparing posttest scores for participants who were and were not pretested, researchers can see whether the pretest had any effect on the results of the experiment.

Even when pretests do not sensitize participants to the independent variable, they sometimes cue participants in to the topic or purpose of the experiment. As we will discuss later, participants often have difficulty responding naturally if they know (or think they know) precisely what a study is about or what behavior the researcher is measuring. Pretests can alert participants to the focus of an experiment and lead them to behave unnaturally.

I want to stress again that, although pretest–posttest designs are sometimes useful, they are by no means necessary. A posttest-only design provides all of the information needed to determine whether the independent variable has an effect on the dependent variable. Assuming that participants are assigned to conditions in a random fashion or that a repeated measures design is used, posttest differences between conditions indicate that the independent variable had an effect on participants' responses.

In brief, we have described three basic one-way designs: the randomized groups design, the matched-subjects design, and the repeated measures (or within-subjects) design. Each of these designs can be employed as a posttest-only design or as a pretest–posttest design, depending on the requirements of a particular experiment.

FACTORIAL DESIGNS

Researchers have known for many years that people's expectations can influence their reactions to things. For example, merely telling medical patients that they have received an effective treatment for a physical or mental condition sometimes produces positive benefits (see Stewart-Williams & Podd, 2004, for a review). Similarly, in consumer research, people who taste meat that is labeled as "75% fat free" report that it tastes better than precisely the same meat labeled as "containing 25% fat" (Levin & Gaeth, 1988). And, as we saw in the previous chapter, participants' beliefs about the effects of an experiment can influence their responses above and beyond the actual effects of the independent variable (which is why researchers sometimes use placebo control groups).

Behavioral researchers who study consumer behavior are interested in expectancy effects because they raise the intriguing possibility that the price that people pay for a product may influence not only how they feel about the product but also the product's actual effectiveness. Not surprisingly, shoppers

judge higher–priced items to be of better quality than lower–priced items. As a result, they may expect items that cost more to be more effective than those that cost less, which may produce a placebo effect that favors higher–priced items. Put simply, paying more for a product, such as a medicine or performance booster, may lead it to be more effective than paying less for exactly the same product.

Furthermore, if this effect is driven by people's expectations about the product's quality, an item's price should exert a stronger effect on its effectiveness when people think consciously about the effectiveness of the product. If people don't think about its effectiveness, their preconceptions and expectancies should not affect their reactions.

Think for a moment about how you might design an experiment to test this idea. According to this hypothesis, the effectiveness of a product is influenced by two factors—(1) its price and (2) whether people think about the product's effectiveness. Thus, testing this hypothesis requires studying the combined effects of these two variables simultaneously.

The one-way experimental designs that we discussed earlier in this chapter would not be particularly useful for testing this hypothesis. A one-way design allows us to test the effects of only one independent variable. Testing the effects of price and thinking about a product's effectiveness requires an experimental design that tests two independent variables simultaneously. Such a design, in which two or more independent variables are manipulated, is called a **factorial design**. Often the independent variables are referred to as **factors**. (Do not confuse this use of the term *factors* with the use of the term in *factor analysis*. In experimental research, a factor is an independent variable.)

In an experiment designed to test this hypothesis, Shiv, Carmon, and Ariely (2005) studied the effects of SoBe Adrenalin Rush®—a popular "energy drink" that, among other things, claims to increase mental performance. The researchers used a factorial design in which they manipulated two independent variables: the price of the SoBe (full price versus discounted price) and expectancy strength (participants were or were not led to think about SoBe's effects). In this experiment, 125 participants were randomly assigned to purchase SoBe Adrenalin Rush® at either full price ($1.89) or at a discounted price ($.89). Then, after watching a video for 10 minutes, ostensibly to allow SoBe to be absorbed into their system, participants were given 30 minutes to solve 15 anagrams (scrambled word puzzles).

However, just before starting to work on the anagrams, participants were randomly assigned either to think about how effective SoBe is at improving concentration and mental performance (this was called the *high expectancy strength condition*) or to solve the puzzles without considering SoBe's effects (*low expectancy strength condition*). Then, the number of anagrams that participants solved in 30 minutes was measured.

The experimental design for this study is shown in Figure 10.6. As you can see, two variables were manipulated: price and expectancy strength. The four conditions in the study represent the four possible combinations of these two variables. The hypothesis was that participants who paid full price for SoBe would solve more anagrams than those who bought SoBe at a discounted price and this difference would be greater for participants in the high expectancy strength condition (who were led to think about SoBe's effects) than in the low expectancy strength condition. In a moment we'll see whether the results of the experiment supported these predictions.

Factorial Nomenclature

Researchers use factorial designs to study the individual and combined effects of two or more independent variables (or factors) within a single experiment. To understand factorial designs, you need to become familiar with the nomenclature researchers use to describe the size and structure of such designs. First, just as a one-way design has only one independent variable, a two-way factorial design has two independent variables, a three-way factorial design has three independent variables, and so on. Shiv et al.'s (2005) SoBe experiment involved a two-way factorial design because two independent variables were involved.

Researchers often describe the structure of a factorial design in a way that immediately indicates to a reader how many independent variables were manipulated and how many levels there were of each variable. For example, Shiv et al.'s experiment was an example of what researchers call a *2 × 2* (read as "2 by 2") *factorial design*. The phrase *2 × 2* tells us that the design had two independent variables, each of which had two levels (see Figure 10.7[a]). A 3 × 3 factorial design also involves two independent variables, but each variable has three levels (see Figure 10.7[b]). A 4 × 2 factorial design has two independent variables, one with two levels and one with four levels (see Figure 10.7[c]).

So far, our examples have involved two-way factorial designs, that is, designs with two independent variables. However, experiments can have more than two factors. For example, a 2 × 2 × 2 design has three independent variables; each of the variables has two levels. In Figure 10.8 (a), for example, we see a design that has three independent variables (labeled *A, B,* and *C*). Each of these variables has two levels, resulting in eight conditions that reflect the possible combinations of the three independent variables. In contrast, a 2 × 2 × 4 factorial design also has

Expectancy Strength

FIGURE 10.6   A Factorial Design: Shiv, Carmon, and Ariely's Experiment.   In this experiment, two independent variables were manipulated: price (full vs. discounted price) and expectancy strength (low vs. high). Participants were randomly assigned to one of four conditions that reflected all possible combinations of price and expectancy strength.

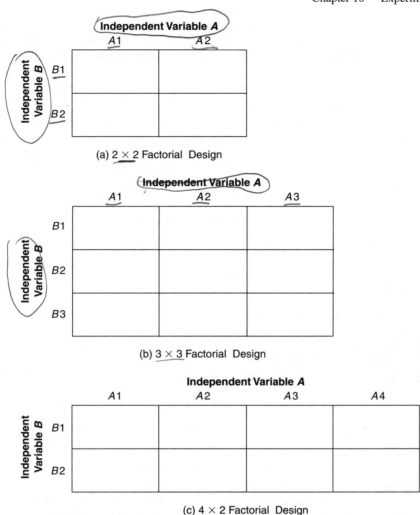

FIGURE 10.7   Examples of Two-Way Factorial Designs.   (a) A 2 × 2 design has two independent variables, each with two levels, for a total of four conditions. (b) In this 3 × 3 design, there are two independent variables, each of which has three levels. Because there are nine possible combinations of variables A and B, the design has nine conditions. (c) In this 4 × 2 design, independent variable A has four levels, and independent variable B has two levels, resulting in eight experimental conditions.

three independent variables, but two of the independent variables have two levels each and the other variable has four levels. Such a design is shown in Figure 10.8 (b); as you can see, this design involves 16 conditions that represent all combinations of the levels of variables A, B, and C.

A four-way factorial design, such as a 2 × 2 × 3 × 3 design, would have four independent variables—two would have two levels, and two would have three levels. As we add more independent

variables and more levels of our independent variables, the number of conditions increases rapidly.

We can tell how many experimental conditions a factorial design has simply by multiplying the numbers in a design specification. For example, a 2 × 2 design has four different cells or conditions—that is, four possible combinations of the two independent variables (2 × 2 = 4). A 3 × 4 × 2 design has 24 different experimental conditions (3 × 4 × 2 = 24), and so on.

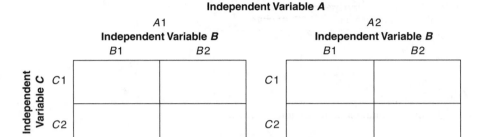

(a) $2 \times 2 \times 2$ Factorial Design

(b) $2 \times 2 \times 4$ Factorial Design

FIGURE 10.8 Examples of Higher-Order Designs. (a) A three-way design such as this one involves the manipulation of three independent variables—*A, B,* and *C.* In a $2 \times 2 \times 2$ design, each of the variables has two levels, resulting in eight conditions. (b) This is a $2 \times 2 \times 4$ factorial design. Variables *A* and *B* each have two levels, and variable *C* has four levels. There are 16 possible combinations of the three variables ($2 \times 2 \times 4 = 16$) and, therefore, 16 conditions in the experiment.

Assigning Participants to Conditions

Like the one-way designs we discussed earlier, factorial designs may include randomized groups, matched-subjects, or repeated measures designs. In addition, as we will see, the split-plot, or between-within, design combines features of the randomized groups and repeated measures designs.

RANDOMIZED GROUPS FACTORIAL DESIGN. In a **randomized groups factorial design** (which is also called a *completely randomized factorial design*) participants are assigned randomly to one of the possible combinations of the independent variables. In Shiv et al.'s study, participants were assigned randomly to one of four combinations of price and expectancy strength.

MATCHED FACTORIAL DESIGN. As in the matched-subjects one-way design, the **matched-subjects factorial design** involves first matching participants into blocks on the basis of some variable that correlates with the dependent variable. There will be as many participants in each matched block as there are experimental conditions. In a 3×2 factorial design, for example, six participants would be matched into each block (because there are six experimental conditions). Then the participants in each block are randomly assigned to one of the six experimental conditions. As before, the primary reason for using a matched-subjects design is to equate more closely the participants in the experimental conditions before introducing the independent variable.

REPEATED MEASURES FACTORIAL DESIGN. A **repeated measures** (or *within-subjects*) **factorial design** requires participants to participate in every experimental condition. Although repeated measures designs are often feasible with small factorial designs (such as a 2 × 2 design), they become unwieldy with larger designs. For example, in a 2 × 2 × 2 × 4 repeated measures factorial design, each participant would serve in 32 different conditions! With such large designs, order effects can become a problem.

MIXED FACTORIAL DESIGN. Because one-way designs involve a single independent variable, they must involve random assignment, matched subjects, or repeated measures. However, factorial designs involve more than one independent variable, and they can combine features of both randomized groups designs and repeated measures designs in a single experiment. Some independent variables in a factorial

experiment may involve random assignment, whereas other variables involve a repeated measure. A design that combines one or more between-subjects variables with one or more within-subjects variables is called a **mixed factorial design**, **between-within design**, or **split-plot factorial design**. (The odd name, *split-plot*, was adopted from agricultural research and actually refers to an area of ground that has been subdivided for research purposes.)

To better understand mixed factorial designs, let's look at a classic study by Walk (1969), who employed a mixed design to study depth perception in infants, using a "visual cliff" apparatus. The visual cliff consists of a clear Plexiglas platform with a checkerboard pattern underneath. On one side of the platform, the checkerboard is directly under the Plexiglas. On the other side of the platform, the checkerboard is farther below the Plexiglas, giving the impression of a sharp drop-off or cliff. In Walk's experiment, the deep side of the cliff consisted of a checkerboard design 5 inches below the clear Plexiglas surface. On the shallow side, the checkerboard was directly under the glass.

Walk experimentally manipulated the size of the checkerboard pattern. In one condition the pattern consisted of $3/4$-inch blocks, and in the other condition the pattern consisted of $1/4$-inch blocks. Participants (who were $6^1/_2$- to 15-month-old babies)

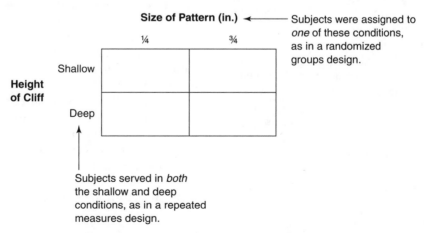

FIGURE 10.9 A Split-Plot Factorial Design. In this 2 × 2 split-plot design, one independent variable (size of the block design) was a between-participants factor in which participants were assigned randomly to one condition or the other. The other independent variable (height of the visual cliff) was a within-participants factor. All participants were tested at both the shallow and deep sides of the visual cliff.

Source: Based on Walk (1969).

were *randomly assigned* to either the $^1/_4$-inch or $^3/_4$-inch pattern condition as in a randomized groups design. Walk also manipulated a second independent variable as in a repeated measures or within-subjects design; he tested each infant on the cliff more than once. Each baby was placed on the board between the deep and shallow sides of the cliff and beckoned by its mother from the shallow side; then the procedure was repeated on the deep side. Thus, each infant served in *both* the shallow and deep conditions.

This is a mixed or split-plot factorial design because one independent variable (size of checkerboard pattern) involved randomly assigning participants to conditions, whereas the other independent variable (shallow vs. deep side) involved a repeated measure. This design is shown in Figure 10.9.

MAIN EFFECTS AND INTERACTIONS

The primary advantage of factorial designs over one-way designs is that they provide information not only about the separate effects of each independent variable but also about the effects of the independent variables when they are combined. That is, assuming that we have eliminated all experimental confounds as discussed in Chapter 9, a one-way design allows us to identify only two sources of the total variability we observe in participants' responses; either the variability in the dependent variable was treatment variance due to the independent variable, or it was error variance.

A factorial design allows us to identify other possible sources of the variability we observe in the dependent variable. When we use factorial designs, we can examine whether the variability in scores was due (1) to the individual effects of each independent variable, (2) to the combined or interactive effects of the independent variables, or (3) to error variance. Thus, factorial designs give researchers a fuller, more complete picture of how behavior is affected by multiple independent variables acting together.

Main Effects

The effect of a single independent variable in a factorial design is called a **main effect**. A main effect reflects the effect of a particular independent variable while ignoring the effects of the other independent variables. When we examine the main effect of a particular independent variable, we pretend for the moment that the other independent variables do not exist and test the overall effect of that independent variable by itself.

A factorial design will have as many main effects as there are independent variables. For example, because a 2×3 design has two independent variables, we can examine two main effects. In a $3 \times 2 \times 2$ design, three main effects would be tested.

In Shiv et al.'s (2005) SoBe experiment, two main effects were tested: the effect of price (ignoring expectancy strength) and the effect of expectancy strength (ignoring price). The test of the main effect of price involved determining whether participants solved a different number of anagrams in the full and discounted price conditions (ignoring whether they had been led to think about SoBe's effects). Analysis of the data showed a main effect of price. That is, averaging across the low and high expectancy strength conditions, participants who paid full price for SoBe solved significantly more anagrams than participants who paid the discounted price. The mean number of problems solved in the full price condition was 9.70 compared to 6.75 in the discounted price condition.

The test of the main effect of expectancy strength examined whether participants in the high expectancy strength condition (who thought about SoBe's effects) solved more anagrams than those in the low expectancy strength condition (who solved the anagrams without thinking explicitly about SoBe). As it turns out, merely thinking about whether SoBe affects concentration and mental performance did not have an effect on performance—that is, no main effect of expectancy strength was obtained. The mean number of problems solved was 8.6 in the low expectancy strength condition and 7.9 in the high expectancy strength condition. This difference in performance is too small to regard as statistically significant.

Interactions

In addition to providing information about the main effects of each independent variable, a factorial design provides information about interactions between the independent variables. An **interaction** is present when the effect of one independent variable differs across the levels of other independent variables. If one independent variable has a different effect at one level of another individual variable than it has at another level of that independent variable, we say that the independent variables *interact* and that an interaction between the independent variables is present. For example, imagine we conduct a factorial experiment with two independent variables, A and B. If the effect of variable A is different under one level of variable B than it is under another level of variable B, an interaction is present. However, if variable A has the same effect on participants' responses no matter what level of variable B they receive, then no interaction is present.

Consider, for example, what happens if you mix alcohol and drugs such as sedatives. The effects of drinking a given amount of alcohol vary depending on whether you've also taken sleeping pills. By itself, a strong mixed drink may result in only a mild "buzz." However, that same strong drink may create pronounced effects on behavior if you've taken a sleeping pill. And mixing a strong drink with two or three sleeping pills will produce extreme, potentially fatal, results. Because the effects of a given dose of alcohol depend on how many sleeping pills you've taken, alcohol and sleeping pills *interact* to affect

behavior. This is an interaction because the effect of one variable (alcohol) differs depending on the level of the other variable (no pill, one pill, or three pills).

Similarly, in the SoBe experiment, Shiv et al. (2005) predicted an *interaction* of price and expectancy strength on participants' anagram performance. According to the hypothesis, although participants who paid full price would solve more anagrams than those who paid the discount price in both the low and high expectancy strength conditions, the difference between full and discount price would be greater when expectancy strength was high rather than low (because participants had stopped to think about their expectancies). The results revealed the predicted pattern. As you can see in Figure 10.10, participants who paid full price outperformed those who paid less whether expectancy strength was low or high. However, as predicted, this effect was stronger in the high expectancy strength condition. The effects of price on performance were different under one level of expectancy strength than the other, so an interaction is present. Because the effect of one independent variable (price) differed depending on the level of the other independent variable (expectancy strength), we say that price and expectancy strength *interacted* to affect the number of anagrams that participants solved successfully.

Expectancy Strength

Price		Low	High
	Full price	9.5	9.9
	Discount price	7.7	5.8

FIGURE 10.10 Effects of Price and Expectancy Strength on Number of Anagrams Solved. These numbers are the average number of anagrams solved in each experimental condition. As predicted, participants who bought SoBe at a discount price solved fewer anagrams than those who paid full price, and this effect was stronger in the high expectancy strength condition. The fact that price had a different effect depending on whether expectancy strength was low or high indicates the presence of an interaction.

Source: From "Placebo Effects of Marketing Actions: Consumers May Get What They Pay For" by B. Shiv, Z. Carmon, and D. Ariely (2005). *Journal of Marketing Research, 42,* 383–393.

Developing Your Research Skills
Graphing Interactions

Researchers often present the results of factorial experiments in tables of means such as shown in Figure 10.10 for the SoBe experiment. Although presenting tables of means provides readers with precise information about the results of an experiment, researchers sometimes graph the means of interactions because visually presenting the data often shows how independent variables interact more clearly and dramatically than tables of numbers.

Researchers graph interactions in one of two ways. One method is to represent each experimental condition as a bar in a bar graph. The height of each bar reflects the mean of a particular condition. For example, we could graph the means from Figure 10.10 as shown in Figure 10.11

FIGURE 10.11 Bar Graph of the Means in Figure 10.10. In this graph, each bar represents an experimental condition. The height of each bar shows the mean number of anagrams solved in that condition.

A second way to graph interactions is with a line graph as shown in Figure 10.12. This graph shows that participants in the full price condition solved more anagrams than those in the discounted price condition when expectancy strength was both low and high. However, it also clearly shows that the discounted price condition performed worse, relative to the full price condition, when expectancy strength was high rather than low.

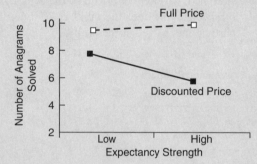

FIGURE 10.12 Line Graph of the Means in Figure 10.10. To make a line graph of the condition means for a two-way interaction, the levels of one independent variable (in this case expectancy strength) are shown on the *x*-axis. The levels of the other independent variable (price) appear as lines that connect the means for that level.

When the means for the conditions of a factorial design are graphed in a line graph, interactions appear as nonparallel lines. The fact that the lines are not parallel shows that the effects of one independent variable differed depending on the level of the other independent variable. In contrast, when line graphs of means show parallel lines, no interaction between the independent variables is present. Looking at the graph of Shiv et al.'s results in Figure 10.12, we can easily see from the nonparallel lines that full and discounted prices produced different reactions in the low versus the high expectancy strength conditions. Thus, price and expectancy strength interacted to affect participants' anagram performance.

Higher-Order Designs

The examples of factorial designs we have seen so far were two-way designs that involved two independent variables (such as a 2×2, a 2×3, or a 3×5 factorial design). As we noted earlier, factorial designs often have more than two independent variables.

Increasing the number of independent variables in an experiment increases not only the complexity of the design and statistical analyses but also the complexity of the information that the study provides. As we saw earlier, a two-way design provides information about two main effects and a two-way interaction. That is, in a factorial design with two independent variables, A and B, we can ask whether there is (1) a main effect of A (an effect of variable A, ignoring B), (2) a main effect of B (ignoring A), and (3) an interaction of A and B.

A three-way design, such as a $2 \times 2 \times 2$ or a $3 \times 2 \times 4$ design, provides even more information. First, we can examine the effects of each of the three independent variables separately—that is, the main effect of A, the main effect of B, and the main effect of C. In each case, we can look at the individual effects of each independent variable while ignoring the other two. Second, a three-way design allows us to look at three two-way interactions—interactions of each pair of independent variables while ignoring the third independent variable. Thus, we can examine the interaction of A by B (while ignoring C), the interaction of A by C (while ignoring B), and the interaction of B by C (while ignoring A). Each two-way interaction tells us whether the effect of one independent variable is different at different levels of another independent variable. For example, testing the B by C interaction tells us whether variable B has a different effect on behavior in Condition $C1$ than in Condition $C2$. Third, a three-way factorial design gives us information about the combined effects of all three independent variables—the three-way interaction of A by B by C. If statistical tests show that this three-way interaction is significant, it indicates that the effect of one variable differs depending on which combination of the other two variables we examine. For example, perhaps the effect of independent variable A is different in Condition $B1C1$ than in Condition $B1C2$, or that variable B has a different effect in Condition $A2C1$ than in Condition $A2C2$.

Logically, factorial designs can have any number of independent variables and, thus, any number of conditions. For practical reasons, however, researchers seldom design studies with more than three or four independent variables. For one thing, when a between-subjects design is used, the number of participants needed for an experiment grows rapidly as we add additional independent variables. For example, a $2 \times 2 \times 2$ factorial design with 15 participants in each of the eight conditions would require 120 participants. Adding a fourth independent variable with two levels (creating a $2 \times 2 \times 2 \times 2$ factorial design) would double the number of participants required to 240. Adding a fifth independent variable with three levels (making the design a $2 \times 2 \times 2 \times 2 \times 3$ factorial design) would require us to collect and analyze data from 720 participants!

In addition, as the number of independent variables increases, researchers find it increasingly difficult to draw meaningful interpretations from the data. A two-way interaction is usually easy to interpret, but four- and five-way interactions are quite complex.

COMBINING INDEPENDENT AND PARTICIPANT VARIABLES

Behavioral researchers have long recognized that behavior is a function of both situational factors and an individual's personal characteristics. A full understanding of certain behaviors cannot be achieved without taking both situational and personal factors into account. Put another way, **participant variables** (also called **subject variables**) such as sex, age, intelligence, ability, personality, and attitudes moderate or qualify the effects of situational forces on behavior. Not everyone responds in the same manner to the same situation. For example, performance on a test is a function not only of the difficulty of the test itself but also of personal attributes, such as how capable, motivated, or anxious a person is. A researcher interested in determinants of test performance might want to take into account these personal characteristics as well as the characteristics of the test itself.

Researchers sometimes design experiments to investigate the combined effects of situational factors and participant variables. These designs involve one or more independent variables that are *manipulated* by the experimenter, and one or more preexisting participant variables that are *measured* rather than manipulated. Unfortunately, we do not have a universally accepted name for these hybrid designs. Some researchers call them *mixed designs*, but we have already seen that this label is also used to refer to designs that include both between-subjects and within-subjects factors—what we have also called *split-plot* or *between-within designs*. Because of this confusion, I prefer to call these designs **expericorr** (or *mixed/expericorr*) **factorial designs**. The label *expericorr* is short for *experimental–correlational;* such designs combine features of an experimental design in which independent variables are manipulated and features of correlational designs in which participant variables are measured. Such a design is shown in Figure 10.13.

USES OF MIXED/EXPERICORR DESIGNS. Researchers use mixed/expericorr designs for two primary reasons. The first is to investigate the generality of an independent variable's effect. Participants who possess different characteristics often respond to the same situation in quite different ways. Therefore, independent variables may have different effects on participants who have different characteristics. Mixed/expericorr designs permit researchers to determine whether the effects of a particular independent variable occur for all participants or only for participants with certain attributes.

For example, one of the most common uses of mixed/expericorr designs is to look for differences in how male and female participants respond to an independent variable. For example, to investigate whether men and women respond differently to success and failure, a researcher might use a 2×3 expericorr design. In this design, one factor would involve a participant variable with two levels, namely gender. The other factor would involve a manipulated independent variable that has three levels: Participants would take a test and then receive either (1) success feedback, (2) failure feedback, or (3) no feedback. When the data were analyzed, the researcher could examine the main effect of participant gender (whether, overall, men and women differ), the main effect of feedback (whether participants respond differently to success, failure, or no feedback), and, most importantly, the interaction of gender and feedback (whether men and women respond differently to success, failure, and/or no feedback).

Second, researchers use expericorr designs in an attempt to understand how certain personal characteristics relate to behavior under varying conditions. The emphasis in such studies is on understanding the measured participant characteristic rather than the manipulated independent variable. For example, a researcher interested in self-esteem might expose persons who scored low or high in self-esteem to various experimental conditions. Or a researcher interested in depression might conduct an experiment in which depressed and nondepressed participants respond to various experimentally manipulated situations. A great deal of research designed to study

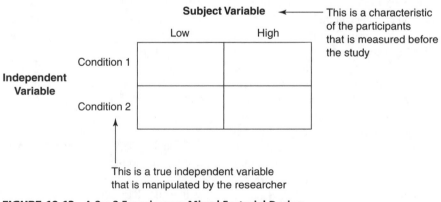

FIGURE 10.13 A 2 × 2 Expericorr or Mixed Factorial Design

gender differences examine how men and women respond to different experimental conditions. Studying how participants who score differently on some participant variable respond to an experimental manipulation may shed light on that characteristic.

CLASSIFYING PARTICIPANTS INTO GROUPS. When researchers use mixed designs, they often classify participants into groups on the basis of the measured participant variable (such as gender or self-esteem), then randomly assign participants within those groups to levels of the independent variable. For discrete participant variables such as gender (male, female), political affiliation (Democrat, Republican, Independent), and race, it is usually easy to assign participants to two or more groups.

However, when researchers are interested in participant variables that are continuous rather than discrete, questions arise about how to classify participants into groups. For example, a researcher may be interested in how self-esteem moderates reactions to success and failure. Because scores on a measure of self-esteem are continuous, the researcher must decide how to classify participants into groups. Traditionally, researchers have typically used either the median-split procedure or the extreme groups procedure.

In the **median-split procedure**, the researcher identifies the median of the distribution of participants' scores on the variable of interest (such as self-esteem). You will recall that the median is the middle score in a distribution, the score that falls at the 50th percentile. The researcher then classifies participants with scores below the median as *low* on the variable and those with scores above the median as *high* on the variable. It must be remembered, however, that the designations *low* and *high* are relative to the researcher's sample. All participants could, in fact, be low or high on the attribute in an absolute sense. In a variation of the median-split procedure, some researchers split their sample into three or more groups rather than only two.

Alternatively, some researchers prefer the **extreme groups procedure** for classifying participants into groups. Rather than splitting the sample at the median, the researcher pretests a large number of potential participants, then selects participants for the experiment whose scores are unusually low or high on the variable of interest. For example, the researcher may use participants whose scores fall in the upper and lower 25% of a distribution of self-esteem scores, discarding those with scores in the middle range.

Researchers interested in how independent variables interact with participant variables have traditionally classified participants into two or more groups using one of these splitting procedures. However, the use of median and extreme group splits is problematic, and using these approaches is discouraged. One reason is that classifying participants into groups on the basis of a measured participant variable throws away valuable information. When we use participants' scores on a continuous variable—such as age, self-esteem, IQ, or depression—to classify them into only two groups (old vs. young, low vs. high self-esteem, low vs. highly intelligent, depressed vs. nondepressed), we discard information regarding the variability in participants' scores. We start with a rich set of data with a wide range of scores and end up with a dichotomy (just low vs. high).

Furthermore, classifying participants into groups on the basis of a participant variable, such as self-esteem or anxiety, can lead to biased results. Depending on the nature of the data, the bias sometimes leads researchers to miss effects that were actually present, and at other times it leads researchers to obtain effects that are actually statistical artifacts (Bissonnette, Ickes, Bernstein, & Knowles, 1990; Cohen & Cohen, 1983; Maxwell & Delaney, 1993). In either case, artificially splitting participants into groups can lead to erroneous conclusions compared to using the full range of continuous scores.

Although median-split and extreme group approaches were commonly used for many years (so you will see them in many older journal articles), these procedures are now known to be problematic. Rather than splitting participants into groups, researchers should use multiple regression procedures that allow them to analyze data from mixed/expericorr designs while maintaining the continuous nature of participants' scores on the measured variable (Aiken & West, 1991; Cohen & Cohen, 1983; Kowalski, 1995).

> ### Behavioral Research Case Study
> *A Mixed/Expericorr Factorial Design: Self-Esteem and Responses to Ego Threats*
>
> Baumeister, Heatherton, and Tice (1993) used a mixed/expericorr design to examine how people with low versus high self-esteem respond to threats to their egos. Thirty-five male participants completed a measure of self-esteem and were classified as low or high in self-esteem on the basis of a median-split procedure.
>
> In a laboratory experiment, the participants set goals for how well they would perform on a computer video game and wagered money on meeting the goals they had set. As with most wagers, they could make "safe" bets (with the possibility of winning or losing little) or "risky" bets (with the potential to win—and lose—more). Just before participants placed their bets, the researcher threatened the egos of half of the participants by remarking that they might want to place a safe bet if they were worried they might choke under pressure or didn't "have what it takes" to do well on the game. Thus, this was a 2 (low vs. high self-esteem) by 2 (ego threat vs. no ego threat) mixed factorial design. Self-esteem was a measured participant variable, and ego threat was a manipulated independent variable.
>
> Participants then made their bets and played the game. The final amount of money won by participants in each of the four conditions is shown in Figure 10.14. Analysis of the data revealed a main effect of self-esteem (low self-esteem participants won more money on average than high self-esteem participants), but no main effect of ego threat (overall participants won roughly the same amount whether or not the researcher threatened their egos).
>
> Most important, the analysis revealed an interaction of self-esteem and ego threat. When participants' egos had not been threatened, the amount of money won by low and high self-esteem participants did not differ significantly; highs won an average of $1.40, and lows won an average of $1.29. However, in the presence of an ego threat, participants with low self-esteem won significantly more money (an average of $2.80) than participants with high self-esteem (an average of $.25). These data suggest that ego threats may lead people with high self-esteem to set inappropriate, risky goals to prove themselves to themselves or to other people.
>
> | | Participant Self-Esteem | | |
> |---|---|---|---|
> | | **Low** | **High** | |
> | **No Ego Threat** | $1.29 | $1.40 | |
> | **Ego Threat** | $2.80 | $ .25 | |
>
> In this mixed/expericorr study, participants who scored low versus high in self-esteem were or were not exposed to an ego threat prior to wagering money on their ability to attain certain scores on a computerized game. As the table shows, participants who were low in self-esteem won more money following an ego threat than when an ego threat had not occurred. In contrast, high self-esteem participants won significantly less money when their egos were threatened than when they were not threatened.
>
> **FIGURE 10.14**

CAUTIONS IN INTERPRETING RESULTS OF A MIXED/EXPERICORR DESIGN. Researchers must exercise care when interpreting results from mixed designs. Specifically, a researcher can draw causal inferences only about the true independent variables in the experiment—those that were manipulated by the researcher. As always, if effects are obtained for a manipulated independent variable, we can conclude that the independent variable *caused* changes in the dependent variable.

When effects are obtained for the measured participant variable, however, the researcher cannot conclude that the participant variable caused changes in the dependent variable. Because the participant variable is measured rather than manipulated, the results are essentially correlational, and (recall from Chapter 7) we cannot infer causality from a correlation. If a main effect of the participant variable is obtained, we can conclude that the two groups differed on the dependent variable, but we cannot conclude that the participant variable caused the difference.

Similarly, if we obtain an interaction between the independent variable and the participant variable, we can conclude that participants who scored low versus high on the participant variable reacted to the independent variable differently, but we cannot say that the participant variable (being male or female, or being depressed, for example) caused participants to respond differently to the levels of the independent variable. Rather, we say that the participant variable *moderated* participants' reactions to the independent variable and that the participant variable is a **moderator variable.** For example, we cannot conclude that high self-esteem caused participants to make risky bets in the ego-threat experiment (Baumeister et al., 1993). Because people who score low versus high in self-esteem differ in many ways, all we can say is that differences in self-esteem were associated with different responses in the ego-threat condition. Or, more technically, self-esteem *moderated* the effects of ego threat on participants' behavior.

Summary

1. A one-way experimental design is an experiment in which a single independent variable is manipulated. The simplest possible experiment is the two-group experimental design.

2. Researchers use three general versions of the one-way design—the randomized groups design (in which participants are assigned randomly to two or more groups), the matched-subjects design (in which participants are first matched into blocks and then randomly assigned to conditions), and the repeated measures or within-subjects design (in which each participant serves in all experimental conditions).

3. Each of these designs may involve a single measurement of the dependent variable after the manipulation of the independent variable, or a pretest and a posttest.

4. Factorial designs are experiments that include two or more independent variables. (Independent variables are sometimes called *factors*, a term not to be confused with its meaning in factor analysis.)

5. The size and structure of factorial designs are described by specifying the number of levels of each independent variable. For example, a 3 × 2 factorial design has two independent variables, one with three levels and one with two levels.

6. There are four general types of factorial designs—the randomized groups, matched-subjects, repeated measures, and mixed (also called *split-plot* or *between-within*) factorial designs.

7. Factorial designs provide information about the effects of each independent variable by itself (the main effects) as well as the combined effects of the independent variables.

8. An interaction between two or more independent variables is present if the effect of one independent variable is different under one level of another independent variable than it is under another level of that independent variable.

9. Expericorr (sometimes called *mixed*) factorial designs combine manipulated independent variables and measured participant variables. Such designs are often used to study participant variables that qualify or moderate the effects of the independent variables.

10. Researchers using an expericorr design sometimes classify participants into groups using a median split or extreme groups procedure, but others use analyses that allow them to maintain the continuity of the measured participant variable. In either case, causal inferences may be drawn only about the variables in the design that were experimentally manipulated.

Key Terms

between-within design (*p. 221*)
expericorr factorial design (*p. 226*)
extreme groups procedure (*p. 227*)
factor (*p. 218*)
factorial design (*p. 218*)
interaction (*p. 223*)
main effect (*p. 222*)
matched-subjects design (*p. 213*)
matched-subjects factorial design
    (*p. 221*)

median-split procedure
    (*p. 227*)
mixed factorial design (*p. 221*)
moderator variable (*p. 229*)
one-way design (*p. 213*)
participant variable (*p. 226*)
posttest-only design (*p. 214*)
pretest–posttest design (*p. 214*)
pretest sensitization (*p. 217*)
randomized groups design (*p. 213*)

randomized groups factorial
    design (*p. 221*)
repeated measures design
    (*p. 213*)
repeated measures factorial
    design (*p. 221*)
split-plot factorial design (*p. 221*)
subject variable (*p. 2256*
two-group experimental design
    (*p. 213*)

Questions for Review

1. How many conditions are there in the simplest possible experiment?
2. Describe how participants are assigned to conditions in randomized groups, matched-subjects, and repeated measures experimental designs.
3. What are the relative advantages and disadvantages of posttest-only versus pretest–posttest experimental designs?
4. What is a factorial design? Why are factorial designs used more frequently than one-way designs?
5. How many independent variables are involved in a 3×3 factorial design? How many levels are there of each variable? How many experimental conditions are there? Draw the design.
6. Describe a $2 \times 2 \times 3$ factorial design. How many independent variables are involved, and how many levels are there of each variable? How many experimental conditions are in a $2 \times 2 \times 3$ factorial design?
7. Distinguish among randomized groups, matched-subjects, and repeated measures factorial designs.

8. Describe a mixed, or split-plot, factorial design. This design is a hybrid of what two other designs?
9. What is a main effect?
10. How many main effects can be tested in a 2×2 design? In a 3×3 design? In a $2 \times 2 \times 3$ design?
11. What is an interaction?
12. How many interactions can be tested in a 2×2 design? In a 3×3 design? In a $2 \times 2 \times 3$ design?
13. If you want to have 20 participants in each experimental condition, how many participants will you need for a $2 \times 3 \times 3$ completely randomized factorial design? How many participants will you need for a $2 \times 3 \times 3$ repeated measures factorial design?
14. How do mixed/expericorr designs differ from other experimental designs?
15. Why do researchers use expericorr designs?
16. Distinguish between an independent variable and a participant variable.

Questions for Discussion

1. Design a randomized groups experiment to test the hypothesis that children who watch an hour-long violent television show subsequently play in a more aggressive fashion than children who watch a nonviolent TV show or who watch no show whatsoever.
2. Explain how you would conduct the study you designed in Question 1 as a matched-subjects design.

3. Build on the design you created in Question 1 to test the hypothesis that the effects of watching violent TV shows will be greater for boys than for girls. (What kind of design is this?)
4. What main effects and interaction could you test with the design you developed for Question 3? Are you predicting that you will obtain an interaction?

5. You have been asked to evaluate the effects of a new educational video that was developed to reduce racial prejudice among adolescents. You plan to administer a pretest measure of racial attitudes to 60 adolescent participants, and then randomly assign these participants to watch either the antiprejudice video, an educational video about volcanoes, or no video. Afterward, the participants will complete the measure of racial attitudes a second time. However, you are concerned that the first administration of the attitudes measure may create pretest sensitization, thereby directly affecting participants' attitudes. Explain how you could redesign the experiment to see whether pretest sensitization occurred. (*Hint:* You will probably use a 3×2 factorial design.) What pattern of results would suggest that pretest sensitization had occurred?

6. Graph the means in Figure 10.14 for the interaction between self-esteem and ego threat. Does the graph *look* like one in which an interaction is present? Why or why not?

.11

ANALYZING
EXPERIMENTAL DATA

An Intuitive Approach to Analysis

Hypothesis Testing

Analysis of Two-Group Experiments: The *t*-Test

Analyses of Matched-Subjects and
Within-Subjects Designs

Computer Analyses

Some of my students are puzzled (or, perhaps more accurately, horrified) when they discover that they must learn about *statistics* in a research methods course. More than one student has asked why we talk so much about statistical analyses in my class, considering that the course is ostensibly about research methods and other courses on campus are devoted entirely to statistics. Given that the next two chapters focus on statistical analyses, it occurred to me that you may be asking yourself the same question.

Statistical analyses are an integral part of the research process. A person who knew nothing about statistics would have difficulty not only conducting research but also understanding other researchers' studies and findings. As a result, most seasoned researchers are quite knowledgeable about statistical analyses, although they sometimes consult with statisticians when their research calls for analyses with which they are not already familiar.

Even if you, as a student, have no intention of ever conducting research, a basic knowledge of statistics is essential for understanding most journal articles. If you have ever read research articles published in scientific journals, you have probably encountered an assortment of mysterious analyses—*t*-tests, ANOVAs, MANOVAs, post hoc tests, simple effects tests, and the like—along with an endless stream of seemingly meaningless symbols and numbers, such as "$F(2, 328) = 6.78, p < .01$." If you're like many of my students, you may skim over these parts of the article until you find something that makes sense. If nothing else, a knowledge of statistics is necessary to be an informed reader and consumer of scientific knowledge.

Even so, for our purposes here, you do not need a high level of proficiency with all sorts of statistical formulas and calculations. Rather, what you need is an understanding of how statistics work. Thus, Chapters 11 and 12 will focus on how experimental data are analyzed from a *conceptual* perspective. Along the way, you will see formulas for demonstrational purposes, but the calculational formulas researchers actually use to analyze data will take a back seat. At this point, it's more important to understand how data are analyzed and what the statistical analyses mean than to learn how to do the analyses. That's what statistics courses are for.

AN INTUITIVE APPROACH TO ANALYSIS

After an experiment is conducted, the researcher must analyze the data to determine whether the independent variable had the predicted effect on the dependent variable(s). Did the manipulation of the independent variable cause systematic changes in participants' responses? Did providing participants with interpretations of the droodles they saw affect their memory of the pictures? Did different patterns of self-reward and self-punishment result in different amounts of weight loss? Was anagram performance affected by the price that participants paid for SoBe?

At the most general level, we can see whether the independent variable has an effect by determining whether the total variance in the data includes any systematic variance due to the manipulation of the independent variable (see Chapter 9). Specifically, the presence of systematic variance in a set of data is determined by comparing the means on the dependent variable for the various experimental groups.

If the independent variable has an effect on the dependent variable, we should find that the means for the experimental conditions differ. Different group averages would suggest that the independent variable had an effect; it created differences in the behavior of participants in the various conditions and, thus, resulted in systematic variance. Assuming that participants assigned to the experimental conditions do not differ systematically before the study and that no confounds are present, the only thing that might have caused the means to differ at the end of the experiment is the independent variable. However, if the means of the conditions do not differ, then no systematic variance is present, and we will conclude that the independent variable had no effect.

In the droodles experiment we described in Chapter 10, for example, participants who were given an interpretation of the droodles recalled an average of 19.6 of the pictures immediately afterward. Participants in the control group (who received no interpretation) recalled an average of only 14.2 of the pictures (Bower Karlin, & Dueck, 1975). On the surface, then, inspection of the means for the two experimental conditions indicates that participants who were given interpretations of the droodles remembered more pictures than those who were not given an interpretation. Unfortunately, this conclusion is not as straightforward as it may appear; we cannot draw conclusions about the effects of an independent variable simply by looking only at the means of the experimental conditions.

The Problem: Error Variance Can Cause Differences Between Means

The problem with merely looking at the differences between the means of the experimental conditions is that means may differ even if the independent variable does *not* have an effect. We discussed one possible cause of such differences in Chapter 9—confound variance. Recall that if something other than the independent variable differs in a systematic fashion between experimental conditions, the differences between the means may be due to this confounding variable rather than to the independent variable.

However, even assuming that the researcher successfully eliminated confounding, the means may differ for yet another reason that is unrelated to the independent variable. Suppose that the independent variable did *not* have an effect in the droodles experiment described earlier; that is, providing an interpretation did not enhance participants' memory for the droodles whatsoever. What would we expect to find when we calculated the average number of pictures remembered by participants in the two experimental conditions? Would we expect the mean number of pictures recalled in the two experimental groups to be *exactly* the same? Probably not. Even if the independent variable did not have an effect, it is unlikely that the means would be identical.

To understand this point, imagine that we randomly assigned participants to two groups, then showed them the same set of droodles while giving interpretations of the droodles to all participants in *both* groups. (That is, we treat both of our groups exactly the same way.) Then we asked participants to recall as many of the droodles as possible. Would the average number of pictures recalled be exactly the same in both groups even if participants in both groups received the same interpretations? Probably not. Even if we created no systematic differences between the two conditions, we would be unlikely to obtain perfectly identical means.

The reason involves error variance. Because of error variance in the data, the average recall of the two groups of participants is likely to differ slightly even if they are treated the same. You will recall that error variance reflects the random influences of variables that remain unidentified in the study, such as individual differences among participants and slight variations in how the researcher treats different participants. These uncontrolled and unidentified variables lead participants to respond differently whether or not the independent variable has an effect. As a result, the means of experimental conditions typically differ even when the independent variable itself does not affect participants' responses.

But if we expect the means of the experimental conditions to differ somewhat even if the independent variable does *not* have an effect, how can we tell whether the difference between the means of the conditions is due to the independent variable (systematic treatment variance) or due to random differences between the groups (error variance)? How big a difference between the means of our conditions must we observe to conclude that the independent variable has an effect and that the difference between means is due to the independent variable rather than to error variance?

The Solution: Inferential Statistics

The solution to this problem is simple, at least in principle. If we can estimate how much the means of the conditions would be expected to differ *even if the independent variable has no effect*, then we can determine whether the difference we observe between the means exceeds this estimate. Put another way, we can conclude that the independent variable has an effect when the difference between the means of the experimental conditions is larger than we expect it to be when that difference is due solely to the effects of error variance. We do this by comparing the difference we obtain between the means of the experimental conditions to the difference we expect to obtain based on error variance alone.

Unfortunately, we can never be absolutely certain that the difference we obtain between group means is not just the result of error variance. Even large differences between the means of the conditions can occasionally be due to error variance rather than to the independent variable. We can, however, specify the *probability* that the difference we observe between the means is due to error variance.

HYPOTHESIS TESTING

The Null Hypothesis

Researchers use **inferential statistics** to determine whether observed differences between the means of the experimental conditions are greater than expected on the basis of error variance alone. If the observed difference between the group means is larger than expected given the amount of error variance in the data, researchers conclude that the independent variable caused the difference.

To make this determination, researchers statistically test the null hypothesis. The **null hypothesis** states that the independent variable *did not* have an effect on the dependent variable. Of course, this is usually the opposite of the researcher's actual **experimental hypothesis**, which states that the independent variable *did* have an effect. For statistical purposes, however, we test the null hypothesis rather than the experimental hypothesis. The null hypothesis for the droodles experiment was that participants provided with interpretations of droodles would remember the same number of droodles as those not provided with an interpretation. That is, the null hypothesis says that the mean number of droodles that participants remembered would be equal in the two experimental conditions.

Based on the results of statistical tests, the researcher will make one of two decisions about the null hypothesis. If analyses of the data show that there is a high probability that the null hypothesis is false, the researcher will reject the null hypothesis. **Rejecting the null hypothesis** means that the researcher concludes that the independent variable *did* indeed have an effect. The researcher will reject the null hypothesis if statistical analyses show that the difference between the means of the experimental groups is larger than would be expected given the amount of error variance in the data.

On the other hand, if the analyses show a very low probability of the null hypothesis being false, the researcher will fail to reject the null hypothesis. **Failing to reject the null hypothesis** means that the researcher concludes that the independent variable had no effect. This would be the case if the statistical analyses indicated that the group means differed about as much as we would expect them to differ based on the amount of error variance in the data. Put differently, the researcher will fail to reject the null hypothesis if analyses show a high probability that the difference between the group means reflects nothing more than the influence of error variance and, thus, the difference is probably not due to the independent variable.

Notice that when the probability that the null hypothesis is false is low, we say that the researcher will *fail to reject* the null hypothesis—not that the researcher will *accept* the null hypothesis. We use this odd terminology because, strictly speaking, we cannot obtain data that allow us to truly accept the null hypothesis as confirmed or verified. Although we can determine whether an independent variable probably has an effect on the dependent variable (and, thus, reject the null hypothesis), we cannot conclusively determine whether an independent variable does not have an effect (and, thus, we cannot accept the null hypothesis).

An analogy may clarify this point. In a murder trial, the defendant is assumed not guilty (a null hypothesis) until the jury becomes convinced by the evidence that the defendant is, in fact, the murderer. If the jury remains unconvinced of the defendant's guilt, it does not necessarily mean the defendant is innocent; it may simply mean there isn't enough conclusive evidence to convict him or her. When this happens, the jury returns a verdict of "not guilty." This verdict does not mean the defendant is innocent; rather, it means only that the current evidence isn't sufficient to find the defendant guilty.

The same logic applies when we test the null hypothesis. If we find that the means of our experimental conditions are not different, we cannot logically conclude that the null hypothesis is true (i.e., that the independent variable had no effect). We can only conclude that the current evidence is not sufficient to reject it. Strictly speaking, then, the failure to obtain differences between the means of the experimental conditions leads us to *fail to reject* the null hypothesis rather than to accept it.

Type I and Type II Errors

Figure 11.1 shows the decisions that a researcher may make about the null hypothesis and the possible outcomes that may result depending on whether the researcher's decision is correct. Four outcomes are possible. First, the researcher may correctly reject the null hypothesis, thereby identifying a true effect of the independent variable. Second, the researcher may correctly fail to reject the null hypothesis, accurately concluding that the independent variable had no effect. In both cases, the researcher reached a correct conclusion.

The other two possible outcomes are the result of two kinds of errors that researchers may make when deciding whether to reject the null hypothesis: Type I and Type II errors. A **Type I error** occurs when a researcher erroneously concludes that the null hypothesis is false and, thus, rejects it. More straightforwardly, a Type I error occurs when a researcher concludes that the independent variable has an effect on the dependent variable when, in fact, the observed difference between the means of the experimental conditions is actually due to error variance.

The probability of making a Type I error—of rejecting the null hypothesis when it is true—is called the **alpha level**. As a rule of thumb, researchers set the alpha level at .05. That is, they reject the null hypothesis when there is less than a .05 chance (i.e., fewer than 5 chances out of 100) that the difference they obtain between the means of the experimental groups is due to error variance rather than to the independent

	Researcher's Decision	
	Reject null hypothesis	Fail to reject null hypothesis
Null hypothesis is false	Correct decision	Type II error
Null hypothesis is true	Type I error	Correct decision

FIGURE 11.1 **Statistical Decisions and Outcomes**

variable. If statistical analyses indicate that there is less than a 5% chance that the difference between the means of our experimental conditions is due to error variance, we reject the null hypothesis and conclude that the independent variable had an effect, knowing there is only a small chance we are mistaken. Occasionally, researchers wish to lower their chances of making a Type I error even further and, thus, set a more stringent criterion for rejecting the null hypothesis. By setting the alpha level at .01 rather than .05, for example, researchers risk only a 1% chance of making a Type I error.

When we reject the null hypothesis with a low probability of making a Type I error, we refer to the difference between the means as **statistically significant**. A statistically significant finding is one that has a low probability (usually < .05) of occurring as a result of error variance alone. We'll return to the important concepts of alpha level and statistical significance later.

The researcher may make a second kind of mistake with respect to the null hypothesis. A **Type II error** occurs when a researcher mistakenly fails to reject the null hypothesis when, in fact, it is false. In this case, the researcher concludes that the independent variable did not have an effect when, in fact, it did. Just as the probability of making a Type I error is called *alpha*, the probability of making a Type II error is called **beta**.

Several factors can increase beta and lead to Type II errors. If researchers do not measure the dependent variable properly or if they use a measurement technique that is unreliable, they might not detect the effects of the independent variable that occur. Mistakes may be made in collecting, coding, or analyzing the data, or the researcher may use too few participants to detect the effects of the independent variable. Excessively high error variance due to unreliable measures, very heterogeneous samples, or poor experimental control can also mask effects of the independent variable and lead to Type II errors. Many things can conspire to obscure the effects of the independent variable and, thus, lead researchers to make Type II errors.

To reduce the likelihood of making a Type II error, researchers try to design experiments that have high power. **Power** is the probability that a study will correctly reject the null hypothesis when the null hypothesis is false. Put another way, power is the probability that the study will obtain a significant result if the researcher's experimental hypothesis is, in fact, true. Power is a study's ability to detect any effect of the independent variable that occurs. Perhaps you can see that power is the opposite of beta—the probability of making a Type II error (i.e., power = 1 − beta). Studies that are low in power may fail to detect the independent variable's effect on the dependent variable.

Among other things, power is related to the number of participants in a study. All other things being equal, the greater the number of participants, the greater the study's power and the more likely we are to detect effects of the independent variable on the dependent variable. Intuitively, you can probably see that an experiment with 100 participants will provide more definitive and clear-cut conclusions about the effect of an independent variable than the same experiment conducted with only 10 participants. Because power is important to the success of an experiment, researchers often conduct a **power analysis** to determine the number of participants that is needed in order to detect the effect of a particular independent variable. Once they set their alpha level (at .05, for example) and specify the power they desire, researchers can calculate the number of participants needed to detect an effect of a particular size. (Larger sample sizes are needed to detect weaker effects of the independent variable.) Generally, researchers aim for power of at least .80 (Cohen, 1988). An experiment with .80 power has an 80% chance of detecting an effect of the independent variable that is really there. Or, stated another way, in a study with .80 power, the probability of making a Type II error, or beta, is .20.

You might wonder why researchers don't aim for even higher power. Why not set power at .99, for example, all but eliminating the possibility of making a Type II error? The reason is that achieving higher power requires an increasing number of participants. For example, if a researcher is designing a two-group experiment and expects the effect of the independent variable to be medium in strength, he or she needs nearly 400 participants to achieve a power of .99 when testing the difference between the condition means (Cohen, 1992). In contrast, to achieve a power of .80, the researcher needs fewer than 70 participants. As with many issues in research, practical considerations must be taken into account when determining sample size.

The formulas for conducting power analyses and calculating sample sizes can be found in many statistics books (Cohen, 1988; Hurlburt, 1998; Lipsey, 1990), and several software programs also exist for power analysis. As we saw in Chapter 5, studies suggest that much research in the behavioral sciences is underpowered and thus Type II error runs rampant. Sample sizes are often too small to detect any but the strongest effects, and small and medium effects are likely to be missed. In fact, when it comes to detecting medium-sized effects, more than half of the studies published in psychology journals have power less than .50 (Cohen, 1988, 1992). And this probably overestimates the power of all research that is conducted because the studies with the lowest power do not obtain any significant effects and, thus, are never published. Conducting studies with inadequate power is obviously a waste of time and effort, so researchers must pay attention to the power of their research designs.

To be sure that you understand the difference between Type I and Type II errors, let us return to our example of a murder trial. After weighing the evidence, the jury must decide whether to reject the null hypothesis of "not guilty." In reaching their verdict, the jury hopes not to make either a Type I or a Type II error. In the context of a trial, a Type I error would involve rejecting the null hypothesis (not guilty) when it was true, or convicting an innocent person. A Type II error would involve failing to reject the null hypothesis when it was false—that is, not convicting a defendant who did, in fact, commit murder. Because greater injustice is done if an innocent person is convicted than if a criminal goes free, jurors are explicitly instructed to convict the defendant (reject the null hypothesis) only if they are convinced "beyond a reasonable doubt" that the defendant is guilty.

Likewise, researchers set a relatively stringent alpha level (of .05, for example) to be certain that they reject the null hypothesis only when the evidence suggests beyond a reasonable doubt that

the independent variable had an effect. Similarly, like jurors, researchers are more willing to risk a Type II error (failing to reject the null hypothesis when it is false) than a Type I error (rejecting the null hypothesis when it is true). Most researchers believe that Type I errors are worse than Type II errors—that concluding that an independent variable produced an effect that it really didn't is worse than missing an effect that is really there. So, we generally set our alpha level at .05 and beta at .20 (or, equivalently, power at .80), thereby making our probability of a Type I error only one-fourth the probability of a Type II error.

Effect Size

When researchers reject the null hypothesis and conclude that the independent variable has an effect on the dependent variable, they usually want to know how strong the independent variable's effect is. They determine the strength of the obtained effect by calculating the **effect size.** For factorial designs—experiments with more than one independent variable—an effect size can be calculated for each effect that is tested. So, for example, if an experiment has two independent variables, A and B, we can calculate the effect size for the main effect of A, the main effect of B, and the interaction of A and B. In each case, the effect size provides information about the strength of the effect.

Two distinct types of effect size indicators are used in experimental research. The first type can be interpreted as the proportion of variability in the dependent variable that is caused by the independent variable. The two effect sizes of this type that are used most commonly in experimental research are eta-squared (η^2) and omega-squared (ω^2). Although these indices differ, for our purposes, the important thing to understand is that they both indicate the proportion of the total variance in the dependent variable that is due to the independent variable (as opposed to error variance). As a proportion, these effect sizes can range from .00, indicating no relationship between the independent variable and the dependent variable, to 1.00, indicating that 100% of the variance in the dependent variable is caused by the independent variable. For example, if we find that the effect size is .37, we know that 37% of the variance in the dependent variable is due to the independent variable.

The second type of effect size is based on the size of the difference between two means relative to the size of the standard deviation of the data. The formula for one such statistic, Cohen's d, is

$$\bar{x}_1 - \bar{x}_2 / s_p$$

Think for a moment about what this number tells us. We said earlier that inferential statistics compare the difference we obtain between the means of the experimental conditions to the difference we would expect to obtain based on error variance alone. The standard deviation, s_p, in this equation reflects the error variance, so d indicates how much the two means differ relative to an index of the error variance.

If $d = .00$, the means do not differ (i.e., $\bar{x}_1 = \bar{x}_2$), but as the absolute value of d increases, a stronger effect is indicated. Importantly, d automatically expresses the size of an effect in standard deviation units. For example, if $d = .5$, the two condition means differ by .5 standard deviations, and if $d = 2.5$, the means differ by 2.5 standard deviations. Because d is on a metric defined by the standard deviation, ds can be compared across studies no matter the size of the means or standard deviation in a particular set of data.

To interpret effect sizes, you need to know whether you are dealing with a proportion-of-variance effect size (such as eta-squared and omega-squared) or a mean difference effect size (such as Cohen's d). As we saw, eta-squared and omega-squared can range from .00 to 1.00, whereas d usually falls in the -3 to $+3$ range (although it can be larger in extreme cases). So, for example, an effect size of .25 might indicate that the independent variable accounts for 25% of the variance in the dependent variable (a reasonably large effect) or that the condition means differ by .25 of a standard deviation (a less impressive effect), depending on what kind of effect size was calculated (a proportion-of-variance effect size or a mean difference effect size).

Developing Your Research Skills
Probability of Replication: The $_{prep}$ Statistic

I want to mention briefly one other statistic that has become popular recently so you will know what it is when you encounter one. The **statistic p_{rep}** estimates the probability of replicating an effect obtained in an experiment. If my experiment finds that participants who were made to feel rejected behaved more aggressively than participants who were led to feel accepted, what is the probability that an identical study would replicate my effect? Or, put differently, if I conducted the same study 100 times, in what percentage would I obtain the same result?

As a probability, p_{rep} can range from .00 (the probability of replication is zero) to 1.00 (the probability of replication is 100%). P_{rep} is related to both the probability of making a Type I error (the smaller the chance that an effect reflects a Type I error, the more likely it is to replicate) and to the effect size (stronger effects are more likely to replicate across studies), but it provides somewhat different information. As a new statistic, use of p_{rep} is somewhat controversial at present (Iverson, Lee, & Wagenmakers, 2009; Killeen, 2005), but you should know what p_{rep} is when you see it used in a study (as you will later in this chapter).

Summary

In analyzing data collected in experimental research, researchers attempt to determine whether the means of the various experimental conditions differ more than they would if the differences were due only to error variance. If the difference between the means is large relative to the error variance, the researcher rejects the null hypothesis and concludes that the independent variable has an effect. Researchers draw this conclusion with the understanding that there is a low probability (usually less than .05) that they have made a Type I error. If the difference in means is no larger than one would expect simply on the basis of the amount of error variance in the data, the researcher fails to reject the null hypothesis and concludes that the independent variable has no effect. When researchers reject the null hypothesis, they often calculate the effect size, which can express either the proportion of variability in the dependent variable that is associated with the independent variable or the difference between the means relative to the error variance depending on what kind of effect size is used.

ANALYSIS OF TWO-GROUP EXPERIMENTS: THE *t*-TEST

Now that you understand the rationale behind inferential statistics, we will look briefly at two statistical tests that are used most often to analyze data collected in experimental research. We will examine *t*-tests in this chapter and *F*-tests in Chapter 12.

Both of these analyses are based on the same rationale. The error variance in the data is calculated to provide an estimate of how much the means of the conditions are expected to differ when differences are due only to random error variance (and the independent variable has no effect). The observed differences between the means are then compared with this estimate. If the observed differences between the means are so large, relative to this estimate, that they are not likely to be the result of error variance alone, the null hypothesis is rejected. As we saw earlier, the likelihood of erroneously rejecting the null hypothesis is held at less than whatever alpha level the researcher has stipulated, usually .05.

Conducting a *t*-Test

Although the rationale behind inferential statistics may seem complex and convoluted, conducting a *t*-test to analyze data from a two-group randomized groups experiment is straightforward. In this section, we will walk through the calculation of one kind of *t*-test to demonstrate how the rationale for comparing mean differences to error variance described previously is implemented in practice.

To conduct a *t*-test, you calculate a value for *t* using a simple formula and then see whether this

calculated value of *t* exceeds a certain critical value that you locate in a table. If it does, the group means differ by more than what we would expect on the basis of error variance alone.

A *t*-test is conducted in the following five steps:

Step 1. Calculate the means of the two groups.

Step 2. Calculate the standard error of the difference between the two means.

Step 3. Find the calculated value of *t*.

Step 4. Find the critical value of *t*.

Step 5. Determine whether the null hypothesis should be rejected by comparing the calculated value of *t* to the critical value of *t*.

Let's examine each of these steps in detail.

Step 1. To test whether the means of two experimental groups are different, we obviously need to know the means. These means will go in the numerator of the formula for a *t*-test. Thus, first we must calculate the means of the two groups, $\bar{x}_1$ and $\bar{x}_2$.

Step 2. Tzo determine whether the means of the two experimental groups differ more than we would expect on the basis of error variance alone, we need an estimate of how much the means are expected to vary if the difference is due only to error variance. The **standard error of the difference between two means** provides an index of this expected difference.

This quantity is based directly on the amount of error variance in the data. As we saw in Chapter 9, error variance is reflected in the variability *within* the experimental conditions. Any variability we observe in the responses of participants who are in the same experimental condition cannot be due to the independent variable because they all receive the same level of the independent variable. Rather, this variance reflects extraneous variables, chiefly individual differences in how participants responded to the independent variable and poor experimental control.

Calculating the standard error of the difference between two means requires us to calculate the pooled standard deviation, which is accomplished in three steps.

2a. First, calculate the variances of the two experimental groups. (You may want to review the section of Chapter 6 that dealt with calculating the variance.) The variance for each condition is calculated from this formula:

$$s^2 = \frac{\sum x_i^2 - \left[(\sum x_i)^2/n \right]}{n - 1}$$

You'll calculate this variance twice, once for each experimental condition.

2b. Then calculate the pooled variance—$s^2{}_p$. This is an estimate of the average of the variances for the two groups:

$$s_p^2 = \frac{(n_1 - 1)s_1^2 + (n_2 - 1)s_2^2}{n_1 + n_2 - 2}$$

In this formula, n_1 and n_2 are the sample sizes for conditions 1 and 2, and $s_1{}^2$ and $s_2{}^2$ are the variances of the two conditions calculated in Step 2a.

2c. Finally, take the square root of the pooled variance, which gives you the pooled standard deviation, s_p.

Step 3. Armed with the means of the two groups ($\bar{x}_1$) and ($\bar{x}_2$), the pooled standard deviation ($_p$), and the sample sizes ($n1$ and $n2$), we are ready to calculate t:

$$t = \frac{\bar{x}_1 - \bar{x}_2}{s_p \sqrt{1/n_1 + 1/n_2}}$$

Step 4. Now we must locate the critical value of t in a table designed for that purpose. To find the **critical value** of t, we need to know the following two things.

4a. First, we need to calculate the degrees of freedom for the t-test. For a two-group randomized design, the degrees of freedom (df) is equal to the number of participants minus 2 (i.e., $n_1 + n_2 - 2$). (Don't concern yourself with what degrees of freedom are from a statistical perspective; simply realize that we need to take the number of scores into account when conducting inferential statistics, and degrees of freedom is a function of the number of scores.)

4b. Second, we need to specify the alpha level for the test. As we saw earlier, the alpha level is the probability we are willing to accept for making a Type I error—rejecting the null hypothesis when it is true. Usually, researchers set the alpha level at .05.

Taking the degrees of freedom and the alpha level, consult the table in Appendix A-1 to find the critical value of t. For example, imagine that we have 10 participants in each condition. The degrees of freedom would be $10 + 10 - 2 = 18$. Then, assuming the alpha level is set at .05, we locate this alpha level in the row labeled 1-tailed, then locate df $= 18$ in the first column, and we find that the critical value of t is 1.734.

Step 5. Finally, we compare our calculated value of t to the critical value of t obtained in the table of t-values. If the absolute value of the calculated value of t (Step 3) exceeds the critical value of t obtained from the table (Step 4), we reject the null hypothesis. The difference between the two means is large enough, relative to the error variance, to conclude that the difference is due to the independent variable and not to error variance alone. As we saw, a difference so large that it is very unlikely to be due to error variance alone is said to be statistically significant. After finding that the difference between the means is significant, we inspect the means themselves to determine the direction of the obtained effect. By seeing which mean is larger, we can determine the precise effect of the independent variable on whatever dependent variable we measured.

However, if the absolute value of the calculated value of t obtained in Step 3 is less than the critical value of t found in Step 4, we do not reject the null hypothesis. We conclude that the probability that the difference between the means is due to error variance is unacceptably high. In such cases, the difference between the means is called *nonsignificant*.

Developing Your Research Skills
Computational Example of a t-Test

To those of us who are sometimes inclined to overeat, anorexia nervosa is a puzzle. People who are anorexic exercise extreme control over their eating so that they lose a great deal of weight, often to the point that their health is threatened. One theory suggests that anorexics restrict their eating to maintain a sense of control over the world; when everything else in one's life seems out of control, one can always control what and how much one eats. One implication of this theory is that anorexics should respond to a feeling of low control by reducing the amount they eat.

To test this hypothesis, imagine that we selected college women who scored high on a measure of anorexic tendencies. We assigned these participants randomly to one of two experimental conditions. Participants in one condition were led to experience a sense of having high control, whereas participants in the other condition were led to experience a loss of control. Participants were then given the opportunity to sample sweetened breakfast cereals under the guise of a taste test. The dependent variable is the amount of cereal each participant eats. The number of pieces of cereal for 12 participants in this study follow:

High Control Condition	Low Control Condition
13	3
39	12
42	14
28	11
41	18
58	16

The question to be addressed is whether participants in the low control condition ate significantly less cereal than participants in the high control condition. We can conduct a *t*-test on these data by following five steps.

Step 1.

Calculate the means of the two groups.

High control=
$$\bar{x}_1 = (13 + 39 + 42 + 28 + 41 + 58)/6 = 36.8$$

Low control=
$$\bar{x}_2 = (3 + 12 + 14 + 11 + 18 + 16)/6 = 12.3$$

Step 2.

2a. Calculate the variances of the two experimental groups (see Chapter 6 for the calculational formula for the variance).

$$s_1^2 = 228.57 \quad s_2^2 = 27.47$$

2b. Calculate the pooled standard deviation, using the formula:

$$s_p^2 = \frac{(n_1 - 1)s_1^2 + (n_2 - 1)s_2^2}{n_1 + n_2 - 2}$$

$$= \frac{(6 - 1)(228.57) + (6 - 1)(27.47)}{6 + 6 - 2}$$

(continued)

(continued)

$$= \frac{(1142.85) + (137.35)}{10}$$

$$= 128.02$$

$$s_p = \sqrt{128.02} = 11.31$$

Step 3.

Solve for the calculated value of t:

$$t = \frac{\bar{x}_1 - \bar{x}_2}{s_p\sqrt{1/n_1 + 1/n_2}}$$

$$= \frac{36.8 - 12.3}{11.31\sqrt{1/6 + 1/6}}$$

$$= \frac{24.5}{11.31\sqrt{.333}}$$

$$= \frac{24.5}{11.31(.577)}$$

$$= \frac{24.5}{6.53}$$

$$= 3.75$$

Step 4.

Find the critical value of t in Appendix A-1. The degrees of freedom equal 10 (6 + 6 − 2); we'll set the alpha level at .05. Looking down the column for a one-tailed test at .05, we see that the critical value of t is 1.812.

Step 5.   Comparing our calculated value of t (3.75) to the critical value (1.812), we see that the calculated value exceeds the critical value. Thus, we conclude that the average amount of cereal eaten in the two conditions differed significantly. The difference between the two means is large enough, relative to the error variance, that we conclude that the difference is due to the independent variable and not to error variance. By inspecting the means, we see that participants in the low control condition ($\bar{x} = 12.3$) ate fewer pieces of cereal than participants in the high control condition ($\bar{x} = 36.8$).

Back to the Droodles Experiment

To analyze the data from their droodles experiment (see p. 212), Bower and his colleagues conducted a t-test on the number of droodles that participants recalled. When the authors conducted a t-test on these means, they calculated the value of t as 3.43. They then referred to a table of critical values of t (such as that in Appendix A-1). The degrees of freedom were $n_1 + n_2 - 2$, or $9 + 9 - 2 = 16$. Rather than setting the alpha level at .05, the researchers were more cautious and used an alpha level of .01. (i.e., they were willing to risk only a 1-in-100 chance of making a Type I error.) The critical value of t when df = 16 and alpha level = .01 is 2.583. Because the calculated value of t (3.43) was larger than the critical value (2.583), the means differed more than would be expected if only error variance were operating. Thus, the researchers rejected the null hypothesis that comprehension does not aid memory for pictures, knowing that the probability that they made a Type I error was less than 1 in 100. As the authors themselves stated in their article:

The primary result of interest is that an average of 19.6 pictures out of 28 (70%) were accurately recalled by the label group . . . , whereas only 14.2 pictures (51%) were recalled by the no-label group. . . .

The means differ reliably in the predicted direction, $t(16) = 3.43$, $p < .01$. Thus, we have clear confirmation that "picture understanding" enhances picture recall. (Bower et al., 1975, p. 218)

In Depth
Directional and Nondirectional Hypotheses

A hypothesis about the outcome of a two-group experiment can be stated in one of two ways. A **directional hypothesis** states which of the two condition means is expected to be larger. That is, the researcher predicts the specific direction of the anticipated effect. A **nondirectional hypothesis** merely states that the two means are expected to differ, but no prediction is ventured regarding which mean will be larger.

When a researcher's prediction is directional—as is most often the case—a **one-tailed test** is used. Each of the examples we've studied involved one-tailed tests because the direction of the difference between the means was predicted. Because the hypotheses were directional, we used the value for a one-tailed test in the table of t values (Appendix A-1). In the droodles experiment, for example, the researchers predicted that the number of droodles remembered would be *greater* in the condition in which the droodle was explained than in the control condition. Because this was a directional hypothesis, they used the critical value for a one-tailed t-test. Had their hypothesis been nondirectional, a **two-tailed test** would have been used.

ANALYSES OF MATCHED-SUBJECTS AND WITHIN-SUBJECTS DESIGNS

The procedure we just described for conducting a t-test applies to a two-group randomized groups design. A slightly different formula, the **paired t-test,** is used when the experiment involves a matched-subjects or a within-subjects design. The paired t-test takes into account the fact that the participants in the two conditions are similar, if not identical, on an attribute related to the dependent variable. In the matched-subjects design, we randomly assign matched pairs of participants to the two conditions; in the within-subjects design, the same participants serve in both conditions.

Either way, each participant in one condition is matched with a participant in the other condition (again, in a within-subjects design, the "matched" participants are the participants themselves). As a result of this matching, the matched scores in the two conditions should be correlated. In a matched-subjects design, the matched partners of participants who score high on the dependent variable in one condition (relative to the other participants) should score relatively high on the dependent variable in the other condition, and the matched partners of participants who score low in one condition should tend to score low in the other. Similarly, in a within-subjects design, participants who score high in one condition should score relatively high in the other condition, and vice versa. Thus, a positive correlation should be obtained between the matched scores in the two conditions.

The paired t-test takes advantage of this correlation to reduce the estimate of error variance used to calculate t. In essence, we can account for the source of some of the error variance in the data: It comes from individual differences among the participants. Given that we have matched pairs of participants, we can use the correlation between the two conditions to estimate the amount of error variance that is due to these differences among participants. Then we can discard this component of the error variance when we test the difference between the condition means.

Reducing error variance in this way leads to a more *powerful* test of the null hypothesis—one that is more likely to detect the effects of the independent variable than the randomized groups t-test. The paired t-test is more powerful because we have reduced the size of s_p in the denominator of the formula for t; and as s_p gets smaller, the calculated value of t gets larger. We will not go into the formula for the paired t-test here. However, a detailed explanation of this test can be found in most introductory statistics books.

Contributors to Behavioral Research
Statistics in the Brewery: W. S. Gosset

One might imagine that the important advances in research design and statistics came from statisticians slaving away in cluttered offices at prestigious universities. Indeed, many of those who provided the foundation for behavioral science, such as Wilhelm Wundt and Karl Pearson, were academicians. However, many methodological and statistical approaches were developed while solving real-world problems, notably in industry and agriculture.

A case in point involves the work of William S. Gosset (1876–1937), whose contributions to research included the t-test. With a background in chemistry and mathematics, Gosset was hired by Guinness Brewery in Dublin, Ireland, in 1899. Among his duties, Gosset investigated how the quality of beer is affected by various raw materials (such as different strains of barley and hops) and by various methods of production (such as variations in brewing temperature). Thus, Gosset conducted experiments to study the effects of ingredients and brewing procedures on the quality of beer and became interested in developing better ways to analyze the data he collected.

Gosset spent a year in specialized study in London, where he studied with Karl Pearson (whom we met in Chapter 7 when we discussed the Pearson correlation coefficient). During this time, Gosset worked on developing solutions to statistical problems he encountered at the brewery. In 1908, he published a paper based on this work that laid out the principles for the t-test. Interestingly, he published his work under the pen name, Student, and to this day, this test is often referred to as *Student's t*.

COMPUTER ANALYSES

In the early days of behavioral science, researchers calculated all of their statistical analyses by hand. Because analyses were time-consuming and cumbersome, researchers understandably relied primarily on relatively simple statistical techniques. The invention of the calculator (first mechanical, then electronic) was a great boon to researchers because it allowed them to perform mathematical operations more quickly and with less error.

However, not until the widespread availability of computers and user-friendly statistical software did the modern age of statistical analysis begin. By the 1970s, analyses that once took many hours (or even days!) to conduct by hand could be performed on a computer in a few minutes. Furthermore, the spread of bigger and faster computers allowed researchers to conduct increasingly complex analyses and test more sophisticated research hypotheses in less and less time. Thus, over the past 40 years, we have seen a marked increase in the complexity of the analyses that researchers commonly use. Analyses that were once considered too complex and laborious to perform by hand are now used regularly.

In the earliest days of the computer, computer programs had to be written from scratch for each new analysis. Researchers either had to be proficient computer programmers or have the resources to hire a programmer to write programs for them. Gradually, however, statistical software packages were developed that any researcher could use by simply writing a handful of commands to inform the computer how their data were entered and which analyses to conduct. With the advent of menu and window interfaces, analyses became as easy as a few keystrokes on a computer keyboard or a few clicks of a computer mouse. Once the researcher has entered his or her data into the computer, named his or her variables, and indicated what analyses to perform on which variables (either by writing a short set of commands or clicking on options on a computer screen), most analyses take only a few seconds. Today, several software packages exist that can perform most statistical analyses. (The most commonly used software statistical packages in the behavioral sciences include *PASW (formerly known as SPSS)*, *SAS*, *BMDP*, *R*, and *Mplus*.) In addition, specialized software exists for many advanced kinds of analyses.

Although computer analyses have greatly enhanced the quality and efficiency of scientific investigation, they have introduced new issues for researchers to consider. First, no matter how well a study is designed and conducted, the results are only as good as the accuracy with which the data are entered into the computer. The individuals who enter the data for analysis must be consistently and uncompromisingly careful in their task. Minor mistakes in inputting data (such as typing a 4 instead of a 5) will result in an increase in error variance in the data that are analyzed, undermining the power of the analyses and the ability to detect significant effects. More serious mistakes (such as entering someone's weight as 230 instead of 130, or entering the value for a variable in the wrong place) can totally compromise the validity of the analyses and any conclusions drawn from them.

For this reason, researchers not only insist on the utmost care when entering data but also check their accuracy before conducting statistical analyses. Often researchers will check the data file—number by number—against the raw data (on the original questionnaires, for example) to be certain that the data were entered accurately. In addition, researchers typically conduct exploratory data analyses to examine data quality before they conduct the primary analyses. For example, they will determine that scores fall within the permitted range for each variable (a score of 415 for the participant's age is presumably an error), examine the frequency distributions of the data to look for anomalies, and see whether the average score for each variable seems reasonable. Only when the researcher is certain that the data are "clean" will he or she proceed to conduct the primary analyses.

A second issue raised by modern user-friendly statistical software is that anyone can now conduct complex statistical analyses even if they know virtually nothing about the analyses they are running, the statistical assumptions that must be met to ensure valid analyses, or how to properly interpret the results they obtain. Now that statistical analyses may require only a few clicks of a mouse button, far less knowledge is required than was once the case. Although this is obviously an advantage, it also opens the possibility that analyses may be conducted or interpreted inappropriately. Researchers should only conduct analyses that they understand.

Although computers have freed researchers from most hand calculations (occasionally, it is still faster to perform simple analyses by hand than to use the computer), researchers must understand when to use particular analyses, what requirements must be met for an analysis to be valid, and what the results of a particular analysis tell them about their data. Computers do not at all diminish the importance or necessity of understanding statistics.

Developing Your Research Skills
Designing and Analyzing Two-group Experiments

At this point, it might be useful for you to review the basics of experimental design and analysis by tackling an example that draws upon material that you have learned in Chapters 9, 10, and 11.

People's judgments of the risk involved in various activities and objects are influenced by many factors. Research has shown that people's assessment of risk is often based on emotional, gut-level reactions rather than a rational consideration of the evidence. As a case in point, an article published in the journal *Psychological Science* tested the hypothesis that stimuli that are difficult to pronounce are viewed as more dangerous than stimuli that are easy to pronounce (Song & Schwartz, 2009). To obtain stimuli that are easy versus difficult to pronounce, the researchers conducted a pilot study in which 15 people rated on a 7-point scale how easily 16 bogus food additives, each consisting of 12 letters, could be pronounced (1 = *very difficult*; 7 = *very easy*). They then picked the five easiest words to pronounce (such as *Magnalroxate*) and the five hardest words to pronounce (such as *Hnegripitrom*) for the experiment. The five easiest names (M = 5.04) were rated as easier to pronounce than the five hardest names (M = 2.15).

(continued)

(continued)

In the experiment itself, 20 students were told to imagine that they were reading food labels and to rate the hazard posed by each food additive on a 7-point scale (1 = *very safe*; 7 = *very harmful*). The 10 names were presented in one of two random orders, and analyses showed that the order in which participants rated the names did not influence their ratings.

Here is the authors' description of the results as stated in the article:

As predicted, participants in Study 1 rated substances with hard-to-pronounce names ($M = 4.12$, $SD = 0.78$) as more harmful than substances with easy-to-pronounce names ($M = 3.7$, $SD = 0.74$), $t(19) = 2.41$, $p < .03$, $p_{rep} = .92$. $d = 0.75$.

1. The researchers conducted a pilot study to develop and test their research materials as we discussed on page 187, and as noted, the five easy-to-pronounce words ($M = 5.04$) were rated as easier to pronounce than the five hard-to-pronounce words ($M = 2.15$). What statistical test would you conduct if you wanted to test whether the easy-to-pronounce words were *significantly* easier to pronounce than the hard-to-pronounce words?
2. Did the researchers assure the equivalence of their two experimental conditions as required in every experiment? If so, what method did they use?
3. Do you see any possible confounds in this description of the experiment?
4. What is the "19" after t?
5. Compare the calculated value of t to the critical value in Appendix A-1.
6. What does "$p < .03$" tell us?
7. Interpret the p_{rep} statistic.
8. What is d, and what does it tell us?

Answers are on page 249.

Summary

1. The data from experiments are analyzed by determining whether the means of the experimental conditions differ. However, because error variance can cause condition means to differ even when the independent variable has no effect, we must compare the difference between the condition means to how much we would expect the means to differ if the difference is due solely to error variance.
2. Researchers use inferential statistics to determine whether the observed differences between the means are greater than would be expected on the basis of error variance alone.
3. If the condition means differ more than expected based on the amount of error variance in the data, researchers reject the null hypothesis (which states that the independent variable does not have an effect) and conclude

that the independent variable affected the dependent variable. If the means do not differ by more than error variance would predict, researchers fail to reject the null hypothesis and conclude that the independent variable does not have an effect.
4. When deciding to reject or fail to reject the null hypothesis, researchers may make one of two kinds of errors. A Type I error occurs when the researcher rejects the null hypothesis when it is true (and, thus, erroneously concludes that the independent variable has an effect); a Type II error occurs when the researcher fails to reject the null hypothesis when it is false (and, thus, fails to detect a true effect of the independent variable).
5. Researchers can never know for certain whether a Type I or Type II error has occurred,

but they can specify the probability that they have made each kind of error. The probability of a Type I error is called *alpha;* the probability of a Type II error is called *beta.*

6. To minimize the probability of making a Type II error, researchers try to design powerful studies. Power refers to the probability that a study will correctly reject the null hypothesis (and, thus, detect true effects of the independent variable). To ensure they have sufficient power, researchers often conduct a power analysis that tells them the optimal number of participants for their study.

7. Effect size indicates the strength of the independent variable's effect on the dependent variable. It is expressed as either the proportion of the total variability in the dependent variable that is accounted for by the independent variable or as the size of the difference between two means expressed in standard deviation units.

8. The *t*-test is used to analyze the difference between two means. A value for *t* is calculated by dividing the difference between the means by an estimate of how much the means would be expected to differ on the basis of error variance alone. This calculated value of *t* is then compared to a critical value of *t*. If the calculated value exceeds the critical value, the null hypothesis is rejected.

9. Hypotheses about the outcome of two-group experiments may be directional (predicting which of the two condition means will be larger) or nondirectional (predicting that the means will differ but not specifying which one will be larger). Whether the hypothesis is directional or nondirectional has implications for whether the critical value of *t* used in the *t*-test is one-tailed or two-tailed.

10. The paired *t*-test is used when the experiment involves a matched-subjects or within-subjects design.

11. The computer revolution has greatly facilitated the use of complex statistical analyses.

Key Terms

alpha level (*p. 235*)
beta (*p. 236*)
critical value (*p. 240*)
directional hypothesis (*p. 243*)
effect size (*p. 237*)
experimental hypothesis (*p. 234*)
failing to reject the null
    hypothesis (*p. 235*)
inferential statistics (*p. 234*)

nondirectional hypothesis (*p. 243*)
null hypothesis (*p. 234*)
one-tailed test (*p. 243*)
paired *t*-test (*p. 243*)
power (*p. 236*)
power analysis (*p. 236*)
p_{rep} statistic (p. 238)
rejecting the null hypothesis
    (*p. 234*)

standard error of the difference
    between two means
    (*p. 239*)
statistical significance
    (*p. 236*)
t-test (*p. 239*)
two-tailed test (*p. 243*)
Type I error (*p. 235*)
Type II error (*p. 236*)

Questions For Review

1. In analyzing the data from an experiment, why is it not sufficient simply to examine the condition means to see whether they differ?
2. Assuming that all confounds were eliminated, the means of the conditions in an experiment may differ from one another for two reasons. What are they?
3. Why do researchers use inferential statistics?
4. Distinguish between the null hypothesis and the experimental hypothesis.

5. When analyzing data, why do researchers test the null hypothesis rather than the experimental hypothesis?
6. Explain the difference between rejecting and failing to reject the null hypothesis. In which case does a researcher conclude that the independent variable has an effect on the dependent variable?
7. Distinguish between a Type I and a Type II error.
8. Which type of error do researchers usually regard as more serious? Why?

9. Explain what it means if a researcher sets the alpha-level for a statistical test at .05.
10. What does it mean if the difference between two means is statistically significant?
11. Do powerful studies minimize alpha or beta? Explain.
12. What information do researchers obtain from conducting a power analysis?
13. What would it mean if the proportion-of-variance effect size in an experiment was .25? .40? .00? What would it mean if the mean difference effect size was .25? .40? .00?
14. Explain the rationale behind the *t*-test.
15. Write the formula for a *t*-test.
16. Once researchers calculate a value for *t*, they compare that calculated value to a critical value of *t*. What two pieces of information must be known in order to find the critical value of *t* in a table of critical values?
17. If the calculated value of *t* is less than the critical value, do you reject or fail to reject the null hypothesis? Explain.
18. If you reject the null hypothesis (and conclude that the independent variable has an effect), what's the likelihood that you have made a Type I error? What is the likelihood that you made a Type II error?
19. Distinguish between one-tailed and two-tailed *t*-tests.
20. Why must a different *t*-test be used for matched-subjects and within-subjects designs than for randomized groups designs?
21. What was W. S. Gosset's contribution to behavioral research?

Questions For Discussion

1. If the results of a *t*-test lead you to reject the null hypothesis, what is the probability that you have made a Type II error?
2. a. Using the table of critical values of *t* in Appendix A-1, find the critical value of *t* for an experiment in which there are 28 participants, using an alpha level of .05 for a one-tailed test.
   b. Find the critical value of *t* for an experiment in which there are 28 participants, using an alpha level of .01 for a one-tailed test.
3. Looking at the table of critical values, you will see that, for any particular degree of freedom, the critical value of *t* is larger when the alpha level is .01 than when it is .05. Can you figure out why?
4. If the difference between two means is not statistically significant, how certain are you that the independent variable really does not affect the dependent variable?
5. Generally, researchers are more concerned about making a Type I error than a Type II error. Can you think of any instances in which you might be more concerned about making a Type II error?

Exercises

1. Professors realize that no matter how much time they give students to complete an assignment many students will not start working on it until the deadline is approaching. This raises the question of whether giving students more time to complete an assignment actually improves the quality of their work. A researcher gave 30 college students an assignment that involved writing a 10-page paper and randomly assigned them to one of two conditions. Half of the students were given two weeks to write the paper, and the other half were given four weeks to write the paper. A professor not involved with the study then graded each paper on a 10-point scale. The grades were as follows:
   a. State the null and experimental hypotheses.
   b. Conduct a *t*-test to determine whether the quality of papers was higher when students had 4 rather than 2 weeks to write them.

2-Week Deadline	4-Week Deadline
6	9
3	4
4	7
7	7
7	6
5	10
7	9
10	8
7	5
4	8
5	7
6	4
3	8
7	7
6	9

2. A researcher was interested in the effects of weather on cognitive performance. He tested participants on either sunny or cloudy days and obtained the following scores on a 10-item test of cognitive performance. Using these data, conduct a *t*-test to see whether performance differed on sunny and cloudy days.

Sunny Day	Cloudy Day
7	7
1	4
3	1
9	7
6	5
6	2
8	9
2	6

Answers to Designing and Analyzing Two-Group Experiments (p. 246)

1. You would conduct a paired *t*-test because this is a within-subjects design. (In fact, the researchers reported conducting such a test in their article, which showed that the easy-to-pronounce words were rated as significantly easier to pronounce than the hard-to-pronounce words.)

2. The researchers assured the equivalence of their two experimental conditions by using a within-subjects or repeated measures design. Each participant rated the harmfulness of both easy- and hard-to-pronounce words.

3. The description of the experiment contains no obvious confounds.

4. The "19" is the degrees of freedom needed interpret the *t*-test.

5. The calculated value of *t* (2.41) is larger than the critical value in the appendix (1.729). To find the critical value, you use a one-tailed test (the researchers made a directional hypothesis), an alpha-level of .05, and 19 degrees of freedom.

6. The notation "*p* < .03" tells us that the probability that we made a Type I error when we rejected the null hypothesis is less than .03 (or 3%).

7. The p_{rep} statistic estimates that the probability of replicating this experiment is .92 (or 92%).

8. The *d* is Cohen's *d* statistic, a mean difference measure of effect size. It tells us that the two condition means differ by .75 standard deviation. This is a reasonably large difference.

Answers to Exercises

1. The calculated value of *t* for these data is -2.08, which exceeds the critical value of 1.701 (alpha level = .05, df = 28, one-tailed *t*-test). Thus, you reject the null hypothesis and conclude that the average grade for the papers in the 4-week deadline condition (mean = 7.2) was significantly higher than the average grade for papers in the 2-week deadline condition (mean = 5.8).

2. The calculated value of *t* is $-.089$, which is less than the critical value of 2.145 (alpha level = .05, df = 14, two-tailed test). Thus, you should fail to reject the null hypothesis and conclude that weather was unrelated to cognitive performance in this study.

12

ANALYZING COMPLEX EXPERIMENTAL DESIGNS

By now, you should have a good understanding of how researchers use the *t*-test to analyze data from experiments that have one independent variable with two levels. Of course, most experiments have more than two conditions, and many have more than one independent variable, so we will now turn our attention to how researchers analyze these more complex designs. We will start with one-way designs that have one independent variable with more than two levels and then look at factorial designs that have more than one independent variable.

In Chapter 10, I described an experiment that investigated the effectiveness of various strategies for losing weight (Mahoney, Moura, and Wade, 1973). In this one-way design, obese adults were randomly assigned to one of five conditions: self-reward for losing weight, self-punishment for failing to lose weight, self-reward for losing combined with self-punishment for not losing weight, self-monitoring of weight (but without rewarding or punishing oneself), and a control condition. At the end of the experiment, the researchers wanted to know whether any of these weight loss strategies were more effective than others in helping participants lose weight.

The means for the number of pounds that participants lost in each of the five conditions are shown in Table 12.1. Given these means, how would you determine whether some of the weight-reduction strategies were more effective than others in helping participants lose weight? Clearly, the average weight loss was greatest in the self-reward condition (6.4 pounds) than in the other conditions, but, as we've seen, we must conduct statistical tests to determine whether the differences among the means are greater than we would expect based on the amount of error variance present in the data. We want to know whether participants lost *significantly* more weight is some conditions than in others.

One possible way to analyze these data would be to conduct 10 *t*-tests, comparing the mean of each experimental group to the mean of every other group: Group 1 versus Group 2, Group 1 versus Group 3, Group 1 versus Group 4, Group 1 versus Group 5, Group 2

TABLE 12.1	Average Weight Loss in the Mahoney et al. Study	
Group	**Condition**	**Mean Pounds Lost**
1	Self-reward	6.4
2	Self-punishment	3.7
3	Self-reward and self-punishment	5.2
4	Self-monitoring of weight	0.8
5	Control group	1.4

versus Group 3, Group 2 versus Group 4, Group 2 versus Group 5, Group 3 versus Group 4, Group 3 versus Group 5, and Group 4 versus Group 5. If you performed all 10 of these *t*-tests, you could tell which means differed significantly from the others and determine whether the strategies differentially affected the amount of weight that participants lost.

THE PROBLEM: CONDUCTING MULTIPLE TESTS INFLATES TYPE I ERROR

Although one could use several *t*-tests to analyze these data, such an analysis creates a serious problem. Recall that when researchers set the alpha level at .05, they run a 5% risk of making a Type I error—that is, erroneously rejecting the null hypothesis when it is actually true—on any particular statistical test they conduct. Put differently, Type I errors will occur on up to 5% of all statistical tests they conduct, and, thus, 5% of all analyses that yield statistically significant results could actually be due to error variance rather than to real effects of the independent variable.

If only one *t*-test is conducted, we have no more than a 5% chance of making a Type I error, and most researchers are willing to accept this risk. But what if we conduct 10 *t*-tests? Or 25? Or 100? Although the likelihood of making a Type I error on any particular *t*-test is .05, the overall Type I error increases as we perform a greater number of tests. As a result, the more *t*-tests we conduct, the more likely it is that one or more of our significant findings will reflect a Type I error, and the more likely it is we will draw invalid conclusions about the effects of the independent variable. Thus, although our

chances of making a Type I error on any one test is no more than .05, our overall chance of making a Type I error across all of our tests is higher.

To see what I mean, imagine that we conduct 10 *t*-tests to analyze differences between each pair of means from the weight-loss data in Table 12.1. The probability of making a Type I error (that is, rejecting the null hypothesis when it is true) on any one of those 10 tests is .05. However, the probability of making a Type I error on *at least one* of the 10 *t*-tests is approximately .40—that is, 4 out of 10—which is considerably higher than the alpha level of .05 for each individual *t*-test we conduct. (When conducting multiple statistical tests, the probability of making a Type I error can be estimated from the formula, $1 - (1 - alpha)^c$, where *c* equals the number of tests [or comparisons] performed.) The same problem occurs when we analyze data from factorial designs. To analyze the interaction from a 4×2 factorial design would require several *t*-tests to test the difference between each pair of means. As a result, we increase the probability of making at least one Type I error as we analyze all those means.

Because researchers obviously do not want to conclude that the independent variable has an effect when it really does not, they must take steps to control Type I error when they conduct many statistical analyses. The most straightforward way to prevent Type I error inflation when conducting many tests is to set a more stringent alpha level than the conventional .05 level. Researchers sometimes use the **Bonferroni adjustment** in which they divide their desired alpha level (such as .05) by the number of tests they plan to conduct. For example, if we wanted to conduct 10 *t*-tests to analyze all pairs of means in the weight-loss study (Table 12.1), we could use an alpha level of .005 rather than .05 for each *t*-test we ran. (We would use an alpha level of .005 because we divide our desired alpha level of .05 by the number of tests we will conduct; .05/10 = .005.) If we did so, the likelihood of making a Type I error on any particular *t*-test would be very low (.005), and the overall likelihood of making a Type I error across all 10 *t*-tests would not exceed our desired alpha level of .05.

Although the Bonferroni adjustment certainly protects us against inflated Type I error when we conduct many tests, it has a drawback: As we make our alpha-level more stringent and lower the probability of a Type I error, the probability of making a Type II error (and missing real effects of the independent variable) increases. By changing the alpha-level from, for example, .05 to .005, we are requiring the condition means to differ from one another by a greater margin in order to declare the difference statistically significant. But if we require the means to be very different before we regard them as significantly different, then small but real differences between the means won't meet our criterion. As a result, our *t*-tests will miss certain effects that they would have detected if a more liberal alpha level of .05 was used for each test. Although we have lowered our chances of making a Type I error, we have increased the likelihood of a Type II error.

Researchers sometimes use the Bonferroni adjustment when they plan to conduct only a few statistical tests but, for the reason just described, they are reluctant to do so when the number of tests is large. Instead, researchers typically use a statistical procedure called *analysis of variance* when they want to test differences among many means. **Analysis of variance**—commonly called **ANOVA**—is a statistical procedure that is used to analyze data from designs that involve more than two conditions.

ANOVA analyzes differences between all condition means in an experiment *simultaneously.* Rather than testing the difference between each pair of means as a *t*-test does, ANOVA determines whether *any* of a set of means differs from another using a single statistical test that holds the alpha level at .05 (or whatever level the researcher chooses) regardless of how many group means are involved in the test. For example, rather than conducting 10 *t*-tests among all pairs of five means (with

the likelihood of making a Type I error being about .40), ANOVA performs a single, simultaneous test on all condition means with only a .05 chance of making a Type I error.

THE RATIONALE BEHIND ANOVA

Imagine that we conduct an experiment in which we know that the independent variable(s) have *absolutely no effect*. In such a case, we can estimate the amount of error variance in the data in one of two ways. Most obviously, we can calculate the error variance by looking at the variability among the participants within each of the experimental conditions; all variance in the responses of participants in a single condition is error variance. Alternatively, if we know for certain that the independent variable has no effect, we can also estimate the error variance in the data from the size of the differences between the condition means. We can do this because, if the independent variable has no effect (and there is no confounding), the only possible reason for the condition means to differ from one another is error variance. In other words, when the independent variable has no effect, the variability among condition means and the variability within groups are both reflections of error variance.

However, to the extent that the independent variable affects participants' responses and creates differences between the experimental conditions, the variability among condition means should be larger than if only error variance is causing the means to differ. Thus, if we find that the variance *between* experimental conditions is markedly greater than the variance *within* the condition, we have evidence that the independent variable is causing the difference (again assuming that there are no confounds in the study).

Analysis of variance is based on a statistic called the **F-test,** which is the ratio of the variance among conditions (between-groups variance) to the variance within conditions (within-groups, or error, variance). Again, if the independent variable has absolutely no effect, the between-groups variance and the within-groups (or error) variance are the same. But the larger the between-groups variance relative to the within-groups variance, the larger the calculated value of F becomes, and the more likely it is that the differences among the condition means reflect effects of the independent variable rather than error variance. By testing this F-ratio, we can estimate the likelihood that the differences between the condition means are due to the independent variable versus error variance.

We will devote most of the rest of this chapter to exploring how ANOVA works. The purpose here is not to show you how to conduct an ANOVA but rather to explain how ANOVA operates. In fact, the formulas used here are intended only to show you what an ANOVA does; researchers use other forms of these formulas to actually compute an ANOVA. The computational formulas for ANOVA appear in Appendix B.

HOW ANOVA WORKS

Recall that the total variance in a set of experimental data can be broken into two parts: systematic variance (which reflects differences among the experimental conditions) and unsystematic, or error, variance (which reflects differences among participants within the experimental conditions).

Total variance = systematic variance
+ error variance.

In a one-way design with a single independent variable, ANOVA breaks the total variance into these two components—systematic variance (presumably due to the independent variable) and error variance.

Total Sum of Squares

We learned in Chapter 2 that the **sum of squares** reflects the total amount of variability in a set of data. We learned also that the **total sum of squares** is calculated by (1) subtracting the mean from each score, (2) squaring these differences, and (3) adding them up. We used this formula for the total sum of squares, which we'll abbreviate SS_{total}:

$$SS_{total} = \Sigma(x_i - \bar{x})^2.$$

SS_{total} expresses the total amount of variability in a set of data. ANOVA breaks down, or partitions, this total variability to identify its sources. One

part—the sum of squares between-groups—involves systematic variance that reflects the influence of the independent variable. The other part—the sum of squares within-groups—reflects error variance:

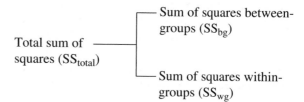

Total sum of squares (SS_{total}) — Sum of squares between-groups (SS_{bg}) — Sum of squares within-groups (SS_{wg})

Let's look at these two sources of the total variability more closely.

Sum of Squares Within-Groups

To determine whether differences between condition means reflect only error variance, we need to know how much error variance exists in the data. In an ANOVA, this is estimated by the **sum of squares within-groups** (or SS_{wg}). SS_{wg} is equal to the sum of the sums of squares for each of the experimental groups. In other words, if we calculate the sum of squares (that is, the variability) separately for each experimental group, then add these group sums of squares together, we obtain SS_{wg}:

$$SS_{wg} = \Sigma(x_1 - \bar{x}_1)^2 + \Sigma(x_2 - \bar{x}_2)^2 + \ldots$$
$$+ \Sigma(x_k - \bar{x}_k)^2.$$

In this equation, we are taking each participant's score, subtracting the mean of the condition that the participant is in, squaring that difference, and then adding these squared deviations for all participants within a condition to give us the sum of squares for each condition. Then, we add the sums for all of the conditions together.

Think for a moment about what SS_{wg} represents. Because all participants in a particular condition receive the same level of the independent variable, none of the variability within any of the groups can be due to the independent variable. Thus, when we add the sums of squares across all conditions, SS_{wg} expresses the amount of variability in our data that is *not* due to the independent variable. This, of course, is error variance.

As you can see, the size of SS_{wg} increases with the number of conditions. Because we need an index of something like the *average* variance within the experimental conditions, we divide SS_{wg} by $n - k$, where n is the total number of participants and k is the number of experimental groups. (The quantity, $n - k$, is called the *within-groups degrees of freedom* or df_{wg}.) By dividing the within-groups variance (SS_{wg}) by the within-groups degrees of freedom (df_{wg}), we obtain a quantity known as the **mean square within-groups** or MS_{wg}:

$$MS_{wg} = SS_{wg}/df_{wg}.$$

It should be clear that MS_{wg} provides us with an estimate of the average within-groups, or error, variance.

Sum of Squares Between-Groups

Now that we've estimated the error variance from the sum of the variability within the groups (MS_{wg}), we must find a way to isolate the variance that is due to the independent variable. ANOVA approaches this task by using the **sum of squares between-groups** (sometimes called the *sum of squares for treatment*).

The calculation of the sum of squares between-groups (or SS_{bg}) is based on a simple rationale. If the independent variable has no effect, we would expect all of the condition means to be roughly equal, aside from whatever differences are due to error variance. Because all of the means are the same, each condition mean would also be approximately equal to the mean of all the group means (the **grand mean**). However, if the independent variable is causing the means of some conditions to be larger or smaller than the means of others, the condition means not only will differ among themselves but some of them will also differ from the grand mean.

Thus, to calculate between-groups variance we first subtract the grand mean from each of the group means. Small differences indicate that the means don't differ very much (and, thus, the independent variable had little, if any, effect). In contrast, large differences between the condition means and the grand mean indicate large differences between the groups and suggest that the independent variable is causing the means to differ.

Thus, to obtain SS_{bg}, we (1) subtract the grand mean (GM) from the mean of each group, (2) square these differences, (3) multiply each squared difference by the size of the group, then (4) sum across groups. This can be expressed by the following formula:

$$SS_{bg} = n_1(\bar{x}_1 - GM)^2 + n_2(\bar{x}_2 - GM)^2 + \cdots + n_k(\bar{x}_k - GM)^2.$$

We then divide SS_{bg} by the quantity $k - 1$, where k is the number of group means that went into the calculation of SS_{bg}. (The quantity $k - 1$ is called the *between-groups degrees of freedom*.) When SS_{bg} is divided by its degrees of freedom ($k - 1$), the resulting number is called the **mean square between-groups** (or MS_{bg}), which is our estimate of between-groups variance:

$$MS_{bg} = SS_{bg}/df_{bg}.$$

MS_{bg}, which is a function of the differences among the group means, reflects two kinds of variance. First, it reflects systematic differences among the groups that are due to the effect of the independent variable. Ultimately, we are interested in isolating this systematic variance to see whether the independent variable had an effect on the dependent variable. However, MS_{bg} also reflects differences among the groups that are the result of random error variance. As noted earlier, the means of the groups would probably differ slightly due to error variance even if the independent variable had no effect.

The *F*-Test

Because we expect to find some between-groups variance even if the independent variables have no effect, we must test whether the between-groups variance is larger than we would expect based on the amount of within-groups (that is, error) variance in the data.

To do this, we conduct an *F*-test. To obtain the value of *F*, we calculate the ratio of between-groups variability to within-groups variability for each effect we are testing. If our study has only one independent variable, we simply divide MS_{bg} by MS_{wg}:

$$F = MS_{bg}/MS_{wg}.$$

If the independent variable has no effect, the numerator and denominator of the F-ratio are estimates of the same thing (the amount of error variance), and the value of F will be around 1.00. However, to the extent that the independent variable is causing differences among the experimental conditions, systematic variance will be produced and MS_{bg} (which contains both systematic and error variance) will be larger than MS_{wg} (which contains only error variance).

The important question is *how much* larger the numerator needs to be than the denominator to conclude that the independent variable truly has an effect. We answer this question by locating a critical value of F, just as we did with the t-test. To find the critical value of F in Appendix A-2, we specify three things: (1) We set the alpha level (usually .05); (2) we calculate the degrees of freedom for the effect we are testing (df_{bg}); and (3) we calculate the degrees of freedom for the within-groups variance (df_{wg}). (The calculations for degrees of freedom for various effects are shown in Appendix B.) With these numbers in hand, we can find the critical value of F in Appendix A-2. For example, if we set our alpha level at .05, and the between-groups degrees of freedom is 2 and the within-groups degrees of freedom is 30, the critical value of F is 3.32.

If the value of F we calculate for an effect exceeds the critical value of F obtained from the table, we conclude that at least one of the condition means differs from the others and, thus, that the independent variable had an effect. More formally, if the calculated value of F exceeds the critical value, we *reject the null hypothesis* that the means do not differ and conclude that at least one of the condition means differs significantly from another. However, if the calculated value of F is less than the critical value, the differences among the group means are no greater than we would expect on the basis of error variance alone. Thus, we fail to reject our null hypothesis and conclude that the independent variable does not have an effect.

In the experiment involving weight loss (Mahoney et al., 1973), the calculated value of F was 4.49. The critical value of F when $df_{bg} = 4$ and $df_{wg} = 48$ is 2.56. Given that the calculated value exceeded the critical value, the authors rejected the null hypothesis and concluded that the five weight-loss strategies were differentially effective.

Extension of ANOVA to Factorial Designs

We have seen that, in a one-way ANOVA, we partition the total variability in a set of data into two components: between-groups (systematic) variance and within-groups (error) variance. Put differently, SS_{total} has two sources of variance: SS_{bg} and SS_{wg}.

In factorial designs, such as those we discussed in Chapter 10, the systematic, between-groups portion of the variance can be broken down further into other components to test for the presence of different main effects and interactions. When our design involves more than one independent variable, we can ask whether any systematic variance is related to each of the independent variables, as well as whether systematic variance is produced by interactions among the variables.

Let's consider a two-way factorial design in which we have manipulated two independent variables, which we'll call A and B. (Shiv et al.'s study on the effects of Sobe energy booster described in Chapter 10 would be an example of such a design.) Using an ANOVA to analyze the data would lead us to break the total variance (SS_{total}) into four parts. Specifically, we could calculate both the sum of squares (SS) and mean square (MS) for the following:

1. the error variance (SS_{wg} and MS_{wg})
2. the main effect of A (SS_A and MS_A)
3. the main effect of B (SS_B and MS_B)
4. the $A \times B$ interaction ($SS_{A \times B}$ and $MS_{A \times B}$)

Together, these four sources of variance would account for all of the variability in participants' responses. That is, $SS_{total} = SS_A + SS_B + SS_{A \times B} + SS_{wg}$. Nothing else could account for the variability in the data other than the main effects of A and B, the interaction of $A \times B$, and the otherwise unexplained error variance.

For example, to calculate SS_A (the systematic variance due to independent variable A), we ignore variable B for the moment and determine how much of the variance in the dependent variable is associated with A alone. In other words, we disregard the fact that variable B even exists and compute SS_{bg} using just the means for the various conditions of variable A. (See Figure 12.1.) If the independent variable has no effect, we will expect the means for the various levels

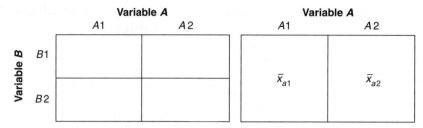

FIGURE 12.1 Testing the Main Effect of Variable A. Imagine we have conducted the 2×2 factorial experiment shown on the left. When we test for the main effect of variable A, we temporarily ignore the fact that variable B was included in the design, as in the diagram on the right. The calculation for the sum of squares for A (SS_A) is based on the means for Conditions $A1$ and $A2$, disregarding variable B.

of A to be roughly equal to the mean of all of the group means (the grand mean). However, if variable A is causing the means of some conditions to be larger than the means of others, the means should differ from the grand mean. Thus, we can calculate the sum of squares for A much as we calculated SS_{bg} earlier:

$$SS_A = n_{a1}(\bar{x}_{a1} - GM)^2 + n_{a2}(\bar{x}_{a2} - GM)^2 + \cdots$$
$$+ n_{aj}(\bar{x}_{aj} - GM)^2.$$

Then, by dividing SS_A by the degrees of freedom for A (df_A = number of conditions of A minus 1), we obtain the mean square for A (MS_A), which provides an index of the systematic variance associated with variable A.

The rationale behind testing the main effect of B is the same as that for A. To test the main effect of B, we subtract the grand mean from the mean of each condition of B, ignoring variable A. SS_B is the sum of these squared deviations of the condition means from the grand mean (GM):

$$SS_B = n_{b1}(\bar{x}_{b1} - GM)^2 + n_{b2}(\bar{x}_{b2} - GM)^2 + \ldots$$
$$+ n_{bk}(\bar{x}_{bk} - GM)^2.$$

Remember that in computing SS_B, we ignore variable A, pretending for the moment that the only independent variable in the design is variable B (See Figure 12.2). Dividing SS_B by the degrees of freedom for B (the number of conditions for B minus 1), we obtain MS_B, the variance due to B.

When analyzing data from a factorial design, we also calculate the amount of systematic variance due to the *interaction* of A and B. As we learned in Chapter 10, an interaction is present if the effects of one independent variable differ as a function of another independent variable. In an ANOVA, the presence of an interaction is indicated if variance is present in participants' responses that can't be accounted for by SS_A, SS_B, and SS_{wg}. If no interaction is present, all the variance in participants' responses can be accounted for by the individual main effects of A and B, as well as error variance (and, thus, $SS_A + SS_B + SS_{wg} = SS_{total}$). However, if the sum of $SS_A + SS_B + SS_{wg}$ is less than SS_{total}, we know that the individual main effects of A and B don't account for all of the systematic variance in the dependent variable. Thus, A and B must combine in a

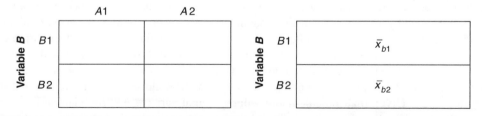

FIGURE 12.2 Testing the Main Effect of Variable B. To test the main effect of B in the design on the left, ANOVA disregards the presence of A (as if the experiment looked like the design on the right). The difference between the mean of $B1$ and the mean of $B2$ is tested without regard to variable A.

nonadditive fashion—that is, they interact. Thus, we can calculate the sum of squares for the interaction by subtracting SS_A, SS_B, and SS_{wg} from SS_{total}. As before, we calculate $MS_{A \times B}$ as well to provide the amount of variance due to the $A \times B$ interaction.

In the case of a factorial design, we then calculate a value of F for each main effect and interaction we are testing. For example, in a 2×2 design, we calculate F for the main effect of A by dividing MS_A by MS_{wg}:

$$F_A = MS_A/MS_{wg}.$$

We also calculate F for the main effect of B:

$$F_B = MS_B/MS_{wg}.$$

To test the interaction, we calculate yet another value of F:

$$F_{A \times B} = MS_{A \times B}/MS_{wg}.$$

Each of these calculated values of F is then compared to the critical value of F in a table such as that in Appendix A-2.

Note that the formulas used in the preceding explanation of ANOVA are intended to show conceptually how ANOVA works. When actually calculating an ANOVA, researchers use formulas that, although conceptually identical to those you have just seen, are easier to use. We are not using these calculational formulas in this chapter because they do not convey as clearly what the various components of ANOVA really reflect. The computational formulas, along with a numerical example, are presented in Appendix B.

Contributors to Behavioral Research
Fisher, Experimental Design, and the Analysis of Variance

No person has contributed more to the design and analysis of experimental research than the English biologist Ronald A. Fisher (1890–1962). After early jobs with an investment company and as a public school teacher, Fisher became a statistician for an experimental agricultural station.

Agricultural research relies heavily on experimental designs in which growing conditions are varied and their effects on crop quality and yield are assessed. In this context, Fisher developed many statistical approaches for analyzing experimental data that have spread from agriculture to behavioral science, the best known of which is the analysis of variance. In fact, the *F*-test was named for Fisher.

In 1925, Fisher wrote one of the first books on statistical analyses, *Statistical Methods for Research.* Despite the fact that Fisher was a poor writer (someone once said that students should not try to read this book unless they had read it before), *Statistical Methods* became a classic in the field. Ten years later, Fisher published *The Design of Experiments,* a landmark in research design. These two books raised the level of sophistication in our understanding of research design and statistical analysis and paved the way for modern behavioral science (Kendall, 1970).

FOLLOW-UP TESTS

When an F-test is statistically significant (that is, when the calculated value of F exceeds the critical value), we know that at least one of the group means differs from one of the others. However, because the ANOVA tests all condition means simultaneously, a significant F-test does not always tell us precisely which means differ: Perhaps all of the means differ from each other; maybe only one mean differs from the rest; or, some of the means may differ significantly from each other but not from other means.

The first step in interpreting the results of any experiment is to calculate the means for the significant effects. For example, if the main effect of A is found to be significant, we would calculate the means for the various conditions of A, ignoring variable B. If the main effect of B is significant, we would examine the means for the various conditions of B. If the interaction of A and B is significant, we would calculate the means for all combinations of A and B.

Main Effects

If an ANOVA reveals a significant effect for an independent variable that has only two levels, no further statistical tests are necessary. The significant F-test tells us that the two means differ significantly, and we can look at the means to understand the direction and size of the difference between them.

However, if a significant main effect is obtained for an independent variable that has more than two levels, further tests are needed to interpret the finding. Suppose an ANOVA reveals a significant main effect that involves an independent variable that has three levels. The significant F-test for the main effect indicates that a difference exists between at least two of the three condition means, but it does not indicate which means differ from which.

To identify which means differ significantly, researchers use **follow-up tests,** often called **post hoc tests** or **multiple comparisons.** Several statistical procedures have been developed for this purpose. Some of the more commonly used are the least significant difference (LSD) test, Tukey's test, Scheffe's test, and Newman-Keuls test. Although differing in specifics, each of these tests is used after a significant F-test to determine precisely which condition means differ from each other.

After obtaining a significant F-test in their study of weight loss, Mahoney et al. (1973) used the Newman-Keuls test to determine which weight-loss strategies were more effective. Refer to the means in Table 12.1 as you read their description of the results of this test:

> Newman-Keuls comparisons of treatment means showed that the self-reward S's [subjects] had lost significantly more pounds than either the self-monitoring ($p < .025$) or the control group ($p < .025$). The self-punishment group did not differ significantly from any other (p. 406).

So, the mean for the self-reward condition (6.4) differed significantly from the means for the self-monitoring condition (0.8) and the control group (1.4). And, the probability that these differences reflect a Type I error are less than .025 (or 2.5%).

Follow-up tests are conducted *only* if the F-test is statistically significant. If the F-test in the ANOVA is not statistically significant, we must conclude that the independent variable has no effect (that is, we fail to reject the null hypothesis) and do not test differences between specific pairs of means.

Interactions

You learned in Chapter 10 that an interaction between two variables occurs when the effect of one independent variable differs across the levels of other independent variables. If a particular independent variable has a different effect at one level of another independent variable than it has at another level of that independent variable, the independent variables *interact* to influence the dependent variable. For example, in an experiment with two independent variables (A and B), if the effect of variable A is different under one level of variable B than it is under another level of variable B, an interaction is present. However, if variable A has the same effect on participants' responses no matter what level of variable B they receive, then no interaction is present.

So, if an ANOVA shows that an interaction is statistically significant, we know that the effects of one independent variable differ depending on the level of another independent variable. However, to understand precisely how the variables interact to produce the effect, we must inspect the condition means and often conduct additional statistical tests.

Specifically, when a significant interaction is obtained, we conduct tests of simple main effects. A **simple main effect** is the effect of one independent variable at a particular level of another independent variable. It is, in essence, a main effect of the variable, but one that occurs *under only one level* of the other variable. If we obtained a significant $A \times B$ interaction, we could examine four simple main effects, which are shown in Figure 12.3:

1. The simple main effect of A at B1. (Do the means of Conditions A1 and A2 differ for participants who received Condition B1?) See Figure 12.3(a).
2. The simple main effect of A at B2. (Do the means of Conditions A1 and A2 differ for participants who received Condition B2?) See Figure 12.3(b).

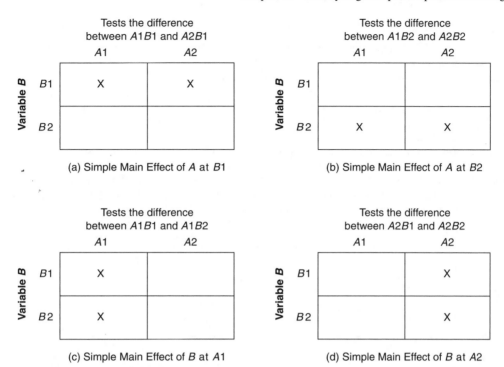

FIGURE 12.3   **Simple Effects Tests.**   A simple main effect is the effect of one independent variable at only one level of another independent variable. If the interaction in a 2 × 2 design such as this is found to be significant, four possible simple main effects are tested to determine precisely which condition means differ.

3. The simple main effect of *B* at *A*1. (Do the means of Conditions *B*1 and *B*2 differ for participants who received Condition *A*1?) See Figure 12.3(c).

4. The simple main effect of *B* at *A*2. (Do the means of Conditions *B*1 and *B*2 differ for participants who received Condition *A*2?) See Figure 12.3(d).

Testing the simple main effects shows us precisely which condition means within the interaction differ from each other.

Behavioral Research Case Study
Liking People Who Eat More than We Do

As an example of a study that used simple effects tests to examine a significant interaction, let's consider an experiment on people's impressions of those who eat more versus less than they do (Leone, Herman, & Pliner, 2008). Participants were 94 undergraduate women who believed that they were participating in a study on the "effects of hunger and satiety on perception tasks." They were randomly assigned to one of two roles—to be an active participant or an observer. Participants who were assigned to be an active participant were given a plate of small pizza slices and told to eat until they were full. (They thought they were asked to eat pizza because they were in the satiety condition of the experiment). After filling up on pizza, the participant received bogus information regarding how many pieces of pizza another participant who was supposedly in the same session had eaten. This information manipulated the independent variable by indicating that the other person had eaten either 50% less pizza than the participant (the *less* condition) or 50% more pizza than the participant (the *more*
(*continued*)

(continued)
condition). For example, if the participant had eaten 6 pieces, the other person was described as eating either 3 pieces (50% less) or 9 pieces (50% more). Participants then rated how much they liked the other person.

Participants who were assigned to the role of observer did not eat any pizza but rather read a description of the study. They read about two female participants, one of whom had eaten 8 pieces of pizza (8 was the modal amount eaten by active participants in the study) and one of whom had eaten either 4 or 12 pieces (50% less or 50% more). The observers then rated how much they liked the second person on the same scales that the active participants used.

The experiment was a 2 × 2 factorial design in which the independent variables involved the *perspective* to which participants were assigned (either active participant or observer) and *eating* (the person to be rated ate either more or less than the active participant). An ANOVA conducted on participants' ratings of how much they liked the person revealed a significant interaction between perspective and eating, $F(1, 90) = 6.97$, $p = .01$, η^2. The mean liking ratings in the four conditions are shown below.

	Eating Condition	
	Less	More
Perspective Condition		
Active participant	4.00	4.78
Observer	4.04	4.24

To understand the interaction, the researchers conducted tests of the simple main effects. First, the simple main effect of eating condition was statistically significant for active participants. Looking at the means for this simple main effect, we can see that active participants liked the other person more when she ate more ($\bar{x} = 4.78$) rather than less ($\bar{x} = 4.00$) than they did. However, the simple main effect of eating condition was not significant for the observers. Observers' liking ratings did not differ significantly depending on whether the person ate more or less (the means were 4.04 and 4.24). Apparently, we like people who eat more than we do, possibly because we look better by comparison, but observers who have not eaten are not similarly affected by how much other people eat.

Putting It All Together: Interpreting Main Effects and Interactions

The last several pages have taken you through the rationale behind analysis of variance. We have seen how ANOVA partitions variability in the data into between-group (systematic) variance and within-group (error) variance, then conducts an F-test to show us whether our independent variable(s) had an effect on the dependent variable. To be sure that you understand how to interpret the results of such analyses, let's turn our attention to a hypothetical experiment involving the effects of darkness on anxiety.

Darkness seems to make things scarier than they are in the light. Not only are people often vaguely uneasy when alone in the dark, but they also seem to find that frightening things are even scarier when the environment is dark than when it is well lit. Imagine that you were interested in studying the effects of ambient darkness on reactions to fear-producing stimuli. You conducted an experiment in which participants sat alone in a room that was either illuminated normally by overhead lights or that was almost pitch dark. In addition, in half of the conditions, a large snake in a glass cage was present in the room, whereas in the other condition, the glass cage was empty. After sitting in the room for 5 minutes, participants rated their current level of anxiety on a scale from 1 (no anxiety) to 10 (extreme anxiety). You should recognize this as a 2 × 2 factorial design in which the two independent variables are the darkness of the room (light vs. dark) and the presence of the snake (absent vs. present). Because this is a factorial design, an ANOVA would test for two main effects (of both darkness and snake presence) and the interaction between darkness and snake presence.

When you analyzed your data, you could potentially obtain many different patterns of results. Let's look at just a few possibilities.

Of course, the unhappiest case would be if the ANOVA showed that neither the main effects nor the interaction was statistically significant. If this happened, we would have to conclude that neither the darkness nor the snake, either singly or in combination, had any effect on participants' reactions.

Imagine, however, that you obtained the following results:

Results of ANOVA

Effect	Results of F-test
Main effect of darkness	Nonsignificant
Main effect of snake	Significant
Interaction of darkness by snake	Nonsignificant

Condition Means (Anxiety)

	Light	Dark	
No snake	2.50	2.40	2.45
Snake	4.50	4.60	4.55
	3.50	3.50	

The ANOVA tells you that only the main effect of snake is significant. Looking at the table of means, you can see that, averaging across the light and dark conditions, the average anxiety rating was higher when the snake was present (4.55) rather than when it was not (2.45). Clearly, the means of the light and dark conditions do not differ overall (so the main effect of darkness is not significant). Nor does the presence of the snake have a markedly different effect in the light versus dark conditions; the snake increases anxiety by about the same margin in the light and dark conditions, confirming the nonsignificant F-test for the interaction.

Now consider how you would interpret the pattern of results in the next two tables. The ANOVA shows that the main effect of snake is significant as before, and the effect is reflected in the difference between the overall means of the no-snake and snake

Results of ANOVA

Effect	Results of F-test
Main effect of darkness	Significant
Main effect of snake	Significant
Interaction of darkness by snake	Nonsignificant

Condition Means (Anxiety)

	Light	Dark	
No snake	2.50	3.80	3.15
Snake	4.50	5.80	5.15
	3.50	4.80	

conditions (3.15 vs. 5.15). In addition, the F-test shows that the main effect of darkness is significant. Looking at the means, we see that participants who were in the dark condition rated their anxiety higher than participants in the light condition (4.80 vs. 3.50).

From looking at the means for all four experimental conditions, you might be tempted to conclude that the interaction is also significant because the combination of snake and darkness produced a higher anxiety rating than any other combination of conditions. Doesn't this show that snake and darkness *interacted* to affect anxiety? No, because an interaction occurs when the effect of one independent variable differs across the levels of the other independent variable (Chapter 10). Looking at the means shows that the snake had precisely the same effect on participants in the light and dark conditions—it increased anxiety by 2.0 units. The high mean for the snake/darkness condition reflects the *additive* influences of the snake and the darkness but *no interaction*. That is, because both darkness and snake increased anxiety, having both together resulted in the highest average anxiety ratings (5.80). But the effect of the snake was the same in the light and dark conditions, so no interaction was present.

Finally, let's consider one more possible pattern of results (although there are potentially many others). The ANOVA on the next page shows that both main effects and the interaction are significant. The significant main effects of snake presence and darkness show that the snake and darkness both increased anxiety. In addition, however, there is an interaction of darkness by snake because the effect of

Results of ANOVA

Effect	Results of *F*-test
Main effect of darkness	Significant
Main effect of snake	Significant
Interaction of darkness by snake	Significant

Condition Means (Anxiety)

	Light	Dark	
No snake	2.50	3.80	2.45
Snake	4.50	7.00	5.75
	3.50	5.40	

the snake differed in the light and dark conditions. In the light condition, the presence of the snake increased anxiety by 2.0 units on the rating scale (4.5 vs. 2.5). However, when it was dark, the snake increased anxiety by 3.2 units (7.0 vs. 3.8).

Because the interaction is statistically significant, we would go on to test the significance of the simple main effects. That is, we would want to see whether the snake had a significant effect in the light (the simple main effect of snake in the light condition), whether the snake had an effect in the dark (the simple main effect of snake in the dark condition), whether the darkness had an effect when no snake was present (the simple main effect of darkness in

the no-snake condition), and whether darkness had an effect when the snake was there (the simple main effect of dark-ness in the snake condition). These four simple effects tests would tell us which of the four condition means differed significantly from each other.

BETWEEN-SUBJECTS AND WITHIN-SUBJECTS ANOVAS

Each of the examples of ANOVA in this chapter involved between-subjects designs—experiments in which participants are randomly assigned to experimental conditions (see Chapter 10). Although the rationale is the same, slightly different computational procedures are used for within-subjects and between-within (or mixed) designs in which each participant serves in more than one experimental condition. Just as we use a paired *t*-test to analyze data from a within-subjects two-group experiment, we use within-subjects ANOVA for multilevel and factorial within-subjects designs and use split-plot ANOVA for mixed (between-within) designs. Like the paired *t*-test, these variations of ANOVA capitalize on the fact that we have repeated measures on each participant that allow us to reduce the estimate of error variance, thereby providing a more powerful statistical test. Full details regarding these analyses take us beyond the scope of this book but may be found in most introductory statistics books.

Developing Your Research Skills

Identifying Main Effects and Interactions: Cultural Differences in Reactions to Social Support

When people are facing a stressful event, they often benefit from receiving support from other people. On one hand, they may receive *explicit* social support in which other people give them advice, emotional comfort, or direct assistance. On the other hand, they may receive *implicit* social support just from having other people around or knowing that others care about them, even if the other people don't actually do anything to help them deal with the stressful event. In a study that examined cultural differences in people's reactions to explicit and implicit social support, Taylor, Welsh, Kim, and Sherman (2007) studied 40 European Americans and 41 Asians and Asian Americans. After providing a baseline rating of how much stress they felt at the moment (1 = not at all; 5 = very much), participants were told that they would perform a stressful mental-arithmetic task and then write and deliver a 5-minute speech, tasks that have been used previously to create stress in research participants.

Participants were then randomly assigned to one of three experimental conditions. In the *implicit-support* condition, participants were told to think about a group that they were close to and to write about the aspects of that group that were important to them. In the *explicit-support* condition, participants were told to think about people they were close to and to write a "letter" asking for support and advice for the upcoming math and speech tasks. In the *no-support* condition, participants were asked to write down their ideas for the locations that a tour of campus should visit. Participants then completed the math and speech tasks. Afterwards, participants rated their stress again on a 5-point scale. The researchers subtracted each participant's pretest, baseline stress rating from his or her stress rating after performing the stressful tasks. A higher difference score indicates that the participant's level of stress was higher at posttest than at pretest.

1. This experiment has a participant variable with two levels (culture) and an independent variable with three levels (support). Draw the design.
2. What kind of experimental design is this? (Be as specific as possible.)
3. What kind of statistical analysis should be used to analyze the data?
4. What effects will be tested in this analysis?

The researchers conducted a 2 (culture: Asian or Asian American vs. European American) by 3 (social-support condition: implicit, explicit, or control) ANOVA on the stress change scores. The average change in stress in each condition is shown below:

Condition Means (Change in Stress Rating)

	Implicit	Explicit	Control
European Americans	.12	−.44	.16
Asians and Asian Americans	−.28	.63	−.19

5. Just from eyeballing the pattern of means, do you think that there is a main effect of cultural group? (Does there appear to be a notable difference between European Americans and Asians/Asian Americans, ignoring social support condition?)
6. Just from eyeballing the pattern of means, do you think that there is a main effect of social support condition? (Does there appear to be a notable difference in the overall means of the three conditions?)
7. Just from eyeballing the means, do you think that there is an interaction? (Do the effects of social support condition appear to differ in the two cultural groups?)
   When Taylor et al. conducted an ANOVA on these data, they obtained a significant interaction, $F(2, 74) = 3.84$, $p = .03$, $\acute{\eta} = .10$.
8. Explain what the F, p, and $\acute{\eta}$ tell us in the earlier sentence.
9. What kind of test is needed to interpret this significant interaction?
10. From these data, would you conclude that European Americans and Asians/Asian Americans differ in their reactions to thinking about implicit and explicit support when they are in a stressful situation?

MULTIVARIATE ANALYSIS OF VARIANCE

We have discussed the two inferential statistics most often used to analyze differences among means of a single dependent variable: the t-test (to test differences between two conditions) and the analysis of variance (to test differences among more than two conditions). For reasons that will be clear in a moment, researchers sometimes want to test differences between conditions on several dependent variables simultaneously. Because t-tests and ANOVAs cannot do this, researchers turn to multivariate analysis of variance.

Whereas an analysis of variance tests differences among the means of two or more conditions on one dependent variable, a **multivariate analysis of variance,** or **MANOVA**, tests differences between the means of two or more conditions on two or more dependent variables simultaneously.

A reasonable question to ask at this point is, Why would anyone want to test group differences on *several* dependent variables at the same time? Why not simply perform several ANOVAs—one on each dependent variable? Researchers turn to MANOVA rather than ANOVA for the following two reasons.

Conceptually Related Dependent Variables

One reason for using MANOVA arises when a researcher has measured several dependent variables, all of which tap into the same general construct. When several dependent variables measure different aspects of the same construct, the researcher may wish to analyze the variables as a set rather than individually.

Suppose you were interested in determining whether a marriage enrichment program improved married couples' satisfaction with their relationships. You conducted an experiment in which couples were randomly assigned to participate for two hours in either a structured marriage enrichment activity, an unstructured conversation on a topic of their own choosing, or no activity together. (You should recognize this as a randomized groups design with three conditions; see Chapter 10.) One month after the program, members of each couple were asked to rate their marital satisfaction on 10 dimensions involving satisfaction with finances, communication, ways of dealing with conflict, sexual relations, social life, recreation, household chores, and so on.

If you wanted, you could analyze these data by conducting 10 ANOVAs—one on each dependent variable. However, because all 10 dependent variables reflect various aspects of general marital satisfaction, you might want to know whether the program affected satisfaction *in general* across all of the dependent measures. If this were your goal, you might use MANOVA to analyze your data. MANOVA combines the information from all 10 dependent variables into a new composite variable, and then analyzes whether participants' scores on this new composite variable differ among the experimental groups.

Inflation of Type I Error

A second use of MANOVA is to control Type I error. As we saw earlier, the probability of making a Type I error (rejecting the null hypothesis when it is true) increases with the number of statistical tests we perform. For this reason, we conduct one ANOVA rather than many *t*-tests when our experimental design involves more than two conditions (and, thus,

more than two means). Type I error also becomes inflated when we conduct *t*-tests or ANOVAs *on many dependent variables*. The more dependent variables we analyze in a study, the more likely we are to obtain significant differences that are due to Type I error rather than to the independent variable.

To use an extreme case, imagine that we conduct a two-group study in which we measure 100 dependent variables, then test the difference between the two group means on each of these variables with 100 *t*-tests. You may be able to see that if we set our alpha level at .05, we could obtain significant *t*-tests on as many as five of our dependent variables even if our independent variable has no effect. Although few researchers use as many as 100 dependent variables in a single study, Type I error increases whenever we analyze more than one dependent variable.

Because MANOVA tests differences among the means of the groups across all dependent variables simultaneously, the overall alpha level is held at .05 (or whatever level the researcher chooses) no matter how many dependent variables are tested. Although most researchers don't worry about analyzing a few variables one by one, many use MANOVA to guard against Type I error whenever they analyze many dependent variables.

How MANOVA Works

MANOVA begins by creating a new composite variable that is a weighted sum of the original dependent variables. How this **canonical variable** is mathematically derived need not concern us here. The important thing is that the new canonical variable includes all of the variance in the set of original variables. Thus, it provides us with a single index of our variable of interest (such as marital satisfaction).

In the second step of the MANOVA, a multivariate version of the *F*-test is performed to determine whether participants' scores on the canonical variable differ among the experimental conditions. If the multivariate *F*-test is significant, we conclude that the experimental manipulation affected the *set* of dependent variables as a whole. For example, in our study of marriage enrichment, we would conclude that the marriage enrichment workshop created significant differences in the overall satisfaction in the three experimental groups; we would then conduct additional analyses to understand precisely how the groups differed. MANOVA has allowed us to analyze the dependent variables as a set rather than individually.

In cases in which researchers use MANOVA to reduce the chances of making a Type I error, obtaining a significant multivariate *F*-test allows the researcher to conduct ANOVAs separately on each variable. Having been ensured by the MANOVA that the groups differ significantly on *something,* we may perform additional analyses without risking an increased chance of Type I error. However, if the MANOVA is not significant, examining the individual dependent variables using ANOVAs would run the risk of making Type I errors.

Behavioral Research Case Study
Fear and Persuasion: An Example of MANOVA

Since the 1950s, dozens of studies have investigated the effects of fear-inducing messages on persuasion. Put simply, when trying to persuade people to change undesirable behaviors (such as smoking, excessive suntanning, and having unprotected sexual intercourse), should one try to scare them with the negative consequences that may occur if they fail to change? Keller (1999) tested the hypothesis that the effects of fear-inducing messages on persuasion depend on the degree to which people already follow the recommendations advocated in the message. In her study, Keller examined the effects of emphasizing mild versus severe consequences on women's reactions to brochures that encouraged them to practice safe sex.

Before manipulating the independent variable, Keller assessed the degree to which the participants typically practiced safe sex, classifying them as either safe-sex adherents (those who always or almost always used a condom) or nonadherents (those who used condoms rarely, if at all). In the study, 61 sexually active college women read a brochure about safe sex that either described relatively mild or relatively serious consequences of failing to practice safe sex. For example, the brochure in the mild consequences condition mentioned the possibility of herpes, yeast infections, and itchiness, whereas the brochure in the serious consequences condition warned participants about AIDS-related cancers, meningitis, syphilis, dementia, and death. In both conditions, the brochures gave the same recommendations for practicing safe sex and reducing one's risk for contracting these diseases. After reading either the mild or severe consequences message, participants rated their reactions on seven dependent variables, including the likelihood that they would follow the recommendations in the brochure, the personal relevance of the brochure to them, the severity of the health consequences that were listed, and the degree to which participants thought they were able to follow the recommendations.

Because she measured several dependent variables, Keller conducted a multivariate analysis of variance. Given that this was a 2 (safe-sex adherents vs. nonadherents) by 2 (low vs. moderately serious consequences) factorial design, the MANOVA tested the main effect of adherent group, the main effect of consequence severity, and the group by severity interaction. Of primary importance to her hypotheses, the multivariate interaction was statistically significant. Having protected herself from inflated Type I error by using MANOVA (I guess we could say she practiced "safe stats"), Keller conducted ANOVAs separately on each dependent variable. (Had the MANOVA not been statistically significant, she would not have done so.)

Results showed that participants who did not already practice safe sex (the nonadherents) were less convinced by messages that stressed severe consequences than messages that stressed low severity consequences. Paradoxically, the safe-sex nonadherents rated the moderately severe consequences as less severe than the low severity consequences and more strongly refuted the brochure's message when severe consequences were mentioned. In contrast, participants who already practiced safe sex were more persuaded by the message that mentioned moderately severe rather than low severe consequences. These results suggest that messages that try to persuade people to change unhealthy behaviors should not induce too high a level of fear if the target audience does not already comply with the message's recommendations.

EXPERIMENTAL AND NONEXPERIMENTAL USES OF INFERENTIAL STATISTICS

Most of the examples of *t*-tests, ANOVA, and MANOVA we have discussed involved data from true experimental designs in which the researcher randomly assigned participants to conditions and manipulated one or more independent variables. A *t*-test, ANOVA, or MANOVA was then used to test the differences among the means of the experimental conditions.

Although the *t*-test and analysis of variance were developed in the context of experimental research, they are also widely used to analyze data from nonexperimental studies. In such studies, participants are not randomly assigned to groups (as in an experiment) but rather are categorized into naturally occurring groups. Then a *t*-test, ANOVA, or MANOVA is used to analyze the differences among the means of these groups. For example, if we want to compare the average depression scores for a group of women and a group of men, we can use a *t*-test even though the study is not a true experiment.

As a case in point, Butler, Hokanson, and Flynn (1994) obtained a measure of depression for 73 participants on two different occasions five months apart. On the basis of these two depression scores, they categorized participants into one of five groups: (1) unremitted depression—participants who were depressed at both testing times; (2) remitted depression—participants who were depressed at Time 1 but not at Time 2; (3) new cases—participants who were not depressed at Time 1 but fell in the depressed range at Time 2; (4) nonrelapsers—participants who had once been depressed but were not depressed at both Time 1 and Time 2; and (5) never depressed. The researchers then used MANOVA and ANOVA (as well as post hoc tests) to analyze whether these five groups differed in average self-esteem, depression, emotional lability, and other measures. Even though this was a nonexperimental design and participants were classified into groups rather than randomly assigned, ANOVA and MANOVA were appropriate analyses.

Summary

1. When research designs involve more than two conditions (and, thus, more than two means), researchers analyze their data using ANOVA rather than *t*-tests because conducting many *t*-tests increases the chances that they will make a Type I error.
2. ANOVA partitions the total variability in participants' responses into between-groups variance (MS_{bg}) and within-groups variance (MS_{wg}). Then an *F*-test is conducted to determine whether the between-groups variance exceeds what we would expect based on the amount of within-groups variance in the data. If it does, we reject the null hypothesis and conclude that at least one of the means differs from the others.
3. In a one-way design, a single *F*-test is conducted to test the effects of the lone independent variable. In a factorial design, an *F*-test is conducted to test each main effect and interaction.
4. For each effect being tested, the calculated value of *F* (the ratio of MS_{bg}/MS_{wg}) is compared to a critical value of *F*. If the calculated value of *F* exceeds the critical value, we know that at least one condition mean differs from the others. If the calculated value is less than the critical value, we fail to reject the null hypothesis and conclude that the condition means do not differ.
5. If the *F*-tests show that the main effects or interactions are statistically significant, follow-up tests are often needed to determine the precise effect of the independent variable. Main effects of independent variables that involve more than two levels require post hoc tests, whereas interactions are decomposed using simple effects tests.

6. Special varieties of ANOVA and MANOVA are used when data from within-subjects designs or mixed designs are being analyzed.
7. Multivariate analysis of variance (MANOVA) is used to test the differences among the means of two or more conditions on a set of dependent variables. MANOVA is used in two general cases: when the dependent variables all measure aspects of the same general construct (and, thus, lend themselves to analysis as a set), and when the researcher is concerned that perform-

ing separate analyses on several dependent variables will increase the possibility of making a Type I error.
8. In either case, MANOVA creates a new composite variable—a canonical variable—from the original dependent variables and then determines whether participants' scores on this canonical variable differ across conditions.
9. ANOVA and MANOVA may be used to analyze data from both experimental and nonexperimental designs.

Key Terms

analysis of variance (ANOVA) (*p. 252*)
Bonferroni adjustment (*p. 251*)
canonical variable (*p. 264*)
follow-up tests (*p. 258*)
F-test (*p. 252*)
grand mean (*p. 254*)

mean square between-groups (MS_{bg}) (*p. 254*)
mean square within-groups (MS_{wg}) (*p. 254*)
multiple comparisons (*p. 258*)
multivariate analysis of variance (MANOVA) (*p. 263*)
post hoc tests (*p. 258*)

simple main effect (*p. 258*)
sum of squares (*p. 253*)
sum of squares between-groups (SS_{bg}) (*p. 254*)
sum of squares within-groups (SS_{wg}) (*p. 253*)
total sum of squares (SS_{total}) (*p. 253*)

Questions for Review

1. What's so bad about making a Type I error?
2. How does the Bonferroni adjustment control for Type I error when many statistical tests are conducted?
3. Why do researchers use ANOVA rather than *t*-tests to analyze data from experiments that have more than two groups?
4. If the independent variable has absolutely no effect on the dependent variable, will the means of the experimental conditions be the same? Why or why not?
5. An ANOVA for a one-way design partitions the total variance in a set of data into two components. What are they?
6. What kind of variance does the mean square within-groups (MS_{wg}) reflect?
7. The sum of squares between-groups (SS_{bg}) reflects the degree to which the condition means vary around the

_____.
8. What is the name of the statistic used in an ANOVA?
9. If the independent variable has no effect, the calculated value of F will be around 1.00. Why?

10. In an experiment with two independent variables, an ANOVA partitions the total variance into four components. What are they?
11. MS_{wg} appears in the denominator of every F-test. Why?
12. If the calculated value of F is found to be significant for the main effect of an independent variable with more than two levels, what tests does the researcher conduct? Why are such tests not necessary if the independent variable has only two levels?
13. When are tests of simple main effects used, and what do researchers learn from them?
14. Who developed the rationale and computations for the analysis of variance?
15. Under what two circumstances would you use a multivariate analysis of variance?
16. Imagine that you conduct a study to test the average level of guilt experienced by Christians, Jews, Buddhists, Muslims, and Hindus. Could you use an ANOVA to analyze your data? Why or why not?

Questions for Discussion

1. Go to the library and find a research article in a psychology journal that used analysis of variance. (This should not be difficult; ANOVA is perhaps the most commonly used analysis. If you have problems, try *Developmental Psychology, Journal of Personality and Social Psychology,* and *Journal of Experimental Psychology.*) Read the article and see whether you understand the results of the ANOVAs that were conducted.

2. When researchers set their alpha level at .05, they reject the null hypothesis (and conclude that the independent variable has an effect) only if there is less than a 5% chance that the differences among the means are due to error variance. Does this mean that 5% of all results reported in the research literature are, in fact, Type I errors rather than real effects of the independent variables?

13 QUASI-EXPERIMENTAL DESIGNS

Pretest–Posttest Designs
Time Series Designs
Comparative Time Series Design
Longitudinal Designs

Cross-Sequential Cohort Designs
Program Evaluation
Evaluating Quasi-Experimental Designs

To reduce the incidence of fatal traffic accidents, most states have passed laws requiring passengers in automobiles to wear seat belts. Proponents of such laws claim that wearing seat belts significantly decreases the likelihood that passengers will be killed or seriously injured in a traffic accident. Opponents of these laws argue that wearing seat belts does not decrease traffic fatalities. Instead, they say, it may even pose an increased risk because seat belts may trap passengers inside a burning car. Furthermore, they argue that such laws are useless because they are difficult to enforce and many people do not obey them anyway. Who is right? Do laws that require people to wear seat belts actually reduce traffic fatalities?

This question seems simple enough until we consider the kind of research we would need to conduct to show that such laws actually *cause* a decrease in traffic fatalities. To answer such a question would require an experimental design such as those we discussed in Chapters 9 and 10. We would have to assign people randomly to either wear or not wear seat belts for a prolonged period of time and then measure the injury and fatality rates for these two groups.

The problems of doing such a study should be obvious. First, we would find it very difficult to assign people randomly to wear or not wear seat belts and even more difficult to ensure that our participants actually follow our instructions. Second, the incidence of serious traffic accidents is so low, relative to the number of drivers, that we would need a gigantic sample to obtain even a few serious accidents within a reasonable period of time. A third problem is an ethical one: Would we want to assign half of our participants to not wear seat belts, knowing that we might cause them to be injured or killed if they have an accident? I hope you can see that it would not be feasible to design a true experiment to determine whether seat belts are effective in reducing traffic injuries and fatalities.

From the earliest days of psychology, behavioral researchers have shown a distinct preference for experimental designs over other approaches to doing research. In experiments, we can manipulate one or more independent variables and carefully control other factors that might affect the outcome of the study, allowing us to draw relatively confident conclusions about whether the independent variables cause changes in the dependent variables.

However, many real-world questions, such as whether seat-belt legislation reduces traffic fatalities, can't be addressed within the narrow strictures of experimentation. Often researchers do not have sufficient control over their participants to randomly assign them to experimental conditions. In other cases, they may be unable or unwilling to manipulate the independent variable of interest. In such instances, researchers often use **quasi-experimental designs**. If the researcher lacks control over the assignment of participants to conditions and/or does not manipulate the causal variable of interest, the design is quasi-experimental.

Because such designs do not involve random assignment of participants to conditions, the researcher is not able to determine which participants will receive the various levels of the independent variable. In fact, in many studies the researcher does not manipulate the independent variable at all; researchers do not have the power to introduce legislation regarding seat-belt use, for example. In such cases, the term **quasi-independent variable** is sometimes used to indicate that the variable is not a true independent variable that is manipulated by the researcher but rather is an event that participants experienced for other reasons.

The strength of the experimental designs we examined in the preceding few chapters lies in their ability to demonstrate that the independent variables cause changes in the dependent variables. As we saw, experimental designs do this by eliminating alternative explanations for the findings that are obtained. Experimental designs generally have high internal validity; researchers can conclude that the observed effects are due to the independent variables rather than to other extraneous factors (see Chapter 9).

Generally speaking, quasi-experimental designs do not possess the same degree of internal validity as experimental designs. Because participants are not randomly assigned to conditions and the researcher may have no control over the independent variable, potential threats to internal validity are present in most quasi-experiments. Even so, a well-designed quasi-experiment that eliminates as many threats to internal validity as possible can provide strong circumstantial evidence about cause-and-effect relationships.

The quality of a quasi-experimental design depends on how many threats to internal validity it successfully eliminates. As we will see, quasi-experimental designs differ in the degree to which they control threats to internal validity. Needless to say, the designs that eliminate most of the threats to internal validity are preferable to those that eliminate only a few threats. In this chapter, we will discuss several basic quasi-experimental designs. We will begin with the weakest, least preferable designs in terms of their ability to eliminate threats to internal validity and then move to stronger quasi-experimental designs.

In Depth
The Internal Validity Continuum

Researchers draw a sharp distinction between experimental designs (in which the researcher controls both the assignment of participants to conditions and the independent variable) and quasi-experimental designs (in which the researcher lacks control over one or both of these aspects of the design). However, this distinction should not lead us to hastily conclude that experimental designs are unequivocally superior to quasi-experimental designs. Although this may be true in general, both experimental and quasi-experimental designs differ widely in terms of their internal validity. Indeed, some quasi-experiments are more internally valid than some true experiments.

A more useful way of conceptualizing research designs is along a continuum of low to high internal validity. Recall from Chapter 9 that *internal validity* refers to the degree to which a researcher draws accurate conclusions about the effects of an independent variable on participants' responses. At the low validity pole of the continuum are studies that lack the necessary controls to draw any meaningful conclusions about the effects of the independent variable whatsoever. As we move up the continuum, studies have increasingly tighter experimental control and, hence, higher internal validity. At the high validity pole of the continuum are studies in which exceptional design and tight control allow us to rule out every reasonable alternative explanation for the findings.

There is no point on this continuum at which we can unequivocally draw a line that separates studies that are acceptable from the standpoint of internal validity from those that are unacceptable. Most studies—whether experimental or quasi-experimental—possess some potential threats to internal validity. The issue in judging the quality of a study is whether the most serious threats have been eliminated, thereby allowing a reasonable degree of confidence in the conclusions we draw. As we will see, well-designed quasi-experiments can provide rather conclusive evidence regarding the effects of quasi-independent variables on behavior.

PRETEST–POSTTEST DESIGNS

As we said, researchers do not always have the power to assign participants to experimental conditions. This is particularly true when the research is designed to examine the effects of an intervention or event on a group of people in the real world. For example, a junior high school may introduce a schoolwide program to educate students about the dangers of drug abuse, and the school board may want to know whether the program is effective in reducing drug use among the students. In this instance, random assignment is impossible because *all* students in the school were exposed to the program. If you were hired as a behavioral researcher to evaluate the effectiveness of the program, what kind of study would you design?

How NOT to Do a Study: The One-Group Pretest–Posttest Design

One possibility would be to measure student drug use before the drug education program and again afterward to see whether drug use decreased. Such a design could be portrayed as

$$O1 \quad X \quad O2$$

where $O1$ is a pretest measure of drug use, X is the introduction of the antidrug program (the quasi-independent variable), and $O2$ is the posttest measure of drug use one year later. (O stands for observation.)

I hope you can see that this design, the **one-group pretest–posttest design**, is a very poor research strategy because it fails to eliminate most threats to internal validity. Many other things might have affected any change in drug use that we might observe other than the drug education program. If you observe a change in students' drug use between $O1$ and $O2$, how sure are you that the change was due to the program as opposed to some other factor?

Many other factors could have contributed to the change. For example, the students may have matured from the pretest to the posttest (maturation effects). In addition, events other than the program may have occurred between $O1$ and $O2$ (history effects); perhaps a popular rock musician died of an overdose, the principal started searching students' lockers for drugs, or the local community started a citywide *Just Say No to Drugs* or *DARE* campaign. Another possibility is that the first measurement of drug use ($O1$) may have started students thinking about drugs, resulting in lower use independently of the educational program (testing effect). Extraneous factors such as these may have occurred at the same time as the antidrug education program and may have been responsible for decreased drug use. The one-group pretest–posttest design does not allow us to distinguish the effects of the antidrug program from other possible influences.

In some studies, the internal validity of one-group pretest–posttest designs may also be threatened by **regression to the mean**—the tendency for extreme scores in a set of data to move, or regress, toward the mean of the distribution with repeated testing. In many studies, participants are selected because they have extreme scores on some variable of interest. For example, we may want to examine the effects of a drug education program on students who are heavy drug users. Or perhaps we are examining the effects of a remedial reading program on students who are poor readers. In cases such as these, a researcher may select participants who have extreme scores on a pretest (of drug use or reading ability, for example), expose them to the quasi-independent variable (the antidrug or reading program), and then remeasure them to see whether their scores changed (drug use declined or reading scores improved, for example).

The difficulty with this approach is that when participants are selected because they have extreme scores on the pretest, their scores may change from pretest to posttest because of the statistical artifact called *regression to the mean*. As we learned in Chapter 3, all scores contain measurement error that causes participants' observed scores to differ from their true scores. Overall, measurement error produces random fluctuations in participants' scores from one measurement to the next; thus, if we test a sample of participants twice, participants' scores are as likely to increase as to decrease randomly from the first to the second test.

However, although the general effect of measurement error on the scores in a distribution is random, the measurement error present in extreme scores tends to bias the scores in an extreme direction—that is, away from the mean. For example, if we select a group of participants with very low reading scores, these participants are much more likely to have observed scores that are *deflated* by measurement error (because of fatigue or illness, for example) than to have observed scores that are higher than their true scores. When participants who scored in an extreme fashion on a pretest are retested, many of the factors that contributed to their artificially extreme scores on the pretest are unlikely to be present; for example, students who performed poorly on a pretest of reading ability because they were ill are likely to be healthy at the time of the posttest. As a result, their scores on the posttest are likely to be more moderate than they were on the pretest; that is, their scores are likely to *regress toward the mean* of the distribution. Unfortunately, a one-group pretest–posttest design does not allow us to determine whether changes in participants' scores are due to the quasi-independent variable or to regression to the mean.

Strictly speaking, the one-group pretest–posttest design is called a **preexperimental design** rather than a quasi-experimental design because it lacks control, has no internal validity, and thereby fails to meet any of the basic requirements for a research design at all. Many alternative explanations of observed changes in participants' scores can be suggested, undermining our ability to document the effects of the quasi-independent variable itself. As a result, such designs should *never, ever* be used.

Nonequivalent Control Group Design

One partial solution to the weaknesses of the one-group design is to obtain one or more control groups for comparison purposes. Because we can't randomly assign students to participate or not participate in the drug education program, a true control group is not possible. However, the design would benefit from adding a *nonequivalent* control group. In a **nonequivalent control group design**, the researcher looks for one or more groups of participants that appear to be reasonably similar to the group that received the quasi-independent variable. A nonequivalent control group design comes in two varieties, one that involves only a posttest and another that involves both a pretest and a posttest.

NONEQUIVALENT GROUPS POSTTEST-ONLY DESIGN. One option is to measure both groups after one of them has received the quasi-experimental treatment. For example, you could assess drug use among students at the school that used the antidrug program and among students at another roughly comparable school that did not use drug education. This design, the **nonequivalent groups posttest-only design** (which is also called a *static group comparison*), can be diagramed like this:

Quasi-experimental group $\quad X \quad O$

Nonequivalent control group $\quad - \quad O$

Unfortunately, this design also has many weaknesses. Perhaps the most troublesome is that we have no way of knowing whether the two groups were actually similar *before* the quasi-experimental group received the treatment. If the two groups differ at time *O*, we don't know whether the difference was caused by variable *X* or whether the groups differed even before the quasi-experimental group received *X* (this involves biased assignment of participants to conditions or **selection bias**). Because we have no way of being sure that the groups were equivalent before participants received the quasi-independent variable, the nonequivalent control group posttest-only design is very weak in terms of internal validity and should rarely be used. However, as the following case study shows, such designs can sometimes provide convincing data.

Behavioral Research Case Study
Nonequivalent Control Group Design: Perceived Responsibility and Well-Being Among the Elderly

Older people often decline in physical health and psychological functioning after they are placed in a nursing home. Langer and Rodin (1976) designed a study to test the hypothesis that a portion of this decline is due to the loss of control that older people feel when they move from their own homes to an institutional setting. The participants in their study were 91 people, ages 65 to 90, who lived in a Connecticut nursing home. In designing their study, Langer and Rodin were concerned about the possibility of **experimental contamination**. When participants in different conditions of a study interact with one another, the possibility exists that they may talk about the study among themselves and that one experimental condition becomes "contaminated" by the other. To minimize the likelihood of contamination, the researchers decided not to randomly assign residents in the nursing home to the two experimental conditions. Rather, they randomly selected two floors in the facility, assigning residents of one floor to one condition and those on the other floor to the other condition. Residents on different floors did not interact much with one another, so this procedure minimized contamination. However, the decision not to randomly assign participants to conditions resulted in a quasi-experimental design—specifically, a nonequivalent control group design.

An administrator gave different talks to the residents on the two floors. One talk emphasized the residents' responsibility for themselves and encouraged them to make their own decisions about their lives in the facility; the other emphasized the staff's responsibility for the residents. Thus, one group was made to feel a high sense of responsibility and control, whereas the other group experienced lower responsibility and control. In both cases, the responsibilities and options stressed by the administrator were already available to all residents, so the groups differed chiefly in the degree to which their freedom, responsibility, and choice were explicitly stressed.

The residents were assessed on a number of measures a few weeks after hearing the talk. Compared with the other residents, those who heard the talk that emphasized their personal control and responsibility were more active and alert, happier, and more involved in activities within the nursing home. In addition, the nursing staff rated them as more interested, sociable, self-initiating, and vigorous than the other residents. In fact, follow-up data collected 18 months later showed long-term psychological and physical effects of the intervention, including a lower mortality rate among participants in the high responsibility group (Rodin & Langer, 1977).

The implication is, of course, that giving residents greater choice and responsibility *caused* these positive changes. However, in considering these results, we must remember that this was a quasi-experimental design. Not only were participants not assigned randomly to conditions, but also they lived on different floors of the facility. To some extent, participants in the two groups were cared for by different members of the nursing home staff and lived in different social groups. Perhaps the staff on one floor was more helpful than that on another floor, or social support among the residents was greater on one floor than another. Because of these differences, we cannot eliminate the possibility that the obtained differences between the two groups were due to other variables that differed systematically between the groups.

Most researchers do not view these alternative explanations to Langer and Rodin's findings as particularly plausible. (In fact, their study is highly regarded in the field.) We have no particular reason to suspect that the two floors of the nursing home differed in some way that led to the findings they obtained. Even so, the fact that this was a quasi-experiment should make us less confident of the findings than if a true experimental design, in which participants were assigned randomly to conditions, had been used.

NONEQUIVALENT GROUPS PRETEST–POSTTEST DESIGN. Some of the weaknesses of the nonequivalent control group design are eliminated by measuring the two groups twice, once before and once after the quasi-independent variable. The **nonequivalent groups pretest–posttest design** can be portrayed as follows:

Quasi-experimental group $O1$ X $O2$
Nonequivalent control group $O1$ $-$ $O2$

This design lets us see whether the two groups scored similarly on the dependent variable (e.g., drug use) before the introduction of the treatment at point X.

Even if the pretest scores at $O1$ aren't identical for the two groups, they provide us with baseline information that we can use to determine whether the groups changed from $O1$ to $O2$. If the scores change between the two testing times for the quasi-experimental group but not for the nonequivalent control group, we have somewhat more confidence that the change was due to the quasi-independent variable. For example, to evaluate the drug education program, you might obtain a nonequivalent control group from another school that does not have an antidrug program under way. If drug use changes from pretest to posttest for the quasi-experimental group but not for the nonequivalent control group, we might assume the program had an effect.

Even so, the nonequivalent groups pretest–posttest design does not eliminate all threats to internal validity. For example, a **local history effect** may occur. Something may happen to one group that does not happen to the other (Cook & Campbell, 1979). Perhaps some event that occurred in the experimental school but not in the control school affected students' attitudes toward drugs—a popular athlete was kicked off the team for using drugs, for example. If this happens, what appears to be an effect of the antidrug program may actually be due to a local history effect. This confound is sometimes called a **selection-by-history interaction** because a "history" effect occurs in one group but not in the other.

In brief, although the nonequivalent groups design eliminates some threats to internal validity, it doesn't eliminate all of them. Even so, with proper controls and measures, this design can provide useful information about real-world problems.

Behavioral Research Case Study
Nonequivalent Groups Pretest–Posttest Design: Motivational Climate in Youth Sports

When people are motivated to succeed in a particular area, such as academics or sports, they may adopt one of two goal orientations by which they judge whether they are successful. On one hand, people may adopt a mastery orientation in which they focus on developing skills, mastering the task, and working hard. On the other hand, they may adopt an ego orientation (also called a performance orientation) where their focus is on outperforming other people to attain recognition or status. Research suggests that teachers and coaches can promote one goal orientation or the other by how they structure situations and react to students' successes and failures.

Because a mastery goal orientation has many benefits that an ego goal orientation does not, coaches may desire to promote a mastery orientation among their players. Smoll, et al. (2007) used a nonequivalent groups pretest–posttest design to test the effects of a program for training youth coaches how to coach in a way that fosters a mastery orientation among their players. The researchers recruited 37 coaches and 225 youth athletes (mean age = 11.5 years) who participated in community-based basketball programs in a large city. The coaches were split into two groups, one of which received training in how to create a motivational climate that promoted mastery goal orientation and one of which did not. However, because the researchers were concerned that coaches who received the training might share the information they learned with coaches in the control group, thereby creating experimental contamination, coaches were not randomly assigned to conditions as they would be in a true experimental design. Instead, the researchers put coaches from one area of the city in the condition that received training and those from another area of the city in the control condition.

At the start of the basketball season, the youth athletes completed pretest measures of mastery and ego goal orientations in sport. Then, a week later, the coaches in the training condition participated in a 75-minute "Mastery Approach to Coaching" workshop in which they learned how to create a motivational climate that would lead their players to develop a mastery orientation. The coaches in the control group did not participate in such a workshop. Near the end of the season, about 12 weeks later, all of the players again completed the measures of mastery and ego goal orientations.

The results of the study are shown in Figure 13.1. Before the season started, the athletes who played for coaches in the two groups did not differ on the pretest measures of mastery and ego orientation. However, at the end of the season, the average mastery orientation score of the players whose coaches participated in the training program was significantly higher than that of the players of the untrained coaches. Furthermore, the ego orientation scores of players of trained coaches decreased significantly over the season, whereas the scores of players of untrained coaches did not.

These results show that a brief workshop can train youth coaches to create a motivational climate that promotes a mastery goal orientation among their players. Keep in mind, however, that this was a quasi-experiment in which coaches and players were not randomly assigned to the two conditions. Although no differences between the two groups were detected before the start of coaches' training, the design of the study does not eliminate the possibility that the groups differed in some other way that was responsible for the results, a point that the authors acknowledged in the published article that describes this study. Even so, the results strongly support the conclusion that the training program was effective in teaching coaches how to foster a mastery orientation in their players.

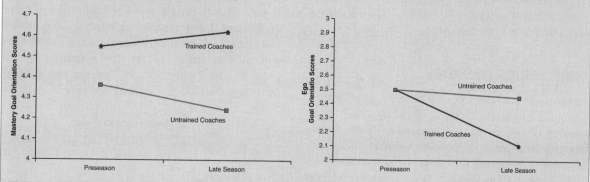

FIGURE 13.1 Goal Orientations of Youth Athletes Who Played for Trained and Untrained Coaches. The athletes who played for coaches who participated in the special workshop on motivational climate showed an increase in their mastery goal orientation scores (left graph) and a decrease in their ego goal orientation scores (right graph). *Source:* Smoll, F. L., Smith, R. E., & Cumming, S. P. (2007). Effects of a motivational climate intervention for coaches on changes in young athletes' achievement goal orientations. *Journal of Clinical Sport Psychology, 1,* 23–46.

In order for nonequivalent control designs to be useful, researchers must make every effort to be sure that they are similar in every possible way. Only if we have strong reasons to think that the quasi-experimental group and the nonequivalent control group are comparable can we have any confidence that the quasi-independent variable created observed differences in the dependent variable. For example, Langer and Rodin (1976) had to be reasonably confident that the elderly residents in the nursing home did not differ between the two floors of the facility, and Smoll, Smith, and Cumming (2007) had to assume that their two groups of coaches and players did not differ in some systematic way before one group of coaches participated in the coaching workshop.

Researchers tackle this problem in two ways. First, they often search for nonequivalent control groups that appear to be as similar to the quasi-experimental group as possible. A researcher studying

the effects of a school drug education program would look for comparison schools that were as similar to the target school as possible in terms of size, student demographics, academic quality, proportion of various racial and ethnic groups, curriculum, and so on. The more closely the control groups match the characteristics of the quasi-experimental group, the more confidence we have in the results.

Second, even after locating control groups that appear similar to the target group, researchers collect as much information about the participants as they can in order to further explore possible differences between the groups. For example, in their study of mastery oriented coaching, Smoll et al. (2007) found that the two areas of the city from which their two samples of coaches were drawn were similar in socioeconomic status, and the youth sports programs in those communities had similar sex and age distributions. The teams used in the study also did not differ in their win–loss records or in the amount of time they practiced each week. And, the players did not initially differ in mastery or ego goal orientation.

Of course, when using nonequivalent control group designs, researchers have no way of knowing whether the groups differ on some important variable that they did not measure, and this uncertainly makes the internal validity of these designs lower than it would be if participants had been randomly assigned to conditions. However, to the extent that researchers show that the groups do not differ on as many relevant variables as possible, they increase our confidence in the results.

TIME SERIES DESIGNS

Some of the weaknesses of the nonequivalent control group designs are further eliminated by a set of procedures known as *time series designs*. **Time series designs** measure the dependent variable on several occasions before and on several occasions after the quasi-independent variable occurs. By measuring the target behavior on several occasions, further threats to internal validity can be eliminated.

Simple Interrupted Time Series Design

The **simple interrupted time series design** involves taking several pretest measures before introducing the independent (or quasi-independent) variable and then taking several posttest measures afterward. This design can be diagramed as follows:

$$O1 \quad O2 \quad O3 \quad O4 \quad X \quad O5 \quad O6 \quad O7 \quad O8$$

As you can see, repeated measurements of the dependent variable have been *interrupted* by the occurrence of the quasi-independent variable (X). For example, we could measure drug use every three months for a year before the drug education program starts and then every three months for a year afterward. If the program had an effect on drug use, we should see a marked change between $O4$ and $O5$.

The rationale behind this design is that by taking multiple measurements both before and after the quasi-independent variable, we can examine the effects of the quasi-independent variable against the backdrop of other changes that may be occurring in the dependent variable. For example, using this

design, we should be able to distinguish changes due to aging or maturation from changes due to the quasi-independent variable. If drug use is declining because of changing norms or because the participants are maturing, we should see gradual changes in drug use from one observation to the next, not just between the first four and the last four observations.

To see what I mean, compare the two graphs in Figure 13.2. Which of the graphs seems to show that the drug education program lowered drug use? In Figure 13.2(a), drug use is lower after the program than before it, but it is unclear whether the decline is associated with the program or is part of a downward pattern that began *before* the initiation of the program. In Figure 13.2(b), on the other hand, the graph shows that a marked decrease in drug use

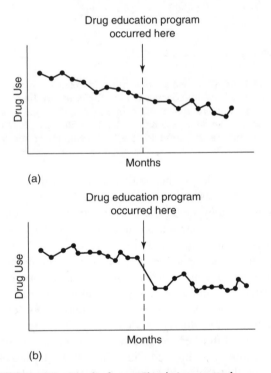

(a)

(b)

FIGURE 13.2 Results from a Simple Interrupted Time Series Design. It is difficult to determine from Figure 13.2 (a) whether the drug education program reduced drug use or whether the lower use after the program was part of a general decline in drug use that started before the program. In contrast, the pattern in Figure 13.2 (b) is clearer. Because the decrease in drug use occurred immediately after the program, we have greater confidence that the change was due to the program.

occurred immediately after the program. Although we can't conclude for certain that the program was, in fact, responsible for the change in drug use, the evidence is certainly stronger in 13.2(b) than in 13.2(a).

The central threat to internal validity with a simple interrupted time series design is **contemporary history**. We cannot rule out the possibility that the observed effects were due to another event that occurred at the same time as the quasi-independent variable. If a rock star died from drugs or an athlete was barred from the team at about the time that the drug education program began, we would not know whether the change between $O4$ and $O5$ was due to the program or to the contemporaneous outside influence.

Behavioral Research Case Study
A Simple Interrupted Time Series Design: The Effects of No-Fault Divorce

Traditionally, for a married couple to obtain a divorce, one member of the couple had to accuse the other of failing to meet the obligations of the marriage contract (by claiming infidelity or mental cruelty, for example). In the past few decades, many states have passed no-fault divorce laws that allow a couple to end a marriage simply by agreeing to, without one partner having to sue the other.

Critics of these laws have suggested that no-fault divorce laws make it too easy to obtain a divorce and have contributed to the rising number of divorces in the United States. To examine whether this claim is true, Mazur-Hart and Berman (1977) used an interrupted time series analysis to study the effects of the passing of a no-fault divorce law in Nebraska in 1972.

Mazur-Hart and Berman obtained the number of divorces in Nebraska from 1969 to 1974. As in all interrupted time series analyses, these years were interrupted by the introduction of the quasi-independent variable (the new no-fault divorce law). Their results are shown in Figure 13.3. This figure shows the number of divorces per month for each of the 6 years of the study, as well as the point at which the new law went into effect.

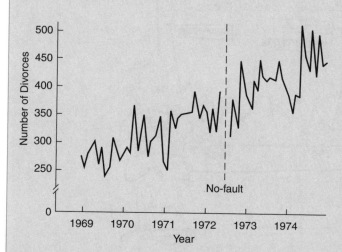

FIGURE 13.3 Effects of No-Fault Divorce Laws on the Number of Divorces. This graph shows the results of an interrupted time series analysis of divorce rates before and after the Nebraska no-fault divorce law. Although the divorce rate was higher after the law went into effect than before, the increase was clearly part of an upward trend that started before the law went into effect. Thus, the law does not appear to have affected the divorce rate. *Source:* Reprinted with permission from the *Journal of Applied Social Psychology,* Vol. 7, No. 4, p. 306. Copyright © V. H. Winston & Son, Inc., 360 South Ocean Boulevard, Palm Beach, FL 33480. All rights reserved.

On first glance, one might be tempted to conclude that divorces did increase after the law was passed. The number of divorces was greater in 1973 and 1974 than in 1969, 1970, and 1971. However, if you look closely, you can see that the divorce rate was increasing even *before* the new law was passed; there is an upward slope to the data for 1969–1972. The data for 1973–1974 continue this upward trend, but there is no evidence that the number of divorces increased an unusual amount after the law went into effect. In fact, statistical analyses showed that there was no discontinuity in the slope of the line after the introduction of the law. The authors concluded,

(continued)

(continued)
"During the period of time studied divorces did systematically increase but . . . the intervention of no-fault divorce had no discernible effect on that increase."

This study demonstrates one advantage of a time series design over designs that compare only two groups or only two points in time. Had the researchers used a simple pretest–posttest design and analyzed data for only 1971 and 1973 (the years before and after the new law), they probably would have concluded that the law increased the divorce rate. By taking several measures before and after the law went into effect, they were able to tell that the increase in divorces after the new legislation was part of an upward trend that had begun at least 3 years before the law went into effect.

Interrupted Time Series with a Reversal

In special instances, the influence of extraneous factors may be discounted by observing what happens to participants' behavior when the quasi-independent variable or treatment is first introduced and then removed. The **interrupted time series design with a reversal** may be portrayed like this:

$$O1 \quad O2 \quad O3 \quad O4 \quad X \quad O5 \quad O6 \quad O7 \quad O8$$
$$-X \quad O9 \quad O10 \quad O11 \quad O12$$

You can think of this as two interrupted time series designs in succession. The first examines the effects of the quasi-independent variable (X) on changes in the target behavior (O). As before, we can see whether X is associated with an unusual increase or decrease in the dependent variable (O) between $O4$ and $O5$. Then, after X has been in place for a while, we can remove it (at point $-X$) and observe what happens to O. Under some circumstances, we would expect the behavior to return to its pre-X level. If this occurs, we

Just as Santa suspected, an interrupted time series design showed that the month of December is associated with a predictable change in children's behavior.
Source: © David A. Hills.

are more confident that X produced the observed changes. It would be unlikely that some external historical influence occurred with X and then disappeared when X was removed. Of course, such an effect is logically possible, but in most instances it is unlikely.

To further increase our confidence that the quasi-independent variable, and not outside historical events, created the observed changes at X and $-X$, we could then *reintroduce* the independent variable, observe its effects, and then remove it a second time. This is known as an **interrupted time series design with multiple replications** and can be diagramed as follows:

$O1$ $O2$ $O3$ X $O4$ $O5$ $O6$
$-X$ $O7$ $O8$ $O9$ X $O10$ $O11$
$O12$ $-X$ $O13$ $O14$ $O15$

Quasi-experimental designs in which the variable of interest is introduced and then removed have three major limitations. The primary one is that researchers often do not have the power to remove the quasi-independent variable—to repeal seat-belt laws or no-fault divorce laws, for example. Second, the effects of some quasi-independent variables remain even after the variable itself is removed. For example, the effects of a community-wide program to reduce racial prejudice should persist even after the program itself is discontinued. Third, the removal of a quasi-independent variable may produce changes that are not due to the effects of the variable per se. For example, if we were interested in the effects of a new incentive system on employee morale, removing work incentives might dampen morale because the employees would be angry about having the system removed (Cook & Campbell, 1979).

Control Group Interrupted Time Series Design

So far, we have discussed time series designs that measure a single group of participants before and after the quasi-independent variable. Adding comparison groups strengthens these designs by eliminating additional threats to internal validity. By measuring more than one group on several occasions, only one of which receives the quasi-independent variable, we can examine the plausibility of certain alternative interpretations of the results. For example, we could perform an interrupted time series analysis on the group that received the quasi-independent variable and on a nonequivalent control group that did not receive the quasi-independent variable:

Quasi-experimental group:
$O1$ $O2$ $O3$ $O4$ X $O5$ $O6$ $O7$ $O8$

Nonequivalent control group:
$O1$ $O2$ $O3$ $O4$ $-$ $O5$ $O6$ $O7$ $O8$

This design helps us rule out certain history effects. If both groups experience the same outside events but a change is observed only for the quasi-experimental group, we can be more certain (though not positive) that the change was due to X rather than to an outside influence. Of course, local history effects are possible in which the quasi-experimental group experiences extraneous events that the nonequivalent control group does not.

Behavioral Research Case Study
Control Group Interrupted Time Series Design: Traffic Fatalities After 9/11

After the terrorist attacks on New York and Washington on September 11, 2001, many Americans avoided flying out of the fear that terrorists might hijack their flight. Some writers suggested that this reaction increased the number of traffic fatalities in the months after 9/11 because many people drove long distances in their cars to avoid flying. To examine this question, Su, Tran, Wirtz, Langteau, and Rothman (2009) analyzed changes in flying, driving, and traffic fatalities, comparing patterns before 9/11 with those afterward. This was a quasi-experimental time series design because they examined changes across years to examine possible effects of the 9/11 attacks (the quasi-independent variable).

(continued)

(continued)

First, they examined the number of miles that travelers flew in October, November, and December of 1999, 2000, and 2001. As expected, the number of miles flown in the last quarter of 2001 (right after the attacks) was significantly lower than miles flown in the last quarter of 1999 and 2000. However, this decrease in flying was *not* associated with increased driving. When they analyzed driving data from 1970–2004, they found that the number of miles driven in the 3 months following the terrorist attacks was about on par with what would be expected based on historical trends. When compared to the previous 2 years, driving after the 9/11 attacks did not differ from how much people drove in 1999 and 2000. So, people did not compensate for less flying with more driving—they simply traveled less after the attacks.

However, analysis of traffic fatalities told a different story. Assuming that the effects of 9/11 would be greatest in the areas of the country in which the attacks occurred, the researchers analyzed traffic fatalities separately for three regions—the northeast (which included New York), the northern south Atlantic region (which included Washington, D.C.), and the rest of the country. This approach used a *control group interrupted time series design* in which the effects of the attacks can be compared across groups. The table below shows the percentage change in traffic fatalities during the last 3 months of each year compared to the number of fatalities during the same 3 months of the previous year.

	1999	2000	2001
Northeast	−2.99	−1.17	18.10
Northern South Atlantic	4.60	6.50	0.78
Rest of country	2.22	−6.41	6.77

This table shows that traffic fatalities were significantly higher in the northeast in the last 3 months of 2001 (the 3 months immediately after the 9/11 attacks)—an increase of 18.10% compared to the previous year. By having two other regions as comparison groups, we can see that this pattern was not obtained in other areas of the country. Thus, the increase observed in fatalities in the northeast was unique to that area.

But, if people were not driving more, why were there more traffic fatalities? The researchers suggested two possibilities. First, research shows that people drive more poorly when they are under stress, partly because they are preoccupied and distracted by thoughts about the stressful event. Perhaps people in the northeast were more upset by the attacks on New York and, thus, drove more poorly. In addition, people who are under stress may use alcohol and other drugs at a higher rate, which would impede their driving. To test the latter hypothesis, the researchers examined data on the number of alcohol- and drug-related citations given for fatal traffic accidents before and after 9/11. These analyses showed that police in the northeast gave out 109.72% more citations after 9/11 than in the previous 2 years, whereas the rate for the country as a whole was unchanged.

This study by Su et al. provides an excellent example of how studies that include comparison or control groups in an interrupted time series design can address interesting and important questions that could not be studied in other ways.

COMPARATIVE TIME SERIES DESIGN

A final time series design, known as a **comparative time series design** (or comparative trend analysis) examines two or more variables over time in order to understand how changes in one variable are related to changes in another variable. Showing that changes in one variable are associated with changes in another variable provides indirect evidence that one variable

may be causing the other. For example, many theorists have proposed that people's political attitudes become more rigid, intolerant, and authoritarian when they feel under military or economic threat (Stenner, 2005). To test this hypothesis, we could measure both perceived threat and authoritarian attitudes over time. Then, we could see whether times in which perceived threat was high were associated with increases in authoritarian attitudes. That is, we can compare the trend for perceived threat with the trend for authoritarianism over the same time span. The hypothesis would predict that we should see authoritarian attitudes increase during times when perceived threat is high. As always with quasi-experimental designs, we cannot conclude for certain that threat causes authoritarianism because other, unmeasured variables may be playing a role. Even so, seeing time series trends on multiple variables change together may provide some insight into the processes underlying the effects.

Behavioral Research Case Study
Comparative Time Series Design: Effects of Graduated Driver's License Laws

Because new drivers account for a disproportional number of traffic accidents, many states began to institute graduated license rules for young drivers in the mid-1990s. Although the details of these rules vary by state, they all set stricter rules for teenage drivers, rules that are then relaxed as the driver becomes older and more experienced. For example, in my state, for the first 6 months after getting his or her learner's permit, a new driver may drive only with a licensed adult between 5 A.M. and 9 P.M. Then, after 6 months of the limited hours, the teen can drive during any time of day or night with a licensed adult. After 12 months without any traffic violations or accidents, the teen may get a provisional license that allows him or her to drive alone between 5 A.M. and 9 P.M. with no more than one other teenager in the car (unless with a licensed adult supervisor or unless the other passengers are family members). After 6 months with the provisional license and a clean driving record, the driver may drive at any hour of day or night without a licensed adult.

The question is this: Do graduated license laws help to reduce fatal traffic accidents among new drivers? The results of a study to address this question are shown below. This graph depicts two time series trends. One trend shows the number of states with graduated licensing laws, and the other trend shows the rate of fatal car accidents among 16-year-olds. Between 1995 and 2003, the number of states with graduated license laws increased from 0 to 47. During this same time, the rate of fatal traffic accidents among 16-year-olds fell from 35 per 100,000 people to 23 per 100,000 people. Comparing these two trends offers support for the idea that graduated license laws reduce traffic fatalities among new drivers.

Like all quasi-experiments, this one is open to alternative interpretations. For example, one could argue that during this span of time, driver's education programs improved, cars became safer, or global warming reduced the severity of winter weather (and, thus, the number of weather-related accidents). Even so, these data support the idea that implementing graduated license laws was associated with a decrease in fatal accidents.

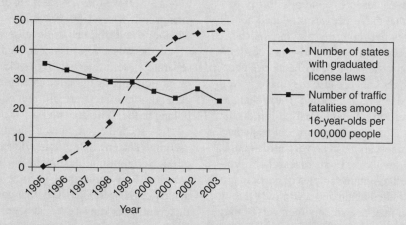

Source: Insurance Institute for Highway Safety, National Highway Traffic Safety Administration.

LONGITUDINAL DESIGNS

Closely related to time series designs are **longitudinal designs**, but in the case of longitudinal designs, the quasi-independent variable is time itself. That is, nothing has occurred between one observation and the next other than the passage of time.

$$O1 \quad O2 \quad O3 \quad O4 \quad O5$$

Longitudinal designs are used most frequently by developmental psychologists to study age-related changes in how people think, feel, and behave. For example, we might use a longitudinal design to study how the strategies that children use to remember things change as they get older. To do so, we could follow a single group of children over a period of several years, testing their memory strategies when they were 4, 8, and 12 years old.

Typically, the goal of longitudinal research is to uncover developmental changes that occur as a function of age, but researchers must be alert for the possibility that something other than age-related development has produced the observed changes. Imagine, for example, that we are interested in how children's hand–eye coordination changes with age. We get a sample of 3-year-old children and study their hand–eye coordination at ages 3, 6, 9, and 12, finding that hand–eye coordination increases markedly with age, particularly between ages 6 and 9. Is this change due to a natural developmental progression, or could something else have caused it? One possibility that comes to mind is that the effect was produced not by age-related changes but rather by playing sports. If participating in sports increases hand–eye coordination, older children would have better hand–eye coordination than younger kids because they have played more baseball, basketball, and soccer. Thus, changes across time observed in a longitudinal design do not necessarily reflect a natural developmental sequence.

Longitudinal research can be very informative, but it has three drawbacks. First, researchers typically find it difficult to obtain samples of participants who agree to be studied again and again over a long period of time. (In fact, researchers themselves may have trouble mustering enough interest in the same topic over many years to maintain their own involvement in the study.) Second, even if they find such a sample, researchers often have trouble keeping track of the participants, many of whom invariably move and, particularly if one is studying developmental changes in old age, may even die. Third, repeatedly testing a sample over a period of years requires a great deal of time, effort, and money, and researchers often feel that their time is better spent doing several shorter studies rather than devoting their resources to a single longitudinal design.

Given these drawbacks, you may wonder why researchers use longitudinal designs instead of **cross-sectional designs** that compare groups of different ages at a single point in time. For example, rather than tracking changes in memory strategies in one group of children over many years, why not test the memory strategies of different groups of 4-, 8-, and 12-year-olds at the same time? In fact, researchers do use cross-sectional designs to study age-related changes. However, cross-sectional designs have a shortcoming when studying development in that they cannot distinguish age-related changes from **generational effects**. Put simply, people of different ages differ not only in age per se but also in the conditions under which their generation grew up. As a result, people who are of different ages today may differ in ways that have nothing to do with age per se. For example, a group of 70-year-olds who grew up during World War II and a group of 50-year-olds who grew up in the 1960s differ not only in age but also in the events experienced by members of their generation. Thus, if we find a systematic difference between groups of 70- and 50-year-olds, we do not know whether the difference is developmental or generational because a cross-sectional design cannot separate these influences. By tracking a single group of participants as they age in a longitudinal design, generational effects are eliminated because they all belong to the same generation.

A second advantage of longitudinal over cross-sectional designs for studying developmental change is that longitudinal designs allow the researcher to examine how individual participants change with age. A cross-sectional study that compares groups of different ages may reveal a significant difference between the groups even though only a small proportion of the participants differs between the groups. For example, cross-sectional studies show that, on average, older people have poorer memories than middle-aged people. However, such an effect could be obtained even if only a relatively small percentage of the older people had impaired memories and the rest were indistinguishable from the middle-aged participants; just a few forgetful participants could pull down the average memory score for the whole older group. As a result, we might be misled into concluding that memory generally declines in old age. Yet, a longitudinal design that tracked participants from middle to old age would allow us to examine how individual participants changed, possibly revealing that memory decrements occurred in only a small number of the older participants.

Longitudinal designs can provide important information about the effects of time and aging on development. However, like all quasi-experimental designs, their results must be interpreted with caution, and researchers must carefully consider alternative explanations of the observed changes.

Behavioral Research Case Study
Longitudinal Design: The Stability of Personality in Infancy and Childhood

Lemery, Goldsmith, Klinnert, and Mrazek (1999) used a longitudinal design to examine the degree to which personality remains stable during infancy and early childhood. To obtain a sample of young infants who could be studied over time, the researchers recruited pregnant women who agreed to allow their children to be measured several times after birth. In this way, a sample of 180 infants was studied at 3, 6, 12, 18, 24, 36, and 48 months of age. At each age, measures were taken of four characteristics—positive emotionality, fear, distress–anger, and activity level.

The researchers were interested in the degree to which these indices of temperament remained stable with age. This is a more difficult question to answer than it might seem because the behavioral manifestations of these characteristics change with age. For example, a 3-month-old expresses positive emotionality in a very different and much simpler way than a 4-year-old. Similarly, a 3-year-old is obviously more active than a 6-month-old. Thus, it makes little sense simply to compare average scores on measures of these characteristics (as could be done if one studied stability on some attribute during adulthood).

Instead, the researchers calculated correlations between scores on each measure across the various ages. High correlations across time would indicate that the participants' personalities remained relatively stable from one measurement period to another, whereas low correlations would show that participants' personalities changed a great deal over time. The correlations for the measures of fear are as follows:

				Age (in months)			
Age	**3**	**6**	**12**	**18**	**24**	**36**	**48**
3	—						
6	.59	—					
12	.42	.49	—				
18	.33	.39	.68	—			
24	.22	.35	.58	.68	—		
36	.21	.22	.48	.61	.70	—	
48	.16	.24	.49	.60	.60	.66	—

Source: Lemery, K. S., Goldsmith, H. H., Klinnert, M. D., & Mrazek, D. A. (1999). Developmental models of infant and childhood temperament. *Developmental Psychology, 35,* 189–204. Copyright © 1999 by the American Psychological Association. Adapted with permission.

This pattern of correlations suggests that the tendency to experience fear becomes more stable with age. As you can see, the tendency to experience fear at 3 months correlates .42 with the tendency to experience fear 9 months later (at 12 months). In contrast, fearfulness at 12 months correlates .58 with fearfulness at 24 months, and

(*continued*)

(continued)

fear correlates .70 between 24 and 36 months. (The correlation of .66 between 36 and 48 months is not significantly different from the 24–36-month correlation.) The same pattern was obtained for the measures of distress–anger and activity level. Clearly, greater stability across time is observed in these characteristics during childhood than in infancy.

CROSS-SEQUENTIAL COHORT DESIGNS

I noted earlier that, when using a cross-sectional design to compare people of different ages, researchers cannot determine the degree to which any differences they observe are due to age or to generational cohort. For example, if we are interested in knowing whether people become more religious as they get older, comparing 70-year-olds, 50-year-olds, and 30-year-olds does not allow us to answer the question. Not only are the 70-year-old participants older than the other cohorts, but they also grew up at a different time in which the prevailing views of religion in society were somewhat different than they were for people who grew up 20 and 40 years later. Thus, any differences we observe in religiosity may have nothing to do with age per se.

A **cross-sequential cohort design** allows researchers to tease apart age and cohort effects. In a cross-sequential cohort design, two or more age cohorts are measured at two or more times. In essence, you can think of this design as a combination of a cross-sectional comparison of two or more age cohorts with a longitudinal design in which each cohort is tested two or more times. For example, we could have three age groups, each of which is measured at four times:

Age Cohort 1	O1	O2	O3	O4
Age Cohort 2	O1	O2	O3	O4
Age Cohort 3	O1	O2	O3	O4

Such a design can help to separate age-related effects from cohort and history effects.

For example, Whitbourne, Sneed, and Sayer (2009) were interested in how people change during early and middle adulthood with respect to Erikson's stages of psychosocial development. Knowing that personality development is influenced not only by age but also by societal conditions, the researchers studied two age cohorts, one group that was born around 1946 and another group that was born around 1957. Although both of these groups fall into the "baby boomer" generation, their experiences were quite different. The older cohort, born just after World War II, grew up in a society that was characterized by rapid post-war growth, with rather traditional values and social stability. By the time they entered college in the mid-1960s, however, society was rapidly changing, and their college experience was affected by the Vietnam War, political unrest (including assassinations), and an upheaval of traditional values with the counterculture movement. The younger cohort grew up during the turmoil of the 1960s and early 1970s, but by the time they went to college in the mid-1970s, things had calmed down quite a bit and society seemed much more stable by the time they graduated from college around 1980.

Given the large differences in the developmental experiences of these two cohorts, Whitbourne et al. (2009) used a cross-sequential cohort design in which they obtained data for both of these groups when they entered college and again two more times until they were about 43 years old (the older cohort also completed the measures an additional time). Many of the variables they studied showed similar age-related changes for the two cohorts. But some changed differently for the older and younger cohorts. For example, for integrity—a sense of satisfaction and contentment with life that arises from finding meaning and feeling connected with social values—decreased after college for both groups and then increased again in middle adulthood. But the degree of later increase was greater for the participants who were born earlier. Using a cross-sequential cohort design allowed the researchers to separate the effects of age and cohort.

PROGRAM EVALUATION

Quasi-experimental designs are commonly used in the context of program evaluation research. **Program evaluation** uses behavioral research methods to assess the effects of interventions or programs designed to influence behavior. For example, a program may involve a new educational intervention designed to raise students' achievement test scores, a new law intended to increase seat-belt use, an incentive program designed to increase employee morale, a marketing campaign implemented to affect the public's image of a company, or a training program for youth basketball coaches. Because these kinds of programs are usually not under researchers' control, they must use quasi-experimental approaches to evaluate their effectiveness.

Although program evaluations often contribute to basic knowledge about human behavior, their primary goal is often to provide information to those who must make decisions about the target programs. Often, the primary audience for a program evaluation is not the scientific community (as is the case with basic research) but rather decision makers such as government administrators, legislators, school boards, and company executives. Such individuals need information about program effectiveness to determine whether program goals are being met, to decide whether to continue certain programs, to consider how programs might be improved, and to allocate money and other resources to programs.

In some instances, program evaluators are able to use true experimental designs to assess program effectiveness. Sometimes they are able to randomly assign people to one program or another and have control over the implementation of the program (which is, in essence, the independent variable). In educational settings, for example, new curricula and teaching methods are often tested using true experimental designs. More commonly, however, program evaluators have little or no control over the programs they evaluate. When evaluating the effects of new legislation, such as the effects of no-fault divorce laws or seat-belt laws, researchers cannot use random assignment or control the independent variable. In industrial settings, researchers have little control over new policies regarding employees. Even so, companies often want to know whether new programs and policies reduce absenteeism, increase morale, or bolster productivity. By necessity, then, program evaluation often involves quasi-experimental designs.

Contributors to Behavioral Research
Donald Campbell and Quasi-Experimentation

Few researchers have made as many groundbreaking methodological contributions to social and behavioral science as Donald T. Campbell (1916–1996) who, among other things, popularized the use of quasi-experimental designs. Campbell's graduate education in psychology was interrupted by World War II when he left school to join the research unit of the Office of Strategic Services (OSS). At OSS, he applied behavioral research methods to the study of wartime propaganda and attitudes, an experience that drew him to a lifelong interest in applied research. After the war, Campbell completed his dissertation and obtained his PhD. Because many of his primary research interests—such as political attitudes, prejudice, and leadership—involved topics of real-world relevance, he became interested in applying traditional experimental designs to research settings in which full experimental control was not possible (Campbell, 1981). For example, he was interested in studying leadership processes in real military groups, which did not permit the strict control that was possible in laboratory experiments on leadership.

In the early 1960s, Campbell invited Julian Stanley to coauthor a brief guide to research designs that, for the first time, delved deeply into quasi-experimental research. Campbell and Stanley's (1966) *Experimental and Quasi-Experimental Designs for Research* has become a classic text for generations of behavioral researchers and is among the most cited works in the social and behavioral sciences. Later, Campbell was among the first to urge researchers to apply quasi-experimental designs to the evaluation of social and educational programs (Campbell, 1969, 1971). Throughout his illustrious career, Campbell made many other important contributions to measurement and methodology, including important work on validity (he was the first to make the distinction between internal and external validity), unobtrusive measures, interviewing techniques, and the philosophy of science. In addition to his work on problems in behavioral measurement and research design, Campbell also published extensively on topics such as leadership, stereotyping, perception, attitudes, conformity, and cross-cultural psychology.

EVALUATING QUASI-EXPERIMENTAL DESIGNS

For many years, most behavioral scientists held a well-entrenched bias against quasi-experimental designs. For many, the tightly controlled experiment was the benchmark of behavioral research, and anything less than a true experiment was regarded with suspicion. Most contemporary behavioral researchers tend not to share this bias against quasi-experimentation, recognizing that the limitations of quasi-experimental designs are compensated by a notable advantage. In particular, true experimentation that involves random assignment and researcher-manipulated independent variables is limited in the questions it can address. Often we want to study the effects of certain variables on behavior but are unable or unwilling to conduct a true experiment that will allow unequivocal conclusions about causality. Faced with the limitations of the true experiment, we have a choice. We can abandon the topic, leaving potentially important questions unanswered, or we can conduct quasi-experimental research that provides us with tentative answers. Without quasi-experimental research, we would have no way of addressing many important questions. In many instances, we must be satisfied with making well-informed decisions on the basis of the best available evidence, while acknowledging that a certain degree of uncertainty exists.

Threats to Internal Validity

One way to think about the usefulness of quasi-experimental research is to consider what is required to establish that a particular variable *causes* changes in behavior. As we discussed earlier, to infer causality, we must be able to show that

1. The presumed causal variable preceded the effect in time.
2. The cause and the effect covary.
3. All other alternative explanations of the results are eliminated through randomization or experimental control.

Quasi-experimental designs meet the first two criteria. First, even if we did not experimentally manipulate the quasi-independent variable, we usually know whether it preceded the presumed effect. Second, it is easy to determine whether two variables covary. A variety of statistical techniques, including correlation and ANOVA, allow us to demonstrate that variables are related to one another. Covariance can be demonstrated just as easily whether the research - design is correlational, experimental, or quasi-experimental.

The primary weakness in quasi-experimental designs involves the degree to which they eliminate the effects of extraneous variables on the results. Quasi-experimental designs seldom allow us the same degree of control over extraneous variables that we have in experimental designs. As a result, we can never rule out all alternative rival explanations of the findings. As we have seen, however, a well-designed quasi-experiment that eliminates as many threats to internal validity as possible can provide important, convincing information.

Thus, judgments about the quality of a particular quasi-experiment are related to the number of threats to internal validity that we think have been eliminated. Table 13.1 lists several common threats to internal validity that we have mentioned in this chapter. Some of these threats arise when we look at the effect of a quasi-independent variable on changes in the behavior of a single group of participants; others occur when we compare one group of participants to another.

Increasing Confidence in Quasi-Experimental Results

Because they do not have enough control over the environment to structure the research setting - precisely as they would like, researchers who use quasi-experimentation adopt a pragmatic approach to research—one that attempts to collect the most meaningful data under circumstances that are often less than ideal (Condray, 1986). The best quasi-experiments are those in which the researcher uses whatever procedures are available to devise a reasonable test of the research hypotheses. Thus, rather than adhering blindly to one particular design, quasi-experimentalists creatively "patch up" basic designs to provide the most meaningful and convincing data possible.

| **TABLE 13.1** | Common Threats to Internal Validity in Quasi-Experimental Designs |

Designs That Study One Group Before and After the Quasi-Independent Variable

History—something other than the quasi-independent variable that occurred between the pretest and posttest caused the observed change

Maturation—normal changes that occur over time, such as those associated with development, may be mistakenly attributed to the quasi-independent variable

Regression to the mean—when participants were selected because they had extreme scores, their scores may change in the direction of the mean between pretest and posttest even if the quasi-independent variable had no effect

Pretest sensitization—taking the pretest changes participants' reactions to the posttest

Designs That Compare Two or More Nonequivalent Groups

Selection bias—the researcher erroneously concludes that the quasi-independent variable caused the difference between the groups when, in fact, the groups differed even before the occurrence of the quasi-independent variable; in a true experiment, random assignment eliminates this confound

Local history—an extraneous event occurs in one group but not in the other(s); this event, not the quasi-independent variable, caused the difference between the groups; also called a selection by history interaction

Thus, researchers often measure not only the effects of the quasi-independent variable on the outcome behavior but also assess the *processes* that are assumed to mediate their relationship. In many cases, simply showing that a particular quasi-independent variable was associated with changes in the dependent variable may not convince us that the quasi-independent variable itself caused the dependent variable to change. However, if the researcher can also demonstrate that the quasi-independent variable was associated with changes in processes assumed to mediate the change in the dependent variable, more confidence is warranted.

For example, rather than simply measuring students' drug use to evaluate the effects of a school's antidrug campaign, a researcher might also measure other variables that should mediate changes in drug use, such as students' knowledge about and attitudes toward drugs. Unlike some extraneous events (such as searches of students' lockers by school authorities), the program should affect not only drug use but also knowledge and attitudes about drugs. Thus, if changes in knowledge and attitudes are observed at the experimental school (but not at a nonequivalent control school), the researcher has more confidence that the drug education program, and not other factors, produced the change.

By patching up basic quasi-experimental designs with additional quasi-independent variables, comparison groups, and dependent measures, researchers increase their confidence in the inferences they draw about the causal link between the quasi-independent and dependent variables. Such patched-up designs are inelegant and may not conform to any formal design shown in research methods books, but they epitomize the way scientists can structure their collection of data to draw the most accurate conclusions possible (Condray, 1986). Researchers should never hesitate to invent creative strategies for analyzing whatever problem is at hand.

As I mentioned previously, our confidence in the conclusions we draw from research comes not only from the fact that a particular experiment was tightly designed but also from seeing that the accumulated results of several different studies demonstrate the same general effect. Thus, rather than reaching conclusions on the basis of a single study, researchers often piece together many strands of information that were accumulated by a variety of methods, much the way Sherlock Holmes would piece together evidence in breaking a case (Condray, 1986). For example, although the results of a single quasi-experimental investigation of a drug education program at one school may be open to criticism, demonstrating the effects of the program at five or ten schools gives us considerable confidence in concluding that the program was effective.

Because our confidence about causal relationships increases as we integrate many diverse pieces of evidence, quasi-experimentation is enhanced by **critical multiplism** (Shadish, Cook, & Houts, 1986). The critical multiplist perspective argues that researchers should critically consider many ways of obtaining evidence relevant to a particular hypothesis and then employ several different approaches. In quasi-experimental research, no single research approach can yield unequivocal conclusions. However, evidence from multiple approaches may converge to yield conclusions that are as concrete as those obtained in experimental research. Like a game of chess in which each piece has its strengths and weaknesses and in which no piece can win the game alone, quasi-experimentation requires the coordination of several different kinds of research strategies (Shadish et al., 1986). Although any single piece of evidence may be suspect, the accumulated results may be quite convincing. Therefore, do not fall into the trap of thinking that the data provided by quasi-experimental designs are worthless. Rather, simply interpret such data with greater caution.

Summary

1. Many important research questions are not easily answered using true experimental designs. Quasi-experimental designs are used when researchers cannot control the assignment of participants to conditions or cannot manipulate the independent variable. Instead, comparisons are made between people in groups that already exist or within one or more existing groups of participants before and after a quasi-independent variable has occurred.

2. The quality of a quasi-experimental design depends on its ability to minimize threats to internal validity.

3. One-group pretest–posttest designs possess little internal validity and should never be used.

4. In the nonequivalent control group designs, a group that receives the quasi-independent variable is compared with a nonequivalent comparison group that does not receive the quasi-independent variable. The effectiveness of this design depends on the degree to which the groups can be assumed to be equivalent and the degree to which local history effects can be discounted.

5. In time series designs, one or more groups are measured on several occasions both before and after the quasi-experimental variable occurs. Time series designs that include comparison groups allow researchers to document not only that the quasi-independent variable was associated with a change in behavior but also that groups that did not receive the quasi-independent variable did not show a change. A comparative time series design examines changes in two or more variables within the same group to see whether changes in one variable are associated with changes in the other.

6. Longitudinal designs examine changes in behavior over time, essentially treating time as the quasi-independent variable.

7. To separate age effects from cohort effects, researchers sometimes conduct a longitudinal study on different age groups—the cross-sequential cohort design.

8. Quasi-experimental designs are frequently used in program evaluation research that is designed to assess the effects of interventions or programs on people's behavior.

9. Although quasi-experimental designs do not allow the same degree of certainty about cause-and-effect relationships as an experiment does, a well-designed quasi-experiment that controls as many threats to internal validity as possible can provide convincing circumstantial evidence regarding the effects of one variable on another.

Key Terms

comparative time series design (*p. 280*)
contemporary history (*p. 277*)
critical multiplism (*p. 288*)
cross-sectional designs (*p. 282*)
cross-sequential cohort design (*p. 284*)
experimental contamination (*p. 273*)
generational effects (*p. 282*)
interrupted time series design with a reversal (*p. 277*)

interrupted time series design with multiple replications (*p. 279*)
local history effect (*p. 274*)
longitudinal design (*p. 280*)
nonequivalent control group design (*p. 272*)
nonequivalent groups posttest-only design (*p. 272*)
nonequivalent groups pretest–posttest design (*p. 274*)
one-group pretest–posttest design (*p. 271*)

preexperimental design (*p. 272*)
program evaluation (*p. 284*)
quasi-experimental designs (*p. 270*)
quasi-independent variable (*p. 270*)
regression to the mean (*p. 271*)
selection bias (*p. 273*)
selection-by-history interaction (*p. 274*)
simple interrupted time series design (*p. 276*)
time series design (*p. 276*)

Questions for Review

1. How do quasi-experimental designs differ from true experiments?
2. Under what circumstances would a researcher use a quasi-experimental rather than an experimental design?
3. Why should researchers never use the one-group pretest–posttest design?
4. What threats to internal validity are present when the nonequivalent control group posttest-only design is used? Which of these threats are eliminated by the pretest–posttest version of this design?
5. What is experimental contamination? Why does a concern with contamination sometimes lead researchers to use quasi-experimental designs?
6. Does a nonequivalent groups pretest–posttest design eliminate local history as a potential explanation of the results? Explain.
7. Explain the rationale behind time series designs.
8. Describe the simple interrupted time series design.
9. Why is contemporary history a threat to internal validity in a simple interrupted time series design?
10. Discuss how the interrupted time series design with a reversal and the control group interrupted time series design improve on the simple interrupted time series design.
11. Distinguish between a longitudinal design and a cross-sectional design.
12. When a longitudinal design reveals a change in behavior over time, why can we not conclude that the change is due to development?
13. What are generational (or cohort) effects, and why do they sometimes create a problem in cross-sectional designs? How does the cross-sequential cohort design help to solve this problem?
14. What is program evaluation? Why do program evaluators rely heavily on quasi-experimental designs in their work?
15. What were some of Donald Campbell's contributions to behavioral research?
16. What three criteria must be met to establish that one variable causes changes in behavior? Which of these criteria are met by quasi-experimental designs? Which of these criteria are not met, and why?
17. Why does quasi-experimentation sometimes require the use of "patched-up" designs?

Questions for Discussion

1. Although quasi-experimental designs are widely accepted in behavioral science, some researchers are troubled by the fact that the evidence provided by quasi-experiments is seldom as conclusive as that provided by true experiments. Imagine you are trying to convince a dubious experimentalist of the merits of quasi-experimental research. What arguments would you use to convince him or her of its value?
2. Imagine that your town or city has increased its night-time police patrols to reduce crime. Design two

quasi-experiments to determine whether this intervention has been effective, one that uses some variation of a nonequivalent control group design and one that uses some variation of a time series design. For each design, discuss the possible threats to internal validity, as well as the ways in which the design could be patched up to provide more conclusive evidence.

3. The Centers for Disease Control and Prevention released a report that attributed part of the increase in youth smoking in the 1980s to the use of the cartoon character, Joe Camel, in cigarette advertising. Using annual data going back to 1965, the report showed that the number of people under the age of 18 who started smoking increased markedly in 1988, the same year that Joe Camel first appeared in tobacco ads ("Daily Smoking by Teens Has Risen Sharply," 1998).

a. What kind of a quasi-experimental design was used in this study?

b. What potential threats to internal validity are present in this design?

c. From these data, how confident are you that Joe Camel was responsible for increases in youth smoking?

14

SINGLE-CASE RESEARCH

When I describe the results of a particular study to my students, they sometimes respond to the findings by pointing out exceptions. "That study can't be right," they object. "I have a friend (brother, aunt, roommate, or whomever) who does just the opposite." For example, if I tell my class that first-born children tend to be more achievement-oriented than later-born children, I can count on some student saying, "No way. I'm the third-born in my family, and I'm much more achievement-oriented than my older brothers." If I mention a study showing that anxiety causes people to prefer to be with other people, someone may retort, "But my roommate withdraws from people when she's anxious."

What such responses indicate is that many people do not understand the probabilistic nature of behavioral science. Our research uncovers generalities and trends, but we can nearly always find exceptions to the general pattern. Overall, achievement motivation declines slightly with birth order, but not every first-born child is more achievement-oriented than his or her younger siblings. Overall, people tend to seek out the company of other people when they are anxious or afraid, but some people prefer to be left alone when they are upset.

Behavioral science is not unique in this regard. Many of the principles and findings of all sciences are probabilities. For example, when medical researchers state that excessive exposure to the sun causes skin cancer, they do not mean that *every person* who suntans will get cancer. Rather, they mean that more people in a group of regular suntanners will get skin cancer than in an equivalent group of people who avoid the sun. Suntanning and skin cancer are related in a probabilistic fashion, but there will always be exceptions to the general finding. But these exceptions do not violate the general finding that, overall, people who spend more time in the sun are more likely to get skin cancer than people who don't.

Although specific exceptions do not invalidate the findings of a particular study, these apparent contradictions between general findings and specific cases raise an important point for researchers to consider. Whenever we obtain a general finding based on a large number of participants, we must recognize that the effect we obtained is not likely to be true of everybody in the world or even of every participant in the sample under study. We may find large differences between the average responses of participants in various experimental conditions, for example, even if the independent variable affected the behavior of only some of our participants. This point has led some to suggest that researchers should pay more attention to the behavior of individual participants.

Since the earliest days of behavioral science, researchers have debated the merits of a nomothetic versus idiographic approach to understanding behavior. Most researchers view the scientific enterprise as an inherently **nomothetic approach**, seeking to establish general principles and broad generalizations that apply across individuals. However, as we have seen, these general principles do not always apply to everyone. As a result, some researchers have argued that the nomothetic approach must be accompanied by an **idiographic approach** (see, for example, Allport, 1961). Idiographic research seeks to describe, analyze, and compare the behavior of *individual* participants. According to proponents of the idiographic approach, behavioral scientists should focus not only on general trends—the behavior of the "average" participant—but also on the unique behaviors of specific individuals.

An emphasis on the study of individual organisms has been championed by two quite different groups of behavioral researchers with different interests and orientations. On one hand, some experimental psychologists interested in basic psychological processes

have advocated the use of single-case (or single-subject) experimental designs. As we will see, these are designs in which researchers manipulate independent variables and exercise strong experimental control over extraneous variables, then analyze the behavior of *individual participants* rather than grouped data.

On the other hand, other researchers have advocated the use of case studies in which the behavior and personality of a single individual or group are described in detail. Unlike single-case experiments, case studies usually involve uncontrolled impressionistic descriptions rather than controlled experimentation. Case studies have been used most widely in clinical psychology, psychiatry, and other fields that specialize in the treatment of individual problems.

Despite the fact that many noted behavioral researchers have used single-case approaches, single-case research has a mixed reputation in contemporary psychology. Some researchers insist that research involving the study of individuals is essential for the advancement of behavioral science, whereas other researchers see such approaches as having limited usefulness. In this chapter, we explore the rationale behind these two varieties of single-case research, along with the advantages and limitations of each.

Contributors To Behavioral Research
Single-Case Researchers

Single-case research—whether single-case experiments or case studies—has had a long and distinguished history in behavioral science. In fact, in the early days of behavioral science, it was common practice to study only one or a few participants. Only after the 1930s did researchers begin to rely on larger samples as most researchers do today (Boring, 1954; Robinson & Foster, 1979).

Many advances in behavioral science came from the study of single individuals in controlled experimental settings. Ebbinghaus, who began the scientific study of memory, conducted his studies on a single individual (himself). Stratton, an early researcher in perception, also used himself as a participant as he studied the effects of wearing glasses that reversed the world from left to right and top to bottom. (He soon learned to function quite normally in his reversed and inverted environment.) Many seminal ideas regarding conditioning were discovered and tested in single-case experiments; notably, both Pavlov and Skinner used single-case experimental designs. Many advances in psychophysiology, such as Sperry's (1975) work on split-brain patients, have come from the study of individuals undergoing brain surgery.

Case studies, often taken from clinical practice, have also contributed to the development of ideas in behavioral science. Kraepelin, who developed an early classification system of mental disorders that was the forerunner to the psychiatric diagnostic system used today, based his system on case studies (Garmezy, 1982). Most of the seminal ideas of Freud, Jung, Adler, and other early personality theorists were based on case studies. In developmental psychology, Piaget used case studies of children in developing his influential ideas about cognitive development. Case studies of groups have also been used by social psychologists, as in Festinger's study of a group that expected the world to end.

Thus, although single-case research is less common than research that involves groups of participants, such studies have had a long and distinguished tradition in behavioral science.

SINGLE-CASE EXPERIMENTAL DESIGNS

In each of the experimental and quasi-experimental designs we have discussed so far, researchers assess the effects of variables on behavior by comparing the average responses of two or more groups of participants. In these designs, the unit of analysis is always grouped data. In fact, in analyzing the data obtained from these designs, information about the responses of individual participants is usually ignored.

Group designs, such as those we have been discussing, reflect the most common approach to research in behavioral science. Most experiments and quasi-experiments conducted by psychologists and other behavioral scientists involve group designs. Even so, group designs have their critics, some as notable as the late B. F. Skinner, who offer an alternative approach to experimental research.

In the **single-case experimental design**, the unit of analysis is not the experimental group, as it is in group designs, but rather the individual participant. Often more than one participant is studied (typically three to eight), but each participant's responses are analyzed separately and the data from individual participants are rarely averaged. Because averages are not used, the data from single-participant experiments cannot be analyzed using inferential statistics such as *t*-tests and *F*-tests.

At first, the single-participant approach may strike you as an odd, if not ineffective, way to conduct and analyze behavioral research. However, before you pass judgment, let's examine several criticisms of group experiments and how they may be resolved by using single-participant designs.

Criticisms of Group Designs and Analyses

Proponents of single-participant designs have suggested that group experimental designs fail to adequately handle three important research issues— error variance, generalizability, and reliability.

ERROR VARIANCE. We saw earlier that all data contain error variance, which reflects the influence of unidentified factors that affect participants' responses in an unsystematic fashion. We also learned that researchers must minimize error variance because error variance can mask the effects of the independent variable (see Chapter 9).

Group experimental designs, such as those we discussed in earlier chapters, provide two partial solutions to the problem of error variance. First, although the responses of any particular participant are contaminated by error variance in unknown ways, *averaging* the responses of several participants should provide a more accurate estimate of the typical effect of the independent variable. In essence, many random and idiosyncratic sources of error variance cancel each other out when we calculate a group mean. Presumably, then, the mean for a group of participants is a better estimate of the typical participant's response to the independent variable than the score of any particular participant.

Second, by using groups of participants we can estimate the amount of error variance in our data. This is what we did when we calculated the denominator of *t*-tests and *F*-tests (see Chapters 11 and 12). With this estimate, we can test whether the differences among the means of the groups are greater than we would expect if the differences were due only to error variance. Indeed, the purpose of using inferential statistics is to separate error variance from systematic variance to determine whether the differences among the group means are likely due to the independent variable or only to error variance.

Although group data provide these two benefits, proponents of single-participant designs criticize the way group designs and inferential statistics handle error variance. They argue that, first, much of the error variance in group data does not reflect variability in behavior per se but rather is *created* by the group design itself, and second, researchers who use group designs accept the presence of error variance too blithely.

As we noted earlier, much of the error variance in a set of data is due to individual differences among the participants. However, in one sense, this **interparticipant variance** is *not* the kind of variability that behavioral researchers are usually trying to understand and explain. Error variance resulting from individual differences among participants is an artificial creation of the fact that, in group designs, we pool the responses of many participants.

Single-participant researchers emphasize the importance of studying **intraparticipant variance**— variability in *an individual's* behavior when he or she is in the same situation on different occasions. This is true behavioral variability that demands our attention. What we typically call error variance is, in one sense, partly a product of individual differences among participants in our sample rather than real variations in a participant's behavior.

Because data are not aggregated across participants in single-participant research, individual differences do not contribute to error variance. Error variance in a single-participant design shows up when a particular participant responds differently under various administrations of the same experimental condition.

Most researchers who use group designs ignore the fact that their data contain a considerable amount of error variance. Ignoring error variance is, for single-participant researchers, tantamount to being content with sloppy experimental design and one's ignorance (Sidman, 1960). After all, error variance is the result of factors that have remained unidentified and uncontrolled by the researcher. Proponents of single-participant designs maintain that, rather than accepting error variance, researchers should design studies in a way that allows them to seek out its causes and eliminate them. Through tighter and tighter experimental control, more and more intraparticipant error variance can be eliminated, and in the process, we can learn more and more about the factors that influence behavior.

GENERALIZABILITY.   In the eyes of researchers who use group designs, averaging across participants serves an important purpose. By pooling the scores of several participants, the researcher minimizes the impact of the idiosyncratic responses of any particular participant. They hope that by doing so they can identify the general, overall effect of the independent variable, an effect that should generalize to most of the participants most of the time.

In contrast, single-participant researchers argue that the data from group designs do not permit us to identify the general effect of the independent variable as many researchers suppose. Rather than reflecting the typical effect of the independent variable on the average participant, results from group designs represent an average of many individuals' responses that may not accurately portray the response of *any* particular participant. Consider, for example, the finding that women in the United States have an average of 2.09 children. Although we all understand what this statistic tells us about childbearing in this country, personally, I don't know any woman who has 2.09 kids. The mean does not reflect the behavior of any individual.

Given that group averages may not represent any particular participant's response, attempts to generalize from overall group results may be misleading. Put differently, group means may have no counterpart in the behavior of individual participants (Sidman, 1960). This point is demonstrated in the accompanying box, "How Group Designs Misled Us About Learning Curves."

In addition, exclusive reliance on group summary statistics may obscure the fact that the independent variable affected the behavior of some participants but had no effect (or even opposite effects) on other participants. Researchers who use group designs rarely examine their raw data to see how many participants showed the effect and whether some participants showed effects that were contrary to the general trend.

RELIABILITY.   A third criticism of group designs is that, in most cases, they demonstrate the effect of the independent variable a single time, and no attempt is made to determine whether the observed effect is reliable—that is, whether it can be obtained again. Of course, researchers may replicate their and others' findings in later studies, but replication *within a single experiment* is rare.

When possible, single-participant experiments replicate the effects of the independent variable in two ways. As I will describe later, some designs introduce an independent variable, remove it, and then reintroduce it. This procedure involves **intraparticipant replication**—replicating the effects of the independent variable with a single participant.

In addition, most single-participant research involves more than one participant, typically three to eight. Studying the effects of the independent variable on more than one participant involves **interparticipant replication**. Through interparticipant replication, the researcher can determine whether the effects obtained for one participant generalize to other participants. Keep in mind that even though multiple participants are used, their data are examined individually. In this way, researchers can see whether all participants respond similarly to the independent variable. To put it differently, unlike group experimental designs, single-case designs allow the generality of one's hypothesis to be assessed through replication on a case-by-case basis.

In Depth
How Group Designs Misled Us About Learning Curves

With certain kinds of tasks, learning is an all-or-none process (Estes, 1964). During early stages of learning, people thrash around in a trial-and-error fashion. However, once they hit on the correct answer or solution, they subsequently give the correct response every time. Thus, their performance jumps from *incorrect* to *correct* in a single trial.

The performance of a single participant on an all-or-none learning task can be graphed as shown in Figure 14.1. This participant got the answer wrong for eight trials and then hit on the correct response on Trial 9. Of course, after obtaining the correct answer, the participant got it right on all subsequent trials.

Different participants will hit on the correct response on different trials. Some will get it right on the first trial, some on the second trial, some on the third trial, and so on. In light of this, think for a moment of what would happen if we averaged the responses of a large number of participants on a learning task such as this. What would the graph of the data look like? Rather than showing the all-or-none pattern we see for each participant, the graph of the averaged group data will show a smooth curve like that in Figure 14.2.

On the average, the probability of getting the correct response starts low, then gradually increases until virtually every participant obtains the correct answer on every trial. However, using group data obscures the fact that at the level of the individual participant, the learning curve was discontinuous rather than smooth. In fact, the results from the averaged group data *do not reflect the behavior of any participant.* In instances such as this, group data can be quite misleading, whereas single-participant designs show the true pattern.

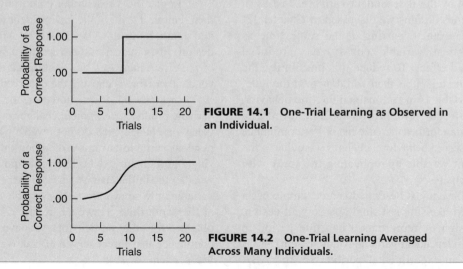

FIGURE 14.1 One-Trial Learning as Observed in an Individual.

FIGURE 14.2 One-Trial Learning Averaged Across Many Individuals.

Basic Single-Case Experimental Designs

In this section, we examine the three basic single-case experimental designs: the ABA, multiple-I, and multiple baseline designs.

ABA DESIGNS. The most common single-participant research designs involve variations of what is known as the **ABA design**. The researcher who uses these designs attempts to demonstrate that an independent variable affects behavior, first by showing that the variable causes a target behavior to occur, and then by showing that removal of the variable causes the behavior to cease. For obvious reasons, these are sometimes called **reversal designs**.

In ABA designs, the participant is first observed in the absence of the independent variable (the baseline or control condition). The target behavior is measured many times during this phase to establish an adequate baseline for comparison. Then, after the target behavior is seen to be relatively stable, the independent variable is introduced and the behavior is observed again. If the independent variable influences behavior, we should see a change in behavior from the baseline to the treatment period. (In many ways, the ABA design can be regarded as an interrupted time series design performed on a single participant.)

However, even if behavior changes when the independent variable is introduced, the researcher should not be too hasty to conclude that the effect was caused by the independent variable. Just as in the time series designs we discussed in Chapter 13, some other event occurring at the same time as the independent variable could have produced the observed effect. To reduce this possibility, the independent variable is then withdrawn. If the independent variable is in fact maintaining the behavior, the behavior may return to its baseline level. The researcher can further increase his or her confidence that the observed behavioral changes were due to the independent variable by replicating the study with other participants.

The design just described is an example of an ABA design, the simplest single-participant design. In this design, A represents a baseline period in which the independent variable is not present, and B represents an experimental period. So, the ABA design involves a baseline period (A), followed by introduction of the independent variable (B), followed by the reversal period in which the independent variable is removed (A). Many variations and elaborations of the basic ABA design are possible. To increase our confidence that the changes in behavior were due to the independent variable, a researcher may decide to introduce the same level of the independent variable a second time. This design would be labeled an *ABAB design*.

Deitz (1977) used an ABAB design to examine the effects of teacher reinforcement on the disruptive behavior of a student in a special education class. To reduce the frequency with which this student disrupted class by talking out loud, the teacher made a contract with the student, saying that she would spend 15 minutes with him after class (something he valued) if he talked aloud no more than 3 times during the class. Baseline data showed that, before the treatment program started, the student talked aloud between 30 and 40 times per day. The reinforcement program was then begun, and the rate of disruptive behavior dropped quickly to 10 outbursts, then to 3 or fewer (see Figure 14.3). When the reinforcement program was withdrawn, the number of outbursts increased, although not to their original level. Then, when it was reinstated, the student virtually stopped disrupting class. These data provide rather convincing evidence that the intervention was successful in modifying the student's behavior.

Logically, a researcher could reintroduce and then remove a level of the independent variable again and again, as in an ABABABA or ABABABABA design. Each successive intraparticipant replication of the effect increases our confidence that the independent variable is causing the observed effects.

In many instances, however, the independent variable produces *permanent* changes in participants' behavior, changes that do not reverse when the independent variable is removed. When this happens, a single participant's data do not unequivocally show whether the initial change was due to the independent variable or to some extraneous variable that occurred at the same time. However, if the same pattern is obtained for other participants, we have considerable confidence that the observed effects were due to the independent variable.

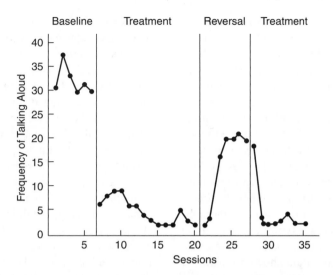

FIGURE 14.3   Decreasing Disruptive Behavior.   During the 6 days of baseline recording, this student engaged in a high level of disruptive behavior, talking aloud at least 30 times each class period. When the teacher promised to give the student special attention if he didn't disrupt, the number of disruptions dropped to less than 3 per session. However, when the teacher stopped the program (the reversal phase), disruptions increased to approximately 20 per session. When the treatment was again implemented, disruptions were nearly eliminated. The pattern of results across the four phases of this ABAB design demonstrates that the teacher's treatment program successfully controlled the student's disruptive behavior.   *Source:* Reprinted from *Behavior Research and Therapy,* Vol. 15, S. M. Dietz, An analysis of programming DRL schedules in educational settings, pp. 103–111, 1977, with permission from Elsevier Science.

MULTIPLE-I DESIGNS.   ABA-type designs compare behavior in the absence of the independent variable (during A) with behavior in the presence of a nonzero level of an independent variable (during B). However, other single-participant designs test differences among *levels* of an independent variable. Single-case experimental designs that present varying nonzero levels of the independent variable are called **multiple-I designs**.

In one such design, the **ABC design**, the researcher obtains a baseline (A) and then introduces one level of the independent variable (B) for a certain period of time. Then, this level is removed and another level of the independent variable is introduced (C). Of course, we could continue this procedure to create an ABCDEFG . . . design.

Often researchers insert a baseline period between each successive introduction of a level of the independent variable, resulting in an **ABACA design**. After obtaining a baseline (A), the researcher introduces one level of the independent variable (B)

and then withdraws it (A) as in an ABA design. Then a second level of the independent variable is introduced (C) and then withdrawn (A). We could continue to manipulate the independent variable by introducing new levels of it, returning to baseline each time. Such designs are commonly used in research that investigates the effects of drugs on behavior. Participants are given different dosages of a drug, with baseline periods occurring between the successive dosages. In one such study, Dworkin, Bimle, and Miyauchi (1989) tested the effects of cocaine on how rats react to punished and nonpunished responding. Over several days, four different dosages of cocaine were administered to five pairs of rats, with baseline sessions scheduled between each administration of the drug. While under the influence of the drug, one rat in each pair received punishment, whereas the other did not. (We'll return to the results of this experiment in a moment.)

Sometimes combinations of treatments are administered at each phase of the study. For example,

Jones and Friman (1999) tested the separate and combined effects of graduated exposure and reinforcement on a 14-year-old boy, Mike, who had been referred by his school principal because his class performance was severely disrupted by an insect phobia. Whenever he saw an insect in the classroom or his classmates teased him about bugs ("Mike, there's a bug under your chair"), Mike stopped working, pulled the hood of his jacket over his head, and started yelling. To begin, the researchers assessed Mike's ability to complete math problems under three baseline conditions—when he knew there were no bugs in the room, when the therapist told him there were bugs in the room (but he couldn't see any), and when three live crickets were released in the room. The baseline data showed that Mike could complete only about half as many problems when the crickets were loose than when the room was free of bugs. After 10 baseline sessions, the therapists implemented a graduated exposure procedure in which Mike experienced a series of increasingly more difficult encounters with crickets until he could hold a cricket in each hand for 20 seconds. Interestingly, despite his increased courage with crickets, Mike's ability to complete math problems while insects were in the room did not improve during this phase. Then, as graduated exposure continued, the researchers also began to reward Mike with points for each correct math answer, points that he could trade for candy and toys. At that point, Mike's math performance with crickets loose in the room increased to the level he had shown initially when he knew no bugs were present. Then a second baseline period was instituted for several sessions to see whether his math performance dropped. (It did, but only slightly.) When the combined treatment of graduated exposure and reinforcement was reinstituted, his math performance increased to an all-time high. The authors described this as an A-B-BC-A-BC design, where A was baseline, B was graduated exposure, and C was reinforcement.

MULTIPLE BASELINE DESIGNS.   As noted earlier, the effects of an independent variable do not always disappear when the variable is removed. For example, if a clinical psychologist teaches a client a new way to cope with stress, it is difficult to "unteach" it. When this is so, how can we be sure the obtained effects are due to the independent variable as opposed to some extraneous factor?

One way is to use a multiple baseline design. In a **multiple baseline design**, two or more behaviors are studied simultaneously. After obtaining baseline data on all behaviors, an independent variable is introduced that is hypothesized to affect *only one of the behaviors*. In this way, the selective effects of a variable on a specific behavior can be documented. By measuring several behaviors, the researcher can show that the independent variable caused the target behavior to change but did not affect other behaviors. If the effects of the independent variable can be shown to be specific to certain behaviors, the researcher has increased confidence that the obtained effects were, in fact, due to the independent variable.

Data from Single-Participant Designs

As I noted earlier, researchers who use single-participant designs resist analyzing their results in the forms of means, standard deviations, and other descriptive statistics based on group data. Furthermore, because they do not average data across participants, those who use such designs do not use statistics such as *t*-tests and *F*-tests to test whether the means of the experimental conditions are significantly different.

The preferred method of presenting the data from single-participant designs is with graphs that show the results individually for each participant. Rather than testing the significance of the experimental effects, single-participant researchers employ **graphic analysis** (also known simply as *visual inspection*).

Put simply, single-participant researchers judge whether the independent variable affected behavior by visually inspecting graphs of the data for individual participants. If the behavioral changes are pronounced enough to be discerned through a visual inspection of such graphs, the researcher concludes that the independent variable affected the participant's behavior. If the pattern is not clear enough to conclude that a behavioral change occurred, the researcher concludes that the independent variable did not have an effect.

Ideally, the researcher would like to obtain results like those shown in Figure 14.4. As you can see in this ABA design, the behavior was relatively stable during the baseline period, changed quickly when the independent variable was introduced, and then returned immediately to baseline when the independent variable was removed.

Unfortunately, the results are not always this clear-cut. Look, for example, at the data in Figure 14.5. During the baseline period, the participant's responses were fluctuating somewhat. Thus, it is difficult to tell whether the independent variable caused a change in behavior during the treatment period or whether the observed change was a random fluctuation such as those that occurred during baseline. (This is why

single-participant researchers try to establish a stable baseline before introducing the independent variable.) Furthermore, when the independent variable was removed, the participant's behavior changed but did not return to the original baseline level. Did the independent variable cause changes in behavior? In the case of Figure 14.5, the answer to this question is uncertain.

Figure 14.6 shows the results from two participants in the study of the effects of cocaine on reactions to punishment described earlier (Dworkin et al., 1989). In the case of the Dworkin et al. study, graphic analysis revealed marked differences in how participants in the

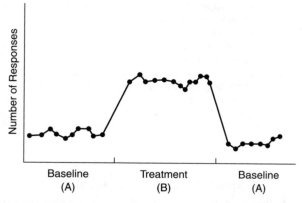

FIGURE 14.4 Results from an ABA Design—I. In this ABA design, the effect of the independent variable is clear-cut. The number of responses increased sharply when the treatment was introduced and then returned to baseline when it was withdrawn.

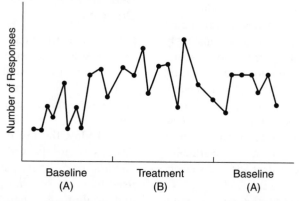

FIGURE 14.5 Results from an ABA Design—II. In this ABA design, whether the independent variable affected the number of responses is unclear. Because responding was not stable during the baseline (A), it is difficult to determine the extent to which responding changed when the treatment was introduced (B). In addition, responding did not return to the baseline level when the treatment was withdrawn.

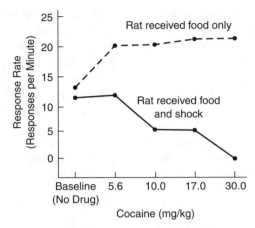

FIGURE 14.6 **Effects of Varying Dosages of Cocaine on Punished and Nonpunished Responding.**
This graph shows the behavior of two rats in the Dworkin et al. study. One rat received only food
when it pressed a bar (nonpunished); the other rat received food and shock (punished). The graph
shows that increasing dosages of cocaine had quite different effects on the response rates for these
two animals. Increasing dosages resulted in increased responding for the nonpunished rat but resulted
in decreased responding for the punished rat. Dworkin et al. replicated this pattern on four other pairs
of rats, thereby demonstrating the interparticipant generalizability of their findings.   *Source:* Adapted
from "Differential Effects of Pentobarbital and Cocaine on Punished and Nonpunished Responding," by
S. I. Dworkin, C. Bimle, and T. Miyauchi, 1989, *Journal of the Experimental Analysis of Behavior, 51,*
pp. 173–184. Used with permission of the Society for the Experimental Analysis of Behavior.

punished and nonpunished conditions responded under
different dosages of cocaine. Furthermore, inspection
of the graphs for the other participants in the study
revealed exactly the same pattern, thereby providing
converging evidence of the effects of various doses of
cocaine on punished and nonpunished responding.

Compared to the complexities of inferential
statistics, graphic analysis may appear astonishingly
straightforward and simple. Furthermore, many
researchers are disturbed by the looseness of using
visual inspection to assess whether an independent
variable influenced behavior; eyeballing, they argue, is
not sufficiently sensitive or objective as a means of data
analysis. Many researchers criticize graphic analysis
because of the ambiguity of the criteria for determining
whether an effect of the independent variable was obtained. How big of an effect is *big enough*?

Proponents of single-participant research
counter that, on the contrary, visual inspection is
preferable to inferential statistics. Because graphic
analysis is admittedly a relatively insensitive way
to examine data, only the strongest effects will be

accepted as real (Kazdin, 1982). This is in contrast to
group data, in which very weak effects may be found
to be statistically significant.

Uses of Single-Case Experimental Designs

During the earliest days of psychology, single-case
research was the preferred research strategy. As we've
seen, many of the founders of behavioral science—
Weber, Wundt, Pavlov, Thorndike, Ebbinghaus,
and others—relied heavily on single-participant
approaches.

Today, the use of single-case experimental
designs is closely wedded to the study of operant
conditioning. Single-participant designs have been
used to study operant processes in both humans
and nonhumans, including rats, pigeons, mice,
dogs, fish, monkeys, and cats. Single-participant
designs have been widely used to study the effects
of various schedules of reinforcement and punishment on behavior. In fact, virtually the entire

research literature involving schedules of reinforcement is based on single-participant designs. Furthermore, most of Skinner's influential research on operant conditioning involved single-participant designs. Single-case experimental designs are also used by researchers who study psychophysiological processes, as well as by those who study sensation and perception.

In applied research, single-participant designs have been used most frequently to study the effects of behavior modification—techniques for changing problem behaviors that are based on the principles of operant conditioning. Such designs have been used extensively, for example, in the context of therapy to study the effects of behavior modification on phenomena as diverse as bed-wetting, delinquency, catatonic schizophrenia, aggression, depression, self-injurious behavior, shyness, and, as we saw earlier, insect phobia (Jones, 1993; Kazdin, 1982).

Single-participant research has also been used in industrial settings (to study the effects of various interventions on a worker's performance, for example) and in schools (to study the effects of token economies on learning).

Finally, single-participant designs are sometimes used for demonstrational purposes simply to show that a particular behavioral effect can be obtained. For example, developmental psychologists have been interested in whether young children can be taught to use memory strategies to help them remember better. Using a single-participant design to show that five preschool children learned to use memory strategies would demonstrate that young children can, in fact, learn such strategies. The causal inferences one can draw from such demonstrations are often weak, and the effects are of questionable generalizability, but such studies can provide indirect, anecdotal evidence that particular effects can be obtained.

Behavioral Research Case Study
Treatment of Stuttering: A Single-Case Experiment

Among the most effective treatments for stuttering are procedures that teach stutterers to consciously regulate their breathing as they speak. Wagaman, Miltenberger, and Arndorfer (1993) used a single-case experimental design to test a simplified variation of such a program on eight children ranging in age from 6 to 10 years.

The study occurred in three phases consisting of baseline, treatment, and posttreatment—an ABA design. To obtain a baseline measure of stuttering, the researchers tape-recorded the children talking to their parents. The researchers then counted the number of words the children spoke, as well as the number of times they stuttered. Using these two numbers, the researchers calculated the percentage of words on which each child stuttered. Analyses showed that interrater reliability was acceptably high on these measures; two researchers agreed in identifying stuttering 86% of the time.

In the treatment phase of the study, the children were taught how to regulate their breathing so that they would breathe deeply and slowly through their mouths as they spoke. The children practiced speaking while holding their fingertips in front of their mouths to ensure that they were, in fact, exhaling as they talked. They also learned to stop talking immediately each time they stuttered, then to consciously implement the breathing pattern they had learned. Parents were also taught these techniques so they could practice them with their children. Conversations between the children and their parents were tape-recorded at the beginning of each treatment session, and the rate of stuttering was calculated. Treatment occurred in 45- to 60-minute sessions three times a week until the child stuttered on less than 3% of his or her words (normal speakers stutter less than 3% of the time). After the rate of stuttering had dropped below 3% for a particular child, treatment was discontinued for that participant. However, posttreatment measures of stuttering were taken regularly for over a year to be sure the effects of treatment were maintained.

In the article describing this study, Wagaman et al. (1993) presented graphs showing the percentage of stuttered words separately for each of the eight children across the course of the study. The data for the eight partici-

(continued)

(continued)

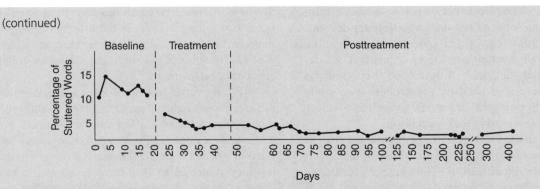

FIGURE 14.7 Effects of a Treatment for Stuttering. This graph shows the percentage of words on which Jake stuttered during the baseline, treatment, and posttreatment phases. His initial rate of stuttering during baseline was over 10% but dropped quickly to less than 5% after treatment started. After treatment stopped, Jake's rate of stuttering remained less than 3% for the remainder of the study. *Source:* From "Analysis of a Simplified Treatment for Stuttering in Children," by J. R. Wagaman, R. G. Miltenberger, and R. E. Arndorfer, 1993, *Journal of Applied Behavior Analysis, 26,* p. 58.

pants showed precisely the same pattern. Figure 14.7 shows the data for one of the children (Jake). During baseline, Jake stuttered on over 10% of his words. When the treatment began, his rate of stuttering dropped sharply to less than 3% and stayed at this low rate for at least a year after treatment was discontinued. Given that the pattern of data was identical for all eight participants, this single-case experiment provides convincing evidence that this treatment is effective in permanently reducing stuttering.

Critique of Single-Participant Designs

Well-designed single-participant experiments can provide convincing evidence regarding the causal effects of independent variables on behavior. They have been used quite effectively in the study of many phenomena, particularly the study of basic learning processes.

However, despite the argument that the results of single-participant studies are more generalizable than the results of group designs, single-participant experiments do not inherently possess greater external validity. Generalizability depends heavily on the manner in which participants are selected. Even when strong experimental effects are obtained across all of the participants in a single-participant experiment, these effects may still be limited to others who are like one's participants. It is certainly true, however, that single-participant designs permit researchers to see how well the effects of the independent variable generalize across participants in a way that is rarely possible with group designs.

Importantly, one reason that single-case experiments are often used by animal researchers is that the results obtained on one participant are more likely to generalize to other potential participants than in the case of human beings. This is because the animals used for laboratory research (mostly rats, mice, pigeons, and rabbits) are partially or fully inbred, thereby minimizing genetic variation. Furthermore, the participants used in a particular study are usually of the same age, have been raised in the same controlled environment, fed the same food, and then tested under identical conditions. As a result, all possible participants are "clones or near-clones, both with respect to genetics and experiential history" (Denenberg, 1982, p. 21). Thus, unlike human research, in which the individual participants differ greatly (and in which one participant's response may or may not resemble another's), the responses of only two or three nonhuman animals may be representative of many others.

One limitation of single-participant designs is that they are not well suited for studying *interactions* among variables. Although one could logically test a participant under all possible combinations of the levels of two or more independent variables, such studies are often difficult to implement (see Kratochwill, 1978).

Finally, ethical issues sometimes arise when ABA designs are used to assess the effectiveness of clinical interventions. Is it ethical to withdraw a potentially helpful treatment from a troubled client to assure the researcher that the treatment was, in fact, effective? For example, we might hesitate to withdraw the treatment that was introduced to reduce depression in a suicidal patient simply to convince ourselves that the treatment did, in fact, ameliorate the client's depression.

CASE STUDY RESEARCH

We now turn our attention to a very different kind of single-case research—the case study. A **case study** is a detailed study of a single individual, group, or event. Within behavioral research, case studies have been most closely associated with clinical psychology, psychiatry, and other applied fields, where they are used to describe noteworthy cases of psychopathology or treatment. For example, a psychotherapist may describe the case of a client who is a sociopath or detail the therapist's efforts to use a particular treatment approach on a client who is afraid of thunderstorms. Similarly, psychobiographers have conducted psychological case studies of famous people, such as Jesus, Lincoln, and van Gogh (see Runyan, 1982).

Although case studies of individuals are most common, researchers sometimes perform case studies of *groups*. For example, in his attempt to understand why groups sometimes make bad decisions, Janis (1982) conducted case studies of several political and military decision-making groups. Within educational research, studies are sometimes made of exemplary schools, with an eye toward understanding why these particular schools are so good (U.S. Department of Education, 1991). A great deal of social anthropology involves case studies of non-Western social groups, and ethologists have conducted case studies of troupes of baboons, chimpanzees, gorillas, and other nonhuman animals.

The data for case studies can come from a variety of sources, including observation, interviews, questionnaires, news reports, and archival records (such as diaries, minutes of meetings, or school records). Typically, the researcher culls the available information together into a **narrative description** of the person, group, or event. In some instances, the researcher's subjective impressions are supplemented by objective measures (such as measures of personality or behavior). The available information is then interpreted to explain how and why the individual or group under study behaved as it did, and conclusions, solutions, decisions, or recommendations are offered (Bromley, 1986).

Uses of the Case Study Method

Although used far less commonly by researchers than the other approaches we have examined, the case study method has at least four uses in behavioral research.

AS A SOURCE OF INSIGHTS AND IDEAS.   Perhaps the most important use of case studies is as a source of ideas in the early stages of investigating a topic. (Doing an intensive case study was recommended as one approach to obtaining research ideas in Chapter 1.) Studying a few particular individuals in detail can provide a wealth of ideas for future investigation.

In fact, many seminal ideas in behavioral science emerged from intensive case studies of individuals or groups. For example, Freud's ideas emerged from his case studies of clients who came to him for therapy, and Piaget's groundbreaking work on cognitive development was based on the case studies he performed on his own children. Within social psychology, Janis's case studies of high-level decision-making groups paved the way for his theory of groupthink, and Festinger's case study of a group that predicted the end of the world led to the theory of cognitive dissonance.

TO DESCRIBE RARE PHENOMENA.   Some behavioral phenomena occur so rarely that researchers are unlikely to obtain a large number of participants displaying the phenomenon for study. For example, if we were interested in the psychology of presidential assassins, we would be limited to case studies of the few people who have killed or tried to kill

U.S. presidents (Weisz & Taylor, 1969). Similarly, studies of mass murderers require a case study approach. Luria (1987) used a case study approach to describe the life of a man who had nearly perfect memory—another rare phenomenon. In a case study in psychophysiology, Witelson, Kigar, and Harvey (1999) conducted an intensive case study of Einstein's brain. Although they found that Einstein's brain was no larger than average, one part of his parietal lobes was wider and uniquely structured when compared to those of 91 other individuals of normal intelligence. The literature in psychology and psychiatry contains many case studies of people with unusual psychological problems or abilities, such as multiple personalities, phobic reactions to dead birds, and "photographic memory."

Neuropsychologists, psychophysiologists, neurologists, and other neuroscientists sometimes conduct case studies of people who—because of unusual injuries, diseases, or surgeries—have sustained damage to their nervous systems. Although they would never purposefully damage people's brains, researchers sometimes take advantage of unusual opportunities to study the effects of brain trauma on personality and behavior.

PSYCHOBIOGRAPHY. **Psychobiography** involves applying concepts and theories from psychology in an effort to understand the lives of famous people. Psychobiographies have been written about many notable individuals, including Leonardo da Vinci (Freud's analysis of da Vinci is regarded as the first psychobiography), Martin Luther, Mahatma Ghandi, Nathaniel Hawthorne, and Richard Nixon (McAdams, 1988). In some cases, the psychobiographer tries to explain the person's entire life, but in other instances, only specific aspects of the individual's behavior are studied. For example, Simonton (1998) used biographical and historical data to study the impact of stressful events on the mental and physical health of "Mad" King George III between 1760 and 1811. His results showed that the king's health consistently deteriorated following periods of increased stress after a 9-month delay.

Psychobiographies necessarily involve post hoc explanations, with no opportunity to test one's hypotheses about why particular events occurred.

Even so, biography has always involved speculations about psychological processes, usually by writers who were not trained as psychologists. Even though interpretations of case study evidence are always open to debate, the systematic study of historical figures from psychological perspectives adds a new dimension to biography and history.

ILLUSTRATIVE ANECDOTES. Real, concrete examples often have more power than abstract statements of general principles. Researchers and teachers alike often use case studies to illustrate general principles to other researchers and to students. Although this use of case studies may seem of minor importance in behavioral science, we should remember that scientists must often convince others of the usefulness and importance of their findings. Supplementing "hard" empirical data with illustrative case studies may be valuable in this regard. Such case studies can never be - offered as proof of a scientist's assertion, but they can be used to provide concrete, easy-to-remember examples of abstract concepts and processes.

Limitations of the Case Study Approach

Although the case study approach has its uses, it also has noteworthy limitations as a scientific method.

FAILURE TO CONTROL EXTRANEOUS VARIABLES. First, case studies are virtually useless in providing evidence to test behavioral theories or psychological treatments. Because case studies deal with the informal observation of isolated events that occur in an uncontrolled fashion and without comparison information, researchers are unable to assess the viability of alternative explanations of their observations. No matter how plausible the explanations offered for the individual's behavior or for the effectiveness of a given treatment, alternative explanations cannot be ruled out.

Too often, however, people use case studies as evidence for the accuracy of a particular explanation or for the effectiveness of a particular intervention. I once heard on the radio that a particular member of Congress had spoken out against a proposal to tighten restrictions for the purchase of handguns.

According to this member of Congress, such legislation was bound to be ineffective. His reasoning was based on the case of Washington, D.C., a city that has relatively strict handgun controls yet a very high murder rate. Clearly, he argued, the case of Washington shows that gun controls do not reduce violent crime. Can you see the problem with this argument?

His argument is based on case study evidence about a single city rather than on scientific data, and we have absolutely no way of knowing what the effect of handgun control is on the murder rate in Washington, D.C. Perhaps the murder rate would be *even higher* if there were no controls on the purchase of guns. For that matter, it's logically possible that the rate would be lower if there were no gun control. The point is that, without relevant comparison information and control over other variables associated with murder (such as poverty and drug use), no conclusions about the effects of handgun control are possible from case study evidence.

OBSERVER BIASES.   Most case studies rely on the observations of a single researcher. In behavioral science, the researcher is often the participant's psychotherapist. In light of this, we often have no way of determining the reliability or validity of the researcher's observations or interpretations. In addition, because the researcher–observer often has a stake in the outcome of the investigation (such as whether a therapeutic procedure works), we must worry about self-fulfilling prophecies and demand characteristics (see Chapter 9).

Behavioral Research Case Study
A Case Study of a Case Study

Case study approaches to research have been commonly used to describe particular cases of psychopathology or to document the effects of specific psychotherapeutic approaches. In many instances, case studies may be the only way to collect information about unusual phenomena.

Take, for example, the case of Jeffrey, a 28-year-old Israeli who developed posttraumatic stress disorder (PTSD) in the aftermath of a terrorist attack that left him seriously burned and disabled. PTSD is a prolonged psychological reaction to highly traumatic events and is characterized by anxiety, irritability, withdrawal, insomnia, confusion, depression, and other signs of extreme stress. Jeffrey's case was quite severe; he had stopped working, had isolated himself from family and friends, and had become depressed and withdrawn. In their case study of Jeffrey, Bar-Yoseph and Witztum (1992) first described Jeffrey's psychological and behavioral reactions to the attack that nearly killed both his father and him three years earlier. They then presented their approach to helping Jeffrey overcome his problems through psychotherapy.

In the first phase of therapy, the primary goal was to establish a therapeutic relationship with Jeffrey. Because he was so depressed, withdrawn, and pessimistic about the prospect of getting better, the therapists proceeded slowly and carefully, focusing initially on only one of his problems (insomnia) rather than on all of them at once. Interestingly, because his symptoms did not emerge until a year after the attack (such a delay is common in PTSD), he continually refused to acknowledge that his problems were caused by the attack itself. After Jeffrey saw that he was improving, therapy entered a second phase. Week by week, the therapists encouraged Jeffrey to take up one activity that his physical injuries, depression, and apathy had led him to abandon after the attack. Thus, for the first time in three years, he began to mow the yard, go shopping, play soccer, and go to the library. In the third phase of therapy, the therapists helped Jeffrey take yet another step toward psychological recovery—returning to full-time work. Although he had difficulty relating to his coworkers, he found he was again able to face the daily stresses of the working world. Even so, he continued to agonize over the fact that his life was not the way it had been before his problems began. As a result, he viewed the positive changes that had occurred as a result of therapy as simply not good enough.

(continued)

(continued)

Along the way, Jeffrey continued to deny that the terrorist attack was the cause of his difficulties. For whatever reason, he found it too threatening to acknowledge that he was unable to cope with this particular misfortune. Believing that it was essential for Jeffrey to see the connection between the attack and his problems, the therapists tried a number of approaches to show him the link. However, Jeffrey found such efforts too upsetting and insisted that the therapists stop. The therapists finally concluded that it was not in Jeffrey's best interests to force the issue further, and Jeffrey terminated treatment. Periodic follow-ups showed that, even three years later, Jeffrey had maintained the improvements he made during therapy, and he continued to get better.

After describing Jeffrey's case, Bar-Yoseph and Witztum (1992) discussed its implications for understanding and treating PTSD. As we've seen, the conclusions that can be drawn from such studies are tenuous at best. Yet, a carefully documented case can provide other psychotherapists with novel approaches for their own practice, as well as generate hypotheses to be investigated using controlled research strategies.

Summary

1. The principles and empirical findings of behavioral science are probabilistic in nature, describing the reactions of most individuals but recognizing that not everyone will fit the general pattern.

2. Single-case research comes in two basic varieties, single-case experimental designs and case studies, both of which can be traced to the earliest days of behavioral science.

3. Single-case experiments investigate the effects of independent variables on individual research participants. Unlike group designs, in which data are averaged across participants for analysis, each participant's responses are analyzed separately and the data from individual participants are not combined.

4. The most common single-participant designs, variations of the ABA design, involve a baseline period, followed by a period in which the independent variable is introduced. Then the independent variable is withdrawn. More complex designs may involve several periods in which the independent variable is successively reintroduced and then withdrawn.

5. In multiple-I designs, several levels of the independent variable are administered in succession, often with a baseline period between each administration.

6. Multiple baseline designs allow researchers to document that the effects of the independent variable are specific to particular behaviors. Such designs involve the simultaneous study of two or more behaviors, only one of which is hypothesized to be affected by the independent variable.

7. Because averages are not used, the data from single-participant experiments cannot be analyzed using inferential statistics. Rather, effects of the independent variable on behavior are detected through graphic analysis.

8. Single-case experiments are used most frequently to study the effects of basic learning processes and to study the effectiveness of behavior modification in treating behavioral and emotional problems.

9. A case study is a detailed, descriptive study of a single individual, group, or event. The case is described in detail, and conclusions, solutions, or recommendations are offered.

10. Case studies rarely allow a high degree of confidence in the researcher's interpretations of the data because extraneous variables are never controlled and the biases of the researcher may influence his or her observations and interpretations. Even so, case studies are useful in generating new ideas, studying rare phenomena, doing psychological studies of famous people (psychobiography), and serving as illustrative anecdotes.

Key Terms

ABA design (*p. 296*)
ABACA design (*p. 297*)
ABC design (*p. 297*)
case study (*p. 303*)
graphic analysis (*p. 298*)
group design (*p. 293*)
idiographic approach
  (*p. 292*)

interparticipant replication
  (*p. 295*)
interparticipant variance
  (*p. 294*)
intraparticipant replication
  (*p. 295*)
intraparticipant variance (*p. 294*)
multiple baseline design (*p. 298*)

multiple-I design (*p. 297*)
narrative description (*p. 303*)
nomothetic approach
  (*p. 292*)
psychobiography (*p. 304*)
reversal design (*p. 296*)
single-case experimental
  design (*p. 293*)

Questions for Review

1. Distinguish between the nomothetic and idiographic approaches to behavioral science.
2. What criticisms do proponents of single-case experimental designs level against group designs?
3. Is the use of single-case studies a new approach to research in psychology? Explain.
4. Why do single-case researchers believe that the data from individual participants should not be combined, as when we compute a group mean?
5. What is the difference between interparticipant and intraparticipant variance? Which of these types of variance is more closely related to error variance in group experimental designs? Which type is of primary interest to researchers who conduct single-case experiments?
6. Researchers who use group designs replicate their findings by repeating the same (or a similar) experiment on other samples of participants. How do single-case researchers replicate their findings?
7. What is the rationale behind the ABA design?
8. Why is it essential for researchers to establish a stable baseline of behavior during the initial A phase of an ABA design?

9. Under what circumstances is an ABA design relatively useless as a way of testing the effects of an independent variable?
10. Can single-case experimental designs be used to test the effects of various levels of an independent variable (as in a one-way group design)? Explain.
11. How many levels of the independent variable are there in an ABACADA design?
12. What is a multiple baseline design, and when are such designs typically used?
14. How do researchers analyze the data from single-case experiments?
14. In what areas have single-case experiments been primarily used?
15. Discuss the advantages and disadvantages of single-case experimental designs, relative to group designs.
16. What is a case study? Are case studies an example of descriptive, correlational, experimental, or quasi-experimental research?
17. What are four primary reasons that behavioral researchers use case studies?
18. What is a psychobiography?
19. Why are behavioral scientists reluctant to trust case studies as a means of testing hypotheses?

Questions for Discussion

1. Single-case experiments are controversial. Many researchers argue that they are the preferred method of experimental research, but others reject them as being of limited usefulness. Write a paragraph arguing in favor of single-case experiments. Then write a paragraph arguing against their usefulness.

2. How researchers feel about single-case experiments appears to stem, in part, from their personal areas of expertise. Single-case experimental designs lend themselves well to certain areas of investigation, whereas they are difficult, if not impossible, to implement in other areas. What do you see as

some topics in behavioral science for which single-case designs might be most useful? What are some topics for which such designs would be difficult or impossible to use, and why? Are there topics for which group and single-case designs would be equally appropriate?

3. Locate a published experiment that used a group design, and redesign it, if possible, using a single-case approach. Remember that many group designs do not convert easily to single-case experiments.

4. Locate a published experiment that used a single-case design (the *Journal of Applied Behavior Analysis* is a particularly good source of such studies). Redesign the experiment, if possible, as a group experimental design.

5. Conduct a psychobiography of someone you know well. Select a life choice the person has made (such as whom to date or marry, where to attend school, or what career to pursue), and gather as much information as possible to help to *explain* why the person made the choice he or she did. For example, you could delve into factors such as the person's background, previous experiences, personality, relationships, and situational pressures. (Don't rely too heavily on the reasons the person gives; people don't always know why they do things.) When possible, use concepts and theories you have learned in psychology. Write a brief report explaining the person's decision in light of these factors.

6. Having written the case study in Question 5, critically evaluate it. How certain are you that your observations and interpretations are valid? Can you generate alternative, equally plausible explanations of the person's behavior?

15

ETHICAL ISSUES IN BEHAVIORAL RESEARCH

Imagine that you are a student in an introductory psychology course. One of the course requirements is that you participate in research being conducted by faculty in the psychology department. When the list of available studies is posted, you sign up for a study titled "Decision Making." You report to a laboratory in the psychology building and are met by a researcher who tells you that the study in which you will participate involves how people make decisions. You will work with two other research participants on a set of problems and then complete questionnaires about your reactions to the task. The study sounds innocuous and mildly interesting, so you agree to participate.

You and the other two participants then work together on a set of difficult problems. As the three of you reach agreement on an answer to each problem, you give your group's answer to the researcher. After your group has answered all of the problems, the researcher says that, if you wish, he'll tell you how well your group performed on the problems. The three of you agree, so the researcher gives you a score sheet that shows that your group scored in the bottom 10% of all groups he has tested. Nine out of every 10 groups of participants performed better than your group! Not surprisingly, you're somewhat deflated by this feedback.

Then, to make things worse, one of the other participants offhandedly remarks to the researcher that the group's poor performance was mostly *your* fault. Now, you're not only depressed about the group's performance but embarrassed and angry as well. The researcher, clearly uneasy about the other participant's accusation, quickly escorts you to another room where you complete a questionnaire on which you give your reactions to the problem-solving task and the other two participants.

When you finish the questionnaire, the researcher says, "Before you go, let me tell you more about the study you just completed. The study was *not,* as I told you earlier, about decision making. Rather, we are interested in how people respond when they are blamed for a group's failure by other members of the group." The researcher goes on to tell you that your group did not really perform poorly on the decision problems; in fact, he did not even score your group's solutions. You were assigned randomly to the failure condition of the experiment, so you were told your group had performed very poorly. Furthermore, the other two participants were not participants at all but rather confederates—accomplices of the researcher—who were instructed to blame you for the group's failure.

This hypothetical experiment, which is similar to some studies in psychology, raises a number of ethical questions. For example, was it ethical

- for you to be required to participate in a study to fulfill a course requirement?
- for the researcher to mislead you regarding the purpose of the study? (After all, your agreement to participate in the experiment was based on false information about its purpose.)
- for you to be led to think that the other individuals were participants, when they were actually confederates of the researcher?
- for the researcher to lie about your performance on the decision-making test, telling you that your group performed very poorly?
- for the confederate to appear to blame you for the group's failure, making you feel bad?

In brief, you were lied to and humiliated as part of a study in which you had little choice but to participate. As a participant who had participated in this study, how would you feel about how you were treated? As an outsider, how do you evaluate the ethics of this study? Should people be required to participate in research? Is it acceptable to mislead and deceive participants if necessary to obtain needed information? How much distress—psychological or physical—may researchers cause participants in a study?

Behavioral scientists have wrestled with ethical questions such as these for many years. In this chapter, we'll examine many of the ethical issues that behavioral researchers address each time they design and conduct a study.

APPROACHES TO ETHICAL DECISIONS

Most ethical issues in research arise because behavioral scientists have two sets of obligations that sometimes conflict. On one hand, the behavioral researcher's job is to provide information that enhances our understanding of behavioral processes and leads to the improvement of human or animal welfare. This obligation requires that scientists pursue research they believe will be useful in extending knowledge or solving problems. On the other hand, behavioral scientists also have an obligation to protect the rights and welfare of the human and nonhuman participants that they study. When these two obligations coincide, few ethical issues arise. However, when the researcher's obligations to science and society conflict with obligations to protect the rights and welfare of research participants, the researcher faces an ethical dilemma.

The first step in understanding ethical issues in research is to recognize that well-meaning people may disagree—sometimes strongly—about the ethics of particular research procedures. People not only disagree over specific research practices but also often disagree over the fundamental ethical principles that should be used to make ethical decisions. Ethical conflicts often reach an impasse because of basic disagreements regarding how ethical decisions should be made and, indeed, whether they can be made at all.

People tend to adopt one of three general approaches to resolving ethical issues about research. These three approaches differ in terms of the criteria that people use to decide what is right and wrong (Schlenker & Forsyth, 1977). An individual operating from a position of **deontology** maintains that ethics must be judged in light of a universal moral code. Certain actions are inherently unethical and should never be performed regardless of the circumstances. A researcher who operates from a deontological perspective might argue, for example, that lying is immoral in all situations and, thus, that deception in research is always unethical.

In contrast, **ethical skepticism** asserts that concrete and inviolate moral codes such as those proclaimed by the deontologist cannot be formulated. Given the diversity of opinions regarding ethical issues and the absence of consensus regarding ethical standards, skeptics resist those who claim to have an inside route to moral truth. Skepticism does not deny that ethical principles are important but rather insists that ethical rules are arbitrary and relative to culture and time. According to ethical skepticism, ethical decisions must be a matter of each person's own conscience: One should do what one thinks is right and refrain from doing what one thinks is wrong. The final arbiters on ethical questions are individuals themselves. Thus, a skeptic would claim that research ethics cannot be imposed from the outside but rather are a matter of the individual researcher's conscience.

The third approach to ethical decisions is **utilitarian**, one that maintains that judgments regarding the ethics of a particular action depend on the *consequences* of that action. An individual operating from a utilitarian perspective believes that the potential benefits of a particular action should be weighed against the potential costs. If the benefits are sufficiently large relative to the costs, the action is ethically permissible. Researchers who operate from this perspective base decisions regarding whether a particular research procedure is ethical on the benefits and costs associated with using the procedure. As we will discuss, the official guidelines for research enforced by the federal government and most professional organizations, including the American Psychological Association(APA), are essentially utilitarian.

People with different ethical ideologies often have a great deal of difficulty agreeing on which research procedures are permissible and which are not. As you can see, these debates involve not only the ethics of particular research practices, such as deception, but also disagreements about the fundamental principles that should guide ethical decisions. Thus, we should not be surprised that well-meaning people sometimes disagree about the acceptability of certain research methods.

Basic Ethical Guidelines In Depth
What Is Your Ethical Ideology?

To what extent do you agree or disagree with the following statements?

1. Weighing the potential benefits of research against its potential harm to participants could lead to sacrificing the participants' welfare and, hence, is wrong.
2. Scientific concerns sometimes justify potential harm to research participants.
3. If a researcher can foresee any type of harm, no matter how small, he or she should not conduct the study.
4. What is ethical varies from one situation and society to the next.
5. Lying to participants about the nature of a study is always wrong, irrespective of the type of study or the amount of information to be gained.
6. It is possible to develop codes of ethics that can be applied without exception to all psychological research.

A deontologist would agree with statements 1, 3, 5, and 6, and disagree with statements 2 and 4. A skeptic would agree with statement 4 and disagree strongly with statements 5 and 6. How a skeptic would respond to statements 1, 2, and 3 would depend on his or her personal ethics. A utilitarian would agree with statements 2, 4, and 6, and disagree with statements 1, 3, and 5.

Source: From Schlenker and Forsyth, 1977. Reprinted with permission of Barry R. Schlenker and Academic Press.

BASIC ETHICAL GUIDELINES

Whatever their personal feelings about such matters, behavioral researchers are bound by two sets of ethical guidelines. The first involves principles formulated by professional organizations such as the American Psychological Association (APA). The APA's *Ethical Principles of Psychologists and Code of Conduct* (1992) sets forth ethical standards that psychologists must follow in all areas of professional life, including therapy, evaluation, teaching, and research. To help researchers make sound decisions regarding ethical issues, the APA has also published a set of guidelines for research that involves human participants, as well as regulations for the use and care of nonhuman animals in research. Also, the division of the APA for specialists in developmental psychology has set additional standards for research involving children.

Behavioral researchers are also bound by regulations set forth by the federal government, as well as by state and local laws. Concerned about the rights of research participants, the surgeon general of the United States issued a directive in 1966 that required certain kinds of research to be reviewed to ensure the welfare of human research participants. Since then, a series of federal directives has been instituted to protect the rights and welfare of the humans and other animals who participate in research.

The official approach to research ethics in both the APA principles and federal regulations is essentially a utilitarian or pragmatic one. Rather than specifying a rigid set of do's and don'ts, these guidelines require that researchers weigh potential benefits of the research against its potential costs and risks. Thus, in determining whether to conduct a study, researchers must consider its likely benefits and costs. Weighing the pros and cons of a study is called a **cost–benefit analysis**.

Potential Benefits

Behavioral research has five potential benefits that should be considered when a cost–benefit analysis is conducted.

BASIC KNOWLEDGE.   The most obvious benefit of research is that it enhances our understanding of behavioral processes. Of course, studies differ in the degree to which they are expected to enhance knowledge. In a cost–benefit analysis, greater potential risks and costs are considered permissible when the contribution of the research to knowledge is expected to be high.

IMPROVEMENT OF RESEARCH OR ASSESSMENT TECHNIQUES.   Some research is conducted to improve the procedures that researchers use to measure and study behavior. The benefit of such research is not to extend knowledge directly but rather to improve the research enterprise itself. Of course, such research has an indirect effect on knowledge by providing more reliable, valid, useful, or efficient research methods.

PRACTICAL OUTCOMES.   Some studies provide practical benefits by directly improving the welfare of human beings or other animals. For example, research in clinical psychology may improve the quality of psychological assessment and treatment, studies of educational processes may enhance learning in schools, tests of experimental drugs may lead to improved drug therapy, and investigations of prejudice may reduce racial tensions.

BENEFITS FOR RESEARCHERS.   Those who conduct research usually stand to gain from their research activities. First, research serves an important educational function. Through conducting research, students gain firsthand knowledge about the research process and about the topic they are studying. Indeed, college and university students are often required to conduct research for class projects, senior research, master's theses, and doctoral dissertations. Experienced scientists also benefit from research. Not only does research fulfill an educational function for them as it does for students, but also many researchers must conduct research to maintain their jobs and advance in their careers.

BENEFITS FOR RESEARCH PARTICIPANTS.   The people who participate in research may also benefit from their participation. Such benefits are most obvious in clinical research in which participants receive experimental therapies that help them with a particular problem. Research participation also can serve an educational function as participants learn about behavioral science and its methods. Finally, some studies may, in fact, be enjoyable to participants.

Potential Costs

Benefits such as these must be balanced against potential risks and costs of the research. Some of these costs are relatively minor. For example, research participants invest a certain amount of time and effort in a study; their time and effort should not be squandered on research that has limited value.

More serious are risks to participants' mental or physical welfare. Sometimes, in the course of a study, participants may suffer social discomfort, threats to their self-esteem, stress, boredom, anxiety, pain, or other aversive states. Participants may also suffer if the confidentiality of their data is compromised and others learn about their responses. Most serious are studies in which human and nonhuman animals are exposed to conditions that may threaten their health or lives. We'll return to these kinds of costs and how we protect participants against them in a moment.

In addition to risks and costs to the research participants, research has other kinds of costs as well. Conducting research costs money in terms of salaries, equipment, and supplies, and researchers must determine whether their research is justified financially. In addition, some research practices may be detrimental to the profession or to society at large. For example, the use of deception may promote a climate of distrust toward behavioral research.

Balancing Benefits and Costs

The issue facing the researcher, then, is whether the benefits expected from a particular study are sufficient to warrant the expected costs. A study with only limited benefits warrants only minimal costs and risks, whereas a study that may have important benefits may permit greater costs.

Of course, researchers themselves may not be the most objective judges of the merits of a piece of research. For this reason, federal guidelines require that research be approved by an Institutional Review Board (IRB).

The Institutional Review Board

Many years ago, decisions regarding research ethics were left to the conscience of the individual investigator. However, after several cases in which the welfare of human and nonhuman participants was compromised (most of these cases were in medical rather than psychological research), the U.S. government ordered all research involving human participants to be reviewed by an **Institutional Review Board (IRB)** at the investigator's institution. All institutions that receive federal funds (which includes virtually every college and university in the United States) must have an IRB that reviews research conducted with human participants.

To ensure maximum protection for participants, the members of an institution's IRB must come from a variety of both scientific and nonscientific disciplines. In addition, at least one member of the IRB must be a member of the local community who is not associated with the institution in any way.

Researchers who use human participants must submit a written proposal to their institution's IRB for approval. This proposal describes the purpose of the research, the procedures that will be used, and the potential risks to research participants. Although the IRB may exempt certain pieces of research from consideration by the board, most research involving human participants should be submitted for consideration. Research cannot be conducted without the prior approval of the institution's IRB.

Six issues dominate the discussion of ethical issues in research that involves human participants (and, thus, the discussions of the IRB):

- lack of adequate informed consent
- invasion of privacy
- coercion to participate
- potential physical or mental harm
- deception, and
- violation of confidentiality.

In addition, studies that use certain vulnerable groups of people as participants—such as children, prisoners, and pregnant women—may receive special attention. In the following sections, we will discuss each of these issues.

THE PRINCIPLE OF INFORMED CONSENT

One of the primary ways of ensuring that participants' rights are protected is to obtain their informed consent prior to participating in a study. As its name implies, **informed consent** involves informing research participants of the nature of the study and obtaining their explicit agreement to participate. Obtaining informed consent ensures that researchers do not violate people's privacy and that prospective research participants are given enough information about the nature of a study to make a reasoned decision about whether they want to participate.

Obtaining Informed Consent

The general principal governing informed consent states:

> Using language that is reasonably understandable to participants, psychologists inform participants of the nature of the research; they inform participants that they are free to participate or to decline to participate or to withdraw from the research; they explain the foreseeable consequences of declining or withdrawing; they inform participants of significant factors that may be expected to influence their willingness to participate (such as risks, discomforts, adverse effects, or limitations on confidentiality) . . . ; and they explain other aspects about which the prospective participants inquire. (*Ethical Principles*, 1992, p. 1608)

Note that this principle does not require that the investigator divulge everything about the study. Rather, researchers are required to inform participants about features of the research that might influence their willingness to participate in it. Thus, researchers may withhold information about the hypotheses of the study, but they cannot fail to tell participants that they will experience pain or discomfort. Whenever researchers choose to be less than fully candid with a participant, they are obligated to later inform the participant of all relevant details.

To document that informed consent was obtained, an **informed consent form** is typically used.

This form provides the required information about the study and must be signed by the participant or by the participant's legally authorized representative (such as parents if the participants are children). In some cases, informed consent may be given orally but only if a witness is present to attest that informed consent occurred.

Problems with Obtaining Informed Consent

Although few people would quarrel in principle with the notion that participants should be informed about a study and allowed to choose whether or not to participate, certain considerations may either make researchers hesitant to use informed consent or preclude informed consent altogether.

COMPROMISING THE VALIDITY OF THE STUDY. The most common difficulty arises when fully informing participants about a study would compromise the validity of the data. People often act quite differently when they are under scrutiny than when they don't think they are being observed. Furthermore, divulging the nature of the study may sensitize participants to aspects of their behavior of which they normally are not aware. It would be fruitless, for example, for a researcher to tell participants, "This is a study of nonverbal behavior. During the next 5 minutes, researchers will be rating your expression, gestures, body position, and movement. Please act naturally." Thus, researchers sometimes wish to observe people without revealing to the participants that they are being observed, or at least without telling them what aspect of their behavior is being studied.

PARTICIPANTS WHO ARE UNABLE TO GIVE INFORMED CONSENT. Certain classes of people are unable to give valid consent. Children, for example, are neither cognitively nor legally able to make such informed decisions. Similarly, individuals who are mentally retarded or who are out of touch with reality (such as people who are psychotic) cannot be expected to give informed consent. When one's research calls for participants who cannot provide valid consent, consent must be obtained from the parent or legal guardian of the participant.

LUDICROUS CASES OF INFORMED CONSENT. Some uses of informed consent would be ludicrous because obtaining participants' consent would impose a greater burden than not obtaining it. For a researcher who was counting the number of people riding in cars that passed a particular intersection, obtaining informed consent would be both impossible and unnecessary.

Federal guidelines permit certain limited kinds of research to be conducted without obtaining informed consent. An IRB may waive the requirement of informed consent if (1) the research involves no more than minimal risk to participants, (2) the waiver of informed consent will not adversely affect the rights and welfare of participants, and (3) the research could not feasibly be carried out if informed consent were required. For example, a researcher observing patterns of seating on public buses would probably not be required to obtain participants' informed consent because the risk to participants is minimal, failure to obtain their consent would not adversely affect their welfare and rights, and the research could not be carried out if people riding buses were informed in advance that their choice of seats was being observed.

Developing Your Research Skills
Elements of an Informed Consent Form

An informed consent form should contain each of the following elements:

- a brief description of why the study is being conducted
- a description of the activities in which the participant will engage
- a brief description of the risks entailed in the study, if any
- a statement informing participants that they may refuse to participate in the study and may withdraw from the study at any time without being penalized
- a statement regarding how the confidentiality of participants' responses will be protected
- encouragement for participants to ask any questions they may have about their participation in the study
- instructions regarding how to contact the researcher after the study is completed
- signature lines for both the researcher and the participant

A sample informed consent form containing each of these elements follows:

Experiment #15

The experiment in which you will participate is designed to study people's reactions to various kinds of words. If you agree to participate, you will be seated in front of a computer monitor. Strings of letters will be flashed on the screen in pairs; the first string of letters in each pair will always be a real word, and the second string of letters may be either a real word or a nonword. You will push the blue key if the letters spell a real word and the green key if the letters do not spell a word.

There are no risks associated with participating in this study. You are under no pressure to participate in this study and should feel free to decline to participate if you wish. Furthermore, even if you agree to participate, you may withdraw from the study at any time. You will not be penalized in any way if you decide not to participate or stop your participation before the end of the study. No information that identifies you personally will be collected; thus, your responses are anonymous and fully confidential.

Please feel free to ask the researcher if you have questions. If you have questions, comments, or concerns after participating today, you may contact the researcher at 636-4099 or the researcher's supervisor (Dr. R. Hamrick) at 636-2828.

If you agree to participate in the study today, sign and date this form on the lines below.

_____
Participant's signature   Today's date

_____
Researcher's signature

INVASION OF PRIVACY

The right to privacy is a person's right to decide "when, where, to whom, and to what extent his or her attitudes, beliefs, and behavior will be revealed" to other people (Singleton, Straits, Straits, & McAllister, 1988, p. 454). The APA ethical guidelines do not offer explicit guidelines regarding **invasion of privacy**, noting only that "the ethical investigator will assume responsibility for undertaking a study involving covert investigation in private situations only after very careful consideration and consultation" (American Psychological Association, 1992, p. 39). Thus, the circumstances under which researchers may collect data without participants' knowledge is left to the investigator (and the investigator's IRB) to judge.

Most researchers believe that research involving the observation of people in *public places* (shopping in a store or sitting in a park, for example) does not constitute invasion of privacy. However, if people are to be observed under circumstances in which they reasonably expect privacy, invasion of privacy may be an issue.

Developing Your Research Skills
You Be the Judge: What Constitutes Invasion of Privacy?

In your opinion, which, if any, of these actual studies constitute an unethical invasion of privacy?

- Men using a public restroom are observed surreptitiously by a researcher hidden in a toilet stall, who records the time they take to urinate (Middlemist, Knowles, & Matter, 1976).
- A researcher pretends to be a lookout for gay men having sex in a public restroom. On the basis of the men's car license plates, the researcher tracks down the participants through the Department of Motor Vehicles. Then, under the guise of another study, he interviews them in their homes (Humphreys, 1975).
- Researchers covertly film people who strip the parts from seemingly abandoned cars (Zimbardo, 1969).
- Participants waiting for an experiment are videotaped, but not observed, without their prior knowledge or consent. However, they are given the option of erasing the tapes if they do not want their tapes to be used for research purposes (Ickes, 1982).
- Researchers stage a shoplifting episode in a drugstore, and shoppers' reactions are observed (Gelfand, Hartmann, Walder, & Page, 1973).
- Researchers hide under dormitory beds and eavesdrop on college students' conversations (Henle & Hubbell, 1938).
- Researchers approach members of the other sex on a college campus and ask them to have sex (Clark & Hatfield, 1989).

What criteria did you use to decide which, if any, of these studies are acceptable to you?

COERCION TO PARTICIPATE

All ethical guidelines insist that potential participants must not be coerced into participating in research. **Coercion to participate** occurs when participants agree to participate because of real or implied pressure from some individual who has authority or influence over them. One common example involves cases in which professors ask their students to participate in research. Other examples include employees in business and industry who are asked to participate in research by their employers, military personnel who are required to serve as participants, prisoners who are asked to volunteer for research, and clients who are asked by their therapists or physicians to provide data. What all of these classes of participants have in common is that they may believe, correctly or incorrectly, that refusing to participate will have negative consequences for them—a lower course grade, putting one's job in jeopardy, being reprimanded by one's superiors, a loss of privileges, or simply displeasing an important person.

Researchers must respect an individual's freedom to decline to participate in research or to discontinue participation at any time. Furthermore, to ensure that participants are not indirectly coerced by offering exceptionally high incentives, the guidelines state that researchers cannot "offer excessive or inappropriate financial or other inducements to obtain research participants, particularly when it might tend to coerce participation" (*Ethical Principles,* 1992, Principle 6.14). In other words, researchers may not offer unreasonably large sums of money to get people to volunteer.

Furthermore, when research participation is part of a course requirement or opportunity for students to earn extra credit in a class, students must be given the choice of alternative activities for filling the requirement or earning the credit (*Ethical Principles,* 1992, Principle 6.11d). So, when university and college students are asked to participate in research, they must be given the option of fulfilling the requirement in an alternative fashion, such as by writing a paper that would require as much time and effort as serving as a research participant.

Although most universities permit students to participate in research as part of course requirements (assuming that an alternative is available for those who do not wish to participate), IRBs hesitate to allow college professors to ask students in their own courses to participate in their own research. If I walk into my own class and ask my students to volunteer for a study that I am conducting, the students might reasonably wonder whether their decision will affect how I view them and possibly even their grade. Thus, many of them may feel compelled to participate in my study. Typically, students should be given a selection of studies from which to choose, and professors should not know who does and does not participate in their own studies.

PHYSICAL AND MENTAL STRESS

Most behavioral research is innocuous, and the vast majority of participants are not at any risk of physical or psychological harm. However, because many important topics in behavioral science involve how people or other animals respond to unpleasant physical or psychological events, researchers sometimes design studies to investigate the effects of experiences such as stress, failure, fear, and pain. Researchers find it difficult to study such topics if they are prevented from exposing their participants to at least small amounts of physical or mental stress. But how much discomfort may a researcher inflict on participants?

At the extremes, most people tend to agree regarding the amount of discomfort that is permissible. For example, most people agree that an experiment that leads participants to think they are dying would be highly unethical. (One study did just that by injecting participants, without their knowledge, with a drug that caused them to stop breathing temporarily [Campbell, Sanderson, & Laverty, 1964]). On the other hand, few people object to studies that involve only minimal risk. **Minimal risk** is "risk that is no greater in probability and severity than that ordinarily encountered in daily life or during the performance of routine physical or psychological examinations or tests" (*Official IRB Guidebook,* 1986). We all experience mildly negative events in the course of our daily lives—annoyances, awkward social interactions, frustration, mild fears, minor failures, and so on—so exposing participants to these kinds of events is generally not a problem.

Between these extremes, however, considerable controversy arises regarding the amount of physical and mental distress that should be permitted in research. In large part, the final decision must be left to individual investigators and the IRB at their institutions. The decision is often based on a cost–benefit analysis of the research. Research procedures that cause stress or pain may be allowed only if the potential benefits of the research are extensive and only if the participant agrees to participate after being fully informed of the possible risks.

Even if the study does not seem to involve more than minimal risk, certain participants may find something about the procedure troubling, so researchers should always be vigilant for unexpected adverse effects. For example, a participant in a study of mood may become upset when viewing photographs depicting violent scenes because of a personal experience. Researchers are obligated to report any adverse effects that the study may have on participants to the IRB immediately.

When a study is deemed to involve more than minimal risk to participants, certain additional safeguards are often used. For example, the lead investigator may be required to monitor the participants more closely, follow-up with participants even after the study is over, and make ongoing reports to the IRB about whether any evidence of adverse effects of the study is detected.

DECEPTION

Perhaps no research practice has evoked as much controversy among behavioral researchers as **deception**. Fifty years ago methodological deception was rare, but the use of deception increased dramatically during the 1960s (Christensen, 1988). Although some areas of behavioral research use deception rarely, if at all, it is common in other areas (Adair, Dushenko, & Lindsay, 1985; Gross & Fleming, 1982).

Behavioral scientists use deception for a number of reasons. The most common one is to prevent participants from learning the true purpose of a study so that their behavior will not be artificially affected. In addition to presenting participants with a false purpose of the study, deception may involve:

- using an experimental confederate who poses as another participant or as an uninvolved bystander
- providing false feedback to participants
- presenting two related studies as unrelated
- giving incorrect information regarding stimulus materials

In each instance, researchers use deception because they believe it is necessary for studying the topic of interest.

Objections to Deception

The objections that have been raised regarding the use of deception can be classified roughly into two basic categories. The most obvious objection is a strictly ethical one. Some researchers maintain that lying and deceit are immoral and reprehensible acts, even when they are used for good purposes such as research. Baumrind (1971) argued, for example, that "fundamental moral principles of reciprocity and justice are violated" when researchers use deception. She added that "scientific ends, however laudable they may be, do not themselves justify the use of means that in ordinary transactions would be regarded as reprehensible" (p. 890). This objection is obviously a deontological one, based on the violation of moral rules.

The second objection is pragmatic. Even if deception can be justified on the grounds that it leads to positive outcomes (the utilitarian perspective), it may lead to undesirable consequences. For example, because of widespread deception, research participants may enter research studies already suspicious of what the researcher tells them. In addition, participants who learn that they have been deceived may come to distrust behavioral scientists and the research process in general, undermining the public's trust in psychology and related fields. Smith and Richardson (1983) found that people who participated in research that involved deception perceived psychologists as less trustworthy than those who participated in research that did not involve deception.

Although the first objection is a purely ethical one for which there is no objective resolution, the second concern has been examined empirically. Several studies have tested how research participants react when they learn they have been deceived by a researcher. In most studies that assessed reactions to deception, the vast majority of participants (usually over 90%) say they realize that deception is sometimes necessary for methodological reasons and report positive feelings about their participation in the study. Even Milgram (1963), who has been soundly criticized for his use of deception, found that less than 2% of his participants reported having negative feelings about their participation in his experiment on obedience. (See the box, "The Milgram Experiments" later in the chapter.)

Interestingly, researchers are typically more concerned about the dangers of deception than are research participants themselves (Fisher & Fryberg, 1994). Research participants do not seem to regard deception in research settings in the same way they view lying in everyday life. Instead, they view it as a necessary aspect of certain kinds of research (Smith & Richardson, 1983). As long as they are informed about details of the study afterward, participants generally do not mind being misled for good reasons (Christensen, 1988). In fact, research shows that, assuming they are properly debriefed, participants report *more* positive reactions to their participation and higher ratings of a study's scientific value if the study includes deception (Coulter, 1986; Smith & Richardson, 1983; Straits, Wuebben, & Majka, 1972). Findings such as these should not be taken to suggest that deception is always an acceptable practice. However, they do show that, when properly handled, deception per se need not have negative consequences for research participants.

Both APA and federal guidelines state that researchers should not use deception unless they have determined that the use of deception is justified by the research's possible scientific, educational, or applied value, and that the research could not be feasibly conducted without the use of deception. Importantly, researchers are never justified in deceiving participants about aspects of the study that might affect their willingness to participate. In the process of obtaining participants' informed consent, the researcher must accurately inform participants regarding possible risks, discomfort, or unpleasant experiences.

Whenever deception is used, participants must be informed about the subterfuge "as early as it is feasible" (*Ethical Principles,* 1992, Principle 6.15c). Usually participants are debriefed immediately after they participate, but occasionally researchers wait until the entire study is over and all of the data have been collected.

CONFIDENTIALITY

The information obtained about research participants in the course of a study is confidential. **Confidentiality** means that the data that participants provide may be used only for purposes of the research and may not be divulged to others. When others have access to participants' data, confidentiality is violated.

Admittedly, in most behavioral research, participants would experience no adverse consequences if confidentiality were violated and others obtained access to their data. (Would you care if other people learned that your reaction time to a visual stimulus was 208 milliseconds?) In some

cases, however, the information collected during a study may be quite sensitive, and disclosure could have negative repercussions for the participant. For example, issues of confidentiality have been paramount among health psychologists who study people who have tested positive for HIV or AIDS (Rosnow, Rotheram-Borus, Ceci, Blanck, & Koocher, 1993).

The easiest way to eliminate concerns with confidentiality is to ensure that participants' responses are *anonymous.* Data are anonymous if they include no information that could be used to identify a particular participant. Confidentiality will obviously not be a problem if participants cannot be identified. Keep in mind, however, that participants can be identified by many kinds of information—not only their name but also their address, telephone number, social security number, and other characteristics. For example, if a small college has only five students from Greece, and only two of them (a male and a female) are participating in research, collecting information about participants' nationality and gender would allow those participants to be identified personally, so the data are not anonymous.

In some instances, researchers need to know the identity of a research participant. For example, they may need to collate data collected in two different research sessions. To do so, they must know which participants' data are which, but they must take steps to protect the confidentiality of the data even while having access to participants' identities. Several practices are used to solve this problem. Sometimes participants are given codes to label their data that allow researchers to connect different parts of their data without divulging their identities. In cases in which the data are in no way potentially sensitive or embarrassing, names may be collected. In such cases, however, researchers must remove all information that might identify a participant after that information is no longer needed.

Confidentiality sometimes becomes an issue when researchers report the results of a study, for example, in a journal article or conference presentation. Occasionally, researchers wish to present information about a particular individual, either because the research is a case study of that person or because they wish to use the person to illustrate a point. Researchers in clinical psychology, for example, may wish to describe aspects of a particular client's case. When descriptions of real people are used, researchers must ensure that the person's privacy and confidentiality are strictly protected. Typically, this is done by changing details to disguise the case, but one must be careful not to change the description of variables that are psychologically relevant to the case. Another option is for the researcher to write the description of the case he or she wishes to use (protecting privacy as much as possible), show it to the person being described, and obtain written permission from the individual to use the case material (*APA Publication Manual,* 2009; Clifft, 1986).

Behavioral Research Case Study
The Milgram Experiments

Perhaps no research has been the center of as much ethical debate as Stanley Milgram's (1963) studies of obedience to authority. Milgram was interestedin factors that affect the degree to which people obey an authority figure's orders, even when those orders lead them to harm another person. To examinethis question, he tested participants' reactions to an experimenter who ordered them to harm another participant.

THE STUDY

Participants were recruited by mail to participate in a study of memory and learning. Upon arriving at a laboratory at Yale University, the participant met an experimenter and another participant who was participating in the same experimental session.

The experiment was described as a test of the effects of punishment on learning. Based on a drawing, one participant was assigned the role of teacher and the other participant was assigned the role of learner. The teacher watched as the learner was strapped into a chair and fitted with an electrode on his wrist. The teacher was then taken to an adjoining room and seated in front of an imposing shock generator that would deliver electric shocks to the other participant. The shock generator had a row of 30 switches, each of which was marked with a voltage level, beginning with 15 volts and proceeding in 15-volt increments to 450 volts.

The experimenter told the teacher to read the learner a list of word pairs, such as *blue–box* and *wild–duck*. After reading the list, the teacher would test the learner's memory by giving him the first word in each pair. The learner was then to say the second word in the pair. If the learner remembered the word correctly, the teacher was to go to the next word on the list. However, if the learner answered incorrectly, the teacher was to deliver a shock by pressing one of the switches. The teacher was to start with the switch marked *15 volts,* and then increase the voltage one level each time the learner missed a word.

Once the study was under way, the learner began to make a number of errors. At first, the learner didn't react to the shocks, but as the voltage increased, he began to object. When the learner received 120 volts, he simply complained that the shocks were painful. As the voltage increased, he first asked and then demanded that the experimenter unstrap him from the chair and stop the study. However, the experimenter told the teacher that "the experiment requires that you continue." With increasingly strong shocks, the learner began to yell, then pound on the wall, and after 300 volts, scream in anguish. Most of the teachers were reluctant to continue, but the experimenter insisted that they follow through with the experimental procedure. After 330 volts, the learner stopped responding altogether; the teacher was left to imagine that the participant had fainted or, worse, died. Even then, the experimenter instructed the teacher to treat no response as a wrong answer and to deliver the next shock to the now silent learner.

As you probably know (or have guessed), the learner was in fact a confederate of the experimenter and received no shocks. The real participants, of course, thought they were actually shocking another person. Yet 65% of the participants delivered all 30 shocks—up to 450 volts—even though the learner had protested, screamed in anguish, and then fallen silent. This level of obedience was entirely unexpected and attests both to the power of authority figures to lead people to perform harmful actions and to the compliance of research participants.

THE ETHICAL ISSUES

Milgram's research sparked an intense debate on research ethics that continues today. Milgram's study involved virtually every ethical issue that can be raised.

- Participants were misled about the purpose of the study.
- A confederate posed as another participant.
- Participants were led to believe they were shocking another person, a behavior that, both at the moment and in retrospect, may have been very disturbing to them.
- Participants experienced considerable stress as the experiment continued: They sweated, trembled, stuttered, swore, and laughed nervously as they delivered increasingly intense shocks.
- Participants' attempts to withdraw from the study were discouraged by the experimenter's insistence that they continue.

What is your reaction to Milgram's experiment? Did Milgram violate basic ethical principles in this research?

DEBRIEFING

At the end of most studies, researchers spend a few minutes debriefing the participants. A good **debriefing** accomplishes four goals. First, the debriefing clarifies the nature of the study for participants. Although the researcher may have withheld certain information at the beginning of the study, the participant should be more fully informed after it is over. This does not require that the researcher give a lecture regarding the area of research, only that the participant leave the study with a sense of what was being studied and how his or her participation contributed to knowledge in an area.

If the study involved deception, the researcher must divulge it. Occasionally, participants are angered or embarrassed when they find they were fooled by the researcher. Of course, if a researcher seems smug about the deception, the participant is likely to react negatively. Thus, researchers should be sure to explain the reasons for any deception that occurred, express their apologies for misleading the participant, and allow the participant to express his or her feelings about being deceived.

The second goal of debriefing is to remove any stress or other negative consequences that the study may have induced. For example, if participants were provided with false feedback about their performance

on a test, the deception should be explained. In cases in which participants have been led to perform embarrassing or socially undesirable actions, researchers must be sure that participants leave with no bad feelings about what they have done.

A third goal of debriefing is for the researcher to obtain participants' reactions to the study itself. Often, if carefully probed, participants will reveal that they didn't understand part of the instructions, were suspicious about aspects of the procedure, were disturbed by the study, or had heard about the study from other people. Such revelations may require modifications in the procedure.

The fourth goal of debriefing is more intangible. Participants should leave the study feeling good about their participation. Researchers should convey their genuine appreciation for participants' time and cooperation, and give participants the sense that their participation was important.

COMMON COURTESY

A few years ago I conducted an informal survey of students who had participated in research as part of a course requirement in introductory psychology. In this survey, I asked what problems they had encountered in their participation. The vast majority of their responses did not involve violations of basic ethical principles involving coercion, harm, deception, or violation of confidentiality. Rather, their major complaints had to do with how they were treated *as people* during the course of the study. Their chief complaints were that (1) the researcher failed to show up or was late, (2) the researcher was not adequately prepared, (3) the researcher was cold, abrupt, or downright rude, and (4) the researcher failed to show appreciation for the participant.

Aside from the formal guidelines, ethical research requires a large dose of common courtesy. The people who participate in research are contributing their time and energy, often without compensation. They deserve the utmost in common courtesy.

VULNERABLE POPULATIONS

Each of the ethical considerations that I have described apply to all studies that involve human participants, but research that uses participants from certain **vulnerable populations** carry some additional safeguards. Federal regulations require that IRBs give special consideration to protecting the welfare of certain protected groups, such as children, prisoners, people who have impaired decisional capacity, people who are at risk for suicide, and pregnant women, fetuses, and newborns.

We have already mentioned that children and adolescents below the age of legal consent may not participate in research without permission from a parent or legal guardian because they may not fully understand the risks associated with research and may be easily pressured to participate. However, even though an adult's permission is required, minors who are over the age of 12 should be given the right to assent or decline to participate. In other words, minors over 12 years cannot be forced to participate in research against their will even if a parent or guardian gives their consent.

Prisoners are singled out as a special case for three reasons. First, because their lives are controlled by prison officials, they must be protected from the possibility of being forced to participate in studies against their will. Second, prisoners' daily lives are so deprived that even very small induce-

ments to participate in research, which would not influence people on the outside, may lead them to consent to participate in studies they would really rather not do. Third, steps must be taken to be sure that prisoners do not erroneously believe that agreeing to participate in research will positively affect how they are treated by prison staff or parole boards.

Special attention is given to people who have a mental disability or cognitive impairment to be certain that they are capable of understanding the research well enough to give their informed consent. If so, they should be treated like other adults; if not, permission must be obtained from a legal guardian if possible. In many cases, however, adults may be impaired yet have no one who is legally responsible for them.

Many complex issues surround studies that involve participants who might be at risk for committing suicide. For example, imagine that we are conducting research on an intervention for depressed patients who are known to be suicidal. Is it ethical to assign some of our participants to a control group that receives no treatment? Similarly, researchers normally must allow participants to withdraw from a study whenever they wish without question, but what about suicidal participants whose premature withdrawal from a treatment study might increase the likelihood that they will kill themselves? As with most ethical issues in research, there are no easy answers, but investigators and IRBs are charged with considering them carefully.

Protections for pregnant women, fetuses, and newborn babies apply mostly to biomedical studies in which certain drugs or procedures might harm the woman, the fetus, or the baby. Occasionally, however, such concerns arise in behavioral research. For example, we might hesitate to expose a pregnant woman to the same levels of stress or physical exertion that we would otherwise use in a study, and we might not want to use pregnant women in studies of the effects of substances such as caffeine, alcohol, or hormones. Researchers must also be careful regarding the procedures they use on newborns. Procedures that might be fine for a 1-year-old child might be dangerous with a neonate.

In Depth
Internet Research Ethics

An increasing amount of behavioral research is being conducted using the Internet. Many researchers use the Internet to collect data, having participants complete questionnaires or participate in experiments online rather than in a research laboratory. In addition, the Internet itself provides new sources of data in the form of what people write in blogs, chat rooms, and social networking sites (such as Facebook). Of course, all of the ethical issues that we have discussed so far apply equally to research conducted using the Internet, but Internet studies also introduce some new ethical concerns for researchers to consider. Let me mention just a few:

- All ethical guidelines require that studies that include participants younger than 18 years obtain consent from a parent or legal guardian. But, how do we know how old our participants are when we conduct an online study?
- Researchers are required to protect the confidentiality of participants' responses, but is any exchange of information over the Internet ever truly secure? Not only can data be intercepted between the participant and the researcher, but computer systems are always vulnerable to hackers.
- Unlike paper questionnaires and computer disks that researchers can lock in a secure location to protect participants' information, data that are collected online often reside on a computer server that is owned and managed by some third party. Thus, the researcher must depend on others to protect the confidentiality of the data.
- Earlier I mentioned that when data are collected face-to-face, researchers can make participants' responses anonymous by removing all information that identifies them personally. This can also be done with online data, but usually special steps must be taken to erase the IP address that identifies the computer on which the participant completed the study.

None of these problems are insurmountable, but researchers who are accustomed to conducting research face-to-face with participants must think carefully about how collecting data via the Internet raises new ethical issues.

Developing Your Research Skills
Ethical Decisions

After reading the description of each case study that follows, consider whether the study raises any ethical issues. If so, what steps could a researcher take to ensure that participants were treated ethically? Would these steps affect the validity of the study? Try to redesign the study so that it addresses the original research question while eliminating any questionable ethical practices.

Case 1. To study the effects of an unpleasant and demeaning social experience, Farina, Wheeler, and Mehta (1991) sent unsuspecting participants to a faculty member's office rather than to a research lab. When the participant arrived, a male professor in the office expressed anger and annoyance, criticized the participant for mistakenly reporting to the wrong room, and harshly directed the participant to the "correct" laboratory where his or her reactions were assessed.

Case 2. Festinger and Carlsmith (1959) had participants engage in a very boring task, and then asked them whether they would help the researcher by telling the next participant that the task was actually interesting and exciting. Participants were told they would be paid either $1 or $20 for telling this lie. All participants agreed to lie to the other person. (The experiment was designed to see if the amount of money they were paid to lie affected participants' attitudes toward the boring task.)

Case 3. To study learned helplessness in animals, Seligman, Maier, and Geer (1968) subjected dogs to inescapable electric shock. Four dogs were suspended in a cloth hammock and shocked for 64 trials through electrodes taped to their hind feet. A day later, they were placed in shuttle boxes from which they could escape when

(continued)

(continued)

shocked, but because they had developed learned helplessness, the dogs passively accepted the shock rather than escape. The researchers then used conditioning to teach the dogs to escape the shock.

Case 4. In a study of embarrassment, Leary, Landel, and Patton (1996) instructed participants to sing "Feelings" (a sappy song from the 1970s that even good singers sound foolish singing) into a tape-recorder while they were alone in a soundproof chamber, assuring participants that no one could hear them singing. When the participant was finished, however, the researcher returned and played back a portion of the tape, ostensibly to see whether the recorder had functioned properly, but the real reason was to embarrass the participants.

Case 5. As male participants walked alone or in groups along a path to a parking lot, Harari, Harari, and White (1995) simulated a rape. A male confederate grabbed a screaming female confederate, put his hand over her mouth, and dragged her into the bushes. Observers recorded the number of participants who offered help. (Before participants could actually intervene, a researcher stopped them and told them that the "rape" was part of a study.)

Case 6. In a study of attitude change following counterattitudinal behavior, Schlenker, Forsyth, Leary, and Miller (1980) asked participants to make a persuasive videotaped speech on a topic with which they personally disagreed (not wearing seat belts in cars) that would supposedly be shown to elementary school children. After participants were paid for their help, they found out that observers questioned their morality, saying that the participant had been "bribed" to make the anti–seat belt speech.

Case 7. To study the effects of social rejection on judgments of other people, Twenge, Baumeister, Tice, and Stucke (2001) gave college-age participants feedback, supposedly based on a questionnaire that they had completed earlier, that said: "You're the type who will end up alone later in life. You may have friends and relationships now, but by your mid-20s most of these will have drifted away. You may even marry or have several marriages, but these are likely to be short-lived and not continue into your 30s. Relationships don't last, and when you're past the age where people are constantly forming new relationships, the odds are you'll end up being alone more and more." After receiving this feedback, participants rated another individual who was applying for a job as a research assistant.

ETHICAL PRINCIPLES IN RESEARCH WITH NONHUMAN ANIMALS

The APA *Ethical Principles* contain standards regarding the ethical treatment of animals, and the APA has published a more detailed discussion of these issues in *Guidelines for Ethical Conduct in the Care and Use of Animals*. These guidelines are noticeably less detailed than those involving human participants, but they are no less explicit regarding the importance of treating nonhuman animals in a humane and ethical fashion.

These guidelines stipulate that all research that uses nonhuman animals must be monitored closely by a person who is experienced in the care and use of laboratory animals and that a veterinarian must be available for consultation. Furthermore, all personnel who are involved in animal research, including students, must be familiar with these guidelines and adequately trained regarding the use and care of animals. Thus, if

you should become involved with such research, you are obligated to acquaint yourself with these guidelines and abide by them at all times.

The facilities in which laboratory animals are housed are closely regulated by the National Institutes of Health, as well as federal, state, and local laws. Obviously, animals must be housed under humane and healthful conditions. The facilities should be inspected by a veterinarian at least twice a year.

Advocates of animal rights are most concerned, of course, about the experimental procedures to which the animals are subjected during research. APA guidelines direct researchers to "make reasonable efforts to minimize the discomfort, infection, illness, and pain of animal participants," and require the investigator to justify the use of all procedures that involve more than momentary or slight pain to the animal: "A procedure subjecting animals to pain, stress, or privation is used only when an alternative procedure is unavailable and the goal is justified by its prospective scientific, educational, or applied value" (*Ethical Principles*, 1992, p. 1609, Standard 6.20). Procedures that involve more than minimal pain or distress require strong justification.

The APA regulations also provide guidelines for the use of surgical procedures, the study of animals in field settings, the use of animals for educational (as opposed to research) purposes, and the disposition of animals at the end of a study.

In Depth
Behavioral Research and Animal Rights

During the 1980s, several animal rights organizations were formed to protest the use of animals for research purposes. Some animal rights groups have simply pressured researchers to treat animals more humanely, whereas others have demanded that the practice of using animals in research be stopped entirely. For example, People for the Ethical Treatment of Animals (PETA)—the largest animal rights organization in the world—opposes animal research of all kinds, arguing that animals should not be eaten, used for clothing, or experimented on. Although PETA does not endorse violence, members of certain other groups have resorted to terrorist tactics, burning or bombing labs, stealing or releasing lab animals, and ruining experiments. For example, members of the Animal Liberation Front vandalized animal research labs at the University of Michigan, causing $2 million worth of damage, destroying data, and abducting animals (Azar, 1999). (Ironically, the animals were released in a field near the university, and, unprepared to live outside a lab, many died before being rescued by researchers.)

Like most ethical issues in research, debates involving the use of animals in research arise because of the competing pressures to advance knowledge and improve welfare on one hand and to protect animals on the other. Undoubtedly, animals have been occasionally mistreated, either by being housed under inhumane conditions or by being subjected to unnecessary pain or distress during the research itself. However, most psychological research does not hurt the animals, and researchers who conduct research on animals argue that occasional abuses should not blind us to the value of behavioral research that uses animal participants. The vast majority of animal researchers treat their nonhuman participants with great care and concern.

Upon receiving the APA's Award for Distinguished Professional Contributions, Neal Miller (1985) chronicled in his address the significant contributions of animal research. In defending the use of animals in behavioral research, Miller noted that animal research has contributed to the rehabilitation of neuromuscular disorders, understanding and reducing stress and pain, developing drugs for the treatment of various animal problems, exploring processes involved in substance abuse, improving memory deficits in the elderly, increasing the survival rate for premature infants, and the development of behavioral approaches in psychotherapy. To this list of contributions from behavioral science, Joseph Murray, a 1990 winner of the Nobel Prize, adds the many advances in medicine that would have been impossible without animal research, including vaccines (for polio, smallpox, and measles, for example), dialysis, organ transplants, chemotherapy, and insulin (Monroe, 1991). Even animal welfare has been improved through research using animals; for example, dogs and cats today live longer and healthier lives than they once did because of research involving vaccines and medicines for pets (Szymczyk, 1995).

To some animal rights activists, the benefits of the research are beside the point. They argue that, like people, nonhuman animals have certain moral rights. As a result, human beings have no right to subject nonhuman animals to pain, stress, and sometimes death, or even to submit animals to any research against their will.

In an ideal world, we would be able to solve problems of human suffering without using nonhuman animals in research. But in our less than perfect world, most behavioral researchers subscribe to the utilitarian view that the potential benefits of animal research often outweigh the potential costs. Several scientific organizations, including the American Association for the Advancement of Science and the APA, have endorsed the use of animals in research, teaching, and education while, of course, insisting that research animals be treated with utmost care and respect ("APA Endorses Resolution," 1990).

SCIENTIFIC MISCONDUCT

In addition to principles governing the treatment of human and animal participants, behavioral researchers are bound by general ethical principles involving the conduct of scientific research. Such principles are not specific to behavioral research but apply to all scientists regardless of their discipline. Most scientific organizations have set ethical standards for their members to guard against **scientific misconduct**.

The National Academy of Sciences identifies three major categories of scientific misconduct. The first category involves the most serious and blatant forms of scientific dishonesty, such as fabrication (invention of data or cases), falsification (intentional distortion of data or results), and plagiarism (claiming credit for another's work). The APA *Ethical Principles* likewise addresses these issues, stating that researchers must not fabricate data or report false results. Furthermore, if they discover significant errors in their findings or analyses, researchers are obligated to take steps to correct such errors. Likewise, researchers do not plagiarize others' work, presenting "substantial portions or elements of another's work or data as their own . . . " (*Ethical Principles,* 1992, Standard 6.22).

A study of graduate students and faculty members in chemistry, civil engineering, microbiology, and sociology found that between 6% and 9% of the 4,000 respondents reported that they had direct knowledge of faculty members who had plagiarized or falsified their data. (This statistic does not indicate that 6–9% of researchers plagiarize or falsify; a single instance of dishonesty may be known by several people.) A meta-analysis of 18 studies of research misconduct revealed that, across studies, about 2% of scientists admit that they have falsified or fabricated data at least once (which almost certainly underestimates the true prevalence), and 14% report that they know of colleagues who have done so (Fanelli, 2009). (Again, this does not indicate that 14% of scientists have engaged in fraud.) Among the graduate students, between 10% and 20% (depending on the discipline) reported that their student peers had falsified data, and over 30% of the faculty reported knowledge of student plagiarism (Swazey, Anderson, & Lewis, 1993).

"THEY DISCOVERED THAT YOUR RESEARCH IS FRAUDULENT, SO YOUR GRANT WILL BE FUNDED IN COUNTERFEIT BILLS."

Source: SCIENCECARTOONSPLUS.COM © 2000 by Sidney Harris.

Although not rampant, such abuses are disturbingly common. Most behavioral scientists agree with former director of the National Science Foundation, Walter Massey, who observed that "Few things are more damaging to the scientific enterprise than falsehoods—be they the result of error, self-deception, sloppiness, and haste, or, in the worst case, dishonesty" (Massey, 1992). Because science relies so heavily on honesty and is so severely damaged by dishonesty, the penalties for scientific misconduct, whether by professional researchers or by students, are severe.

A particularly egregious case of scientific misconduct came to light in 2001 when a young psychology professor at a leading university was accused of fabricating data. After two articles that reported fraudulent results were published in leading journals, a graduate student who had collaborated on the research asked the professor for notes that he had taken while helping to conduct the studies. When the professor refused to turn over the notes, the student became suspicious and reported her to university authorities. After admitting that she had fabricated some of the data, the professor was fired from her faculty position, was forced to publish retractions in the journals in which the studies were published, and faced the possibility of criminal prosecution because the research was funded partly by a federal grant (Lisheron, 2001). A promising career was ended by the cardinal sin in science—fraud.

Everyone agrees that fabricating data is wrong, but is a researcher permitted to "massage" his or her data to make them better? For example, is one allowed to delete the data of participants who did not appear to understand the instructions, who acted bizarrely during the study (suggesting that they were under the influence of alcohol or drugs), or whose data appear unusual or suspicious? Researchers regularly ignore the data of certain participants, and students understandably want to know whether such researchers are cheating.

The answer depends on whether the researcher's treatment of the data increases or decreases the validity of the results. Sometimes it is absolutely essential to disregard certain participants' data in order to ensure the integrity of the final results. If a participant did not follow the instructions—for whatever reason—it makes no sense to include his or her data in the analyses. If the researcher has reason to suspect that the participant was under the influence of drugs or purposefully responded bizarrely (to shock the researcher or damage the study), that participant's data should be eliminated. If a participant's responses are so extreme that they compromise the statistical analyses that will be conducted (because they violate statistical assumptions that must be met in order for the analyses to be valid), those data should be deleted. In each case, the researcher's goal is to ensure that the data are not contaminated by extraneous factors. Doing so clearly enhances the validity of the results.

In contrast, a researcher is never allowed to discard data or disregard results simply because they are contrary to his or her hypotheses. Doing so undermines the validity of the results and is a serious breach of scientific ethics. Thus, data manipulation to clean the data file in advance of analyzing it is usually permitted, but manipulating the data after seeing preliminary results is not.

When one confronts these kinds of gray areas in research ethics, one rule of thumb is to ask whether other scientists, on learning that you treated the data in a particular way, would regard your findings as more accurate or less accurate than before. In many cases, other researchers wholeheartedly support, if not insist, on data cleaning and manipulation, but in other cases, they would consider it to damage the conclusions one can draw from the study. Ask yourself, *would I hesitate to tell other researchers what I did to my data?* If so, it's probably ill-advised.

A second category of ethical abuses involves questionable research practices that, although not constituting scientific misconduct per se, are problematic. For example, researchers should take credit for work only in proportion to their true contribution to it. This issue sometimes arises when researchers must decide whom to include as authors on research articles or papers and in what order to list them (in psychology journals, authors are usually listed in descending order of their scientific or professional contributions to the project). Problems of "ownership" can occur in both directions: In some cases, researchers have failed to properly acknowledge the contributions of other people, whereas in other cases researchers have awarded authorship to people who didn't contribute substantially to the project (such as a boss or a colleague who loaned them a piece of equipment).

Other ethically questionable research practices include failing to report data inconsistent with one's own views and refusing to make one's data available to other competent professionals who wish to verify the researcher's conclusions by reanalyzing the data. In the study described previously, for example, 15% of the respondents reported knowing researchers who did not present results that were inconsistent with their own previous research. Many opportunities for scientific misconduct arise when grant money is at stake; there have been instances in which researchers have sabotaged other researchers' grant applications in order to improve their or their friends' chances of obtaining grants as well as cases in which researchers misused research grant money for other purposes (Bell, 1992).

A third category of ethical problems in research involves unethical behavior that is not unique to scientific investigation, such as sexual harassment (of research assistants or research participants), abuse of power, discrimination, or failure to follow government regulations. Not surprisingly, such unethical behaviors occur in science as they do in all human endeavors (Swazey et al., 1993).

In the wake of widely-publicized cases of misconduct, universities, institutes, hospitals, and research centers have implemented new programs to teach researchers and students how to conduct research responsibly. In addition, many research teams now operate in an environment of "collective openness" in which everyone on the team is privy to all aspects of the data collection and analyses, which should deter certain kinds of abuses. In addition, most institutions have policies for reporting scientific misconduct, along with protection for those who blow the whistle on researchers who commit scientific sins (Price, 2010).

SUPPRESSION OF SCIENTIFIC INQUIRY AND RESEARCH FINDINGS

History is filled with many examples of scientific findings being ridiculed, suppressed, and even punished by political and religious authorities. When Copernicus offered evidence that the earth revolved around the sun, church authorities declared that he was wrong and condemned Galileo for teaching the Copernican view. (The church officially withdrew its condemnation of Galileo only in the twentieth century.) Starting in the 1920s, many states passed laws that prohibited studying or teaching evolution, and prosecuted teachers who defied these laws, including John Scopes in the famous "Scopes Monkey Trial."

Although one might think that we now live in a more open, enlightened atmosphere in which science operates freely without outside interference, scientists and teachers continue to come under pressure to avoid studying certain topics and to sweep controversial theories and findings under the rug. Because the results of behavioral research touch upon controversial and sensitive topics such as child care, sexuality, gender differences, morality, evolution, religious beliefs, racial differences, and intimate relationships, university administrators, the public, and even some scientists have attempted to squelch research that they find personally objectionable.

For example, in 2002, a university president ruled that a psychologist's research project dealing with sexual behavior was not appropriate even though the study had been unanimously approved by the university's Institutional Review Board (Wilson, 2002). At the national level, elected officials have interfered with scientific investigations with which they disagreed on many occasions. The most well-known examples are Senator William Proxmire's attacks on several psychological studies involving topics such as interpersonal attraction, the link between heat and aggression, and the evolution of facial expressions. More recently, members of Congress introduced legislation to halt studies that examined marital stability and divorce during the early years of marriage, drug use and other behaviors that put prostitutes at risk for HIV, visual perception using pigeons as models, and the mental and physical health benefits of focusing on positive life goals through journal writing (Azar, 1997; Navarro, 2004). In other instances, efforts have been made to abolish the arm of the National Science Foundation that supports the social, behavioral, and economic sciences and to condemn the APA for publishing a peer-reviewed article suggesting that the long-term effects of childhood sexual abuse are less serious than had been assumed (see *In Depth* below).

Such actions raise ethical questions regarding the degree to which science should operate freely without outside interference. The issue is a complex one. Some people argue that because the results of scientific investigations can have negative outcomes, science must be regulated. For example, some suggest that research that reflects badly on members of a particular group, challenges people's deeply held religious convictions, or deals with sensitive or controversial topics should not be conducted. Likewise, university administrators worry that controversial research, no matter how important or well-designed, might bring unfavorable publicity to their institution.

In contrast, most researchers believe that they ought to be free to pursue knowledge in whatever direction it takes them and that only other scientists—not university administrators, local officials, or elected representatives—are in the position to judge the scientific merits of their research. They note that their work is already scrutinized by Institutional Review Boards that are charged with weighing the risks of a study against its scientific merit. Furthermore, in the case of federally funded projects that have been targeted by some members of Congress, research goes through many layers of scientific review, and Congress is not in a good position to decide what is good versus bad science compared to the panels of scientific experts that review each grant. Suppression of knowledge is, in the eyes of many researchers, inherently unethical.

In Depth

Should Scientists Consider the Ethical Implications of Controversial Findings?

The scientific enterprise is often regarded as an objective search for the truth, or at least as a careful, systematic search for the most reasonable conclusions that can be drawn from current data. Thus, researchers should presumably state the facts as they see them, without concern for whether their conclusions are popular and without regard for how people might use the information they publish. But what should researchers do if publication of their findings might lead to people being harmed or might appear to condone unacceptable behavior? And how should journal reviewers and editors react if they think publication of a well-designed investigation will have a negative impact? To suppress the publication of well-designed research would violate the fundamental tenets of scientific investigation, yet its publication may create undesirable effects, so an ethical dilemma arises.

A case in point involves an article that involved a meta-analysis of 59 previous studies that examined the long-term effects of childhood sexual abuse among people who were currently enrolled in college (Rind, Tromovitch, & Bauserman, 1998). (You may recall from Chapter 2 that meta-analysis statistically summarizes and analyzes the results of several studies on the same topic.) Across the studies, students who reported being sexually abused as children were slightly less well adjusted than students who had not been abused, as we might expect. However, the meta-analysis revealed that this effect was due primarily to differences in the kinds of families in which the students grew up rather than to the sexual abuse itself. The article concluded that the effects of childhood sexual abuse on later adjustment are not as strong as people commonly believe. In fact, the authors suggested that researchers discard the term *sexual abuse* for a "value neutral" term such as *adult–child sex*.

The article was published in *Psychological Bulletin,* one of the most prestigious, rigorous, and demanding journals in behavioral science. It underwent the standard process of peer review in which other experts examined the quality of the study's methodology and conclusions, and recommended that it be published. However, upon publication, the article provoked considerable controversy. Some of the criticisms focused on the conceptualization and methodology of the meta-analysis and the original studies on which it was based. For example, some authors questioned the meta-analytic coding strategy, the symptoms of child sexual abuse that were examined, the limited number of studies that involved male participants, and the shortcomings of using retrospection to study sexual abuse (Dallam, 2001; Tice, Whittenburg, Baker, & Lemmey, 2001). Rind and his collaborators rebutted these criticisms of their meta-analysis in subsequent articles (Rind, Bauserman, & Tromovitch, 2000; Rind, Tromovitch, & Bauserman, 2001). This, of course, is precisely the way that science is

(continued)

(continued)

supposed to operate, with arguments for and against researchers' methods and conclusions supported by scientific logic and evidence.

However, much of the criticism was not of this variety. A number of conservative social commentators and mental health practitioners condemned the article because they said that it condoned pedophilia. The outcry eventually reached the U.S. House of Representatives where a resolution was introduced condemning the article and, by association, the American Psychological Association, which publishes *Psychological Bulletin*. Under attack, the APA released a statement clarifying its position against sexual abuse and promised to have the article's scientific quality reevaluated (Martin, 1999; McCarty, 1999).

Many behavioral scientists were dismayed that scientific findings were repudiated by members of Congress and others on the basis of the study's conclusions rather than the quality of its methodology. (They were also troubled that APA buckled under political pressure and instituted an unprecedented reevaluation of a published article.) What should the researchers have done? Lied about their results? Suppressed the publication of their unpopular findings? This particular case highlights the ethical issues that may arise when behavioral research reaches controversial conclusions that may have implications for public policy. It also demonstrates that science does not operate in a vacuum but is influenced by social and political forces.

A FINAL NOTE

The general consensus is that major kinds of ethical abuses, such as serious mistreatment of participants and outright data fabrication, are rare in behavioral science (Adler, 1991). However, the less serious kinds of ethical violations discussed in this chapter are more common. By and large, the guidelines discussed in this chapter provide only a framework for making ethical decisions about research practices. Rather than specifying a universal code of do's and don'ts, they present the principles by which researchers should resolve ethical issues. No unequivocal criteria exist that researchers can use to decide how much stress is too much, when deception is and is not appropriate, or whether data may be collected without participants' knowledge in a particular study. As a result, knowledge of APA principles and federal regulations must be accompanied by a good dose of common sense.

Summary

1. Ethical issues must be considered whenever a study is designed. Usually the ethical issues are minor ones, but sometimes the fundamental conflict between the scientific search for knowledge and the welfare of research participants creates an ethical dilemma.

2. Researchers sometimes disagree not only regarding the ethicality of specific research practices but also regarding how ethical decisions should be made. Researchers operating from the deontological, skeptical, and utilitarian perspectives use very different standards for judging the ethical acceptability of research procedures.

3. Professional organizations and the federal government have provided regulations for the protection of human and nonhuman participants.

4. Six basic issues must be considered when human participants are used in research: informed consent, invasion of privacy, coercion to participate, potential physical or psychological harm, deception, and confidentiality. Although APA and federal guidelines provide general guidance regarding these issues, in the last analysis individual researchers must weigh the potential benefits of their research against its potential costs.

5. Federal regulations require an Institutional Review Board (IRB) at an investigator's institution to approve research involving human beings to protect research participants.

6. Generally, researchers must inform participants about features of a study that might affect their willingness to participate and then obtain their explicit agreement to participate. In cases in which participants cannot give informed consent (such as when researchers

study children or people who have certain cognitive impairments), consent must be obtained from those who have legal responsibility for the individual.

7. Obtaining informed consent also ensures that researchers do not invade participants' privacy by studying private aspects of their behavior without their knowledge.

8. People may not be coerced into participating in research by real or implied pressure from authority figures or the promise of very large incentives.

9. Although researchers may expose participants to small amounts of physical and mental stress, they may inflict greater amounts of pain or stress only when the cost-benefit analysis shows that the potential contributions of the research warrant it, the research could not otherwise be conducted, the IRB agrees with the research procedure, and steps are taken to protect the welfare of the participants.

10. Researchers sometimes deceive participants by misleading them about the purpose of a study, providing them with false information about themselves, having a confederate pose as another participant or an uninvolved bystander, presenting two related studies as unrelated, or giving incorrect information about other aspects of the study. Deception should be used only when the study could not be conducted without it.

11. All data must be treated with utmost confidentiality.

12. Federal regulations require that special attention be devoted to the welfare of vulnerable populations, such as children, pregnant women (and their unborn babies), prisoners, people with a reduced capacity for decision-making, and people at risk for suicide.

13. Professional and governmental regulations also govern the use and care of nonhuman animals in research.

14. Scientific misconduct involves behaviors that compromise the integrity of the scientific enterprise, including dishonesty (fabrication, falsification, and plagiarism), questionable research practices, and otherwise unethical behavior (such as sexual harassment and misuse of power).

15. Efforts by politicians, university administrators, and others to suppress scientific inquiry or the publication of certain research findings also raise a variety of ethical issues.

Key Terms

coercion to participate (*p. 316*)
confidentiality (*p. 319*)
cost–benefit analysis (*p. 312*)
debriefing (*p. 321*)
deception (*p. 318*)
deontology (*p. 310*)

ethical skepticism (*p. 311*)
informed consent (*p. 310*)
informed consent form (*p. 314*)
Institutional Review Board (IRB) (*p. 313*)
invasion of privacy (*p. 316*)

minimal risk (*p. 317*)
scientific misconduct (*p. 326*)
utilitarian (*p. 311*)
vulnerable population (p. *322*)

Questions for Review

1. Distinguish among deontology, skepticism, and utilitarianism as approaches to making decisions.
2. Which of these three ethical philosophies comes closest to the official ethical guidelines expressed by federal regulatory agencies and the American Psychological Association?
3. What factors should be considered when doing a cost–benefit analysis of a proposed study?
4. What is the purpose of the Institutional Review Board?
5. According to the principle of informed consent, what must participants be told before soliciting their agreement to participate in a study?

6. When is it not necessary to obtain informed consent?
7. What must be done if a research participant is unable to give valid informed consent, as in the case of children or people who are very psychologically disturbed?
8. Why may researchers not offer potential participants large incentives (e.g., a large amount of money) to participate in research?
9. In general, how much mental or physical risk is permissible in research?
10. Describe the concept of *minimal risk.*
11. Why do researchers use deception?

12. Why do some people object to the use of deception in research?
13. What four goals should a debriefing accomplish?
14. How do researchers maintain the confidentiality of participants' responses?
15. Describe the Milgram (1963) study and discuss the ethical issues it raised.
16. What are the basic ethical principles that animal researchers must follow?
17. Discuss the pros and cons of using nonhuman animals in behavioral research.
18. What are some examples of scientific misconduct?

Questions for Discussion

1. How much distress or pain may researchers inflict on participants who freely agree to participate in a study after being fully informed about the pain or distress they will experience?
2. Milgram conducted his experiments on obedience in the days before all research was scrutinized by an Institutional Review Board (IRB). Imagine, however, that Milgram had submitted his research proposal to an IRB of which you were a member. What ethical issues would you raise as a member of the board? Would you have voted to approve Milgram's

research? In thinking about this question, keep in mind that no one expected participants to obey the researcher as strongly as they did (see Schlenker & Forsyth, 1977).
3. To gain practice writing an informed consent form, write one for the Milgram study described in this chapter. Be sure to include all of the elements needed in an informed consent form.
4. Do you think that governmental agencies should exercise more or less control over behavioral research? Why?

16 | SCIENTIFIC WRITING

How Scientific Findings Are Disseminated

Elements of Good Scientific Writing

Avoiding Biased Language

Parts of a Manuscript

Citing and Referencing Previous Research

Other Aspects of APA Style

Writing a Research Proposal

Using *PsycINFO*

Sample Manuscript

As a system for advancing knowledge, science requires that investigators share their findings with the rest of the scientific community. Only if one's findings are made public can knowledge accumulate as researchers build on, extend, and refine one another's work. As we discussed in Chapter 1, a defining characteristic of science is that, over the long haul, it is self-correcting; and self-correction can occur only if research findings are widely disseminated. To this end, informing others of the outcome of one's work is a critical part of the research process.

In this chapter we will examine how researchers distribute their work to other scientists, students, and the general public. Because the effective communication of one's research nearly always involves writing, much of this chapter will be devoted to scientific writing. We will discuss criteria for good scientific writing and help you improve your own writing skills. We will also examine the guidelines that behavioral researchers use to prepare their research reports, a system of rules known as *APA style*. To begin, however, we'll take a look at the three main routes by which behavioral scientists disseminate their research to others.

HOW SCIENTIFIC FINDINGS ARE DISSEMINATED

Researchers disseminate the results of their investigations among themselves in three ways: journal publications, presentations at professional meetings, and personal contact.

Journal Publication

Journal publication is the primary route by which research findings are disseminated to the scientific community. Scientific journals serve not only as a means of communication among researchers (most researchers subscribe to one or more journals in their fields) but also as the basis for the permanent storage of research findings in library collections.

Traditionally, journals were published only in printed form, but today many journals are published in digital format as PDF files and on the Internet.

Before most journals will publish a research paper, it must undergo the process of **peer review**. In peer review, a paper is evaluated by other scientists who have expertise in the topic under investigation. Although various journals use slightly different systems of peer review, the general process is as follows.

1. The author submits copies of his or her paper to the editor of a relevant journal. (The editor's name and address typically appear on the inside front cover of the journal and on the journal's Web site.) Although a few journals still ask authors to submit paper copies of their manuscripts, most journals have on-line systems by which authors submit their work by sending word processing files. Authors are permitted to submit a particular piece of work to only one journal at a time.

2. The editor (or an associate editor designated by the editor) then sends a copy of the paper to two or more peer reviewers who are known to be experts in the area of research covered in the paper.

3. Each of the reviewers reads and critiques the paper, evaluating its conceptualization, methodology, analyses, results, interpretations, and contribution to the field. Each reviewer then sends a written review, typically a page or two in length (and, often, several pages), which provides the editor with feedback regarding the manuscript's strengths and weaknesses. Sometimes the reviewer makes a specific recommendation regarding whether the paper ought to be published.

4. Having received the reviewers' comments, suggestions, and recommendations, the editor considers their input and reads the paper him- or herself. The editor then makes one of four editorial decisions. First, he or she may decide to publish the paper as it is. Editors rarely make this decision, however; even if the paper is exceptional, the reviewers virtually always suggest ways in which it can be improved. Second, the editor may accept the paper for publication contingent on the author making certain minor revisions. Third, the editor may decide *not* to accept the paper for publication in the journal but asks the authors to revise the

paper in line with the reviewers' recommendations and to resubmit it for reconsideration. Editors make this decision when they think the paper has potential merit but see too many problems to warrant publication of the original draft. The fourth decision an editor may make is to reject the paper, with no opportunity for the authors to resubmit the paper to that particular journal. However, once the manuscript is rejected by one journal, the author may revise and submit it for consideration at another journal.

The most common editorial decision is the fourth one—rejection. In the leading journals in behavioral science, between 65% and 85% of the submitted manuscripts are rejected for publication (*Summary Report of Journal Operations*, 2009). Even if they are ultimately accepted for publication, most submitted papers undergo one or more rounds of reviews and revisions before they are published, so researchers must become accustomed to receiving critical feedback about their work. (The entire process, from submission to publication, usually takes a year or two.) Although no one likes having their work criticized or rejected, seasoned researchers realize that tight quality control is essential in science. Critical feedback from reviewers and editors helps to ensure that published articles meet minimum standards of scientific acceptability. In addition, critical feedback may actually help the researcher by ensuring that his or her flawed studies and poorly written manuscripts are not published, thereby preventing even greater criticism and embarrassment in the long run.

Students are often surprised to learn that researchers are not paid for the articles they publish. Conducting and publishing research is part of many researchers' jobs at colleges and universities, hospitals, research institutes, government agencies, and other research organizations. Thus, they are compensated for the research they conduct as part of their normal salaries and do not receive any extra pay when their articles are published.

Presentations at Professional Meetings

The second route by which scientific findings are distributed is through presentations at professional meetings. Most behavioral researchers belong to one or more professional organizations, such as the

American Psychological Association, the Association for Psychological Science, the American Educational Research Association, the Psychonomic Society, regional organizations (such as the Southeastern, Midwestern, and Western Psychological Associations), and a number of other groups that cater to specific areas of behavioral science (such as neuroscience, law and psychology, social psychology, health psychology, developmental psychology, and so on). Most of these organizations hold annual meetings at which researchers present their latest work.

In most instances, researchers who wish to present their research submit a short proposal (usually 200–500 words) that is peer-reviewed by other researchers. The acceptance rate for professional meetings is much higher than that for journal publication; typically 50% to 80% of the submitted proposals are accepted for presentation at the conference or convention.

Depending on the specific organization and on the researcher's preference, the presentation of a paper at a professional meeting can take one of two forms. One mode of presentation involves giving a talk to an audience. Typically, papers on related topics are included in the same **paper session** or **symposium**, in which each speaker has 15 or 20 minutes to present his or her research and to answer questions from the audience.

A second mode of presentation is the poster session. In a **poster session**, researchers display summaries of their research on poster boards, providing the essential details of its background, methodology, results, and implications. The researchers then stand with their posters to provide details, answer questions, and discuss their work with interested persons. They also have copies of a longer research report on hand to distribute to interested parties. Many researchers prefer poster sessions over verbal presentations because more people typically attend a particular poster session than a paper session (thus, the research gets wider exposure), and poster sessions allow more one-on-one interactions between researchers. Poster sessions not only give the researchers who are presenting their studies an opportunity to meet others who are interested in their topic, but they also often serve as a social hour in which convention attendees gather to interact with one another.

Personal Contact

A great deal of communication among scientists occurs through informal channels, such as personal contact. After researchers have been actively involved in an area of investigation for a few years, they get to know others around the world who are interested in the same topic. They talk with one another at professional meetings, sharing their latest ideas and findings; and they often send prepublication drafts of their latest papers to these individuals and may even collaborate on research projects. Most researchers also stay in contact with one another through e-mail.

This network of researchers from around the world, which has been called the "hidden university," is an important channel of scientific communication that allows researchers to stay informed about the latest advances in their fields. Researchers who are linked to these informal networks often become aware of advances in their fields a year or more before those advances are published in scientific journals.

In Depth
Peer Review, the Media, and the Internet

As we have seen, the dissemination of research findings among members of the scientific community occurs primarily through journal publication, presentations at professional meetings, and personal contact. However, information about research is sometimes released in two additional ways—in the popular media and on the World Wide Web.

Researchers are sometimes interviewed about their work by reporters and writers. You have probably seen articles about behavioral research in newspapers and magazines and heard stories about research, if not interviews with the researchers themselves, on television and radio. Although most scientists believe that researchers

(continued)

(continued)

are obligated to share their findings with the public, the drawback of reporting research in the general media is that the audience who reads, hears, or sees the report has no way of judging the quality of the research or the accuracy of the interpretations. Researchers can talk about their research whether it meets minimum standards of scientific acceptability or passes the test of peer review. For this reason, researchers in some sciences, though not in psychology, are discouraged from talking publicly about research that has not been peer-reviewed.

Furthermore, even if research has the scientific stamp of approval of peer review, popular reports of research are notoriously inaccurate. News reporters and writers typically focus on the study's most interesting conclusion without addressing the qualifications and limitations of the study that one would find in a journal article.

The same problem of quality control arises when researchers post reports of their research on the World Wide Web. Because anyone can create a Web site and post whatever they wish on it, we often have no way of knowing that research posted on the Web was properly conducted, analyzed, and interpreted. (For this reason, many teachers do not allow students to use the Web to locate previous research on a topic except when the research has been published in a peer-reviewed journal.) Sometimes researchers post manuscripts after they have been peer-reviewed and accepted for publication, which is a different matter. As long as the research passed the critical process of peer review, we have at least minimum assurance that other experts viewed it as acceptable. However, if research posted on the Web has not been peer-reviewed, you should be wary about using or citing it.

ELEMENTS OF GOOD SCIENTIFIC WRITING

Good writing skills are essential for researchers. No matter how insightful, creative, or well-designed particular studies may be, they are not likely to have an impact on behavioral science if researchers do not convey their ideas and findings in a clear, accurate, and engaging manner. In fact, research shows that influential papers in psychology are more readable than less influential ones. When they systematically compared 72 influential journal articles with matched control articles, Hartley and Sotto (2001) found that the influential papers had significantly shorter sentences that were easier to understand.

Unfortunately, good writing cannot be taught as easily as experimental design or the calculation of a correlation coefficient. It develops only through conscious attention to the details of good writing, coupled with practice and feedback from others. Very few people are good scientific writers without working on it; most researchers continue to improve their writing skills throughout their careers.

Although you will not suddenly learn to become an effective writer from the material in the next few pages, I hope that I can offer some suggestions that will help you to develop your own scientific writing skills. Specifically, this section will focus on the importance of organization, clarity, and conciseness, and offer you hints on how to achieve them.

Organization

The first prerequisite for clear writing is *organization*—the order in which one's ideas are expressed. The general organization of research reports in behavioral science is dictated by guidelines established by the American Psychological Association. Among other things, these guidelines stipulate the order in which sections of a paper must appear. In light of these guidelines (which we will examine in detail later in this chapter), you will have few problems with the general organization of a research paper.

Problems are more likely to arise in the organization of ideas *within* sections of the paper. If the order in which ideas are expressed is faulty, readers are likely to become confused. Someone once said that good writing is like a road map; the writer should take the reader from point A to point B—from beginning to end—using the straightest possible route, without backtracking, without detours, and without getting the reader lost along the way. To do this, you must present your ideas in an orderly and logical progression. One thought should follow from and build on another in a manner that will be easily grasped by the reader.

Before you start writing, make a rough outline of the major points you wish to express. This doesn't necessarily need to be one of those detailed, multi-level outlines you learned to make in high school; just a list of major points will usually suffice. Be sure the major points in your outline progress in an orderly fashion. Starting with an outline may alert you to the fact that your ideas do not flow coherently or that you need to add certain points to make them progress more smoothly.

As you write, be sure that the transitions between one idea and another are clear. If you move from one idea to another too abruptly, the reader may miss the connection between them and lose your train of thought. Pay particular attention to the transitions from one paragraph to another. Often, you'll need to write transition sentences that explicitly lead the reader from one paragraph to the next.

Clarity

Perhaps the fundamental requirement of scientific writing is *clarity*. Unlike some forms of fiction in which vagueness enhances the reader's experience, the goal of scientific writing is to communicate information. It is essential, then, that the information is conveyed in a clear, articulate, and unclouded manner.

This is a very difficult task, however. You don't have to read many articles published in scientific journals to know that not all scientific writers express themselves clearly. Often writers find it difficult to step outside themselves and imagine how readers will interpret their words. Even so, clarity must be a writer's first and foremost goal.

Two primary factors contribute to the clarity of one's writing: sentence construction and word choice.

SENTENCE CONSTRUCTION. The best way to enhance the clarity of your writing is to pay close attention to how you construct your sentences; awkwardly constructed sentences distract and confuse the reader. First, state your ideas in the most explicit and straightforward manner possible. One way to do this is to avoid the passive voice. For example, compare the following sentences:

> The participants were told by the experimenter to press the button when they were finished (passive voice).

> The experimenter told the participants to press the button when they finished (active voice).

I think you can see that the second sentence, which is written in the active voice, is the better of the two.

Second, avoid overly complicated sentences. Be *economical* in the phrases you use. For example, the sentence, "There were several different participants who had not previously been told what their IQ scores were," is terribly convoluted. It can be streamlined to, "Several participants did not know their IQ scores." (In a moment, I'll share with you one method I use to identify wordy and awkwardly constructed sentences in my own writing.)

WORD CHOICE. A second way to enhance the clarity of one's writing is to choose one's words carefully. Choose words that convey *precisely* the idea you wish to express. "Say what you mean and mean what you say" is the scientific writer's dictum.

In everyday language, we often use words in ways that are discrepant from their dictionary definition. For example, we tend to use *theory* and *hypothesis* interchangeably in everyday language, but they mean different things to researchers. Similarly, people talk informally about seeing a therapist or counselor, but psychologists draw a distinction between therapists and counselors. Can you identify the problem in this sentence?

> Many psychologists feel that the conflict between psychology and psychiatry is based on fundamental differences in their theoretical assumptions.

In everyday language, we loosely interchange *feel* for *think;* in this sentence, *feel* is the wrong choice.

Use specific terms. When expressing quantity, avoid loose approximations such as *most* and *very few*. Be careful with words, such as *significant*, that can be interpreted in two ways (that is, *important* vs. *statistically significant*). Use verbs that convey precisely what you mean. The sentence, "Smith *argued* that earlier experiments were flawed" connotes greater animosity on Smith's part than does the sentence, "Smith *suggested* that earlier experiments were flawed." Use the most accurate word. It would be impossible to identify all of the pitfalls of poor

Calvin and Hobbes

by Bill Watterson

word choice; just remember to consider your words carefully to be sure you "say what you mean."

Finally, avoid excessive jargon. As in every discipline, psychology has a specialized vocabulary for the constructs it studies—such as operant conditioning, cognitive dissonance, and preoperational stage—constructs without which behavioral scientists would find communication difficult. However, refrain from using jargon when a more common word exists that conveys the desired meaning. In other words, don't be like Calvin in the accompanying cartoon; don't use jargon when everyday language will do the job.

Conciseness

A third important consideration in scientific writing is *conciseness*. Say what you are going to say as economically as possible. Like you, readers are busy people. Think how you feel when you must read a 26-page journal article that could have conveyed all of its points in only 15 pages. Have mercy on your readers! Conciseness is also important for practical reasons. Scientific journals are able to publish only a limited number of pages each year, so papers that are unnecessarily long rob the field of badly needed journal space.

However, do not use conciseness as an excuse for skimpy writing. Research papers must contain all necessary information. Ideas must be fully developed, methods described in detail, results examined carefully, and so on. The advice to be concise should be interpreted as an admonition to include only the necessary information and to express it as succinctly (yet clearly) as possible.

Developing Your Research Skills
What's Wrong with These Sentences?

Like all writers, scientists are expected to use words and grammar correctly to convey their ideas. Each of the sentences below contains one or more common writing or grammatical errors. Can you spot them?

1. Since this finding was first obtained on male participants, several researchers have questioned its generalizability.

   Error: The preferred meaning of *since* is "between a particular past time and the present," and it should not be used as a synonym for *because*. In this example, the meaning of *since* is ambiguous—does it mean *because* or *in the time after?*

2. This phenomena has been widely studied.

> Error: *Phenomena* is plural; the singular form is *phenomenon*.

3. While most researchers have found a direct relationship between incentives and performance, some studies have obtained a curvilinear relationship.

> Error: *While* should be used to mean *during the same time as*. The proper word here is *whereas* or *although*.

4. Twenty females served as participants.

> Error: *Female* (and *male*) are generally to be used as adjectives, not as nouns. As such, they must modify a noun (female students, male employees, for example).

5. After assigning participants to conditions, participants in the experimental group completed the first questionnaire.

> Error: The phrase *after assigning participants to conditions* is a dangling modifier that has no referent in the sentence. One possible remedy would be to write, "After the experimenter assigned participants to conditions, participants in the experimental group completed the first questionnaire."

6. The data was analyzed with a *t*-test.

> Error: *Data* is plural; *datum* is singular. Thus, the sentence should be, "The data *were* analyzed. . . . "

7. It is hypothesized that shy participants will participate less fully in the group discussion.

> Error: As a pronoun, *it* must refer to some noun. In this sentence, *it* has no referent. The sentence could be rewritten in a number of ways, such as:
>
> This study tested the hypothesis that . . .
> The hypothesis tested in this study was that . . .
> Based on previous research, one would expect that . . .

8. When a person is in a manic state, they often have delusions of grandeur.

> Error: Pronouns must agree in number with their corresponding nouns. In this case, *person* is singular but *they* is plural. The sentence could be written in one of two ways:
>
> When people are in a manic state, they often have delusions of grandeur. (The noun and pronoun are both plural.)
> When a person is in a manic state, he or she often has delusions of grandeur. (The noun and pronoun are both singular.)

9. The participants scored the questionnaire which they had completed.

> Error: Use "that" rather than "which" when the phrase includes essential information and is not separated from the rest of the sentence by commas. In this example, "that" is the correct word. In contrast, in the following sentence, "which" is correct because it is used in a phrase that contains nonessential information and is separated from the rest of the sentence by commas: "The participants gave the questionnaire, which was printed on blue paper, to the researcher."

10. The researcher that administered the drug was blind to the participant's experimental condition.

> Error: Use "who" for people, "that" for things or groups.
>
> The researcher who administered the drug was blind to the participant's experimental condition.
> The test that the participants completed contained 20 questions.

Proofreading and Rewriting

Good writers are *rewriters*. Writers whose first draft is ready for public distribution are extremely rare, if they exist at all. Most researchers revise their papers many times before they allow anyone else to see them (unlike the students I've known who hand in their first draft!).

When you reread your own writing, do so with a critical eye. Have you included everything necessary to make your points effectively? Is the paper organized? Are ideas presented in a logical and orderly progression, and are the transitions between them clear? Is the writing clear and concise? Have you used precise vocabulary throughout?

When you proofread your paper, *read it aloud*. I often imagine that I am a television newscaster and that my paper is the script of a documentary I am narrating. If you feel silly pretending to be a newscaster, just read your paper aloud slowly as if you were reading a speech that was written by someone else and listen to how it sounds. Reading a paper aloud is the best way I know to spot awkward constructions. Sentences that look fine on paper often sound stilted or convoluted when they are spoken.

Allow yourself enough time to write and revise your paper and then set it aside for a few days. After a period away from a paper, I am always able to see weaknesses that I had missed earlier. Many researchers also seek feedback from colleagues and students. They ask others to critique a polished draft of the paper. Typically, other people will find areas of confusion, awkwardness, poor logic, and other problems. If you ask for others' feedback, be prepared to accept their criticisms and suggestions graciously. After all, that's what you asked them to give you! Whatever tactics you use, proofread and revise your writing not once but several times, until it reads smoothly from beginning to end.

AVOIDING BIASED LANGUAGE

Gender-Neutral Language

Consider the following sentence: "The therapist who owns his own practice is as much a businessman as a psychologist." Many people regard such writing as unacceptable because it involves sexist language—language that reinforces sexism by treating men and women differently. In the preceding sentence, the use of *he* and *businessman* seems to imply that all therapists are men.

In the 1970s, the American Psychological Association was one of several organizations and publishers to adopt guidelines for the use of **gender-neutral** (or *nonsexist*) **language**. Using gender-neutral language is important for two reasons. First, careless use of gender-related language may promote sexism. For example, consider the sentence, "Fifty fraternity men and 50 sorority girls were recruited to serve in the study." The use of the nonparallel words *men* and *girls* reinforces stereotypes about and status differences between men and women. Second, sexist language can create ambiguity. For example, does the sentence, "Policemen experience a great deal of job-related stress," refer only to police*men* or to both male and female police officers?

The APA *Publication Manual* (2009) discusses many variations of sexist language and offers suggestions on how to use gender-neutral substitutes in your writing. I'll discuss three common cases of sexist language.

GENERIC PRONOUNS.   Historically, writers have used generic pronouns such as *he, him*, and *his* to refer to both men and women, as in the sentence, "Every citizen should exercise his right to vote." However, the use of generic masculine pronouns to refer to people of both sexes is problematic on two counts.

First, using masculine pronouns can create ambiguity and confusion. Consider the sentence, "After each participant completed his questionnaire, he was debriefed." Are the participants described here both men and women, or men only? Second, many writers have argued that the use of generic masculine pronouns is inherently male centered and sexist (see Pearson, 1985). What is the possible justification, they ask, for using masculine pronouns to refer to women?

Writers deal with gender-relevant pronouns in one of two ways. On one hand, phrases that include both *he or she* or *his or her* can be used: "After each participant completed his or her questionnaire, he or she was debriefed." However, the endless repetition of *he or she* in a paper can become very tiresome. A better way to avoid sexist language is to use plural nouns and pronouns; the plural form of generic pronouns, such as *they, them*, and *theirs* are gender free: "After participants completed their questionnaires, they were debriefed." Incidentally, APA style discourages use of the forms *he/she* and *s/he* to refer to both sexes.

THE WORD MAN.   Similar problems arise when the word *man* and its variations (e.g., *mankind, the average man, manpower, businessman, policeman, mailman*) are used to refer to both men and women. Man-linked words not only foster confusion but also maintain a system of language that has become outmoded. Modern awareness of and sensitivity to sexism force us to ask ourselves why words such as *policeman* were traditionally used to refer to female police officers.

In most instances, gender-neutral words can be substituted for man-linked words. For example, terms such as *police officer, letter carrier, chairperson, fire fighter*, and *supervisor* are preferable to *policeman*,

mailman, chairman, fireman, and *foreman*. Such gender-neutral terms are not only sometimes more descriptive than the man-linked version (the term *fire fighter* more clearly expresses the nature of the job than does *fireman*) but also avoid the absurdity of reading about firemen who take time off from work each day to breast-feed their babies.

NONEQUIVALENT FORMS.   Other instances of sexist language involve using words that are not equivalent for women and men. The earlier example involving "fraternity men and sorority girls" is an example of this inequity. Furthermore, some words that seem structurally equivalent for men and women have different connotations. For example, a person who *mothered* a child did something quite different from the person who *fathered* a child. If caretaking behavior is meant, gender-neutral words such as *parenting* or *nurturing* are preferred over mothering. Other words, such as *coed*, that do not have an equivalent form for the other gender (that is, what is a *male coed* called?) should be avoided.

In Depth
Sexist Language: Does It Really Matter?

Some writers object to being asked to use gender-neutral language. Some argue that so-called non-exist language is really unnecessary because everyone knows that *he* refers to both men and women and that *mankind* includes everybody. Others point out that nonsexist language leads to awkwardly constructed sentences and distorts the English language.

At one level, the arguments for and against gender-neutral language are philosophical or political: Should we write in ways that discourage sexism and promote egalitarianism? At another level, however, the debate regarding nonsexist language can be examined empirically. Several researchers have investigated the effects of sexist and nonsexist language on readers' comprehension.

Kidd (1971) examined the question whether readers interpret the word *man* to refer to everyone as opponents of gender-neutral language maintain. In her study, participants read sentences that used the word *man* or a variation and then answered questions in which they identified the gender of the person referred to in each sentence. Although the word *man* was used in the generic sense, participants interpreted it to refer specifically to men 86% of the time. If you want to demonstrate this effect on your own, ask 10 people to draw a picture of a *caveman* and see how many opt to draw a cave*woman*. People do not naturally assume that *man* refers to everybody (see also McConnell & Gavanski, 1994).

In another study, Stericker (1981) studied the effects of gender-relevant pronouns on students' attitudes toward jobs. Participants read descriptions of several jobs (such as lawyer, interior decorator, high school teacher). In these descriptions, Stericker experimentally manipulated the words *he, he or she*, or *they* in job descriptions. Her results

(continued)

(continued)

showed that female participants were more interested in jobs when *he or she* was used in the description than when only *he* was used, but that male participants' preferences were unaffected by the pronouns being used. More recently, McConnell and Fazio (1996) showed that using man-suffix words (such as *chairman of the board*) led readers to draw different inferences about the person being described than did gender-neutral words (such as *chair of the board*).

In brief, studies have shown that using sexist or gender-neutral language *does* make a difference in the inferences readers draw (see Adams & Ware, 1989; McConnell & Fazio, 1996; Pearson, 1985). In the eyes of most readers, *man, he,* and other masculine pronouns are not generic, gender-neutral designations that refer to men and women equally.

Other Language Pitfalls

AVOID LABELS.   Writers should avoid labeling people when possible and particularly when the label implies that the person is characterized in terms of a single defining attribute. For example, writing about "depressives" or "depressed people" seems to define the individuals solely in terms of their depression. To avoid the implication that a person as a whole is depressed (or disabled in some other way), APA style suggests using phrases that put people first, followed by a descriptive phrase about them. Thus, rather than writing about "depressed people," write about "people who are depressed." Similarly, "individuals with epilepsy" is preferred over "epileptics," "a person who has a disability" is preferred over "disabled person," "people with a mental illness" is preferred over "mentally ill people" (or, worse, "the mentally ill"), and so on.

RACIAL AND ETHNIC IDENTITY.   When describing people in terms of their racial or ethnic identity, writers must use the most accurate and specific terms and should be sensitive to any biases that their terms contain. Preferences for nouns that refer to racial and ethnic groups change frequently, and writers should use the words that the groups in question prefer (assuming, of course, that they are accurate). The APA *Publication Manual* includes guidelines regarding the most appropriate designations for various racial, ethnic, and cultural groups.

PARTS OF A MANUSCRIPT

In 1929, the American Psychological Association adopted a set of guidelines regarding the preparation of research reports. This first set of guidelines, which was only 7 pages long, was subsequently revised and expanded several times. The most recent edition of these guidelines—the *Publication Manual of the American Psychological Association* (6th edition)—was published in 2009 and runs more than 240 pages.

Most journals that publish behavioral research—not only in psychology but in other areas as well, such as education and communication—require that manuscripts conform to **APA style**. In addition, most colleges and universities insist that students use APA style as they write theses and dissertations, and many professors ask that their students write class papers in APA style. Thus, a basic knowledge of APA style is an essential part of the behavioral researcher's toolbox.

The guidelines in the APA *Publication Manual* serve three purposes. First, many of the guidelines are intended to help authors write more effectively. Thus, the manual includes discussions of grammar, clarity, word usage, punctuation, and so on. Second, some of the guidelines are designed to make published research articles uniform in certain respects. For example, the manual specifies the sections that every paper must include, the style of reference citations, and the composition of tables and figures. When writers conform to a single style, readers are spared from a variety of idiosyncratic styles that may distract them from the content of the paper itself. Third, some of the guidelines are designed to facilitate the conversion of manuscripts typed using word processing software into printed journal articles. Certain style conventions assist the editors, proofreaders, and typesetters who prepare manuscripts for publication.

The APA *Publication Manual* specifies the parts that every research report must have, as well as the order in which they appear. Generally speaking, a research paper should have a minimum of seven major sections:

- title page
- abstract
- introduction
- method
- results
- discussion
- references

In addition, papers may have sections for footnotes, tables, figures, and/or appendixes, all of which appear at the end of the typed manuscript. Each of these sections is briefly discussed next.

Title Page

The title page of a research paper should include the title, the authors' names, the authors' affiliations, and a running head.

The title should state the central topic of the paper clearly yet concisely. As much as possible, it should mention the major variables under investigation. Titles should generally be no more than 12 words. The title is centered in the upper half of the first page of the manuscript.

Good Titles

Effects of Caffeine on the Acoustic Startle Response
Parenting Styles and Children's Ability to Delay Gratification
Probability of Relapse after Recovery from an Episode of Depression

Poor Titles

A Study of Memory
Effects of Feedback, Anxiety, Cuing, and Gender on Semantic and Episodic Memory under Two Conditions of Threat: A Test of Competing Theories

---

In the examples of poor titles, the first one is not sufficiently descriptive, and the phrase "A study of" is unnecessary. The second title is way too long and involved.

One double-spaced line beneath the title are the author's name and affiliation. Most authors use their first name, middle initial, and last name. The affiliation identifies the institution where the researcher is employed or is a student.

The *Author Note* is located at the bottom of the title page. In the Author Note, the authors provide their complete departmental affiliation at the time of the study and any changes in affiliation that may have occurred after the study was completed. They can also thank those who helped with the study, acknowledge grants and other financial support for the research, and discuss any special circumstances that may be relevant. The note also provides the mailing address and e-mail address for the contact author.

In the header of the title page is the running head, an abbreviated form of the title. For example, the title "Effects of Social Exclusion on Dysphoric Emotions" could be reduced to the running head, "Effects of Exclusion." The running head is typed flush left at the top of the page in uppercase letters. When an article is typeset for publication in a journal, the running head appears at the top of every other page of the printed article.

Abstract

The second page of a manuscript consists of the **abstract**, a brief summary of the content of the paper. The abstract should be 150–250 words depending on the policy of a particular journal. The abstract for the report of an empirical study should describe the following items:

- the problem under investigation
- the participants used in the study
- the research procedures
- the findings
- the conclusions or implications of the study

Because this is a great deal of information to convey in so few words, many researchers find it difficult to write an accurate and concise abstract that is coherent and readable. However, in some ways, the abstract is the single most important part of a journal article because most readers decide whether to read an article on the basis of its abstract. Furthermore, the abstract is retrieved by computerized literature search services such as *PsycINFO*. Although the abstract is usually the last part of a paper to be written, it is by no means the least important section.

Introduction

The body of a research report begins on page 3 of the manuscript. The title of the paper is repeated at the top of page 3, followed by the introduction itself. (The heading *Introduction* does not appear, however.)

The *Introduction* section describes for the reader the problem under investigation and presents a background context in which the problem can be understood. The author discusses aspects of the existing research literature that pertain to the study—not an exhaustive review of all research that has been conducted on the topic but rather a selective review of previous work that deals specifically with the topic under investigation.

When reviewing previous research, write in the past tense. Not only does it make sense to use past tense to write about research that has already been conducted ("Smith's findings *showed* the same pattern") but also writing in the present tense often leads to awkward sentences in which deceased persons seem to speak from the grave to make claims in the present ("Freud suggests that childhood memories may be repressed"). Throughout the paper, but particularly in the introduction, you will cite previous research conducted by others. We'll return later to how to cite previous studies using APA style.

After addressing the problem and presenting previous research, discuss the purpose and rationale of your research. Typically, this is done by explicitly stating the goals of the study or describing the hypotheses that were tested.

In stating their hypotheses, researchers must be wary of HARKing—Hypothesizing After the Results are Known (Kerr, 1998). Occasionally, researchers will present a "hypothesis" in the introduction that they developed after seeing the results of the study as if it was derived a priori. In essence, they imply that the research was designed to test a particular hypothesis when, in fact, the so-called hypothesis did not occur to them until after the study was conducted and

they saw the results. HARKing creates a number of problems for science. Among other things, presenting post hoc hypotheses as if they were a priori can transmute flukes into theories. A true a priori hypothesis is based on an existing theoretical foundation that is independent of the results of the study, whereas HARKing gives us a hypothesis that may be based on an anomalous finding (such as a Type I error). In addition, HARKed hypotheses are not subject to disconfirmation because they came after rather than before the study. Given that scientific theories must be disconfirmable (Chapter 1), HARKing violates a basic tenet of scientific investigation. Furthermore, HARKing hides ideas and hypotheses that did not work, leaving other researchers open to the risk of committing the same mistakes. For these and other reasons, HARKing in the introduction of a paper is typically discouraged, although it is certainly appropriate for researchers to offer ideas and "hypotheses" that dawned on them later as long as they are identified as post hoc.

The introduction should proceed in an organized and orderly fashion. You are presenting, systematically and logically, the conceptual background that provides a rationale for your particular study. In essence, you are building a case for why your study was conducted and what you expected to find. After writing the introduction, ask yourself:

- Did I adequately orient the reader to the purpose of the study and explain why it is important?
- Did I review the literature adequately, using appropriate, accurate, and complete citations?
- Did I deal with both theoretical and empirical issues relevant to the topic?
- Did I clearly state the research question or hypothesis?

Method

The *Method* section describes precisely how the study was conducted. A well-written method allows readers to judge the adequacy of the procedures that were used and provides a context for them to interpret the findings. A complete description of the method is essential so that readers may assess what a study does and does not demonstrate. The method section also allows other researchers to replicate the study if they wish. Thus, the method should describe, as precisely, concisely, and clearly as possible how the study was conducted.

The method section is typically subdivided into three sections, labeled *Participants, Apparatus* (or *Materials*), and *Procedure*. The participants and procedure sections are nearly always included, but the apparatus or materials section is optional.

PARTICIPANTS. The *Participants* section describes the participants and how they were selected. (As you will notice when you read older journal articles, until 1994, this section was labeled *Subjects*. Today, *participants* is the preferred term for the people or animals that were studied.) When human participants are used, researchers typically report the number, sex, and age of the participants, along with their general demographic characteristics. In many cases, the manner in which the participants were obtained is also described. When nonhuman animals are used, researchers report the number, genus, species, and strain, as well as their sex and age. Often relevant information regarding housing, nutrition, and other treatment of the animals is included as well.

APPARATUS OR MATERIALS. If special equipment or materials were used in the study, they are described in a section labeled *Apparatus* or *Materials*. For example, sophisticated equipment for presenting stimuli or measuring responses should be described, as well as special instruments or inventories. This section is optional, however, and is included only when special apparatus or materials were used. If an apparatus or measure can be described very briefly—in a sentence or two—many authors simply describe it at the appropriate place in the *Procedure*.

PROCEDURE. The procedure section describes in a step-by-step fashion precisely how the study was conducted. Included here is information regarding instructions to the participants, experimental manipulations, all research procedures, and even the debriefing. The procedure must be presented in sufficient detail that another researcher could replicate the study in its essential details.

After writing the method section, ask yourself:

- Did I describe the method adequately and clearly, including all information that would be needed for another investigator to replicate the study?
- Did I fully identify the people or animals who participated?
- Did I describe the apparatus and materials fully?
- Did I report the research procedure fully in a step-by-step fashion?

Results

The *Results* section reports the statistical analyses of the data collected in the study. Generally, writers begin by reporting the most important results and then work their way to secondary findings. Researchers are obligated to describe all relevant results, even those that are contrary to their predictions. However, you should not feel compelled to include every piece of data obtained in the study. Most researchers collect and analyze more data than needed to make their points. However, you are not permitted to present only those data selected to support your hypothesis!

When reporting the results of statistical tests, such as *t*-tests or *F*-tests, include information about the kind of analysis that was conducted, the degrees of freedom for the test, the calculated value of the statistic, its statistical significance, and the effect size. If an experimental design was involved, also include the means and standard deviations for each condition. (Because it is difficult to type the conventional symbol for the mean, $\bar{x}$ on many word processors, the symbol *M* is used for the mean.) The results of statistical analyses are typically separated from the rest of the sentence by commas, as in the following sentence:

A *t*-test revealed that participants exposed to uncontrollable noise made more errors ($M = 7.5$, SD = .67) than participants who were exposed to controllable noise ($M = 4.3$, *SD* = .56), $t(39) = 4.77$, $p = .012$, eta = .29.

Note that this sentence includes the name of the analysis, the condition means and standard deviations, the degrees of freedom (39), the calculated value of *t* (4.77), the *p* value for the test (.012), and the effect size (.29). Specific *p* values should be reported whenever possible (to the second or third decimal place); however, if a *p* value is less than .001, it should be reported as $p < .001$. (You may notice that older journal articles often report all *p* values as less than a particular value, such as "$p < .05$." However, the most recent edition of APA style recommends that precise *p* values be reported, such as "$p = .043$" or "$p = .075$".)

When the results of an analysis are not significant, the APA *Publication Manual* recommends that researchers report a power analysis. As discussed in Chapter 10, a power analysis tells us the likelihood of making a Type II error—of failing to detect an effect that was actually present (or failing to reject the null hypothesis when it was false). When power is low, the failure to obtain a significant effect may be due to insufficient power. Thus, the nonsignificant effect may reflect a Type II error. However, when power is high, it is unlikely that a nonsignificant finding reflects a Type II error, and it is more likely that the effect truly did not occur. Readers are better able to interpret the meaning of a nonsignificant result when they know whether statistical power was low or high.

When you need to report a large amount of data—many correlations or means, for example—consider putting some of the data in tables or in figures (graphs). APA style requires that tables and figures be appended to the end of the manuscript, with a reference to the table or figure at an appropriate place in the text. Tables and figures are often helpful in presenting data, but they should be used only when the results are too complex to describe in the text itself. Furthermore, avoid repeating the same data in both the text and in a table or figure. Remember to be economical.

The results should be reported as objectively as possible with minimal interpretation, elaboration, or discussion. The material included in the results section should involve what your data showed but *not* your interpretation of the data. After writing the results section, ask yourself:

- Did I clearly describe how the data were analyzed?
- Did I include all results that bear on the original purpose of the study?
- Did I include all necessary information when reporting statistical tests?

- Did I describe the findings objectively, with minimal interpretation and discussion?

Discussion

Having described the results, you are free in the *Discussion* to interpret, evaluate, and discuss your findings. As a first step, discuss the results in terms of the original purpose or hypothesis of the study. Most researchers begin the discussion with a statement of the central findings and how they relate to the goals or hypotheses of the study. They then move on to discuss other findings.

In your discussion, integrate your results with existing theory and previous findings, referencing others' work where appropriate. Note inconsistencies between your results and those of other researchers, and discuss alternative explanations of your findings, not just the one you prefer. Also mention qualifications and limitations of your study; however, do not feel compelled to dwell on every possible weakness or flaw in your research. All studies have shortcomings; it is usually sufficient simply to note yours in passing. Often, researchers conclude the Discussion with ideas for future research—the next steps that need to be taken to pursue the topic further. After writing the discussion section, ask yourself:

- Did I state clearly what I believe are the major contributions of my research?
- Did I integrate my findings with both theory and previous research, citing others' work where appropriate?
- Did I discuss alternative explanations or interpretations of my findings?
- Did I note possible qualifications and limitations of my study?

CITING AND REFERENCING PREVIOUS RESEARCH

Citations in the Text

Throughout the text of the paper, you will cite previous work that is relevant to your study. APA guidelines specify the form that such citations must take. APA style uses the **author–date system** in which others' work is cited by inserting the last name of the author and the year of publication at the appropriate point in the text. The book you are reading uses the author–date system.

The author–date system allows you to cite a reference in one of two ways. The first way is to include the author's last name, followed by the date of publication in parentheses, as part of the sentence, as shown in the following examples:

Jones (2009) showed that participants . . .

In a recent review of the literature, Jones (2009) concluded . . .

This finding was replicated by Jones (2009).

If the work being cited has two authors, cite both names each time:

Jones and Williams (2010) showed . . .

After reviewing the literature, Jones and Williams (2010) concluded . . .

If the work has more than two authors but fewer than six, cite all authors the *first* time you use the reference. Then, if the reference is cited again, include only the first author, followed by *et al.* (an abbreviation of Latin for "and others") and the year:

Jones, Williams, Isner, Cutlip, and Bell (2007) showed that participants . . .

Jones et al. (2007) revealed . . . [subsequent citations]

The second way of citing references in the text is to place the authors' last names, along with the year of publication, within parentheses at the appropriate point:

Other studies have obtained similar results (Jones & Smith, 2005).

If several works are cited in this fashion, alphabetize them by the last name of the first author and separate them by semicolons:

The effects of stress on decision making have been investigated in several studies (Anderson,

1997; Cohen & Bourne, 1988; Smith, Havert, & Menken, 2004; Williams, 2008).

The Reference List

All references cited in the text must appear in a reference list that begins on a new page labeled *References* immediately after the discussion section. References are listed in alphabetical order by the first author's last name. The APA *Publication Manual* presents 95 variations of reference style, depending on whether the work being referenced is a book, journal article, newspaper article, dissertation, film, abstract on a CD-ROM, government report, or whatever. However, the vast majority of citations involve five types of sources— journal articles, books, book chapters, papers presented at professional meetings, and Internet sources—so I'll limit my examples to these five types of references.

JOURNAL ARTICLE. The reference to a journal article includes the following items, in the order listed:

1. last name(s) and initials of author(s)
2. year of publication (in parentheses), followed by a period
3. title of the article, with only the first word of the title capitalized (with the exception of words that follow colons, which are also capitalized), followed by a period
4. name of the journal, followed by a comma (All important words in the title are capitalized, and the title is italicized.)
5. volume number of the journal (italicized), followed by a comma
6. page numbers of the article, followed by a period
7. direct object identifier (doi) number, if available (I will explain the doi in a moment)

Here are two examples of references to articles. Note that the second and subsequent lines of each reference are indented. (This is called hanging indentation.)

Smith, M. B. (2010). The effects of research methods courses on student depression. *Journal of Cruelty to Students, 15*, 67–78. doi: 10.1267/0568-6354.23.1.564

Smith, M. B., Jones, H. H., & Long, I. M. (2007). The relative impact of *t*-tests and *F*-tests on student mental health. *American Journal of Unfair Teaching, 7*, 235–240. doi: 10.4532/9856-3424.56.3.234.

BOOKS. References to books include the following items, in the order listed:

1. last name(s) and initials of author(s)
2. year of publication (in parentheses), followed by a period
3. title of the book (only the first word of the title is capitalized, and the title is italicized), followed by a period
4. city and state in which the book was published, followed by a colon
5. name of the publisher, period

Leary, M. R. (1995). *Self-presentation: Impression management and interpersonal behavior.* Boulder, CO: Westview Press.

BOOK CHAPTER. References to a book chapter in an edited volume include the following, in the order listed:

1. last name(s) and initials of author(s)
2. year of publication (in parentheses), followed by a period
3. title of the chapter, followed by a period
4. the word "In," followed by the first initial(s) and last name(s) of the editor(s) of the book, with "Eds." in parentheses, followed by a comma
5. title of the book (only the first word of the title is capitalized, and the title is italicized)
6. page numbers of the chapter in parentheses, followed by a period
7. city and state in which the book was published (followed by a colon)
8. name of the publisher, period

Smith, K. L. (2009). Techniques for inducing statistical terror. In J. Jones & V. Smith (Eds.), *A manual for the sadistic teacher* (pp. 45–67). Baltimore, MD: Neurosis Press.

PAPER PRESENTED AT A PROFESSIONAL MEETING. References to a paper or poster that was presented at a professional meeting include the following, in the order listed:

1. last name(s) and initials of author(s)
2. year and month in which the paper was presented (in parentheses), followed by a comma

3. title of the paper (italicized), followed by a period
4. phrase "Paper presented at the meeting of . . ." followed by the name of the organization, comma
5. city and state in which the meeting occurred, period

Wilson, H. K., & Miller, F. M. (1988, April). *Research methods, existential philosophy, schizophrenia, and the fear of death.* Paper presented at the meeting of the Society for Undergraduate Teaching, Dallas, TX.

INTERNET SOURCES. References to material obtained on the Internet vary depending on the specific nature of the source. In general, references to Internet sources should provide as much information as possible regarding the following items:

1. the author or organization responsible for the document
2. a date (either the date of publication of the document or, if no publication date is shown, the date you retrieved it from the Internet)
3. a title or description of the document
4. the Internet address (the URL or uniform resource locator). If the URL extends to another line, break it after a slash or period and do not hyphenate it at the break (shown later).

In many cases, some of this information will be unknown (such as when a Web page lists no author or sponsor). In all cases, however, provide enough information to allow others to access the document if desired.

Internet journal or archive:

Blaha, S. (2002, Feb. 9) A classical probabilistic computer model of consciousness. Cogprints, No. 2077. Retrieved from http://cogprints.ecs.soton.ac.uk/archive/00002077/

Newspaper article—electronic version:

Squires, S. (2002, Oct. 9). Study finds that in U.S., 1 in 3 is obese. Washington Post. Retrieved from http://www.washingtonpost.com/wp-dyn/articles/A62930–2002Oct8.html

Stand-alone document (no author listed):

Brain anticipates events to learn routines (2002). Retrieved October 16, 2002 from http://www.eu-rekalert.org/pub_releases/2002–10/bcom-bae100802.php

The APA *Publication Manual* contains examples of how to cite other types of Internet sources, including government reports, messages posted to news-groups, e-mail messages, and data files obtained via the Internet.

In Depth
Electronic Sources and Locator Information: URL and DOI

In the latest version of the APA *Publication Manual*, new attention was given to electronic publishing and to referencing material that was obtained online. Publishing in the online, digital environment has led to easier and faster access to research findings, space for storing supplemental files that are relevant to an article (such as appendices containing supplemental data), and the possibility of making corrections to an article after it is published. As a result of these changes, some styles of referencing have become outdated, and new methods have become necessary. In particular, locator information is now necessary for any article found on the Internet or in a digital database. Providing locator information helps readers locate references and differentiate between articles that might have different versions on the Internet and in print.

For sources that are published online, providing a **Uniform Resource Locator** or **URL** allows readers to locate the material and ensures that they are directed to the same version of the article that you are citing in the paper. A URL is an Internet address that allows readers to locate the article on the Web and should be included in the references whenever possible.

Before the digital revolution, researchers obtained virtually all of the scientific articles that they read from printed journals. Today, however, they can obtain articles from printed journals, a variety of digital databases (such as *PsycINFO* and *Medline*), and from Web sites. For that reason, scholarly publishers developed a **direct object identifier (DOI)** system that provides a unique number for every article. With this number in hand, readers can locate a particular article without knowing the specific method of accessing the article used by the authors. Authors should include the DOI in reference citations whenever it is available.

The Web site Crossref.org offers resources to assist researchers in finding DOI numbers for specific articles as well as using DOI numbers to locate articles. DOI numbers are typically found on the first page of a print or PDF version of all new articles.

SECONDARY SOURCES. By and large, you should cite only sources that you have personally read. Citing someone else's work implies that you have read it and attest that it is relevant and accurate with regard to the point that you are making in your paper. Trusting that you understand another author's work by reading someone else's brief description of it is risky. All seasoned researchers have had the experience of looking up a reference cited in a paper only to find that the reference does not actually draw the conclusion that the author of the paper suggested. Clearly, the author had not actually read the original paper but rather relied on a secondary source that had cited it.

Even so, situations occasionally arise in which a writer wishes to cite an article or book that he or she found in a secondary source but is unable to locate the original. In such cases, this fact should be reflected in both the citation in the text and the entry in the reference list. For example, if you wished to mention Amsterdam's (1972) study of children's reactions to their self-reflections that you saw in Courage and Howe's (2002) article about infant cognition but were unable to locate Amsterdam's original article, you would cite it in the text of your paper as:

Amsterdam (as cited in Courage & Howe, 2002) . . .

Note that you do not include the year of Amsterdam's study because you are citing Courage and Howe as your source rather than Amsterdam.

Then in the reference list you would enter not the Amsterdam study (because you didn't really read or cite it directly) but rather the Courage and Howe article, which you would cite like any other journal article:

Courage, M. L., & Howe, M. L. (2002). From infant to child: The dynamics of cognitive change in the second year of life. *Psychological Bulletin, 128*, 250–277. doi:10.1037/0033-2909.128.2.250

A reader who was interested in the Amsterdam study would know that you found it in the Courage and Howe article and that's where the original reference citation is located. Use secondary citations sparingly, if at all.

OTHER ASPECTS OF APA STYLE

Optional Sections

In addition to the title page, abstract, introduction, method, results, discussion, and references, all of which are required in research reports, many research papers include one or more of the following sections.

FOOTNOTES.   In APA style, footnotes are rarely used. They are used to present ancillary information and are typed at the end of the paper. In the published article, however, they appear at the bottom of the page on which the footnote superscript appears.

TABLES AND FIGURES.   As noted earlier, tables and figures are often used to present results. A table is an arrangement of words or numbers in columns and rows; a figure is any type of illustration, such as a graph, photograph, or drawing. The APA *Publication Manual* provides extensive instructions regarding how tables and figures should be prepared. In the typed manuscript they appear at the end of the paper, but in the published article they are inserted at the appropriate places in the text.

APPENDICES.   Occasionally, authors wish to include detailed information in a manuscript that does not easily fit into the text itself. In this case, the information can be contained either in an appendix (in the printed version of the article) or in a supplemental file that is maintained online by the publisher of the article.

Appendices are useful when the additional information is relatively brief, such as a list of stimuli used in the study or a detailed description of materials. In the case of multiple appendices, each appendix is labeled with a letter—Appendix A, Appendix B, and so on. In some cases, the additional material is too long for a printed article, not easily conveyed in print format, or is more helpful in downloaded form (such as a piece of software used in the study). In these cases, authors may decide to present the additional information as a supplemental file that is accessible on the Web.

Both appendices and supplemental materials are considered part of the published article and cannot be changed or deleted. As such, most journals require that these materials also go through the peer review process. Appendices and supplemental files have the potential to help readers understand or replicate the study design; however, they should be included only if they are essential to the manuscript.

Headings, Spacing, Pagination, and Numbers

HEADINGS.   With the exception of the introduction, each section we have discussed is labeled. For the other major sections of the paper—abstract, method, results, discussion, and references—the section heading is centered in the middle of the page and bolded, with only the first letter of the word capitalized. For subsections of these major sections (such as the subsections for participants, apparatus, and procedure), a side heading is used. A side heading is typed flush with the left margin and bolded. If a third-level heading is needed, a paragraph heading is used. A paragraph heading is indented and bolded, with the first word capitalized and ending in a period; the text of the paragraph then begins on the same line. For example, the headings for the method section typically look like this:

Method   ←   Center major headings.

Participants
Apparatus   ←   Use side heads for subsections.
Procedure

This is a paragraph heading.   ←   Use paragraph headings for third-level sections.

The title and abstract appear on the first two pages of every manuscript. The introduction then begins on page 3. The method section does *not* start on a new page but rather begins directly wherever the introduction ends. Similarly, the results and discussion sections begin immediately after the method and results sections, respectively. Thus, the text begins with the introduction on page 3, but the next three sections do not start on new pages. However, the references, footnotes, tables, figures, and appendixes each begin on a new page.

SPACING. The main text of research reports written in APA style are *double-spaced* from start to finish. Set your word processor on double spacing and leave it there.

PAGINATION. Pages are numbered in the upper right corner, starting with the title page as page 1.

In APA style, *the running head* is typed in the upper left corner of each page, with the page number in the upper right corner. The running head also appears on the title page following the label Running head; however, on subsequent pages the label is removed.

NUMBERS. In APA style, whole numbers less than 10 are generally expressed in words ("the data for two participants were omitted from the analysis"), whereas numbers 10 and above are expressed in numerals ("Of the 20 participants who agreed to participate, 10 were women"). However, numbers that begin a sentence must be expressed in words ("Twenty rats were tested"). Furthermore, numbers that precede units of measurement should be expressed in numerals (the temperature was 8 degrees), as should numbers that represent time, dates, ages, and sample sizes (2 weeks; November 29, 1954; 5-year-olds; $n = 7$).

In Depth
Who Deserves the Credit?

As researchers prepare papers for publication or presentation, they often face the potentially thorny question of who deserves to be listed as an author of the paper. Many people contribute to the success of a research project—the principal investigator (P.I.) who initiates and oversees the project, research assistants who help the P.I. design the study, other researchers not directly involved in the research who nonetheless offer suggestions, the clerical staff who types questionnaires and manuscripts, the individuals who collect the data, statistical consultants who help with analyses, technicians who maintain equipment and computers, and so on. Which of these individuals should be named as an author of the final paper?

According to the *Publication Manual of the American Psychological Association* (2009), authorship is reserved for those individuals who have made substantial scientific contributions to a study. Substantial scientific contributions include formulating the research problem and hypotheses, designing the study, conducting statistical analyses, interpreting results, and writing major parts of the research report—activities that require scientific knowledge about the project. Generally, supportive functions—such as maintaining equipment, writing computer programs, recruiting participants, typing materials, or simply collecting data—do not by themselves constitute a "substantial scientific contribution" because they do not involve specialized knowledge about the research. However, individuals who contribute in these ways are often acknowledged in the author note that appears on the title page.

In psychology, the authors' names are usually listed on the paper in order of decreasing contribution. (The norms about the order of authorship are different across sciences.) Thus, the principal investigator—typically the faculty member or senior scientist who supervised the project—is listed first, followed by the other contributors. However, when an article is substantially based on a student's thesis or dissertation, the student is usually listed as first author. If two or more authors have had equal roles in the research, they sometimes list their names in a randomly chosen order and then state that they contributed equally in the author's note.

The order in which authors are listed is based on the magnitude of their scientific and professional contributions to the project and not on the sheer amount of time that each person devoted to the project. Thus, although the P.I. may spend less time on the project than assistants who collect data, the P.I. will probably be listed as first author because his or her contributions—designing the study, conducting statistical analyses, writing the manuscript, and overseeing the entire project—are more crucial to the scientific merit of the research.

To the new researcher, APA style is complex and confusing; indeed, veteran researchers are not familiar with every detail in the APA *Publication Manual*. Even so, these guidelines are designed to enhance effective communication among researchers, and behavioral researchers are expected to be familiar with the basics of APA style. When preparing a manuscript for submission, researchers often refer to the *Publication Manual* when they are uncertain of how the manuscript should look.

WRITING A RESEARCH PROPOSAL

In some cases, researchers write about their research *before* rather than after it is conducted. For example, students who are designing a research project for a course, investigators applying for a research grant, and student researchers writing proposals for honors, thesis, or dissertation research must describe their plans in advance in a **research proposal**. In most cases, a proposal is written to convince other people of the importance, feasibility, and methodological quality of the planned research. The goal of a proposal is to demonstrate that the research idea is a good one, that the study is well conceived, and that the design and analyses will adequately address the question under investigation.

In most regards, a research proposal follows the same format as a research report. For example, all proposals include an introduction that reviews the existing literature and provides a rationale for the study, and, like research reports, they are usually written in APA style. However, proposals involving future research differ from reports of completed research in a few important ways.

First, parts of a research proposal are written in future tense. Unlike a research report, which describes a completed study using the past tense, the abstract and method of a research proposal are written in future tense because they describe a study that may be conducted in the future. The elements of a proposal's method section are the same as those of a research report, but the participants, materials, and procedure are described in future tense.

Second, a research proposal does not include a results or discussion section because there are no results to describe or discuss. Instead, proposals often include a *Planned Analyses* section that describes how the data will be analyzed and a *Predicted Results* section that describes the predictions in detail. (Sometimes these two sections are combined into a single *Planned Analyses and Predicted Results* section.) The author's goals are to convey that he or she knows how to analyze the data that will be collected and has thought carefully about his or her predictions of what the results will reveal.

In brief, in addition to a title page (and often an abstract), a typical research proposal consists of the following sections:

- An introduction that presents the rationale for the study, including an overview of the topic, a review of other relevant research, and a description of how the study will add to our knowledge. Typically the Introduction ends with a statement of the research goals or major hypotheses.
- A method section that provides clear and specific descriptions of the participants, materials or apparatus (if any), and procedure. Enough detail should be provided so that another researcher could run the study according to your specifications simply from reading the method. The method section of a proposal is written in future tense.
- A brief section labeled *Planned Analyses* should describe how the data will be analyzed.
- A *Predicted Results* section describes the specific patterns of findings that the author expects. In addition, alternative patterns that might reasonably be obtained are sometimes noted.
- The references section lists all sources that were cited.

USING PSYCINFO

An important part of scientific writing—whether one is writing a manuscript for publication, a research proposal, or a paper for a course—involves becoming familiar with the published literature on the paper's topic. Thus, researchers and students must be able to locate articles, books, chapters, and other documents that are relevant to whatever they are writing.

Not too many years ago, researchers and students who wanted to locate published articles on a particular topic had to engage in a laborious and time-consuming search through years and years of *Psychological Abstracts*—a set of volumes that listed all of the articles that were published in psychology journals each year. Today, however, they rely on *PsycINFO*, a computerized database for finding journal articles, books, book chapters, dissertations, and other scholarly documents in the behavioral sciences. *PsycINFO* includes not only material in psychology per se but also publications involving psychological aspects of other fields such as communication, marketing, nursing, education, physiology, public health, psychiatry, sociology, law, and management. The database contains citations and summaries for over 2 million sources published since 1887.

Most universities and colleges have subscriptions to *PsycINFO* that allow students and faculty members to use the database. Typically, access to *PsycINFO* is managed by the college or university library, and many public libraries have access as well. Sometimes, students and faculty members can log on to *PsycINFO* from their own computer over the Internet, but often users must use a computer terminal in the library. The specific way that users access *PsycINFO* differs depending on the institution, so you should check on your library's Web site or contact a reference librarian for details.

Once users are logged on to *PsycINFO*, they can search for publications by entering search terms such as the topic (perhaps you are looking for articles about *moral development*), the author's name (maybe you want to see every publication by a particular researcher), the year of publication (if you want only recent publications), or a particular journal's name (because it publishes articles on the topic that you are writing about). As when doing any kind of computerized search, the trick is to select exactly the right terms that will give you the number and kinds of citations that you want. Thus, you must think carefully about the terms that authors tend to use when they write about your topic of interest. If you don't use the right terms, you may miss many important citations or perhaps find none at all.

On the other hand, if you use terms that are too broad, you may be overwhelmed by too many citations. For example, imagine that you are interested in finding publications that deal with the relationship between depression and eating disorders. What terms would you use? If you search for articles about depression, you will get more than 90,000 hits, so that doesn't seem to be a useful approach. If you narrow your search for articles that are about both depression and eating disorders, you get about 700 citations, which is more manageable but, depending on how deeply you want to delve into the topic, may still be too many to wade through. So, you could search for articles that have both *depression* and *eating disorders* in the title of the article. That search will yield about 100 citations, which might be a reasonable number for starters. But before you start looking at the summaries of those articles, chapters, and books, consider the possibility that a search that looked for citations with *depression* and *eating disorder* in their titles would miss an article with a title such as "The relationship between depression, anorexia, and bulimia," which is obviously relevant to your interests. So, you would want to also conduct searches for articles with *depression and anorexia* and with *depression and bulimia* in their titles as well.

When *PsycINFO* gives you too many potentially relevant references but you cannot think of terms that allow you to narrow the scope, you have a number of other ways to limit your search. For example, you can choose the kinds of publications you wish to consider (do you want books and dissertations to be included, or just articles and chapters?), the age of the participants used in the study, the language in which the article was published (there's not much sense getting things you can't read), and the year of publication (perhaps you want to focus only on research conducted in the last 20 years).

Once you have a reasonable number of citations to examine, read through the summaries of the publications that *PsycINFO* provides, looking for those that are most closely aligned with your interests. Although all of the citations contain your search terms, many of them will nonetheless be irrelevant to your specific concerns. When you find one that you want to explore further, you can mark it. When you are finished reading all of the summaries, you can instruct *PsycINFO* to print the citations and summaries of all papers that you marked, save the citations and summaries to your computer, or e-mail them to you. Then it's time to start reading the sources.

Conducting a useful search on *PsycINFO* requires a good deal of thought and patience, and usually involves conducting many searches that try different combinations of terms. You can find many good guides to *PsycINFO* on the Internet, and your library may have instructions as well.

And, if you ever get frustrated using *PsycINFO*, just remember how researchers and students used to look for articles in the days before computerized searching.

SAMPLE MANUSCRIPT

What follows is an example of a research report that has been prepared according to APA style.[1] This is a manuscript that an author might submit for publication; the published article would, of course, look very different. I've annotated this manuscript to point out some of the basic guidelines that we have discussed in this chapter.

---

[1] The sample manuscript is a shortened and edited version of a longer article by Ashley Batts Allen and Mark Leary entitled "Reactions to others' selfish actions in the absence of tangible consequences" that was published in *Basic and Applied Social Psychology* (2010).

The title page includes five things: the running head, the manuscript title, the authors' names, the authors' institutional affiliations, and the author note.

The running head is included in the header of the paper and is a shortened version of the title. Note that on subsequent pages, the running head is still present, but the label has been dropped.

Running head: REACTIONS TO SELFISH ACTIONS   1

Reactions to Others' Selfish Actions in the

Absence of Tangible Consequences

Ashley Batts Allen Mark R. Leary

Duke University

Author Note

Ashley Batts Allen, Department of Psychology and Neuroscience; Mark R. Leary, Department of Psychology and Neuroscience, Duke University.

Correspondence concerning this article should be addressed to: Ashley Batts Allen, Department of Psychology and Neuroscience, Box 90085, Duke University, Durham, NC, 27708. E-mail: xxx@duke.edu

The abstract summarizes the study in 150–250 words (depending on the journal) and appears on page 2. The word "Abstract" is centered with only the first letter capitalized, and the first line of the abstract is not indented.

                                Abstract

This research assessed the role of perceived selfishness in people's reactions to events that do not have any tangible consequences. Participants were assigned to complete a boring task by another person who gave a selfish, legitimizing, or exculpatory explanation for the decision. However, half of the participants knew that the other's decision was irrelevant and that they would personally complete the task regardless of the other person's decision. Results showed that participants who received a selfish explanation responded strongly whether or not the person's decision had tangible consequences for them.

        Keywords: selfishness, egoism, anger

Authors may list a few key-words that describe the topic of the paper.
The keywords should be centered and the label *Keywords* should be italicized.

Reactions to Others' Selfish Actions in the
Absence of Tangible Consequences

The introduction starts on page 3 with the title of the paper centered at the top of the page. The text begins one double-space below the title.

The paper starts with a general introduction to the topic under investigation—people's reactions to others' selfish actions. The author–date system is used to cite references to previous work.

People understandably react strongly to events that threaten their well-being. When people are attacked, discriminated against, taken advantage of, or treated unfairly, they often act to defend themselves, minimize the negative outcomes, and punish those who have hurt or disadvantaged them (Aquino, Tripp, & Bies, 2001; Folger, Baron, VandenBos, & Bulatao, 1996). Less understandably, people sometimes react just as strongly to events that have few, if any, tangible implications for their well-being. In such instances, the actual threat is minimal (if there is one at all), yet people respond as if they are facing genuine danger or harm. Wood (2006) suggested that modern American culture encourages excessively strong reactions to trivial events, but the general phenomenon appears widespread across cultures and history.

Our focus in this research is on people's reactions to others' behaviors that, although selfishly motivated, have no direct or tangible consequences for the individual. In everyday life, people generally respond strongly to those who behave selfishly because selfishness usually has direct negative consequences for them, but people also may react to selfish actions that have no implications for their well-being. Although reactions to selfish actions have not been studied in their own right, insights regarding people's reactions to selfishness can be gleaned from other work. Research shows that the strength of people's reactions to another person's behavior often bears little direct relationship to its objective impact but rather depends on their construals of the perpetrator's motives (Reeder, Kumar, Hesson-McInnis, & Trafimow, 2002). For example, people's perceptions of the degree to which another person intended to harm them sometimes predict their desire for retribution more strongly than the degree to which they were actually harmed (Batson, Bowers, Leonard, & Smith, 2000).

However, when another person's selfish behavior does not directly affect them, people may believe that the perpetrator acted out of self-interest without taking their interests into account, but they do not necessarily infer that he or she intended to harm them. Even so, victims usually regard selfishness as unfair (Mikula, Petri, & Tanzer, 1990), and people react strongly to events that they view as unfair even when those events have no effect on their well-being (Lind & Tyler, 1988). Furthermore, even when another person's behavior does not notably affect them, people may nonetheless react strongly to the violation of norms involving politeness and respect (Cohen, Nisbett, & Bowdle, 1996; Greenberg, 1994; Lind & Tyler, 1988).

In the previous paragraph, the citation to Wood (2006) was incorporated into the sentence. In this paragraph, the citation to Reeder, Kumar, Hesson-McInnis, and Trafimow (2002) is included in parentheses.

When several references are given in parentheses, they are alphabetized by the first author's last name and separated by semicolons.

Even when another person's selfish behavior does not objectively matter, reacting strongly may be functional when one's reactions have the potential to deter future transgressions and establish one's identity as a person who should not be mistreated. Because strong, irrational, and overblown displays of emotion may serve deterrence and reputation-maintaining functions better than a measured response, people may be prone to react more strongly to seemingly trivial infractions than would otherwise seem rational (Frank, 1991). Many violent reactions to insignificant signs of disrespect and selfishness appear designed to serve this deterrence function (Cohen et al., 1996; Tedeschi & Felson, 1994; Toch, 1992).

In real-life cases in which people react to others' selfish actions, identifying the source of the reaction is difficult because the provocation includes both an objectively negative outcome and an indication that the perpetrator selfishly disregarded the person's well-being. The present study disentangled these two effects by examining people's reactions to selfish actions when nothing tangible was at stake and their reactions had no possible deterrence function. Because reacting to others' actions when they do not matter wastes energy and creates new problems, one might predict that people should not react to selfishness that has no tangible consequences. On the other hand, because other people's

---

The Cohen et al. reference used here was already cited in the previous paragraph. Because the Cohen, Nisbett, and Bowdle article had more than two authors, subsequent citations are listed as Cohen et al.

The introduction typically states the research questions or hypotheses under investigation.

selfishness often has negative effects, people may be sensitive to any indication that another person does not have their interests at heart and thus react strongly even when nothing tangible is at stake. Along these lines, evolutionary psychologists suggest that human beings possess cognitive systems that sensitize them to the possibility that others are taking advantage of them (Cosmides, 1989).

When people are treated badly, even in minor ways, they expect others to account for their actions (Bies & Shapiro, 1987; Shapiro, Buttner, & Barry, 1994). If the perpetrator can explain a seemingly selfish or unfair action, the target is more likely to forgive the person (Lind & Tyler, 1988; Sitkin & Roth, 1993). However, if an adequate and acceptable account is not given, people may respond not only to the initial infraction but also to the perpetrator's unwillingness to provide an accept-able account. We expected that when no account is pro-vided, people will assume that a person who behaved selfishly was, at best, unconcerned about their well-being, or worse, intentionally trying to harm them. In either case, people should respond as strongly to those who do not explain their selfish actions as those who acknowledge that their actions were selfish. However, when the individual who acts in a selfish manner offers an explanation that legitimizes his or her actions, peo-ple should react less strongly.

The method section begins immediately after the end of the introduction, with the heading "Method" centered on the page and bolded. The subheadings "Participants" and "Procedure" appear as bolded side-headings, typed flush with the left margin. Because no specialized materials or apparatus were used in this study, an Apparatus or Materials section is not included in this particular paper.

The number, sex, and age of participants are given. Note that the number, 128, is expressed as a word because it begins a sentence, but the other numbers (all over 10) are expressed in numerals.

The procedure is described in enough detail that it could be replicated by another researcher.

The labels for the experimental conditions are italicized the first time they are mentioned. After an italicized term has been used once, do not italicize it again.

REACTIONS TO SELFISH ACTIONS   7

Method

Participants

One-hundred and twenty-eight participants (64 male, 64 female) between the ages of 18 and 22 participated in partial fulfillment of a research requirement for an introductory psychology course.

Procedure

Multiple participants signed up to participate in each session, but they reported to separate lab rooms and never met one another. Participants were told that the study was investigating processes involved in how managers assign tasks in work groups. They were told that they and another participant (referred to as their "work partner") would make decisions regarding which of them would work on a task. After signing an informed consent form, participants were told that their work partner had been randomly chosen to decide which of the two of them would perform a tedious attentional task that involved counting "beeps" occurring at irregular intervals on a tape recording for 25 minutes.

Participants in the *high implication condition* were told that the person chosen by the partner to perform the onerous task would perform the task for 25 minutes, whereas the other person would complete a short questionnaire and leave immediately (thereby spending less

than 10 minutes in the study). In contrast, participants in the *low implication condition* were told that,
although the work partner believed that his or her
decision would determine who performed the tedious
task, in fact the participant had already been randomly
selected to spend 25 minutes counting beeps no matter
what decision the partner made. Thus, for participants
in the low implication condition, the work partner's
decision had absolutely no consequences for them
although they believed that their work partner thought
that it did.

The researcher then gave the participant a form
ostensibly filled out by the work partner indicating
that he or she had assigned the participant to do the
tedious task. In addition to showing that the partner
had checked the option "The other participant will perform the tedious task" rather than the option "I will
personally perform the tedious task," the form included
a handwritten note, supposedly written by the partner,
in response to the prompt, "Explain briefly why you
made this decision regarding who will perform the
task." Participants were assigned randomly to one of
four conditions that differed in the explanation that
the partner offered for his or her decision. In the
selfish explanation condition, the note said: "I don't
see why *I* should sit here and waste *my* time;" in the
legitimizing explanation condition, the note said,
"I woke up with the flu this morning and feel like I'm

REACTIONS TO SELFISH ACTIONS   9

about ready to pass out;" and in the *random selection explanation condition*, the note said "The researcher told me to flip a coin so the choice would be random, so I did." Participants in a fourth, *no explanation control condition* did not receive an explanation for the partner's decision. Thus, the design was a 2 (*implication of the decision for the participant*: low vs. high) × 4 (*explanation*: selfish, legitimizing, random, none) randomized factorial.

The design is a 2×4 factorial. Notice that the 2 and the 4 are indicated with numerals because they express a mathematical function.

Participants then completed a questionnaire that assessed their reactions. First, participants rated their feelings of anger on four adjectives—angry, irritated, annoyed, and mad (1 = *not at all*; 7 = *extremely*). Participants then gave their impressions of the work partner on twelve 9-point bipolar scales that assessed four dimensions—competence (competent-incompetent, unintelligent-intelligent, foolish-wise), friendliness (friendly-unfriendly, warm-cold, unlikeable-likeable), self-centeredness (unselfish-selfish, humble-conceited, self centered-other centered), and morality (ethical-unethical, moral-immoral, bad-good). They also rated how they felt on 7-point scales that reflected positive (warmth, kindness, friendliness, tenderness) and negative feelings (dislike, anger, resentment, hatred) toward the partner.

Italicize anchors of a scale. Here, participants rated how angry they were on a scale that went from 1 (*not at all*) to 7 (*extremely*).

REACTIONS TO SELFISH ACTIONS   10

     Participants were then asked to imagine interact-
ing with the partner face-to-face after receiving his
or her decision and to indicate how tempted they would
be to do each of 16 behaviors adapted from the
Conflict Tactics Scale (Straus, 1979). These items
were selected to assess temptations to physically
aggress (e.g., slapping the other person, pushing or
shoving the other person, throwing something at the
other person) and psychologically aggress (e.g.,
humiliating the other person, insulting or swearing
at the other person, shouting or yelling at the other
person). Participants rated how tempted they would
feel to do each behavior on 9-point scales (1 = *not
at all tempted*; 9 = *very tempted*). As a check on the
explanation manipulation, participants were asked why
the partner made the decision that he or she did.
After completing the questionnaire, participants were
debriefed and informed that they would not actually
perform the task, there was no work partner, and all
decisions had been randomly determined by the researcher.

Results

    Data were screened for outliers and adherence to
statistical assumptions, then analyzed with 2 × 4
analyses of variance (ANOVAs) as appropriate with
implication (low, high) and explanation (selfish,
legitimizing, random, none) as between-subjects factors.

The source of materials or measures adapted from other studies must be cited. Here, the source of the items from the Conflict Tactics Scale is given.

The Results section starts immediately after the Method ends. Do not start a new page or use extra spacing.

Abbreviations (such as ANOVA) must be spelled out the first time they appear in a paper.

The Results section does not need to be broken into subsections as it is here, but doing so often improves readability. If used, the subsections are labeled with bolded side-headings.

Manipulation Check

Participants rated the likelihood that the other person assigned them to complete the task for each of the following reasons: (a) randomly, (b) because of their mood, (c) out of selfishness, (d) to be hurtful, and (e) because the situation required it. An ANOVA showed a significant main effect of explanation for ratings of "selfishness," $F(3, 120) = 8.96$, $p < .001$, $\eta_p^2 = .18$, indicating that participants in the selfish ($M = 8.3$, $SD = 3.2$) and no explanation ($M = 8.1$, $SD = 2.6$) conditions rated selfishness higher as a reason than participants in the legitimizing ($M = 5.2$, $SD = 3.0$) and random ($M = 5.7$, $SD = 3.2$) conditions, $ps < .05$. A main effect of explanation also showed that participants in the random explanation condition ($M = 8.8$, $SD = 3.8$) rated "random selection" as a reason for the decision higher than participants in the other explanation conditions (Legitimate $M = 2.0$, $SD = 1.5$; Selfish $M = 2.5$, $SD = 2.6$; None $M = 3.5$, $SD = 2.9$, $ps < .05$), $F(3, 120) = 39.68$, $p < .001$, $\eta_p^2 = .50$. These patterns show that participants clearly understood the work partner's explanation for his or her decision.

When describing statistical tests, such as the *F*-test, the degrees of freedom, calculated value of the statistic, probability level, and effect size are included.

Provide exact *p* values (include three decimal places) unless the *p* value is less than .001, in which case indicate it as *p* < .001.

Perceptions of the Partner

The 12 ratings of the partner were summed within sets to create measures of friendliness, competence, self-centeredness, and morality. ANOVAs showed that the effect of explanation was obtained on three

Greek letters such as η (eta) are not italicized.

scales—friendliness, F (3, 126) = 8.26, p < .001, η_p^2 =.18, morality, F (3, 126) = 8.39, p < .001, η_p^2 =.18 and self-centeredness, F (3,126) = 17.30, p < .001, η_p^2 =.31. Participants in the selfish explanation condition (M = 18.4, SD = 3.6) thought that their partners were more unfriendly than participants in the random (M = 14.6, SD = 4.9), legitimizing (M = 14.9, SD = 3.5), and no explanation (M = 16.4, SD = 2.9) conditions, ps < .05. Participants in the no explanation condition perceived their partner to be more unfriendly than participants in the random and legitimizing conditions, which did not differ. Participants in the selfish explanation condition (M = 16.6, SD = 2.6) also thought that their partners were more immoral/unethical than participants in the random (M = 12.7, SD = 3.9) and legitimizing (M = 14.5, SD = 2.9) explanation conditions, ps < .05. The legitimizing and no explanation (M = 15.6, SD = 3.3) conditions did not differ from one another.

Condition means are labeled as M and standard deviations are labeled as SD.

The main effect of explanation on ratings of self-centeredness showed that participants in the selfish explanation condition (M = 21.6, SD = 3.1) thought their partners were more self-centered than participants in the other three explanation conditions, ps < .05. In addition, participants rated the work partner as more self-centered in the no explanation condition (M = 19.0, SD = 3.3) than in the legitimizing explanation condition

(M = 17.5, SD = 3.0), suggesting that, in the absence of any information, participants assumed that the decision had been motivated by selfishness. Participants in the random explanation condition (M = 15.7, SD = 3.9) rated the other person as the least selfish.

Feelings toward the Work Partner

After reverse-scoring the negative ratings, participants' ratings of their feelings toward their work partner were summed, with higher values representing more positive/less negative feelings. A main effect of explanation, F (3, 120) = 7.24, $p < .001$, η_p^2 =.15, showed that participants in the selfish explanation condition (M = 3.4, SD = .87) had more negative feelings toward their partner than participants in the random (M = 4.2, SD = .94) and legitimizing (M = 4.3, SD = .81) explanation conditions. Participants in the no explanation condition (M = 3.9, SD = .83) did not differ significantly from the others.

The main effect of explanation was qualified by a significant interaction as shown in Table 1, F(3, 120) = 2.98, p = .034, η_p^2 =.07. Participants in the no explanation condition expressed less positive feelings toward their partners when the implications of the decision were high rather than low, whereas participants in the random explanation condition expressed more positive feelings toward their partner when the implications of the decision were high rather than low. These findings

Table 1 is included at the end of the paper, although it would appear about here in the Results section of the published version of the article.

When tables are used, the text describes the patterns of results shown in the table but does not repeat the data (such as the means) that the table contains.

suggest that participants in the no explanation and random conditions judged their partner on the basis of the
consequences of his or her decision but that, in both
the selfish and legitimizing explanation conditions,
participants' feelings were unaffec-ted by the implications of the partner's decision. In the selfish and
legitimizing conditions, participants' feelings
reflected only the nature of the explanation without
respect to whether the partner's decision objectively
mattered. Most relevant to the hypotheses, participants
felt significantly more negatively toward the partner in
the selfish than legitimizing condition even when the
partner's decision did not affect them and, in fact,
they felt as negatively when the decision had no implications as when it did, showing that the partner's
selfish action evoked negative responses even when it
had no consequences whatsoever.

Anger

An ANOVA was conducted on the sum of the four
anger ratings. A main effect of explanation, $F(3, 119) = 4.30$, $p = .006$, $\eta_p^2 = .10$, showed that
participants who received a selfish explanation ($M = 12.9$, $SD = 6.5$) felt more angry than participants in
all other conditions. Participants in the no
explanation condition ($M = 11.1$, $SD = 5.6$) also felt
angrier than participants in the random ($M = 8.5$, $SD = 5.3$) and legitimizing explanation ($M = 9.2$, $SD = 4.6$)

REACTIONS TO SELFISH ACTIONS   15

conditions, *ps* < .05. Importantly, the two-way
interaction was not significant, indicating that
participants were as angered by the selfish explanation
when the partner's decision had no implications for
them as when the implications were high.

Behavioral Inclinations

Participants' ratings of how they felt like
responding toward the work partner were summed to create
separate measures of the degree to which they felt
tempted to physically and psychologically aggress.
A 2 × 4 ANOVA revealed a significant implication by
explanation interaction for physical aggression,
$F(3, 114) = 2.77$, $p = .045$, $\eta_p^2 = .07$. As seen in Table 2,
aggressive urges were low except when participants
received a selfish explanation for a decision with low
implications.

Discussion

Compared to participants who received an
explanation that legitimized their decision
(by appealing to illness or the researcher's
instructions to decide randomly), participants who
received a selfish explanation for being assigned to
perform the tedious task were more angry, perceived
the other person more negatively, expressed fewer
positive feelings toward the partner, and felt
more tempted to aggress. Importantly, most of these
effects were obtained whether or not the partner's
decision

Table 2 appears at the end
of the paper.

The Discussion section
begins immediately after
the Results section.

The Discussion usually
begins by describing and
interpreting the major
findings.

had any consequences for the participant, showing that participants reacted to selfish intent regardless of whether the partner's behavior made any real difference to them.

Although we anticipated that participants might react as strongly to the selfish explanation when the decision did not have any consequences as when it did, we had not expected that they might react even more strongly when there were no implications. One possible explanation for this finding is that, when the partner's actions had implications for them, participants may have focused primarily on the upcoming tedious task. However, when the selfish decision had no consequences, participants may have focused on the selfish decision itself. In any case, this pattern shows that people react to selfishness even when the other person's selfishness has no tangible effect on them.

That people react strongly when others selfishly disadvantage them is not surprising (Miller, 2001; Vidmar, 2000). The current findings are intriguing because participants reacted negatively to another's selfish decision even when it had absolutely no tangible effect on them. In fact, participants reacted as strongly to selfishness that had no tangible consequences as to selfish disregard that led them to waste time working on a tedious task, and on one measure—temptations to physically aggress—they reacted more strongly to selfish decisions that did not have consequences for

In the Discussion, the author tries to explain the patterns of results that were obtained.

In this sentence, connections are drawn between the findings of this study and other research.

them than to those that did. By either legitimizing the
situation (by claiming to be ill) or eliminating responsibility (by noting that the process had been random),
the partner redeemed him- or herself in the eyes of the
participant, reducing negative perceptions, emotions,
and aggressive urges. In contrast, the selfish explanation confirmed participants' suspicions that the partner
was self-centered and inconsiderate. Under such circumstances, explaining one's negative behaviors is not only
ineffective but may lead to more negative emotions than
had an explanation not been provided.

The emotional reactions and ratings of the partner
that participants reported on the questionnaire could
not serve the function of expressing displeasure or
deterring him or her from behaving selfishly in the
future. Not only did participants not expect to work
again with their partner, but they did not even know
who the partner was. In light of these patterns, the
data suggest that people react negatively to perceived
selfishness even when it absolutely does not matter
and support the idea that people are highly sensitive
to selfish and egoistic behavior on the part of other
people (Reeder, Vonk, Ronk, Ham, & Lawrence, 2004).

Limitations of the current study should be noted.
First, the implication manipulation involved an outcome
that par ticipants already expected to receive.
Participants signed up to participate in a 30-minute

Often, researchers
mention considerations
that limit the generalizability
of the findings.

study, so being told that they would not be able to leave after 10 minutes may not have seemed consequential. However, this consideration only makes the results more surprising given that participants still reacted strongly to an event without any implications. Second, participants were asked to make judgments about a person about whom they had not met and about whom they had little information, and they may have logically used the limited information they had about him or her —that is, the partner's decision and explanation. However, in the no explanation condition, participants were provided with even less information with which to make a decision, and in this condition, their responses suggest they attributed selfish motives to their partner.

People often react strongly to events that have no important implications for them. This study shows that an important ingredient in these reactions is the perception that another person has behaved selfishly. This research has implications for understanding instances in which people overreact in everyday life. For example, many cases of physical violence, including road rage and domestic and child abuse, occur when people overreact to a trivial incident of perceived selfishness or disrespect. Future research should focus on factors that moderate these reactions and on the functions that they serve in interpersonal life.

REACTIONS TO SELFISH ACTIONS   19

The references begin on a new page. Like the rest of the manuscript, the references are double-spaced.

References

Aquino, K., Tripp, T. M., & Bies, R. J. (2001). How employees respond to personal offense: The effects of blame attribution, victim status, and offender status on revenge and reconciliation in the workplace. *Journal of Applied Psychology, 86,* 52-59. doi:10.1037/0021-9010.86.1.52

Batson, C. D., Bowers, M. J., Leonard, E. A., & Smith, E. C. (2000). Does personal mortality exacerbate or restrain retaliation after being harmed? *Personality and Social Psychology Bulletin, 26,* 35-45. doi:10.1177/0146167200261004

Bies, R. J., & Shapiro, D. L. (1987). Interactional fairness judgments: The influence of causal accounts. *Social Justice Research, 1,* 199-218. doi:10.1007/BF01048016

Cohen, D., Nisbett, R. E., & Bowdle, B. F. (1996). Insult, aggression, and the southern culture of honor: An 'experimental ethnography.' *Journal of Personality and Social Psychology, 70,* 945-960. doi:10.1037/0022-3514.70.5.945

Cosmides, L. (1989). The logic of social exchange: Has natural selection shaped how humans reason? Studies with the Wason selection task. *Cognition, 31,* 187-276. doi:10.1016/0010-0277(89)90023-1

Folger, R., Baron, R. A., VandenBos, G. R., & Bulatao, E. Q. (1996). Violence and hostility at

The Cosmides reference is to a journal article. It includes the author's name, year of publication (in parentheses), title of the article, journal (italicized), volume (italicized), and page numbers. The reference concludes with the article's direct object identification (doi) number.

work: A model of reactions to perceived injustice. In *Violence on the job: Identifying risks
and developing solutions.* (pp. 51-85). Washington,
D.C.: American Psychological Association.
doi:10.1037/10215-002

Frank, R. H. (1991). *Passions within reason.* New York:
W. W. Norton.

Greenberg, J. (1994). Using social fair treatment to
promote acceptance of a work site smoking ban.
Journal of Applied Psychology, 79, 288-297.
doi:10.1037/0021-9010.79.2.288

Lind, E. A., & Tyler, T. R. (1988). The *social psychology of procedural justice.* New York: Plenum.

Mikula, G., Petri, B., & Tanzer, N. K. (1990). What
people regard as unjust: Types and structures of
everyday experiences of injustice. *European
Journal of Social Psychology, 20,* 133-149.
doi:10.1002/ejsp.2420200205

Miller, D. T. (2001). Disrespect and the experience of
injustice. *Annual Review of Psychology, 52,* 527-
553. doi:10.1146/annurev.psych.52.1.527

Reeder, G. D., Kumar, S., Hesson-McInnis, M. S.,
& Trafimow, D. (2002). Inferences about the morality of an aggressor: The role of perceived motive.
Journal of Personality and Social Psychology, 83,
789-803. doi:10.1037/0022-3514.83.4.789

Reeder, G. D., Vonk, R., Ronk, M. J., Ham, J., &
Lawrence, M. (2004). Dispositional attribution:

The Lind and Tyler reference is to a book. It includes the author's names, year of publication (in parentheses), title of the book (italicized), city of publication, and publisher.

Multiple inferences about motive-related traits. *Journal of Personality and Social Psychology, 86*, 530-544. doi:10.1037/0022-3514.86.4.530

Shapiro, D. L., Buttner, E. H., & Barry, B. (1994). Explanations: What factors enhance their perceived adequacy? *Organizational Behavior and Human Decision Processes, 58,* 346-368. doi:10.1006/obhd.1994.1041

Sitkin, S. B. & Roth, N. L. (1993). Explaining the limited effectiveness of legalistic remedies for trust/distrust. *Organization Science, 4,* 367-392. oi:10.1287/orsc.4.3.367

Strauss, M. A. (1979). Measuring intrafamily conflict and violence: The Conflict Tactics Scales. *Journal of Marriage and the Family, 41,* 75-81. doi:10.2307/351733

Tedeschi. J. T., & Felson, R. (1994). *Violence, aggression, and coercive actions.* Washington, DC: American Psychological Association. doi:10.1037/10160-000

Toch, H. (1992). *Violent men: An inquiry into the psychology of violence.* Washington, DC: American Psychological Association. doi:10.1037/10135-000

Vidmar, N. (2000). Retribution and revenge. In J. Sanders & V. L. Hamilton (Eds.), *Handbook of justice research in law* (pp. 31-63). New York: Kluwer.

Wood, P. (2006). *A bee in the mouth: Anger in American now.* New York: Encounter Books.

The Vidmar reference is to a chapter in an edited book. It includes the author's name, year of publication (in parentheses), title of the chapter, the word "In," editors of the book, "Eds." In parentheses, title of the book (italicized), page numbers (in parentheses), city of publication, and publisher.

Tables and figures appear at the end of the manuscript. When the article is published, they will be inserted at the appropriate place in the Results section.

TABLE 1

Feelings toward the Partner

	Explanation Condition			
Implication	Random	Selfish	Legitimizing	None
Low				
M	3.8_{ae}	3.5_b	4.3_{cd}	4.1_{ce}
SD	1.03	.46	.49	.82
High				
M	4.6_d	3.3_b	4.3_{cd}	3.6_{ab}
SD	.68	1.15	1.05	.80

Note. Means that share a common subscript do not differ significantly at $\alpha = .05$. Higher numbers represent more positive feelings.

TABLE 2

Aggressive Inclinations

| Implication | Explanation Condition | | | |
	Random	Selfish	Legitimizing	None
Low				
M	1.1_{ab}	1.9_c	1.0_a	1.2_{ab}
SD	.18	1.5	.13	.53
High				
M	1.2_{ab}	1.2_{ab}	1.1_{ab}	1.3_b
SD	.43	.39	.20	.74

Note. Means that share a common subscript do not differ significantly at $\alpha = .05$.

Key Terms

abstract (*p. 343*)
APA style (*p. 342*)
author–date system (*p. 346*)
direct object identifier (DOI) (*p. 349*)

gender-neutral language (*p. 340*)
paper session (*p. 335*)
peer review (*p. 334*)
poster session (*p. 334*)
PsycINFO (*p. 344*)

research proposal (*p. 352*)
Uniform Resource Locator (URL) (*p. 349*)

Questions for Review

1. What are the three primary ways in which scientists share their work with the scientific community?
2. Why is peer review so important to science?
3. When an author submits a manuscript to a journal, what is the general process by which the decision is made whether or not to publish the paper?
4. Distinguish between a paper session and a poster session.
5. Why should we be cautious about reports of research that are published in the popular media and posted on the World Wide Web?
6. What are the three central characteristics of good writing?
7. Why should authors avoid using gender-biased language?
8. List in order the major sections that all research papers must have.
9. What is the purpose of the introduction of a paper?
10. What information should be included in the method section of a paper? What subsections does the method section typically have?
11. When presenting the results of statistical analyses, what information should be presented?
12. Write each of the following references in APA style:

   a. a book written by Donelson R. Forsyth entitled *Group Dynamics* that was published by Wadsworth (based in Belmont, CA) in 2006
   b. a journal article entitled "Interpersonal Reactions to Displays of Depression and Anxiety" that was published in the *Journal of Social and Clinical Psychology* in 1990; the authors were Michael B. Gurtman, Kathryn M. Martin, and Noelle M.

   Hintzman, and the article appeared on pages 256 to 267 of Volume 9 of the journal; the DOI is 10.6766/9876-65543.23.87.234
   c. a chapter entitled "We always hurt the ones we love" written by Rowland S. Miller, that appeared on pages 13 to 29 of an edited book entitled *Aversive Interpersonal Behaviors;* the book was edited by Robin M. Kowalski and published in 1997 by Plenum Press in New York City
   d. a paper presented by Mark R. Leary at the meeting of the American Psychological Association that was held in Boston in August of 1999; the paper was titled "The social and psychological importance of self-esteem"

   Answers to Question 12 appear in the next page.

13. Find the violations of APA style in each of the following sentences:

   a. Research suggests that attributions have an effect on relationship satisfaction over time (Wilson, 1987; Anderson and Camby, 1992).
   b. Atkinson (1991) noted that "previous studies confounded disease severity with the cost of medical care."
   c. Wilson, Ebbet, and Demorest (1986) were unable to replicate the earlier finding.
   d. Carter and Steinmore (1994) manipulated the brightness of the stimuli presented on the monitor screen. However, when analyzing their data, Carter et al. deleted all participants with reaction times greater than 1500 ms.

   Answers to Question 13 appear in the next page.

Exercises

1. If your college or university has *PsycINFO*, find out how to access it and then play around with it until you feel comfortable with how it works. Try different kinds of searching, using different terms and search fields, and then practice limiting your searches by type of document, participants, year of publication, and other criteria.

Don't worry—you can't break it—so try all of *PsycINFO*'s features to see what happens with each one.

2. Once you feel comfortable that you understand PsycINFO's basic features, search for publications on the following topics:

a. Search for all publications on the topic of jealousy.
b. Now limit your search to publications that deal specifically with differences in jealousy between men and women. (Consider what terms you will use. Sex differences? Gender differences? Differences between men and women? Others?) Try different ways of searching for relevant publications.
c. Eliminate publications that are not in English and dissertations from your search above (in b).
d. Read the summaries for a few of the citations that your search produced.

e. Search for peer-reviewed articles that deal with the evolution of jealousy. Try different search strategies. For example, try a search for (1) both *jealousy* and *evolution* in the article's title, (2) both *jealousy* and *evolution* in the article's abstract, and then (3) *jealousy* in the title and *evolution* in the abstract. Which strategy seems to provide the best results? See what happens if you use the word *evolutionary* rather than *evolution* in the abstract. Read a few of the summaries.
f. Search for articles and chapters on cultural differences in jealousy. Read a few of the summaries.
g. Search for publications on jealousy by Peter Salovey.
h. Search for publications specifically on jealousy in infants and children.

Answers to Question 12

a. Book Reference
Forsyth, D. R. (2006). *Group dynamics*. Belmont, CA: Wadsworth.
b. Journal Reference
Gurtman, M. B., Martin, K. M., & Hintzman, N. M. (1990). Interpersonal reactions to displays of depression and anxiety. *Journal of Social and Clinical Psychology, 9*, 256–267. doi: 10.6766/9876-65543.23.87.234.
c. Chapter Reference

Miller, R. S. (1997). We always hurt the ones we love. In R. M. Kowalski (Ed.), *Aversive interpersonal behaviors* (pp. 13–29). New York: Plenum Press.
d. Paper Reference
Leary, M. R. (1999, August). *The social and psychological importance of self-esteem*. Paper presented at the meeting of the American Psychological Association, Boston, MA.

Answers to Question 13

a. This sentence contains two violations of APA style: The "and" in "Anderson and Camby" should be an ampersand (&), and "Anderson & Camby" should precede "Wilson."

Research suggests that attributions have an effect on relationship satisfaction over time (Anderson & Camby, 1992; Wilson, 1987).

b. When quoting, the page number of the quotation must be given.

Atkinson (1991) noted that "previous studies confounded disease severity with the cost of medical care" (p. 456).

c. This sentence is perfectly okay as it is.
d. Because there are only two authors, both names should be given each time the study is cited; use "et al." only when referencing sources that have more than two authors.

Carter and Steinmore (1994) manipulated the brightness of the stimuli presented on the monitor screen. However, when analyzing their data, Carter and Steinmore deleted all participants with reaction times greater than 1500 ms.

GLOSSARY

ABA design a single-case experimental design in which baseline data are obtained (A), the independent variable is introduced and behavior is measured again (B), then the independent variable is withdrawn and behavior is observed a third time (A)

ABACA design a multiple-I single-case experimental design in which baseline data are obtained (A), one level of the independent variable is introduced (B), this level of the independent variable is withdrawn (A), a second level of the independent variable is introduced (C), and this level of the independent variable is withdrawn (A)

ABC design a multiple-I single-case experimental design that contains a baseline period (A), followed by the introduction of one level of the independent variable (B), followed by the introduction of another level of the independent variable (C)

abstract a summary of a journal article or research report

acquiescence the tendency for some people to agree with statements regardless of their content

alpha level the maximum probability that a researcher is willing to make a Type I error (rejecting the null hypothesis when it is true); typically, the alpha level is set at .05

analysis of variance (ANOVA) an inferential statistical procedure used to test differences between means

APA style guidelines set forth by the American Psychological Association (APA) for preparing research reports; these guidelines may be found in the *Publication Manual of the American Psychological Association* (6th ed.)

applied research research designed to investigate real-world problems or improve the quality of life

a priori prediction a prediction made about the outcome of a study before data are collected

archival research research in which data are analyzed from existing records, such as census reports, court records, or personal letters

attrition the loss of participants during a study

author–date system in APA style, the manner of citing previous research by providing the author's last name and the date of publication

bar graph a graph of data on which the variable on the x-axis is measured on a nominal or ordinal scale of measurement; because the x-variable is not continuous, the bars do not touch one another

basic research research designed to understand psychological processes without regard for whether that understanding will be immediately applicable in solving real-world problems

beta the probability of committing a Type II error (failing to reject the null hypothesis when it is false)

between-groups variance the portion of the total variance in a set of scores that reflects systematic differences between the experimental groups

between-subjects or between-groups design an experimental design in which each participant serves in only one condition of the experiment

between-within design an experimental design that combines one or more between-subjects factors with one or more within-subjects factors; also called *mixed factorial* or *split-plot design*

biased assignment a threat to internal validity that occurs when participants are assigned to conditions in a nonrandom manner, producing systematic differences among conditions prior to introduction of the independent variable

Bonferroni adjustment a means of preventing inflation of Type I error when more than one statistical test is conducted; the desired alpha level (usually .05) is divided by the number of tests to be performed

canonical variable in MANOVA, a composite variable that is calculated by summing two or more dependent variables that have been weighted according to their ability to differentiate among groups of participants

carryover effects effects that may occur in a within-subjects experiment when the effect of a particular level of the independent variable persists even after the treatment ends; carryover effects may lead researchers to conclude that a particular level of the independent variable had an effect on participants' responses when the effect was actually caused by a level that was administered earlier

case study an intensive descriptive study of a particular individual, group, or event

checklist a measuring instrument on which a rater indicates whether particular behaviors have been observed

class interval a subset of a range of scores; in a grouped frequency distribution, the number of participants who fall into each class interval is shown

cluster sampling a probability sampling procedure in which the researcher first samples clusters or groups of participants, and then obtains participants from the selected clusters

coefficient of determination the square of the correlation coefficient; indicates the proportion of variance in one variable that can be accounted for by the other variable

coercion to participate the situation that arises when people agree to participate in a research study because of real or implied pressure from some individual who has authority or influence over them

comparative time series design a quasi-experimental design that examines two or more variables over time to understand how changes in one variable are related to changes in another variable; also called comparative trend analysis

computerized experience sampling methods the use of small, portable computers, personal digital assistants, or smartphones to allow participants to record information about experiences in their daily lives soon after they happen

conceptual definition an abstract, dictionary-type definition (as contrasted with an operational definition)

concurrent validity a form of criterion-related validity that reflects the extent to which a measure allows a researcher to distinguish between respondents at the time the measure is taken

condition one level of an independent variable

confederate an accomplice of an experimenter whom participants assume to be another participant or an uninvolved bystander

confidence interval (CI) the range of scores around a sample mean in which the means of other samples from the same population are likely to fall with a certain probability (usually 95%)

confidentiality maintaining the privacy of participants' responses in a study

confounding a condition that exists in experimental research when something other than the independent variable differs systematically among the experimental conditions

confound variance the portion of the total variance in a set of scores that is due to extraneous variables that differ systematically between the experimental groups; also called *secondary variance*

construct validity the degree to which a measure of a particular construct correlates as expected with measures of other constructs

contemporary history a threat to the internal validity of a quasi-experiment that develops when another event occurs at the same time as the quasi-independent variable

content analysis procedures used to convert written or spoken information into data that can be analyzed and interpreted

contrived observation the observation of behavior in settings that have been arranged specifically for observing and recording behavior

control group participants in an experiment who receive a zero level of the independent variable

convenience sample a nonprobability sample that includes whatever participants are readily available

convergent validity documenting the validity of a measure by showing that it correlates appropriately with measures of related constructs

converging operations using several measurement approaches to measure a particular variable

correlational research research designed to examine the nature of the relationship between two measured variables

correlation coefficient an index of the direction and magnitude of the relationship between two variables; the value of a correlation coefficient ranges from 21.00 to 11.00

cost–benefit analysis a method of making decisions in which the potential costs and risks of a study are weighed against its likely benefits

counterbalancing a procedure used in within-subjects designs in which different participants receive the levels of the independent variable in different orders; counterbalancing is used to avoid systematic order effects

criterion-related validity the extent to which a measure allows a researcher to distinguish among respondents on the basis of some behavioral criterion

criterion variable the variable being predicted in a regression analysis; the dependent or outcome variable

critical multiplism the philosophy that researchers should use many ways of obtaining evidence regarding a particular hypothesis rather than relying on a single approach

critical value the minimum value of a statistic (such as t or F) at which the results would be considered statistically significant

Cronbach's alpha coefficient an index of interitem reliability

cross-lagged panel correlation design a research design in which two variables are measured at two points in time and correlations between the variables are examined across time

cross-sectional design a research design in which a group of respondents is studied once

cross-sequential cohort design a quasi-experimental design in which two or more age cohorts are measured at two or more times; in essence, it is a longitudinal design with multiple age groups that allows researchers to separate the effects of age and cohort

debriefing the procedure through which research participants are told about the nature of a study after it is completed

deception misleading or lying to participants for research purposes

deduction the process of reasoning from a general proposition to a specific implication of that proposition; for example, hypotheses are often deduced from theories

demand characteristics aspects of a study that indicate to participants how they are expected to respond

demographic research descriptive research that studies basic life events in a population, such as patterns of births, marriages, deaths, and migrations

deontology an ethical approach maintaining that right and wrong should be judged according to a universal moral code

dependent variable the response measured in a study, typically a measure of participants' thoughts, feelings, behavior, or physiological reactions

descriptive research research designed to describe in an accurate and systematic fashion the behavior, thoughts, or feelings of a group of participants

descriptive statistics numbers that summarize and describe the behavior of participants in a study; the mean and standard deviation are descriptive statistics, for example

diary methodology a method of data collection in which participants keep a daily record of their behavior, thoughts, or feelings

differential attrition the loss of participants during a study in a manner such that the loss is not randomly distributed across conditions

directional hypothesis a prediction that explicitly states the direction of a hypothesized effect; for example, a prediction of which two means will be larger

direct object identifier (doi) the unique number assigned to a journal article that assists with its retrieval from electronic databases and on-line sources

discriminant validity documenting the validity of a measure by showing that it does not correlate with measures of conceptually unrelated constructs

disguised observation observing participants' behavior without their knowledge

double-blind procedure the practice of concealing the purpose and hypotheses of a study both from the participants and from the researchers who have direct contact with the participants

duration a measure of the amount of time that a particular reaction lasts from its onset to conclusion

economic sample a sample that provides a reasonable degree of accuracy at a reasonable cost in terms of money, time, and effort

effect size the strength of the relationship between two or more variables, usually expressed as the proportion of variance in one variable that can be accounted for by another variable

empirical generalization a hypothesis that is based on the results of previous studies

empiricism the practice of relying on observation to draw conclusions about the world

environmental manipulation an independent variable that involves the experimental modification of the participant's physical or social environment

epidemiological research research that studies the occurrence of disease in different groups of people

error bar a vertical line used in a bar graph or histogram to indicate the confidence interval around a group mean

error of estimation the degree to which data obtained from a sample are expected to deviate from the population as a whole; also called *margin of error*

error variance that portion of the total variance in a set of data that remains unaccounted for after systematic variance is removed; variance that is unrelated to the variables under investigation in a study

ESM see *experience sampling method*

ethical skepticism an ethical approach that denies the existence of concrete and inviolate moral codes

evaluation research the use of behavioral research methods to assess the effects of programs on behavior; also called *program evaluation*

expericorr factorial design an experimental design that includes one or more manipulated independent variables and one or more preexisting participant variables that are measured rather than manipulated; also called *mixed factorial design*

experience sampling method (ESM) a method of collecting data in which participants record information about their thoughts, emotions, or behaviors as they occur in everyday life

experiment research in which the researcher assigns participants to conditions and manipulates at least one independent variable

experimental contamination a situation that occurs when participants in one experimental condition are indirectly affected by the independent variable in another experimental condition because they interacted with participants in the other condition

experimental control the practice of eliminating or holding constant extraneous variables that might affect the outcome of an experiment

experimental group participants in an experiment who receive a nonzero level of the independent variable

experimental hypothesis the hypothesis that the independent variable will have an effect on the dependent variable; equivalently, the hypothesis that the means of the various experimental conditions will differ from one another

experimental research research designed to test whether certain variables cause changes in behavior, thoughts, or feelings; in an experiment, the researcher assigns participants to conditions and manipulates at least one independent variable

experimenter expectancy effect a situation in which a researcher's expectations about the outcome of a study influence participants' reactions; also called *Rosenthal effect*

experimenter's dilemma the situation in which, generally speaking, the greater the internal validity of an experiment, the lower its external validity, and vice versa

external validity the degree to which the results obtained in one study can be replicated or generalized to other samples, research settings, and procedures

extreme groups procedure creating two groups of participants that have unusually low or unusually high scores on a particular variable

face validity the extent to which a measurement procedure appears to measure what it is supposed to measure

factor (1) in experimental designs, an independent variable; (2) in factor analysis, the underlying dimension that is assumed to account for observed relationships among variables

factor analysis a class of multivariate statistical techniques that identifies the underlying dimensions (factors) that account for the observed relationships among a set of measured variables

factorial design an experimental design in which two or more independent variables are manipulated

factor loading in factor analysis, the correlation between a variable and a factor

factor matrix a table that shows the results of a factor analysis; in this matrix the rows are variables and the columns are factors

failing to reject the null hypothesis concluding on the basis of statistical evidence that the null hypothesis is true—that the independent variable does not have an effect

falsifiability the requirement that a hypothesis must be capable of being falsified

fatigue effects effects that may occur in a within-subjects experiment when participants' performance declines during the study because they become tired, bored, or unmotivated as they serve in more than one experimental condition; fatigue effects may lead researchers to conclude that participants' poor performance in a particular experimental condition was due to the independent variable when it was actually due to fatigue, disinterest, or lack of motivation

field notes a researcher's narrative record of a participant's behavior

file drawer problem the possibility that studies that failed to support a particular hypothesis have not been published, leading researchers to overestimate the amount of support for an effect based on only the published evidence

fit index in structural equations modeling, a statistic that indicates how well a hypothesized model fits the data

fixed-alternative response format a response format in which participants answer a questionnaire or interview item by choosing one response from a set of possible alternatives; also called a multiple choice response format

fMRI see *functional magnetic resonance imaging*

follow-up tests inferential statistics that are used after a significant *F*-test to determine which means differ from which; also called *post hoc tests* or *multiple comparisons*

free-response format a response format in which the participant provides an unstructured answer to a question; also called an open-ended question

frequency the number of participants who obtained a particular score

frequency distribution a table that shows the number of participants who obtained each possible score on a measure

frequency polygon a form of line graph

F-test an inferential statistical procedure used to test for differences among condition means; the *F*-test is used in ANOVA

functional magnetic resonance imaging (fMRI) a brain imaging technology that allows researchers to view the structure and activity of the brain; used to study the relationship between brain activity and psychological phenomena, such as perception, thought, and emotion

gender-neutral language language that treats men and women equally and does not perpetuate stereotypes about men and women

generational effects differences among people of various ages that are due to the different conditions under which each generation has grown up rather than age differences

grand mean the mean of all of the condition means in an experiment

graphical method presenting and summarizing data in pictorial form (e.g., graphs and pictures)

graphic analysis in single-case experimental research, the visual inspection of graphs of the data to determine whether the independent variable affected the participant's behavior

group design an experimental design in which several participants serve in each condition of the design, and the data are analyzed by examining the average responses of participants in these conditions

grouped frequency distribution a table that indicates the number of participants who obtained each of a range of scores

hierarchical multiple regression a multiple regression analysis in which the researcher specifies the order that the predictor variables will be entered into the regression equation

histogram a form of bar graph in which the variable on the x-axis is on a continuous scale

history effects changes in participants' responses between pretest and posttest that are due to an outside, extraneous influence rather than to the independent variable

hypothesis a proposition that follows logically from a theory; also, a prediction regarding the outcome of a study

hypothetical construct an entity that cannot be directly observed but that is inferred on the basis of observable evidence; intelligence, status, and anxiety are examples of hypothetical constructs

idiographic approach research that describes, analyzes, and attempts to understand the behavior of individual participants; often contrasted with the nomothetic approach

independent variable in an experiment, the variable that is varied or manipulated by the researcher to assess its effects on participants' behavior

induction the process of reasoning from specific instances to a general proposition about those instances; for example, hypotheses are sometimes induced from observed facts

inferential statistics mathematical analyses that allow researchers to draw conclusions regarding the reliability and generalizability of their data; t-tests and F-tests are inferential statistics, for example

informed consent the practice of informing participants regarding the nature of their participation in a study and obtaining their explicit consent to participate

informed consent form a document that describes the nature of participants' participation in a study (including all possible risks) and provides an opportunity for participants to indicate in writing their willingness to participate

Institutional Review Board (IRB) a committee mandated by federal regulations that must evaluate the ethics of research conducted at institutions that receive federal funding

instructional manipulation an independent variable that is varied through verbal information that is provided to participants

interaction the combined effect of two or more independent variables such that the effect of one independent variable differs across the levels of the other independent variable(s)

interbehavior latency the time that elapses between the occurrence of two behaviors

interitem reliability the consistency of respondents' responses on a set of conceptually related items; the degree to which a set of items that ostensibly measure the same construct are intercorrelated

internal validity the degree to which a researcher draws accurate conclusions about the effects of an independent variable

Internet survey a survey in which respondents access and respond to research materials on the World Wide Web

interparticipant replication in single-case experimental research, documenting the generalizability of an experimental effect by demonstrating the effect on other participants

interparticipant variance variability among the responses of the participants in a particular experimental condition

interrater reliability the degree to which the observations of two independent raters or observers agree; also called *interjudge* or *interobserver reliability*

interrupted time series design with a reversal a study in which (1) the dependent variable is measured several times; (2) the independent variable is introduced; (3) the dependent variable is measured several more times; (4) the independent variable is then withdrawn; and (5) the dependent variable is again measured several times

interrupted time series design with multiple replications a study in which (1) the dependent variable is measured several times; (2) the independent variable is introduced; (3) the dependent variable is measured again; (4) the independent variable is withdrawn; (5) the dependent variable is measured; (6) the independent variable is introduced a second time; (7) more measures of the dependent variable are taken; (8) the independent variable is once again withdrawn; and (9) the dependent variable is measured after the independent variable has been withdrawn for the second time

interval scale a measure on which equal distances between scores represent equal differences in the property being measured

interview a method of data collection in which respondents respond verbally to a researcher's questions

interview schedule the series of questions and accompanying response formats that guides an interviewer's line of questioning during an interview

intraparticipant replication in single-case experimental research, the attempt to repeatedly demonstrate an experimental effect on a single participant by alternatively introducing and withdrawing the independent variable

intraparticipant variance variability among the responses of a participant when tested more than once in a particular experimental condition

invasion of privacy violation of a research participant's right to determine how, when, or where he or she will be studied

invasive manipulation an independent variable that directly alters the participant's body, such as surgical procedures or the administration of chemical substances

item any prompt that leads a participant to provide an answer, rating, or other verbal response on a questionnaire or in an interview

item-total correlation the correlation between respondents' scores on one item on a scale and the sum of their responses on the remaining items; an index of interitem reliability

knowledgeable informant someone who knows a participant well enough to report on his or her behavior

latency the amount of time that elapses between a particular event and a behavior

Latin Square design an experimental design used to control for order effects in a within-subjects design

level one value of an independent variable

local history effect a threat to internal validity in which an extraneous event happens to one experimental group that does not happen to the other groups

longitudinal design a study in which a single group of participants is studied over time

main effect the effect of a particular independent variable, ignoring the effects of other independent variables in the experiment

manipulation check a measure designed to determine whether participants in an experiment perceived different levels of the independent variable differently

margin of error see *error of estimation*

matched random assignment a procedure for assigning participants to experimental conditions in which participants are first matched into homogeneous blocks and then participants within each block are assigned randomly to conditions

matched-subjects design an experimental design in which participants are matched into homogeneous blocks, and participants in each block are randomly assigned to the experimental conditions

matched-subjects factorial design an experimental design involving two or more independent variables in which participants are first matched into homogeneous blocks and then, within each block, are randomly assigned to the experimental conditions

maturation changes in participants' responses between pretest and posttest that are due to the passage of time rather than to the independent variable; aging, fatigue, and hunger may produce maturation effects, for example

mean the mathematical average of a set of scores; the sum of a set of scores divided by the number of scores

mean square between-groups an estimate of between-groups variance calculated by dividing the sum of squares between-groups by the between-groups degrees of freedom

mean square within-groups the average variance within experimental conditions; the sum of squares within-groups divided by the degrees of freedom within-groups

measurement error the deviation of a participant's observed score from his or her true score

measures of central tendency descriptive statistics that convey information about the average or typical score in a distribution; the mean, median, and mode are measures of central tendency

measures of variability descriptive statistics that convey information about the spread or variability of a set of data; the range, variance, and standard deviation are measures of variability

median the score that falls at the 50th percentile; the middle score in a rank-ordered distribution

median-split procedure assigning participants to two groups depending on whether their scores on a particular variable fall above or below the median of that variable

meta-analysis a statistical procedure used to analyze and integrate the results of many individual studies on a single topic

methodological pluralism the practice of using many different research approaches to address a particular question

minimal risk risk to research participants that is no greater than they would be likely to encounter in daily life or during routine physical or psychological examinations

misgeneralization generalizing results from a study to a population that differs in important ways from the one from which the sample was drawn

mixed factorial design (1) an experimental design that includes one or more between-subjects factors and one or more within-subjects factors; also called *between-within design;* (2) also refers to an experimental design that includes both manipulated independent variables and measured participant variables; also called *expericorr design*

mode the most frequent score in a distribution

model an explanation of how a particular process occurs

moderator variable a variable that qualifies or moderates the effects of another variable on behavior

multi-item scale a set of questionnaire or interview items that are intended to be used and analyzed as a set

multilevel modeling an approach to analyzing data that have a nested structure in which variables are measured at different levels of analysis; for example, when researchers study several preexisting groups of participants, they use multilevel modeling to analyze the influence of group-level variables and individual-level variables simultaneously

multiple baseline design a single-case experimental design in which two or more behaviors are studied simultaneously

multiple choice response format a response format in which participants answer a questionnaire or interview item by choosing one response from a set of possible alternatives; also called a *fixed-alternative response format*

multiple comparisons inferential statistics that are used after a significant F-test to determine which means differ from which; also called *post hoc tests* or *follow-up tests*

multiple correlation coefficient the correlation between one variable and a set of other variables; often used in multiple regression to express the strength of the relationship between the outcome variable and the set of predictor variables

multiple-I design a single-case experimental design in which levels of an independent variable are introduced one at a time

multiple regression analysis a statistical procedure by which an equation is derived that can predict one variable (the criterion or outcome variable) from a set of other variables (the predictor variables)

multistage cluster sampling a variation of cluster sampling in which large clusters of participants are sampled, followed by smaller clusters from within the larger clusters, followed by still smaller clusters, until participants are sampled from the small clusters

multivariate analysis of variance (MANOVA) a statistical procedure that simultaneously tests differences among the means of two or more groups on two or more dependent variables

narrative description a descriptive summary of an individual's behavior, often with interpretations and explanations, such as is generated in a case study

narrative record a full description of a participant's behavior as it occurs

naturalistic observation observation of ongoing behavior as it occurs naturally with no intrusion or intervention by the researcher

nay-saying the tendency for some participants to disagree with statements on questionnaires or in interviews regardless of the content

negative correlation an inverse relationship between two variables such that participants with high scores on one variable tend to have low scores on the other variable, and vice versa

negatively skewed distribution a distribution in which there are more high scores than low scores

nested design a research design in which participants are drawn from various groups, such as students being recruited from classrooms; in a nested design, the responses of participants who come from a single group are not independent of one another, which raises special analysis issues

neuroimaging techniques, such as fMRI and Computed Axial Tomography (CAT), that allow researchers to see images of the structure and activity of the brain

neuroscience an interdisciplinary field involving chemistry, biology, psychology, and other disciplines that studies biochemical, anatomical, physiological, genetic, and developmental processes involving the nervous system; within psychology, neuroscientists study how processes occurring in the nervous system are related to sensation, perception, thought, emotion, and behavior

neuroscientific measure a measure that assesses processes occurring in the brain or other parts of the nervous system; also called a *psychophysiological measure*

nominal scale a measure on which the numbers assigned to participants' characteristics are merely labels; participant sex is on a nominal scale, for example

nomothetic approach research that seeks to establish general principles and broad generalizations; often contrasted with the idiographic approach

nondirectional hypothesis a prediction that does not express the direction of a hypothesized effect—for example, which of two means will be larger

nonequivalent control group design a quasi-experimental design in which the group of participants that receives the quasi-independent variable is compared to one or more groups of participants who do not receive the treatment

nonequivalent groups posttest-only design a quasi-experimental design in which two preexisting groups are studied—one that has received the quasi-independent variable and one that has not

nonequivalent groups pretest–posttest design a quasi-experimental design in which two preexisting groups are tested—one that has received the quasi-independent variable and one that has not; each group is tested twice—once before and once after one group receives the quasi-independent variable

nonprobability sample a sample selected in such a way that the likelihood of any member of the population being chosen for the sample cannot be determined

nonresponse problem the failure of individuals who are selected for a sample to agree to participate or answer all questions; nonresponse is a particular problem when probability samples are used because it destroys their representativeness

normal distribution a distribution of scores that rises to a rounded peak in the center with symmetrical tails descending to the left and right of the center

null finding failing to obtain a statistically significant effect in a study

null hypothesis the hypothesis that the independent variable will not have an effect; equivalently, the hypothesis that the means of the various experimental conditions will not differ

numerical method presenting and summarizing data in numerical form (e.g., means, percentages, and other descriptive statistics)

observational measure a method of measuring behavior by directly observing participants

one-group pretest–posttest design a preexperimental design in which one group of participants is tested before and after a quasi-independent variable has occurred; because it fails to control for nearly all threats to internal validity, this design should never be used

one-tailed test a statistic (such as *t*) used to test a directional hypothesis

one-way design an experimental design with a single independent variable

operational definition defining a construct by specifying precisely how it is measured or manipulated in a particular study

order effects effects that may occur in a within-subjects experiment when participants' responses are affected by the order in which they receive various levels of the independent variable; order effects may lead researchers to conclude that a particular level of the independent variable had an effect when, in fact, the effect was produced by administering the levels of the independent variable in a particular order

ordinal scale a measure on which the numbers assigned to participants' responses reflect the rank order of participants from highest to lowest

outcome variable the variable being predicted in a multiple regression analysis; also called *criterion* or *dependent variable*

outlier an extreme score; typically scores that fall farther than 3 standard deviations from the mean are considered outliers

paired *t*-test a *t*-test performed on a repeated measures two-group design

panel survey design a study in which a single group of participants is studied over time; also called *longitudinal survey design*

paper session a session at a professional conference in which researchers give oral presentations about their studies

partial correlation the correlation between two variables with the influence of one or more other variables removed

participant observation a method of data collection in which researchers engage in the same activities as the participants they are observing

participant variable a personal characteristic of research participants, such as age, gender, self-esteem, or extraversion; also called a *subject variable*

Pearson correlation coefficient the most commonly used measure of correlation

peer review the process by which experts evaluate research papers to judge their suitability for publication or presentation

perfect correlation a correlation of −1.00 or +1.00, indicating that two variables are so closely related that one can be perfectly predicted from the other

phi coefficient a statistic that expresses the correlation between two dichotomous variables

physiological measure a measure of bodily activity; in behavioral research, physiological measures generally are used to assess processes within the nervous system

pilot test a preliminary study that examines the usefulness of manipulations or measures that later will be used in an experiment

placebo control group participants who receive an ineffective treatment; this is used to identify and control for placebo effects

placebo effect a physiological or psychological change that occurs as a result of the mere suggestion that the change will occur

point-biserial correlation the correlation between a dichotomous and a continuous variable

positive correlation a direct relationship between two variables such that participants with high scores on one variable tend also to have high scores on the other variable, whereas low scorers on one variable tend also to score low on the other

positively skewed distribution a distribution in which there are more low scores than high scores

poster session a session at a professional conference at which researchers display information about their studies on posters

post hoc explanation an explanation offered for a set of findings after the data are collected and analyzed

post hoc tests inferential statistics that are used after a significant F-test to determine which means differ; also called *follow-up tests* or *multiple comparisons*

posttest-only design an experiment in which participants' responses are measured only once—after introduction of the independent variable

power the degree to which a research design is sensitive to the effects of the independent variable; powerful designs are able to detect effects of the independent variable more easily than less powerful designs

power analysis a statistic that conveys the power or sensitivity of a study; power analysis is often used to determine the number of participants needed to achieve a particular level of power

practice effects effects that may occur in a within-subjects experiment when participants' performance improves merely because they complete the dependent variable more than once; practice effects may lead researchers to conclude that participants' performance was due to the independent variable when it was actually caused by completing the dependent variable multiple times (i.e., practice)

predictive validity a form of criterion-related validity that reflects the extent to which a measure allows a researcher to distinguish between respondents at some time in the future

predictor variable in a regression analysis, a variable used to predict scores on the criterion or dependent variable

preexperimental design a design that lacks the necessary controls to minimize threats to internal validity; typically preexperimental designs do not involve adequate control or comparison groups

p_{rep} a statistic that estimates the probability of replicating an effect obtained in an experiment

pretest–posttest design an experiment in which participants' responses are measured twice—once before and once after the introduction of the independent variable

pretest sensitization the situation that occurs when completing a pretest affects participants' responses on the posttest

primary variance that portion of the total variance in a set of scores that is due to the independent variable; also called *treatment variance*

probability sample a sample selected in such a way that the likelihood of any individual in the population being selected can be specified

program evaluation the use of behavioral research methods to assess the effects of programs on behavior; also called *evaluation research*

proportionate sampling method a variation of stratified random sampling in which cases are selected from each stratum in proportion to their prevalence in the population

pseudoscience claims of knowledge that are couched in the trappings of science but that violate the central criteria of scientific investigation, such as systematic empiricism, public verification, and testability

psychobiography a biographical case study of an individual, with a focus on explaining the course of the person's life using psychological constructs and theories

psychometrics the field devoted to the study of psychological measurement; experts in this field are known as *psychometricians*

psychophysiological measure a measure that assesses processes occurring in the brain or other parts of the nervous system

public verification the practice of conducting research in such a way that it can be observed, verified, and replicated by others

purposive sample a sample selected on the basis of the researcher's judgment regarding the "best" participants to select for research purposes

quasi-experimental design a research design in which the researcher cannot assign participants to conditions and/or manipulate the independent variable; instead, comparisons are made between groups that already exist or within a single group before and after a quasi-experimental treatment has occurred

quasi-experimental research research in which the researcher cannot assign participants to conditions or manipulate the independent variable

quasi-independent variable the independent variable in a quasi-experimental design; the designator *quasi*-independent is used when the variable is not manipulated by the researcher

questionnaire a method of data collection in which respondents provide written answers to written questions

quota sample a sample selected to include specified proportions of certain kinds of participants

random digit dialing a method of obtaining random samples by dialing telephone numbers at random

randomized groups design an experimental design in which each participant serves in only one condition of the experiment; also called *between-groups* or *between-subjects design*

randomized groups factorial design an experimental design involving two or more independent variables in which each participant serves in only one condition of the experiment

range a measure of variability that is equal to the difference between the largest and smallest scores in a set of data

rating scale response format a response format on which participants rate the intensity or frequency of their behaviors, thoughts, or feelings

ratio scale a measure on which scores possess all of the characteristics of real numbers, including a true zero point

raw data the original data collected on a sample of participants before they are summarized or analyzed

reaction time the time that elapses between a stimulus and a participant's response to that stimulus

reactivity the phenomenon that occurs when a participant's knowledge that he or she is being studied affects his or her responses

regression analysis a statistical procedure by which an equation is developed to predict scores on one variable based on scores from another variable

regression coefficient the slope of a regression line

regression constant the y-intercept in a regression equation; the value of y when $x = 0$

regression equation an equation from which one can predict scores on one variable from one or more other variables

regression to the mean the tendency for participants who are selected on the basis of their extreme scores on some measure to obtain less extreme scores when they are retested

rejecting the null hypothesis concluding on the basis of statistical evidence that the null hypothesis is false

relative frequency the proportion of participants who obtained a particular score or fell in a particular class interval

reliability the consistency or dependability of a measuring technique; reliability is inversely related to measurement error

repeated measures design an experimental design in which each participant serves in more than one condition of the experiment; a within-subjects design

repeated measures factorial design an experimental design involving two or more independent variables in which each participant serves in all conditions of the experiment

representative sample a sample from which one can draw accurate, unbiased estimates of the characteristics of a larger population

research proposal a description of research that an investigator would like to conduct written to convince decision makers (such as funding agencies or faculty committees) of the importance, feasibility, and methodological quality of the project

response format the manner in which respondents indicate their answers to questions

restricted range a set of data in which participants' scores are confined to a narrow range of the possible scores

reversal design a single-case experimental design in which the independent variable is introduced and then withdrawn

sample a subset of a population; the group of participants who are selected to participate in a research study

sampling the process by which a sample is chosen from a population to participate in research

sampling error the difference between scores obtained on a sample and the scores that would have been obtained if the entire population had been studied

sampling frame a list of the members of a population

scales of measurement properties of a measure that reflect the degree to which scores obtained on that measure reflect the characteristics of real numbers; typically, four scales of measurement are distinguished—nominal, ordinal, interval, and ratio

scatter plot a graphical representation of participants' scores on two variables; the values of one variable are plotted on the *x*-axis and those of the other variable are plotted on the *y*-axis

scientific misconduct unethical behaviors involving the conduct of scientific research, such as dishonesty, data fabrication, and plagiarism

secondary variance the variance in a set of scores that is due to systematic differences between the experimental groups that are not due to the independent variable; also called *confound variance*

selection bias a threat to internal validity that arises when the experimental groups were not equivalent before the manipulation of the independent or quasi-independent variable

selection-by-history interaction see *local history effect*

self-report measure a measure on which participants provide information about themselves, on a questionnaire or in an interview, for example

sensitization effects effects that may occur in a within-subjects experiment when participants become aware of (sensitized to) the purpose of the experiment as they serve in more than one experimental condition; sensitization

effects may lead researchers to conclude that participants' performance was due to the independent variable when it was actually caused by serving in multiple conditions of the experiment

simple frequency distribution a table that indicates the number of participants who obtained each score

simple interrupted time series design a quasi-experimental design in which participants are tested on many occasions—several before and several after the occurrence of the quasi-independent variable

simple main effect the effect of one independent variable at a particular level of another independent variable

simple random assignment placing participants in experimental conditions in such a way that every participant has an equal chance of being placed in any condition

simple random sample a sample selected in such a way that every possible sample of the desired size has the same chance of being selected from the population

simultaneous multiple regression a multiple regression analysis in which all of the predictors are entered into the regression equation in a single step; also called *standard multiple regression*

single-case experimental design an experimental design in which the unit of analysis is the individual participant rather than the experimental group; also called *single-subject design*

single-item measure a questionnaire or interview item that is intended to be analyzed and used by itself; compare to *multi-item scale*

social desirability response bias the tendency for people to distort their responses in a manner that portrays them in a positive light

Spearman rank-order correlation a correlation coefficient calculated on variables that are measured on an ordinal scale

split-half reliability the correlation between respondents' scores on two halves of a single instrument; an index of interitem reliability

split-plot factorial design a factorial design that combines one or more between-subjects factors with one or more within-subjects factors; also called *mixed factorial design* and *between-within design*

spurious correlation a correlation between two variables that is not due to any direct relationship between them but rather to their relation to other variables

standard deviation a measure of variability that is equal to the square root of the variance

standard error of the difference between two means a statistical estimate of how much two condition means would be expected to differ if their difference is due only to error variance and the independent variable had no effect

standard multiple regression see *simultaneous multiple regression*

statistical notation a system of symbols that represents particular mathematical operations, variables, and statistics; for example, in statistical notation, $\overline{x}$ stands for the mean, Σ means to add, and s^2 is the variance

statistical significance a finding that is very unlikely to be due to error variance

stepwise multiple regression a multiple regression analysis in which predictors enter the regression equation in order of their ability to predict unique variance in the outcome variable

strategy of strong inference designing a study in such a way that it tests competing predictions from two or more theories

stratified random sampling a sampling procedure in which the population is divided into strata, then participants are sampled randomly from each stratum

stratum a subset of a population that shares a certain characteristic; for example, a population could be divided into the strata of men and women

structural equations modeling a statistical analysis that tests the viability of alternative causal explanations of variables that correlate with one another

subject variable a personal characteristic of research participants, such as age, gender, self-esteem, or extraversion; also called a *participant variable*

successive independent samples survey design a survey design in which different samples of participants are studied at different points in time

sum of squares the sum of the squared deviations between individual participants' scores and the mean; $\Sigma(x - \overline{x})^2$

sum of squares between-groups the variance in a set of scores that is associated with the independent variable; the sum of the squared differences between each condition mean and the grand mean

sum of squares within-groups the sum of the variances of the scores within particular experimental conditions

symposium a session at a scientific conference that includes several presentations on a single topic

systematic sampling a probability sampling procedure that involves taking every nth individual from a sampling frame

systematic variance the portion of the total variance in a set of scores that is related in an orderly, predictable fashion to the variables the researcher is investigating

table of random numbers a table containing numbers that occur in a random order that is often used to select random samples or to assign participants to experimental conditions in a random fashion

task completion time the amount of time it takes a research participant to complete a test, problem, or other task

test bias the characteristic of a test that is not equally valid for different groups of people

test–retest reliability the consistency of respondents' scores on a measure across time

theory set of propositions that attempts to explain the relationships among a set of concepts

time series design a class of quasi-experimental designs in which participants are tested on many occasions—several before and several after the occurrence of a quasi-independent variable

total mean square the variance of a set of data; the sum of squares divided by its degrees of freedom

total sum of squares the total variability in a set of data; calculated by subtracting the mean from each score, squaring the differences, and summing them

total variance the total sum of squares divided by the number of scores minus 1

treatment variance that portion of the total variance in a set of scores that is due to the independent variable; also called *primary variance*

true score the hypothetical score that a participant would obtain if the attribute being measured could be measured without error

t-test an inferential statistic that tests the difference between two means

two-group experimental design an experiment with two conditions; the simplest possible experiment

two-tailed test a statistical test for a nondirectional hypothesis

Type I error erroneously rejecting the null hypothesis when it is true; concluding that an independent variable had an effect when, in fact, it did not

Type II error erroneously failing to reject the null hypothesis when it is false; concluding that the independent variable did not have an effect when, in fact, it did

undisguised observation observing participants with their knowledge of being observed

uniform resource locator (URL) an Internet (Web site) address

unobtrusive measure a dependent variable that can be measured without affecting participants' responses

utilitarian an ethical approach maintaining that right and wrong should be judged in terms of the consequences of one's actions

validity the extent to which a measurement procedure actually measures what it is intended to measure

variability the degree to which scores in a set of data differ or vary from one another

variance a numerical index of the variability in a set of data

Web-based research research that is conducted using the World Wide Web

within-groups variance the variability among scores within a particular experimental condition

within-subjects design an experimental design in which each participant serves in more than one condition of the experiment; also called *repeated measures design*

z-score a statistic that expresses how much a particular participant's score varies from the mean in terms of standard deviations; also called *standard score*

APPENDIX A

Statistical Tables

Appendix A-1 Critical Values of t

Appendix A-2 Critical Values of F

| APPENDIX A-1 | Critical Values of t |

1-tailed	0.25	0.1	0.05	0.025	0.01	0.005	0.001	0.0005
2-tailed	0.5	0.2	0.1	0.05	0.02	0.01	0.002	0.001
df 1	1.000	3.078	6.314	12.706	31.821	63.657	318.310	636.620
2	0.816	1.886	2.920	4.303	6.965	9.925	22.327	31.598
3	.765	1.638	2.353	3.182	4.541	5.841	10.214	12.924
4	.741	1.533	2.132	2.776	3.747	4.604	7.173	8.610
5	0.727	1.476	2.015	2.571	3.365	4.032	5.893	6.869
6	.718	1.440	1.943	2.447	3.143	3.707	5.208	5.959
7	.711	1.415	1.895	2.365	2.998	3.499	4.785	5.408
8	.706	1.397	1.860	2.306	2.896	3.355	4.501	5.041
9	.703	1.383	1.833	2.262	2.821	3.250	4.297	4.781
10	0.700	1.372	1.812	2.228	2.764	3.169	4.144	4.587
11	.697	1.363	1.796	2.201	2.718	3.106	4.025	4.437
12	.695	1.356	1.782	2.179	2.681	3.055	3.930	4.318
13	.694	1.350	1.771	2.160	2.650	3.012	3.852	4.221
14	.692	1.345	1.761	2.145	2.624	2.977	3.787	4.140
15	0.691	1.341	1.753	2.131	2.602	2.947	3.733	4.073
16	.690	1.337	1.746	2.120	2.583	2.921	3.686	4.015
17	.689	1.333	1.740	2.110	2.567	2.898	3.646	3.965
18	.688	1.330	1.734	2.101	2.552	2.878	3.610	3.922
19	.688	1.328	1.729	2.093	2.539	2.861	3.579	3.883
20	0.687	1.325	1.725	2.086	2.528	2.845	3.552	3.850
21	.686	1.323	1.721	2.080	2.518	2.831	3.527	3.819
22	.686	1.321	1.717	2.074	2.508	2.819	3.505	3.792
23	.685	1.319	1.714	2.069	2.500	2.807	3.485	3.767
24	.685	1.318	1.711	2.064	2.492	2.797	3.467	3.745
25	0.684	1.316	1.708	2.060	2.485	2.787	3.450	3.725
26	.684	1.315	1.706	2.056	2.479	2.779	3.435	3.707
27	.684	1.314	1.703	2.052	2.473	2.771	3.421	3.690
28	.683	1.313	1.701	2.048	2.467	2.763	3.408	3.674
29	.683	1.311	1.699	2.045	2.462	2.756	3.396	3.659
30	0.683	1.310	1.697	2.042	2.457	2.750	3.385	3.646
40	.681	1.303	1.684	2.021	2.423	2.704	3.307	3.551
60	.679	1.296	1.671	2.000	2.390	2.660	3.232	3.460
120	.677	1.289	1.658	1.980	2.358	2.617	3.160	3.373
∞	.674	1.282	1.645	1.960	2.326	2.576	3.090	3.291

Note: From Table 12 of *Biometrika Tables for Statisticians* (Vol. 1, ed. 1) by E. S. Pearson and H. O. Hartley, 1966, London: Cambridge University Press, p. 146. Adapted by permission of the publisher and the Biometrika Trustees.

APPENDIX A-2 Critical Values of F

		df associated with the numerator (df_{bg})								
	1	**2**	**3**	**4**	**5**	**6**	**7**	**8**	**9**	**10**
1	161.40	199.50	215.70	224.60	230.20	234.00	236.80	238.90	240.50	241.90
2	18.51	19.00	19.16	19.25	19.30	19.33	19.35	19.37	19.38	19.40
3	10.13	9.55	9.28	9.12	9.01	8.94	8.89	8.85	8.81	8.79
4	7.71	6.94	6.59	6.39	6.26	6.16	6.09	6.04	6.00	5.96
5	6.61	5.79	5.41	5.19	5.05	4.95	4.88	4.82	4.77	4.74
6	5.99	5.14	4.76	4.53	4.39	4.28	4.21	4.15	4.10	4.06
7	5.59	4.74	4.35	4.12	3.97	3.87	3.79	3.73	3.68	3.64
8	5.32	4.46	4.07	3.84	3.69	3.58	3.50	3.44	3.39	3.35
9	5.12	4.26	3.86	3.63	3.48	3.37	3.29	3.23	3.18	3.14
10	4.96	4.10	3.71	3.48	3.33	3.22	3.14	3.07	3.02	2.98
11	4.84	3.98	3.59	3.36	3.20	3.09	3.01	2.95	2.90	2.85
12	4.75	3.89	3.49	3.26	3.11	3.00	2.91	2.85	2.80	2.75
13	4.67	3.81	3.41	3.18	3.03	2.92	2.83	2.77	2.71	2.67
14	4.60	3.74	3.34	3.11	2.96	2.85	2.76	2.70	2.65	2.60
15	4.54	3.68	3.29	3.06	2.90	2.79	2.71	2.64	2.59	2.54
16	4.49	3.63	3.24	3.01	2.85	2.74	2.66	2.59	2.54	2.49
17	4.45	3.59	3.20	2.96	2.81	2.70	2.61	2.55	2.49	2.45
18	4.41	3.55	3.16	2.93	2.77	2.66	2.58	2.51	2.46	2.41
19	4.38	3.52	3.13	2.90	2.74	2.63	2.54	2.48	2.42	2.38
20	4.35	3.49	3.10	2.87	2.71	2.60	2.51	2.45	2.39	2.35
21	4.32	3.47	3.07	2.84	2.68	2.57	2.49	2.42	2.37	2.32
22	4.30	3.44	3.05	2.82	2.66	2.55	2.46	2.40	2.34	2.30
23	4.28	3.42	3.03	2.80	2.64	2.53	2.44	2.37	2.32	2.27
24	4.26	3.40	3.01	2.78	2.62	2.51	2.42	2.36	2.30	2.25
25	4.24	3.39	2.99	2.76	2.60	2.49	2.40	2.34	2.28	2.24
26	4.23	3.37	2.98	2.74	2.59	2.47	2.39	2.32	2.27	2.22
27	4.21	3.35	2.96	2.73	2.57	2.46	2.37	2.31	2.25	2.20
28	4.20	3.34	2.95	2.71	2.56	2.45	2.36	2.29	2.24	2.19
29	4.18	3.33	2.93	2.70	2.55	2.43	2.35	2.28	2.22	2.18
30	4.17	3.32	2.92	2.69	2.53	2.42	2.33	2.27	2.21	2.16
40	4.08	3.23	2.84	2.61	2.45	2.34	2.25	2.18	2.12	2.08
60	4.00	3.15	2.76	2.53	2.37	2.25	2.17	2.10	2.04	1.99
120	3.92	3.07	2.68	2.45	2.29	2.17	2.09	2.02	1.96	1.91
∞	3.84	3.00	2.60	2.37	2.21	2.10	2.01	1.94	1.88	1.83

df associated with the denominator (df_{wg})

			df associated with the numerator (df$_{bg}$)					
12	**15**	**20**	**24**	**30**	**40**	**60**	**120**	**∞**
243.90	245.90	248.00	249.10	250.10	251.10	252.20	253.30	254.30
19.41	19.43	19.45	19.45	19.46	19.47	19.48	19.49	19.50
8.74	8.70	8.66	8.64	8.62	8.59	8.57	8.55	8.53
5.91	5.86	5.80	5.77	5.75	5.72	5.69	5.66	5.63
4.68	4.62	4.56	4.53	4.50	4.46	4.43	4.40	4.36
4.00	3.94	3.87	3.84	3.81	3.77	3.74	3.70	3.67
3.57	3.51	3.44	3.41	3.38	3.34	3.30	3.27	3.23
3.28	3.22	3.15	3.12	3.08	3.04	3.01	2.97	2.93
3.07	3.01	2.94	2.90	2.86	2.83	2.79	2.75	2.71
2.91	2.85	2.77	2.74	2.70	2.66	2.62	2.58	2.54
2.79	2.72	2.65	2.61	2.57	2.53	2.49	2.45	2.40
2.69	2.62	2.54	2.51	2.47	2.43	2.38	2.34	2.30
2.60	2.53	2.46	2.42	2.38	2.34	2.30	2.25	2.21
2.53	2.46	2.39	2.35	2.31	2.27	2.22	2.18	2.13
2.48	2.40	2.33	2.29	2.25	2.20	2.16	2.11	2.07
2.42	2.35	2.28	2.24	2.19	2.15	2.11	2.06	2.01
2.38	2.31	2.23	2.19	2.15	2.10	2.06	2.01	1.96
2.34	2.27	2.19	2.15	2.11	2.06	2.02	1.97	1.92
2.31	2.23	2.16	2.11	2.07	2.03	1.98	1.93	1.88
2.28	2.20	2.12	2.08	2.04	1.99	1.95	1.90	1.84
2.25	2.18	2.10	2.05	2.01	1.96	1.92	1.87	1.81
2.23	2.15	2.07	2.03	1.98	1.94	1.89	1.84	1.78
2.20	2.13	2.05	2.01	1.96	1.91	1.86	1.81	1.76
2.18	2.11	2.03	1.98	1.94	1.89	1.84	1.79	1.73
2.16	2.09	2.01	1.96	1.92	1.87	1.82	1.77	1.71
2.15	2.07	1.99	1.95	1.90	1.85	1.80	1.75	1.69
2.13	2.06	1.97	1.93	1.88	1.84	1.79	1.73	1.67
2.12	2.04	1.96	1.91	1.87	1.82	1.77	1.71	1.65
2.10	2.03	1.94	1.90	1.85	1.81	1.75	1.70	1.64
2.09	2.01	1.93	1.89	1.84	1.79	1.74	1.68	1.62
2.00	1.92	1.84	1.79	1.74	1.69	1.64	1.58	1.51
1.92	1.84	1.75	1.70	1.65	1.59	1.53	1.47	1.39
1.83	1.75	1.66	1.61	1.55	1.50	1.43	1.35	1.25
1.75	1.67	1.57	1.52	1.46	1.39	1.32	1.22	1.00

Values of F (for alpha level = .05)

(*continued*)

APPENDIX A-2 Continued

df associated with the numerator (df$_{bg}$)

	1	2	3	4	5	6	7	8	9	10
1	4052.00	4999.50	5403.00	5625.00	5764.00	5859.00	5928.00	5981.00	6022.00	6056.00
2	98.50	99.00	99.17	99.25	99.30	99.33	99.36	99.37	99.39	99.40
3	34.12	30.82	29.46	28.71	28.24	27.91	27.67	27.49	27.35	27.23
4	21.20	18.00	16.69	15.98	15.52	15.21	14.98	14.80	14.66	14.55
5	16.26	13.27	12.06	11.39	10.97	10.67	10.46	10.29	10.16	10.05
6	13.75	10.92	9.78	9.15	8.75	8.47	8.26	8.10	7.98	7.87
7	12.25	9.55	8.45	7.85	7.46	7.19	6.99	6.84	6.72	6.62
8	11.26	8.65	7.59	7.01	6.63	6.37	6.18	6.03	5.91	5.81
9	10.56	8.02	6.99	6.42	6.06	5.80	5.61	5.47	5.35	5.26
10	10.04	7.56	6.55	5.99	5.64	5.39	5.20	5.06	4.94	4.85
11	9.65	7.21	6.22	5.67	5.32	5.07	4.89	4.74	4.63	4.54
12	9.33	6.93	5.95	5.41	5.06	4.82	4.64	4.50	4.39	4.30
13	9.07	6.70	5.74	5.21	4.86	4.62	4.44	4.30	4.19	4.10
14	8.86	6.51	5.56	5.04	4.69	4.46	4.28	4.14	4.03	3.94
15	8.68	6.36	5.42	4.89	4.56	4.32	4.14	4.00	3.89	3.80
16	8.53	6.23	5.29	4.77	4.44	4.20	4.03	3.89	3.78	3.69
17	8.40	6.11	5.18	4.67	4.34	4.10	3.93	3.79	3.68	3.59
18	8.29	6.01	5.09	4.58	4.25	4.01	3.84	3.71	3.60	3.51
19	8.18	5.93	5.01	4.50	4.17	3.94	3.77	3.63	3.52	3.43
20	8.10	5.85	4.94	4.43	4.10	3.87	3.70	3.56	3.46	3.37
21	8.02	5.78	4.87	4.37	4.04	3.81	3.64	3.51	3.40	3.31
22	7.95	5.72	4.82	4.31	3.99	3.76	3.59	3.45	3.35	3.26
23	7.88	5.66	4.76	4.26	3.94	3.71	3.54	3.41	3.30	3.21
24	7.82	5.61	4.72	4.22	3.90	3.67	3.50	3.36	3.26	3.17
25	7.77	5.57	4.68	4.18	3.85	3.63	3.46	3.32	3.22	3.13
26	7.72	5.53	4.64	4.14	3.82	3.59	3.42	3.29	3.18	3.09
27	7.68	5.49	4.60	4.11	3.78	3.56	3.39	3.26	3.15	3.06
28	7.64	5.54	4.57	4.07	3.75	3.53	3.36	3.23	3.12	3.03
29	7.60	5.42	4.54	4.04	3.73	3.50	3.33	3.20	3.09	3.00
30	7.56	5.39	4.51	4.02	3.70	3.47	3.30	3.17	3.07	2.98
40	7.31	5.18	4.31	3.83	3.51	3.29	3.12	2.99	2.89	2.80
60	7.08	4.98	4.13	3.65	3.34	3.12	2.95	2.82	2.72	2.63
120	6.85	4.79	3.95	3.48	3.17	2.96	2.79	2.66	2.56	2.47
∞	6.63	4.61	3.78	3.32	3.02	2.80	2.64	2.51	2.41	2.32

(left axis label: df associated with the denominator (df$_{wg}$))

Note: From Table 18 of *Biometrika Tables for Statisticians* (Vol. 1, ed. 1) by E. S. Pearson and H. O. Hartley, 1966, London: Cambridge University Press, pp. 171–173. Adapted by permission of the publisher and the Biometrika Trustees.

			df associated with the numerator (df$_{bg}$)					
12	**15**	**20**	**24**	**30**	**40**	**60**	**120**	**∞**
6106.00	6157.00	6209.00	6235.00	6261.00	6287.00	6313.00	6339.00	6366.00
99.42	99.43	99.45	99.46	99.47	99.47	99.48	99.49	99.50
27.05	26.87	26.69	26.60	26.50	26.41	26.32	26.22	26.13
14.37	14.20	14.02	13.93	13.84	13.75	13.65	13.56	13.46
9.89	9.72	9.55	9.47	9.38	9.29	9.20	9.11	9.02
7.72	7.56	7.40	7.31	7.23	7.14	7.06	6.97	6.88
6.47	6.31	6.16	6.07	5.99	5.91	5.82	5.74	5.65
5.67	5.52	5.36	5.28	5.20	5.12	5.03	4.95	4.86
5.11	4.96	4.81	4.73	4.65	4.57	4.48	4.40	4.31
4.71	4.56	4.41	4.33	4.25	4.17	4.08	4.00	3.91
4.40	4.25	4.10	4.02	3.94	3.86	3.78	3.69	3.60
4.16	4.01	3.86	3.78	3.70	3.62	3.54	3.45	3.36
3.96	3.82	3.66	3.59	3.51	3.43	3.34	3.25	3.17
3.80	3.66	3.51	3.43	3.35	3.27	3.18	3.09	3.00
3.67	3.52	3.37	3.29	3.21	3.13	3.05	2.96	2.87
3.55	3.41	3.26	3.18	3.10	3.02	2.93	2.84	2.75
3.46	3.31	3.16	3.08	3.00	2.92	2.83	2.75	2.65
3.37	3.23	3.08	3.00	2.92	2.84	2.75	2.66	2.57
3.30	3.15	3.00	2.92	2.84	2.76	2.67	2.58	2.49
3.23	3.09	2.94	2.86	2.78	2.69	2.61	2.52	2.42
3.17	3.03	2.88	2.80	2.72	2.64	2.55	2.46	2.36
3.12	2.98	2.83	2.75	2.67	2.58	2.50	2.40	2.31
3.07	2.93	2.78	2.70	2.62	2.54	2.45	2.35	2.26
3.03	2.89	2.74	2.66	2.58	2.49	2.40	2.31	2.21
2.99	2.85	2.70	2.62	2.54	2.45	2.36	2.27	2.17
2.96	2.81	2.66	2.58	2.50	2.42	2.33	2.23	2.13
2.93	2.78	2.63	2.55	2.47	2.38	2.29	2.20	2.10
2.90	2.75	2.60	2.52	2.44	2.35	2.26	2.17	2.06
2.87	2.73	2.57	2.49	2.41	2.33	2.23	2.14	2.03
2.84	2.70	2.55	2.47	2.39	2.30	2.21	2.11	2.01
2.66	2.52	2.37	2.29	2.20	2.11	2.02	1.92	1.80
2.50	2.35	2.20	2.12	2.03	1.94	1.84	1.73	1.60
2.34	2.19	2.03	1.95	1.86	1.76	1.66	1.53	1.38
2.18	2.04	1.88	1.79	1.70	1.59	1.47	1.32	1.00

Values of *F* (for alpha level = .01)

APPENDIX B

Computational Formulas for ANOVA

Appendix B-1 Calculational Formulas for a One-Way ANOVA
Appendix B-2 Calculational Formulas for a Two-Way Factorial ANOVA

APPENDIX B-1

Calculational Formulas for a One-Way ANOVA

The demonstrational formulas for a one-way ANOVA presented in Chapter 12 help to convey the rationale behind ANOVA, but they are unwieldy for computational purposes. Appendix B-1 presents the calculational formulas for performing a one-way ANOVA on data from a between-groups (completely randomized) design.

The data used in this example are from a hypothetical study of the effects of physical appearance on liking. In this study, participants listened to another participant talk about him- or herself over an intercom for 5 minutes. Participants were led to believe that the person they listened to was either very attractive, moderately attractive, or unattractive. To manipulate perceived attractiveness, the researcher gave each participant a digital photograph that was supposedly a picture of the other participant. In reality, the pictures were prepared in advance and were *not* of the person who talked over the intercom.

After listening to the other person, participants rated how much they liked him or her on a 7-point scale (where 1 = *disliked greatly* and 7 = *liked greatly*). Six participants participated in each of the three conditions. The ratings for the 18 participants follow.

Attractive Picture	Unattractive Picture	Neutral Picture
7	4	5
5	3	6
5	4	6
6	4	4
4	3	5
6	5	5

Step 1. For each condition, compute:

1. the sum of all of the scores in each condition (Σx)
2. the mean of the condition ($\bar{x}$)
3. the sum of the squared scores (Σx^2)
4. the sum of squares ($\Sigma x^2 - [(\Sigma x)^2/n]$)

You'll find it useful to enter these quantities into a table such as the following:

	Attractive Picture	Unattractive Picture	Neutral Picture
Σx	33	23	31
$\bar{x}$	5.5	3.8	5.2
Σx^2	187	91	163
SS	5.5	2.83	2.83

Steps 2–4 calculate the within-groups portion of the variance.

Step 2. Compute SS_{wg}—the sum of the SS of each condition:

$$SS_{wg} = SS_{a1} + SS_{a2} + SS_{a3}$$
$$= 5.50 + 2.83 + 2.83$$
$$= 11.16$$

Step 3. Compute df_{wg}:

$$df_{wg} = N - k, \quad \text{where } N = \text{total number of participants and}$$
$$= 18 - 3 \qquad\qquad k = \text{number of conditions}$$
$$= 15$$

Step 4. Compute MS_{wg}:

$$MS_{wg} = SS_{wg}/df_{wg}$$
$$= 11.16/15$$
$$= .744$$

Set MS_{wg} aside momentarily as you calculate SS_{bg}.

Steps 5–7 calculate the between-groups portion of the variance.

Step 5. Compute SS_{bg}:

$$SS_{bg} = \frac{\left(\Sigma x_{a1}\right)^2 + \left(\Sigma x_{a2}\right)^2 + \ldots + \left(\Sigma x_{ak}\right)^2}{n} - \frac{\left(\Sigma x\right)^2}{N}$$
$$= \frac{(33)^2 + (23)^2 + (31)^2}{6} - \frac{(33 + 23 + 31)^2}{18}$$
$$= \frac{1089 + 529 + 961}{6} - \frac{(87)^2}{18}$$
$$= 429.83 - 420.50$$
$$= 9.33$$

Step 6.   Compute df_{bg}:

$$df_{bg} = k - 1, \quad \text{where } k = \text{number of conditions}$$
$$= 3 - 1$$
$$= 2$$

Step 7.   Compute MS_{bg}:

$$MS_{bg} = SS_{bg}/df_{bg}$$
$$= 9.33/2$$
$$= 4.67$$

Step 8.   Compute the calculated value of F:

$$F = MS_{bg}/MS_{wg}$$
$$= 4.67/.744$$
$$= 6.28$$

Step 9.   Determine the critical value of F using Appendix A-2. For example, the critical value of F when $df_{bg} = 2$, $df_{wg} = 15$, and alpha $= .05$ is 3.68.

Step 10.   If the calculated value of F (Step 8) is equal to or greater than the critical value of F (Step 9), we reject the null hypothesis and conclude that at least one mean differed from the others. In our example, 6.28 was greater than 3.68. Thus, we reject the null hypothesis and conclude that at least one mean differed from the others. Looking at the means, we see that participants who received attractive pictures liked the other person most ($\bar{x} = 5.5$), those who received moderately attractive photos were second ($\bar{x} = 5.2$), and those who received unattractive pictures liked the other person least ($\bar{x} = 3.8$). We would need to conduct post hoc tests to determine which means differed significantly (see Chapter 12).

If the calculated value of F (Step 8) is less than the critical value (Step 9), we fail to reject the null hypothesis and conclude that the independent variable had no effect on participants' responses.

APPENDIX B-2

Calculational Formulas for a Two-Way Factorial ANOVA

The conceptual rationale and demonstrational formulas for factorial analysis of variance are discussed in Chapter 12. The demonstrational formulas in Chapter 12 help to convey what each aspect of factorial ANOVA reflects, but they are unwieldy for computational purposes. Appendix B-2 presents the calculational formulas for performing factorial ANOVA on data from a between-groups factorial design.

The data are from a hypothetical study of the effects of audience size and composition on speech disfluencies, such as stuttering and hesitations. Twenty participants told the story of Goldilocks and the Three Bears to a group of elementary school children or to a group of adults. Some participants spoke to an audience of 5; others spoke to an audience of 20. This was a 2×2 factorial design, the two independent variables being audience composition (children vs. adults) and audience size (5 vs. 20). The dependent variable was the number of speech disfluencies—stutters, stammers, misspeaking, and the like—that the participant displayed while telling the story.

The data were as follows:

		B	
		AUDIENCE SIZE	
		Small (b_1)	Large (b_2)
	Children (a_1)	3 1 2 5 4	7 2 5 3 4
A AUDIENCE COMPOSITION	Adults (a_2)	3 8 4 2 6	13 9 11 8 12

Step 1. For each condition (each combination of a and b), compute:

1. the sum of all of the scores in each condition (Σx)
2. the mean of the condition ($\bar{x}$)
3. the sum of the squared scores (Σx^2)
4. the sum of squares ($\Sigma x^2 - [(\Sigma x)^2/n]$)

You'll find it useful to enter these quantities into a table such as the following:

		B	
		b_1	b_2
a_1	Σx	15	21
	$\bar{x}$	3.0	4.2
	Σx^2	55	103
	SS	10	14.8
A a_2	Σx	23	53
	$\bar{x}$	4.6	10.6
	Σx^2	129	579
	SS	23.2	17.2

Also, calculate $\Sigma\, (\Sigma x)^2/N$—the square of the sum of the condition totals divided by the total number of participants:

$$\Sigma\left(\Sigma x\right)^2/N = (15 + 21 + 23 + 53)^2/20$$

$$= (112)^2/20$$

$$= 12544/20$$

$$= 627.2$$

This quantity appears in several of the following formulas.

Steps 2–4 compute the within-groups portion of the variance.

Step 2.   Compute SS_{wg}:

$$SS_{wg} = SS_{a1b1} + SS_{a1b2} + SS_{a2b1} + SS_{a2b2}$$

$$= 10 + 14.8 + 23.2 + 17.2$$

$$= 65.2$$

Step 3.   Compute df_{wg}:

$$df_{wg} = (j \times k)\,(n-1), \quad \text{where } j = \text{levels of } A$$

$$= (2 \times 2)(5 - 1) \qquad\quad k = \text{levels of } B$$

$$= 16 \qquad\qquad\qquad\quad n = \text{participants per condition}$$

Step 4.   Compute MS_{wg}:

$$MS_{wg} = SS_{wg}/df_{wg}$$

$$= 65.2/16$$

$$= 4.075$$

Set MS_{wg} aside for a moment. You will use it in the denominator of the F-tests you perform to test the main effects and interaction that follow.

Steps 5–8 calculate the main effect of A.

Step 5.   Compute SS_A:

$$SS_A = \frac{\left(\Sigma x_{a1b1} + \Sigma x_{a1b2}\right)^2 + \left(\Sigma x_{a2b1} + \Sigma x_{a2b2}\right)^2}{(n)(k)} - \frac{\left[\Sigma\left(\Sigma x\right)\right]^2}{N}$$

$$= \frac{(15 + 21)^2 + (23 + 53)^2}{(5)(2)} - 627.2$$

$$= \frac{(36)^2 + (76)^2}{10} - 627.2$$

$$= \frac{1296 + 5776}{10} - 627.2$$
$$= 707.2 - 627.2$$
$$= 80.0$$

Step 6. Compute df_A:

$$df_A = j - 1, \quad \text{where } j = \text{levels of } A$$
$$= 2 - 1$$
$$= 1$$

Step 7. Compute MS_A:

$$MS_A = SS_A/df_A$$
$$= 80.0/1$$
$$= 80.0$$

Step 8. Compute F_A:

$$F_A = MS_A/MS_{wg}$$
$$= 80.0/4.075$$
$$= 19.63$$

Step 9. Determine the critical value of F using Appendix A-2. The critical value of F (alpha level = .05) when $df_A = 1$ and $df_{wg} = 16$ is 4.49.

Step 10. If the calculated value of F (Step 8) is equal to or greater than the critical value of F (Step 9), we reject the null hypothesis and conclude that at least one mean differed from the others. In our example, 19.63 was greater than 4.49, so we reject the null hypothesis and conclude that a_1 differed from a_2. To interpret the effect, we would inspect the means of a_1 and a_2 (averaging across the levels of B). When we do this, we find that participants who spoke to adults ($\bar{x} = 7.6$) emitted significantly more disfluencies than those who spoke to children ($\bar{x} = 3.6$).

If the calculated value of F (Step 8) is less than the critical value (Step 9), we fail to reject the null hypothesis and conclude that the independent variable had no effect on participants' responses.

Steps 11–14 calculate the main effect of B.

Step 11. Compute SS_B:

$$SS_B = \frac{\left(\Sigma x_{a1b1} + \Sigma x_{a2b1} \right)^2 + \left(\Sigma x_{a1b2} + \Sigma x_{a2b2} \right)^2}{(n)(j)} - \frac{\left[\Sigma \left(\Sigma x \right) \right]^2}{N}$$

$$= \frac{(15 + 23)^2 + (21 + 53)^2}{(5)(2)} - 627.2$$

$$= \frac{(38)^2 + (74)^2}{10} - 627.2$$

$$= \frac{1444 + 5476}{10} - 627.2$$

$$= 692 - 627.2$$

$$= 64.8$$

Step 12. Compute df_B:

$$df_B = k - 1, \quad \text{where } k = \text{levels of } B$$

$$= 2 - 1$$

$$= 1$$

Step 13. Compute MS_B:

$$MS_B = SS_B/df_B$$

$$= 64.8/1$$

$$= 64.8$$

Step 14. Compute F_B:

$$F_B = MS_B/MS_{wg}$$

$$= 64.8/4.075$$

$$= 15.90$$

Step 15. Determine the critical value of F using Appendix A-2. The critical value of F $(1, 16) = 4.49$.

Step 16. If the calculated value of F (Step 14) is equal to or greater than the critical value of F (Step 15), we reject the null hypothesis and conclude that at least one mean differed from the others. In our example, 15.90 was greater than 4.49, so the main effect of B—audience size—was significant. Looking at the means for b_1 and b_2 (averaged across levels of A), we find that participants emitted more speech disfluencies when they spoke to large audiences than when they spoke to small audiences; the means for the large and small audiences were 7.4 and 3.8, respectively.

If the calculated value of F (Step 14) is less than the critical value (Step 15), we fail to reject the null hypothesis and conclude that the independent variable had no effect on participants' responses.

Steps 17–23 Calculate the A × B interaction.   The simplest way to obtain $SS_{A×B}$ is by subtraction. If we subtract SS_A and SS_B from SS_{bg} (the sum of squares between-groups), we get $SS_{A×B}$.

Step 17.   Compute SS_{bg}:

$$
\begin{aligned}
SS_{bg} &= \frac{\left(\Sigma x_{a1b1}\right)^2 + \left(\Sigma x_{a1b2}\right)^2 + \left(\Sigma x_{a2b1}\right)^2 + \left(\Sigma x_{a2b2}\right)^2}{n} - \frac{\Sigma\left(\Sigma x\right)^2}{N} \\
&= \frac{(15)^2 + (21)^2 + (23)^2 + (53)^2}{5} - 627.2 \\
&= \frac{225 + 441 + 529 + 2809}{5} - 627.2 \\
&= 800.8 - 627.2 \\
&= 173.6
\end{aligned}
$$

Step 18.   Compute $SS_{A×B}$:

$$
\begin{aligned}
SS_{A×B} &= SS_{bg} - SS_A - SS_B \\
&= 173.6 - 80.0 - 64.8 \\
&= 28.8
\end{aligned}
$$

Step 19.   Compute $df_{A×B}$:

$$
\begin{aligned}
df_{A×B} &= (j - 1)(k - 1) \\
&= (2 - 1)(2 - 1) \\
&= (1)(1) \\
&= 1
\end{aligned}
$$

Step 20.   Compute $MS_{A×B}$:

$$
\begin{aligned}
MS_{A×B} &= SS_{A×B}/df_{A×B} \\
&= 28.8/1 \\
&= 28.8
\end{aligned}
$$

Step 21.   Compute $F_{A×B}$:

$$
\begin{aligned}
F_{A×B} &= MS_{A×B}/MS_{wg} \\
&= 28.8/4.075 \\
&= 7.07
\end{aligned}
$$

Step 22.   Determine the critical value of *F* using Appendix A-2. We've seen already that for *F* (1, 16), the critical value is 4.49.

Step 23.   If the calculated value of *F* (Step 21) is equal to or greater than the critical value of *F* (Step 22), we reject the null hypothesis and conclude that at least one mean differed from the others. In our example, 7.07 was greater than 4.49, so we conclude that the *A* × *B* interaction was significant.

Looking at the means we calculated in Step 1, we see that participants who spoke to a large audience of adults emitted a somewhat greater number of speech disfluencies than those in the other three conditions.

	Audience Size	
Audience Composition	**Small**	**Large**
Children	3.0	4.2
Adults	4.6	10.6

To determine precisely which means differed from one another, we would conduct tests of simple main effects.

If the calculated value of *F* (Step 21) is less than the critical value (Step 22), we fail to reject the null hypothesis and conclude that variables *A* and *B* (audience composition and size) did not interact.

APPENDIX C

Choosing the Proper Statistical Analysis

Even after students learn how to perform various statistical analyses, they often have difficulty knowing which analysis is appropriate for a particular set of data. This question is usually easily resolved by thinking about the number and nature of the variables to be analyzed.

All analyses involve efforts to understand the nature of the relationship between two or more variables. In most cases, these variables may be either discrete or continuous. A discrete variable is a variable that has a limited number of possible values. For example, an independent variable with three levels is a discrete variable (because it can have only three values), as is gender (because it has only two values—male and female). In general, all nominal variables (Chapter 3) are discrete.

A continuous variable is one whose values fall on a continuum and can potentially have a large number of values. Scores on an IQ test, ratings of anxiety, the number of times a rat presses a bar, heart rate, and participants' ages or weights are all continuous variables. In general, variables that are measured on an interval or ratio scale can be regarded as continuous.

Analyses Involving Two Variables

Imagine that you wish to analyze the relationship between two variables, X and Y, both of which are continuous. Consulting the following table shows that correlation is the analysis of choice. (Simple linear regression, which is not on the table, is another option.)

However, if one variable is discrete and the other is continuous, then you need to conduct either a t-test or a one-way analysis of variance, depending on whether the discrete variable has two levels (t-test) or more than two levels (one-way ANOVA).

X Variable	Y Variable	Suggested Analysis
1 continuous	1 continuous	Pearson correlation
1 discrete (2 levels only)	1 continuous	t-test
1 discrete	1 continuous	One-way analysis of variance

Analyses Involving More Than Two Variables

If you have more than two variables in a single analysis, you need to think about them as two sets. One set (X) will include one or more variables that you conceptualize as predictors, antecedents, or independent variables. The other set (Y) will include one or more variables that you conceptualize as outcomes, consequences, or dependent variables.

So, for example, if you were predicting scores on an eating disorders inventory from participants' ages, self-esteem scores, weights, and numbers of siblings, the X set would include the predictors (age, self-esteem, weight, and number of siblings) and the Y set would include only the scores on the eating disorders inventory. Given that all of the variables in both the X and Y sets are continuous, consulting the table would lead you to conduct a multiple regression analysis. (The kind of regression analysis you conducted—simultaneous, stepwise, or hierarchical—would depend on your goal.)

When the X variables are independent variables in an experiment, you have two or more discrete X variables. Assuming that the dependent variable (Y) is continuous, you would conduct a factorial analysis of variance.

If you have one or more discrete X variables (as in an experiment) but more than one continuous dependent variable (Y), you would choose multivariate analysis of variance.

Factor analysis is a strange creature because you have only one set of variables to factor analyze. In essence, you are analyzing a set of continuous Y variables to identify the latent, underlying X variables (that is, the factors) that account for the relationships among them.

These tables include only those analyses that are discussed in this book and there are, of course, many other statistics available. In addition, in some cases, more than one analysis can be used (for example, multiple regression can do almost everything that ANOVA does, but it is often more cumbersome), and there are

X Variable(s)	Y Variable(s)	Suggested Analysis
2 or more continuous	1 continuous	Multiple regression
2 or more discrete	1 continuous	Factorial analysis of variance
1 or more discrete	2 or more continuous	Multivariate analysis of variance
0	2 or more continuous	Factor analysis
2 or more continuous	2 or more continuous	Structural equations modeling

occasional exceptions to these general guidelines. Finally, these examples do not apply to data that are ordinal (such as ranks), which require other statistics.

REFERENCES

Adair, J. G., Dushenko, T. W., & Lindsay, R. C. L. (1985). Ethical regulations and their impact on research. *American Psychologist, 40,* 59–72.

Adams, K. L., & Ware, N. C. (1989). Sexism and the English language: The linguistic implications of being a woman. In J. Freeman (Ed.), *Women: A feminist perspective* (pp. 470–484). Mountain View, CA: Mayfield.

Adler, T. (1991, December). Outright fraud rare, but not poor science. *APA Monitor,* p. 11.

Agocha, V. B., & Cooper, M. L. (1999). Risk perceptions and safer-sex intentions: Does a partner's physical attractiveness undermine the use of risk-relevant information? *Personality and Social Psychology Bulletin, 25,* 746–759.

Aiken, L. S., & West, S. G. (1991). *Multiple regression: Testing and interpreting interactions.* Newbury Park, CA: Sage.

Allport, G. W. (1961). *Pattern and growth in personality.* New York: Holt, Rinehart, and Winston.

American Psychological Association. (1992). *Ethical principles in the conduct of research with human participants.* Washington, DC: Author.

American Psychological Association. (2009). *Publication manual of the American Psychological Association* (6th ed.). Washington, DC: American Psychological Association.

Anderson, C. A. (1989). Temperature and aggression: Ubiquitous effects of heat on occurrence of human violence. *Psychological Bulletin, 106,* 74–96.

Anderson, T., & Kanuka, H. (2003). *e-Research: Methods, strategies, and issues.* Boston: Allyn & Bacon.

APA endorses resolution on the use of animals. (1990, October–November). *APA Science Agenda,* p. 8.

Archer, D., Iritani, B., Kimes, D. D., & Barrios, M. (1983). Face-ism: Studies of sex differences in facial prominence. *Journal of Personality and Social Psychology, 45,* 725–735.

Asendorpf, J. (1990). The expression of shyness and embarrassment. In W. R. Crozier (Ed.), *Shyness and embarrassment* (pp. 87–118). Cambridge: Cambridge University Press.

Ayala, F. J., & Black, B. (1993). Science and the courts. *American Scientist, 81,* 230–239.

Azar, B. (1997, August). When research is swept under the rug. *APA Monitor,* p. 18.

Azar, B. (1999, July–August). Destructive lab attack sends a wake-up call. *APA Monitor,* p. 16.

Baldwin, E. (1993). The case for animal research in psychology. *Journal of Social Issues, 49,* 121–131.

Bales, R. F. (1970). *Personality and interpersonal behavior.* New York: Holt, Rinehart & Winston.

Baron, R. A., & Bell, P. A. (1976). Aggression and heat: The influence of ambient temperature, negative affect, and a cooling drink on physical aggression. *Journal of Personality and Social Psychology, 33,* 245–255.

Barrett, L. F., & Barrett, D. J. (2001). An introduction to computerized experience sampling in psychology. *Social Science Computer Review, 19,* 175–185.

Bar-Yoseph, T. L., & Witztum, E. (1992). Using strategic psychotherapy: A case study of chronic PTSD after a terrorist attack. *Journal of Contemporary Psychotherapy, 22,* 263–276.

Bauer, H. H. (1992). *Scientific literacy and the myth of the scientific method.* Urbana, IL: University of Illinois Press.

Baumeister, R. F., Heatherton, T. F., & Tice, D. M. (1993). When ego threats lead to self-regulation failure: Negative consequences of high self-esteem. *Journal of Personality and Social Psychology, 64,* 141–156.

Baumeister, R. F., & Steinhilber, A. (1984). Paradoxical effects of supportive audiences on performance under pressure: The home disadvantage in sports championships. *Journal of Personality and Social Psychology, 47,* 85–93.

Baumrind, D. (1971). Principles of ethical conduct in the treatment of subjects: Reactions to the draft report of the committee on ethical standards in psychological research. *American Psychologist, 26,* 887–896.

Bell, C. R. (1962). Personality characteristics of volunteers for psychological studies. *British Journal of Social and Clinical Psychology, 1,* 81–95.

Bell, R. (1992). *Impure science: Fraud, compromise, and political influence in scientific research.* New York: John Wiley & Sons.

Berelson, B. (1952). *Content analysis in communication research.* New York: The Free Press.

Biemer, P. B., & Lyberg, L. E. (2003). *Introduction to survey quality.* Hoboken, NJ: John Wiley & Sons.

Bissonnette, V., Ickes, W., Bernstein, I., & Knowles, E. (1990). Personality moderating variables: A warning about statistical artifact and a comparison of analytic techniques. *Journal of Personality, 58,* 567–587.

Bolger, N., Davis, A., & Rafaeli, E. (2003). Diary methods: Capturing life as it is lived. *Annual Review of Psychology, 54,* 579–616.

Boring, E. G. (1954). The nature and history of experimental control. *American Journal of Psychology, 67,* 573–589.

Botwin, M., Buss, D. M., & Shackelford, T. (1997). Personality and mate preferences: Five factors in mate selection and marital satisfaction. *Journal of Personality, 65,* 107–136.

Bower, G. H., Karlin, M. B., & Dueck, A. (1975). Comprehension and memory for pictures. *Memory and Cognition, 3,* 216–220.

Braginsky, B. M., Braginsky, D. D., & Ring, K. (1982). *Methods of madness: The mental hospital as a last resort.* Lanham, MD: University Press of America.

Brennan, P. A., Grekin, E. R., & Mednick, S. A. (1999). Maternal smoking during pregnancy and adult male criminal outcomes. *Archives of General Psychiatry, 56,* 215–219.

Bringmann, W. (1979, Sept/Oct). Wundt's lab: "humble . . . but functioning" [Letter to the editor]. *APA Monitor,* p. 13.

Bromley, D. B. (1986). *The case-study method in psychology and related disciplines.* Chichester: John Wiley & Sons.

Brown, A. S. (1988). Encountering misspellings and spelling performance: Why wrong isn't right. *Journal of Educational Psychology, 80,* 488–494.

Bryan, J. H., & Test, M. A. (1967). Models and helping: Naturalistic studies in aiding behavior. *Journal of Personality and Social Psychology, 6,* 400–407.

Buchanan, C. M., Maccoby, E. E., & Dornbusch, S. M. (1996). *Adolescents after divorce.* Cambridge, MA: Harvard University Press.

Butler, A. C., Hokanson, J. E., & Flynn, H. A. (1994). A comparison of self-esteem lability and low trait self-esteem as vulnerability factors for depression. *Journal of Personality and Social Psychology, 66,* 166–177.

Campbell, D., Sanderson, R. E., & Laverty, S. G. (1964). Characteristics of a conditioned response in human subjects during extinction trials following a single traumatic conditioning trial. *Journal of Abnormal and Social Psychology, 68,* 627–639.

Campbell, D. T. (1969). Reforms as experiments. *American Psychologist, 24,* 409–429.

Campbell, D. T. (1971, September). *Methods for the experimenting society.* Paper presented at the meeting of the American Psychological Association, Washington, DC.

Campbell, D. T. (1981). Comment: Another perspective on a scholarly career. In M. Brewer & B. E. Collins (Eds.), *Scientific inquiry and the social sciences* (pp. 454–501). San Francisco: Jossey-Bass.

Campbell, D. T., & Stanley, J. C. (1966). *Experimental and quasi-experimental designs for research.* Skokie, IL: Rand McNally.

Cassandro, V. J. (1998). Explaining premature mortality across fields of creative endeavor. *Journal of Personality, 66,* 805–833.

Cheek, J. M. (1982). Aggregation, moderator variables, and the validity of personality tests: A peer-rating study. *Journal of Personality and Social Psychology, 43,* 1254–1269.

Chevalier-Skolnikoff, S., & Liska, J. (1993). Tool use by wild and captive elephants. *Animal Behavior, 46,* 209–219.

Christensen, L. (1988). Deception in psychological research: When is its use justified? *Personality and Social Psychology Bulletin, 14,* 664–675.

Clark, R. D., & Hatfield, E. (1989). Gender differences in receptivity to sexual offers. *Journal of Psychology and Human Sexuality, 2,* 39–55.

Clifft, M. A. (1986). Writing about psychiatric patients. *Bulletin of the Menninger Clinic, 50,* 511–524.

Cochran, W. G., Mosteller, F., & Tukey, J. W. (1953). Statistical problems in the Kinsey report. *Journal of the American Statistical Association, 48,* 673–716.

Cohen, J. (1977). *Statistical power analysis for the behavioral sciences* (Rev. ed.). New York: Academic Press.

Cohen, J. (1988). *Statistical power analysis for the behavioral sciences.* Hillsdale, NJ: Lawrence Erlbaum Associates.

Cohen, J. (1992). Statistical power analysis. *Current Directions in Psychological Science, 1,* 98–101.

Cohen, J., & Cohen, P. (1983). *Applied multiple regression/correlation analysis for the behavioral sciences* (2nd ed.). Hillsdale, NJ: Erlbaum.

Condray, D. S. (1986). Quasi-experimental analysis: A mixture of methods and judgment. In W. M. K. Trochim (Ed.), *Advances in quasi-experimental design and analysis* (pp. 9–28). San Francisco: Jossey-Bass.

Cook, T. D., & Campbell, D. T. (1979). *Quasi-experimentation.* Boston: Houghton Mifflin.

Coon, D. (1992). *Introduction to psychology* (6th ed.). St. Paul, MN: West Publishing Company.

Cooper, H. (1990). Meta-analysis and the integrative research review. In C. Hendrick & M. S. Clark (Eds.), *Research methods in personality and social psychology* (pp. 142–163). Newbury Park, CA: Sage.

Cordaro, L., & Ison, J. R. (1963). Psychology of the scientist: X. Observer bias in classical conditioning of the planaria. *Psychological Reports, 13,* 787–789.

Coulter, X. (1986). Academic value of research participation by undergraduates. *American Psychologist, 41,* 317.

Cowles, M. (1989). *Statistics in psychology: An historical perspective.* Hillsdale, NJ: Erlbaum.

Cronbach, L. J. (1970). *Essentials of psychological testing* (3rd ed.). New York: Harper & Row.

Cronbach, L. J., & Meehl, P. E. (1955). Construct validity in psychological tests. *Psychological Bulletin, 52,* 281–302.

Dabbs, J. M., Jr., Frady, R. L., Carr, T. S., & Besch, N. F. (1987). Saliva testosterone and criminal violence in young adult prison inmates. *Psychosomatic Medicine, 49,* 174–182.

Daily smoking by teens has risen sharply. (1998, Oct. 9). *Washington Post,* p. A3.

Dallam, S. J. (2001). Science or propaganda? An examination of Rind, Tromovitch, and Bauserman (1998). *Journal of Child Sexual Abuse, 9,* 109–134.

Deitz, S. M. (1977). An analysis of programming DRL schedules in educational settings. *Behaviour Research and Therapy, 15,* 103–111.

Denenberg, V. H. (1982). Comparative psychology and single-subject research. In A. E. Kazdin & A. H. Tuma (Eds.), *Single-case research designs* (pp. 19–31). San Francisco: Jossey-Bass.

Dijksterhuis, A. (2004). Think different: The merits of unconscious thought in preference development and decision making. *Journal of Personality and Social Psychology, 87,* 586–598.

Domjan, M., & Purdy, J. E. (1995). Animal research in psychology: More than meets the eye of the general psychology student. *American Psychologist, 50,* 496–503.

Dworkin, S. I., Bimle, C., & Miyauchi, T. (1989). Differential effects of pentobarbital and cocaine on punished and nonpunished responding. *Journal of the Experimental Analysis of Behavior, 51,* 173–184.

Else-Quest, N. M., Hyde, J. S., & Linn, M. C. (2010). Cross-national patterns of gender differences in mathematics: A meta-analysis. *Psychological Bulletin, 136,* 103-127.

Eron, L. D., Huesmann, L. R., Lefkowitz, M. M., & Walder, L. O. (1972). Does television violence cause aggression? *American Psychologist, 27,* 253–263.

Estes, W. K. (1964). All-or-none processes in learning and retention. *American Psychologist, 19,* 16–25.

Ethical Principles of Psychologists and Code of Conduct. (1992). *American Psychologist, 47,* 1597–1611.

Fanelli, D. (2009) How many scientists fabricate and falsify research? A systematic review and meta-analysis of survey data. PLoS ONE 4(5): e5738. doi:10.1371/journal.pone.0005738.

Farina, A., Wheeler, D. S., & Mehta, S. (1991). The impact of an unpleasant and demeaning social interaction. *Journal of Social and Clinical Psychology, 10,* 351–371.

Ferraro, F. R., Kellas, G., & Simpson, G. B. (1993). Failure to maintain equivalence of groups in cognitive research: Evidence from dual-task methodology. *Bulletin of the Psychonomic Society, 31,* 301–303.

Festinger, L., & Carlsmith, J. M. (1959). Cognitive consequences of forced compliance. *Journal of Abnormal and Social Psychology, 58,* 203–210.

Festinger, L., Riecken, H. W., & Schachter, S. (1956). *When prophecy fails.* Minneapolis: University of Minnesota Press.

Feyerabend, P. K. (1965). Problems of empiricism. In R. Colodny (Ed.), *Beyond the edge of certainty.* Englewood Cliffs, NJ: Prentice-Hall.

Fiedler, F. E. (1967). *A theory of leadership effectiveness.* New York: McGraw- Hill.

Fisher, C., & Fryberg, D. (1994). College students weigh the costs and benefits of deceptive research. *American Psychologist, 49,* 417–427.

Fiske, S. T. (2004). Mind the gap: In praise of informal sources of formal theory. *Personality and Social Psychology Review, 8,* 132–137.

Frank, M. G., & Gilovich, T. (1988). The dark side of self-and social perception: Black uniforms and aggression in professional sports. *Journal of Personality and Social Psychology, 54,* 74–85.

Frone, M. (2001). Gallup data: A lesson in research methods? Posted to the SPSP listserve, September 19, 2001.

Gahan, C., & Hannibal, M. (1998). *Doing qualitative analysis with QSR NUD*IST.* London: Sage Publications.

Garmezy, N. (1982). The case for the single case in research. In A. E. Kazdin & A. H. Tuma (Eds.), *Single-case research designs* (pp. 5–17). San Francisco: Jossey-Bass.

Gelfand, D. M., Hartmann, D. P., Walder, P., & Page, B. (1973). Who reports shoplifters: A field-experimental study. *Journal of Personality and Social Psychology, 25,* 276–285.

Gentile, D. (2009). Pathological video-game use among youth ages 8 to 18. *Psychological Science, 20,* 594-602.

Gershoff, E. T. (2002). Corporal punishment by parents and associated child behaviors and experiences: A meta-analysis and theoretical review. *Psychological Bulletin, 128,* 539–579.

Glass, G. V. (1976). Primary, secondary, and meta-analysis of research. *Educational Researcher, 5,* 3–8.

Gosling, S. D., Vazire, S., Srivastava, S., & John, O. (2004). Should we trust Web-based studies? A comparative analysis of six preconceptions about Internet questionnaires. *American Psychologist, 59,* 93–104.

Gottman, J. M., & Levenson, R. W. (1992). Marital processes predictive of later dissolution: Behavior, physiology, and health. *Journal of Personality and Social Psychology, 63,* 221–233.

Gottschalk, L. A., Uliana, R., & Gilbert, R. (1988). Presidential candidates and cognitive impairment measured from behavior in campaign debates. *Public Administration Review, 48,* 613–618.

Grady, K. E. (1981). Sex bias in research design. *Psychology of Woman Quarterly, 5,* 628–636.

Green A. S., Rafaeli E., Bolger N., Shrout P. E., & Reis H. T. (2006). Paper or plastic? Data equivalence in paper and electronic diaries. *Psychological Methods, 11,* 87–105.

Gross, A. E., & Fleming, I. (1982). Twenty years of deception in social psychology. *Personality and Social Psychology Bulletin, 8,* 402–408.

Haig, B. D. (2002). Truth, method, and postmodern psychology. *American Psychologist, 57,* 457–458.

Hansel, C. E. M. (1980). *ESP and parapsychology: A critical re-evaluation.* Buffalo, NY: Prometheus Books.

Harari, H., Harari, O., & White, R. V. (1985). The reaction to rape by American male bystanders. *Journal of Social Psychology, 125,* 653–658.

Hartley, J., & Sotto, E. (2001, March). *Style and substance in psychology: Are influential articles more readable than less influential ones?* Paper presented to the Centennial Conference of the British Psychological Society, Glasgow.

Hempel, C. G. (1966). *Philosophy of natural science.* Englewood Cliffs, NJ: Prentice-Hall.

Henle, M., & Hubbell, M. B. (1938). "Egocentricity" in adult conversation. *Journal of Social Psychology, 9,* 227–234.

Herschel, J. F. W. (1987). *A preliminary discourse of the study of natural philosophy.* Chicago: University of Chicago Press.

Hite, S. (1987). *Women and love.* New York: Alfred A. Knopf.

Hodges, E. V. E., & Perry, D. G. (1999). Personal and interpersonal antecedents and consequences of victimization by peers. *Journal of Personality and Social Psychology, 76,* 677–685.

Huck, S. W., & Sandler, H. M. (1979). *Rival hypotheses: Alternative explanations of data-based conclusions.* New York: Harper & Row.

Huff, D. (1954). *How to lie with statistics.* New York: W. W. Norton.

Humphreys, L. (1975). *Tearoom trade: Impersonal sex in public places.* Chicago: Aldine.

Hunt, M. (1974). *Sexual behavior in the 1970s.* Chicago: Playboy Press.

Hurlburt, R. T. (1998). *Comprehending behavioral statistics* (2nd ed.). Pacific Grove, CA: Brooks/Cole.

Hyde, J. S., Fennema, E., & Lamon, S. J. (1990). Gender differences in mathematics performance: A meta-analysis. *Psychological Bulletin, 107,* 139–155.

Ickes, W. (1982). A basic paradigm for the study of personality, roles, and social behavior. In W. Ickes & E. S. Knowles (Eds.), *Personality, roles, and social behavior* (pp. 305–341). New York: Springer-Verlag.

Ickes, W., Bissonnette, V., Garcia, S., & Stinson, L. L. (1990). Implementing and using the dyadic interaction paradigm. In C. Hendrick & M. S. Clark (Eds.), *Research methods in personality and social psychology* (pp. 16–44). Newbury Park, CA: Sage.

Iverson, G., Lee, M. D., & Wagenmakers, E. J. (2009). p_{rep} misestimates the probability of replication. *Psychonomic Bulletin and Review, 16,* 424–429.

Janis, I. L. (1982). *Groupthink.* Boston: Houghton Mifflin.

Jaynes, J. (1976). *The origin of consciousness in the breakdown of the bicameral mind.* Boston: Houghton Mifflin.

Jones, E. E. (1993). Introduction to special section: Single-case research in psychotherapy. *Journal of Consulting and Clinical Psychology, 61,* 371–372.

Jones, K. M., & Friman, P. C. (1999). A case study of behavioral assessment and treatment of insect phobia. *Journal of Applied Behavioral Analysis, 32,* 95–98.

Jung, J. (1971). *The experimenter's dilemma.* New York: Harper & Row.

Kaplan, R. M. (1982). Nader's raid on the testing industry. *American Psychologist, 37,* 15–23.

Kaptchuk, T. J., Stason, W. B., Davis, R. B., Legedza, A. R. T., Schnyer, R. N., Kerr, C. E., Stone, D. A., Nam, B. H., Kirsch, I., & Goldman, R. H. (2006). Sham device v inert pill: Randomised controlled trial of two placebo treatments. *British Medical Journal, 332,* 391–397.

Kazdin, A. E. (1982). *Single-case research designs.* New York: Oxford.

Keeter, S., Kennedy, C., Clark, A., Tompson, T., & Mokrzycki, M. (2007). What's missing from national landline RDD surveys? The impact of the growing cell-only population. *Public Opinion Quarterly, 71,* 772–792.

Keller, P. A. (1999). Converting the unconverted: The effect of inclination and opportunity to discount health-related fear appeals. *Journal of Applied Psychology, 84,* 403–415.

Kendall, M. G. (1970). Ronald Aylmer Fisher, 1890–1962. In E. S. Pearson & M. G. Kendall (Eds.), *Studies in the history of probability and statistics* (pp. 439–453). London: Charles Griffin.

Keppel, G. (1982). *Design and analysis: A researcher's handbook.* Englewood Cliffs, NJ: Prentice-Hall.

Kerr, N. L. (1998). HARKing: Hypothesizing after the results are known. *Personality and Social Psychology Review, 2,* 196–217.

Kidd, V. (1971). A study of the images produced through the use of the male pronoun as the generic. *Moments in Contemporary Rhetoric and Communication, 1,* 25–30.

Killeen, P. R. (2005). An alternative to null–hypothesis significance tests. P*sychological Science, 16,* 345–353.

Kinsey, A. C., Pomeroy, W. B., & Martin, C. E. (1948). *Sexual behavior in the human male.* Philadelphia: Saunders.

Kinsey, A. C., Pomeroy, W. B., Martin, C. E., & Gebhard, P. H. (1953). *Sexual behavior in the human female.* Philadelphia: Saunders.

Kirby, D. (1977). The methods and methodological problems of sex research. In J. S. DeLora & C. A. B. Warren (Eds.), *Understanding sexual interaction.* Boston: Houghton Mifflin.

Klinesmith, J., Kasser, T., & McAndrew, F. T. (2006). Guns, testosterone, and aggression. *Psychological Science, 17,* 568–571.

Kneip, R. C., Delamater, A. M., Ismond, T., Milford, C., Salvia, L., & Schwartz, D. (1993). Self- and spouse ratings of anger and hostility as predictors of coronary heart disease. *Health Psychology, 12,* 301–307.

Kowalski, R. M. (1995). Teaching moderated multiple regression for the analysis of mixed experimental designs. *Teaching of Psychology, 22,* 197–198.

Kramer, A. F., Coyne, J. T., & Strayer, D. L. (1993). Cognitive function at high altitude. *Human Factors, 35,* 329–344.

Kratochwill, T. R. (1978). *Single subject research.* New York: Academic Press.

Kraut, R., Olson, J., Banaji, M., Bruckman, A., Cohen, J., & Couper, M. (2004). Psychological research online: Report of Board of Scientific Affairs' Advisory Group on the Conduct of Research on the Internet. *American Psychologist, 59,* 105–117.

Kruger, D. J., & Neese, R. M. (2004). Sexual selection and the male:female mortality ratio. *Evolutionary Psychology, 2,* 66–85.

Kuhn, T. S. (1962). *The structure of scientific revolutions.* Chicago: University of Chicago Press.

Langer, E. J., & Rodin, J. (1976). The effects of choice and enhanced personal responsibility for the aged: A field experiment in an institutional setting. *Journal of Personality and Social Psychology, 34,* 191–198.

Laumann, E. O., Gagnon, J. H., Michael, R. T., & Michaels, S. (1994). *The social organization of sexuality in the United States.* Chicago: University of Chicago Press.

Leary, M. R. (1983). Social anxiousness: The construct and its measurement. *Journal of Personality Assessment, 47,* 66–75.

Leary, M. R. (1995). *Self-presentation: Impression management and interpersonal behavior.* Boulder, CO: Westview Press.

Leary, M. R., & Kowalski, R. M. (1993). The interaction anxiousness scale: Construct and criterion-related validity. *Journal of Personality Assessment, 61,* 136–146.

Leary, M. R., Landel, J. L., & Patton, K. M. (1996). The motivated expression of embarrassment following a self-presentational predicament. *Journal of Personality, 64,* 619–636.

Leary, M. R., & Meadows, S. (1991). Predictors, elicitors, and concomitants of social blushing. *Journal of Personality and Social Psychology, 60,* 254–262.

Leary, M. R., Rogers, P. A., Canfield, R. W., & Coe, C. (1986). Boredom in interpersonal encounters: Antecedents and social implications. *Journal of Personality and Social Psychology, 51,* 968–975.

Lemery, K. S., Goldsmith, H. H., Klinnert, M. D., & Mrazek, D. A. (1999). Developmental models of infant and childhood temperament. *Developmental Psychology, 35,* 189–204.

Levesque, R. J. R. (1993). The romantic experience of adolescents in satisfying love relationships. *Journal of Youth and Adolescence, 22,* 219–251.

Levin, I. P., & Gaeth, G. J. (1988). How consumers are affected by the framing of attribute information before and after consuming the product. *Journal of Counsumer Research, 15,* 374–378.

Levin, I., & Stokes, J. P. (1986). An examination of the relation of individual difference variables to loneliness. *Journal of Personality, 54,* 717–733.

Lewinsohn, P. M., Hops, H., Roberts, R. E., Seeley, J. R., & Andrews, J. A. (1993). Adolescent psychopathology: I. Prevalence and incidence of depression and other *DSM-III-R* disorders in high school students. *Journal of Abnormal Psychology, 102,* 133–144.

Link, M. W., Battaglia, M. P., Frankel, M. R., Osborn, L., & Mokdad, A. H. (2007). Reaching the U.S. cell phone generation: Comparison of cell phone survey results with an ongoing landline telephone survey. *Public Opinion Quarterly, 71,* 814–839.

Lipsey, M. W. (1990). *Design sensitivity: Statistical power for experimental research.* Newbury Park, CA: Sage.

Lisheron, M. (2001, Nov. 18). Fraud shakes the walls of academia's ivory tower. *Austin American-Statesman* (www.statesman.com).

Little, A. C., Burt, D. M., & Perrett, D. I. (2006). Assortative mating for perceived facial personality traits. *Personality and Individual Differences, 140,* 973–984.

Löckenhoff, C. E., De Fruyt, F., Terracciano, A., McCrae, R. R., De Bolle, M., Costa, Jr., P. T., et al. (2009). Perceptions of aging across 26 cultures and their culture-level associates. *Psychology and Aging, 24,* 941–954.

Lord, C. G., Ross, L., & Lepper, M. R. (1979). Biased assimilation and attitude polarization: The effects of prior theories on subsequently considered evidence. *Journal of Personality and Social Psychology, 37,* 2098–2109.

Luria, A. R. (1987). *The mind of a mnemonist.* Cambridge, MA: Harvard University Press.

Mahoney, M. J., Moura, N. G. M., & Wade, T. C. (1973). Relative efficacy of self-reward, self-punishment, and self-monitoring techniques for weight loss. *Journal of Consulting and Clinical Psychology, 40,* 404–407.

Martin, S. (1999, July–August). APA defends stance against the sexual abuse of children. *APA Monitor,* p. 47.

Massey, W. (1992). *National Science Foundation Annual Report 1991.* Washington, DC: National Science Foundation.

Maxwell, S. E. (2004). The persistence of underpowered studies in psychological research: Causes, consequences, and remedies. *Psychological Methods, 9,* 147–163.

Maxwell, S. E., & Delaney, H. D. (1993). Bivariate median splits and spurious statistical significance. *Psychological Bulletin, 113,* 181–190.

Mazur-Hart, S. F., & Berman, J. J. (1977). Changing from fault to no-fault divorce: An interrupted time series analysis. *Journal of Applied Social Psychology, 7,* 300–312.

McAdams, D. P. (1988). Biography, narrative, and lives: An introduction. *Journal of Personality, 56,* 2–18.

McCall, R. (1988). Science and the press. *American Psychologist, 43,* 87–94.

McCarty, R. (1999, July–August). Impact of research on public policy. *APA Monitor,* p. 20.

McConnell, A. R., & Fazio, R. H. (1996). Women as men and people: Effects of gender-marked language. *Personality and Social Psychology Bulletin, 22,* 1004–1013.

McConnell, A. R., & Gavanski, I. (1994, May). *Women as men and people: Occupation title suffixes as primes.* Paper presented at the 66th meeting of the Midwestern Psychological Association, Chicago.

McCrae, R. R., & Costa, P. T., Jr. (1987). Validation of the five-factor model of personality across instruments and observers. *Journal of Personality and Social Psychology, 52,* 81–90.

McGuire, W. J. (1997). Creative hypothesis generating in psychology: Some useful heuristics. In J. T. Spence (Ed.), *Annual Review of Psychology, 48,* 1–30.

Melis, A. P., Hare, B., & Tomasello, M. (2006). Chimpanzees recruit the best collaborators. *Science, 311,* 1297–1300.

Meyer, G. J., Finn, S. E., Eyde, L. D., Kay, G. G., Moreland, K. L., Dies, R. R., Eisman, E. J., Kubiszyn, T. W., & Read, G. M. (2001). Psychological testing and psychological assessment: A review of evidence and issues. *American Psychologist, 56,* 128–165.

Middlemist, R. D., Knowles, E. S., & Matter, C. F. (1976). Personal space invasion in the lavatory: Suggestive evidence for arousal. *Journal of Personality and Social Psychology, 35,* 541–546.

Milgram, S. (1963). Behavioral study of obedience. *Journal of Abnormal and Social Psychology, 67,* 371–378.

Miller, N. E. (1985). The value of behavioral research on animals. *American Psychologist, 40,* 423–440.

Minium, E. (1978). *Statistical reasoning in psychology and education* (2nd ed.). New York: John Wiley & Sons.

Mischel, W. (1968). *Personality and assessment.* New York: Wiley.

Monroe, K. (1991, April 21). Nobel prize winner is convincing in defense of animal research. *Winston-Salem Journal,* p. A17.

Mook, D. G. (1983). In defense of external invalidity. *American Psychologist, 38,* 379–387.

Moscowitz, D. S. (1986). Comparison of self-reports, reports by knowledgeable informants, and behavioral observation data. *Journal of Personality, 54,* 294–317.

Munro, G. D. (2010). The scientific impotence excuse: Discounting belief-threatening scientific abstracts. *Journal of Applied Social Psychology, 40,* 579–600.

Musch, J., & Reips, U. D. (2000). A brief history of Web experimenting. In M. H. Birnbaum (Ed.), *Psychological experiments on the Internet* (pp. 61–87). San Diego, CA: Academic Press.

National Institute of Mental Health. (2006, August). *The numbers count: Mental illness in America.* [Online report]. Available: www.nimh.nih.gov/publicat/numbers.cfm.

National Science Board. (2002). *Science and engineering indicators 2002.* Washington, DC: National Science Foundation.

Navarro, M. (2004, July 11). Experts in sex field say conservatives interfere with health and research. *New York Times,* p. 1.16.

Neale, J. M., & Liebert, R. M. (1980). *Science and behavior.* Englewood Cliffs, NJ: Prentice-Hall.

News from ACT. (2004, Aug. 21). Iowa City, IA: ACT.

Nicol, A. A. M., & Pexman, P. M. (2003). *Displaying your findings: A practical guide for creating figures, posters, and presentations.* Washington, D. C.: American Psychological Association.

NISAD (Neuroscience Institute of Schizophrenia and Allied Disorders). (2004, June). *Research News.* Available: www.nisad.org.au/newsEvents/resNews/street%20drugs.asp.

Nisbett, R. E., & Wilson, T. D. (1977). Telling more than we can know: Verbal reports on mental processes. *Psychological Review, 84,* 231–259.

Nosek, B. A., Banaji, M., & Greenwald, A. G. (2002). Harvesting implicit group attitudes and beliefs from a demonstration Web site. *Group Dynamics, 6,* 101–115.

Nunnally, J. C. (1978). *Psychometric theory* (2nd ed.). New York: McGraw-Hill.

Official IRB guidebook. (1986). The President's Commission for the Study of Ethical Problems in Medicine and Biomedical and Behavioral Research. Washington, DC: Government Printing Office.

Olshansky, S. J., Goldman, D. P., Zheng, Y., & Rowe, J. W. (2009). Aging in America in the twenty-first century: Demographic forecasts from the McArthur Foundation Research Network on an Aging Society. *The Milbank Quarterly, 87,* 842–862.

Orne, M. T., & Scheibe, K. E. (1964). The contribution of nondeprivation factors in the production of sensory deprivation effects: The psychology of the "panic button." *Journal of Abnormal and Social Psychology, 68,* 3–12.

Paulhus, D. L., Lysy, D. C., & Yik, M. S. M. (1998). Self-report measures of intelligence: Are they useful as proxy IQ tests? *Journal of Personality, 66,* 525–554.

Pearson, E. S., & Kendall, M. G. (1970). *Studies in the history of statistics and probability.* London: Griffin.

Pearson, J. C. (1985). *Gender and communication.* Dubuque, IA: Wm. C. Brown.

Pennebaker, J. W. (1990). *Opening up: The healing power of confiding in others.* New York: William Morrow.

Pennebaker, J. W., Francis, M. E., & Booth, R. J. (2001). *Linguistic inquiry and word count (LIWC) software.* Hillsdale, NJ: Lawrence Erlbaum Associates.

Pennebaker, J. W., Kiecolt-Glaser, J. K., & Glaser, R. (1988). Disclosure of traumas and immune function: Health implications for psychotherapy. *Journal of Consulting and Clinical Psychology, 56,* 239–245.

Peterson, R. A. (2001). On the use of college students in social science research: Insights from a second-order meta-analysis. *Journal of Consumer Research, 28,* 450–461.

Piaget, J. (1951). *Play, dreams, and imitation in childhood* (C. Gattegno & F. M. Hodgson, Trans.). New York: Norton.

Piliavin, I. M., Rodin, J., & Piliavin, J. A. (1969). Good Samaritanism: An underground phenomenon? *Journal of Personality and Social Psychology, 13,* 289–299.

Platt, J. R. (1964). Strong inference. *Science, 146,* 347–353.

Popper, K. R. (1959). *The logic of scientific discovery.* New York: Basic Books.

Powell, R. (1962). *Zen and reality.* New York: Taplinger Publishing.

Prescott, H. M. (2002). Using the student body: College and university students as research subjects in the United States during the twentieth century. *Journal of the History of Medicine and Allied Sciences, 57,* 3–38.

Price, M. (2010). Sins against science. *Monitor on Psychology,* July/August, 44–47.

Proctor, R. W., & Capaldi, E. J. (2001). Empirical evaluation and justification of methodologies in psychological science. *Psychological Bulletin, 127,* 759–772.

Prussia, G. E., Kinicki, A. J., & Bracker, J. S. (1993). Psychological and behavioral consequences of job loss: A covariance structure analysis using Weiner's (1985) attribution model. *Journal of Applied Psychology, 78,* 382–394.

Radner, D., & Radner, M. (1982). *Science and unreason.* Belmont, CA: Wadsworth.

Reardon, P., & Prescott, S. (1977). Sex as reported in a recent sample of psychological research. *Psychology of Women Quarterly, 2,* 57–61.

Reis, H. T., & Gable, S. L. (2000). Event sampling and other methods for studying daily experience. In H. T. Reis & C. M. Judd (Eds.), *Handbook of research methods in social and personality psychology* (pp. 190–222). New York: Cambridge University Press.

Reis, H. T., & Wheeler, L. (1991). Studying social interaction with the Rochester Interaction Record. In M. P. Zanna (Ed.), *Advances in experimental social psychology* (Vol. 24, pp. 270–318). San Diego: Academic Press.

Rind, B., Bauserman, R., & Tromovitch, P. (2000). Science versus orthodoxy: Anatomy of the congressional condemnation of a scientific article and reflections for future ideological attacks. *Applied and Preventive Psychology, 9,* 211–226.

Rind, B., Tromovitch, P., & Bauserman, R. (1998). A meta-analytic examination of assumed properties of child sexual abuse using college samples. *Psychological Bulletin, 124,* 22–53.

Rind, B., Tromovitch, P., & Bauserman, R. (2001). The validity and appropriateness of methods, analyses, and conclusions in Rind et al. (1998): A rebuttal of victimological critique from Ondersma et al. (2001) and Dallem et al. (2001). *Psychological Bulletin, 127,* 734–758.

Robinson, J. P., Shaver, P. R., & Wrightsman, L. S. (1991). *Measures of personality and social psychological attitudes.* San Diego: Academic Press.

Robinson, P. W., & Foster, D. F. (1979). *Experimental psychology: A small-N approach.* New York: Harper & Row.

Rodin, J., & Langer, E. J. (1977). Long-term effects of a control-relevant intervention with the institutionalized aged. *Journal of Personality and Social Psychology, 35,* 897–902.

Rosen, K. S., & Rothbaum, F. (1993). Quality of parental caregiving and security of attachment. *Developmental Psychology, 29,* 358–367.

Rosen, L. A., Booth, S. R., Bender, M. E., McGrath, M. L., Sorrell, S., & Drabman, R. S. (1988). Effects of sugar (sucrose) on children's behavior. *Journal of Consulting and Clinical Psychology, 56,* 583–589.

Rosenberg, A. (1995). *Philosophy of science* (2nd ed.). Boulder, CO: Westview Press.

Rosengren, K. E. (1981). *Advances in content analysis.* Beverly Hills, CA: Sage.

Rosnow, R. L., Rotheram-Borus, M. J., Ceci, S. J., Blanck, P. D., & Koocher, G. P. (1993). The institutional review board as a mirror of scientific and ethical standards. *American Psychologist, 48,* 821–826.

Runyan, W. M. (1982). *Life histories and psychobiography: Explorations in theory and method.* New York: Oxford University Press.

Sales, S. M. (1973). Threat as a factor in authoritarianism: An analysis of archival data. *Journal of Personality and Social Psychology, 28,* 44–57.

Sawyer, H. G. (1961). *The meaning of numbers.* Speech before the American Association of Advertising Agencies, as cited in E. J. Webb, D. T. Campbell, R. D. Schwartz, & L. Sechrest, *Unobtrusive measures* (1966). Skokie, IL: Rand McNally.

Scarr, S., Webber, P. L., Weinberg, R. A., & Wittig, M. A. (1981). Personality resemblance among adolescents and their parents in biologically related and adoptive families. *Journal of Personality and Social Psychology, 40,* 885–898.

Schachter, S., & Singer, J. (1962). Cognitive, social, and physiological determinants of emotional state. *Psychological Review, 65,* 379–399.

Scheier, M. F., & Carver, C. S. (1985). Dispositional optimism and physical well-being: The influence of generalized outcome expectancies on health. *Journal of Personality, 55,* 169–210.

Schlenker, B. R., & Forsyth, D. R. (1977). On the ethics of psychological research. *Journal of Experimental Social Psychology, 13,* 369–396.

Schlenker, B. R., Forsyth, D. R., Leary, M. R., & Miller, R. S. (1980). A self-presentational analysis of the effects of incentives on attitude change following counterattitudinal behavior. *Journal of Personality and Social Psychology, 39,* 553–577.

Schuman, H., & Kalton, G. (1985). Survey methods. In G. Lindzey & E. Aronson (Eds.), *Handbook of social psychology* (3rd ed., Vol. 1). New York: Random House.

Schwarz, N. (1999). Self-reports: How the questions shape the answers. *American Psychologist, 54,* 93–105.

Schwarz, N., Hippler, H. J., Deutsch, B., & Strack, F. (1985). Response categories: Effects on behavioral reports and comparative judgments. *Public Opinion Quarterly, 49,* 388–395.

Schwarz, N., Knäuper, B., Hippler, H. J., Noelle-Neumann, E., & Clark, F. (1991). Rating scales: Numeric values may change the meaning of scale labels. *Public Opinion Quarterly, 55,* 570–582.

Sedikides, C. (1993). Assessment, enhancement, and verification determinants of the self-evaluation process. *Journal of Personality and Social Psychology, 65,* 317–338.

Seligman, M. E., Maier, S., & Geer, J. H. (1968). Alleviation of learned helplessness in the dog. *Journal of Abnormal Psychology, 73,* 256–262.

Shadish, W. R., Cook, T. D., & Houts, A. C. (1986). Quasi-experimentation in a critical multiplist mode. In W. M. K. Trochim (Ed.), *Advances in quasi-experimental design and analysis* (pp. 29–46). San Francisco: Jossey-Bass.

Shiffman, S. (2005). Dynamic influences on smoking relapse process. *Journal of Personality, 73,* 1715–1748.

Shiv, B., Carmon, Z., & Ariely, D. (2005). Placebo effects of marketing actions: Consumers may get what they pay for. *Journal of Marketing Research, 42,* 383–393.

Sidman, M. (1960). *Tactics of scientific research.* New York: Basic Books.

Simonton, D. K. (1984). *Genius, creativity, and leadership.* Cambridge, MA: Harvard University Press.

Simonton, D. K. (1994). *Greatness: Who makes history and why.* New York: Guilford Press.

Simonton, D. K. (1998). Mad King George: The impact of personal and political stress on mental and physical health. *Journal of Personality, 66,* 443–466.

Simonton, D. K. (2009). Cinematic success criteria and their predictors: The art and business of the film industry. *Psychology and Marketing, 26,* 400–420.

Singleton, R., Jr., Straits, B. C., Straits, M. M., & McAllister, R. J. (1988). *Approaches to social research.* New York: Oxford University Press.

Smith, S. S., & Richardson, D. (1983). Amelioration of deception and harm in psychological research: The important role of debriefing. *Journal of Personality and Social Psychology, 44,* 1075–1082.

Smoll, F. L., Smith, R. E., & Cumming, S. P. (2007). Effects of a motivational climate intervention for coaches on changes in young athletes' achievement goal orientations. *Journal of Clinical Sport Psychology, 1,* 23–46.

Song, H., & Schwarz, N. (2009). If it's difficult to pronounce, it must be risky. *Psychological Science, 20,* 135–138.

Sperry, R. W. (1975). Lateral specialization in the surgically separated hemispheres. In B. Milner (Ed.), *Hemispheric specialization and interaction.* Cambridge: MIT Press.

Stanovich, K. E. (1996). *How to think straight about psychology* (5th ed.). Chicago: Scott, Foresman.

Steinberg, L., Fegley, S., & Dornbusch, S. M. (1993). Negative impact of part-time work on adolescent adjustment: Evidence from a longitudinal study. *Developmental Psychology, 29,* 171–180.

Stenner, K. (2005). *The authoritarian dynamic.* New York: Cambridge University Press.

Stericker, A. (1981). Does this "he or she" business really make a difference? The effect of masculine pronouns as generics on job attitudes. *Sex Roles, 7,* 637–641.

Stewart-Williams, S., & Podd, J. (2004). The placebo effect: Dissolving the expectancy versus conditioning debate. *Psychological Bulletin, 130,* 324–340.

Stigler, S. M. (1986). *The history of statistics.* Cambridge, MA: Belknap Press.

Stiles, W. B. (1978). Verbal response modes and dimensions of interpersonal roles: A method of discourse analysis. *Journal of Personality and Social Psychology, 36,* 693–703.

Straits, B. C., Wuebben, P. L., & Majka, T. J. (1972). Influences on subjects' perceptions of experimental research situation. *Sociometry, 35,* 499–518.

Su, J. C., Tran, A. G. T. T., Wirtz, J. G., Langteau, R. A., & Rothman, A. J. (2009). Driving under the influence (of stress): Evidence of a regional increase in impaired driving and traffic fatalities after the September 11 terrorist attacks. *Psychological Science, 20,* 59–65.

Summary report of journal operations, 2009. (2009). *American Psychologist, 65,* 524–525.

Swazey, J. P., Anderson, M. S., & Lewis, K. S. (1993). Ethical problems in academic research. *American Scientist, 81,* 542–553.

Szymczyk, J. (1995, August 14). Animals, vegetables, and minerals: I love animals and I can still work with them in a research laboratory. *Newsweek,* p. 10.

Terkel, J., & Rosenblatt, J. S. (1968). Maternal behavior induced by maternal blood plasma injected into virgin rats. *Journal of Comparative and Physiological Psychology, 65,* 479–482.

Thrane, L. E., Hoyt, D. R., Whitbeck, L. B., & Yoder, K. A. (2006). Impact of family abuse on running away, deviance, and street victimization among homeless rural and urban youth. *Child Abuse and Neglect, 30,* 1117–1128.

Tice, P. P., Whittenburg, J. A., Baker, G. L., & Lemmey, D. E. (2001). The real controversy about child sexual abuse research: Contradictory findings and critical issues not addressed by Lind, Tromovitch, and Bauserman in their 1998 outcomes meta-analysis. *Journal of Child Sexual Abuse, 9,* 157–182.

Timms, M. W. H. (1980). Treatment of chronic blushing by paradoxical intention. *Behavioral Psychotherapy, 8,* 59–61.

Underwood, B. J. (1957). *Psychological research.* New York: Appleton-Century-Crofts.

U.S. Department of Education. (1991). *Effective compensatory education sourcebook* (Vol. 5). Washington, DC: Government Printing Office.

U. S. Department of Education. (2009). National Center for Educational Statistics, National Assessment of Educational Progress (NAEP), *NAEP 1999 Long-term trend reading summary data tables.* Downloaded from: http://nces.ed.gov/programs/youthindicators/Indicators.asp?PubPageNumber=13&ShowTablePage=TablesHTML/13.asp

U.S. Justice Department. (2005). *National Crime Victimization Survey for 2005.* Washington, DC: Government Printing Office.

Viney, L. L. (1983). The assessment of psychological states through content analysis of verbal communications. *Psychological Bulletin, 94,* 542–563.

von Daniken, E. (1970). *Chariots of the Gods?* New York: Bantam.

Wagaman, J. R., Miltenberger, R. G., & Arndorfer, R. E. (1993). Analysis of a simplified treatment for stuttering in children. *Journal of Applied Behavior Analysis, 26,* 53–61.

Walk, R. D. (1969). Two types of depth discrimination by the human infant with five inches of visual depth. *Psychonomic Society, 14,* 251–255.

Watson, R. I. (1978). *The great psychologists* (4th ed.). Philadelphia: J. B. Lippincott.

Weber, R. P. (1990). *Basic content analysis* (2nd ed.). Newbury Park, CA: Sage.

Weick, K. E. (1968). Systematic observational methods. In G. Lindzey & E. Aronson (Eds.), *The handbook of social psychology* (2nd ed., Vol. 2, pp. 357–451). Reading, MA: Addison-Wesley.

Weisz, A. E., & Taylor, R. L. (1969). American presidential assassinations. *Diseases of the Nervous System, 30,* 659–668.

What's the DIF? Helping to insure test question fairness. (1999, August). *Research@ets.org* [On-line report], pp. 1–3. Available: www.ets.org/research/dif.html.

Wheeler, L., Reis, H., & Nezlek, J. (1983). Loneliness, social interaction, and sex roles. *Journal of Personality and Social Psychology, 45,* 943–953.

Wichman, A. L., Rodgers, J. L., & MacCallum, R. C. (2006). A multilevel approach to the relationship between birth order and intelligence. *Personality and Social Psychology Bulletin, 32,* 117–127.

Wichman, A. L., Rodgers, J. L. & MacCallum, R. C. (2007). Birth order has no effect on intelligence: A reply and extension of previous findings. *Personality and Social Psychology Bulletin, 33,* 1195–1200.

Wilson, R. (2002, August 2). An ill-fated sex survey. *The Chronicle of Higher Education,* pp. A10–A12.

Wintre, M. G., North, C., & Sugar, L. A. (2002). Psychologists' response to criticisms about research based on undergraduate participants: A developmental perspective. *Canadian Psychology,* http://findarticles.com/p/articles/mi_qa 3711/is_200108/ai_n8992746/?tag=content;col1

Witelson, S. F., Kigar, D. L., & Harvey, T. (1999). The exceptional brain of Albert Einstein. *The Lancet, 353,* 2149–2153.

Zeskind, P. S., Parker-Price, S., & Barr, R. G. (1993). Rhythmic organization of the sound of infant crying. *Developmental Psychobiology, 26,* 321–333.

Zimbardo, P. G. (1969). The human choice: Individuating reason, and order versus deindividuation, impulse, and chaos. In W. J. Arnold & D. Levine (Eds.), *Nebraska symposium on motivation, 1969.* Lincoln, NE: University of Nebraska Press.

INDEX